P9-CEO-972

THE GEOGRAPHY OF ECONOMIC ACTIVITY

McGRAW-HILL SERIES IN GEOGRAPHY

John C. Weaver, Consulting Editor

Bennett *Soil Conservation*

Cressey *Asia's Lands and Peoples*

Cressey *Land of the 500 Million: A Geography of China*

Finch, Trewartha, Robinson, and Hammond *Elements of Geography: Physical and Cultural*

Finch, Trewartha, Robinson, and Hammond *Physical Elements of Geography* (a republication of Part I of the above)

Pounds *Europe and the Mediterranean*

Pounds *Political Geography*

Raisz *General Cartography*

Raisz *Principles of Cartography*

Thoman *The Geography of Economic Activity*

Trewartha *An Introduction to Climate*

Trewartha, Robinson, and Hammond *Fundamentals of Physical Geography*

Van Riper *Man's Physical World*

Vernor C. Finch was Consulting Editor of this series from its inception in 1934 to 1951.

THE GEOGRAPHY OF

AN INTRODUCTORY

NEW YORK TORONTO LONDON

ECONOMIC ACTIVITY

WORLD SURVEY

Richard S. Thoman

DEPARTMENT OF GEOGRAPHY, QUEEN'S UNIVERSITY

McGraw-Hill BOOK COMPANY, INC. *1962*

Library of Congress Catalog Card Number 61-11396

64200

456789-VH-9876

To Robert S. Platt – scholar, teacher, exemplar

PREFACE

THIS BOOK IS AN introduction to economic geography. It has been written chiefly for the student who has had access to little or no geography since childhood, and is designed to provide him with both an insight into the field of economic geography and a better understanding of the complex and tense world in which we live today. These objectives are by no means unrelated, as we shall verify in succeeding chapters.

Economic geography has ties to both economics and geography. It exists as a subject of study chiefly because of a need to recognize and understand more fully the location and functioning of economic activity in a world that varies so conspicuously from place to place in both human and natural features. In the past, the field of economic geography has been somewhat of a collection of loosely related facts rather than a unified body of thought, but much work has been done recently to sift and refine its subject matter. No small part of that work has involved the incorporation of more economic concepts into a subject which has its oldest and deepest roots in geography.

This volume is intended to reflect both the newer effort and the lasting qualities of the field's earlier content. In the Introduction and Parts One to Three the world patterns of selected types of economic activity, as well as selected human and natural features associated with that activity, are mapped and examined. Some national, regional, and local patterns also are considered. Where possible, the explanations of those patterns include specific principles or theories. Care has been taken, however, to avoid the forcing of a valid explanation into an unverified law or principle. Part Four, a separate section treating energy, is an innovation to textbooks in economic geography. Traditionally, inanimate energy has been considered a handmaiden of the manufacturing with which it emerged from the early and mature phases of the Industrial Revolution and with which it still is closely associated. However, inanimate energy now is used so extensively by several economic activities that it cannot be discussed logically in the manufacturing section alone. In Part Five the approach shifts from the general to the specific. There, single commodities are used as instruments with which to probe deeper into the book's central theme that man, viewing the world through the eyeglasses of his own culture, picks and chooses from a varied natural endowment to satisfy his endless economic needs and wants. Only a comparatively few commodities are examined in detail. Each exemplifies some particular aspect of the location and functioning of the world's economies within the world's cultural and natural setting. Other commodities which are important quantitatively but which are analogous to a selected commodity as to manner of production and utilization, are given shorter treatment. Such a policy avoids the snares and pitfalls which all too frequently transform textbooks into encyclopedias.

Our concern with economic activity is not limited to the traditional production and exchange. Consumption is presented as a major activity in the Introduction, is discussed more fully in Chapter 3, and is never far from the forefront of consideration. Economic geographers are beginning to give more attention to consumption, and its treatment here is in keeping with a methodological trend. Attention also is given in appropriate places to the service activities that are becoming increasingly important in technically advanced economies and in some underdeveloped economies as well.

Throughout the book, the stated or implied focus of emphasis is upon *man* who, whether initiating monumental economic, political, and social movements or merely striving for physical existence, is a paramount force in changing this changing world. The non-Communist and Communist groups of nations, the technically advanced and underdeveloped economies of both groups, the declining colonial systems, the growing number of sovereign states—these are but a few of the ingredients of economic geography resulting from present and past human decision and interaction.

Nevertheless, the natural environment cannot be overlooked. We have devoted a section of the book to that environment, not as an entity, but as one basic part of the field's subject matter. Among the objectives is appreciation of the subtleties of nature's varied endowment—subtleties which all too frequently are abstracted into a trite sentence, or even a phrase. The inclusion of this section is in keeping with a firm conviction that the development of such an appreciation by the student is one of the most necessary objectives of a course in economic geography.

If it is to be of value, a textbook in economic geography must contain a generous supply of numerical data. These have been procured for the latest possible year—usually 1958 or 1959 for United Nations information, and later for data from sources published by individual nations. Where earlier years are used, they were the latest available at the time the book went to press or the drawings to paper.

The book is designed for use in both single-term and full-year courses. Instructors in single-term courses who wish to emphasize the commodity approach will find the section on the roles of selected commodities to be relatively self-sufficient. To help make it so, three short explanatory chapters have been inserted there. These are Chapters 16, 24, and 28, treating, respectively, agriculture, mining, and manufacturing as economic activities.

A debt of gratitude is owed to many associates, both professional and otherwise. The earliest ideas received stimulating comment from Professors Jesse H. Wheeler, Jr., J. Trenton Kostbade, and Philip L. Wagner. Initial drafts were further improved by reactions from Professors Chauncy D.

Harris, Harold M. Mayer, Raymond E. Murphy, Wesley C. Calef, Clyde F. Kohn, Neil E. Salisbury, and George Murphy. Particularly valuable comments on late drafts came from Professors Richard I. Ruggles, Donald J. Patton, and Howard J. Nelson. Mr. Philip A. True offered excellent suggestions throughout the writing period. Also important have been opinions from Professors Clemens Thoman, Duane Hill, Thomas Bonner, and James Kenyon. Professor Arthur H. Robinson kindly granted permission to use the Flat Polar Quartic Equal-area Projection, which he had adapted for use in another book and which the author has altered further, however slightly, for use as the base for most of the world maps in this volume. Also, Figures 5.1, 6.1, 6.5, and 7.1 are modeled after Plates 2, 5, 6, and 8 of *Elements of Geography* by Vernor C. Finch, Glenn T. Trewartha, Arthur H. Robinson, and Edwin H. Hammond (New York: McGraw-Hill Book Company, 1957). Professor Donald Hudson and representatives of Encyclopaedia Britannica, Inc., kindly granted permission to use their transportation maps and to adapt them to the three-color form of this book. The Office of Area Development of the Department of Commerce made available some of their publications for inspection and use. Their excellent published classification of county-by-county distribution of specific industries in the United States, based on a special tabulation from the 1954 Census of Manufactures, has been the source for the several maps of plant size and location. The Office of the Geographer in the Department of State has been extremely helpful. The Foreign Statistics Section of the Division of Foreign Activities of the Bureau of Mines also has given excellent cooperation. Mrs. Clara Louise Lewis and Mrs. Virginia Gallahue have worked long and arduously in preparing special material. Last but by no means least, Mrs. Evelyn Z. Thoman and Gordon R. Thoman have been most helpful—and patient. The author, alas, must assume responsibility for any errors or deficiencies.

RICHARD S. THOMAN

CONTENTS

THE ROLES OF SELECTED COMMODITIES

INTRODUCTION

THE SUBJECT MATTER OF THIS BOOK MAY BE BETTER UNDERSTOOD BY CONSIDERing the etymology of the term *economic geography*, in which there is an adjective from one field of knowledge and a noun from another. The adjective is from economics, a specialized social science focused primarily upon man's efforts to earn a daily living—upon his attempts to provide himself and his dependents with food, shelter, clothing, and if Fortune smiles, a few luxuries.[1] Man is born a creature of need. As he matures, want is added to need. Economic *needs* are spontaneous and, in their crudest sense, limited. Man, like all living things, needs a minimum of nourishment; like some other living things, he needs a type of shelter; and, unlike any other living being, he needs essential clothing. Economic *wants*, however, are for nonessentials and hence are limitless. Unlike basic needs, wants are not spontaneous and not characteristic of the lower animals; they arise not from an inner desire for preservation of self or species but from a desire for satisfaction above the level of absolute necessity. To satisfy his material needs and wants, man consumes. To consume, he must first produce. In earning his daily living, man thus attempts to satisfy as many as possible of his material needs and wants by producing goods and transporting them to places of exchange and ultimate consumption. Economic wants are not, however, restricted to goods. To a limited degree in the simpler societies, and to a greater degree in the more technically advanced societies, an economy is expected to provide specialized *services*. These include a substantial number of professional, trade, transportational, administrative, and other services. Basically, economics is a study of man's attempts to maximize his utilization of both goods and services.

The noun in the term *economic geography* denotes a broad field of knowledge that has arisen largely from man's curiosity about his own community and the world beyond that community. It involves questions about other men and societies, about their ways of life, and about the natural surroundings in which they live. Fundamentally, it is a consideration of *areas*, the many areas that make up the earth's surface

[1] *Economics* is also defined by some authorities as a study of the allocation of resources—of the relative apportionment among all men of all natural and human advantages available to a given civilization at a given time. Such a definition is not markedly unlike the one offered in this book; in gaining a living, man in effect is maximizing his share of available resources.

on the basis of criteria concerning man himself, his cultures, and his natural environment. The areas studied by geographers may be smaller than a portion of a village or larger than an entire continent. Indeed, the largest area of geographical concern is the earth's entire surface. In studying an area, some geographers may be primarily interested in its inhabitants, others in its culture or civilization, and yet others in its natural environment. If all these geographers work together, they should be able to develop an understanding not only of the human, cultural, and natural features of that area but also of pertinent interrelationships among these features. As a group, they should also be able to note the *similarities* and *differences* between the area they are studying and other areas, near and far, on the earth's surface. Geography is therefore not so highly specialized as economics but extends to both the natural sciences and the social sciences.

THE FIELD OF ECONOMIC GEOGRAPHY

As implied by its title, the field of economic geography is related to both parent disciplines. From economics it derives a primary consideration for man's production, exchange, and consumption of commodities—a concern, in other words, for the methods used by man to gain a living. Economic distribution[2] traditionally has been of only indirect interest in economic geography, but it is becoming more important. To a somewhat limited degree, economic geography is concerned with services as well as goods, but less so than economics is. From geography the subject receives emphasis upon the many areas of the earth, and upon the human, cultural, and natural components of those areas.

Economic geography may be defined, therefore, as an inquiry into the production, exchange, and consumption of goods by people in different areas of the world. Particular emphasis is placed upon the location of economic activity—upon asking just why economic functions are situated where they are in this world. Historical as well as current considerations are important, the former especially as an aid to understanding the latter.

Consumption

Consumption is the using up of commodities.[3] The goods consumed are usually grouped in two categories: *consumer goods* and *producer goods.* The first are utilized mainly by individuals and include such items as food, shelter, clothing, and other commodities used directly to satisfy man's needs and wants. Being consumed by individuals, consumer goods are found in all societies, ranging from the primitive to the complex. Producer goods, in contrast, are consumed in the act of further production and include the raw materials and tools of production. They are not consumed directly by individuals but are intended to facilitate production of consumer goods. Currently they are restricted largely to societies using technically advanced tools and methods. The total volume of consumption for any nation involves both consumer and producer goods over a given period; and, for the entire world, it necessarily includes all materials used up directly by the world's inhabitants, plus the wear and tear on the world's instruments of production.

Production

Production is the fashioning by man of producer and consumer goods, chiefly from natural resources. We consider here that there are six *productive occupations:* agriculture, grazing, forest-products industries, fishing and hunting, mining and quarrying, and manufacturing. Although these are well known,

[2] The word *distribution* has different meanings in different fields. In economics, it refers to the respective shares which different groups in a society receive of all goods produced and services rendered. In business organization, it refers to the actual transfer of commodities from places of production to those of consumption. (An economist includes this function in his term *production.*) In geography the term *distribution* has an entirely different denotation; here it indicates a spatial pattern of features as expressed, for example, in the phrase "the distribution of cities in the United States." The word will be used in all three ways in this book, but its meaning should be clear from the context.

[3] Unless otherwise noted, *consumption* is used in this book in its broadest possible interpretation as synonymous with *disappearance,* and includes waste as well as use.

they are defined below because some are used in a particular sense in this book.

Agriculture is here defined as the growing and raising, under human supervision, of plants and animals. Besides the more common activities, it includes truck gardening, planting and harvesting tree crops, planting grasses and legumes regularly for either direct harvest or pasture, raising fish in farm ponds, and raising mink on mink farms.

Grazing is here considered as the use of *natural* vegetation for animal forage, the animals being under direct or indirect human supervision. In some places the natural forage may be reseeded by man, but such reseeding is not done regularly.

Forest-products industries are here considered to involve the gathering by man of every *natural* forest product useful to him. Timber, naval stores, latex, maple sirup, cinchona bark, carnauba wax, palm leaves, quebracho extract, and numerous other commodities are so gathered. As is true with grazing, the plant life in question is predominantly natural and is not planted regularly by man. The maintaining of a farm wood lot, for example, is here considered as agriculture.

Fishing is here considered to consist of the taking of fauna from water bodies and waterways. It includes exploitation of water fauna which have been raised artificially in fish hatcheries to replenish dwindling supplies but excludes the taking of fish from regularly stocked farm ponds. *Hunting* is the killing or capturing of undomesticated game.

Mining and quarrying involve the taking of mineral and rock resources from nature, usually from the land. However, some minerals are obtained from the earth's water and air.

Manufacturing is the changing of single materials, or the combining of different materials, into more useful or desirable products. We consider here that manufacturing involves handicraft industries as well as factory production.

Interrelationships among Productive Occupations. The first five of these occupations are directly and rather closely oriented to certain aspects of nature—agriculture expressly to climate, landforms, soil, and water; grazing to climate, flora, fauna, and water; forest industries to climate and flora; fishing to fauna and water; and mining to mineral and rock resources. Manufacturing, in contrast, is largely dependent upon the other five productive occupations, securing most of its raw materials from farms, grazing lands, forests, fishing and hunting grounds, and mines and quarries.

Labor Force. Normally, at least 30 per cent of a nation's population is actively employed in a *labor force,* involving personnel not only in the productive occupations but also in such *service* or *secondary* occupations[4] as wholesale and retail trade,

[4] Some writers, particularly economists, group occupations in *primary, secondary,* and *tertiary* classifications. The first usually includes occupations closely oriented to nature—agriculture, grazing, forest-products industries, and fishing and hunting; the second, manufacturing and mining; the third, various service occupations. One advantage of such a classification is that it implies the dependence of manufacturing upon the primary group. However, the inclusion of mining with manufacturing in the secondary group is misleading, for mining is as closely oriented to nature as is any of the four occupations here classified as primary. Furthermore, some manufacturing is scarcely, if at all, dependent upon any of the other occupations for the supply of raw materials or energy. Hence, in this book, we consider all six occupations as in one category rather than two. The productive occupations of our classification include both the primary and secondary occupations in some other classifications. Our secondary occupation group includes all activities elsewhere classified as tertiary.

On the following pages are illustrations of the six productive occupations. The upper row shows each occupation in a technically advanced economy that has benefited from the Industrial Revolution, and the lower row shows the same occupation in an underdeveloped economy that as yet has not benefited very much from that revolution. Notice the large number of people usually shown at work in the underdeveloped group, in contrast to the small number of workers and large number of machines in the technically advanced group.

Planting spinach on the Seabrook farms near Bridgton, New Jersey (Standard Oil Company of New Jersey).

Topping a coniferous tree in British Columbia, Canada (National Film Board of Canada).

Plowing an experimental farm near Saha in Egypt (International Cooperation Administration).

Cutting timber in Sierra Leone (British Information Services).

Range cattle around a water pond in Nebraska (U.S. Forest Service); Bedouins and livestock at a water hole at Turaif, Saudi Arabia (Standard Oil Company of New Jersey).

Fishing for salmon near Quathiaski, British Columbia, Canada (National Film Board of Canada).

Natives fishing in northern Nigeria (British Information Services).

Stripping iron ore with power equipment in the Hull-Rust-Mahoning open-pit mine near North Hibbing, Minnesota (Standard Oil Company of New Jersey).

Hand stripping of tin ore at the Pengal mine in northern Nigeria (British Information Services).

Making hydrogen by hydrogenation in the United Kingdom (British Information Services).

Making sandals in South Vietnam (International Cooperation Administration).

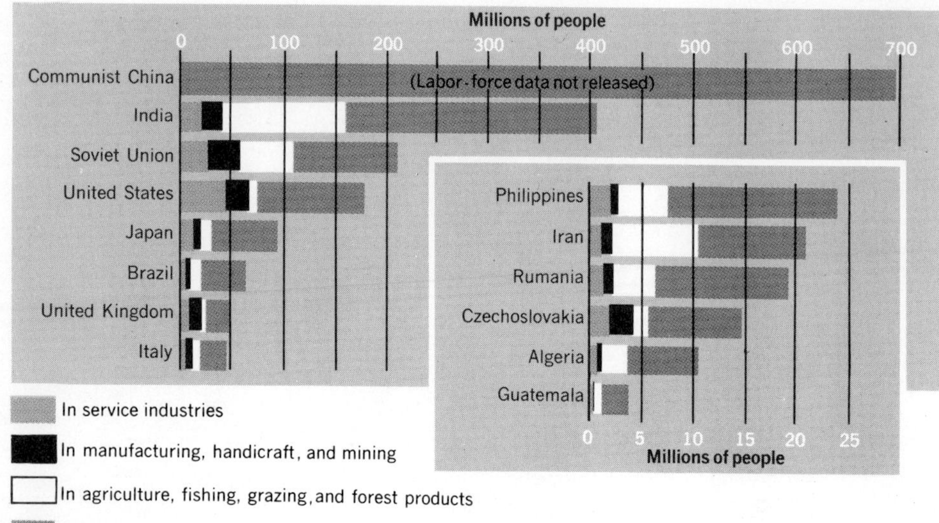

Population and labor-force relationships of selected nations. *The data for some nations are official estimates only. Both the estimated and the reported figures are complicated somewhat by the fact that some people work in at least two occupations and women and children are included in the labor forces of some countries but not of others. The labor forces for India, Brazil, the Philippines, Iran, Rumania, Algeria, and Guatemala, although the data are from official sources, are probably larger than indicated.*

transportation, communication, law, medicine, teaching, government, and domestic work. These occupations exist to perform services rather than to produce goods.

Nations differ markedly in the percentage of their labor forces employed in productive and secondary occupations. Those nations that emphasize inanimate energy, mechanized production, and specialized labor skills tend to produce enough goods so that over one-half of their labor forces need not be engaged in actual production but can devote full time to services. Those nations in which animate energy and hand methods still dominate the productive occupations tend to have only a few personnel in the service occupations, and each productive worker is more or less a Jack-of-all-trades, providing his own services as well as his own goods.

Population and labor-force projections for the United States, 1955 to 1975.

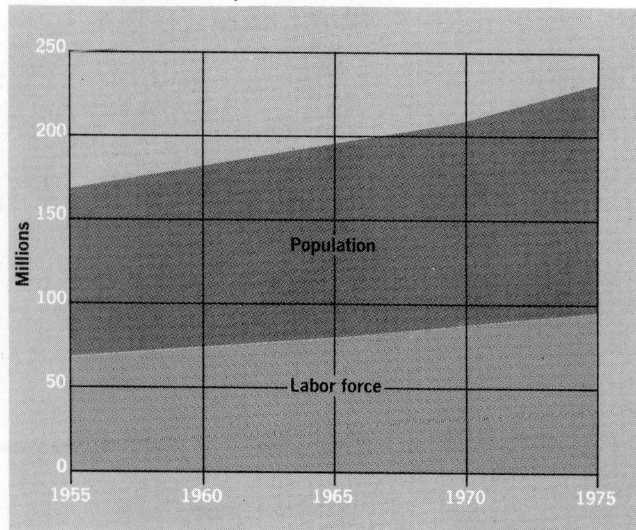

Exchange

In its most rigid interpretation, *exchange* refers to the sale of goods in a market place. In economic geography, the word is not used so frequently as in economics; but economic geographers frequently study both the domestic and international movements of commodities. Their interest is not so much in brokerage offices, stock and grain markets, and other mechanisms of exchange as in the actual movement of the exchanged materials from and to specific places following specific routes, and in the importance of different types of transportation media in facilitating such movement.

Nations in which the factory is well established tend to have higher percentages of their labor forces engaged in transportation, communication, and trade than other countries do. The United States ranks first in this respect among nations for which data are available, with about 30 per cent of its labor force so engaged. In contrast, the reported percentage of some countries is almost nothing.

Reduced to a definition, economic geography appears deceptively simple. Indeed, it is comparatively simple when applied to primitive societies, particularly those wherein the population pressure is light, nature is kind, and little or no contact with the outside world exists. Under such conditions, man can satisfy most of his material needs by hunting, fishing, and extracting from wild plants.

Most of the world's societies, however, are not primitive, nor are they sparsely peopled, nor located in idyllic natural surroundings, nor isolated. Instead, most societies possess at least some cultural advancement, they cope with serious natural obstacles, and they are quite dependent upon other societies, both near and far. Economic geography becomes more intricate when applied to these societies, particularly when they are characterized by such features as dense population pressure, differing levels of living, use of involved machinery and of inanimate energy, specialization of labor, efficient warehousing facilities, varying forms of money, discriminating tariffs, differing modes of ownership of entire systems of production and distribution, and natural surroundings of sharply varied beneficence and abundance. Economic geography becomes most complex when it is studied with respect to all of the world's societies, large and small, advanced and primitive, and to the inevitable relationships among those societies—relationships that are evidenced by the numerous transport and communication routes, global and local, of the land, sea, and air.

THE SCOPE OF ECONOMIC GEOGRAPHY

Number and distribution of people

Economic geography is complicated partially by sheer numbers of people. Nearly 3 billion—3,000 million—human beings now live on this earth, and these are rapidly multiplying. Fifty years ago the total was 1,571 million, and a century ago 1,091 million. By the year 2000, it may well become 6,000 million or even more. Each person is a consumer, and at least one in every three either produces commodities or provides services for those who do.

To persistently increasing numbers may be added the uneven distribution of mankind over the face of the earth. Man has crowded into the choicest locations of the earth's surface, preferring these to the tolerable but not so favorable areas that are only moderately populated and shunning the excessively cold, or hot, or dry, or wet, or mountainous lands. Moreover, the locations that have been favored by nature are unevenly populated. Many older civilizations, notably some Asian cultures that have not been so active in colonization, have tended to experience increasingly high population pressures. Even in Europe, where emigration has been heavy, population densities are high. Conversely, most of the territory colonized from Europe has not as yet acquired numbers of people comparable with those in Asia and Europe. Today, over four-fifths of the world's residents are in the Eastern Hemisphere. More than five-sixths live north of the equator. Nearly two-thirds reside in the seven largest nations—Communist China, India, the Soviet Union, the United States, Japan, Indonesia, and Pakistan. About two-fifths are jammed into Communist China and India alone. Over one-seventh are in Europe (excluding the Soviet Union). Obviously, under such circumstances the world's needs and wants, and the means of satisfying them, are numerous and unevenly distributed.

Role of political units

Political units, by which people are governed and through which their economies are either owned or controlled, add yet another dimension to economic geography.

Number and Distribution. Over one hundred sovereign nations and a host of subordinate states, cities, and territorial dependencies provide political administration for the world's billions. Independent nations range from the tiny Vatican city-state with

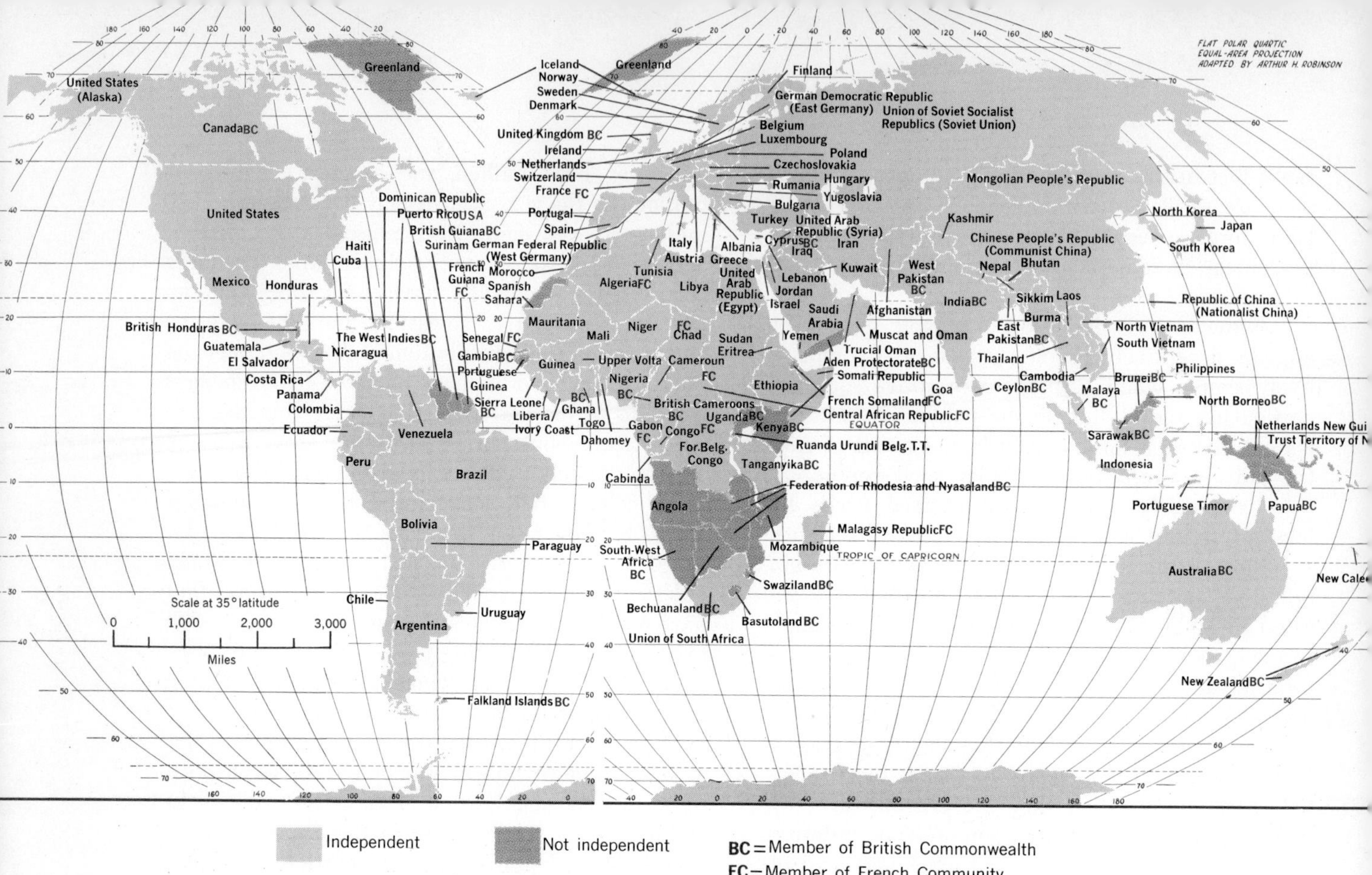

The world's political units. *Only the highest level of government for each part of the world, large or small, is indicated. Kashmir is claimed by both India and Pakistan, and since 1948 has been divided by a UN-supervised cease-fire line. Bhutan is nominally independent, although under protection of India. For additional information on the world's political units, see the table of political units at the back of the book.*

slightly more than 1,000 inhabitants to Communist China with a reported population of almost 700 million. Most nations contain more than 1 million and fewer than 60 million inhabitants.

Political units are comprised of people—of the same 3 billion people already stated to be very unevenly distributed over the earth's surface. The pattern of political units is also uneven, and its irregularities do not coincide with those of population distribution. When, therefore, the patterns of population distribution and political units are combined, there appears all too often a compartmentalization in which some nations, like Libya, are essentially devoid of population, while others, like Belgium and the Netherlands, are almost unidentifiable portions of large population clusters, and still others, like Canada and Australia, are lopsided imbalances of heavy population on one side and wide open spaces on the other.

Self-concern of Political Units. A nation tends to be self-oriented. Except when there is aggression by other nations, its existence depends upon the wishes of its citizens and/or its administrators, all of whom tend to place their own welfare above that of other countries. Hence a national boundary line, which appears unimpressive on a map and which is often unfenced on the earth's surface, can be a serious barrier to otherwise unhindered movement of *commodities, currency*, and *people* and, under extreme conditions, to *communication*. The major obstacles encountered at a political border include import,

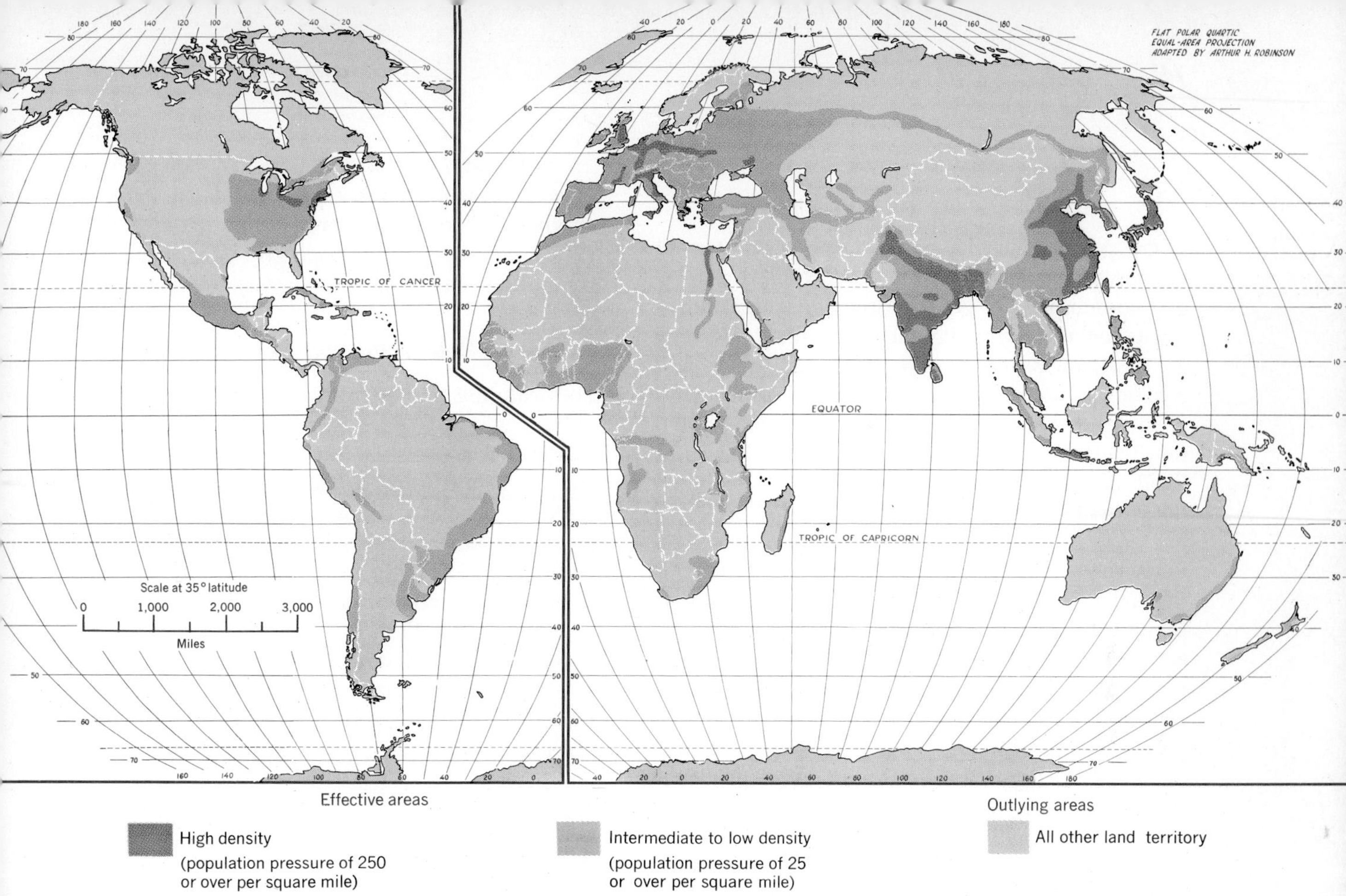

Density of world population. *In this book, places of moderate-to-heavy population density are called* effective areas, *because they are the vital cores of their respective countries. Other places are called* outlying areas.

transit, and export tariffs; quotas; disease inspection (of both commodities and people); currency control; and immigration laws. These usually, but not always, restrict or limit *incoming* commodities and people, and *outgoing* currency. Whatever the restriction, it is usually intended to benefit the nation that brought it into being.

Effect upon Exchange. The division of the world's people into political units may or may not hinder their efforts toward economic cooperation, since a political boundary line is no stronger an obstacle than may be decreed by participating governments. If, therefore, a nation follows a policy of complete cooperation with all other political units, the "barrier effect" of its boundary lines is eliminated. If, on the other hand, the policy is of selective cooperation or of some form of isolation, the boundary obstacles may become almost insurmountable. In practice, the economic policies of the world's political units range from almost complete isolationism to almost unrestricted cooperation, and the complexity of the world's economic geography is thereby increased.

Still more intricacy is added by the existence of political units that are not independent but occupy a subordinate political and economic status in the world scheme of things. In international affairs the colonies and other absolute dependencies obey the decree of their respective mother countries, and the quasi-independent political units follow their mother countries' guidance.

Role of economies

Every political unit has its economy—its system of orderly arrangements for the production, exchange, and consumption of goods. Although such arrangements include day-to-day labor of individuals, they are centered primarily upon group objectives and conflicts in man's attempts to satisfy as many as possible of his needs and wants. Particular attention is given to the regulation or administration of fiscal affairs, as well as to the functions of production, distribution, etc.

Dominating and Dominated Economies. A few independent nations are so strong economically that they tend to chart the pathways and set the pace for economic affairs, not only for themselves but also for weaker nations and for dependencies. In the economic world of today, the United States, the Soviet Union, and the United Kingdom are predominant. Other nations, most of them in northwestern Europe, have been able to preserve their economic independence and in some cases to exert appreciable economic influence beyond their own boundaries. However, most of the world's one hundred or more sovereign states and all its political dependencies are either so completely reliant upon other nations for raw materials, markets, and/or investments of capital, or are so assuredly under the political domination of other nations, that they abide necessarily by decisions from those nations. Generally, the same countries that exercise direct control over the economies of dependencies wield strong influence over the economies of the weaker independent states.

Interdependence of Economies. A detailed census of foreign trade of any major nation reveals at least a minor exchange with almost every other nation. In this exchange, some political units, whether voluntarily or involuntarily, remain rather consistently oriented toward a single country or group of countries, whereas others tend to be more versatile, trading on a day-by-day basis with any political unit offering a temporarily attractive bargain.

International trade, however, is not uniformly necessary. Some countries must trade for economic survival; others, with a large domestic demand and great internal resources, need give only casual attention to the world market.

Role of the cultural environment

Political units and economies are but two aspects of *culture,* a word which in this book designates the totality of a society's ideals and ideas, including such diverse features as mores, folkways, laws, arts, sciences, religious beliefs, highways, and cities—in short, including the lasting accumulation of human learning and thought in that society. In this sense, a culture is a recognizable way of life of a group of people, regardless of the size of that group. It is a summary of what that group believes to be of positive and of negative importance, and includes the objectives, the problems, and the achievements of the group.

Significance in Economic Geography. Culture is pertinent to economic geography especially in that the different peoples of the world do not have identical objectives, including economic objectives, in this life, nor do they have identical means of reaching their goals. Certainly most members of primitive societies do not consider seriously the possibility of owning refrigerators or automobiles, nor are they able currently to produce and maintain such commodities, which are conceptually far beyond their levels of intimate understanding. Their entire grasp of need and want, as well as the means of supplying both, is limited to the horizons of elementary cultures derived from the comparatively few experiences of lasting effect that they and their ancestors have had. On the other hand, members of certain technically advanced societies have ceased to look upon automobiles and refrigerators as objects of want, and now consider them necessary. The cultures of such societies obviously contain not only an understanding of how an automobile is produced and maintained but also an incentive for ownership of this costly gadget. Still other societies, also advanced, may not regard ownership of an automobile as a worthy goal in this life. Cultural objectives and methods of a society are thus very important in shaping that society's needs and wants and the means of their satisfaction.

Cultural Objectives and National Objectives. These cultural objectives are reflected in *national* consumption. Although cultural boundaries do not necessarily coincide with political boundaries, nations do differ in taste, style, and volume of consumption, production, and exchange; and a sizable but immeasurable portion of their differences can be ascribed to dissimilar cultural objectives.

Role of the natural environment

Man's economies and political units, like his other creations, have been superimposed upon, and meshed into, a natural (physical and biological) environment composed of varying and numerous organic and inorganic earth features. Viewed broadly, as they are here applied to global economic geography, such features may be grouped in eight categories: (1) landforms, (2) minerals, (3) climates, (4) water, (5) air, (6) flora, (7) fauna, and (8) soils. Such categories do not exist independently but occur in varying combinations.

Change in the Natural Environment. The natural environment is not permanent or static but is constantly changing. Much of this change is a process so slow that it is scarcely recognizable within the span of one man's lifetime. By way of illustration, the reader, regardless of his age, will realize that the landform, mineral, climate, water, floral, faunal, and soil conditions of his birthplace are essentially the same now as when he first became aware of them; and if he were to formulate a judgment on the basis of his own experience, he might assume that these features are virtually unchanging. With the passage of centuries and particularly of millenniums, however, these features do change—some of them to such a degree that they would have been scarcely recognizable a thousand years ago. Those that are least altered are, in all probability, the world's landforms, and yet most of these have undergone severe deformation and erosion throughout geologic time. Some change in natural environment, however, is more hurried, and this is usually associated with seasons of the year. The coming of spring signifies that snows will give way to rains, and that warmer temperatures will stimulate the anticipated flowering of the world's plant life and the reappearance of much of its fauna, whether microscopic, Gargantuan, or in between. Other hurried changes in nature are usually the result of sudden violence—of fractures in the earth's crust causing earthquakes and perhaps tidal waves, and of forest fires, floods, avalanches, disease plagues, and similar catastrophes.

Significance in Economic Geography. The natural environment is particularly important to economic geography in two respects: (1) it is a storehouse of certain *source materials* that will be consumed ultimately by man, and (2) it provides certain *physical and biological conditions* within and on which man's production, exchange, and consumption occur.

THE NATURAL ENVIRONMENT AS A STOREHOUSE OF MATERIALS. The earth is a gigantic repository of materials that man, through the ages, has learned and is learning to utilize to his advantage. Nearly every commodity that man has produced and consumed existed originally in the natural environment. In addition, nearly all the energy used in production and distribution comes from nature. Extraction from that environment is usually the first stage of production. The more common forms of extraction, such as the mining of coal and iron or the logging of forests, are well known. Even more refined practices, however, such as the creation in the laboratory and subsequent factory of plutonium from uranium, or the production of plastics from coal, petroleum, and other substances, or the recovery of nitrogen from the air, represent ultimate dependence by man upon some facet of nature. Man therefore turns necessarily to his natural surroundings for his raw materials and for substances that he uses as agents of production. Some of these are renewable—especially air, water, flora, fauna, and soils. They are not necessarily exhausted with use but can be returned to a natural reservoir, or reproduced, or revitalized. Others, particularly the minerals, have been accumulating within and upon the earth's surface over a long period of geologic time, are restricted as to total reserves, and yet, with a few exceptions, can be used only once under present-day technology. They are nonrenewable, limited resources.

Man looks to nature not only for raw materials and agents of production but also for most of the energy without which the Industrial Revolution would have been impossible. We shall have much to say later of energy. Suffice it to say now that the sun, directly or indirectly, is currently believed to be the source of all earthly energy except that derived in atomic reactions.

NATURAL ENVIRONMENTAL CONDITIONS. Besides being the origin of key materials, man's natural surroundings provide certain conditions within which man lives and works. Each major category of natural surroundings considered in this book—landforms, minerals, climate, water, air, flora, fauna, and soils—is an integral part of such conditions. These conditions may be positive or negative—favorable or unfavorable—with respect to man's livelihood. For example, the flat land of most plains normally may be a decided asset, and undulating and hilly land may be distinct liabilities, to the production and transportation of most commodities. Conversely, in times of flood the flat land may be a liability and the undulating and hilly lands an asset. Climates are important also to man's economies, for every type of production and transportation has its own optimum and marginal climatic conditions. Likewise, as will be shown later, the other six categories of natural environment are somehow relevant to man's earning a living in different areas of the world.

Interactions of man, culture, and nature

Man draws most of his sustenance from nature. Partially for this purpose, he has developed over the centuries a series of cultures that, although not oriented wholly to sustenance, nevertheless provide him with certain basic tools and instruments toward that end. Thus, for example, in agriculture he has improved upon the crooked stick to make a succession of increasingly efficient plowshares and today in certain societies has mounted those shares on wheels with rubber tires and pulls them with rubber-tired tractors. Similarly, in the other productive occupations he has made outstanding progress: in fishing, from the use of hollow logs to skiffs, to schooners, and finally to large floating canneries with which the fish are caught and processed in the open seas; in mining, from elementary hand picking of minerals in natural caves to mechanized loading in well-ventilated mines; in grazing, from foot-wearying shepherd conditions to use of fenced pastures served by motor, railway, and other carriers; in forest-products exploitation, from the use of stones with jagged edges to reliance upon both portable and stationary sawmills; in manufacturing, from dependence upon handicraft needles made of bone to operation of modern textile mills on the verge of automation. These are but a few changes in instruments and methods that man has adapted in his progress toward a more abundant livelihood. Thus he is learning that limitations imposed by nature are not absolute but retreat as the human mind recognizes them and devises means of overcoming them.[5] The seriousness of the limitations depends largely upon the depth and versatility of the minds that try to recognize and nullify them, and the richness of the cultural legacy upon which those minds rely for instruments to do the job. In this manner, throughout human history a series of what once appeared to be natural limitations have been overcome by successive advances of the frontiers of knowledge. Serious interruptions to the smooth functioning of economies usually are due not so much to natural obstacles as to human actions that frequently appear illogical when viewed objectively but are quite understandable when viewed in terms of current events. Vested interest is still very much with us.

Location, size, and shape in economic geography

Throughout this discussion we have been treating implicitly three universal qualities applicable to

[5] And in the process sometimes creates others.

human, natural, or cultural features: location, size, and shape. In economic geography, as in the entire field of geography, these qualities are never far from the forefront of consideration. For example, a map of the world's political units indicates that every nation and dependency has an exact location, a certain size, and a specific shape. At first glance, these may appear rather obvious and perhaps even trivial, but they assume a measure of importance—sometimes a very large measure—when, by way of further example, the political units are compared as to economic activity. Consider only the mining of iron ore: Is the ore situated in a tiny, a medium-sized, or a very large country? Are the shape of the nation and the position of the ore within that nation sufficiently in harmony so that the ore can be shipped at reasonable cost to the domestic market? To a foreign market? These are but a few questions arising from size, shape, and location as considered in economic geography, and they are focused upon only one geographic feature—the political unit. When the reader remembers the variety of human, cultural, and natural features that might be compared and otherwise examined on the basis of size, shape, and location, he can readily appreciate both the significance and the complexity of these aspects of economic geography.

REFERENCES

Ballabon, M. B.: "Putting the 'Economic' into Economic Geography," *Economic Geography,* **33:**217–223, 1957.

Berry, Brian, J. L.: "Recent Studies Concerning the Role of Transportation in the Space Economy," *Annals of the Association of American Geographers,* **49:**328–342, 1959.

Fisher, C. A.: "Economic Geography in a Changing World," *Transactions and Papers of the Institute of British Geographers,* **14:**69–85, 1948.

Gregor, Howard F.: "German vs. American Economic Geography," *Professional Geographer,* **9** (1):12–13, 1957.

Lukermann, F.: "Toward a More Geographic Economic Geography," *Professional Geographer,* **10** (4):2–10, 1958.

McCarty, H. H.: "An Approach to a Theory of Economic Geography," *Economic Geography,* **30:**95–101, 1954.

———: "Toward a More General Economic Geography," *Economic Geography,* **35:**283–289, 1959.

McNee, Robert B.: "The Changing Relationships of Economics and Economic Geography," *Economic Geography,* **35:**189–198, 1959.

Murphy, Raymond E.: "The Fields of Economic Geography," in *American Geography: Inventory and Prospect,* Preston E. James and Clarence F. Jones (Eds.), Syracuse University Press for the Association of American Geographers, Syracuse, N. Y., 1954, pp. 240–245.

Stamp, J. C.: "Geography and Economic Theory," *Geography,* **22:**1–13, 1937.

Thoman, Richard S.: "Recent Methodological Contributions to German Economic Geography," *Annals of the Association of American Geographers,* **48:**92–96, 1958.

Thomas, William L., Jr. (Ed.): *Man's Role in Changing the Face of the Earth,* University of Chicago Press for the Wenner-Gren Foundation for Anthropological Research and the National Science Foundation, Chicago, 1956.

Warntz, William: "Contributions toward a Macroeconomic Geography: A Review," *Geographical Review,* **47:**420–424, 1957.

Weaver, John C.: "A Design for Research in the Geography of Agriculture," *Professional Geographer,* **10** (1):2–8, 1958.

PART ONE THE HUMAN BEING AND HIS ECONOMIES

Man is born a creature of need. As he matures, want is added to need. INTRODUCTION, PAGE 3

1 PEOPLE, COUNTRIES, AND ECONOMIES

THE INTRODUCTION TO THIS BOOK CONTAINS THE SUGGESTIONS THAT MAN HAS learned the advantages of group organization and action in achieving his varied economic objectives from a varied natural environment and that the most effective organizations for this purpose are political units and their associated economies. Sheer numbers of people are also significant, as is the distribution of those people in cities, towns, and open countrysides over the earth's surface. In this chapter, which begins a part of the book devoted to the human being and his economies, we shall examine the growing world population, its rural-to-urban trend, and the sometimes dynamic, sometimes almost stagnant political units and economies that have evolved for governing the population and providing for its general welfare.

POPULATION

There are now nearly 3 billion people in this world. At current natural-increase rates, there will probably be between 6 billion and 7 billion by the year A.D. 2000. The world's billions are only now beginning to reap the harvest of centuries of "fertility investment"; the momentum of demographic change, like other momentums, begins with almost imperceptible sluggishness, intensifies slowly but gradually over long periods of time, and finally bursts into fruition almost all at once. We are now at the bursting point (Fig. 1.1). The recent popular accounts of a looming population "explosion" are not overly dramatic when trends are viewed in perspective.

However, concern with man-land balance is by no means restricted to our times but is traceable at least to the late eighteenth century and the writings of Malthus.

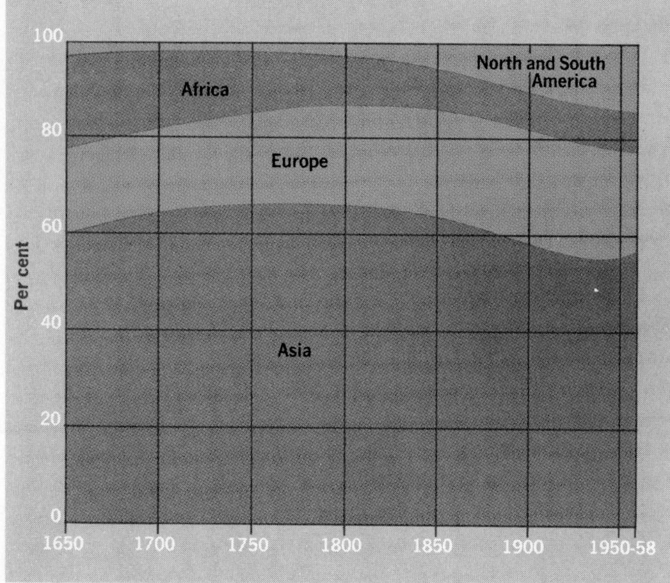

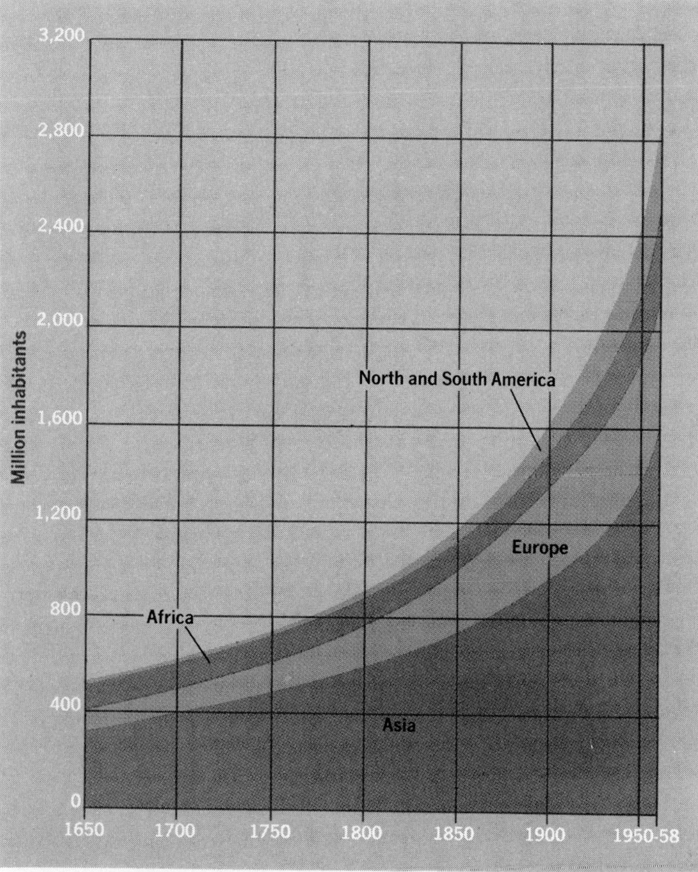

Figure 1.1 ***Growth of the world's population,*** *in numbers and per cent. The population "explosion" is just beginning.*

THE MALTHUSIAN DOCTRINE

The essence of the doctrine

In 1798, when the world's population totaled slightly over 900 million, an English economist and ordained minister whose name was Thomas Robert Malthus published a book-length treatise entitled, *An Essay on the Principle of Population as It Affects the Future Improvement of Society*. From the time of its initial appearance, the Malthusian doctrine, as it has come to be known, provoked controversy—and it reappears consistently in both scholarly and popular literature. Basically, Malthus stated in this and revised versions of his work that populations tend to increase much faster than do their means of support and, if not held in preventive check by war, vice, or, preferably, moral restraint, they soon exceed the productive capacities of the land. Malnutrition, exposure to the elements, disease, and other agents of decimation then begin to take their respective tolls. Finally outright famine, the most efficient reaper of them all, stalks the countryside until the man-land balance is restored.

Demographic conditions in Malthus's time

Malthus wrote at the early dawn of an industrial and scientific age that was to render some of his major assumptions obsolescent, even obsolete. He could not have been expected to foresee some of the effects of that age, especially those that increasingly enlightened mankind as to nature's potential of endowment for human use and those that permitted man to gain control over his own potential for reproduction. To Malthus, "land" was mainly agricultural acres fertilized, under optimum conditions, by natural manures. The more advanced agricultural practices were then largely unknown, and the factory had not yet come to dominate the English landscape. Small wonder that he was concerned as to whether the 16 million inhabitants of the United Kingdom of his day might become excessive! (One can only conjecture what his reaction would have been had he been informed prophetically that this population, despite wholesale emigration to other continents, would experience more than a threefold increase in less than a century and a half!) His basic principle, therefore, that populations invariably outgrow their means of subsistence, is now recognized as invalid, for many population increases have stopped short of the catastrophes that he set down as checking agents. Man's increased efficiency in utilizing nature and in controlling his own rate of reproduction have offset, in some countries, the extreme predictions of the Malthusian doctrine. And yet, even though the principle is not universally applicable, the possibility remains that it still sheds appreciable light on population growth, especially in countries that have been affected only slightly, if at all, by the Industrial Revolution.

Post-Malthusian population trends

The 900 million people inhabiting the earth when Malthus published his treatise were distributed about as unevenly as the population is today. Over 85 per cent were in Asia (including Asian Russia) and Europe, with the former alone accounting for approximately two-thirds of the world's total (Fig. 1.1). In the years that followed, the population of Europe grew rapidly in association with the embryonic Industrial Revolution. Furthermore, millions of emigrants left Europe in response to new opportunities beckoning from across the oceans. As a result of this population growth and emigration, Europeans living at home and abroad made up a higher percentage of the world's population than previously. By 1900, Asia contained only about 57 per cent of the world's people, and Europe slightly over 25 per cent. The remainder was accounted for chiefly by recent immigrants to the Americas and by a rather rapidly growing native population in Africa.

The twentieth century witnessed a slowing down of population growth in Europe (although the records of individual nations vary sharply) and a speeding up in certain other areas, notably Asia. The major gains have been most dramatic in lands sometimes classified as underdeveloped[1]—lands

How many people are there in the world? If every man, woman, and child were mounted on bicycles like those shown in the photograph and the bicycles were placed end to end in a single line, the line would reach 120 times around the world at the equator. How fast is that population growing? By the turn of the next century, that line could well reach around the world at the equator at least 240 times, and perhaps more. (British Information Services)

along the eastern and southern rim of Asia, in Africa, and in Latin America. The most serious aspects of these increases are their recency and their scope. They are now in process, and they evidence no indication of reduction in intensity. They are so dynamic that even conservative estimates declare that, for example, the population of Asia (excluding the Soviet Union) will increase by 50 per cent within another half century. Other estimates place the increase at an even higher rate. If these predictions are fulfilled, as they may well be, Asia's current

[1] We shall have much more to say about underdeveloped and advanced countries in the latter portion of this chapter and in Chap. 2.

54 per cent of the world's people will become even higher than it is now, as will percentages in most other economically underdeveloped regions.

These increases, although foreboding, are interesting in view of the Malthusian doctrine. It is well known that the hardships of misery, disease, malnutrition, and periodic famine have long been active in underdeveloped lands, and many scholars have assumed that these were preventing overwhelming increases in populations there. This apparently has been a correct assumption. In recent years, well-known techniques and instruments of combating diseases and other bodily infirmities have been applied to the inhabitants of some underdeveloped lands with almost instantaneous results. These techniques include the use of DDT and other efficient insecticides, vaccines, drugs, antibiotics, and similar preventives. In a surprisingly large number of cases where they have been put to use in underdeveloped lands, the death rates have declined, whereas births have maintained at least their normal rates. The almost appalling natural increases resulting from these conditions now constitute problems of major importance for associated political units and economies, many of which are young and comparatively unstable. The problems focus basically upon a simply worded and yet difficult question: How are the new mouths to be fed and the new bodies to be clothed adequately, in order to keep the Malthusian famine from coming forth to stalk the countrysides?

RURAL AND URBAN OCCUPANCE

Most human beings reside, worship, work, market their produce, purchase their desired commodities, and play in a manner peculiar to their own culture. They lay out transportation and communication routes within and among the buildings, fields, and other artifacts of life and livelihood. They set down arbitrary property and political boundary lines which serve as a framework for these artifacts. In short, when man lives in an area, he establishes a *pattern of occupance* there.

Although occupance patterns vary throughout the world, all can be classified into rural and urban types. This is usually done rather arbitrarily, either by law or by decision of some executive agency of the government, or by both. Since this action is almost invariably taken at the national level, there is an appreciable difference among nations concerning the definition of *rural* and *urban*. In the United States, urban units are incorporated places of 2,500 or more inhabitants (with certain exceptions that do not fit this classification easily, and yet are obviously urban). This is a moderate definition as compared with others: Canada considers as urban all places of 1,000 or more in population; Egypt, all primary towns of provinces and districts; Italy, all places with less than one-half of their populations employed in agriculture; Belgium, communities of 5,000 or more residents; the Netherlands, municipalities of 20,000 or more residents; Japan, municipalities of 30,000 or more residents. Because of the disparity among these and other definitions, demographers and other scholars are turning increasingly to the size of urban units regardless of their domestic classifications for both local study and international comparison.

Historical urbanization

One of the most interesting aspects of urbanization is its recency. Rather conclusive evidence exists to indicate that only very few sizable cities existed before the classical ages, and that even the Greek and Roman cities accommodated only small portions of the countryside. Indeed, one authority, Kingsley Davis, estimates that, even as late as the beginning

TABLE 1.1

Per cent of the world's population living in cities, by years

Year	Cities of 20,000 or more	Cities of 100,000 or more
1800	2.4	1.7
1850	4.3	2.3
1900	9.2	5.5
1950	20.9	13.1

SOURCE: Kingsley Davis, "The Origin and Growth of Urbanization in the World," *The American Journal of Sociology*, **60**:433, 1955. Percentages in the center column include those in the right-hand column.

You are looking at a photograph of an entire country—the Vatican City. How much of the Soviet Union could be included in such a photograph? (Pan American World Airways)

of the nineteenth century, less than 2.5 per cent of the world's people were living in cities of 20,000 or more, and less than 2 per cent in cities of 100,000 or more (Table 1.1). With the Industrial Age, however, came the urbanization of much of Europe, marked by the mushrooming of cities not only on the continent itself but also in outlying European offshoots. Urban percentages of total populations approximately doubled each succeeding half century for the world as a whole and multiplied even faster where machines became commonplace. By the mid-twentieth century, over one-fifth of the world's people lived in cities of 20,000 or more, and over one-eighth in metropolises of at least 100,000.

Current urbanization

At least three significant points mark present-day urbanization: (1) it is still concentrated in Europeanized areas, (2) it is increasing at an extremely rapid rate, and (3) it is shifting slightly in relative importance from Europe to Asia and other heretofore predominantly rural areas.

Urbanization and European Culture. The first of these points is illustrated in Table 1.2. The most highly urbanized regions are currently either in Europe (including the European section of the Soviet Union) or its former colonies—Oceania,

Anglo-America, Latin America. Asia and Africa are the least urbanized of major world regions.

Increasingly Rapid Urbanization. The rate of increase in urbanization is outdistancing even the current growth of over-all populations. Davis has estimated that, at existing trends, over one-fourth of the world's people will be living in cities of 100,000 or more, and nearly one-half in cities of 20,000 or more, by the year 2000. Fifty years from that date, in 2050, the respective portions could well be 50 per cent and 90 per cent. The march to the cities is in progress (Fig. 1.2).

Urbanization and Traditionally Agrarian Countries. The increase in tempo of urbanization in countries that until now have been primarily agricultural is even more sobering, because a means of support for many of the newly arrived urban immigrants is not always to be had. In other words, the factories, retail and wholesale trade organizations, etc., which provide the key economic support for most cities in

TABLE 1.2

Per cent of population living in cities, by regions (1950)

	Cities of 20,000 or more	*Cities of 100,000 or more*
World	21	13
Oceania	47	41
North America (Canada and the United States)	42	29
Europe (except the Soviet Union)	35	21
Soviet Union	31	18
South America	26	18
Middle America and the Caribbean	21	12
Asia (except the Soviet Union)	13	8
Africa	9	5

SOURCE: Kingsley Davis, "The Origin and Growth of Urbanization in the World," *The American Journal of Sociology*, **60**:434, 1955. Percentages in the center column include those in the right-hand column.

Man's future home is in the city. This one is Vancouver, in Canada. However, the city now is found in nearly all parts of the inhabited world, and is growing in size and stature. (Photographic Surveys, Canada)

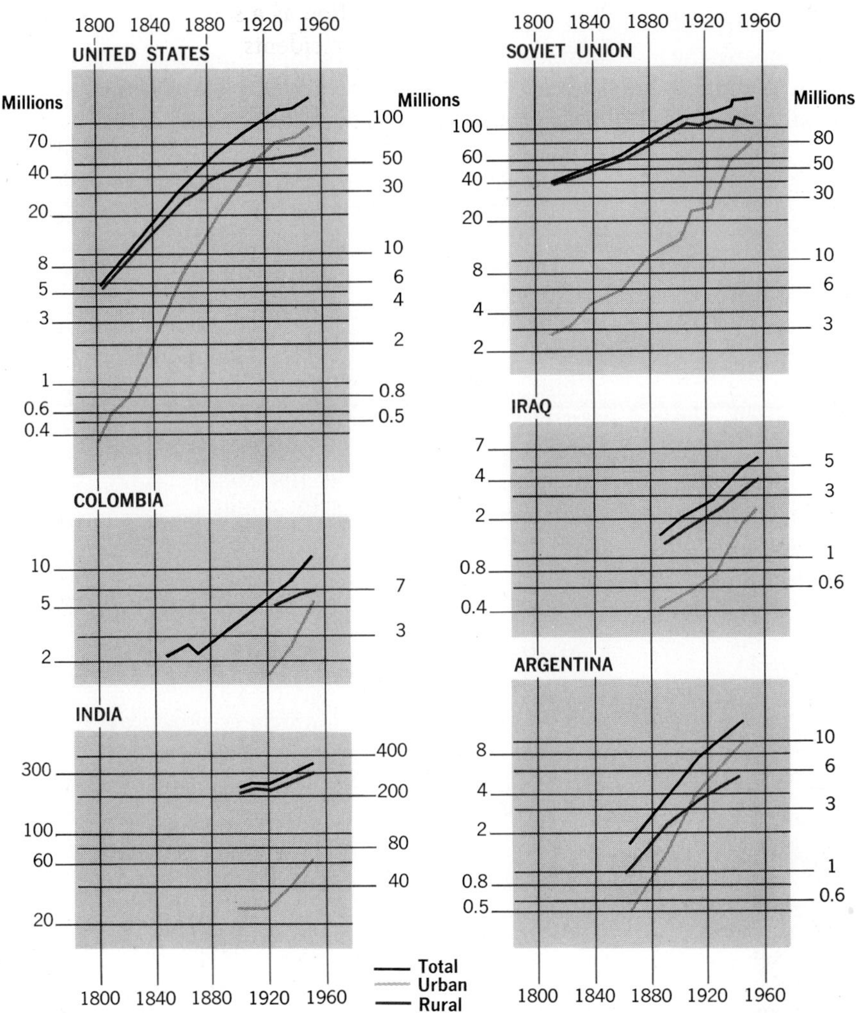

Figure 1.2 ***Trends in urban, rural, and total populations in selected nations.*** *The graph is on a semilogarithmic scale. Note the rise of urban populations in all countries, whether technically advanced or underdeveloped. In the United States and Argentina, urban populations now exceed rural populations. (Keep in mind, however, that each country has its own definition of "urban.") (After* The State of Food and Agriculture, 1959, *FAO, p. 131)*

Europe and its offshoots are not always being established in sufficient quantity and quality to provide livelihood for the growing urban populations of such countries. Davis has estimated that all countries now usually classified as underdeveloped have more people living in cities than do all countries usually classified as technically advanced. Furthermore, in many such traditionally agrarian countries, the urban immigrants are where they are not so much because cities attract as because countrysides repel. There is no longer room for them in many rural areas; and since emigration to other countries is almost impossible because of immigration quotas set up by nations to which they might go, their only alternative is the city or town of their own country. Here too there is no real place for them, and as a group they become a problem of the greatest magnitude. This new "enforced urbanization" is especially characteristic of the rimlands of southern and eastern Asia, where rural populations have grown beyond the means of support under existing conditions.

Not all urbanization of underdeveloped areas, of course, is enforced. The growth of modern domestic industries in many such areas, notably of food-processing and textile plants, has meant the need for labor. Such factories as these are comparatively new to underdeveloped areas. Doubtless they will receive close attention as a solution to both the problem of jobless city residents and that of general scarcity of commodities with which to supply life's basic economic needs in such areas.

COUNTRIES

THE PATTERN OF POLITICAL UNITS

As suggested in the introduction to this book, the earth's land surface is organized politically into a hierarchy of domestic and overseas political units ranging in size and level of authority from the hamlet and the tribe to the largest nation. The hierarchy seldom is rigidly defined—i.e., seldom does one level of unit have absolute authority over another. (Witness the perennial controversy over Federal versus states' rights in the United States.) Nor is it consistent throughout all of the world's many areas. One form of this hierarchy might be as shown in the following diagram:

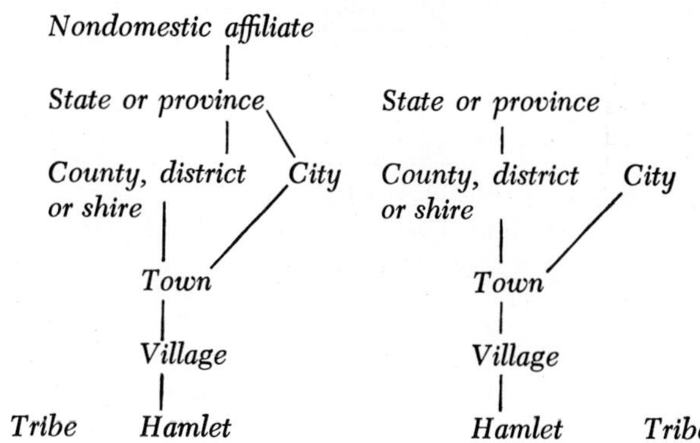

Except for nomadic tribes (and not by any means are all tribes nomadic), all these political units are sedentary and occupy specific areas of the earth's surface. Considered as a whole the units are numerous, and a world map of all would be complex indeed. Each unit has jurisdiction over certain functions of significance in economic geography; but since the scale of this book is global, we shall focus mainly on only the highest level of the political units and the most coarse of the political patterns—that of nations and their overseas dependencies. These are outlined in the table of political units at the end of the book.

Some political boundary lines, like this one between Alaska and British Columbia, scarcely leave an imprint upon the landscape. Others result in sharp changes of land use. (National Film Board of Canada)

EFFECTIVE AND OUTLYING AREAS

Populations are unevenly distributed, not only for the world as a whole, but also for individual countries. Most political units are comprised of one or more *effective areas* and one or more *outlying areas*. The former are invariably populated very intensively and are usually highly urbanized.[2] Together with their immediate fringe territories, they enclose the portion of a political unit where things are happening—where the basic decisions are being made for the entire unit. The outlying areas, outnumbered in population and usually outdistanced in technical, social, and artistic development, are weaker in voice regardless of the type of government in power. Their chief contribution to decision making tends to be that of a brake; they are usually opposed to change, notably drastic change.

It is generally erroneous, therefore, to think of the pattern of political units in the traditional sense, as shown in the figure on page 12. Instead, if one wishes to be realistic, he should visualize the pattern of effective areas of the world (page 13). This pattern, interestingly, is even less uniform in distribution than that of the political units themselves.[3]

A very few nations, very small, very intensively populated, like Belgium and the Netherlands, do not exhibit effective-area–outlying-area relationships when viewed on a global scale; but even these break down into such components when the scale is enlarged.

The significance of effective areas to economic geography is enormous. Regardless of the scale of political units—whether nations and overseas dependencies, component states, provinces, districts, counties, townships, cities, villages, or hamlets—an effective area is usually discernible. Effective areas, therefore, are the mainsprings of consumption, production, and exchange for each political unit in question.

[2] Because they usually are urbanized, effective areas can be confused with nodal regions, which are discussed at some length in Chap. 10. A *nodal region* is a specific portion of the earth's surface, whether large or small, organized for a specific purpose and focusing upon a definite location where vital decisions for it are made. A firm's trading territory, for example, focuses upon the head office of the firm. Another example is found in a metropolitan area's trading territory, in so far as it can be delimited. Studies exist to demonstrate that both rural and urban land use of that territory tend to become more intense as the focal point, the metropolitan area itself, is approached, and that this change of intensity is due at least partially to organization arrangements between the territory and the metropolitan area. The reader can easily see that such nodal regions would be the vitals of most effective areas as defined above, especially for highly urbanized nations. However, there are rural nations containing clustered populations but lacking such a focal point. An oasis in the desert may attract many rural dwellers, organized only loosely if at all but clustered because land in the oasis is productive whereas land beyond the oasis is sterile for lack of water. Nodality—certainly urban nodality—may be lacking in such an oasis; yet it contains the majority of a nation's population—may be, in other words, its effective area in terms of actual political, economic, social, and religious functions. For this reason, the term *effective area* is preferable to *nodal region* for global concentrations of people and human activity.

[3] In reality, of course, there is a transition from very intense conditions at the cores of the effective areas to almost a vacuum in the most distant reaches of the outlying areas. We have classified this transition rather crudely into effective areas and outlying areas, largely for emphasis. Had we desired, we could easily have provided several classifications, graduating them by level of intensity—by, for example, specific population per square mile.

ECONOMIES

Rural and urban occupance signify the presence of man in an area. The varying hierarchies of political units suggest organized cooperation, voluntary or enforced, toward governmental objectives that are too large or too complex to be solved satisfactorily by individuals acting only for themselves. But, important though they may be, these features, like man himself, are all ultimately dependent for their existence upon economies—upon man's arrangements for either simple or specialized livelihood.

Whether happily or not, economies are invariably associated with governments, regardless of type of level. Every political unit, in other words, can be said to have an economy—expressly and bureaucratically so where economies are actually owned outright or very closely controlled by governments, and more indefinitely so where that ownership is partially private and governmental control or influence less potent. Thus, particularly where some form of socialist government prevails, economies tend to be in a hierarchical order like their associated political units, the jurisdiction at any given level usually exceeding that of the smaller though more numerous lower-level units. In this book, with its global perspective, we are interested primarily in the highest level of jurisdiction—that of nations and their overseas affiliates.

CLASSIFICATIONS OF ECONOMIES

A bit of classification, like a bit of knowledge, can be a dangerous thing. Yet, like knowledge, classification is necessary to bring order from seeming chaos and for this purpose is vital—if the reader never forgets that all classifications are but arbitrary groupings by frail human minds of certain facts and figures for purposes of generalization.

So it is with the classification of economies. It would be possible to fill the rest of this book, however unprofitably, with a seemingly endless chain of such classifications (doubtless losing most of the readers, quite justifiably, along the way!). The chain would include, however, a few groupings that are vital to understanding the nature of economies, among which almost certainly would be one categorization by per capita propensity to exchange, a second by level of economic development, and a third by political-economic affiliation. There exists a generally positive correlation between components of the first two classifications, since most countries evidencing a high per capita propensity to exchange also evidence a high level of technical and economic advancement, and vice versa.

Not all of the most desirable information for such classifications is available, because some countries either do not gather or do not publish adequate census material. However, estimates have been made by specialists for most countries lacking official data.

CLASSIFICATION BY PER CAPITA PROPENSITY TO EXCHANGE

Per capita propensity to exchange involves desire plus capability to exchange on the part of an average member of an economy. No satisfactory index for this exists, but a somewhat crude approximation can be made by examining per capita (1) money income and (2) real income. The first of these indicates the average amount of money actually received by each member of an economy over a given period. This amount usually is translated into one particular currency for easy international comparison. The second indicates the actual value of average money income to each person expressed in terms of what that money will buy in the economy of which he is a member. This is the more revealing of the two yardsticks, because economies vary from each other in matters of domestic commodity price.

We are interested here in the propensity of each person to exchange goods in his own country as well as in the world markets; therefore, using per capita real income as the master criterion, we have classified the world's economies in Fig. 1.3 in three categories: commercial, commercial-subsistence, and subsistence-with-some-commerce. This represents a declining order of propensity to exchange. The reader should bear in mind that the classification does not necessarily indicate the extent to which *entire economies* depend upon the world markets but only evidences the extent to which *individuals* depend upon any kind of market—local, subnational, national, or international. Political affiliates and sovereign nations are mapped only with respect to their domestic economies, regardless of status. Thus, for example, *France* denotes only the traditional France of Europe, whereas *Algeria* refers to the domestic economy of that northern African political unit.

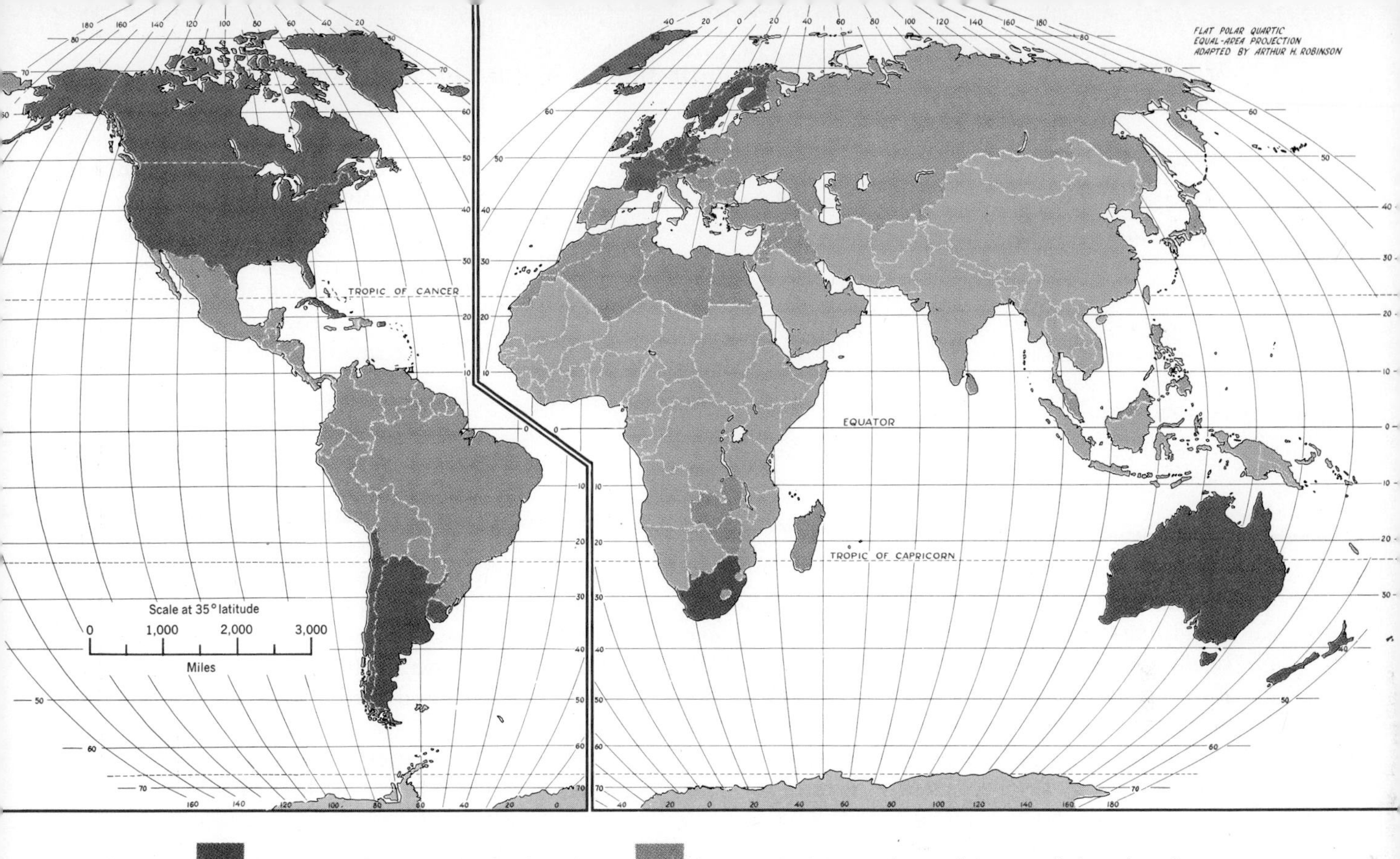

Commercial (high propensity to exchange)

Commercial-subsistence (intermediate propensity to exchange)

Subsistence with some commercial
(low or very low propensity to exchange)

Figure 1.3 ***World levels of per capita propensity to exchange.*** *This map suggests the degree to which individuals are inclined to purchase goods in home or foreign markets. The classifications are based upon real income (what a currency will buy in its own economy). Note that most Latin American economies are in the intermediate category, whereas most economies of Africa and Asia are in the low category. Commercial enterprises, such as mining in the Central African Federation, yield returns sufficiently high to lift some economies from the lowest to the intermediate category. Such returns are not always distributed to all participants, however, and to that extent the map may be somewhat misleading.*

Commercial economies

The reader doubtless has anticipated correctly that the countries with the highest per capita propensity to exchange, nearly all of which are politically independent, are the manufacturing and commercial nations of northwestern Europe and their younger offshoots in North America, southern Africa, and Oceania. Only the Latinized political units of Cuba, Argentina, Chile, Uruguay, and Puerto Rico, and special-status units such as the Canal Zone, Hong Kong, and Macao are highly commercial and yet not traceable to northwestern Europe as to prevailing culture. The Latin American political units have achieved their status by exchanging prodigious amounts of agricultural surpluses for needed finished commodities. All in all, the commercial economies account for nearly one-fifth of the world's people (Table 1.3).

TABLE 1.3

Allocation of population among respective types of economies

Type of economy	*Percentage of world population*
Commercial	20
Commercial-subsistence	33
Subsistence with some commerce	47

SOURCE: Classified from various reports and estimates of global real income.

Commercial-subsistence economies

The commercial-subsistence economies, involving about one-third of the world's population, are particularly conspicuous in Latin America, the Middle East including northern Africa, eastern Europe, the Soviet Union, and the island nations of the Far East. Politically they tend to be either entirely or partially independent; few are controlled completely from foreign capitals, and the times favor more self-authority for even these few.

Within the commercial-subsistence category is found a pronounced range of per capita propensity to exchange. The Soviet Union, Italy, Japan, and Mexico are among a group of countries that are almost sufficiently active to qualify for the higher commercial classification. In contrast, such countries as Egypt, Northern Rhodesia, Guatemala, and Turkey exhibit such a low per capita propensity to exchange that they are precariously near the subsistence-with-some-commerce category. The leading nations of the commercial-subsistence group indicate a per capita exchange propensity which is approximately five times as high as the least active countries of that group.

The effective areas, as defined earlier in this chapter, of commercial-subsistence economies are usually comprised of cores of commercial activity, whereas the outlying areas are dominated by subsistence conditions. Stated differently, per capita propensity to exchange tends to increase with proximity to effective areas. Such a tendency also is rather easily recognizable in subsistence economies that carry on some types of commercial activity (and nearly all do). It is discernible in commercial economies but frequently is not so vividly displayed there, because the outlying areas of such economies generally exhibit higher per capita propensities to exchange than is true of outlying areas in economies of any of the other two classifications. This is particularly true in the small nations of northwestern Europe.

Subsistence economies with some commerce

The nearly one-half of the world's people living under subsistence or subsistence-with-some-commerce conditions are found largely in the low latitudes of Africa and in eastern and southern Asia. There is a lower percentage of sovereign states in this category than in the other two, but current world trends towards nationalism are affecting even many of these, however deficient they may be in the wherewithal for existence that a viable state should have. Among the large countries that do contain the basic ingredients for raising their levels of economic activity are those two giants, Communist China and India, and such sizable countries as Indonesia and Pakistan.

As suggested in the title of this classification, the people involved depend less upon world, regional, and local markets for sustenance than upon their own abilities to produce directly from the natural environmental conditions of their immediate vicinities. Their per capita cash income is much lower than in either of the two other classifications. Their taste of modern commercial life is limited essentially to opportunities afforded in a few seaport or rail cities. Most of them live a hand-to-mouth existence. They make up the lion's share of the world's underfed, ill-clothed, ill-housed, and yet rapidly multiplying inhabitants about whom so much is now being written in both scholarly and popular literature.

Man has at his command the means through which to transform such conditions into something that, by twentieth-century standards, is usually considered much more desirable—in other words, to lift these human beings out of the semianimal existence in which they now find themselves and enable them to live much better in terms of modern conveniences and material goods. The basic question is, "Who is to do the job?" Outsiders, whether for profit, or for political reasons, or out of altruism? If all responsibility is assumed by strangers, have members of such low-level economies basically gained? On the other hand, most members of such economies have neither sufficient capital nor know-how to do the job themselves. The answer appears to lie in a combination of marked determination and rigid short-term planning on the parts of such economies with technical and financial aid from their more fortunate world neighbors. The two largest nations in this classification, Communist China and India, have adopted just such measures with varying degrees of success, as we shall explain in more detail in the next chapter.

CLASSIFICATION BY LEVEL OF ECONOMIC DEVELOPMENT

Background

The Second World War and its immediate aftermath marked the *coup de grâce* of European colonialism as a major movement. In eastern and southern Asia, Japan humiliated the colonialist nations temporarily but effectively before going down to ultimate defeat. In the wake of that humiliation, appeals were made by local leaders to end the movement, and in large measure it was done. The once all-powerful colonialist nations, weakened by two world wars and outdistanced economically by larger, younger, and more powerful countries, could either withdraw, resist, or compromise. The wiser ones chose a combination of the first and last of these alternatives; others futilely chose the second.

Twentieth-century Concern with Underdeveloped Economies. The attitude of the world's leading nations toward the Asian and other outlying areas has changed abruptly in recent years. In the heyday of colonialism, both the political dependencies and the independent but economically weak nations were regarded as objects of exploitation by the more powerful nations. (They were scarcely regarded at all by that sleeping giant, the United States.) Abruptly, a new-found interest in these areas has taken form in the mid-twentieth century—an interest stemming partially from the anticolonial movement, partially from a heightened sense of responsibility toward these areas by the former colonialist nations but also from the cold war, which has overshadowed in magnitude even the rebellion against colonial rule. The rapid growth of the Communist bloc of nations—a growth generally coincident in time with the fundamental causes and aspects of the anticolonial movement but not otherwise intrinsically related to it—has resulted in a grim struggle, as yet undecided, between that bloc and non-Communist countries acting under the general leadership of the United States. The cold-war struggle began in earnest after the last world war, with both groups of participants eyeing warily not only each other but also the areas around and between them—the Soviet Union and its cohorts, by all appearances and by announced intent, in order to transfer these areas to the Communist way of life, and the United States and its allies to preserve at least the political *status quo*. Thus the heretofore casually regarded political units along the rim of Asia, in Africa, and, to a degree, in Latin America almost overnight have become objects of concern.

Importance of Location near the Iron Curtain. In this cold war, all areas are of concern to both groups of participants; but those along the outer periphery of the iron curtain are regarded more closely than are the others, for these are in the immediate paths of the outward-reaching Communist bloc. Somewhat more attention, therefore, has been accorded to them by cold-war leaders than to the outlying areas farther removed from the iron curtain.

Roles of the League of Nations and the United Nations. As has been suggested, twentieth-century concern with the welfare of outlying areas is not wholly attributable to the anticolonial movement or to the cold war. It has roots also in other movements and changes in outlook, perhaps most notably in man's increasing awareness of his responsibilities for his fellow man. One result of this awareness has been the creation, in this century, of the League of Nations and its successor, the United Nations. These organizations, however imperfect when compared with an ideal, represent man's first attempts to place reasoned, collective thought and negotiation above the calculated interests of single nations or blocs of nations, and to do this on a continuing basis by way of a permanent organization. Their several temporary and permanent representatives, committees, agencies, and other suborganizations are engaging not only in the more highly publicized efforts to arbitrate disagreements but also, without fanfare, in the much more difficult and laborious tasks of inventorying the world's people, cultures, and natural environments, and of applying to selected representations of all three some part of existing knowledge for the betterment of human life.

Classification

Terminology. Although the task of inventorying the basic components of the world's economic geography is by no means complete—and indeed, in these rapidly changing times, it never will be—enough information does exist to classify economies crudely in at least two developmental levels: (1) those which are economically and technically advanced and (2) those which are economically and technically underdeveloped.[4] The classification could be, and has been, broken down into still more groupings, but these two have become generally familiar and serve satisfactorily to emphasize the basic ideas. Furthermore, as we have noted, precise data on quite a number of countries are lacking, and further breakdowns would be made on an appreciable measure of conjecture.

Meaning. Now that we have some terminology regarding developmental levels of economies, what is the meaning of our terms? The clue lies in the word *developed,* which is implied in the first category (economically and technically advanced) and stated in the second. What is a *developed* economy? Basically, it is one in which the natural and human resources are being utilized at a relatively high level of efficiency at any given time. Developmental levels vary, of course, from economy to economy, from culture to culture, from one set of natural environmental conditions to another. For a single country, a developmental level varies also over a span of time; for, as we have indicated previously, man's ability to maximize the utility of his surroundings increases more or less directly with enlargement in his fund of knowledge, including tools and methods. How high, then, should a developmental level be for an economy to qualify as economically and technically advanced? At present, we do not have a generally accepted, omnipotent model against which all economies are gauged, and neither do we have an iron-clad rule for such a purpose. Existing classifications rest at this point on carefully selected criteria that are generally accepted by researchers as indicative.

Criteria. A multitude of criteria have been employed to determine level of economic development.[5] Of these, two appear to generalize the results rather satisfactorily. The first involves the percentage of a country's labor force in agriculture, and the second

[4] Some authorities prefer to use the term *less developed* rather than *underdeveloped* to designate countries in the second category. Their reasoning is based mainly upon psychological reaction, i.e., upon the thought that inhabitants of such countries will not resent so much having their economies termed *less developed* as having them called *underdeveloped.* However, it would seem that the truly incisive and industrious minds of such countries—minds that want to get on with the work and not haggle about details—would not take offense; indeed, that these minds would see a kind of challenge in accepting, temporarily, the term *underdeveloped* for their economies inasmuch as the term implies existence of a potential. So we shall use *underdeveloped.* Furthermore, we shall use *technically* and *economically* as synonymous when referring to developmental level, since the one implies the other in practice.

[5] Including per capita indices of freight and passenger traffic, transportation-route distance, motor vehicles owned, telephones used, domestic and international mail flows, newspaper circulation, energy consumed and produced, foreign trade, urbanization, cultivated land; per unit area indices of crop yields, cultivated land, population density, transportation-route mileage, total population, birth and death rates, and infant mortality rates. This list is indicative rather than complete.

the per capita gross national product.[6] High percentages of labor-force allocation to agriculture suggest technical and economic underdevelopment by modern standards, as does a low per capita gross national product.

Reservations. Three reservations need be stated, however. In the first place, the term *development* refers to specific economies, the potential of which is not uniform throughout the world. In other words, if all economies were fully developed, they would not be yielding similar returns to all the world's inhabitants. Among the most outstanding differences in the potential of economies is in land, or natural environment. One country may have at its command a plethora of natural resources, and another almost none. Under such circumstances, the per capita production and income of the two countries, even if fully developed, would be at much different levels.

Secondly, a nation that is categorized as technically or economically advanced usually is not so throughout its entire territory. Its land area may well contain pockets of occupance were conditions are definitely underdeveloped, considered by any criteria. These usually are in the outlying areas, as we have used the term earlier in this chapter. Conversely, nations that are classified as technically or economically underdeveloped may well contain pockets of occupance that are technically and economically advanced—cities, plantation districts, mining areas, etc. Classifications are usually based upon generalized census data supplied for whole countries, and such generalizations mask regional and local variations.

Thirdly, economic and technical advance or underdevelopment does not necessarily imply *cultural* advance or underdevelopment. Each reader of this book doubtless can call to mind some person who is a "whiz" at mechanics or finance but who knows precious little about, let us say, the humanities or philosophy. So it is with cultures. Some contain more specialized knowledge in the precise disciplines, whereas others are accumulations of mental effort toward very different objectives. Still others, of course, are advanced in many and varied channels of learning. The point is that certain technically and economically underdeveloped countries may well be advanced in certain cultural components in which certain technically advanced nations may be deficient or even lacking.

[6] The value, per person, of all goods sold and services performed within a country over a given period.

The Classification. Figure 1.4 is a map of the world's economies drawn on the basis of percentage of labor force in agriculture and adjusted in the legend on the basis of per capita gross national product. Both indices yield rather similar results except in Chile, Argentina, Uruguay, and Japan, where labor-force allotment indicates technical advance but per capita gross national product currently indicates underdevelopment, and in Venezuela and Kuwait, where, if per capita gross national product were the measuring criterion, petroleum revenues would lend an aura of technical advance to otherwise underdeveloped countries. Poland also might qualify as technically advanced on a gross national product basis, chiefly because of the active manufacturing there.

A word of caution about interpreting the map: In a twofold classification such as this, many nations, especially in eastern and southern Europe, were included in the underdeveloped category because they did not quite measure up to the standards of the higher classification. Nevertheless, they are only a cut below Ireland or Italy, which barely qualified for the higher category. Others in the underdeveloped category, of course, are much farther down the scale of economic development.

Level of economic and technical advance compared with per capita propensity to exchange

The reader doubtless has anticipated a rather close and direct correlation between level of economic and technical advance and per capita propensity to exchange (Figs. 1.3 and 1.4). All the sovereign states at the highest level of propensity to exchange also are classified here as economically advanced.

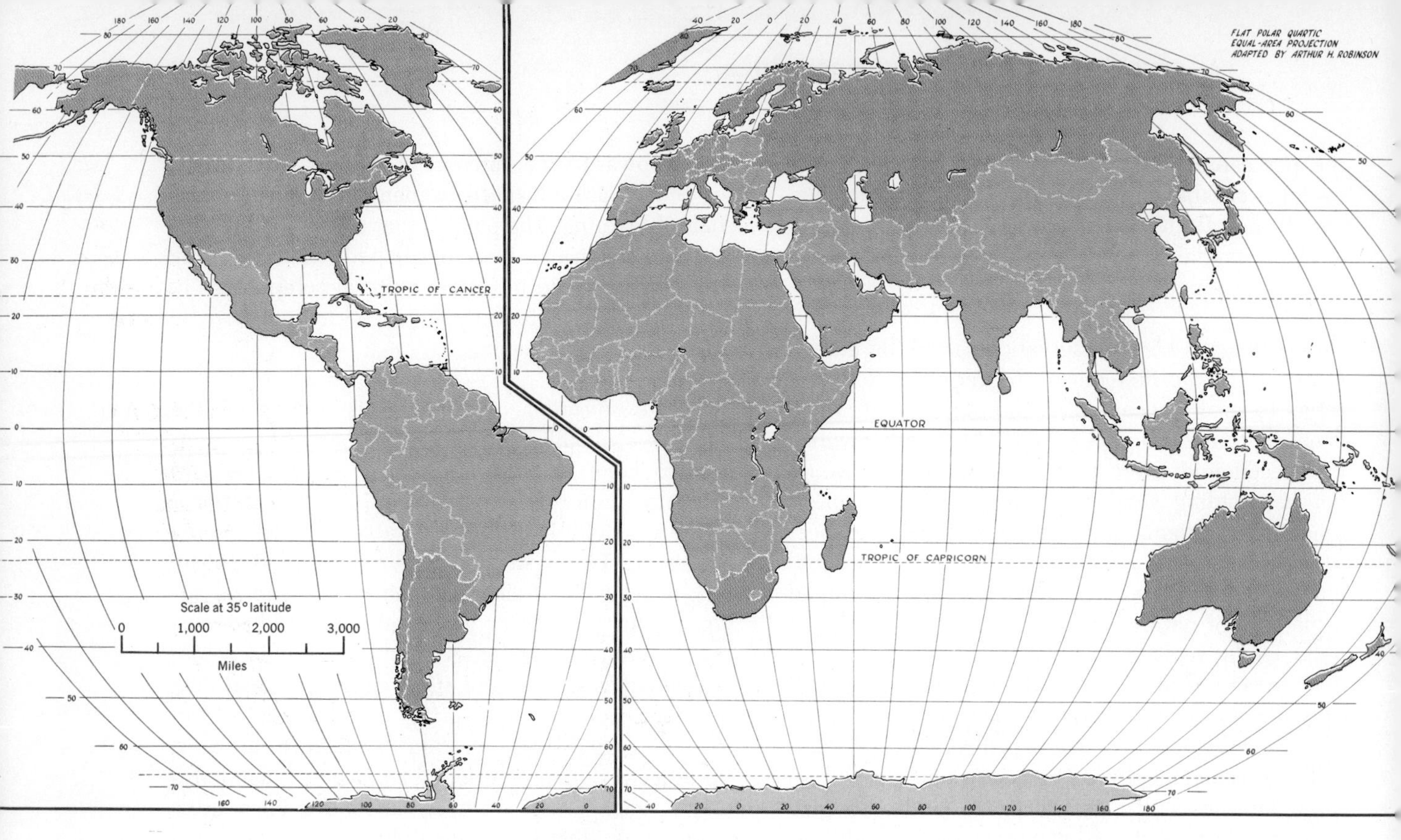

Technically advanced economies (with 45 per cent or less of their labor forces in agriculture)

Underdeveloped economies (with 46 per cent or more of their labor forces in agriculture)

Figure 1.4 ***The world's technically advanced and underdeveloped economies,*** *classified by per cent of labor forces in agriculture. A classification by per capita gross national product might place Chile, Argentina, Uruguay, and Japan into the underdeveloped category, and Poland, Venezuela, and Kuwait into the technically advanced group. Compare with Fig. 1.3.*

Only Italy, Japan, and the core sections of the Soviet Union are classified as technically advanced and yet not at the highest level of per capita propensity to exchange, and these are at the second-highest, or commercial-subsistence, level. Furthermore, all three nations are recovering from severe economic and physical damage of the last world war and may soon qualify for the highest category.

Except for isolated pockets of plantation or mining occupance, much of which is financed by foreign capital and maintained by foreign administrators, most of the economies at the commercial-subsistence and lower levels are technically and economically underdeveloped.

CLASSIFICATION BY POLITICAL-ECONOMIC AFFILIATION

Preliminary consideration of the control of the means of production and exchange can be on a two-fold basis: (1) economies of subordinate political-economic affiliates, mainly owned by, or controlled from, other countries—in other words, economies of countries which are not actually independent—and (2) economies of sovereign nations (page 12). In the second category, and by implication also in the first, we are interested in the degree of public and private ownership of key features of economies.

Economies of subordinate affiliates

Economies of subordinate affiliates are controlled mainly from their mother countries, with the rigidity and degree of that control varying with the status of the dependency.

Affiliates of Non-Communist Countries. Those non-Communist countries that are controlled almost absolutely from their mother countries, such as colonies and overseas territories, may be considered essentially as adjuncts to the economies of their mother countries. Other politically affiliated economies, such as overseas departments, which send representatives to the parliaments of their mother countries, may be considered as possessing some vestige of local autonomy. Although the amount of autonomy varies, it generally is not great because of the economic as well as political power of the mother country.

Affiliates of Communist Countries. Theoretically, no Communist nation has any significant political affiliate subordinate to it; all Communist nations operate independently. Controls from higher authority, notably from Moscow, do exist, however. They take their form not so much through governmental arrangements as through the monolithic Communist Party. Since this is the only legal political party in all Communist nations and since strong efforts are made from the Soviet Union to maintain the structure of that party as a single pyramid with the Soviet rulers at the apex, some of the Communist, non-Russian nations are indeed satellites of the Soviet Union. The ruthless stamping out of the 1956 Hungarian revolt by Soviet armed forces indicates conclusively not only that such control exists but that it will be maintained by force of arms if necessary. Despite these efforts at centralization, however, deviants do exist at the present time. Yugoslavia, Communist China, and Poland are outstanding examples of such deviants who, while stopping short of the kind of abortive revolution that was attempted in Hungary, are by no means ruled by Moscow.

Economies of sovereign nations

Among the world's sovereign states, ownership of the means of production and exchange is primarily public or semipublic. The United States alone stands out as a major nation where private ownership of such facilities is outstandingly championed, and even here public control and sometimes even public ownership are very much in evidence. In Communist nations ownership by the state is essentially absolute, although control of production and exchange is delegated in varying degree to the management of collective farms and of industrial and service enterprises. However, such seeming independence is largely theoretical, for these local sectors of the economy are controlled both through the hierarchy of government agencies and through the Communist Party organization, which is active at every level from the national to the local community. The non-Communist European nations, almost without exception, are characterized by government ownership or close control of key transportation facilities, particularly the railroads. Shipping and trucking lines and many channels of production are owned both publicly and privately, but those that are privately owned tend to be controlled very closely by their associated governments, so that government policy is important if not dominant in formulating and executing economic arrangements. The same generalization may be made of most of the smaller outlying economies of all hemispheres.

ECONOMIC DOMINATION BY TECHNICALLY ADVANCED SOCIETIES

Although they contain less than one-third of the world's people, the technically advanced countries tend to dominate economic affairs, using their methods and instruments of scientific and technological know-how, of capital accumulation, of a heightened standard of living, and—occasionally—of outright political ownership, for this purpose. Expressed more forthrightly, they tend to control not only the world's markets but also the means of production and exchange of much more of the world than they occupy. Of the four basic components of an economy, they possess most of the world's available capital, most of its labor that is educated or trained in tune with this Industrial Age, and most of its entrepreneurship. They are deficient only in land (with land interpreted here in its broadest sense as synonymous with natural resources) and must look to some of the underdeveloped societies only for some of this land.

The underdeveloped countries contain an aggregate of about two-thirds of the world's population and over 85 per cent of its agricultural population—its inhabitants who depend primarily upon agriculture for survival. Yet, with such a large agricultural population, these societies encompass only about one-half of all cultivated land, which they work with methods and tools that too often are antiquated. Although they account for nearly one-half of the world's labor force in manufacturing and handicrafts, most of their workers are in the latter category, as is shown by the fact that the underdeveloped societies consume less than 20 per cent of all the inanimate energy used each year.

Domination of markets

The prevailing control over the world's markets by technically advanced societies—and it is a pronounced control—is discussed at length in later chapters, notably Chapters 9 and 10.

Domination of capital accumulation

The technically advanced societies tend to control not only the majority of the world's markets but also the primary stocks of capital, whether of goods or money.

Domination in capital goods

The paramount position of technically advanced societies in capital goods is suggested by their very high proportionate consumption of the world's inanimate energy—over 80 per cent of the current total. It is further emphasized by the concentration of the world's means of production and exchange either within their own political territory or under their auspices in political affiliates and in foreign nations.

Domination in money capital

The degree of control by technically advanced societies over the world's money capital is also pronounced. The nature of accumulation of money capital is a nebulous thing, imperfectly understood even by the professionals, many of whom are in fundamental disagreement about it. This much, however, appears certain: money-capital accumulation cannot be wrought magically overnight in indigent nations. A continued momentum over a rather prolonged period is necessary for significant amounts of accumulation in these or any other nations. Psychological factors, such as a feeling of confidence on the part of other nations in the economy of the nation aspiring to accumulate the currency, or in sections of that economy, are as important as the actual gathering of some collateral or other assurance to support the credit forms of the money being accumulated. All this takes time, and technically advanced societies currently enjoy an investment of time that dates back several centuries, whereas the underdeveloped nations are just beginning to build that investment.

Most of the world's capital available for investment, therefore, is traceable mainly to technically advanced societies—regardless of whether that capital is in the form of public or private, direct or indirect, long-term or short-term investment, of outright financial aid, or of loans from such international organizations as the International Monetary Fund and the International Bank for Reconstruction and Development (the World Bank). (Lest the reader misinfer, these last are subscribed to by a rather large group of nations, both technically advanced and underdeveloped, and their loan privileges are available to any nation, underdeveloped or not, that can qualify; however, the major amount of actual money supporting these organizations comes from technically advanced nations, whose need for loans from such organizations, while definitely real, usually is not so pronounced as that of underdeveloped nations.)

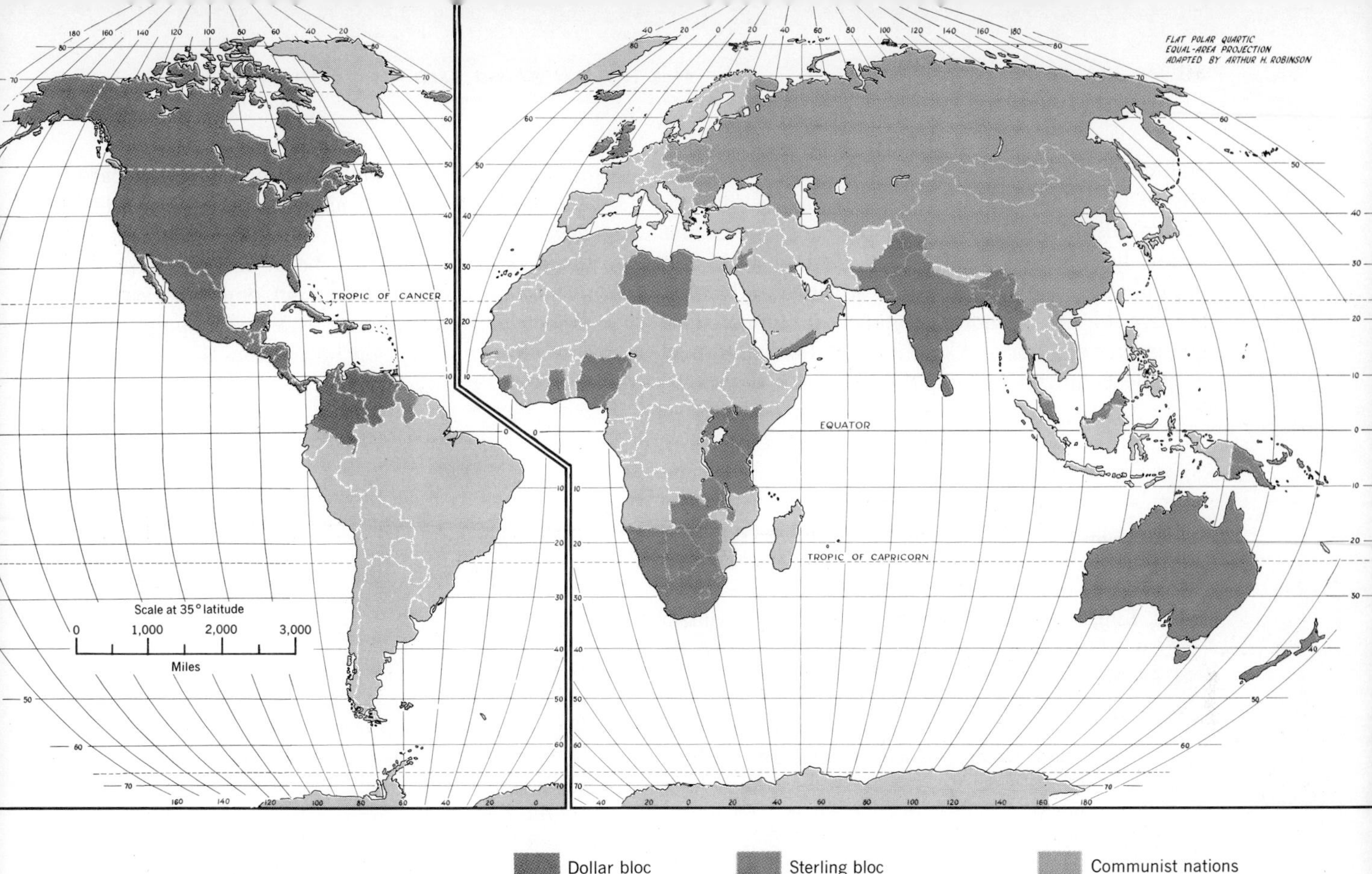

Figure 1.5 ***Major money blocs of the world.*** *A money bloc involves a group of economies whose currencies are freely interchangeable with the currency of the economy after which the bloc is named. Rates of exchange within the bloc frequently are based on that same currency. Some blocs, especially the sterling bloc, maintain a common reserve of hard-to-get foreign currencies upon which all members can draw in an emergency. The French community sometimes is also considered as a separate bloc, as are unions between smaller European nations and their overseas political affiliates. Kuwait sometimes is considered as part of the sterling bloc.*

Money capital for foreign investment or aid originates largely in the United States, Western Europe, and lately, to a much smaller degree, the Soviet Union. Although there are major exceptions (for example, West Germany, with no money bloc, who is an outstanding source of such capital), the geographical distribution of such investment coincides quite closely with that of major currency blocs (Fig. 1.5). The United States invests particularly heavily in the dollar bloc, the United Kingdom in the sterling bloc, and the Soviet Union in neighboring Communist countries. Thus the technically advanced nations dominate both the blocs and the investment.

Role of Communist nations

Communist nations, especially the Soviet Union, have spent their embryonic years in rapid capital accumulation. This has been done mainly through rigid central control in which every available part and parcel of profits from all economic ventures are returned to the economy as producer goods (an interesting exploitation of the workers, not unlike eighteenth- and nineteenth-century capitalist methods so harshly decried by that founder of modern Communism, Karl Marx!). As a result, the Soviet Union has "pulled itself up by its bootstraps" to preliminary stages of technical advance and is beginning to invest more capital—both money and goods—in neighboring Communist nations and even in some countries beyond the orbit of strict Communist control. Communist China now appears to be employing methods similar to those used in the early stages of Russian Communism. The results of this activity cannot yet be foreseen, particularly because government policy in Communist nations is subject to quick and unexpected change, but it would appear that their future roles in world investment will be important.

REFERENCES

Clark, Colin: *The Conditions of Economic Progress,* The Macmillan Company, New York, 1957. (Especially chaps. 1 and 11.)

Davis, Kingsley: "The Origin and Growth of Urbanization in the World," *The American Journal of Sociology,* **60:**429–437, 1955.

———: "The Unpredicted Pattern of Population Change," *Annals of the American Academy of Political and Social Science,* **305:**53–59, 1956.

———, and Hilda Hertz Golden: "Urbanization and the Development of Pre-industrial Areas," *Economic Development and Cultural Change,* **3:**6–24, 1954.

Ginsburg, Norton: "Natural Resources and Economic Development," *Annals of the Association of American Geographers,* **47:**196–212, 1957.

Hoselitz, Bert F.: "Nationalism, Economic Development, and Democracy," *Annals of the American Academy of Political and Social Science,* **305:**1–11, 1956.

Malthus, Thomas R.: *Essay on the Principle of Population as It Affects the Future Improvement of Society,* J. Johnson (St. Paul's Church Yard), London, 1798.

Nelson, Howard J.: "The Spread of an Artificial Landscape over Southern California," *Annals of the Association of American Geographers,* **49** (3, part 2):80–98, 1959.

The Objectives of the United States Economic Assistance Programs, United States Senate Special Committee to Study the Foreign Aid Program, 1957.

Rostow, W. W.: *The Process of Economic Growth,* W. W. Norton & Company, Inc., New York, 1952.

Thomas, William L., Jr. (ed.): *Man's Role in Changing the Face of the Earth,* University of Chicago Press for the Wenner-Gren Foundation for Anthropological Research and the National Science Foundation, Chicago, 1956.

Woytinsky, W. S., and E. S. Woytinsky: *World Commerce and Governments,* The Twentieth Century Fund, Inc., New York, 1955. (Especially chaps. 5 and 6.)

———, and ———: *World Population and Production,* The Twentieth Century Fund, Inc., New York, 1953. (Especially chaps. 2, 4, 7, and 13.)

2 TECHNICALLY ADVANCED AND UNDERDEVELOPED ECONOMIES

THIS CHAPTER IS AN ELABORATION AND A PARTIAL DOCUMENTATION OF ECOnomic or technical advance and economic or technical underdevelopment. Its title is somewhat of a misnomer, because our primary concern is with selected underdeveloped economies. The reasons for this emphasis are two: (1) presumably most readers are familiar with the outer trimmings of technically advanced economies inasmuch as they are active participants in such economies, and (2) later in this book much attention will be given to technically advanced economies, which dominate the commercial aspects of global consumption, production, and exchange of most commodities.

TECHNICALLY ADVANCED ECONOMIES

At least eleven features usually are observable in advanced economies: (1) comparatively small allocation of the labor force to agriculture; (2) comparatively high levels of per capita gross national production; (3) comparatively high levels of per capita consumption; (4) energy available in large amounts at low cost per unit; (5) diversified manufacturing that accounts for an important part of the labor force; (6) numerous secondary occupations; (7) specialization in both physical and mental labor and surpluses of both goods and services; (8) modern, complex facilities for transportation, communication, and exchange; (9) media and methods for experiment, and consistent application of the positive results of such experimenting to nearly all aspects of an economy; (10) an urbanization based upon production as well as exchange; (11) an internal range of economic conditions varying from definite advance to equally definite underdevelopment. Most of these are treated at some length elsewhere in this book, and here we shall confine our efforts largely to accentuating their relationship to economic and technical advance.

Labor-force allocation to agriculture and high per capita gross national product

The reader will recall that these are the main criteria upon which we based our separation of advanced from underdeveloped economies (Fig. 1.4) and they are included here for the obvious reason that they should head this particular list. Both these features should be familiar to the reader who is an inhabitant of a land with an economy usually classified as advanced. It remains for us to add that, generally, the proportion of labor force allocated to agriculture is declining rather dramatically in many advanced economies whereas per capita gross national product is on the rise. Among the most forceful of the many explanations is the familiar argument that human and animal muscle, operating within a rather limited horizon of traditionally acquired know-how, are rapidly being replaced by mechanical energy used with increasing efficiency and by more specialized and effective methods.

High levels of per capita consumption

Certainly the reader who lives in the United States, Canada, northwestern Europe, or any of the other countries whose economies are classified as technically advanced is well aware of the high level of per capita consumption in his country. Individuals living in certain technically advanced economies have well over fifty times as much money to spend each year as do individuals in certain underdeveloped economies. Such a statement does not give adequate consideration of varying price levels among nations and allowances for goods produced at home in many underdeveloped economies, but it nonetheless serves to illustrate our point. We shall have much more to say concerning per capita consumption in the next chapter.

Availability of energy at low cost

We shall demonstrate in more detail in Chapter 11 that the world's technically advanced economies use a share of all energy far in excess of their share of all people—in other words, that their per capita consumption is much higher than is the world average. With increases in volume of energy production at any specific time, and with increases in know-how of increasingly efficient production over a span of time, the costs per unit to the consumer are reduced. The modern home has so many gadgets that it is veritably a factory, and the lady of the house, once tied to the kitchen range and the mop, is now largely free to give her attention to other matters—social, community, political, etc. (Whether this transition represents progress remains yet to be seen.) The modern factory in many cases consumes so much energy that it scarcely can be compared with the handicraft shop whence it sprang and which characterizes many economies, most of them underdeveloped, of the present day.

Diversified manufacturing

It has been said that a truly dynamic economy must be active in the production of primary metals (notably iron and steel), chemicals, textiles, and food. These are certainly prerequisite materials upon which further output is based. The output of fabricated products, transportation equipment, buildings, etc., is based upon primary metals; upon chemicals, an almost innumerable and rapidly growing list of diverse items; upon textiles, the output of apparel, upholstery, and related fabrics and nonfabrics; and human existence itself upon food. Perhaps we should add to this list the growing electronics industry, which, in all its ramifications, is assuming a pronounced importance in modern industrial output. An economy deficient in any of these industries would find competition difficult with an economy containing a complement.[1] This would be particularly true in wartime.

These five, however, are but the foundation industries. Upon them rest a marked number and variety of specialized activities, each of which has a definite destiny to fulfill in a modern economy.

[1] To those who think otherwise, particularly in respect to food industries, and cite the United Kingdom as an example, we answer: (1) although that country imports much food, it processes a large quantity of that food domestically, and (2) lack of adequate domestic food supply *has* been a handicap in the United Kingdom's recent ability to compete, as is partially evidenced by the long period of austerity and rationing after the last war.

Individual factories may specialize, but a truly competitive economy in today's scheme of things must have a diversified manufacturing structure.

Numerous secondary occupations

A recheck of the graph on page 10 will indicate the extent to which secondary, or service, occupations characterize technically advanced economies and do not characterize underdeveloped economies. The resident of a technically advanced country sometimes takes for granted the number or variety of services available for himself, his family, even his dog and cat.

Specialization

The presence of secondary occupations is made possible largely through specialization and consequent surplus production in the productive occupations; and, once brought into existence, the secondary occupations themselves have become highly specialized. The trend, which is continuing, is based on the very simple idea that a specialist can do a job better and, in the long run, less expensively (especially when aided by a machine) than can the generalist. So the Jack-of-all-trades, the "Johnathan O" of A. A. Milne's whimsical child's verse, is disappearing in technically advanced countries but is very much present in underdeveloped societies.

Transportation, communication, exchange facilities

The chicken-or-egg analogy can be applied aptly to the evolution of facilities for production and for liaison. Did higher production result from, or cause, increasing efficiency in transport and communication? We shall never know for certain; both production and exchange appear, like Topsy, to have "growed" as the Industrial Age itself emerged from an embryo. Whatever the cause, facilities for exchange and communication are highly developed in technically advanced economies and usually not so highly developed in other economies—except in some that long have been political and/or economic colonies and thus have benefited from the colonial system (a system that all too frequently is denounced today as something wholly sinful rather than something that had a rather logical place in the evolution of political and economic affairs).

Experimentation

Modern production is based upon demonstrated results—whether in factories, on farms, in transportation, in clerical offices, or in any of a sizable list of additional economic ingredients. Although the chemical and electronic industries lead in this respect, most dynamic industries reinvest substantial portions of their gross returns in research. The net result is a continuous change in methods and tools—an unceasing adoption of something just a little bit better. Assuming general stability in an economy, we may take the place of such change as an indication of the degree to which that economy is vibrant and strong, and intends to remain so.

Urbanization

We have indicated in the preceding chapter that more and more of the world's people are going to be born or are being born in metropolitan areas, cities and towns, and that the vanguard of this trend can be found in technically advanced economies. Before the Industrial Revolution, such cities as existed usually depended largely upon surrounding countrysides for existence—they were mainly exchange centers, housing a few artisans who provided the "something extra" for the lucky who could afford to buy their wares. Modern cities in technically advanced lands are still exchange centers—retail and wholesale trade account for sizable portions of labor forces in very many large and small urban units in such lands—but they also generate a large measure of their own production. Such production, of course, comes appreciably from the many factories, large and small, which chambers of commerce seek as eagerly as miners of the old West once sought gold—and for the same general reason.

Range of internal conditions

This point is included chiefly for reemphasis, inasmuch as it has been presented before. Economically and technically advanced nations are not advanced

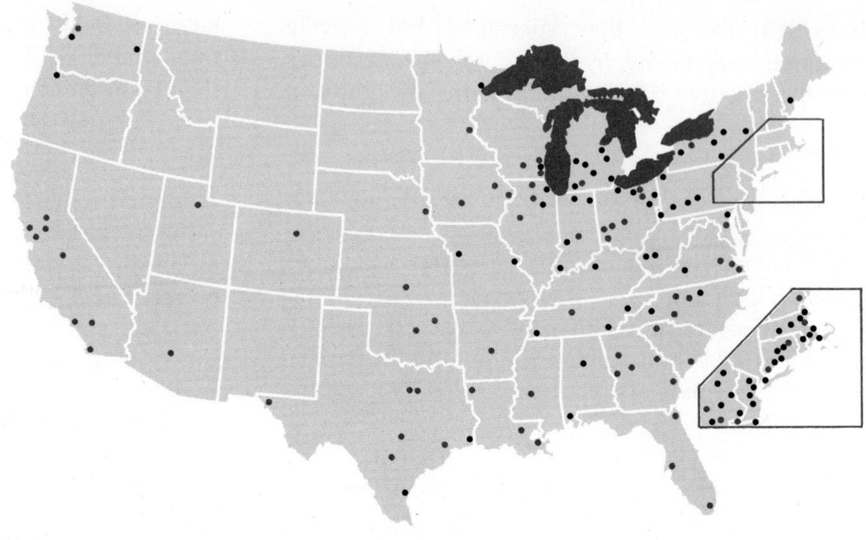

Figure 2.1 ***Unemployment in selected places of the United States in January, 1959.*** *The brown dots show places where unemployment was only slightly above normal, and the black dots show places where unemployment was considerably higher than normal. This map appeared during a time of slight recession in the United States economy. Note the large number of places in the manufacturing belt, which scarcely can be classified as technically or economically underdeveloped. In contrast, many places of consistently low living standards, such as the remote sections of the Appalachian Mountains or some Indian reservations, are not shown. In other words, this map shows temporary change in* status quo *rather than underdevelopment. The two conditions should not be confused. (After* Area Labor Market Trends, *U.S. Department of Labor, January, 1959)*

in all their geographical parts but contain many internal areas of definite underdevelopment—recognizable in the urban and rural slums dotting the landscape all too frequently. Such sore spots are beginning to prove somewhat embarrassing, and some technically advanced nations are giving them increasing attention.

There is a fine point for consideration in this respect: We ought not to confuse areas experiencing *temporary* stress—let us say, areas suffering because of short-run decrease in demand for their product specialties—with areas which, on a long-term basis, either have never been developed to the limit of their capabilities or are experiencing a long-term decline from previously reached developmental levels. A map published not too long ago during an economic "turndown" in the United States listed Detroit as one of the several areas experiencing stress (Fig. 2.1). This, of course, was true—but only because people temporarily weren't buying motor vehicles as feverishly as previously. This type of stress is very different from that found on many Indian reservations, for example, which are on perennially low levels of income and development. There is, of course, an overlap in the two concepts, but they basically are separate and distinct, and need to be recognized as such.

UNDERDEVELOPED ECONOMIES

At least one branch of economics—the institutionalist branch—maintains that an economy cannot be satisfactorily isolated from the remainder of a society, even for observation; it is only one aspect of a society, one that contains many other social institutions, and hence it cannot be judged apart from such considerations as individual and social values. Whether this is true of economies of technically advanced nations has been the focus of considerable debate. There is some evidence, however, that economic affairs in underdeveloped economies, with their varying degrees of subsistence living, are almost inextricably interwoven into the fabric of total human existence there.

This point has been emphasized in the discussion that follows by Paul G. Phillips, an authority familiar not only with some native Indian societies of the United States but also with a wide range of underdeveloped countries beyond our national borders:[2]

In underdeveloped economies, human beings gain a living by direct means. They often actually gather, cultivate, process, store, and then use the products upon which they subsist.

Dearth of markets

Generally, in such economies, pricing and market systems do not enter actively into living and making a living. There is less exchange of products and services than in technically advanced economies, and communication and transportation facilities are comparatively rudimentary or even lacking. Although there are very few, if any, places on earth where manufactured products are not sold (the sun never sets on carbonated drinks), the amount of currency that is circulated in underdeveloped economies is relatively insignificant, and there is a reciprocal predominance of trading and barter. Central financing and fiscal contracts figure relatively little, and the average person may see only a few cents or a few dollars—or their equivalents in local currency—in a year or even a lifetime. Some inhabitants of underdeveloped countries, however, are remarkably astute and discriminating buyers and excellent and skilled entrepreneurs in terms of their own cultures and values. Some have gone to lands of opportunity and established highly active and profitable commercial systems, and many have made fortunes, as have Indians and Arabs along the eastern coast of Africa. Almost every country has its enterprising people who can be traced to the indigenous inhabitants of an underdeveloped country as well as to commercial enclaves implanted from the outside.

Varying degrees of mobility

Inhabitants of underdeveloped lands appear to have combinations of strange and seemingly inconsistent tendencies in respect to mobility. While some of

Three grave problems in underdeveloped economies are filth, disease, and ignorance. A street in the village of Robat Karim in Iran; the polluted water in the foreground is the supply for the village (International Cooperation Administration).

[2] This material and that concerning southeastern Asian tribes, Laotian rural villages, and the Iranian tenant farmer are invited contributions to this book by Dr. Phillips, Chief of the Latin American and African Branch, Community Development Division, International Cooperation Administration.

them may seem rooted to the spot, others are highly mobile and move quickly and eagerly in response to the hope of relatively small economic reward. However, underdeveloped people are generally little inclined to move, except for such seasonal migrations and transhumance as may take place among tribal and fragmented nomadic groups. In village cultures a family head may travel once every year to once every ten years to the neighboring regional city, while some men and many women may travel only to the neighboring villages. Naturally, people who lead such restricted lives are bound to have very closely restricted horizons and outlooks. To them the world beyond is a vague and fearsome thing, while "development," if they know about it at all, may give them an uneasy and uncertain feeling. They tend to cling to tradition and locality for reasons of security (fear) as well as lack of opportunity.

Difficulty in generalization

However, few categorical statements can be made about underdeveloped people. There are more or less combinations, types, and stages of underdevelopment, which must be defined in terms of the level of welfare at which the majority of the people live. In other words, economic underdevelopment is a human condition in which too many people within an area have neither the sufficiencies of life nor the opportunity, means, and motivation to secure them. Its real causes are obscure and not well known. Numerous attempts have been made to explain it, but most of these efforts have resulted only in an enumeration of the superficial symptoms and factors associated with or related to it.

SOME THEORIES OF UNDERDEVELOPMENT

Higgins[3] presents one of the most complete reviews of general theories of underdevelopment. He calls attention to the fact that there are at least two subdisciplinary concepts of economics: equilibrium economics and development economics.[4]

Equilibrium economics

Equilibrium economics is economics in the usual sense of classical economics based on the fundamentals of the market and the laws of supply and demand. The well-known basic premise is that market supply and demand always control and equalize the flow and distribution of goods, and that there is a continuous tendency for supply and demand to return to a balance that represents the greatest benefit to the most people. Higgins points out very significantly that this type of economics may well be valid only for western Europe and the United States during the nineteenth century.

Development economics

The other great branch of economics is just now coming into being and is associated with an increased understanding of the economics of backward societies. It is called *development economics* by Higgins, because out of a closer study of backward people must come theories and practices of planned economic societies.

In the backward societies, the results predicted by classical economists are often diametrically wrong.[5] For example: An increase in wages sometimes creates less, rather than more, demand for jobs in underdeveloped economies; a rise in price

[3] Benjamin Higgins, *Economic Development: Principles, Problems and Policies,* W. W. Norton & Company, Inc., New York, 1959.

[4] Note by the author of the text: The institutionalist school of economic thought would be included in development economics as explained here.

[5] Note by the author of the text: Indeed, this frequently is true in economically advanced societies, although not usually in the same sense as here applied to underdeveloped economies. An economically advanced economy currently does not rely wholly upon market balance of supply and demand but manipulates both supply and demand to secure certain moral, economic, and political objectives. Witness, for example, subsidization of agriculture and shipbuilding and repair in the United States, which outwardly champions perhaps loudest of all nations the laissez-faire aspects of classical economics. At the other pole, the Soviet Union manipulates closely internal markets, all of which are state-owned.

of products may or may not stimulate more output; an increased amount of land made available to farmers may or may not induce them to farm more land than before. On the other hand, backward people sometimes exhibit high motivation and great energy in seeking income advantage. Laborers often will travel long distances for a relatively small wage increase and work long hours under extremely hazardous and uncomfortable conditions for small wages.

The reasons for these seemingly perverse and anomalous reactions are not at all clear, but they evidently are associated with sociopsychological factors such as value systems, feeling about status, individual prestige, and other noneconomic phenomena. Certainly the basic assumption of classical economics that human wants are insatiable does not hold in many cases around the world and throughout history.[6]

As pointed out in a recent African study,[7] caution must be exercised at the time when underdeveloped people are apparently seeking change unreservedly and undergoing change at a rapid rate. In present-day Africa there is drift to newly built urban centers, incorporation of Africans into large-scale schemes, heightened levels of involvement in world trade, increase in number of schools and school populations, nationalistic movements, constitutional reforms, and exposure to, and adoption of, some other European traits. Yet, despite all this and more, there is strong adherence to antecedent tradition. Beneath the innovations are preexisting cultures which are, and continue to be, functioning realities. The power of tradition is manifested everywhere, and at every turn affects economies. There are the pulls of tribal affiliations cutting across present (often artificial) country boundaries, contests between tribal leaders and politicians of the new country governments, contests between parliamentary procedures and indigenous methods of reaching decision. In the economic sphere, problems are encountered when tribal agricultural work patterns are transferred to industry, when the tradition of wealth sharing is confronted with the profit motive, when traditional family and clan social customs encounter systems built on individual initiative.

Geographic determinism

One theory that Higgins discusses is called by him *geographic determinism.* (Geographers would call this *environmentalism* or *environmental determinism.*) It is the old controversial idea that the tropics are detrimental to zestful living.[8] The conclusion is that there is little, if any, demonstrably irreparable

[6] The author of the text would add these two qualifications: (1) the assumption that human wants are insatiable is not limited to classical economics; and (2) although the immediate wants of any individual or group may be easily satiated to the point that, for example, he may stop work until his savings are all gone, there is appreciable evidence that, as societies develop and as individuals become aware of the possibility that material things can be owned or otherwise made available to *them,* their wants for such commodities increase. Certainly it is unthinkable for a resident of an underdeveloped country who earns, let us say, some $15 a year, to consider ownership and maintenance of an automobile. So an automobile is simply not a part of his dream world. This is not to say, however, that it will *never* be a part of his dream world—or, at least, that of his son, or grandson, or great-grandson. The statement made in the text above has been included so that the student can read two viewpoints that are not completely in harmony; however, the author does not alter his position that human wants are insatiable, even though some of them may be temporarily dormant and may require some sort of outer stimulus to awaken them.

[7] "*Africa,*" *Study prepared by the Program of African Studies, Northwestern University, U.S. Senate,* Committee on Foreign Relations, 85th Cong., S.Res. 336, and 86th Cong., S.Res. 31, no. 4. Distributed by Melville J. Herskovits.

[8] Note by the author of the text: Actually, environmentalism is applied other than to the tropics and holds basically that the physical environment is a strong molder, if not a determinant, of human activities in any area. However, human beings, including professionally trained minds, are faddish. Once we thought nature all-powerful. Now, it seems at least to this author, we ascribe too much to man's potential to overcome nature. We cannot escape some measure of environmentalism; and a partial disagreement with Higgins as reported above is hereby registered. Perhaps the tropics can be made very livable; but will this not involve tremendous capital outlay in air conditioning and moisture control—much more than now is allocated to summer cooling and winter heating in the middle latitudes? Perhaps we *can* grow crops beyond the latitudinal limits nature seems to have established, but at what price? Nature may not *determine* our living or way of life, but, make no mistake about it, she is there to be coped with.

A mounted malaria-eradication team with their spraying equipment in South Vietnam (International Cooperation Administration).

effect of the natural environment on productivity and no insurmountable reason why advanced economies cannot be established in the tropical parts of the world.

Dualism

Another theory is called *sociological dualism.* (It might as well be called *economic, political, cultural,* or *geographical* dualism.) This is the existence, resulting from invasion or indigenous growth, of an affluent and economically and socially advanced controlling group side by side with an amorphous mass of underdevelopment. The elite group may be associated with an indigenous royal family (as in Cambodia), clusters of traders (as in Mozambique), landlords (as in Iran), imported colonialism (as in the Cameroons), locally evolved capitalists (as in Japan), or imported management (as in Ethiopia). There may be social differences along class lines (Cuba), language differences (Peru), other cultural differences (numerous examples), and/or combinations of these. However constituted, the elite tend to be located at the central city, with branches in the principal market towns, while the underdeveloped people are scattered over the remaining inhabited portions of the country.

From the standpoint of historical development, there are two main forms of dualism: (1) a type in which the advanced economy is an invading force, causing a breakdown and a certain measure of disintegration to the indigenous economy, and (2) a type in which the advanced economy grew up indigenously within an elite group which established the system, complete with its connections to foreign economic organizations. Representative examples of the former are found in the Philippines, where effects of the Spanish invasion were inherited by the United States, and in former French Indochina, where the effects of the French colonial invasions still persist under independence, although grafted closely to the local elite family patterns. The second form of dualism has been called the *ingrown type.* Several theories have been formulated to relate cultural patterns with sociopsychopolitical fea-

An elementary classroom of Masai children in Kenya (British Information Services).

tures. One of these deals with the *achievement factor,* which postulates that different peoples have different capabilities or tendencies to perform work vigorously and efficiently.[9] Supposedly underdeveloped people have a lesser achievement factor than developed peoples, and for this reason do not work as hard or as efficiently. Other theories stress that only a group that will strive to regain (or gain) status will exert the effort to achieve economic reform and advancement. Some writers attribute economic disintegration to the backwash results of colonial enterprise and exploitation, because of the "spread" effects of the advanced economic operation. These effects come from high turnover of labor, the practice of importing labor and concomitantly discriminating against local labor, and the discouragement of indigenous merchandising and manufacturing.

[9] D. C. McClelland, *Community Development and the Nature of Human Motivation: Some Implications of Recent Research,* paper read to the Conference on Community Development and National Change at the Massachusetts Institute of Technology Center for International Studies, December, 1959.

Circular causation

Population pressures, as they grow and increase, are known to bring about a reduction in level of living, simply because returns are diminished as natural resources are depleted and eventually exhausted in the face of a multiplication of population to support. When extractive industries are superimposed on such deteriorating economic areas and the raw materials thereby won from nature are exported, the domestic deprivation process is thereby speeded up. This condition suggests the *circular causation* concepts of Myrdal,[10] wherein evidence indicates that underdevelopment tends to aggravate itself, because those economic regions that are undergoing active advancement attract resources, management, and investment away from stagnant areas and thus intensify further the latter's stagnation. This works across international boundaries and has deleterious and discriminatory effects on backward people. The expansion of trade gives advantages to the more active areas, because they are able to produce and sell more cheaply per unit.

Isolated enterprises

Another theory[11] implies that economies retrogress or fail to advance partly because commercial enterprises are attempted only as isolated units. If an enterprise is associated with no complementary enterprises to increase buying power for its products, it will fail.

Necessity for more knowledge

There are numerous other theories concerning the reasons for economic stagnation, but none so far that offers satisfactorily complete explanations. Most discussions deal with the symptoms of underdevelopment rather than causes. In fact, symptoms are often mistaken for causes. Correspondingly, many of the so-called remedies for underdevelopment treat only symptoms and do not get to the basic causes. More satisfactory explanations will have to await substantially more study. One can say only that underdevelopment may rest mostly within the minds of the people involved, and within entrenched systems and customs. It is associated with an affinity for familiar things, and ignorance and fear of new things. It is associated also with a fear on the part of the masses of the elite, and with selfishness by that elite and insistence upon traditional privilege and advantage. Above all, there exists a general ignorance as to how to proceed to reform, regardless of sincerity of intention. One thing is certain: underdevelopment does not concern any one scientific discipline alone; it concerns all disciplines and ultimately may become the chief concern of some synthesizing concept such as human ecology.

[10] Gunnar Myrdal, *Economic Theory and Under-Developed Regions*, Gerald Duckworth & Co., Ltd., London, 1957.

[11] P. N. Rosenstein-Rodan, *Notes on the theory of the "Big Push,"* Massachusetts Institute of Technology Center for International Studies, Cambridge, Mass., 1957.

SOME EXAMPLES OF UNDERDEVELOPMENT

So much for generalizations concerning underdevelopment. We shall proceed now to more intimate glimpses of selected societies, some of them tribal, some of them village, and some of them national. In keeping with our primary theme that economic underdevelopment is more fully understandable if presented in context with noneconomic aspects of societies, we shall include intentionally selected noneconomic features that we feel are important. All societies and economies discussed in the remainder of this chapter are at the lowest level of propensity to exchange, as mapped in Fig. 1.3.[12]

Tribes in eastern and southern Asia

In the mountains, piedmonts, and plateaus of eastern and southern Asia lives a complex assemblage of tribal people. Their economies are based mainly on foraging and shifting cultivation, and the chief cash crop of the area is opium.

The people of the *Khamu tribe* inhabit the mountain slopes of Laos, northern Thailand, North Vietnam, and northward into the mountains of Yunnan (Fig. 2.2). These are the aboriginal people of the region. They are darker and shorter than the Lao who came into the area from China 100 to 500 years ago. Their language is a member of the

[12] They represent nearly half the world's people (Table 1.3).

Indonesian family of languages. They have tried to resist cultural integration with the Buddhists and the Lao, but the inevitable process of amalgamation is taking place, especially along zones of contact with the Lao.

The people of the *Meo tribe* live on the mountain tops and high plateaus in the same general regions in scattered settlements consisting of two or three to a dozen wood houses built directly on the ground. The Meo are relatively recent arrivals from the mountains to the north, which are within the present boundaries of Communist China. Their cultural and language ties are to the region extending north across the border into Yunnan, and they identify themselves with the Meo citizens in that area rather than with the Lao of the valleys, whom they tend to look upon as foreigners.

The people of the *Radi tribe* live on the eastern slopes and piedmonts of North and South Vietnam. They live in villages of long, thatched houses with bamboo and wood framing and split-wood and bamboo floors built on pole pillars with a 3- to 4-foot space underneath.

These tribes are animistic and shamanistic, practice part-time shifting agriculture, and supplement this with foraging and hunting for a living.

Agriculture. The shifting agriculture produces both glutinous and nonglutinous rice, maize, potatoes, and other vegetables. The forests produce wood, charcoal, fruits, stick-lac, wild game, skins, bamboo strips, neat packages of banana leaves (for wrapping food sold in the markets), and betel nuts, and special leaves for wrapping and chewing them. The Meo are large producers of opium, which is raised both in small mountain patches and in large fields of the high plateaus and mountain basins under a landlord-plantation-sharecropper-and-laborer system.

Trade. There is considerable trade among the tribal groups and between them and the Lao and Vietnamese. A peculiar feature of this trade is an institution and practice known as *Lam*. This means, briefly, that a person known as a Lam acts as an intermediary between the parties concerned. Usually the Lam is a Lao who comes from a village located so as to be accessible to both the tribal settlements and the outside markets. He is frequently a village or district headman. The tribal people come to the Lam whenever they have some items to trade or sell and procure from him the items they need. These are salt, clothing, iron bars (to take to the blacksmith to be forged into tools), cloth (black cotton broadcloth and locally made blue-black indigo homespun), soap, nails, flashlights and batteries, and such rare luxury items as kerosene and powdered coffee.

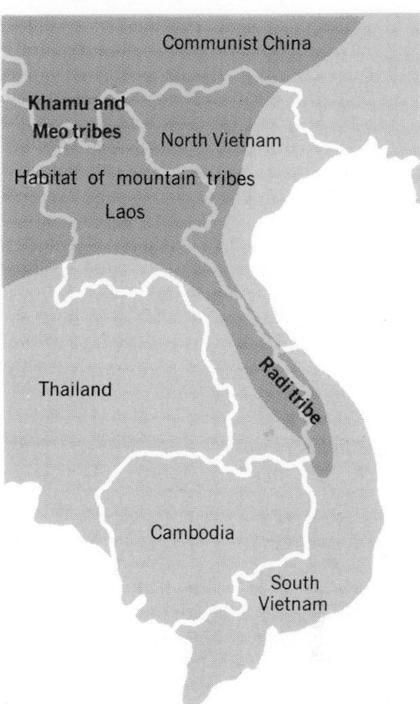

Figure 2.2 ***Location of selected tribes in eastern and southern Asia.*** *The gray color shows uplands and mountains, and the beige color shows lowlands.*

Opium is one of the principal items of Laotian foreign trade and important in the balance of foreign exchange. Formerly it was shipped by pack train over mountain trails to the north into Yunnan, whence it found its way to the cities and ports of mainland China. Processing and packaging took place at various points along the way. Now it is shipped out primarily by small planes that fly between the provincial centers of Laos to unknown points in Yunnan, North and South Vietnam, and perhaps other areas. Some is still traded to the Lao and Chinese middlemen who collect it and ship it by plane, and some is used for barter between the villages and tribal settlements. A considerable amount is used for home consumption.

The tribes still often refuse to accept paper money; they use their own silver currency in the form of small ingots, heavy neck collars, and bracelets. Burmese and Chinese coins are melted down in Luang Prabang and made into bars for trade with the tribes.

Other Sources of Income. Often the tribes lack goods to trade and try to meet their living requirements by working as laborers and servants. Groups of young men come together and frequently walk on long treks over the mountains for more than a week to reach towns and look for jobs. During these walks they sleep under the trees and eat whatever they can find. Usually the trips to towns to seek jobs take place after the farm patches are cleared in February, between weedings during the summer when the crops are growing, and again after harvest in November.

Imprint of Foreign Economy. The Radi tribe is connected with Vietnamese trading points. Radi life has many traditional features: warriors who carry spears and wear the halberd, the practice of sacrificing, and the ceremony of singing and drinking wine through a long cane tube. However, some Radi communities have gone through a period of disruption as a result of the establishment of coffee and rubber plantations in their landscapes by the French. For a time large numbers of Radi were used for plantation labor. Then with the subsequent reduction of plantation activity coincident with the independence of Vietnam, the Radi mostly have returned to tribal life. Many of the plantations have grown up in brush.

Current Change. Currently the tribes are undergoing a process of rapid transition and intermingling of culture with the outside world and are being subjected to the overtures and promotions of their Communist fellow tribesmen from the north. Although changes are taking place, the people hold on to some elements of their traditions with remarkable tenacity.

Laotian rural villages

Physiographically, Laos consists of the valleys of the Upper Mekong River and its tributaries, which are narrow and occupy relatively little area, and of the much more extensive, rugged mountains. The previously discussed Khamu tribe occupies primarily the mountain slopes, and the Meo live on the high mountain tops and plateau areas. The settlements of the Lao tribe, extending along the valleys, are part of an occupance centered in the northern part of neighboring Thailand.

Settlement. The Lao live in villages located for the most part along the river banks, but some settlements extend back to the mountain slopes and are accessible only by narrow cart trails and foot paths. The villages range in size from 10 to 400 households, with the average estimated at about 50. Village population averages about 250, ranging from 50 to 1,800. The average household has about 5 persons.

The Lao houses are built on wooden posts with bamboo-matting walls and thatch or bamboo-matting roofs. The floors are of wood or split bamboo. A few of the wealthier families have walls of wood and tile, and corrugated iron roofs. Under the floors there is considerable space, and here are stored odds and ends of farm tools, vessels, and spare bamboo poles. Here, too, the ubiquitous water buffalo (if the family owns one) has his stall, and a few chickens run in and out, together with an occasional pig or two. Inside the houses are furnishings consisting of a few mats, cups, and a coconut knife. Some houses have two rooms, a large one for receiving guests and eating and a small one for cooking. Sometimes there are one or two partitioned areas for sleeping.

There are local stores which sell such commodities as candles, cigarettes, matches, local crude tobacco, cotton thread, hard candies, beer, canned milk, salt, all-purpose pills, canned fish, blankets, shirts, trousers, soap powder, soft drinks, and miscellaneous items imported from Communist China and Hong Kong. Some villages have a blacksmith shop, usually operated by two men, one to work the bellows and one to hammer out the iron. The shops repair iron tools, and make the much-needed and constantly used machete and ax blades. Wood and bamboo are the universal building and craft materials, and tools for woodworking are indispensable. In the larger villages are found one or two tailors; both men and women work at the trade. They make trousers, shirts, sheets, mosquito nets, etc. Some tailors have been able to acquire foot-pedal or hand-operated sewing machines. One or two members of the community specialize in medicine. They may be classed as herb doctors or midwives. Children and women who live in the village near a traveled road sometimes set out for sale homemade wares such as cakes, noodles, or sugar cane. They place their wares on trays or in baskets and squat in groups along the roads or near the *Wat* (place of worship), especially on holy days, and sell and chat.

Leadership. Discipline and order in village life are maintained by social sanction. Law enforcement as ordinarily conceived in the West is locally unnecessary. The headman is elected for life by public vote and remains in office until he feels he is so old that he should step down and make room for a younger man. He settles family quarrels, witnesses agreements and business transactions, and gives general counsel. Qualities desired in a headman are temperance, industriousness, and adherence to the Buddhist way of life.

Six to ten villages form a canton (township). The canton head is the highest elected official. Each province has a governor appointed by the central government. The province is divided into county-sized districts, the heads of which are appointed for indefinite periods by the provincial governor with the approval of the central government.

Diet. The basic item of diet is glutinous rice. The average individual may consume about a pound a day, or about 150 pounds per family per month. About half of the families eat three meals a day, and half eat two meals a day. Some of the families are able to buy fish, whereas others have only the fish they are able to catch. A few people eat eggs occasionally, and most forage for coconuts, cucumbers, and fruit from time to time. Salt is purchased or bartered for with rice or labor.

For most families, the supply of rice lasts only from September or October, when the crops are harvested, until spring. Almost invariably the supply is exhausted by June, and the family then forages and works out during the period from June to September for whatever it can find to live. Meanwhile, new rice is growing.

Agriculture. Many of the peasant families own their rice fields, the average size of which is less than 3 acres. Many other farmers are tenants, paying from one-third to one-half of their crops as rents to landlords, some of whom also may be farmers. Farming operations are highly seasonal, coinciding with the monsoon rains. Most of the rice fields must depend on direct rainfall. Field work begins in May or June, whenever the rains start. The wooden plowshares are pulled by water buffaloes, or in some cases by human power. The buffaloes often are rented. Earthen borders are placed around the rice fields, which then are subdivided into basins preparatory to plowing. The soil, of course, is very wet. The plowing itself is done in a generally crisscross pattern and a somewhat lackadaisical manner, the farmer letting the buffalo go where he will.

After plowing, the patches are harrowed or dragged with crude wooden implements. As soon as water begins to accumulate in the basins, rice seeds are planted in small flooded beds. When the seedlings are mature, in about six weeks, they are transplanted. This is an extremely arduous, back-bending task. The work is done by both women and men in organized groups. One group picks the rice seedlings, cleans the mud, and ties the seedlings in small bundles with rice stems. Another carries the bunches to the basins, placing them in the corners. Still a third sets the plants.

The better rice lands have been occupied along the rivers and streams where the terrain is flat and where permanent borders and basins can be built.

The richer farms are located in these areas, and it is here that the tenant-farming system predominates.

Most of the small independent farmers live in the still-forested areas extending back from the streams. Here they follow a slash-and-burn system, cutting the brush and small trees in patches, allowing them to dehydrate during the dry season, and burning them just before the rainy season is expected. Many of these areas are extremely hummocky because of large termite and ant mounds and natural undulations. Dikes around the rice basins are very crude and temporary. The slash-and-burn system requires a great amount of labor, inasmuch as a new area must be prepared each year. After the crop is grown, the patches are left fallow until at least partially regrown in natural vegetation (about five years) and then slashed and burned again.

This process of clearing, slashing, and burning keeps families moving about within a restricted area. At first the moving is not complete but is more or less centered upon a fixed location. However, as the land becomes exhausted and populations increase, some families migrate to wholly new areas. There are still extensive untapped reserves of such forested lands that as yet are only sparsely settled.

Exchange. The rural economy is of the rice-barter type while the rice supply lasts; then it becomes largely a credit proposition, at which time borrowing from merchants begins. In Laos, as is true through most of eastern and southern Asia, Chinese expatriate merchants control and handle the local markets and do the trading with the peasants. They operate the local stores and act as buyers of rice for the large central rice mills and wholesalers and exporters. These Chinese merchants have become so integrated into the local economies that the villagers look upon them as necessary sources of supply, credit, and demand. They lend money for cropping and subsistence; repayment is made in rice at harvest time. The farmer, destitute when his rice supply gives out and "flush" at harvest time, is fair game and subject to exorbitant rates of interest.

Rice is traded for salt, fish, tools, clothing, and such services as the midwife's fee. It is used to pay rent for land, for the buffalo, and for the debts accumulated at the stores. Usually the store debts and rents take the crop, and the peasant family, only a month or two after harvest, enters into the credit phase of the year's operation. Home-prepared foods, vegetables, pigs, coconuts, chickens, and eggs also are sold on occasion. Meanwhile, the farmer supplements his rice income and rice diet with forest foraging yielding bamboo, mushrooms, herbs, birds, and small animals, some of which he consumes himself and some of which he sells to the merchants. Nearly everybody hires out to work for whatever is paid when the opportunity is presented.

Transportation. Almost all transportation within the daily living pattern is by foot. Food and water are carried in baskets attached to the ends of a pole balanced across the shoulder. Carriers develop a rhythmic dancing step that synchronizes with the swinging and bending of the pole. Surprisingly small men and women carry from 200 to 300 pounds long distances in this fashion. Shoulder poles are rigged to carry portable workshops, stores, eating stands, large baskets of fish, rice, pigs, sugar cane, wood, bamboo, charcoal, etc.

People who live in villages along the rivers use long dugouts, in which they paddle supplies in and products out to market. Some households own oxcarts and hire out to do hauling.

Motor trucks belonging to central merchandising concerns haul supplies out to larger villages and towns that are located along the roads. From these points the goods are transshipped by oxcart or by pole carrier to the villages.

Passenger travel is by foot, bicycle, and bus. Bus travel is very popular, and people often take a bus trip to Vientiane whenever they can scrape together the price of a ticket.

The agrarian economy of Iran and the Iranian tenant farmer

Another example of underdevelopment is found in Iran, a country of about 21 million inhabitants, of which some 18 million are farmers, farm tenants, sharecroppers, or farm laborers. There are about

60,000 occupied places in Iran, and approximately 40,000 of these may be classified as villages, some 50 as regional market towns, and 10 or so as larger provincial cities; there is one outstanding industrial (oil-refining) city, and there is one metropolitan center. The economy of the country is of the type usually associated in the West with medieval feudalism, in which most of the people live in rural villages and are bound to the land. An overwhelming majority of those people are chronically tired and frustrated—concerned at all times with getting a daily bite to eat. This is particularly true of the tenant farmer, to whose situation the remarks of this section apply if not otherwise specified.

Relevant Natural Features. Terrain and climate govern to some extent the distribution of agricultural land in Iran and consequently the distribution of the prevailingly rural population. From a narrow, hot plain fringing the Persian Gulf there rises a series of rugged escarpments that culminate in mountains extending from the country's northwestern boundary southeastward along the coast of the Persian Gulf and the Arabian Sea (Fig. 2.3). To the north and east of these mountains is a central plateau dotted with mountains and hills that are erosional remnants. The plateau, in turn, is bounded on the north by an arc of moderately high mountains circling parallel to the southern shore of the Caspian Sea and connecting mountainous clusters in northwestern Iran with equally mountainous Afghanistan. Beyond this arc is the low (below sea level) Caspian littoral plain, which is humid on the west but becomes extremely dry to the east. The remainder of the country is arid and semiarid, with the degree of aridity increasing to the southeast. Conditions attractive to settlement are found chiefly where irrigating water is available, and because Iran has no major waterways, most such water occurs in small, sometimes intermittent, rivers and streams located primarily in the northwestern half of the country. These descend from the larger mountain ranges, particularly from slopes receiving more than an average portion of the meager precipitation—slopes located both in the mountains bordering the central plateau and in the erosional remnants within that plateau. In the vicinity of the ancient city of Shiraz there is a winter-rainfall belt that produces grains and fruit without irrigation.

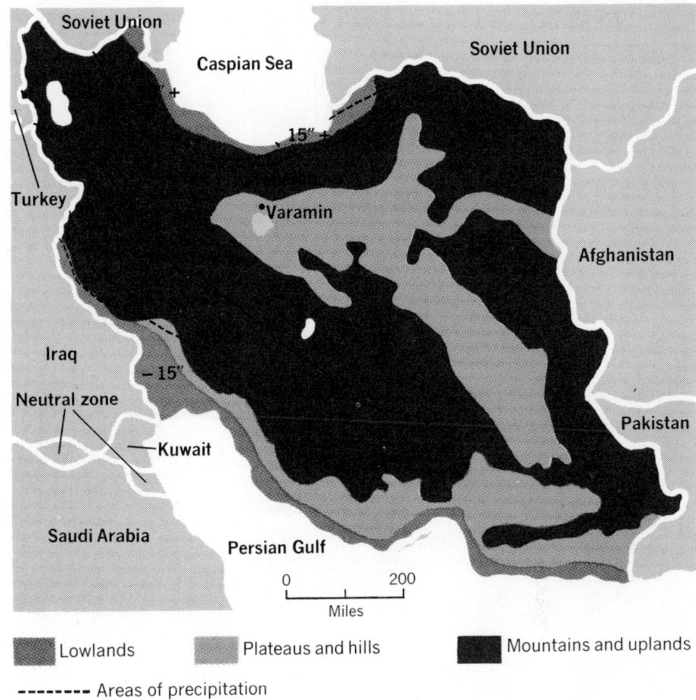

Figure 2.3 ***Selected natural features of Iran.***

Settlement. The farm villages are located primarily at irrigated spots along the rivers and streams or at the mouths of *ganats*, which are long galleries dug by hand into water-bearing gravels and marked by rows of shaft openings surrounded by circular piles of waste dirt and gravel. The agrarian villages have various patterns. Along the moister fringes of the Caspian Sea, they dot the flatlands rather evenly. There, each village is made up of a cluster of wood and thatch buildings surrounded by small kitchen gardens and enclosures for livestock. Radiating patterns of donkey trails connect them to the fields and to nearby villages. Other villages in the country are strung along stream valleys, being compressed by topography and water availability. In forested mountainsides, the comparatively few settlements are marked by small clearings and by columns of smoke where charcoal is being made.

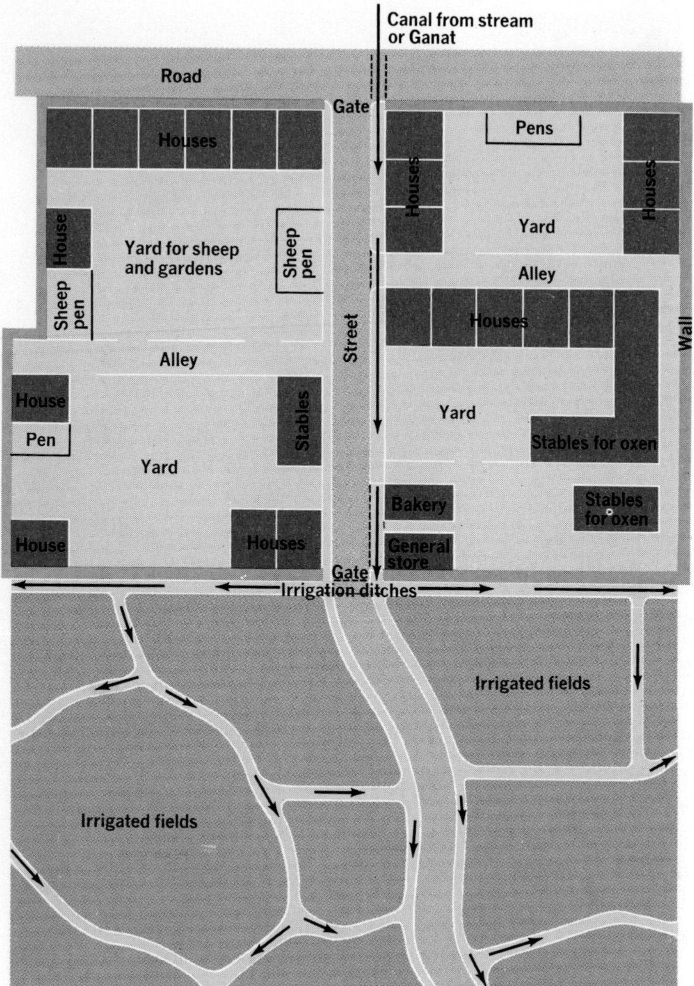

Figure 2.4 ***General plan of a village on the Iranian plateau.*** *This village is similar to the actual village of Varamin, 30 miles to the east and south of Teheran (Fig. 2.3).*

Housing Construction and Arrangement. On the central plateau, the dwellings of the tenant farmer are joined together in rows along narrow streets or around rectangular courts. Sheep, goats, donkeys, oxen, and sometimes even camels are kept in the courts. Oxen also are kept in adjoining compounds which are interspersed with small gardens, refuse heaps, and empty space. Surrounding all these are the fields (Fig. 2.4).

Individual dwelling units are usually constructed of adobe walls topped by cleverly built arched roofs of brick. Each unit consists of an open front room with three walls only, and perhaps a second room (Fig. 2.5). The arched roof covers the entire unit, which measures some 10-12 feet in length and 8 feet in width, and extends some 4 to 10 feet beyond the unit to form an open end. Here the cooking, eating, and group living of the family are carried on. On one side of the room is a clay or brick stove with a grill or sheet-metal top, and on the other there may or may not be some raised platforms and combination seat-tables of clay or brick. Some houses have a second room about 8 feet long and as wide as the house. Here the women remain in seclusion much of the time, carrying on handwork, mending, etc. This also may be the family sleeping room. Bedding consists of goat- and sheepskins which are rolled up during the day and spread out only at night. If the family is relatively rich, some old but remarkably durable rugs replace the skins. The separating wall between the two rooms is usually a partial one, extending upward only as far as the beginning of the arch. There may be curtains hanging over the passageway through the wall.

There are, of course, numerous variations of this house type. Some families have a living space of only 3 by 4 feet, and others have more than the average. The one described above is particularly characteristic of that of the farm tenant–sharecropper.

Village Organization. Each house, and the entire village and the surrounding farm land as well, is usually owned by a landlord, who may also own other villages and their land. Villages have remained in the same family for centuries. The business of the landlord may be transacted by a broker.

Each village is presided over by a mayor, called a *Katkoda*, who is the landlord's or broker's representative and boss of the village life, farm operations, and daily routine. His jurisdiction combines that of a foreman, mayor, judge, and lawgiver. He sees to the work of the tenants and the meticulous care of the irrigation ditches, oxen, and other properties of the landlord. He issues seeds, keeps records, requites work for the landlord himself, disciplines rebellious or recalcitrant tenants, discharges some if necessary, does the talking to visitors (the tenants often will not talk to strangers), makes the decisions, manages the harvests, assigns and reassigns land. He is generally obsequious to his superiors but arrogant toward those under his control. He has authorized prerogatives and functions defined by legislation. He is the key element in the management of the feudal economic system of Iran.

Village Laborers. Besides the farm tenants, there is in most villages a class of laborers and unemployed people. These live in fence corners, between buildings, and under trees. They sometimes are not organized as families but live as individuals, foraging for food in the refuse heaps and any other possible sources. They work when they can get work—often for the tenants—and stand ready to compete for any sharecropping opportunity or to take any sort of odd job. Because of this surplus of labor, numerous peasants are always competing with each other for each parcel of land. Any disagreement between the landowner and the tenant, or a protest by the tenant, is likely to result in the tenant's being displaced, because a substitute is always ready to take his place.

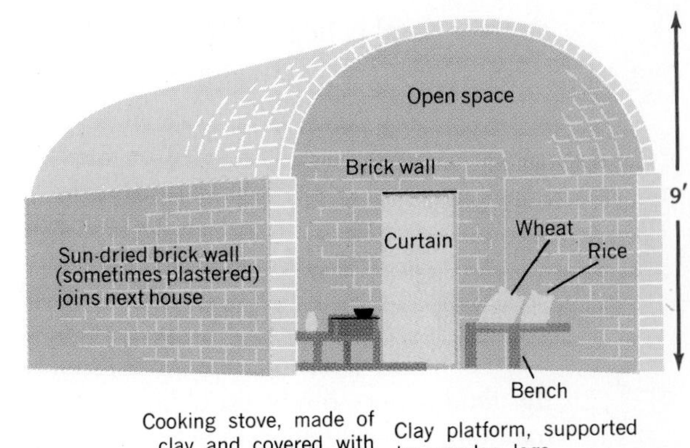

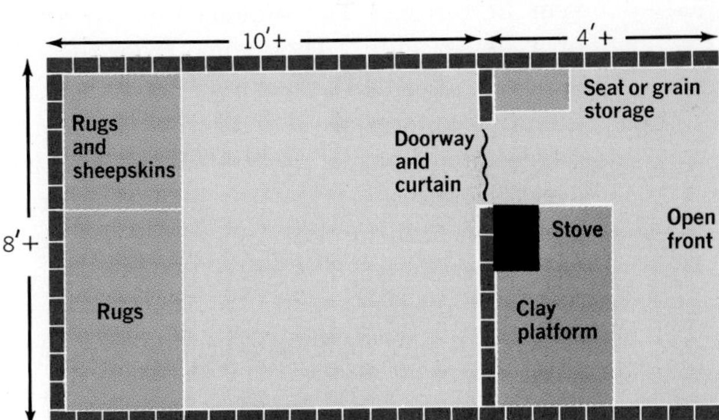

Figure 2.5 ***A sketch and plan of a house in a peasant village located in the Iranian plateau.***

The System of the Fifths. The system of the fifths is the basic sharecropping arrangement. By this system, the five major items needed for production—land, water, seed, oxen, and human labor—form the basis for proportionate division of the final product. The shares of the harvest are divided into fifths, each fifth belonging to the person supplying the corresponding production item. Thus, if the tenant can supply only labor, he gets one-fifth; if he has his oxen, he gets two-fifths; if he can get funds for credit to furnish seed, he gets three-fifths. The landlord always owns and furnishes the land and water, so gets a minimum of two-fifths. Most landlords furnish seed, and many furnish the oxen, although tenants with oxen usually can displace those with no oxen.

Usually the tenant's share is limited to labor, which means the labor of his entire family. In addition, he may be forced to go into debt to his landlord for the barest essentials of subsistence at interest rates often amounting to as much as 200 to 300 per cent. A common result is that the tenant owes the landlord his own share of the harvest long before it is produced and is obligated to pay in usury twice to three times the amount advanced to him.

The Landowners. The landowning families are usually of the large, extended-family type in which relatives combine under a single head who is customarily an older man. He manages the property for the entire family. These families frequently have one or more members as representatives in the Parliament. These are the so-called "100 families" that own virtually all of the productive land of the country. These families are in control of the governmental policy and business, and have successfully resisted thorough reform. Needless to say property taxes are miniscule.

Brokers. The sharecropper system is sometimes combined with a brokerage or middleman system that results in even more hopeless conditions for the tenant and his family. The landowners frequently lease their land to middlemen, who in turn lease it to the peasants. Under these arrangements, the landowners rarely visit their own holdings but maintain several households in villas with numerous servants and may spend a good part of an average year in Europe. The brokers tend to be members of a "lesser elite." They come from the cities, and may be described as business operators, not infrequently connected with larger flour mills, rice-wholesaling firms, etc. Some are full-time land managers. In any case, they are under pressure to show maximum returns, but sometimes are inclined to "play both ends." They may be given to chicanery in their dealings with the landowners and to cruelty in their dealings with the tenants.

Farming Practices. Most agricultural land is irrigated. However, many of the streams from which water is obtained are intermittent, flowing principally during early spring when snow is melting in the mountains and deficient or even dry during much of the remainder of the year. Under these conditions, planting occurs in time to take advantage of the peak water flow. Water from ganats is usually in permanent supply, and the growing season is longer.

Irrigation ditches are raised above the general level of the ground, and are maintained through the use of short-handled hoes. Plots of tilled ground are leveled and formed into small basins with dike borders. Each plot is flood-irrigated for grains and bedded with furrows and intervening ridges for row crops. The furrows are made with hoes or with oxen-drawn plows. In the fall an entire holding is plowed if the dike and basin borders are relatively low so that the topography is relatively uniform. Before irrigating, the dikes are built up again to hold water. Prior to seeding, the plots are dragged with wooden floats made of logs and poles and pulled by oxen, so that they are level once again.

Crops. WHEAT. Wheat is the principal grain raised under irrigation. Some is planted in the fall and some in the spring. The actual seeding is carried out by broadcasting, whereby the seeds are scattered by hand. Sometimes the seed is "irrigated up" by running water over it, and sometimes it is covered by a light dragging or brushing.

At harvest time, the wheat is threshed by flailing or trampling with livestock. The grain is winnowed, swept into piles, sacked, and stored in a village room under the watchful eye of the landlord's representative.

RICE. Rice-producing areas are found in the mild climate of the Caspian littoral, chiefly along the large streams with sustained flow. At the point where these streams strike the flat plain, water is diverted into canals, each of which usually supplies from ten to fifty villages. In the mountains, some rice-growing is found on the sides of canyons, in terracelike basins that are supplied by irrigation canals from sharply descending mountain streams. These fields sometimes extend to considerable heights on the canyon sides, the water passing from basin to basin by means of weirs.

Plowing for the rice planting is done in late winter and early spring, both before and after flooding. After being plowed, the land is leveled by hand or by a flat-board scraper pulled by an ox. The fields are flooded, and the final leveling is done with the aid of water, which acts as both a settling agent and leveling gauge.

Rice plants are started in small beds in the corners of the irrigated basins and are set out in the fields during the month of April. Women perform most of the transplanting work, a back-bending and strenuous job. The men keep them supplied with handfuls of shoots and work on the dikes, ditches, weirs, etc.

In rice culture, more of the work is done by hired laborers than in wheat culture. Many landlords simply hire labor and managers and pay wages, which range from 20 to 30 cents for a full workday. Many laborers are employed only during planting and harvest, thus realizing only two or three months of work in early spring, perhaps sporadic work during the irrigating season, and two months or so during the harvest. During the remainder of the year, they endure unemployment.

The harvesting of rice starts late in summer, at which time the irrigation water is drained away and the ground allowed to dry. The grain is cut by hand sickle and is threshed on the spot—either on hard ground or on canvases or blankets. After it has been winnowed, it is taken to the village headquarters, the shares are divided, and the commercial portion is taken to a rice-polishing mill.

OTHER CROPS. Barley is grown in places usually too dry for wheat. Production of barley is normally smaller than that of wheat but greater than that of rice. Some sorghum, known as *Duva,* also is produced. Essentially no maize (corn) is grown in any part of the country. In the market gardens adjacent to some of the cities and in the numerous smaller gardens of the villages are raised a variety of beans, okra, melons, and other vegetables, and some fruit as well.

Trade. Much of the landlord's portion of grain is traded and a small amount exported. A sizable portion is transported to central markets and warehouses, moving first by donkey or human back to loading points accessible to trucks, and thence to provincial mills or warehouses or to the cities. Some of the wheat is sold to stores in the villages and nearby small towns to be retailed locally. Part of this is milled in small village water-mills, particularly in northern Iran. Rice is a luxury item, channeled mainly into markets catering to higher-income groups. It is also highly prized by the country's many low-income residents, who try to serve it on special occasions that occur once or twice a year.

The traditional center of trade and merchandising in Iran, as it is in most of the countries from Africa to the Far East, is the bazaar. It is found in both small and large centers but is more elaborate in the latter. Physically, it is comprised principally of a series of stalls arranged in rows under one roof, with entrances opening to the center of town and back walls facing the roads leading to open countryside and to other centers. Adjoining the stalls is the traditional camel pen. Usually a bank is nearby.

Within the bazaar are displayed rugs, silverware, jewelry, shoes, tinware, enamelware, porcelain and chinaware, clothing, blankets, bolt cloth goods, yarn, wood articles, brassware, candy, perfume, nuts, grain, beans, rice, imported canned goods, meat, eggs, cheese, milk products such as mast (clabbered milk) and dried curd, spices, coffee, oils, olives, potatoes, seeds, flowers, and ironwork. There are shops for tinning, utensil repair, shoe repair, haircutting, knife sharpening, and many other goods and services—in short, commodities and shops to supply many of the wants of a society. Few of these goods or services, however, find their way to the tenant farmer.

Overview of the Landlord-Broker-Tenant System. The peasant of Iran is the foundation of the country's economic pyramid. His work and production furnish basic commodities for exchange. On the results of his productive labor are elaborated and differentiated the other occupations and levels of living.

The system is generally inimical to general welfare. However, there are instances of benevolent landlordism. One village of about two hundred families is owned by three brothers who reside there, manage the business personally, and deal directly with their tenants in an apparently kind and sympathetic fashion. The families farm about 500 hectares of land, with some tenants working as many as 20 hectares. The village has an elected council which conducts its affairs, a meeting house which has been built by the community as a village center, a school which all children of elementary age can attend. Decisions affecting the whole community are taken jointly after full discussion by all interested parties. There are community projects of cooperatively built roads, bridges, play spaces, windbreaks, etc. The people seem happy, free, and outspoken. The landlord brothers apparently enjoy the mutual understanding and confidence of the villagers, and there seems to be little dissatisfaction.

In contrast, a smaller village of thirty-five tenant families is located not far away from the one described above. Here, as a result of repeated inheritance and fragmentation, there are seventy-five owners. The people are desperate, hopeless, frustrated, bitter, and apparently ready to subscribe to any alternative that would perhaps offer some hope for their relief.

India and Communist China: awakening giants

We have glanced at technical and economic underdevelopment in small nations and societies. But what is its nature and how is it being dealt with in large nations? The following account[13] treats these and related questions.

Of the many nations now classified as underdeveloped, only a very few show promise of maintaining a sufficiently high rate of economic growth to release themselves from the fetters of underdevelopment in the near future. India and Communist China are the two largest nations now struggling to do so. Their combined populations amount to about two-fifths of the world's total. Both are led by vigorous, dynamic governments. The goals that they have set and their methods and rates of realizing those goals are of interest not only to other underdeveloped nations but also to the rest of the world.

Similarities. Many parallels are apparent in the physical and economic features that are given consideration in assessing the economic development of the two countries. The economy of each is largely agricultural and low in total productivity. Factory output currently is relatively unimportant in terms of national product, and much manufacturing is, in effect, handicrafts. Somewhat similar limitations are found in the availability of additional agricultural land and the more efficient use of existing land. However, roughly comparable and somewhat extensive mineral-resource supplies are available in both for the establishment of heavy industry.

Differences. But many contrasts also are apparent. Communist China is attempting a vast economic and social transformation within the next generation, basing its programs largely upon those previously instituted in the Soviet Union. And to implement these far-reaching programs, Chinese leaders have not hesitated to use the ruthless methods of a totalitarian regime with its close control of the individual. Although India shares with Communist China the common goal of the transformation of an impoverished, agrarian society into a modern industrial state, its program calls for a more gradual change that relies upon the voluntary support and assistance of its people. Implementation of Indian programs is based upon Western democratic procedures involving more respect for traditional values and the dignity of the individual than is true in China.

Agricultural Resources. Man has lived long on the land of India and China. No large tracts of virgin land capable of being tilled exist in either country. Irrigation and reclamation projects can increase somewhat the total amount of cultivated land in each nation, but the greatest emphasis in both countries currently is being placed upon more intensive and scientific utilization of the land now under cultivation.

Outwardly, India's natural environment appears favorable for agriculture, with a year-round growing season (except in the highlands) and annual precipitation totals adequate for most crops in the major agricultural areas. However, most of the major agricultural areas receive 80 per cent of their annual precipitation during the four months (June through September) of the summer monsoon. Unfortunately, the monsoon is often erratic in time of occurrence, intensity, and duration, with consequent losses as a result of having too little, too much, or improperly timed rainfall. Water management, then, is a critical problem that must be dealt with before sizable increases in agricultural output can be realized. A second physical factor of consequence

[13] Especially written by Philip A. True, a geographic specialist in the Far East.

is the general unproductiveness of Indian soils, which is reflected in the very low crop yields that are characteristic of Indian agriculture.[14] Although this is in part related in some areas to lack of moisture, most Indian soils are too low in plant nutrients for satisfactory crop production, primarily because of insufficient application of organic fertilizers. India has some 160 million cattle, but much of their dung is dried and used as fuel rather than applied to the land.

Physical factors present serious problems to man's use of the land in Communist China, where only about 12 per cent is actually cropped of a total land area amounting to approximately 3.7 million square miles.[15] Because much of China is too arid, too cold, or too high to support agriculture under present technology, there appears little likelihood that this figure can be increased substantially in the near future.

Internal climatic variation is more pronounced in Communist China than in India. Adequate rainfall and suitable temperatures permit double cropping in most parts of southern Communist China, but northern Communist China receives much less rainfall, and the growing season is mostly under two hundred days. As in India, fluctuations in the amount and distribution of precipitation are frequent, particularly in central and northern Communist China, resulting in droughts, floods, and crop losses. Typhoons frequently lash the southeastern coastal regions, causing considerable damage to ripening rice and other crops. Climate, then, is also a key factor to Communist China's economic development. This has been emphasized by the persistent theme appearing in Chinese Communist geographical literature concerning efforts to "remake nature," and the importance accorded irrigation, flood control, reclamation, soil conservation, afforestation, and related projects that are designed for control and better utilization of Communist China's physical resources.

Mineral Resources. Both India and Communist China possess sufficient quantities of most of the mineral resources generally considered necessary for large-scale industrialization.

Indian reserves of iron ore are very large. Furthermore, much of the ore is high in iron content and easily accessible to existing iron- and steel-manufacturing districts. Although supplies of bituminous and coking coal are small in terms of world quantity, they appear adequate to sustain India's future needs. The country also has large reserves of manganese, bauxite, and many lesser materials. It is a leading producer of manganese. Principal deficiencies are in nonferrous metals and in some nonmetallic minerals such as sulfur, potash, and phosphate. Petroleum also is in short supply, and present needs are met largely through imports.

Communist China exhibits somewhat similar strengths and weaknesses. While iron-ore reserves are believed adequate, most deposits are scattered and small and the ores medium- to low-grade. Communist China contains great coal reserves, ranking third in the world. Its supply of coking coal, like that of India, is modest when compared to supplies in the United States or the Soviet Union and yet adequate for present needs. The country also has an adequate supply of most materials needed for steel production and in addition is an important world producer of tin and antimony. Although petroleum prospecting has received priority of attention, new discoveries apparently have been insufficient to satisfy the country's small but expanding needs.

Population Growth. Recently revised estimates by Indian officials place the country's net population increase at about 2 per cent per year (instead of the previously maintained 1.3 to 1.5 per cent), so that 7 to 8 million persons are added each year to a population that was estimated at about 425 million in 1960. With a larger population of nearly 700 million in 1960, Communist China is estimated to

[14] Average rice yields per acre in India are about one-half of those obtained in Communist China but from one-third to one-fourth of those obtained in Japan.

[15] About 0.42 acre per capita of cultivated land is available in Communist China, and about 0.81 in India. However, these figures should be examined with the additional reservation that about 40 per cent of the cultivated land in Communist China is cropped more than once a year, but only 15 to 20 per cent is so used in India.

increase its population by nearly 15 million people each year. Its rate of increase is thought to be slightly higher than in India—from 2 to 2.5 per cent per year.

Both India and Communist China have attempted to slow the growth of population through education of the average citizen of the desirability of family planning and information and instruction concerning the techniques of birth control. India considers family planning in the larger context of improved health of its people, and family-planning units have been set up in conjunction with primary health centers in rural and urban centers throughout the country. Although Indian officials are fully cognizant of the dangers to future economic development posed by uncontrolled population growth, the enormity of the problem is complicated by the basic conservatism of the Indian peasant and apparently precludes any early, significant slowing of the birth rate.

Institution of population control measures in Communist China has been complicated by the conflict with Marxist dogma, which holds a large working population to be desirable because it constitutes a guarantee of ample production and economic progress. In 1954–1955, when Communist Chinese leaders became fully aware of the enormous size of their population and the nation's high rate of increase, party theoreticians attempted to reconcile Communist ideology with practical measures to combat unrestricted population growth. Between 1956 and 1958, a national campaign was launched that proclaimed the benefits of smaller families (one alleged benefit was that more time could be devoted to the study of political doctrine!) and gave instructions to the populace on the means of birth control. By 1959, however, the more orthodox party line that a large and growing population is of positive economic benefit was reaffirmed from Peking. Despite ideological inhibitions, the hard facts of unchecked population growth are undoubtedly appreciated by the Chinese leadership, and more intensive, perhaps more subtle, means may be employed in the future in an attempt to retard Communist China's ever-quickening population spiral.

Economic Planning. India and Communist China began their economic planning from roughly comparable economic bases and potentials, but strong contrasts are evident in the differing objectives, priorities, and methods employed by each in carrying out planned decisions. In essence, these differences arise from the diametrically opposed political philosophies in which economic development has been conceived by Peking and New Delhi.

Economic development programs in India contain elements of both the socialist and capitalist systems. The private sector (that part of the economy dependent on private capital) contributes a large share of total investment, but increasing emphasis is being placed upon public investment and centralized planning in the development of basic resources and industrial capacity. India views the next decade as preparing the groundwork for a future rapid industrial growth. While on the one hand the government has attempted during its First and Second Five-Year Plans to increase both agricultural and industrial output, it has made simultaneous efforts to improve the standard of living and to increase social and economic opportunities for the average citizen.[16]

Economic planning in Communist China is based upon Marxist-Leninist aims of socialization of the agents of production and distribution, restrictions upon increases in consumption so as to maximize the amount of investment, and expansion of heavy industry. A basic objective of economic policy decisions is to increase output the greatest amount in the shortest possible time. To implement these policies, a vast hierarchy of officials and Party cadres are present at all levels of society to transmit and enforce national programs. Persuasion and exhortation generally have proved sufficient, but the Chinese Communists have also used purges, "labor reform," imprisonment, and execution to force their will upon individuals who have resisted. Although

[16] The primary instrument to attain these goals is the community-development program coupled with the national extension service through which knowledge and means of self-advancement are disseminated and demonstrated in an attempt to breach the barriers of poverty, apathy, and ignorance.

the level of living in Communist China purposely has been kept low and heavy physical demands made upon the individual to increase output, this has been made theoretically palatable by reiterations that the hardships and struggles of the present are but a necessary prelude to the "glorious era of full socialism" soon to be realized.

Development Progress. India was able to meet and even exceed agricultural targets in the First Five-Year Plan, extending from 1952 to 1956 (Table 2.1). Increased output, however, appeared to be largely the result of favorable weather rather than any significant basic improvement in Indian agricultural standards. With a growing realization that population growth is canceling out gains in agricultural output—projections based on present rates of population increase suggest a possible 25-million-ton additional shortage in food grains by 1966—India is presently undertaking a crash program to spur agricultural output. The recommended program of action for Indian agriculture includes (1) centralized governmental control of the program to allocate resources, establish priorities, coordinate programs, and enforce policy decisions; (2) stabilization of farm prices to provide production incentives; (3) availability of credit through cooperatives; (4) a public-works program of land improvements (drainage, leveling, etc.); (5) expanded irrigation and reclamation projects; (6) greater use of chemical fertilizers, particularly nitrogen; (7) more intensive use of the better croplands to gain quick results from increased yields of rice, wheat, and maize; and (8) a progressive reduction in the vast number of cattle.

India has exhibited steady, if slow, progress in meeting its planned goals in the development of industry. It has lagged most notably in the production of iron and steel. Many industrial targets were attained, however, during the First Five-Year Plan, particularly in the production of consumer goods. Future planning allocates a significant part of industrial investment for consumer-goods factories and small-scale industry in keeping with the over-all objective of a gradual rise in the level of living.

During Communist China's First Five-Year Plan, which extended from 1953 to 1957, primary emphasis was placed upon the development of heavy industry and, to a lesser extent, upon transportation, largely at the expense of agriculture and consumer-goods production. Changes in emphasis were made during the early years of the second plan, primarily as the result of the relatively slow growth rate of agricultural output coupled with continued high rates of population increase and the realization that considerable time and large capital outlays were needed to construct and complete heavy industry projects. Consequently, in 1958 a great speed-up (called the "great leap forward" in Communist terminology) was undertaken in both industry and agriculture in an attempt through intensive labor drives to reach many of the Second Five-Year Plan targets in a single year.

To accomplish these goals, a revolutionary institutional change was made in mid-1958 whereby the rural population was organized into more than twenty-five thousand communes. During 1955–1956 Chinese agriculture had been organized into collectives. The announced purposes of the communes organized in 1958 were to merge local government and cooperatives into one entity and to coordinate and integrate agriculture, forestry, industry, trade, education, and military affairs. The communes would also utilize local resources to provide much of their needs through the construction of small-scale industrial establishments and the building of local transportation facilities. In its pure form, the commune would provide living quarters, public mess halls, nurseries, and a multitude of other communal services. In practice, there apparently has been considerable variation in the structure of individual communes—particularly in such matters as living quarters, public eating places, and relinquishment of personal items. Despite the uncertainties as to their eventual form, it appears that the Chinese leaders have been able to solidify in a single entity nearly complete control over all aspects of economic, political, and social life in rural Communist China. With a tight rein over its massive supplies of labor, giant labor projects ranging from water-conservancy to fertilizer collection may be organized and directed by top governmental echelons.

TABLE 2.1

Output of selected industrial and agricultural commodities in Communist China and India (1952, 1957, 1958, 1959)

Commodity	*Communist China*				*India*			
	1952	*1957*	*1958*	*1959*	*1952*	*1957*	*1958*	*1959*
Coal (million metric tons)	63.6	128	270	347.9	36.9	44.2	46.0	47.8
Crude steel (million metric tons)	1.3	5.4	8.0*	13.4*	1.6	1.7	1.8	2.5
Crude petroleum (thousand metric tons)	436	1440	2260	3700	263	429	434	447
Chemical fertilizer (thousand metric tons)	194	750	811	1333	270	530	550	na †
Electric power (billion kilowatt hours)	7.3	19.3	27.5	41.5	6.2	11.4	12.8	14.6
Total food grains ‡ (million metric tons)	154.4	185	250 §	270 §	52.0	69.8	63.5	74.5
Rice ¶ (million metric tons)	68.4	86.8	113.7 §	na	34.3	37.9	45.3	46.3
Wheat (million metric tons)	18.1	23.7	28.9 §	na	6.2	9.5	7.9	9.8

* Excludes 3.1 million tons of off-grade steel in 1958 and several million tons in 1959.
† Not available.
‡ Chinese figures for food grains exclude soybeans but include potatoes; Indian figures include pulses.
§ The 250 and 270 million tons of food grains reported for Communist China in 1958 and 1959, respectively, are believed by most Western experts to be too high—perhaps by 10 to 20 per cent. Likewise, rice and wheat totals reported for 1958 are believed exaggerated. Additionally, unfavorable weather during 1959 makes it problematical whether food-grain output actually increased over 1958 levels.
¶ Rice in terms of rough, or paddy, rice. Indian food-grain totals, however, are based upon milled or cleaned rice.
SOURCE: Basic data derived mainly from United Nations, *Statistical Yearbook, 1959,* supplemented by various official sources.

Communist China recorded steady, often impressive, output gains in both agriculture and industry during the period from 1952 through 1957. In 1958 many record-breaking increases were reported in agricultural and industrial output—some of them verging on the fantastic. Many of these record claims subsequently were reduced in August, 1959—particularly in food grains—as it became apparent that the statistical reporting system had suffered serious damage during 1958, in part because of the administrative upheavals resulting from commune formation and output distortions induced by the unrealistic targets established during the feverish "great leap." Although considerable output increases were made in 1958, and to a lesser extent in 1959, the statistical situation does not appear to be fully recovered from the excesses of 1958.

Although heavy industry is not being neglected, there is considerable present emphasis in Communist China upon small- and medium-scale industry.[17] Such projects are feasible in Communist China in that many of the needed mineral resources for local industry are widely scattered in small deposits—iron ore and coal, for example—and development of these otherwise uneconomic deposits is practical for

[17] According to Peking, in 1959 about one-half of the pig iron was attributable to medium-sized and small blast furnaces; one-fifth of the coal production came from small mines; and more than one-third of the steel production, from medium-sized and small converters.

small-scale local industry. Small-scale industrial projects also offer the advantages of relatively simple and quick construction, early return on investment, and lessened demand on a burdened transportation system.

Problems, Prospects, and Implications. The major problem confronting India and Communist China is that of increasing agricultural output at a rate sufficiently high both to meet the needs of rapidly growing populations and to provide surpluses for investment in industrial expansion. Since curbs on population increases appear unlikely in the near future, a continuous expansion of agricultural output must be maintained. Both countries are pursuing similar programs designed to obtain the maximum benefit from their great rural supplies of manpower to make basic agricultural improvements. Labor-intensive projects such as irrigation works, reclamation, and greater use of locally available fertilizer sources should make possible significant increases in yields per acre (particularly in India). Furthermore, increased governmental direction of agriculture in India will allow experimentation and establishment of pilot projects in which maximum production resources can be concentrated in areas most suitable for greatest yields per acre. Similar experimental programs are under way in Communist China through the medium of the commune. The increases to be gained from these practices are limited; eventually, methods requiring more investment, such as chemical fertilizers, improved seeds, insecticides, and mechanization (in some areas), will be required to continue output growth. In the next few years the margin between food production and consumption will remain thin in both countries, and a succession of poor crop years could slow economic development and prove a serious strain on the stability of existing governments.

Industrial growth will continue in both countries—probably at a continued rapid rate in Communist China and at a slower pace in India. Communist China apparently has experienced some success with its recent emphasis upon small- and medium-scale industry, and its role likely will continue to be an important one at this stage of Communist China's economic development. Communist China boasts of overtaking and surpassing the United Kingdom in industrial production by 1970. Although these goals may be reached in terms of gross output levels, the Chinese press generally fails to indicate that by 1970 estimated per capita output levels of the major industrial commodities in Communist China still will be far less than those of the United Kingdom.

The more rapid rate of economic growth in Communist China as contrasted with India is of considerable significance to other underdeveloped nations who have not as yet embarked upon development programs. Although the rapid rate of progress in Communist China and the promise of an advanced economy within a generation are impressive, outsiders may experience qualms about the totalitarian methods employed, with their disregard for the individual. Even though India is experiencing considerable problems in its development program, the democratic procedures employed and the respect for traditional values and institutions in the slower, more humane Indian program may well prove more attractive to other underdeveloped nations.

Underdevelopment elsewhere

In this chapter, we have emphasized underdevelopment in Asia. Our choice of nations and societies should not lead the reader to misinfer that the problem of underdevelopment is limited to the southern and eastern fringes of this one continent. As indicated in Figure 1.4, it is very much present throughout most of Africa and Latin America, and in portions of other major world divisions. In each of these large and small places, it will differ in certain details from its appearance in our sample studies, but not in over-all form.

REFERENCES

Communist China's Agriculture, U. S. Department of Agriculture, Foreign Agriculture Report 115, 1959.

Daniel, James (ed.): *Private Investment,* McGraw-Hill Book Company, Inc., New York, 1958.

Dey, Sushil: *Industrial Development,* Thacker's Press & Directories, Ltd., Calcutta, 1955.

Du Sautoy, Peter: *Community Development in Ghana,* Oxford University Press, New York, 1958.

Higgins, Benjamin: *Economic Development: Principles, Problems and Policies,* W. W. Norton & Company, Inc., New York, 1959.

Jackson, I. C.: *Advance in Africa,* Oxford University Press, New York, 1956.

Lewis, W. Arthur: *The Theory of Economic Growth,* George Allen & Unwin, Ltd., London, 1955.

Malenbaum, Wilfred: *India and China: Contrasts in Development Performance,* Massachusetts Institute of Technology Center for International Studies, Cambridge, Mass., 1959.

Mayer, Albert, et al.: *Pilot Project, India,* University of California Press, Berkeley, Calif., 1958.

Phillips, Paul G.: "The Community Function in Economic Progress," *Community Development Review,* no. 2, International Cooperation Administration, Washington, D.C., 1956.

———: "Trends in Community Development in the United States," International Cooperation Administration, 1958. (Mimeographed report.)

Redfield, Robert: *The Primitive World and Its Transformation,* Cornell University Press, Ithaca, N. Y., 1953.

Report on India's Food Crisis and Steps to Meet It, Government of India, Ministry of Food and Agriculture and Ministry of Community Development and Cooperation, New Delhi, 1959.

"Rich Mineral Resources Spur Communist China's Bid for Industrial Power," *Mineral Trade Notes,* Special Supplement 59, U. S. Department of the Interior, Bureau of Mines, 1960.

Ross, Murray G.: *Community Organization,* Harper & Brothers, New York, 1955.

Staley, Eugene: *The Future of Underdeveloped Countries,* Harper & Brothers, New York, 1954.

Third Five-Year Plan: A Draft Outline, Government of India, Planning Commission, New Delhi, 1960.

3 CONSUMPTION AND THE FUNCTIONING OF ECONOMIES

WE HAVE STATED IN THE INTRODUCTION TO THIS BOOK THAT CONSUMPTION IS A basic stimulant, if not *the* basic stimulant, to economic activity. Assuming this to be true, we can benefit from examining the geographical distribution of consumption throughout the world, its internal structure within specific nations and economies, and its role in technically advanced and underdeveloped lands. Unfortunately, we are not yet able to secure detailed inventories of consumption on a world-wide basis. Most appraisals are based instead upon income, which indicates general capacity to consume. Even data on income are reported reliably for only about one-half of the world's countries and for less than one-half of its population; we must depend upon estimates for coverage of the remaining economies, nearly all of which are usually classified as underdeveloped. Nevertheless, some interesting implications and indications can be discovered in examining such materials as are available.

UNEVEN GLOBAL DISTRIBUTION

At this stage of our reasoning, we are interested in *absolute*, or *aggregate*, consumption, both in the entire world and in its individual component economies. It does not matter for the time being whether the commodities supplying this consumption to any specific economy are produced domestically or imported. Lacking complete inventories on such consumption, we can approximate it roughly by multiplying per capita income by total population, thus obtaining potential consuming capacity at any given time. The results of one such approximation are shown in Table 3.1.

Although the table must be interpreted cautiously, especially in that it does not allow for differences in purchasing power among economies, it nonetheless contains two very important implications for economic geographers: (1) aggregate consuming capacity depends upon total population as well as per capita income, and (2) technically advanced nations, notably the United States, dominate as potential consumers.

TABLE 3.1

Estimated consuming capacity of selected nations (average, 1952–1954)

Nation	*Population mid-year, 1953 (in millions)*	*Per capita income (in United States dollars)*	*Index of consuming capacity (per capita income multiplied by total population, in billions)*
United States*	159.6	1,870	298.5
United Kingdom*	50.6	780	39.5
France*	42.9	740	31.7
West Germany*	49.0	510	25.0
India	372.0	60	22.3
Canada*	14.8	1,310	19.4
Japan*	86.7	190	16.5
Italy*	47.6	310	14.8
Brazil	55.8	230	12.8
Argentina*	18.4	460	8.5
Australia*	8.8	950	8.4
Belgium*	8.8	800	7.0
Sweden*	7.2	950	6.8
Mexico	28.1	220	6.2
Pakistan	79.3	70	5.6
Netherlands*	10.5	500	5.3
Switzerland*	4.9	1,010	4.9
Turkey	22.5	210	4.7
Union of South Africa*	13.2	300	4.0
Denmark*	4.4	750	3.3
Philippines	21.0	150	3.2
United Arab Republic (Egypt)	22.1	120	2.7
New Zealand*	2.0	1,000	2.0
Cuba*	5.8	310	1.8
South Korea	21.4	70	1.5
Ireland*	2.9	410	1.2
Peru	9.0	120	1.1
Ceylon	8.2	110	0.9
Israel	1.7	470	0.8
Ecuador	3.5	150	0.5
Lebanon	1.4	260	0.4
Uganda	5.3	50	0.3
Honduras	1.6	150	0.2
Paraguay	1.5	140	0.2
Iceland*	0.15	780	0.12

* Nations usually considered to be technically and economically advanced. All others in the table are considered to be underdeveloped.

SOURCE: Computed from *Per Capita National Product of Fifty-Five Countries, 1952–1954,* United Nations Statistical Office, New York, 1957, pp. 8–9. Net national product is considered to be the equivalent of income. Corporate as well as personal income is included in per capita totals. The first twenty nations in the table are the leading nations shown in the original source, whereas the last fifteen nations are selected at random from that source. All are ranked in descending order of capacity to consume. Communist nations are not included.

The importance of total population as well as per capita consumption is indicated by the positions of specific countries, especially in the twenty leaders shown in the table. The United States, with a high per capita income as well as a large population, unquestionably is in the forefront. Most of the other nineteen leaders contain at least moderately high per capita incomes and populations. However, India, Pakistan, Brazil, and Mexico all have per capita incomes of less than $250 per year, and the first two of not more than $70 per year. Yet these also rank among the highest twenty aggregate consumers in the table. Communist China, with its more than one-fifth of the world's population, also would rank high if it had been included in the table. On the other hand, Canada, Australia, and Switzerland have comparatively small populations but are among the leaders in aggregate consuming capacity because of their high per capita incomes.

The dominance of technically advanced nations in aggregate consumption is indicated by the fact that fifteen of the leading twenty countries in Table 3.1 are so classified. Lacking complete data, we cannot be certain just how much of the world's total consumption is accounted for by this group. However, if we assume that average per capita income for the world is $250 per year—a generous figure in view of the data shown in Table 3.1 and of the fact that most nations not in the table are underdeveloped—the index number for the nearly three billion world inhabitants would be about 750. The fifteen technically advanced nations that are among the leaders in Table 3.1, with less than 20 per cent of the world's population, would account for nearly 70 per cent of all consuming capacity. The United States alone, with about 6 per cent of the total population, would account for about 40 per cent of that capacity.

The world's technically advanced nations thus can be visualized as Gargantuan consumers. Their domestic economies supply part of, but not all, the commodities that they consume, and they are substantial importers. (Some, of course, are also substantial exporters.) A marked decrease in their capacities to consume would result in a slowing down of production, not only at home, but also in

Consumption of petroleum products in (a) an underdeveloped economy and (b) a technically advanced economy. (Standard Oil Company of New Jersey)

dependent economies that export to them and receive imports from them.

The relation of United States consumption to the well-being of its own and other economies can scarcely be overemphasized. This one nation's capacity to consume is high enough that, despite its outstanding ability to supply most of that consumption from domestic output, it is still the world leader in international trade. The statement has been made that when the United States sneezes, the world catches pneumonia. This is not too excessive an exaggeration. Until the volume of consumption becomes more evenly distributed throughout the world, the markets of the United States and other technically advanced nations, most of them in the non-Communist realm of political and economic influence, will continue to be key considerations in the functioning of the world's economies.

This state of affairs is being challenged, however, by two movements. One is Marxist communism as exemplified in the Soviet Union, eastern Europe, and parts of the Far East, notably Communist China. As yet, only the Soviet Union, East Germany, Czechoslovakia, and perhaps Poland can be termed moderately high in per capita capacity to consume,[1] but that capacity appears to be on the rise in most Communist nations. At present, much of this capacity involves producer goods—machinery, etc., for further production—and per capita increases are more theoretical than real. However, total consuming capacities are increasing rapidly enough so that the Communist bloc of nations can be said to be challenging the world *status quo* in consumption.

A second challenge is associated especially with underdeveloped nations that are not in the Communist realm of political and economic influence, and it results primarily from their attempts to strengthen themselves economically. Most of these economies are technically underdeveloped, and many are only recently independent. India, Pakistan, Indonesia, the Philippines, and the United Arab Republic are good examples. Also important in this group are nations that long have been politically independent but currently are working ardently for more economic self-sufficiency. Brazil is a good example of this category, which also includes several other Latin American countries. However, economic advance and associated capacity to consume appear to be proceeding at a somewhat slower pace in these nations than in some Communist countries, and their over-all challenge to the dominance of present world leaders is correspondingly less dynamic.

These challenges, however, are offset measurably by expansion of per capita consuming capacities in many of the present world leaders—expansion so rapid that it exceeds population growth. Especially for this reason, such nations offer promise of continued dominance in world aggregate consuming capacity for the foreseeable future.

STRUCTURE

Consumption varies among cultures, nations, and societies, not only in volume, but also in structure. Particularly conspicuous in this context are differences in emphasis upon producer as compared to consumer goods, and upon personal expenditure for necessities as compared to luxuries.

In this Industrial Age, a nation that consumes in large volume usually must first produce in large volume—and modern production requires expensive capital equipment. A substantial share of consumption, therefore, involves producer goods, notably in the technically advanced countries where such goods are concentrated. Technically underdeveloped countries tend to spend higher shares of their incomes on consumer goods.

However, proportionate expenditures upon producer goods within a given economy are only moderately high if that economy enjoys the benefits of past capital accumulation, preferably over a long period. It is when an underdeveloped economy decides to become more advanced, technically and economically, that an extraordinarily high percentage of national income must be diverted to pro-

[1] It must be noted, however, that the countries of eastern Europe were at, or near, their current levels of consuming capacity before the advent of communism there.

ducer goods, especially if that economy is unable to attract substantial amounts of foreign currency in the forms of direct investment, loans, or other aid. This is one important reason why underdeveloped economies find the transition period to technical advance so difficult.

The two-thirds of the world's people living under conditions of technical and economic underdevelopment, and some living under conditions of technical advance, as well, think not so much in terms of producer and consumer goods as in terms of how to get enough to eat each day. Such thinking has been generalized by the German statistician Engel into a so-called *Law of Consumption*, which states that poorer families and societies tend to spend a much higher percentage of their respective incomes on food than do more wealthy individuals and groups. The law is applicable to lower-income groups in technically advanced countries as well as to underdeveloped societies, but it is reflected particularly in national statistics of the latter. Figure 3.1 tends to substantiate Engel's law on a global scale.

Despite their relatively high expenditures on food, over one-half of the world's people do not get as many as 2,250 calories daily, and an additional one-sixth receive fewer than 2,750 calories each day. Only one-third—essentially the same one-third that live in technically advanced societies—receive as many as 2,750 daily calories, the minimum amount considered necessary for minimum health of an average adult twenty-five years old. (Fig. 3.2.)

Consumption in technically advanced countries thus tends not only to be large in volume but also to involve substantial amounts of producer goods and consumer luxuries. Aggregate consumption in underdeveloped countries varies markedly with total population and tends to involve fewer producer goods and more consumer necessities, especially food. Exceptions to these generalizations are most numerous and pronounced in economies in which efforts are being made to move from underdeveloped conditions to the higher levels of livelihood.

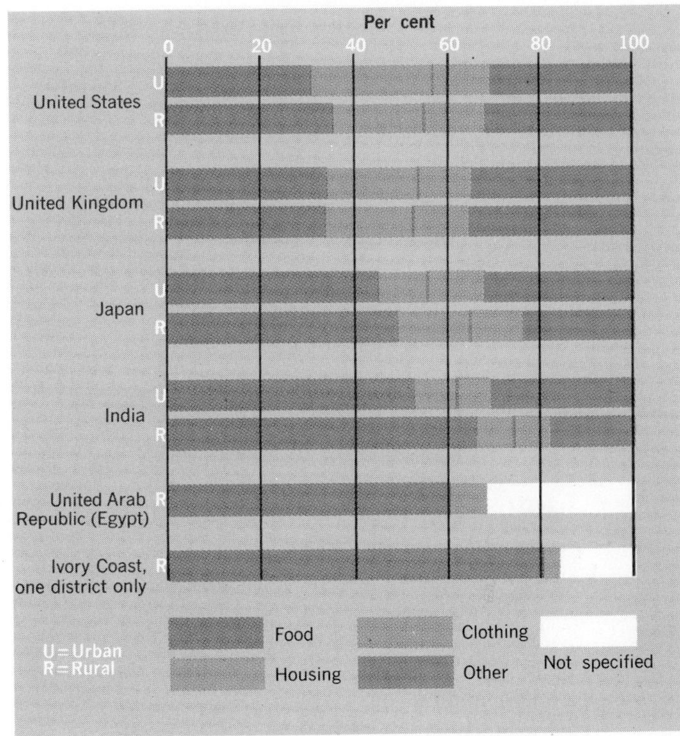

Figure 3.1 ***Percentage of per capita incomes spent for food, housing, clothing, and other purposes in selected countries.*** *The figures include estimated income for agricultural products consumed on farms. This figure can be considered a documentation of Engel's law of consumption. Note that housing, especially, receives a much smaller share of income in underdeveloped than in technically advanced nations.*

UNDERCONSUMPTION AND OVERCONSUMPTION

For technically advanced lands, the Industrial Age is fast becoming an age of automation. Production and exchange are increasingly carried on by electronically controlled machines, and decreasingly by physical and mental labor of human beings. But there is no such thing as push-button consumption—at least, not of most consumer goods. Yet consumption is a major stimulant to economies, and should it

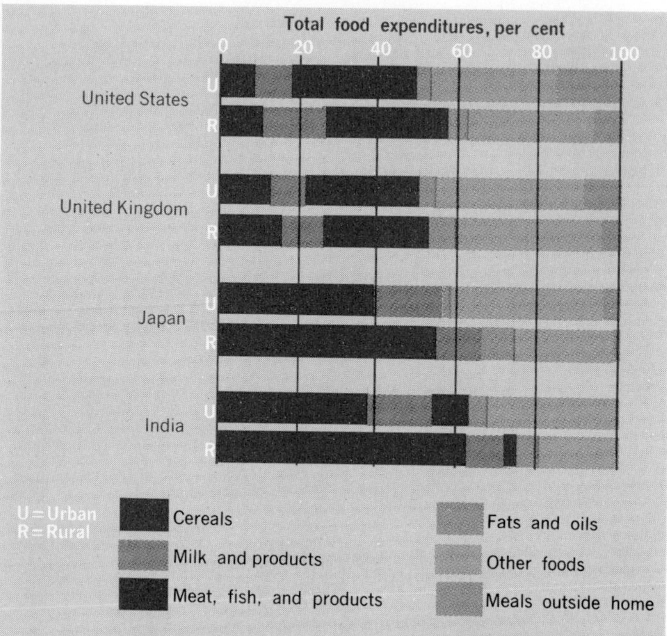

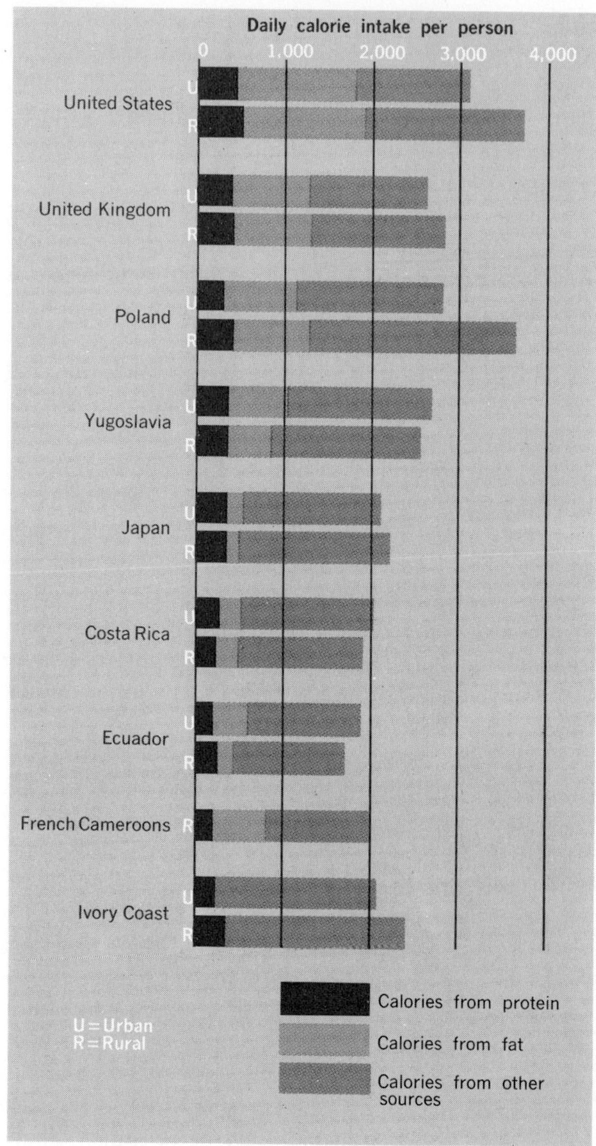

***Figure 3.2* Proportionate expenditure for food, including home-produced food, and per capita calorie intake in selected countries.** *The graph above shows the percentage of food budgets spent for each commodity and commodity group; it does not show the amount of food obtained. Note the rather large percentage spent on milk products in India, where those products are scarce. Note also the high percentage expenditures for cereals in India and Japan. (After* The State of Food and Agriculture, 1959, *FAO, p. 103) In the graph on the right, data for rural Ecuador and the Ivory Coast are from only one village in each country. Calorie intake in rural Poland, the economy of which sometimes is classified as underdeveloped, is almost as high as in rural United States and higher than in the United Kingdom. (After* The State of Food and Agriculture, 1959, *FAO, p. 107)*

decline in technically advanced countries, the productive machinery soon would become glutted by mechanically produced merchandise. The fear of underconsumption is thus more or less constant in some technically advanced societies. Man there virtually has been returned to the garden of Eden, where his major task in life is to consume. Now, however, unless he harvests all the fruit, the orchard will sicken and perhaps die.

Underdeveloped countries, in contrast, are faced with the sobering possibility of continued underproduction. For them, a major problem is not how to keep consumption at a sufficiently high rate to maintain or expand production but how to produce enough—even enough food—to meet life's minimum requirements. For them, the Malthusian doctrine has real meaning.

Only a few nations that, on the one hand, are moving into stages of technical advance and, on the other, are still somewhat deficient in consumer goods are not confronted with either the problem of underconsumption or that of overconsumption.

REFERENCES

Clark, Colin: *The Conditions of Economic Progress,* The Macmillan Company, New York, 1957. (Especially chap. 8.)

Ginsburg, Norton S. (ed.): *Essays on Geography and Economic Development,* University of Chicago Department of Geography Research Paper 62, Chicago, 1962. (Especially chap. 1.)

Higgins, Benjamin: *Economic Development,* W. W. Norton & Company, Inc., New York, 1959.

Samuelson, Paul A.: *Economics,* McGraw-Hill Book Company, Inc., New York, 1958. (Especially chaps. 10–11, 20, 23.)

Woytinsky, W. S., and E. S. Woytinsky: *World Population and Production,* The Twentieth Century Fund, Inc., New York, 1953. (Especially pp. 265–311.)

PART TWO THE NATURAL ENVIRONMENT

The natural environment is particularly important to economic geography in two respects: (1) it is a storehouse of certain source materials that will be consumed ultimately by man; and (2) it provides certain physical and biological conditions within and on which man's production, exchange, and consumption occur. INTRODUCTION, PAGE 15

4 LANDFORMS AND MINERAL RESOURCES

WE HAVE EMPHASIZED THAT THE NATURAL ENVIRONMENT IS ESPECIALLY SIGNIFIcant to man's gaining a living because on the one hand it sets forth certain conditions within which man's economic activities take place and on the other it is the source of most raw materials and energy. Landforms and minerals are two fundamental components of the natural environment from the viewpoint of the economic geographer, since landforms are particularly important as natural conditions and minerals yield raw materials and energy sources.

Landforms are literally the surface forms of the land, the upper irregularities of the earth's solid portion. They have been classified on the basis of relief (the difference between the lowest and highest elevations) and configuration (the arrangement of terrain) in three hierarchal orders. The first separates the world's continents from its ocean basins; the continental shelves are considered as fringes of the continents (Fig. 4.1). The second delimits all plains, plateaus, hill country, and mountains of the continents (Fig. 4.2). The third distinguishes lesser undulations—ravines, small canyons, knolls, etc. It is the second order that is emphasized in this book.

A *mineral* is a natural element or combination of such elements with a specific chemical composition and usually a definite molecular arrangement. Some minerals occur as single elements and others occur as combinations. They usually are solid but may be liquid or gaseous. Most are inorganic, but some may have been derived from the decay or alteration of organic materials. More than 1,600 minerals are now recognized.[1]

A *mineral resource* is a mineral supply capable of exploitation. Whether and to what degree a mineral supply can be exploited depends upon its quality, quantity, and accessibility, as well as upon current technological and economic conditions and arrangements. About two hundred minerals now are classified as economically exploitable.[2]

[1] See especially Alan M. Bateman, *Economic Mineral Deposits*, John Wiley & Sons, Inc., New York, and Chapman & Hall, Ltd., London, 1950, p. 19.
[2] *Ibid.*

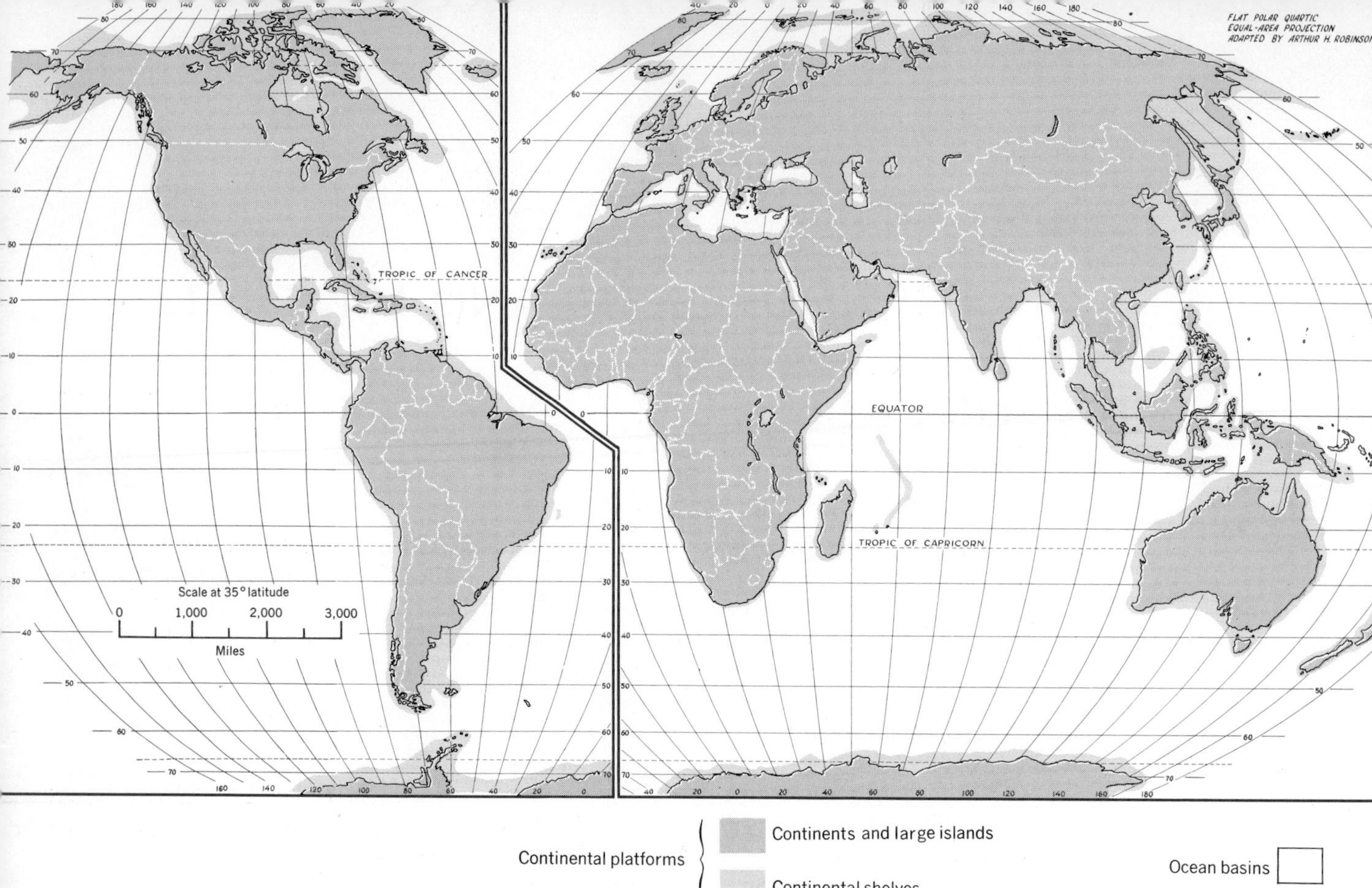

Figure 4.1 ***The first order of relief—continental platforms and ocean basins.*** *The expanse of the ocean basins illustrated is somewhat minimized by the contraction of the map through the Atlantic Ocean. The continental shelves are particularly useful to man in that they attract fish where other natural environmental features are favorable, and in that they place within man's reach certain minerals which would be difficult to extract from ocean basins.*

Landforms and minerals occur in association with geologic *rocks*, and both, as they now exist, are the result of a continuous interplay between subsurface forces of upthrust and surface agents of wear. The former bend, fracture, and otherwise tend to force the rocks upward, whereas the latter act to weather and erode those same rocks. Rocks are defined geologically as solid mineral matter plus minor amorphous materials.[3] They may be rigid like granite and limestone, or loose like sand, or plastic like mud; but by definition, their component particles must be solids. In nature they are associated with both landforms and minerals as is shown in the following diagram:

LANDFORMS

are comprised of

ROCKS

which are comprised of

MINERALS

Rocks thus are the foundations of landforms and the repositories of minerals. However, the pres-

[3] However, only about fifty minerals are classified as rock-making, and only twenty-nine are common rock-making minerals. The remainder occur as mineralized fillings of cracks, fissures, tiny interstices, etc.

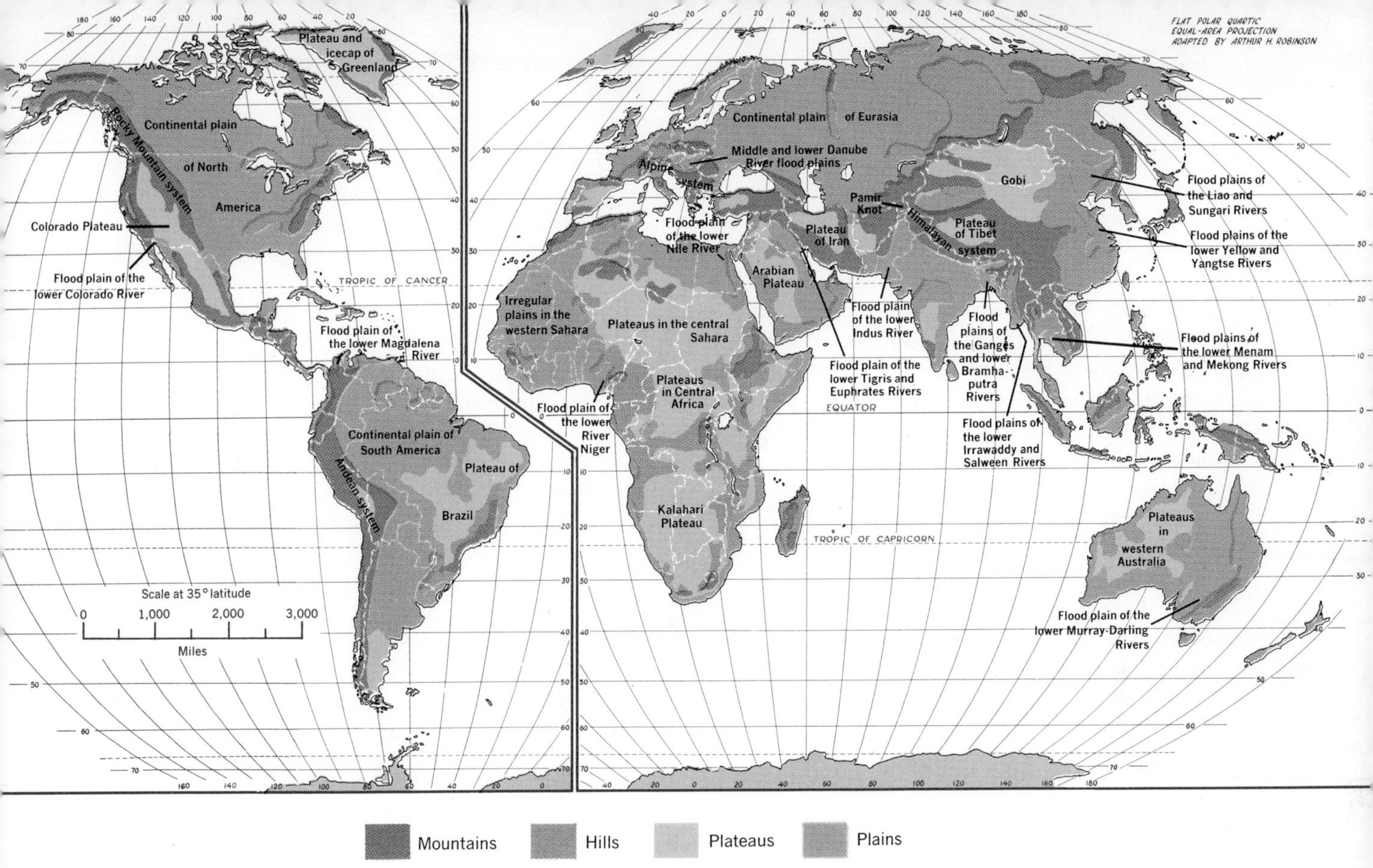

Figure 4.2 ***The second order of relief—plains, plateaus, hill country, and mountains.***

ence of certain types of landforms is not necessarily indicative of the existence of certain minerals, nor is the reverse true. This lack of absolute interrelationship is mostly due to the complexity of the earth's rock structure with which both are associated.

All rocks have been classified by genesis as to whether they are igneous, sedimentary, or metamorphic.

Igneous rocks result from the direct cooling of molten material called *magma*. It is probable that these were the only rocks of the earth's surface after initial crustal solidification. Even today, they comprise essentially all of the earth's solid material beneath an average depth of 1,500 feet, and sometimes actually outcrop at the surface (Fig. 4.3). Most such rocks remain in the places where they hardened. Here and there, however, in response particularly to high temperatures and/or high pressures, igneous rocks remelt into magma and force their way into other rocks, perhaps even breaking through to the open air above. If the magma reaches the surface and is still active, it becomes a *volcanic cone* and/or *lava flow*, eventually hardening. In either case, it is an *extrusive igneous rock*. If, on the other hand, the magma hardens underground while still under pressure, it becomes what is known as an *intrusive igneous rock*. In some places an intrusive igneous rock is now at the earth's surface, having been exposed by the wearing away of other materials that covered it at the time of intrusion.

Igneous materials thus may be classified as (1) initial or residual rocks and magmatic intrusives, and (2) magmatic extrusives. Granite dominates, especially in residual igneous rocks at upper surface levels. Diorite and gabbro are important, the latter particularly at lower levels. Lava, basalt, and various glassy and fragmented rocks are the leading magmatic extrusives.

As their name implies, *sedimentary rocks* are made up of sediment—of materials deposited mechanically or chemically by water, ice, and wind. Many of the component particles exist initially in igneous rocks and are lifted out of their places of origin, reworked, and redeposited by the agents of erosion and deposition. In the reworking process, additional materials from the plant and animal world, from soil, and from direct chemical recombination may be added, so that the types which are ultimately deposited as sedimentary rocks bear little, if any, resemblance to igneous rocks.

Water-formed sedimentary rocks tend to assume a layered structure, whether accumulated as the floors and beaches of water bodies or as the beds of waterways. Sedimentary materials resulting from glacial action tend to be unlayered and unconsolidated, with large boulders and fine-grained debris often dropped side by side where the ice eventually halted and retreated. (Occasionally, however, some glacial debris is reworked by running water from the melting ice and thus has the characteristic layered appearance of water-deposited sediment.) Wind-blown sediments tend to be massive, unlayered, and of uniform texture. In some instances the coarser-grained, heavier materials that form sand dunes are dropped not far from points of initial erosion, and the finer, lighter silt known as *loess* is carried some distance away. In other instances, loess and sand deposits do not appear to be related in origin.

Shales are a common type of sedimentary rock. It is estimated that they comprise more than 80 per cent of all sedimentary rocks. They are derived mainly from mud or clay found in sluggish water-

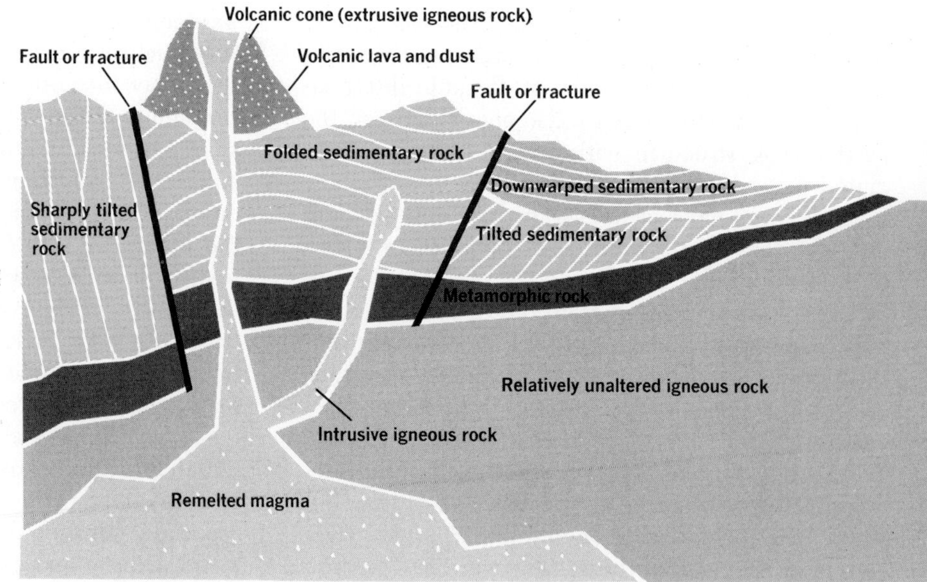

Figure 4.3 ***A hypothetical view of the three basic rock types and some overlying landforms.*** *The orientation of the rock structure may or may not affect that of the landforms. This volcanic cone happens to rise above the other mountains and may rise even higher if the volcano remains active. Metamorphic rock shown here is in an irregular stratum, but it might well be less concentrated, and it also might occur around the magma because of the heat and pressure there. Some of the relatively unaltered igneous rock has been uncovered by erosion and now lies at the land surface at the right of the drawing. Note the variations in form and structure of the rock strata. These are part of a diversity found in nature—a diversity which scarcely can be overemphasized.*

ways and water bodies and subsquently compressed when covered with additional sediment. Sandstones, accounting for about 12 per cent of all sedimentary rocks, can be traced largely to compacted beds of former waterways and beaches of former water bodies. An occasional sandstone can be traced to wind-deposited sand dunes. Limestones, making up about 6 per cent of all sedimentaries, are deposited chiefly on the floors of water bodies and occasionally in the beds or deltas of rivers where the rate of flow is sufficiently slow to permit their formation. They are either precipitated directly from ocean water that is heavily impregnated with calcium or they are formed by the accumulation of skeletons of coral, oysters, and other marine life. Among the remaining sedimentary rocks are the carbonaceous group, which result from partial decomposition under water of plant life. Ultimately, these rocks are changed into grades of coal ranging in quality from lignite to anthracite.

Some igneous and sedimentary rocks are subjected to so much heat and/or pressure in the earth's crustal adjustment that they actually are changed into a third type, known as *metamorphic rock*. This type includes marble (which was originally limestone), slate (originally shale), quartzite (originally sandstone), gneiss (originally granite), and others. This rock does not often underlie sizable regions or even districts, but tends to occur as threadlike intermixtures with igneous and sedimentary rocks, especially the former.

More than three-fourths of the rocks at or near the surface of the earth's land area are sedimentary, and the remainder are igneous and metamorphic.

LANDFORMS

THE WORLD PATTERN OF LANDFORMS

We are concerned here with landforms of the second order of relief—with plains, plateaus, hill country, and mountains. Although the world distribution of these features is uneven, no continent is entirely lacking in any of the four categories.

Attempts to define these terms rigidly have not been successful. General agreement exists, however, on the following explanations:

A *plain* is a sizable land surface of flat to gently undulating terrain. Most plains are low in elevation, but high plains do exist. The stream and river beds of both low and high plains are not incised but are at the approximate floor levels of their respective landscapes. The boundaries of plains which adjoin lower-lying features are not cliffed but graduate them gently downward. In contrast, the boundaries of plains with features of higher elevation may be abrupt. Lowlands are miniature plains.

A *plateau* is a noticeably incised, flat or slightly irregular surface of appreciable extent, usually bounded on at least one side by a steep decline. Occasional plateaus are bounded by upward trending mountains or cliffs. Actually, some plateaus resemble high plains, except that their streams and rivers flow in deep valleys, whereas the drainage of plains is at, or near, the level of the prevailing land surface.

A *hill* and a *mountain* are landforms of appreciable slope and of small summit area. The difference between them is chiefly a matter of elevation, and even this is not rigidly defined. No quantitative standard exists for distinguishing them, and the "hill country" of one specialist is frequently termed "mountain" by another. Often local terminology is accepted with equally unsatisfactory results. Classification of these two landform types is more arbitrary, and there is less agreement than about other components of the second order of relief.

Plains and lowlands

The world's plains and lowlands may be classified in three categories of size: (1) three large continental plains, each of which constitutes at least half the total area of Eurasia, North America, and South

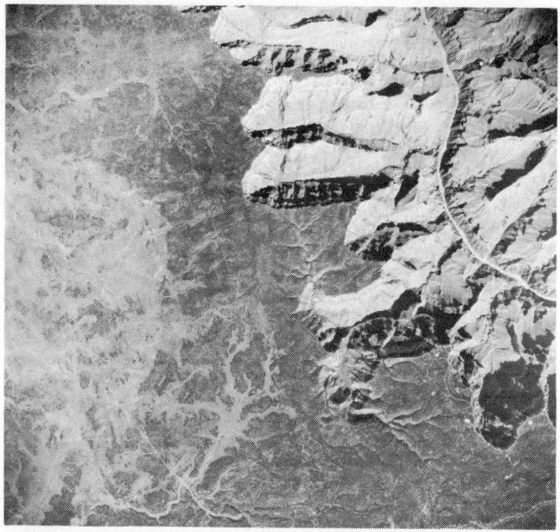

America, respectively; (2) a series of single river flood plains and adjacent countrysides; and (3) numerous coastal lowlands and fringes (Fig. 4.2.).

Continental Plains. The continental plain of Eurasia is the largest. Fringed on the south by the Alpine-Himalayan Cordillera as well as by lesser mountains, it reaches to the North Sea, the Arctic Ocean, and almost to Bering Strait. Conspicuous in north central Europe, it becomes truly extensive in the Soviet Union, where it occupies about one-half of the total territory.

The continental plain of North America contains: (1) the basins of most rivers emptying into the Arctic Ocean and Hudson Bay; (2) most of the drainage basins of the many and diverse tributaries of the Mississippi River, and that of the Mississippi itself; (3) most of the rivers of southeastern United States that reach the Atlantic Ocean and the Gulf of Mexico; and (4) the Great Lakes–St. Lawrence series of water reservoirs and channels. It extends throughout the longitudinal center of the United States and Canada, and reaches to the Atlantic and Arctic Oceans as well as to the Gulf of Mexico.

The continental plain of South America includes essentially all the drainage basins of the Amazon, Orinoco, and Paraguay-Parana Rivers and their tributaries. It encompasses over one-half of Brazil, together with sizable portions of Venezuela, Colombia, Bolivia, Argentina, and Uruguay.

Flood Plains of Individual Rivers. The flood plains of some rivers are not incorporated into continental plains. Most of these are in the Eastern Hemisphere. Among the more conspicuous are (1) the Liao and Sungari Rivers of Manchuria, (2) the lower Yellow and Yangtze Rivers of east central Communist China, (3) the lower Mekong and Menam Rivers

A plain, a plateau, hill country, and a mountain. (a) A view of the Great Plains near Lethbridge, Alberta, Canada (Photographic Surveys of Canada); (b) a portion of the Colorado River and Colorado plateau in Arizona (U.S. Air Force); (c) Hill country (both foreground and background) south of London (Pan American World Airways); (d) Mount Waddington in British Columbia (Royal Canadian Air Force).

of Cambodia and Thailand, (4) the lower Irrawaddy and Salween Rivers of Burma, (5) the entire Ganges River and the lower Indus and Brahmaputra Rivers of India and Pakistan, (6) the Mesopotamian portions of the Tigris and Euphrates Rivers of Iraq and peripheral countries, (7) the middle and lower basins of the Danube River in the Balkans, (8) the lower Nile River of Egypt, (9) the Niger River of Nigeria and neighboring countries, and (10) the Murray-Darling Rivers of Australia. Among the few in the Western Hemisphere are the San Joaquin and Sacramento Rivers and the lower Colorado River in North America and the Magdalena River in South America.

Coastal Lowlands and Fringes. These small features are so inconspicuous on a world map that they can be seen only with some difficulty. They are numerous in Africa, where they form a narrow boundary around an almost continuous series of plateaus. They are found also along nearly all the margins of other continents and of major islands, sometimes merging into larger continental plains.

Plateaus

Many of the world's plateaus are in dry climates, where chemical weathering and erosion is slight. Consequently, their features are more angular than would be true if more moisture were present. Examples are the Colorado Plateau, the Gobi plateau of western Communist China, the Plateau of Iran and the Arabian plateau in the Middle East, the Saharan and Kalaharian plateaus of Africa, and the slightly raised plateau of western Australia (Fig. 4.2). Chemical weathering and erosion, resulting in gently rounded landforms, are more active in humid than in dry climates. Instead of plateaus, these actions tend to produce hill country. Nevertheless, some landforms in humid and boreal climates are classified as plateaus. Examples are the humid plateaus in central Africa and in eastern Brazil, and the boreal plateaus in Greenland and Tibet.

The only continental plateau of significance is in Africa, where it takes the form of a series of relatively unwarped and unfractured sedimentary strata and underlying igneous and metamorphic materials worn down to different levels of elevation by running water and wind. The existence of the plateau—or more accurately, of the coalescing series of plateaus—is reflected in the continent's drainage: each major waterway tumbles to lower ground over a series of falls or rapids.

Hill country

Most of the world's hill country now exists in patches of moderate to small size that lie within humid climates. This landform type is usually found in the transition from mountains or plateaus to plains. It is most conspicuous in eastern Asia, less prominent in Africa, and of intermediate but recognizable occurrence in the other continents (Fig. 4.2).

Mountains

The world's mountains can be envisioned in terms of (1) two Gargantuan axes and (2) numerous outlying systems, chains, ranges, or groups. Each axis is the backbone of a hemisphere.

In the Eastern Hemisphere, the axis is distorted into the shape of an east-west–oriented Y formation, with the Alpine Mountain system of Europe and its projections into the Middle East comprising the stem of the Y and the high mountains of central and eastern Asia forming the two prongs. From the bifurcation point, known as the *Pamir knot,* one prong trends northeastward, initially along the border between the Soviet Union and Communist China, and eventually into the Soviet Union and Japan. The other and larger prong includes the Himalayas and trends southeastward through southwestern Communist China to the islands of Indonesia.

The axis of the Western Hemisphere is that of the Rocky Mountains and Andes Mountains, trending in an offset north-south direction (Fig. 4.2). This differs from the axis of the Eastern Hemisphere in three outstanding respects: (1) it is a true axis, with no large scale bifurcations; (2) it is oriented at an approximate right angle to its Eurasian counterpart—that is, it trends latitudinally instead of longitudinally; and (3) it is situated more nearly to one side of its associated continent or series of continents than is true of the Alpine-Himalayan axis.

Both as to height and as to square miles of surface area, the two axes dwarf the prominences of eastern Labrador, the southern Appalachians, the mountains in eastern Brazil, isolated but occasionally high features in Africa, the Blue Mountains of Australia and the small but rugged ranges in New Zealand, and the crystalline high country of Scandinavia.

LANDFORMS AND ECONOMIC GEOGRAPHY

Population

The people of eastern and southern Asia are located chiefly in the plains, and secondarily in plateaus and hill country (Fig. 4.2 and page 13). Among the most heavily populated plains are the Yangtze-Yellow River plains of east central Communist China and the Ganges–lower Brahmaputra River plains and coastal fringes of India. Almost all the plains, regardless of size or type, are thickly settled. Particularly in the three southern islands of Japan and in Java and Madura in Indonesia, but also in many places in eastern and southern Asia, there are not enough plains to accommodate the swollen populations, and settlement has spread to terraced hillsides. For these predominantly agricultural peoples, plains land is almost a luxury.

The population clusters of northwestern Europe and east central North America are situated on both plains and hill country, and when reviewed on a generalized small-scale map, they appear not to have favored either type of landform when establishing their settlements. When viewed on a large-scale map, however, they evidence a distinct preference for plains and low-lying countrysides. That they are not so rigidly oriented toward plains is due partially to the fact that their production, much of which is factory output, is more highly centralized than in eastern and southern Asia. Unlike agriculture, manufacturing requires only small amounts of space for large amounts of output. Consequently, extensive areas of flat land are not so vital to the industrialized Western World as to places mainly dependent upon agriculture.

The remainder of the world's populations tend also to be settled on flat land. Except in extremely unfavorable natural conditions (other than landforms), they are clustered notably along coasts and nearby valleys. Where such natural features, particularly climate, become adverse in lowlands, settlements may appear in higher, cooler elevations—in the mountain valleys and the more desirable sections of plateaus. This is especially true in the tropics.

Economic activity

The Productive Occupations. Agriculture and manufacturing, which are the mainstays of production, display a marked affinity for plains and hill country. The four remaining industries—grazing, forest exploitation, fishing and hunting, and mining and quarrying—are necessarily oriented directly toward specific natural features other than landforms and therefore are related to landforms only indirectly. Grazing, for example, is carried on where the world's natural forage is to be found. The forage, in turn, may exist on any of the four landform types. Analogous statements can be made for forest exploitation, fishing and hunting, and mining and quarrying.

The Secondary Occupations. The world's service occupations are closely associated in function with people and markets, and their distribution thus coincides almost exactly with the world's population. Such association as they may have with any landform type is largely coincidental.

Transportation. Flat country offers the possibility of transporting goods over land via the shortest route and at a minimum cost. Where the land becomes irregular, the resultant extra costs are due not only to the winding routes, which necessarily are placed in valleys and other gradual inclines, but also to the added energy needed to force the carrier and its load upslope. The world's rail and highway routes adhere closely to plains and hill country, with connections reaching through the least difficult passages of landform obstacles. Water and air carriers, requiring only small amounts of flat land for terminals, are not so closely oriented to landforms as the overland carriers.

Landforms have an indirect as well as a direct significance for economic activity. This rests chiefly upon their capacity to affect other natural environmental features which, in turn, are important to such activity. For example, mountains and other high landforms frequently act as barriers to climates, restricting them to much smaller areas than they would otherwise occupy. In contrast, low plains are essentially unrestrictive in this sense. Natural vegetation and soils, being affected by climate, slope, and drainage as well as other factors thus also are affected indirectly by landforms of an area. Climate, vegetation, and soils are natural environmental features with which man must cope directly in earning a living. By exerting an influence over their distribution and make-up, landforms thus become objects of indirect but definite concern in a study of economic activities.

MINERALS

MINERAL FORMATION

Of the 102 elements now known, 92 are natural and are found in the earth's crust, its water, or its air.[4] Table 4.1 contains an estimate of the elements dominating the earth's crust and their approximate percentages. Eight, it will be noted are outstanding.

We have noted that, of the more than 1,600 minerals now recognized, only about fifty are classified as rock-making. Most of the remainder, while occurring in rocks, are injected into crevasses, fissures, etc. Rock structure is so complex that it would be difficult to relate specific minerals to specific rock types. Most of the metallic minerals, however, appear to be related, directly or indirectly, to igneous rocks.

Table 4.1 emphasizes the very small percentage of the earth's crust that most single elements comprise. Elements, it will be remembered, make up minerals. Most minerals too are poorly represented in that crust—so poorly, in fact, that the exploitation of certain desired minerals may be commercially unfeasible at a given time. To be exploitable, nearly all minerals must have been naturally concentrated. The actual degree of concentration necessary depends upon the substance being sought; for example, shallow ores containing less than 1 per cent of metallic copper now are mined profitably, whereas materials containing 20 per cent or less of iron now are generally considered too lean for exploitation. Until quite recently, iron compounds of less than 50 per cent metal were not considered commercially exploitable, but technological advance has made possible the use of poorer ores.

Although the total geologic history of natural elements can never be known, certain processes of concentration now are understood. Some of these processes occur in the absence of water, and others result from water action. Those involving water appear to be responsible for a majority of minerals now being exploited. Both surface and subsurface water must be considered, and the latter may have been either rising or sinking at the time it acted upon the mineral in question. Coal was deposited by surface water as a sediment and subsequently covered. It thus occurs today as a layer, or stratum, however altered by rock deformation. In contrast, most of the metallic minerals have been removed from their original igneous rocks by either surface or subsurface waters and now occur as deposits in small and large fissures and holes, or even in tiny interstices between the grains of some porous rocks.

The few and simplified illustrations of the preceding paragraph are intended to emphasize a highly important aspect of the natural occurrence of minerals—namely, that they do not exist as a

[4] The remainder are man-made.

TABLE 4.1

*Composition of the earth's crust by dominant elements**

Element	*Percentage*
Oxygen (O)	46.710
Silicon (Si)	27.690
Aluminium (Al)	8.070
Iron (Fe)	5.050
Calcium (Ca)	3.650
Sodium (Na)	2.750
Potassium (K)	2.580
Magnesium (Mg)	2.080
Per cent of 8 dominant elements	98.580
Titanium (Ti)	0.589
Hydrogen (H)	0.140
Phosphorus (P)	0.130
Carbon (C)	0.094
Manganese (Mn)	0.090
Sulfur (S)	0.082
Barium (Ba)	0.050
Chlorine (Cl)	0.045
Chromium (Cr)	0.035
Fluorine (F)	0.029
Zirconium (Zr)	0.025
Nickel (Ni)	0.019
Strontium (Sr)	0.018
Vanadium (V)	0.016
Cerium (Ce), Yttrium (Y)	0.014
Copper (Cu)	0.010
Uranium (U)	0.008
Tungsten (W)	0.005
Lithium (Li)	0.004
Zinc (Zn)	0.004
Columbium (Cb), Tantalum (Ta)	0.003
Hafnium (Hf)	0.003
Thorium (Th)	0.002
Lead (Pb)	0.002
Cobalt (Co)	0.001
Boron (B)	0.001
Glucinum (Gl)	0.001
Total	100.000

* The table shows only the 35 leading elements in the earth's crust, including sea and air. The percentages of all other elements would be very low—for each less than that of glucinum.

SOURCE: Amended from E. B. Branson and W. A. Tarr, rev. by C. C. Branson and W. D. Keller, *Introduction to Geology,* 3d ed., McGraw-Hill Book Company, Inc., New York, 1952, p. 8.

uniform blanket throughout the earth's crust but are very unevenly distributed, both horizontally and vertically. The reader should never lose sight of this point. It is a common fallacy to "take the natural environment as given"—to assume, for purposes of theoretical calculation, that nature's bounty is uniformly distributed. This is simply not true—whether we are concerned with soils, vegetation, plant life, minerals or other natural features. As suggested in Figs. 4.4 and 4.5, minerals are particularly erratic in their distribution—in localities, in states, in nations, in continents, and in the world.

MINERAL RESOURCES AND ECONOMIC GEOGRAPHY

Pattern of exploitation

In later chapters we shall consider the world distribution of specific minerals. Here we are interested only in known areas of unusually heavy mineral exploitation. These areas are shown in Fig. 4.5. Technically advanced nations in North America and Europe and the Soviet Union and a few other countries have actively exploited local reserves, whether on the coasts or inland. In outlying countries, however, the areas of exploitation tend to fringe seacoasts—to be oriented, in other words, to ocean shipping lanes which connect them with technically advanced societies.

Certainly with respect to minerals, the Age of Exploration is not yet ended on this earth. Almost every day brings reports of new mineral discoveries—usually in the more isolated places, but occasionally in areas that have been inhabited for a long, long time. Also, techniques of recovering and processing mineral resources are being improved constantly, and existing materials are always being reexamined to see whether they can qualify as recoverable ore in the light of the most recent technological developments. Furthermore, uses are being found for minerals once considered undesirable, and demand for yet other minerals is declining because superior alternatives are being utilized. The net result of these and lesser considerations is that the areas of mineral extraction are not fixed

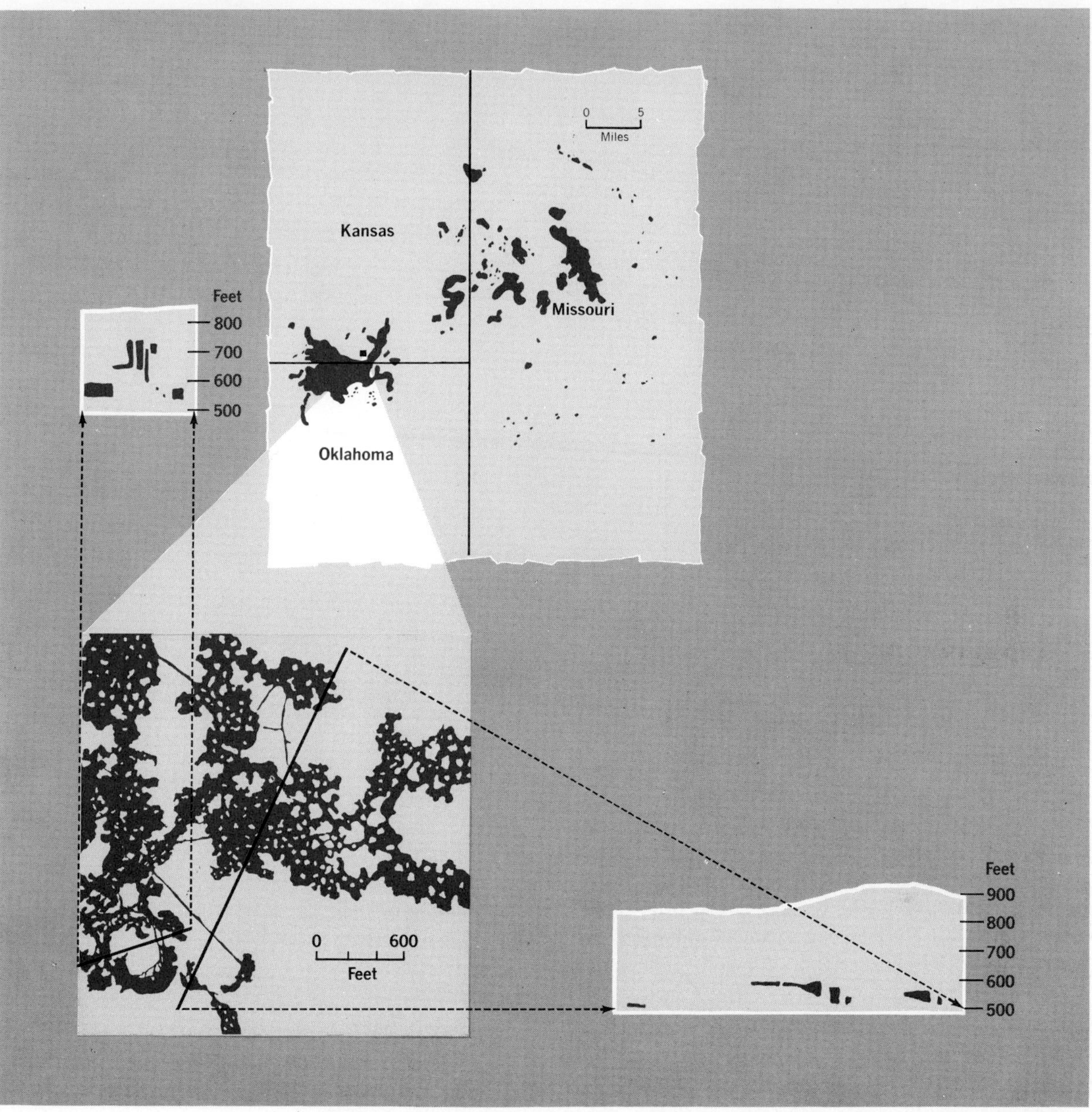

Figure 4.4 ***Water-deposited zinc and lead ore in the tristate district of Missouri, Kansas, and Oklahoma.*** *The upper map shows where most mining has taken place. The lower map shows the extent of underground mining in one of the most actively exploited mines. The cross sections, in which the vertical scale is exaggerated, show different levels of tunneling in this mine. The ore has been deposited by underground water into a porous limestone that dips gently downward to the northwest. It lies essentially at the land surface in Missouri, but is at shallow underground levels in Kansas and Oklahoma. Local geologists disagree as to whether the water depositing this ore was rising or sinking at the time. Whatever its prevailing vertical movement, it tended to carve horizontal circles or arcs and has deposited the ore in them.*

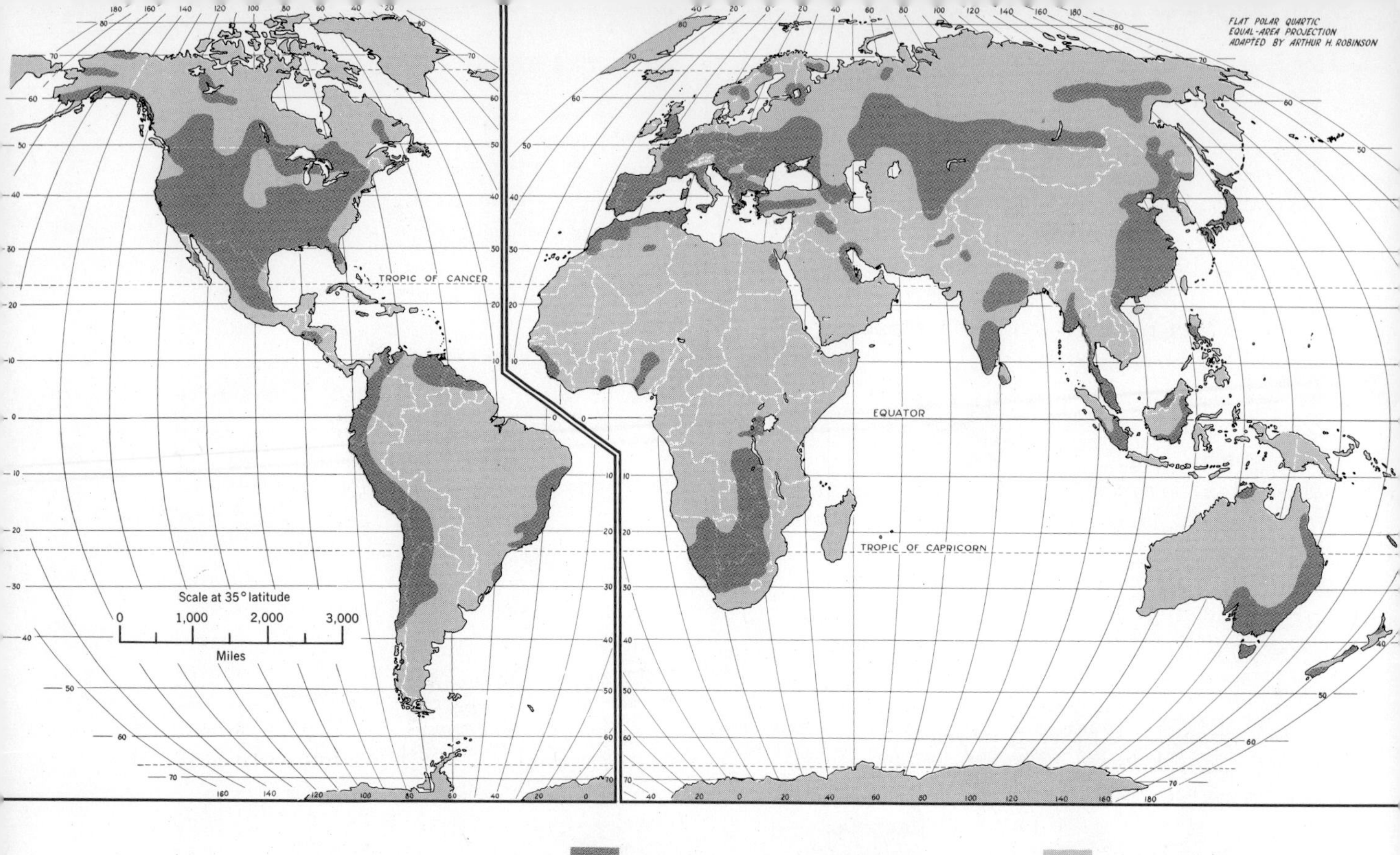

Figure 4.5 ***Major areas of active mineral extraction.*** *Note that technically advanced lands have been and are being thoroughly worked. Technically underdeveloped areas are not yet so thoroughly exploited. Where they are exploited, activity tends to be near coasts from which sea lanes can carry their mineral products to technically advanced countries. Not all areas of exploitation are outstanding producers.*

but change with the passage of time. The areas of heaviest mineral exploitation shown in Fig. 4.5 thus represent a *status quo* already changing. The change is normally sufficiently slow that the status of any single area will not be drastically altered a decade hence, but within a half century it may be altered noticeably.

Minerals and population

We have noted that mineral resources do not always occur in places, quantities, or qualities that man would desire. Neither does man normally migrate in large numbers to mineral resources for the sole purpose of their exploitation.[5] Instead, the existence of sizable populations tends to stimulate local mineral exploitation and to attract minerals from elsewhere. Thus such resources as occur near population clusters tend to be mined more vigorously than those farther removed, unless the quality and accessibility of the more distant resources, or such man-made features as tariffs, offset the advantages of the

[5] Historically, an exception to this generalization has been coal, the location of which has attracted heavy industry, particularly in Europe. With increasing industrial efficiency and with the development of alternative sources of fuel and power, however, the coal fields largely have lost the magnetism they once held for such industry.

local resources. These generalizations are reflected in the distribution of the world's people in comparison to that of areas undergoing extensive mineral exploitation. (Compare Fig. 4.5 and page 13.)

Minerals and economic activity

Mining and quarrying are usually the first stages of a production that continues through several manufacturing stages. Often the second stage, the milling of materials to a quality that can justify the cost of transportation to a manufacturing plant, is located near the mine, but many of the other stages are found in and near the large population clusters constituting the world's markets. In technically advanced societies, both the mining and the milling are highly mechanized. The importance of minerals to the world's economies, therefore, lies not in the labor forces supported directly by their exploitation, for these are small. Nor does it rest in the value of products obtained, for this is also small in comparison to the value of finished products. It lies, instead, in the overwhelming necessity for such minerals in a technical economy. Because of this necessity, many of the world's most heavily traveled routes, regardless of transportation media, exist appreciably for the purpose of freighting minerals to market.

Minerals and political units

Because of their significance in economies, minerals are vital ingredients of economic and political power. Control over them is achieved and maintained most easily when they are located inside the boundaries of an exploiting nation. Consequently, areas of known mineral wealth are regarded covetously by nearly all nations and sometimes actually become political pawns. A nation that is sprawled over a large area—ideally, an unbroken, unfragmented area—is more likely to possess a wide variety of minerals than its smaller neighbors, and is thus likely to be more powerful. At present, the United States and the Soviet Union illustrate this point very effectively, for they are giants among nations in the matter of mineral possession. When the focus is broadened to include respective spheres of influence, the mineral wealth available to each nation becomes even more abundant.

REFERENCES

Bateman, Alan M.: *Economic Mineral Deposits*, John Wiley & Sons, Inc., New York, 1950 and Chapman & Hall, Ltd., London, 1950. (Especially chap. 3.)

Carter, George F.: "Man, Time, and Change in the Far Southwest," *Annals of the Association of American Geographers*, **49** (3, part 2):8–30, 1959.

Finch, Vernor C., et al.: *Elements of Geography*, McGraw-Hill Book Company, Inc., New York, 1957. (Especially chaps. 11–18 and 23–24.)

McGill, John T: "Map of Coastal Landforms of the World," *Geographical Review*, **48**:402–405, 1958. (Accompanied by world map of coastal landforms.)

Peltier, Louis C.: "Geomorphology," in Preston E. James and Clarence F. Jones, (eds.), *American Geography: Inventory and Prospect*, Syracuse University Press for the Association of American Geographers, Syracuse, N. Y., 1954, pp. 362–380.

Spilhaus, Athelstan: "Control of the World Environment," *Geographical Review*, **46**:451–459, 1956.

White, Gilbert F., et al.: *Changes in Urban Occupance of Flood Plains of the United States*, University of Chicago Department of Geography Research Paper 57, Chicago, 1958.

5 CLIMATE, WATER, AND AIR RESOURCES

IN THE PRECEDING CHAPTER WE HAVE DISCUSSED TWO OF THE EIGHT FUNDAmental features of natural environment—landforms and minerals—and their roles in man's economic activities. In the present chapter we discuss the importance of climate, water, and air.

CLIMATE

Climate is unique among the natural environmental features emphasized in this book in that it is an intangible. The term *climate* refers to a series of changes within the atmosphere and involves also, although mainly in gaseous form, moisture contributions to and from the hydrosphere. In other words, climate is a summary (usually taken over a minimum period of one year) of day-to-day weather conditions, the basic elements being (1) *temperature,* (2) *humidity,* including precipitation, (3) *pressure* (weight), and (4) *winds.* These four basic ingredients are constantly changing, both absolutely and relatively, and their changes result in changes of weather and climate—the former on a short-term basis and the latter on a very long-term basis.

CLASSIFICATION AND DISTRIBUTION

The relationships among the four basic elements of a climate, although constantly changing, are well enough systematized to permit general classification. Most of the accepted classifications are based on averages, means, ranges, and seasonal rhythms of temperature and humidity, the two elements of weather and climate that appear to be most directly critical for man and his activities.

Before attempting a study of a specific climate classification, the reader should be aware of the existence of an orderly pattern of global distribution—of an arrangement which tends to repeat itself from continent to continent. Regardless of hemisphere, a climate which occupies a certain position in one continent will tend to be found in an analogous position in all other continents. This is due chiefly to the fact that the climatic elements are affected, directly or indirectly, by a number of climatic controls (incoming solar radiation, wind currents, ocean currents, etc.) which, for the most part, are themselves in orderly arrangement and which have global influence.

Exceptions to the orderly pattern of climates do exist, and these are likewise traceable to climatic controls—but usually to controls that are not in repetitious arrangement. Outstanding among such controls are landform features, which often interrupt the functioning of controls responsible for orderly climatic patterns and hence either void entirely or restrict severely the normal area of a climate's distribution. They are influential over all of the climatic elements. Land masses that are extraordinarily large, like those found especially in the northern portion of the Eastern Hemisphere (where Europe, Asia, and northern Africa tend to heat up and cool off as a single unit), may interfere directly and severely with temperatures, and indirectly with pressures, winds, and precipitation. Landforms situated wholly or partially within the high latitudes, such as Antarctica, Eurasia, and North America, are characterized by cold, even frigid, climates not found elsewhere except at very high altitudes. Landforms of prominent elevation, including nearly all major mountain systems and plateaus, not only reach into cooler temperatures but also cause air to rise and often to precipitate moisture. Consequently, the windward slopes of such landforms are often wet, and the leeward slopes dry.

A classification of thirteen climate types, separated on the basis of temperature and humidity, is presented in Fig. 5.1.

Tropical rain forest

The tropical rain-forest climate occupies continental interiors of low-to-moderate elevation along the equator and reaches discontinuously outward to include a few western coasts and several eastern coasts, of which some are as distant as the Tropic of Cancer and the Tropic of Capricorn (Fig. 5.1). It cores the Amazon River basin of South America and the Congo River basin of Africa, includes the major islands of Indonesia, and sends offshoots from each of these tropical areas toward the subtropical latitudes.

As implied in its name, the temperatures are tropical, never dropping to the freezing point but maintaining a monotonous regularity, day by day and year by year. The temperatures of the strictly equatorial locations usually range from 5°F above and below an annual average of 80°F, and the range increases with latitude. The four seasons scarcely exist as such. In the very low latitudes, temperatures tend to be highest during the months of March to May and September to November, for at these times the noonday sun is directly overhead, and the incoming solar radiation is at its maximum effectiveness along the equator. During the remainder of the year, the noonday sun is perpendicular to the earth's surface at places either to the north or south, and the equatorial temperatures decline slightly. On about June 22, the noonday sun is directly over the Tropic of Cancer, and on approximately December 22 it is over the Tropic of Capricorn. Equatorial locations thus tend to experience a dual temperature maximum, with the highest readings during the vernal and autumnal equinoxes and their lowest during the summer and winter solstices.

The precipitation of tropical rain-forest climate is heavy and regular, amounting to at least 60 inches, and sometimes exceeding 200 inches, each year. Daily rains, in the form of thundershowers, are common, and there is no pronounced dry season. Hurricanes (also called *typhoons*) seldom occur between lat 5° N and S, but they may strike the eastern coasts reaching beyond those very latitudes.

Tropical savanna

Situated on either side of tropical rain-forest climate is the tropical savanna climate, which extends rather continuously to lat 15° N and S, and fragmentally to the Tropics of Cancer and Capricorn (Fig. 5.1). Except where interrupted by prominent landforms, it occupies major areas in South America, Africa, southeastern Asia; portions of the coastal sections of Australia, Madagascar, Java, Ceylon,

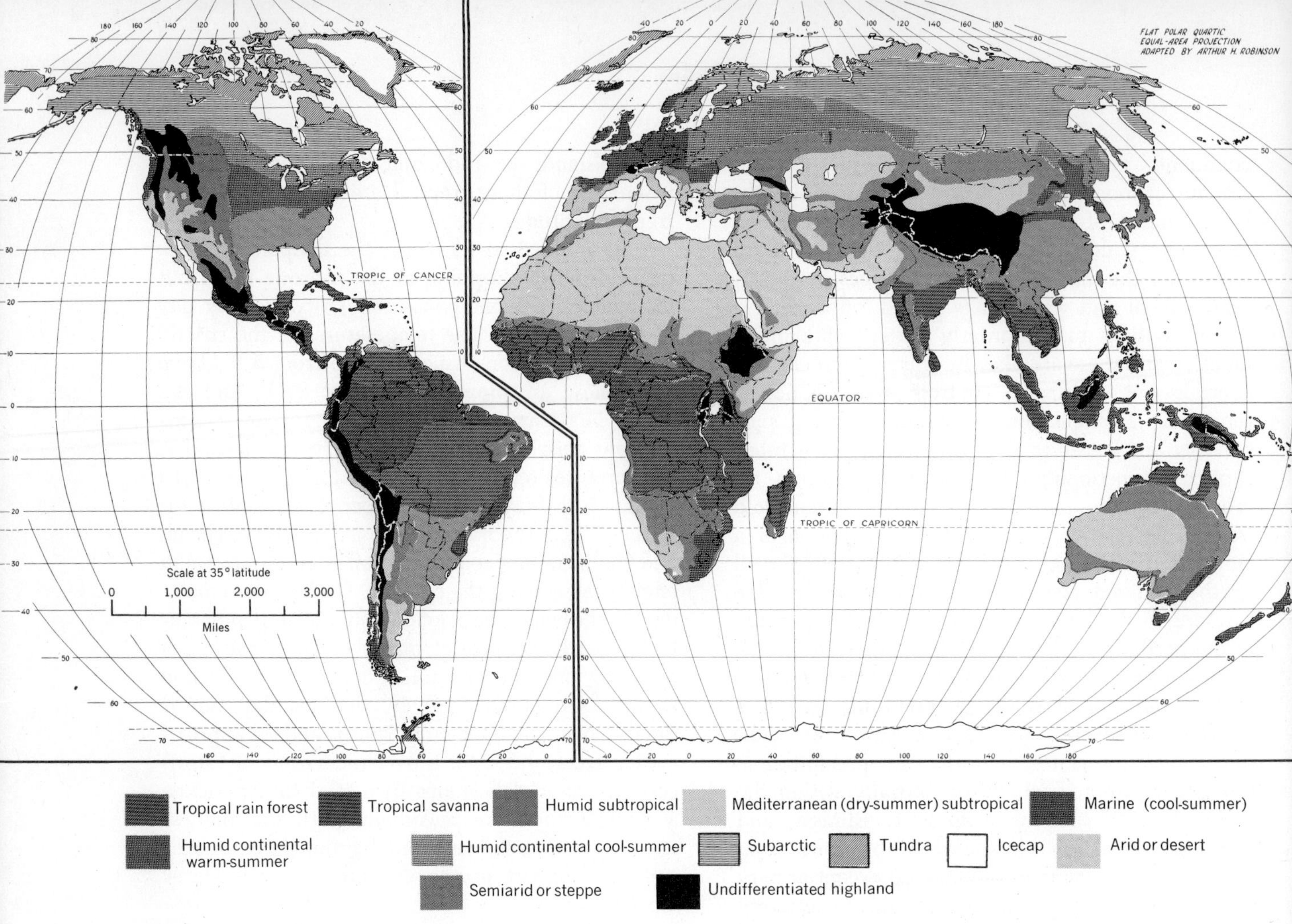

Figure 5.1 ***The world pattern of climates.*** *(After the Koeppen system as modified by Trewartha)*

and Hispaniola; and all of Cuba, as well as numerous smaller islands.

Although temperatures of tropical savanna climate fall into the same classification as those of tropical rain-forest climate, they tend to be slightly cooler and to have a more pronounced annual range than is true in the very low latitudes.

The distinguishing feature of tropical savanna climate is the seasonality of its precipitation, which, although ranging in amount from approximately 30 to 60 inches a year, is concentrated within the summer months. Winters are pronouncedly dry. Hurricanes may strike all eastern coasts in this climate except along the shore of the Atlantic Ocean south of the equator. Here, for reasons not yet fully understood, none occur in any climate type.

Humid subtropical

Moving still farther toward the middle latitudes, one finds the eastern portions of continents occupied by humid subtropical climate, which usually extends latitudinally from the vicinity of the Tropic of Cancer to approximately lat 40° N, and the vicinity of the Tropic of Capricorn to approximately lat 40° S. Excellent examples are found in southeastern United States, in southeastern Asia, and in Uruguay and its neighbors of South America, with smaller examples along the eastern fringes of Australia and South Africa, and in the Adriatic and Balkan countries of Europe. Like the two tropical climates, it is largely in orderly arrangement, the only major exceptions being the European fragments, which are due mainly to local causes. Frost may be expected in this climate, the frequency and severity increasing with latitude. As implied in the term *subtropical,* however, the growing season is still long, and temperatures, even in winter, are not harshly cold (Fig. 5.1).

Precipitation in this climate is quite regular and heavy, amounting usually to no fewer than 40 inches and no more than 70 inches per year. There is no distinctly dry season. Hurricanes and related storms are to be expected, with greatest frequency and intensity in early autumn and in spring.

Mediterranean subtropical

Continental western coasts that are within lat 30°–40° N or S are generally under mediterranean subtropical climate. This climate is developed most adequately along the Mediterranean Sea, for that large indentation is the "western coast" of a land complex which includes Europe, Asia, and Africa north of the equator. The climate is found also on the two "western coasts" of Australia, and in southern Africa, central Chile, and southern California.

The distinguishing aspect of this climate is its precipitation, but not so much the annual amount, which ranges from 5 to 30 inches, as its seasonality. Nearly all the precipitation occurs during the winter months, and summers are deficient in rainfall—indeed, often completely arid. Few hurricanes occur on continental west coasts, and they are virtually absent in areas dominated by this type of climate.

The temperatures are moderate, not greatly unlike those of humid subtropical climate.

Marine

Most regions of marine climate are located poleward from mediterranean subtropical climate, but a few are poleward and/or upslope from humid subtropical climate. Throughout most of the world, this climate is restricted by mountains to narrow strips, usually along western coasts, and to offshore islands. In northwestern Europe, however, it reaches southward to an Alpine system appreciably removed from the Atlantic Ocean, and eastward to the colder continental climates of the remainder of the Eurasian continental plain.

Marine temperatures are cool in both summer and winter, and its growing season, often upward of 180 days, is surprisingly long in consideration of the high latitudes (40°–60° N and S) in which it occurs.

Except along the very humid slopes of certain mountains, its average annual precipitation ranges generally between 25 and 35 inches, with no specific season of drought or deficiency.

Humid continental warm-summer

The large size and high latitudinal extent of Eurasia and North America result in three climates not found in the southern hemisphere—the humid continental warm-summer, the humid continental cool-summer, and the subarctic climates.

In the United States and in southeastern Asia, the humid continental climate is immediately north of the humid subtropical climate. In the Balkan countries of Europe, it is east of the humid subtropical climate.

As implied by its title, this climate is rather moist, with precipitation usually in the range of 25–45 inches annually. Summers are ordinarily but not necessarily the times of highest precipitation, and there is no specific dry season. Temperatures vary markedly during the course of a year in response not only to the "march of the seasons" but also to the pronounced summer heating and subsequent winter chilling of the land masses. This is true despite the fact that all three major regions of this climate type are adjacent to oceans or seas; for westerly winds, which prevail in these latitudes, tend to carry continental influences to the east.[1] The winter season is sufficiently cold and long that the frost-free period ranges from 150 to 180 days.

[1] An exception can be noted during the summer season of southeastern Asia, where a persistent sea-to-land monsoon develops during the warm season; however, the moisture and moderate temperatures of this wind are altered as it passes over the mountains of southern China, Korea, and Japan; and it approaches the humid continental warm-summer climate as a rather hot, drying airflow.

Humid continental cool-summer

This climate is distinguished from its southern neighbor, the humid continental warm-summer climate, especially by cooler temperatures and a shorter growing season (120 to 150 days), and by a slightly reduced precipitation. Its temperature and humidity conditions are harsh enough so that it marks the northern limit of effective agriculture at current levels of science and technology.

Subarctic

On the poleward margins of the humid continental cool-summer climate of the Northern Hemisphere is an extensive area of subarctic climate. Not much precipitation falls in this climate, the annual amount frequently totaling less than 20 inches. However, this reduced precipitation is offset by retarded rates of evaporation in these cool temperatures, so that the climate is considered moist. In some areas there is a summer maximum of precipitation, and in others a winter maximum, but no season is noteworthily deficient in moisture. Summers are short, and the average annual temperatures are not high. An erratic growing season of 60 to 90 days renders agriculture so difficult as to be almost impossible.

Tundra and icecap

These climates are found in the very high latitudes, with the icecap climate coring the sizable land masses of Greenland and Antarctica, and the tundra climate fringing most land masses that reach into these latitudes. Both are very cold and are usually low in precipitation. However, evaporation is retarded to the extent that these climates are classified as humid rather than arid.

Arid, or desert

The world contains a surprisingly consistent "tier" of subtropical deserts that enclose central and western portions of continents, generally between lat 20°–30° N or S. The most prominent of these are the Sahara, the Arabian, and the Thar Deserts, which constitute the "west central" portion of the Eurasian–North African land complex; the desert in western Australia; the Kalahari Desert of South Africa; the Atacama Desert of Chile (an extension of which, because of local conditions, reaches northward through coastal Peru almost to the equator); and the Sonora and related deserts of North America.

Other deserts are due mainly to their situation on the leeward margins of prominent landforms. These include particularly the Turkestan desert east of the Caspian Sea in the Soviet Union; the Tarim River basin and Gobi Desert of western Communist China; the desert in central Iran; and the Patagonian Desert of Argentina.

Average annual temperatures in the subtropical deserts are warm or hot and in the middle-latitude deserts are alternately very hot and very cold. Precipitation seldom exceeds 10 inches per year.

Semiarid, or steppe

Semiarid, or steppe, climates represent a transition from deserts to more humid conditions and consequently are found almost invariably along the outer margins of deserts. Their causes and their global distribution are so similar to those of deserts that further elaboration is unnecessary. They are distinguished from deserts primarily on the basis of precipitation, which tends to range from 10 inches in the cooler areas, where evaporation is somewhat retarded, to 25 inches in areas of very active evaporation.

Undifferentiated highland

Temperatures decrease with elevation at an average rate of 3.3°F per 1,000 feet if air is stagnant or moving horizontally, and usually at a higher rate if air is rising; higher landforms, therefore, experience cooler temperatures than do lower elevations.

Precipitation is also affected by prominent landforms, which tend to have moist conditions on slopes facing a prevailing wind and dry conditions on their leeward slopes.

Because of the marked impact of landform elevation upon climate, the climates of prominent landforms are classified in a specific category known as *undifferentiated highland climate.* The lower margins of this climate are almost indistinguishable from the climates of the surrounding countrysides; but with ascent the temperatures are reduced, and the precipitation may or may not be altered, depending upon local conditions. In reality, therefore, the undifferentiated highland climate represents a catch-all climate—a generalization for a host of tiny, vertically aligned climate zones which are too small to be viewed with understanding on a world map. Where moisture is adequate, there is a tendency for such climates to be arranged in a series of consecutive tiers, not unlike the latitudinal arrangement of the world's moist climates. Thus, for example, if one were to move up the eastern Andes in Ecuador, he might be able to pass through successive zones corresponding to the humid subtropical, humid continental, subarctic, and tundra climates, respectively.

CLIMATE AND ECONOMIC GEOGRAPHY

Being an intangible, climate is directly significant in economic geography as a natural conditioning agent, and not as a source of raw materials for production.

Climate and population

The three major clusters of world population—in southeastern Asia, northwestern Europe, and east central North America—are situated primarily in subtropical and middle-latitude climates, but offshoots extend equatorward in the Far East to include portions of tropical savanna and even tropical rain-forest climates (Fig. 5.1 and page 13). The subarctic, polar, and icecap climates of the high latitudes are very sparsely settled, as are the arid and semiarid climates (except for irrigated oases), most tropical climates, and the undifferentiated highland climate (except for the cooler elevations upslope from the tropics).

Climate and economic activity

Climate is especially important to production and transportation in two respects: (1) it may affect the vigor and productive capacity, whether mental or physical, of a nation's labor force and (2) it may be either an asset or a liability to the work which that labor force performs.

Human Vigor. There is little agreement concerning the influence of climate upon man's physical and mental energy. Perhaps the most ardent advocate of positive influence was a noted geographer, the late Ellsworth Huntington, who conducted prodigious research to demonstrate a causal relationship between certain climates which allegedly stimulated human activity and areas of the world possessing what it terms "very high civilizations." Huntington's "ideal climate" for mental and physical activity was similar to the marine climate described above and included aspects of the humid continental warm- and cool-summer climates. His "very high civilizations" involved northern Europe, together with its cultural offshoots in the brisk, but not paralyzingly cold, portions of North America, South America, South Africa, and Australia—areas that are now usually designated as technically advanced. There is, of course, a rather close global overlap between these two sets of features. Huntington's opponents have maintained, however, (1) that no universally accepted definition of the term *civilization* exists and that Huntington's "very high civilizations" can be more or less arbitrarily delimited; and (2) that highly intricate civilizations once thrived in adverse climates along the eastern and southern Mediterranean Sea, and in Central and South America. If there be a close relationship between civilization and climate, they asked, why did such vigorous civilizations develop under subtropical climate conditions?

Whatever the resolution to this particular debate, one can scarcely deny entirely an effect of weather and climate upon mental and physical activity. Any of us who has attempted either mental or physical labor under extremes of temperature and humidity is well aware that work does have its optimum weather conditions. It is partially for this reason that buildings have long been heated during the winter months and, recently, have been air-conditioned in some regions during the summer.

As time passes, however, this aspect of climate will become decreasingly important to economic geography, for man is already demonstrating a determination and an ability to create artificial climates inside his buildings. Perhaps some day air conditioning for entire cities will not be unfeasible—and thereby man will mark another milestone in his perennial struggle with nature.

The Productive Occupations. Three of the six productive occupations—agriculture, grazing, and forest-products industries—are executed in intimate association with climate. The remainder, while not unaffected by climate, are less directly associated with it.

Climate may be viewed as both favorable and unfavorable for agriculture. It is favorable in that it permits agriculture, as we know it, to exist; being in orderly arrangement both in time and in space, it is conducive to the growth, year after year and century after century, of certain crops and animals in certain areas of the world. It is unfavorable in that it places restrictions upon the growing seasons and growth areas of individual species or types of crops and animals, for each plant and animal has its optimum and marginal growth areas, and each of those areas occupies only a portion of the entire land surface of the earth. To an extent, man can and has overcome such climatic limitations by providing irrigation water in dry regions, by using greenhouses in cold regions, and by developing plants and animals which yield satisfactorily under adverse temperature and/or moisture conditions. He has not yet offset nature entirely in this respect, however; and the population of a given area, if it hopes to maintain an adequate and balanced diet, must usually import some agricultural commodities.

In global distribution, most of the cultivated land occurs in the same climates as do the major clusters of population. Such a situation should not be unexpected, for well over one-half of the world's labor force is engaged in agriculture.

Grazing is here considered as restricted to those natural forage areas which, at least recently, have not been regularly planted. In practice, these areas are predominantly in semiarid and tropical savanna climates, and they also are in erratically distributed sections and fringes of mediterranean, desert, humid subtropical, humid continental, and subarctic climates. The relationship of climate to plant life, including forage, is discussed in more detail in the next chapter; suffice it to say here that certain climates tend to stimulate the growth of forage-type vegetation and that a climate favorable to grazing must have mild enough temperatures for animals to survive and enough moisture to produce drinking water.

The association of the forest-products industries with climate is similar to that of grazing with climate, since both depend upon vegetation types intimately related to local climatic conditions.

Unlike the three productive occupations discussed in the preceding paragraphs, fishing and hunting, mining and quarrying, and manufacturing are not directly dependent upon climate for any condition vital to their existence. Fishermen are at work where sea life is available, miners where minerals are to be exploited, manufacturers where products are to be made. Of course, climate is always a consideration, as it can be a very important convenience and/or cost factor; but with the possible exception of hunting for game, which takes place in certain climate zones because of the natural forage, climate is a secondary factor in the location and functioning of these three industries.

Transportation. Travel by water is seriously hampered, and frequently halted, by winter ice of the middle latitudes and polar regions. In practice, such interruptions occur almost entirely in the Northern Hemisphere, which contains the bulk of the world's sea lanes and inland waterways. Transportation media other than water carriers are sensitive to weather and climate conditions, at least to the extent that service is temporarily interrupted during hazardous storms. This is especially true of aircraft. All in all, however, the association between climate and transportation is rather casual, with the former acting as a noteworthy but not vital direct influence upon the global distribution and functioning of the latter.

Climate and political units

The economic strength of political units depends largely upon their capacity and efficiency for production and transportation of commodities. The significance of climate to them, therefore, is primarily indirect and is to be found in the significance of climate to production and transportation.

The law of averages would suggest that, among specific nations, those which are largest in area would be the most auspiciously endowed with favorable climates. In practice, however, this is not always true. Other factors, particularly location, often offset the theoretical advantages of mere size, as is demonstrated in a comparison of the most extensive political units of the world: the Soviet Union, Canada, Communist China, Brazil, the United States, and Australia—nations ranging downward from over 8 million to fewer than 3 million square miles.

The Soviet Union. The Soviet Union possesses eight climate types: tundra, subarctic, humid continental cool-summer, humid continental warm-summer, mediterranean subtropical, semiarid, desert, and undifferentiated highlands. Unfortunately, the country's location and landform distribution are such that adverse climates aggregately enclose much of its territory. Only the tiny representations of mediterranean subtropical and humid continental warm-summer climates along the shore line of the Black Sea and the rather extensive areas of humid continental cool-summer climate are conducive to extensive settlement, production, and transportation at current levels of world technical advancement.

Canada. With a latitudinal location very much like that of the Soviet Union, Canada is endowed with climates similarly adverse. Six climate types are recognized here; and only the presence of a strip of marine climate on the western coast and the absence of mediterranean subtropical, humid continental warm-summer, and desert climates distinguish Canada's range of climates from that of the Soviet Union. Currently, favorable climatic conditions for Canadian livelihood are found only in the humid continental cool-summer and marine climates.

Communist China. Communist China is in the middle latitudes, and its seven climate types reflect that location. The fringe of subarctic climate continuing into Communist China's Manchuria from across the border of the Soviet Union graduates southward into humid continental cool-summer climate, which soon merges into humid continental warm-summer climate. This, in turn, transits into the humid subtropical climate that encloses much territory in the southeastern portion of the country. Inland are extensive reaches of undifferentiated highland and semiarid climates, which jointly enclose a pocket of desert. Of the seven climates, the first one and the last three may be considered as not favorable for a dynamic economy at existing levels of world science and technology.

Brazil. Among the world's six largest nations, only Brazil is primarily tropical in climate. Tropical rainforest and tropical savanna climates, which encompass at least two-thirds of the country, merge into the small strip of semiarid climate that reaches inland from the northeastern coast, into the fragmentary undifferentiated highland climate near the southeastern shore line, and into the humid subtropical climate of the far south. With so much of its territory engulfed by tropical climates, Brazil cannot be said to possess as favorable an endowment as does Communist China; and yet, as has been shown by residents of southeastern Asia, notably India, the tropics need not be an insurmountable barrier to the development of complex civilizations involving large numbers of people.

The United States. With an excellent cross section of the world's middle latitude and subtropical climates, the United States is without parallel among the world's six largest nations in possession of climates which offer no serious barrier to human growth and development at present levels of civilizations. More than half the country is in humid, seasonally changeable climates, with humid continental warm-summer and cool-summer and humid

Irrigation in both humid and dry places. (a) Drawing water for irrigation in arid fringes of mediterranean climate in Azerbaijan, Iran (International Cooperation Administration); (b) overhead irrigation in marine climate south of London (British Information Services); (c) irrigating in semiarid climate in southern Colorado (U.S. Department of Agriculture).

subtropical climates dominating the landscape eastward from long 100° W, and the mediterranean subtropical and marine climates sharing the western coast. Only in the Mountain West and in the Great Plains have semiarid, desert, and undifferentiated highland climates been a deterrent to settlement and consequent economic activity. Communist China alone, among the six nations compared here, approaches the United States in general climatic amenities.

Australia. Some have said that Australia must have been created as an afterthought out of surplus ingredients from other continents. If this be true, aridity must have been in overwhelming surplus; for about two-thirds of Australia is in desert and steppe climates, which are fringed by mediterranean subtropical, marine, humid subtropical, and tropical savanna climates. Unfortunately, the representation of each is rather small, and the nation suffers accordingly.

WATER

Water functions so closely in conjunction with other natural environmental features that its isolation from them, even for analysis, may seem somewhat artificial. As has been shown in the preceding pages, water is an integral component of climate—so integral, in fact, that climatic classification without careful attention to it would be impossible. It is associated with landforms as a major force of erosion and subsequent deposition, as a series of river drainage basins, and as a gigantic reservoir covering three-fourths of the earth's surface—leaving only a meager one-fourth of that surface protruding above sea level. It is a dynamic agent of mineral deposition, of plant and animal existence, and of soil formation. Indeed, it is a prime requisite for all life, including human life, and might quite properly be added to the economists' classical necessities: food, shelter, and clothing.

Water and population

Most of the world's people are found in areas where the water supply is continuous and adequate but not superfluous—and hence are found in the humid climates of the middle latitudes and the subtropics. Within southeastern Asia, however, the populations have utilized not only such of these climates as they

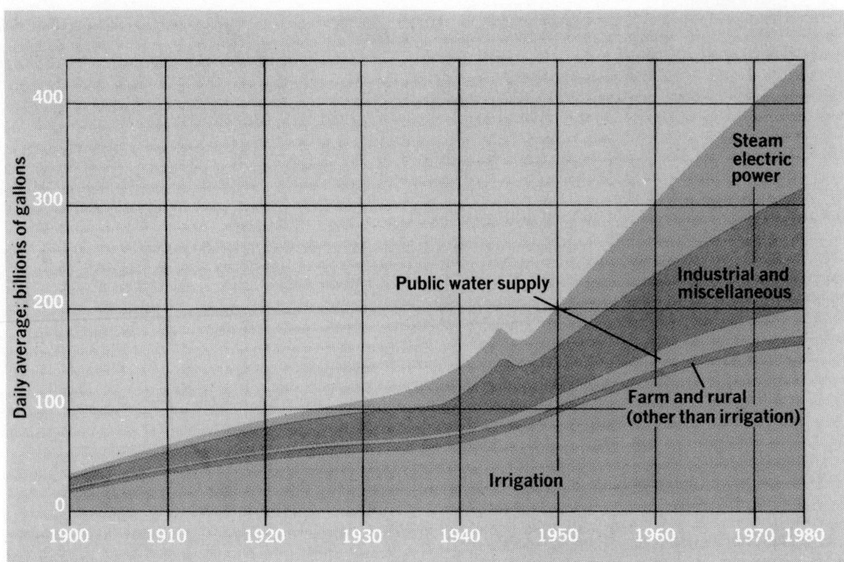

Figure 5.2 ***Utilization of water in the United States,*** *1900–1975. Farm demand is expected to increase, but not so fast as industrial demand. Steam electric (fuel-generated) plants are expected to consume a very large amount of the nation's future water supply. In such technically advanced economies as ours, serious questions are being raised about the adequacy of future water supplies, even in humid climates.* (Area Development Bulletin, *U.S. Office of Area Development)*

possess but also the tropical savanna climate, where precipitation is adequate but seasonally deficient, and much of the tropical rain-forest climate, where water is chronically in excess.

In contrast, the vast, dry areas of the world are either sparsely populated or empty.

Water and production

Water enters into the function of production via two important considerations: (1) it is almost invariably associated in nature with the raw materials to be produced, and (2) it often assumes a dynamic role in man's processes of extracting and producing such raw materials.

Natural Raw Materials. Except in manufacturing, which is mainly dependent upon raw materials supplied by the other five productive occupations, water is an active agent in establishing natural conditions for production. In agriculture it is a major factor in the creation of a soil; in grazing and forestry it is partially accountable for both the underlying soil and the vegetation so necessary to these industries; in fishing it is the very habitat of sea life; in hunting it is a direct necessity for the game which is hunted; and in mining and quarrying it has been responsible for the deposition and/or the concentration of very many mineral deposits.

The Productive Occupations. Water not only makes certain natural raw materials available for extraction and production by man, but it also is an active agent in some of the productive processes. In agriculture and grazing, whether supplied naturally or artificially, it is a necessity for plant and animal growth; in fishing it provides a habitat for all marine life; in mining and milling it is an agent for washing and for dust and fire alleviation; in manufacturing it is assuming increased importance as an agent of processing and a source of hydroelectric power (Fig. 5.2). In all the productive occupations as well as in daily living, water is becoming more significant in removal of waste—indeed, so significant that polluted rivers and streams are not uncommon. Among these is the Potomac River, which is so polluted as it flows by the capital of the United States that swimming in it is prohibited.

Water and transportation

Water carriers, unlike air carriers, float even when at rest, and locomotion is necessary only to provide thrust across a quasi-frictionless water surface. Unlike overland vehicles, most of the world's water carriers follow lanes which are provided free of charge by nature. Moreover, the largest water carriers can transport a greater amount of freight in a single haul than can most overland or air carriers.

Primarily because of these features, transportation by water generally is less expensive than by other means; consequently, it has assumed a commanding position, the significance of which is attested by the thousands of inland waterway, coastal, intercoastal, and overseas shipping craft, which aggregately reach every water port but which concentrate on the routes within and among the world's major clusters of population.

Among the other mechanical carriers, water is less active. It is necessary for the operation of the steam engines of railways where such engines are still used, and it is the major cooling agent for many gasoline-powered vehicles. In air transportation, it provides landing places for a comparatively small number of seaplanes. All these uses, however, while interesting, are definitely secondary when compared with the critical importance of water for shipping vessels, barges, and boats.

AIR

Air, like water, is (1) a vital component of climate and (2) essential to most biological life. In these and many other aspects, therefore, it is indirectly of significance in economic geography. Its direct importance to the subject is at least threefold: (1) in production it is a source of some raw materials, especially nitrogen; (2) it is an agent in various types of manufacturing; and (3) in transportation it is a medium of passage for air carriers.

Unlike other features of the natural environment emphasized in this book, air is ubiquitous. Air, unlike the minerals, need not be sought in out-of-the-way places. As the efficiency of air carriers increases, no point along the earth's land-water surface will be truly inaccessible to approach by air. Moreover, air routes are shorter than most land or water routes. Whereas overland routes seek the world's plains and gentle slopes and water routes detour to circumvent landform obstacles (including whole continents), air routes follow the shortest distance between two points along the earth's curved land-water surface. It is in the realm of transportation that air appears to be of maximum direct importance to economic geography—in the present and, even more decidedly, in the future.

REFERENCES

Borchert, John R.: "The Climate of the Central North American Grassland," *Annals of the Association of American Geographers,* **40:**1–39, 1950.

Climate and Man, Yearbook of Agriculture, 1941, U.S. Department of Agriculture, 1941.

Finch, Vernor C., et al.: *Elements of Geography,* McGraw-Hill Book Company, Inc., New York, 1957. (Especially chaps. 6–10 and 19.)

Hare, Kenneth: "The Westerlies," *Geographical Review,* **50:**345–367, 1960.

Leighly, John: "Climatology," in Preston E. James and Clarence F. Jones (eds.), *American Geography: Inventory and Prospect,* Syracuse University Press for the Association of American Geographers, Syracuse, N. Y., 1954, pp. 335–361.

McIntosh, C. B.: "Atmospheric Conditions and Explosions in Coal Mines," *Geographical Review,* **47:** 155–174, 1957.

Manley, Gordon: "The Revival of Climatic Determinism," *Geographical Review,* **48:**98–105, 1958.

Van Burkalow, Anastasia: "The Geography of New York City's Water Supply: A Study of Interactions," *Geographical Review,* **49:**369–386, 1959.

White, Gilbert F.: "Industrial Water Use: A Review," *Geographical Review,* **50:**412–430, 1960.

6 BIOTIC AND SOIL RESOURCES

WE TURN NOW TO THE REMAINING THREE OF THE EIGHT CATEGORIES OF NATURAL environment that are here considered fundamental to economic geography: plant life, or flora; animal life, or fauna; and soils.

THE FLORA

Botanical life can be said to be either *macroscopic* or *microscopic*—either visible or invisible to the naked eye. Most microscopic plant life is not of major concern to the beginning student of economic geography, as it does not appear to have a direct association with man's efforts to gain a livelihood or with other aspects of man's economies. In contrast, the macroscopic flora of both land and water, especially the former, is of decided interest, because it is used extensively to satisfy human needs and wants. Ranging in size and complexity downward from trees, this and antecedent vegetation once covered the earth's land surface except the cold and dry portions. Despite its removal in large amounts by man, much remains to the present day. Maritime plant life, on the other hand, tends to be restricted to upper water levels that are accessible to sunlight, with the larger, rooted forms growing along the earth's continental shelves and other shallows, and the smaller forms floating freely in water. As yet, man has seen fit to exploit only a small amount of the known maritime plant life, which remains more or less as it would have been if man had not existed.

LAND FLORA

Land vegetation has been classified in three groups: (1) forests, (2) grasses, and (3) shrubs and tundras (Fig. 6.1). Although there are many exceptions, forests tend to be found where climates and soils (especially soils) are moist, grasses where climates and soils are moist to dry, and shrubs and tundras (respectively) where climates and soils are very dry or cold.

The forests

Forests, the most widespread of the three groups, extend discontinuously from lat 70° N southward to the tips of all continents and major islands except polar Antarctica. In northern Anglo-America and Eurasia, they reach without serious interruption from the Pacific to the Atlantic Oceans. Moreover, they are found on most high landforms, regardless of the vegetation below. Today, despite man's exploitation, they occupy over one-fourth of the earth's total land surface (Fig. 6.2).[1]

Low-latitude Forests. The world's tree life is characteristically subdivided into two categories—the low-latitude and the middle-latitude forests. These, in turn, are usually classified into broadleaf-evergreen, deciduous, and narrowleaf-evergreen varieties.

In the low latitudes are dense stands of broadleaf-evergreens containing a wide range of types, frequently more than sixteen per acre. They have been classified mainly by their Latin designations and are not well known in popular terminology. Some appear to be close cousins of mahogany, teak, and ebony trees that flourish in slightly higher latitudes. One of the best known is the palm, which is usually present in one form or another. They are called *broadleaf evergreens* because, in these mild regions, they are never without foliage, which consists of broad, flat leaves. In many cases a changing of leaves occurs, but it is on a continuous basis, so that the trees are never bare. A forest like this, usually referred to as *selva,* or *tropical rain forest,* reaches average heights of 150 to 180 feet, and some trees exceed 200 feet. Not all growth is this tall, however, for the selva is a multilevel forest with shorter trees, shrubs, and parasitic jungle growth notably present along clearings, waterways, and other places where breaks appear in the umbrellalike canopies of the tallest trees. In slightly higher elevations, these forests merge into related varieties of trees which, despite their cooler habitat, remain evergreen.

[1] A recent world land use estimate by the Food and Agricultural Organization of the United Nations: barren land, 48 per cent; forests, 27 per cent; grasslands, 15 per cent; cropland, 10 per cent.

With a few important exceptions, the wood of the selva is hard and difficult to work, the other products are in only moderate demand, and the locations are appreciably inaccessible. For these reasons, the selva has been exploited only preliminarily, except by the overcrowded populations of the older civilizations in the mainland sections of southeastern Asia. The tropical rain forest may be considered, therefore, as a reserve of potentially useful timber which will be tapped if dwindling reserves in other areas become so small that such action is necessary. It is an extensive reserve, accounting for about one-half of the world's existing timber resources classified as productive or capable of exploitation (Fig. 6.1).

Also in the low latitudes are a few semideciduous and deciduous trees which apparently shed their leaves because of regular or sporadic drought. These are erratically distributed from the selva approximately to the Tropics of Cancer and Capricorn, usually merging into low-latitude grasses. Their height and luxuriance decrease latitudinally with decreasing moisture and range from conditions resembling those of the tropical rain forest to isolated, single, stunted trees. These trees are best developed where adjacent to the selva.

Fringing either the low-latitude deciduous trees or the tropical rain forest are erratically distributed stands of scrub or thorn forest, a series of plants that manage to exist in the drier sections of the tropics. Being drought-resistant, most of these have a minimum of foliage, are quite woody and thorny, seldom reach more than 5 or 6 feet in height, and whose only commercial value is limited grazing.

Middle-latitude Forests. Ideally, the latitudinal arrangement of the world's forests would appear to be that of a transition from broadleaf-evergreen to deciduous to narrowleaf-evergreen trees with increasing distance from the equator. In fact, where moisture permits, this distribution is recognizable, but with a major exception: notably in southeastern United States between lat 25°–35° N (and extending even farther northward within the higher eleva-

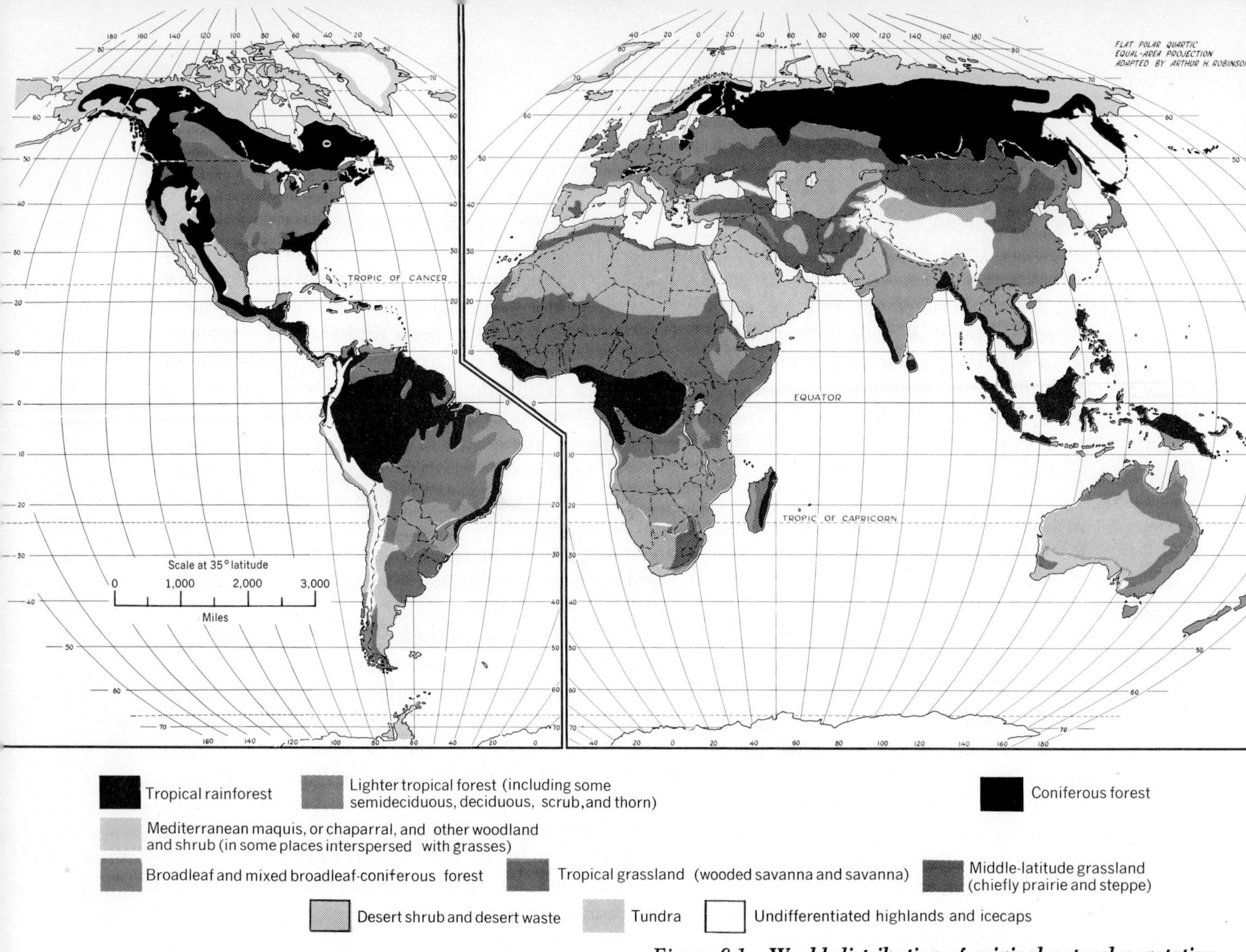

Figure 6.1 **World distribution of original natural vegetation.**

tions of the Appalachian Mountains) is a prodigious growth of pine and associated narrowleaf evergreens. These are longleaf, narrowleaf softwoods that reproduce themselves by bearing and shedding cones, and hence are called *coniferous.* Analogous varieties appear in corresponding positions (the eastern sections of continents roughly between lat 25°–35° N or S) in South America, Africa, Australia, and Asia, but their stands are usually more sparse and more liberally sprinkled with deciduous trees. They are blessings to the regions possessing them, for they can be utilized very intensively for a wide variety of purposes, and because they grow in relatively mild temperatures and under plentiful supplies of moisture, they replace themselves more quickly than do the evergreens of the higher latitudes. If man continues to cut timber with his current prodigious energy, these forests, especially in the United States, may well become the chief source areas of the softwoods.

Beyond these stands of subtropical coniferous trees are middle-latitude broadleaf forests that occupy extensive areas of east central United States, north central and southeastern Canada, northern Europe, west central and east central Asia, and coastal strips of southeastern Australia and southern Chile, as well as a small district in southeastern Brazil. These include a large number of specific types, of which the more common varieties are oak, hickory, chestnut, elm, cottonwood, poplar, ash, walnut, beech, birch, and maple. Most are deciduous, shedding their leaves annually because of seasonal cold.

The reserves of middle-latitude broadleaf forests have been decimated by man to a greater degree than has been true of any other group—not because they are so desirable, for they are mostly hardwoods and are not so suitable for most of man's purposes as are the softwoods—but because they, like the American Indian, once occupied a territory that expanding populations found very much to their liking. It will be noted that, of the world's three major clusters of population, those of Anglo-America and Europe lie almost wholly within this deciduous belt, as does the northern part of the agglomeration in southeastern Asia. Today, these trees constitute only 14 per cent of the productive timber reserves of the world.

High-latitude and High-altitude Forests. Still farther poleward and upslope, as temperatures decrease with higher altitude as well as latitude, are the most widespread stands of coniferous softwoods (Figs. 6.1 and 6.4). This is "Christmas tree" vegetation—pine, spruce, fir, cedar, larch, hemlock. Most of these trees are not only narrowleaf but also shortleaf evergreens. The largest stands are in the Soviet Union, Canada, Alaska, and Fennoscandia. Each forest projects southward, particularly along the higher landforms where temperatures are cooler. In contrast, the Southern Hemisphere is essentially devoid of extensive forests that are exclusively coniferous, except in the intermediate and upper reaches of the uplands. The coniferous forests of the high latitudes and altitudes are the most extensively utilized of all, especially along their equatorward margin. Their reserves have been depleted rather seriously, emphatically so in Anglo-America, where man has not yet experienced the need to achieve a proper cut-growth ratio. Even in Eurasia, where he has exploited forests for a longer period of time, there are nations which have not yet learned through the sometimes disastrous expedient of trial and error that forest depletion can be costly—and that these critical resources, existing as they do under rather cool climates, do not tend to reproduce themselves rapidly in polar reaches of the middle latitudes. Today, coniferous trees constitute 36 per cent of world's productive timber reserves.

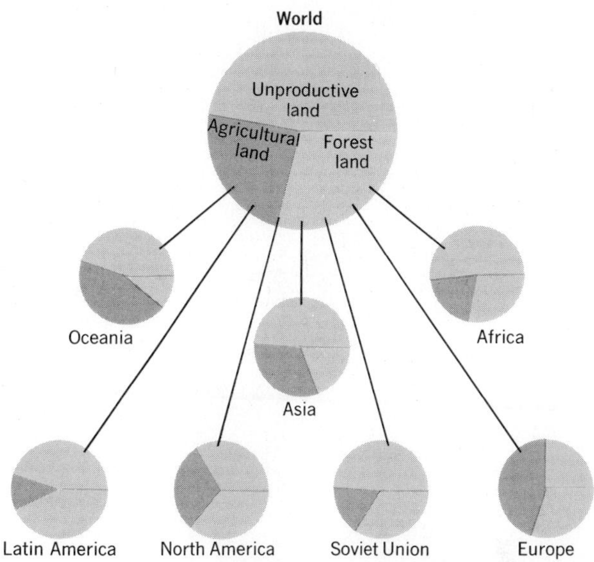

Figure 6.2 ***Gross land use in the world and major divisions.*** *"Agricultural land" actually includes grazing land as well.* (After World Forest Industries, 1955, *FAO, p. 4*)

Mediterranean Vegetation. Continental western coasts between approximately lat 30°–40° in either hemisphere tend to be characterized by a vegetation known as *chaparral* or *maquis*—a series of drought-resistant vegetative types which are smaller than most trees, taller than many shrubs, and more luxuriant than most scrub or thorn forests. Rather surprisingly, the majority of these are broadleaf evergreens successfully withstanding the dry summers of their habitats by resistances other than the shedding of leaves. They are usually quite sparse in stand and may be interspersed with some grasses. Their significance in economic geography lies primarily in their supply of a few gathered commodities and in the limited pasture they provide for animals, notably goats that are sufficiently agile to take advantage of them.

The grasslands

The majority of the world's natural grasslands may be classified in three broad categories: the savanna, the prairie, and the steppe grasses. The first is

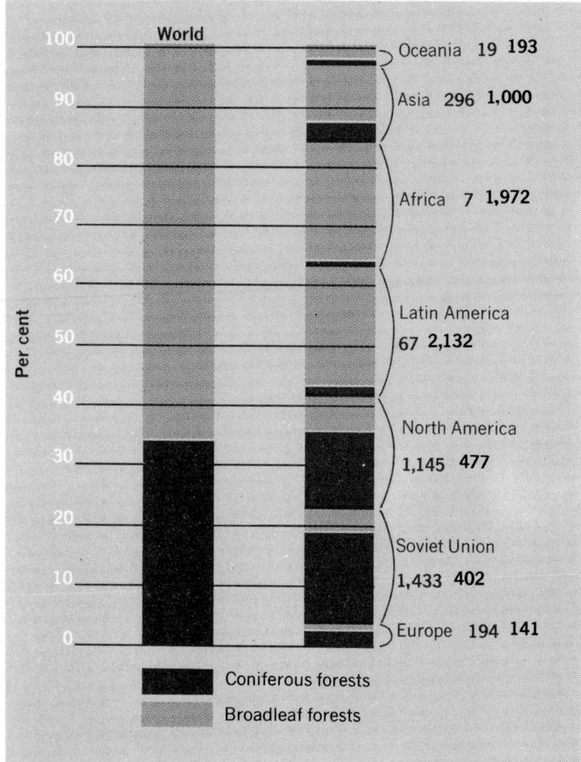

Figure 6.3 ***Distribution of the world's forests by major division.*** The figures at the right denote millions of acres.

restricted almost entirely to the low latitudes, and the remainder to the middle latitudes.

Savanna Grasses. The savanna grasses fringe the low-latitude forests of all continents but Asia, where semideciduous trees tend to replace them. They are reedy plants resembling sorghums, and reach heights of 4 to 12 feet. The tallest varieties tend to be found in the more copious moistures of the low latitudes, fringing the semideciduous forests and occasionally the tropical rain forest. They do not tend to form a compact turf but exist as individual plants. Although perennials, they wither and their stalks die during the dry winters of tropical savanna climate and send forth new shoots when the spring rains come. Their direct economic significance to man is chiefly that of providing forage for grazing purposes—forage which approaches adequacy during the wet season but becomes brittle and difficult, even dangerous, to graze during the dry period, for it tends to inflict rather severe lacerations upon the internal tissues of the animals. Savanna grasses are very widespread, approximately equal in total area to that of the world's steppe lands. Occasionally varieties of intermediate height are interspersed with sparse stands of such trees as the acacia, resulting in a parklike landscape.

Prairie Grasses. Originally occupying extensive regions of Anglo-America and Latin America, and noteworthy territory in European Russia, central Manchuria, the Hungarian basin, and the Transvaal-Orange Free State sections of the Union of South Africa, prairie grasses have been appreciably removed by man. The climates under which they thrived have been excellent for a wide selection of man's crops, so they have been and are being obliterated. They are thin-stemmed, turfed, and thick in stand. Under optimum environmental conditions, they may reach heights exceeding 10 feet. In less favorable habitats, notably where moisture is reduced, they may be only a few inches tall. They are usually perennials but, being located in the middle latitudes, they freeze down in winter and send up new growth in the spring. Only in Latin America are large virgin stands still in existence.

Steppes. The world's steppe grasses usually fringe its middle latitude deserts, providing a transition from them to the more luxuriant vegetation. (Most of the low-latitude climates where steppe grasses might be expected have some form of shrub or thorn forest.) Some are turfed, like the prairie varieties, but are very few inches in height. Others are tufted and are usually somewhat taller, reaching upward from the ground perhaps as much as a foot. They occupy approximately as much of the world's total grassland area as do the savannas and much more area than do the prairies. They have found widest expression in central Asia, with smaller but prominent representations in North America,

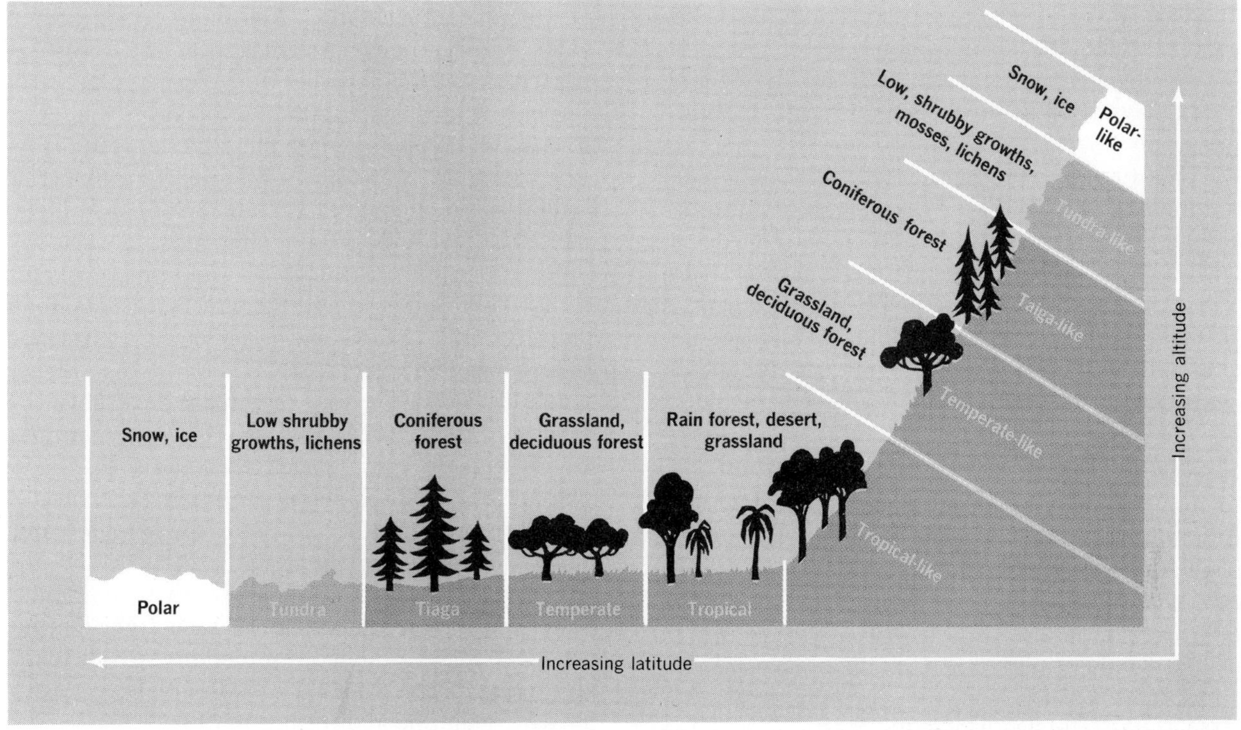

Figure 6.4 ***Vegetational transition and the general correlation between latitude and altitude.*** *The subtropical coniferous forests, not present in all continents, are not shown. (After Paul B. Weisz,* The Science of Biology, *McGraw-Hill Book Company, Inc., New York, 1959, Fig. 5.18, pp. 116–117)*

South America, Africa, and Australia. Their direct economic significance to man has been and is chiefly in the grazing industry, although their soils tend to be fertile for many crops if irrigation water can be had.

Alpine Meadows. In most mountainous and other upland regions, zones of grasses reach above timber line and merge into the tundra. These grasses are usually quite short, turfed, and capable of existing under the erratic high-landform weather and climate conditions which may change quickly and drastically. It is their good fortune to occur where man usually does not desire to plant crops, and their sole contacts with human civilization usually takes place either under the watchful eyes of the shepherd or the awed eyes of the tourist.

The desert shrublands and the tundras

The transitions from warm to very cold climates and from moist to very dry climates are marked by corresponding gradations from tall, thick, intricate vegetation to that which is short, sparse, and of relatively simple pattern. This last stage is reached in both the arid and the frigid regions of the earth. Most of the world's arid deserts—in contrast to the implications of many motion pictures—are rocky and are at least sprinkled with types of drought-resistant bush, shrub, or cactus, all of which are termed *xerophytes.* Most of these either have the capacity to resist transpiration (the releasing of moisture by plants in a manner generally similar to perspiration by some animals) and thus are able to conserve their meager water supply, or else they pass very quickly through the flowering and reproduction cycle after an uncommon bit of precipitation, remaining as dormant seeds for the coming hours, days, months, or even years until moisture reappears.

The tundras, here interpreted as meaning only the mosses and lichens of the very high altitudes and latitudes, are even more stunted than the desert bushes, but they tend to constitute somewhat more of a carpet than the desert plants. Both categories offer very limited grazing possibilities, and the tundras provide some peat for fuel, but generally, both are of little current use to the whole of mankind.

Regions and vertical zones of transition

In the immediately preceding overview of the distribution of general classifications of the world's plant life, attention has been focused upon certain core types of plants so that the reader can envision their distribution. It is perhaps unnecessary to explain that these classifications, like all such categorizations, are arbitrary, that in reality each region merges gradually into its neighboring area, and that often the merging is so subtle that their dividing lines are drawn somewhat subjectively. This is true of vertical as well as horizontal merging; anyone familiar with high mountain country, for example, knows that the term *timber line* usually denotes a myth, and that *timber zone* would be a more accurate description for the increasingly stubby tree growth that tries valiantly to extend itself upward into the alpine meadows.

THE FLORA OF WATER BODIES

Despite the fact that it clings to the peripheries of continents and therefore has been, throughout all of human history, very accessible to man, the flora of the earth's water bodies does not play a direct, vital role in many of man's efforts to gain a livelihood. Botanical water life either has been carried by the world's waterways to the larger repositories or is indigenous; it is either floating or rooted. The floating plants, being mobile, cannot be grouped satisfactorily into areas of prevailing types as is possible with landform vegetation. The rooted plant life of water, while varied, does not appear to exhibit the marked physical differences from place to place that is apparent in the distribution of plant life upon the lithosphere. For both types, photosynthesis is necessary, and both therefore exist at depths sufficiently shallow—generally under 1,500 feet—so that sunlight can reach them. Within this limitation, the floating varieties, especially the microscopic and tiny plankton, move about rather freely but are more numerous along coastal shallows and river mouths. Most botanical water life is classified further as (1) algae, which do not flower and essentially have no well-defined, rigid structure, and (2) the maritime groups that do possess such characteristics. Algae include very small, sometimes microscopic plant life as well as larger flora, of which some is rooted and some is floating. Certain of the larger varieties are sources of iodine, the principal item of economic significance derived directly by man from marine botanical forms. Far more important is tiny plant life, which is the food for a substantial portion of the earth's marine and fresh-water fish.

FLORA AND ECONOMIC GEOGRAPHY

The direct importance of the components of the world's natural plant life to economic man has been suggested at appropriate places in the preceding paragraphs. In review, one might state that the forest-products industries are directly reliant upon certain types of tree life, which man exploits. The industries of grazing, fishing, and hunting are vitally, but not so directly, dependent upon natural vegetation, for in these industries man utilizes the plant life in a roundabout manner by consuming animals and fish, wild or domestic, which first consume the vegetation. The remaining industries—agriculture, mining, and manufacturing—are also at least partially dependent upon wild plant life, but the ties are more tenuous. With respect to agriculture, the ancestors of today's crop plants were once completely undomesticated, and many of them had doubtless gone through a series of naturally selective processes to reach the stage of development they possessed by the time man learned to grow them under his supervision. Moreover, the land which man now tills once sustained wild vegetation that left lasting imprints and effects. Finally, the natural plant life that is still standing performs an outstanding service for all of mankind and all his activities, but especially for farmers, in minimizing the excesses of erosion and subsequent deposition by water and wind—excesses that would be accelerated far beyond their present rates if the natural flora did not exist. For mining, flora is important not only because of erosion and flood control but also because it supplies wood for mine-pit props and other facilities, without which most shaft and tunnel mines could not exist. Manufacturing is also reliant upon the flora, notably for many raw materials and for many of the construction materials in the factories and their fixtures.

In short, flora is a source of raw materials for production, and an essential part of the earth's natural environmental conditions that permeate human existence and its accompanying consumption, production, and exchange.

THE DISTRIBUTION OF FLORA AMONG NATIONS

The nations possessing most of the existing flora are large and yet not so evenly settled that most vegetation has been removed to make room for man. Thus the Soviet Union, Brazil, Canada, and the United States are the leading nations in total acreage of forests (Table 6.1).

The world's grasslands are likewise unevenly shared, with Brazil's dominance in low-latitude savannas not seriously challenged by smaller reserves in neighboring Latin American nations, by those in African tropical dependencies and scattered nations, and by those along Australia's northern rim (Fig. 6.1). The middle-latitude grasslands are found notably in the United States, China, Australia, the Soviet Union, Argentina, and Mexico. All of the world's permanent meadows and pastures, including savanna, prairie, steppe, and alpine meadows, are held by leading nations as follows: Australia, 16 per cent; United States, 12 per cent; Communist China, 9 per cent; Brazil, 6 per cent; the Soviet Union, 6 per cent; Argentina, 5 per cent; Mexico, 5 per cent; Union of South Africa, 4 per cent; all others, 37 per cent.

TABLE 6.1

World forest reserves, in millions of acres

Nation or group	*Total forests*	*Accessible forests*	*Inaccessible forests*
Soviet Union	1,835.0	1,050.2	784.8
Brazil	1,186.3	296.5	889.8
Canada	845.1	321.7	523.4
United States	777.1	450.0	327.1
Total	4,643.5	2,118.4	2,525.1
Europe (excluding Soviet Union)	335.1	327.6	7.5
Other areas	4,503.4	2,037.4	2,466.0
World total	9,482.0	4,483.4	4,998.6

SOURCE: *World Forest Resources,* United Nations, Food and Agriculture Organization, Rome, 1955, pp. 60–68. This report contains the results of an inventory taken in 1953.

THE SOILS

Most of the continental platforms which stand above prevailing water level (and do not, therefore, include continental shelves) are surfaced with a cover of *soil,* the medium through which the earth's land flora is joined, physically and physiologically, with its land surface. Soil, in other words, is the loose land surface material in which vegetation can grow. Genetically, soil is the result of a slow admixing of critical organic and other materials traceable mainly to surface life, with equally necessary minerals and other materials originating in subsurface rock strata. The mixing is carried on through the chemical and mechanical action of underground and surface water and air, and through the activities of myriads of microscopic and macroscopic plants and animals, including the roots of vegetation growing at any particular place. Also very important to this mixing are the slope and the rock make-up of the land on which the soil is being formed, as these influence markedly the degree and rate of chemical and mechanical weathering, erosion, and deposition. Climate is significant both directly and indirectly, as it sets temperature and moisture limits to certain types of plant life, provides the precipitation responsible for much of the water action, and acts in diverse other ways. Indeed, there appears to be a general association among the broad climate, vegetation, and soil regions of the world. This is particularly true where soils have developed in the place in which they are now found.

ESSENTIAL SOIL ELEMENTS AND PROPERTIES

Minerals of the earth's crust

Soils are composed of minerals, organic matter, water, and air. At least half their bulk is derived from minerals, and their composition is appreciably a reflection of the make-up of the underlying *parent materials*—the uppermost layer or layers of rocks. Since almost 98 per cent of the earth's rock structure is comprised of eight elements in combination with each other and with other elements (Table 4.1), these eight tend to predominate in the mineralized portions of the earth's soils, although they differ a great deal in relative amounts from place to place. The remaining mineral accumulation in soils is made up of all other elements.

Most plants require a total of sixteen elements for normal growth—carbon, hydrogen, oxygen, nitrogen, phosphorus, sulfur, potassium, calcium, magnesium, iron, manganese, zinc, copper, molybdenum, boron, and chlorine. All of these are obtained from the soil except carbon, hydrogen, and oxygen, which come mainly from water and air. Nine of the basic sixteen elements are classified as *macronutrients* and must be present in the soil in comparatively substantial quantities for most plant growth. The remaining seven—iron, manganese, zinc, copper, molybdenum, boron, and chlorine—are *micronutrients* (sometimes called *trace elements*) and need be present only in small quantities for normal vegetative growth.

Of the eight abundant elements in the earth's crust and hence in soil minerals, silicon and aluminum are of no apparent value to plant growth. Sodium appears to be equally unnecessary for healthy development of the earth's flora, but it is vital for some of the animal life which graze on it. All the other abundant crustal elements are macronutrients except iron, which is a micronutrient.

Organic materials

Contributions to soil from flora and fauna include organic remains ranging in stage of decomposition from tissues of newly expired life to a more degraded, blackish, spongy, absorbent substance called *humus*. In total, organic contributions make up a comparatively small fraction of an average soil but are a source of nitrogen, calcium, potassium, phosphorus, and sulfur for living plants. Humus also fosters plant growth in various other ways.

Water and air

The amount of *water* and *air* in a soil differs sharply from place to place and depends not only upon their being readily available but also upon the degree to which the nature of a soil permits their penetration. Under optimum conditions, they may constitute nearly half the total bulk (pore space included) of a soil.

Basic properties

Both the mineral and the organic constituents weather and decompose chemically and mechanically until some grains of each pass through the submicroscopic size, eventually becoming *colloids*. Although not yet fully understood, colloids are believed to be forms through which certain elements, especially the soluble salts and some organic chemicals, pass into the roots of vegetative life. They also are somewhat adhesive, and may help larger soil particles to stick together into aggregates known as *floccules*.

The sizes of particles making up a soil determine its *texture*. Fine-textured soils tend to be made up of clay, coarse textures of sand, and intermediate textures of loam, which is a combination of clay and sand. Silts are also of intermediate texture.

The arrangement of a soil's particles constitutes its *structure*, which is dependent largely upon the shape and uniformity of individual soil grains and upon the capacity of such grains to form floccules. If the particles are long and thin, for example, they may be tightly packed with little or no pores for air and water—a condition which would be markedly different if all the particles were roughly circular. The amount of humus in a soil is also a significant determinant of its structure.

Soil texture and structure are very interrelated. In combination they are vital to a soil's compactness and permeability. Both, and especially texture, are at least partially responsible for a soil's *tilth*, or crumbly reaction to a plow. Fine-textured soils tend to form clods, and coarse soils tend to crumble when tilled.

The *color* of soils ranges from black to white and includes yellow, red, rust, brown, and gray. Color may be an indication of other soil qualities such as acidity, alkalinity, or humus content, but its significance varies so sharply with each soil that generalizations must be made cautiously.

The *fertility* of a soil refers to its content of nutrients. Its *productivity* refers to its capacity to yield specific crops under definite conditions of climate and cultivation. These two terms are frequently misused as synonyms.

CLASSIFICATION OF SOILS

One of several soil classifications involves *orders*, *groups*, and many finer subdivisions. A different but overlapping classification involves soil *acidity* and *alkalinity*. We are interested chiefly in the soil groups of the first classification, but can understand these better by first examining soil orders and soil acidity and alkalinity. The three recognized orders are *zonal*, *intrazonal*, and *azonal* soils.

Zonal soils

Most of the world's soils can be categorized into horizontal zones which generally coincide with areas of climate and natural vegetation. Thus, an area or zone with a certain climate and natural vegetation tends also to contain soil characteristics which normally accompany that particular climate and its associated plant life. Such soils are known as *zonal* soils. Invariably, they have formed in the places where they now exist. With the passing of time, they have developed vertical *profiles*, or series of vertically arranged *horizons*, which have been recognized as indicated in Table 6.2.

It is obvious that the *A* and *B* horizons contain most of the organic material. When we speak of zonal-soil characteristics, therefore, we are usually referring to these two horizons, but do not overlook completely the other two horizons.

Intrazonal and azonal soils

Intrazonal soils, while usually evidencing at least the suggestion of a profile, tend to be dominated by soil-forming factors other than climate and natural vegetation. *Azonal* soils do not have well-developed profiles. These frequently are comprised of alluvium, silt, sand or other materials which recently have been deposited by wind, water, or ice. It is difficult to generalize concerning either of these soil orders, as each varies markedly from place to place. However, neither contains a very large portion of the world's soils.

Pedalfers, pedocals, and neutral soils

Some soils are dominated by weak acids derived partially from organic life and partially from chemical reaction of water with solid ingredients. Such soils are notably present under moist conditions. They are called *pedalfers* because of their high content of aluminum (Al) and iron (Fe)—a content resulting from the resistance of these two elements to the acid and water action which removes many other elements. To the economic geographer the significant point about the pedalfers is that they are acid. They exist chiefly in the world's wet areas

TABLE 6.2

The zonal-soil profile

Horizon	*Position and depth*	*Description*
A	From surface downward usually not more than 15 in.	Zone of leaching (chemical withdrawal) and eluviation (mechanical withdrawal) of materials; usually organic, especially in upper portions; organic matter increasingly decomposed with depth
B	Just beneath *A* horizon; usually base of *B* is no deeper than 36 in.	Zone of illuviation or accumulation; materials from both *A* and *C* horizons find their way to *B* horizon
C	Just beneath *B* horizon; usually no deeper than 8 ft	Zone of altered parent materials moving up from below to *B* horizon
D	Just beneath *C* horizon	Zone of unaltered parent materials, usually bedrock

and cool areas. Other soils, found notably under dry conditions, are termed *pedocals* because of their high content of calcium (Ca) and other alkaline, or nonacid, elements. They exist chiefly in the world's arid and semiarid portions. Still other soils are neutral—that is, neither predominantly acid nor alkaline in chemical reaction. These are usually encountered where moist and dry climates meet.

Ideally a soil should not be excessively acid or nonacid for the growth of most crops. The very acid soils are especially unfavorable. The highly pedocalic soils, however, can be made to produce without too much additional cost if proper drainage systems accompany their necessary irrigation.

Association with Vegetation. All the world's luxuriant forests are rooted in pedalferic soils. All desert plants and essentially all short grasses are rooted in pedocalic soils. The tallest of the grasses, usually mixed with trees, tend to exist in soils that are pedalferic, whether in the low latitudes or the middle latitudes. The transition to pedocalic soils is usually found where grasses are of intermediate height, interrupted by tree growth only along the waterways.

The association of vegetation with soils is particularly important in two respects: (1) the vegetative type suggests the degree of moisture in a given climate, and this moisture, in turn, is an active agent in affecting the amount of soluble ingredients and in maintaining this current plant life of a soil; (2) different forms of plant life contribute humus to the soil in sharply varying amounts and ways that affect very markedly the qualities of their respective underlying soils.

Association with Trees. The roots of most trees pass through the more active portion of a soil into the *C* and perhaps even the *D* horizons, for such roots are necessary not only for sustenance but also for support. They are usually sizable in diameter and tubular. When the trees eventually die, they decompose slowly, adding only a small amount of their humus to the soil. Moreover, being tubular, they provide channels of easy access by which water and air can enter the soil and thereby hasten the process of pedalferization. Humus contributions from the part of the tree above the soil is limited to the annual leaf fall, if the tree cover is deciduous, or to a rather consistent but light accumulation of individual leaves if it is evergreen. In either case, the leaves drop only to the surface of the ground, and the humus must enter the soil through slow processes of chemical and mechanical change, during which time it is subjected to continuous oxidation and erosion from surface air and water. Tree

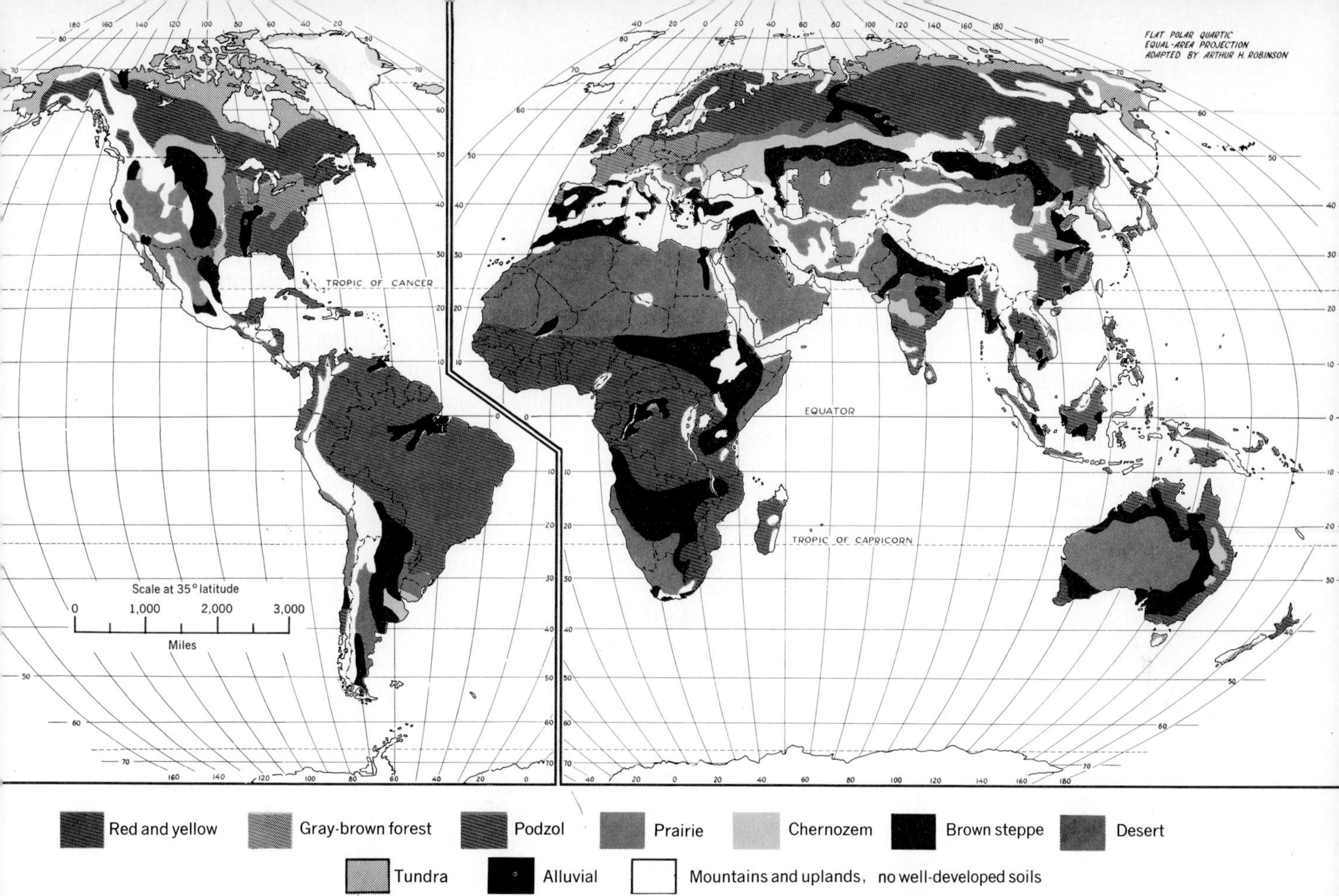

Figure 6.5 ***The world pattern of soil groups.*** *The alluvial soils are azonal. The soil groups shown here are more generalized than in some classifications.*

life cannot be considered, therefore, as the best possible of natural vegetational forms for direct soil maintenance. Still another comparative liability is indirect: trees do not generally attract the larger herbivorous animals, nor the carnivorous animals that feed upon them. Forest soils have thus not benefited from the humus of the manures and decomposing carcasses that accompany such life.

Association with Grasses and Xerophytes. Grasses are generally the best sources of soil humus. Their roots are numerous but thin. When they die, the entire roots decompose quickly into organic soil accumulation. The amount of annual humus contribution from the stalk section varies, of course, with the height of the plants, but it usually exceeds the leaf drop from most trees. Most grasses occur where the stems and leaves wither and die each year, either because of frost or drought, thus returning more humus to the soil than is true of at least evergreen trees. Finally, the grasses attract large animals and benefit by their presence. In contrast, xerophytes add little humus to the highly pedocalic soils in which they occur.

SOIL GROUPS AND THEIR ASSOCIATION WITH CLIMATE AND VEGETATION

Soil orders are subclassified into groups on the basis of depth, color, organic content, acidity and alkalinity, and still other properties. Such groups mainly are subdivisions of zonal soils, described above.

They are shown in Table 6.3, compared with broad regions of climate and natural vegetation in Table 6.4, and mapped in Fig. 6.5.

The red and yellow soils

One of the most widespread of the soil groups, the red and yellow soils are found under the trees of the tropics and subtropics where moisture is copious. They are badly leached (i.e., their soluble materials have been largely removed by chemical weathering and erosion), they do not contain much humus, and they may be considered as generally unproductive. Occasionally, where underlying parent materials provide consistently good supplies of minerals, as occurs in some volcanic and some limestone areas, they are more productive—as indeed are other soils underlain by such materials.

The gray-brown forest soils

These are found largely in Anglo-America, Europe, and eastern Asia, with traces in the Southern Hemisphere. They underlie deciduous hardwoods, are moderately leached, have the richest humus accumulations, and are the most productive of the forest soils. Some, notably in higher latitudes, have *podzol* tendencies (see next paragraph), and are termed *podzolic.*

The podzol soils

The podzol soils (ashen soils) are most extensively distributed in the Soviet Union and Canada. Found under narrowleaf, shortleaf coniferous vegetation (often called taiga), they are ash gray in color, quite acid, shallow, lacking in humus, and comparatively unproductive. Unlike the warmer soils, which owe their acidity to high rainfall, the podzols are acid largely because of retarded evaporation and drainage in cool climates where not much precipitation actually falls and where the subsoils are usually frozen in winter.

The tundras

Occupying cold areas of *permafrost* (permanently frozen subsoils), these soils are usually intrazonal and even azonal, for they are frozen solidly in winter, and are marshy in summer because the frozen subsoils restrict drainage.

The prairie soils

The most naturally fertile soils of the earth are the prairie-chernozem-steppe soils, often mapped and discussed as the *black soils.* This general title applies aptly to the prairies and the chernozems but not so aptly to the steppe varieties, which are brown rather than black in color. They mark the transition from the pedalfers to the pedocals, with the prairies being the least acid of the pedalfers, and the chernozem and steppe soils—notably the chernozems—the least alkaline of the pedocals.

The prairie soils are deep, black, waxy, rich in humus, and productive. They are among the world's most highly prized soils.

TABLE 6.3

Classification of selected soil groups by acidity and alkalinity

Pedalfers (acid)	*Transitional or essentially neutral*	*Pedocals (alkaline)*
Red and yellow soils		
Gray-brown forest soils (including podzolics)		
Prairie soils	Prairie-chernozem soils	Chernozem soils
Podzol soils		Brown steppe soils
Tundras		Arid-desert soils (sierozems)

TABLE 6.4

Associations among the world's climates, natural vegetation, and soil groups

Climate	*Natural vegetation*	*Soil group*
Tropical rain forest	Tropical rain forest	Red and yellow
Tropical savanna	Transition from tropical rain forest to semideciduous trees to tall savanna grasses to short savanna grasses	Transition from red and yellow to prairie to chernozem
Humid subtropical	Prevailingly deciduous hardwoods, replaced in some areas, especially the United States, by longleaf, narrowleaf conifers	Red and yellow; mostly red under deciduous trees; yellow under conifers
Mediterranean subtropical	Chaparral, maquis	Transported (because of coincidental location of most such climates in or near mountains)
Marine	Middle-latitude deciduous trees, sometimes mixed with shortleaf, narrowleaf conifers	Where occurring in mountains, soils are transported as in mediterranean climates, above; where plains prevail in this climate, as in Europe, soils are gray-brown forest, becoming more podzolic with higher latitude as conifers increase in proportion of vegetative cover
Humid continental warm-summer	Primarily middle-latitude deciduous trees in moist portions, transiting to prairie grasses in drier sections	Mainly gray-brown forest soils where under trees; prairie soils under grasses
Humid continental cool-summer	Mixed deciduous forest and shortleaf, narrowleaf conifers, transiting to prairie grasses on drier margins	Gray-brown (podzolic) transiting to true podzols in higher latitudes and to prairie and prairie-chernozem soils on drier margins
Subarctic	Shortleaf, narrowleaf conifers (taiga)	Podzol
Tundra	Tundra	Tundra
Icecap	None	None
Semiarid, or steppe	Steppe grasses, transiting to prairie grasses in wetter sections and to drought-resistant (xerophytic) types on drier margins	Brown steppe, transiting to chernozem on wetter margins and to desert (sierozem) on drier margins
Arid, or desert	Drought-resistant (xerophytic) types	Desert (sierozem)

The chernozem soils

Generally like the prairies, except that their overlying grasses were (or are) shorter and their chemical reaction is slightly alkaline rather than acid, the chernozems (black soils) are also among the world's best in agricultural productivity. Unfortunately, however, lack of ready availability of water at all times is a problem in the utilization of some chernozems—a problem that becomes increasingly acute with transition to the world's drier soils.

The brown steppe soils

Deprived of the prodigious humus accumulations that give color and high fertility to the prairies and chernozems, the brown steppe soils are nonetheless able to produce efficiently if utilized scientifically—especially where irrigation water and proper drainage or the growth of drought-resistant crops are feasible.

The desert soils

Although generally rich in alkaline elements and somewhat poor in humus, the world's desert (sierozem, or white soil) lands can be made also to produce under careful management. The availability of water, however, is a severe restriction, as may be also the superfluity of some salts, the removal of which sometimes becomes troublesome. These are two major problems that arise in attempts to utilize such soils.

SOILS AND ECONOMIC GEOGRAPHY

Soils and agricultural productivity

The major significance of soils in economic geography lies in their association with the productive occupations and most particularly with agriculture, which is responsible for about 90 per cent of the food supply to human beings. Climate tends to set the outer limits of soil productivity and, at current levels of technology, prevents man from effectively using the very cold or very dry lands. Where climates permit agriculture, the natural fertility of the soils becomes more important, and the prairie, chernozem, and more moist brown steppe soils emerge as the most fertile, all other residual soils being of moderate to low quality.

The productivity of soils, however, has been altered sharply by man through analysis and careful replacement of mineral and organic materials—better still, by the addition of such materials to optimum needs of certain crops. This has been done especially where (1) the soils are in great de-

Black soil; there is no better soil for many crops, if the climate is favorable. (a) right, a handful of chernozem soil picked up in McLean County, Illinois (Standard Oil Company of New Jersey); (b) far right, a view on the fringe of chernozem soil near Regina in Saskatchewan, Canada (Hunting Survey Corporation Ltd., Toronto).

mand for feeding clustered populations and (2) where levels of living are high enough to absorb the additional cost of artificial fertilization. The dynamic but land-hungry nations of northwestern Europe and Japan especially utilize such methods (Figs. 6.6 and 6.7). The map of agricultural productivity therefore reflects population pressure and technical advance perhaps more than it reflects natural fertility (Figs. 6.6 and 1.4, p. 13).

Soils, nature, and man

As a component of nature, soils are not exploited directly by man; they supply directly no raw materials for consumption or production. Instead, they constitute one of the most important series of natural conditions with which man must cope in gaining a livelihood.

THE DISTRIBUTION OF SOIL PRODUCTIVITY AMONG NATIONS

In practice, the giants among nations as to possession of arable cropland are the Soviet Union, the United States, and India. The first owns about one-fifth of the world total, and the other two approximately one-sixth apiece. Communist China is next with about one-twelfth, and the remainder of the world's political units are much less favorably endowed.

Of these four nations, the Soviet Union is hampered seriously by both cold and aridity in its attempts to expand the acreage of its farm land; indeed, it has difficulty extracting maximum yields on existing land in the high latitude in which the nation is located. Nevertheless, the nation recently has completed the plowing up of some 93 million acres of land—an amount equal to nearly one-fourth of that nation's cultivated land prior to the plowing —in semiarid climatic conditions not unlike those of the dust bowl in the United States. Those of us who have lived through the dust-bowl conditions can predict some of the problems that will plague this new project. India's soils, depleted over the centuries by bad farming methods, suffer further in places from moisture and temperature excesses accompanying a low latitudinal location. Communist China's land, while in latitudes and climates not unlike those of the United States, involves only

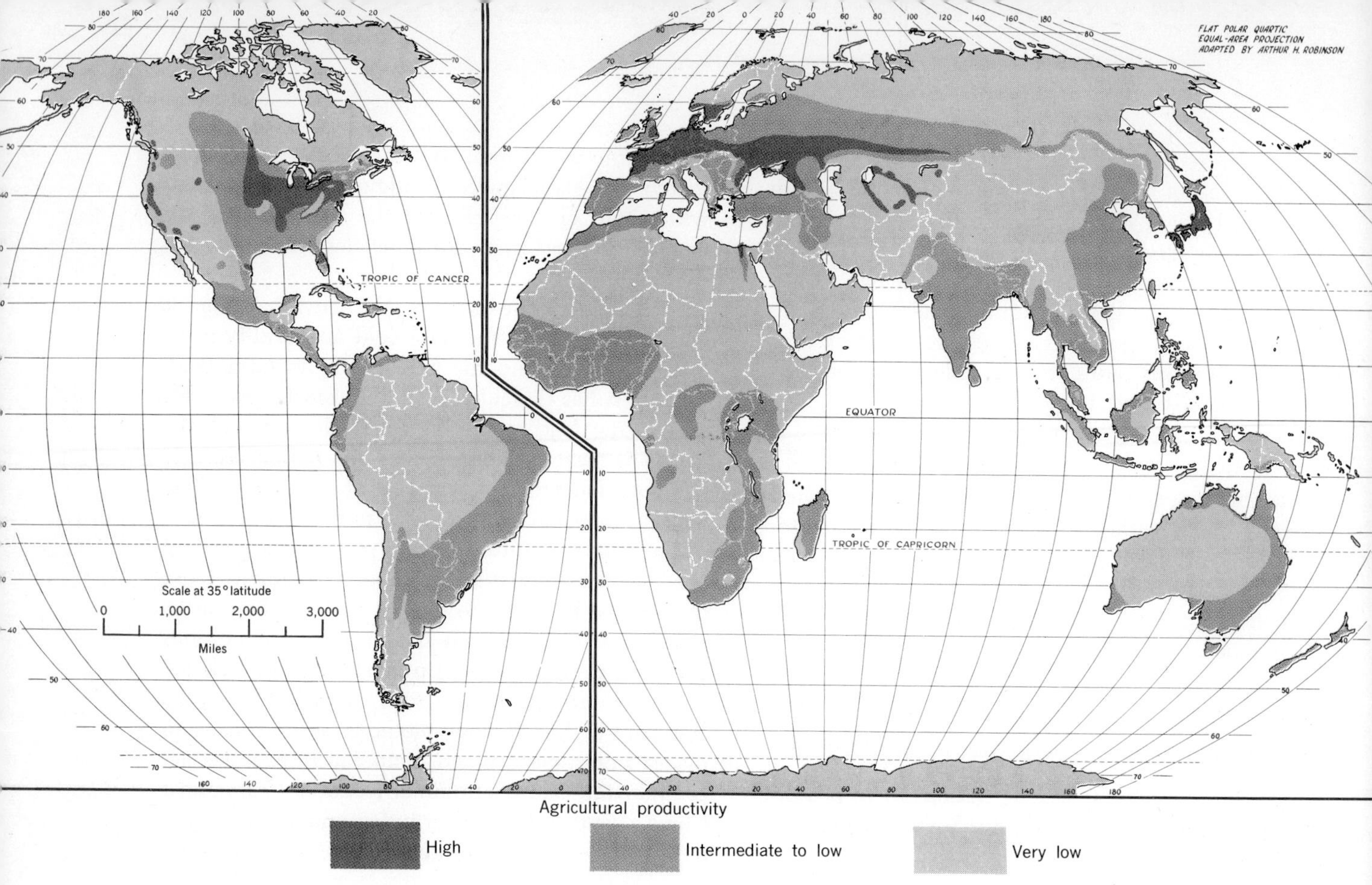

Figure 6.6 ***Agricultural productivity of the world's soils*** *(generalized). Japan and northwestern Europe realize high yields per acre from soils of only moderate natural fertility.*

about one-half as many acres, and many of these have been depleted through inferior methods and tools. Without doubt, the United States possesses the largest amount of naturally excellent farm land of all the world's nations.

However, we have noted that increasing the productivity of soil is possible and that it is largely a matter of added costs of production. The issue thus becomes that of total benefit weighed against total cost over a specified time period, with other considerations such as climate, size, and location of market given particular attention.

THE FAUNA

Animals are more mobile than plants, and their natural life zones are not so well defined. Moreover, man essentially has removed the wild fauna from lands he now occupies intensively, and the animals of outlying areas are of little economic interest other than to small numbers of primitive or quasiprimitive societies. The total number of people dependent upon hunting game is very small.

Zoological water life is much more important to man and may become even vital as human pop-

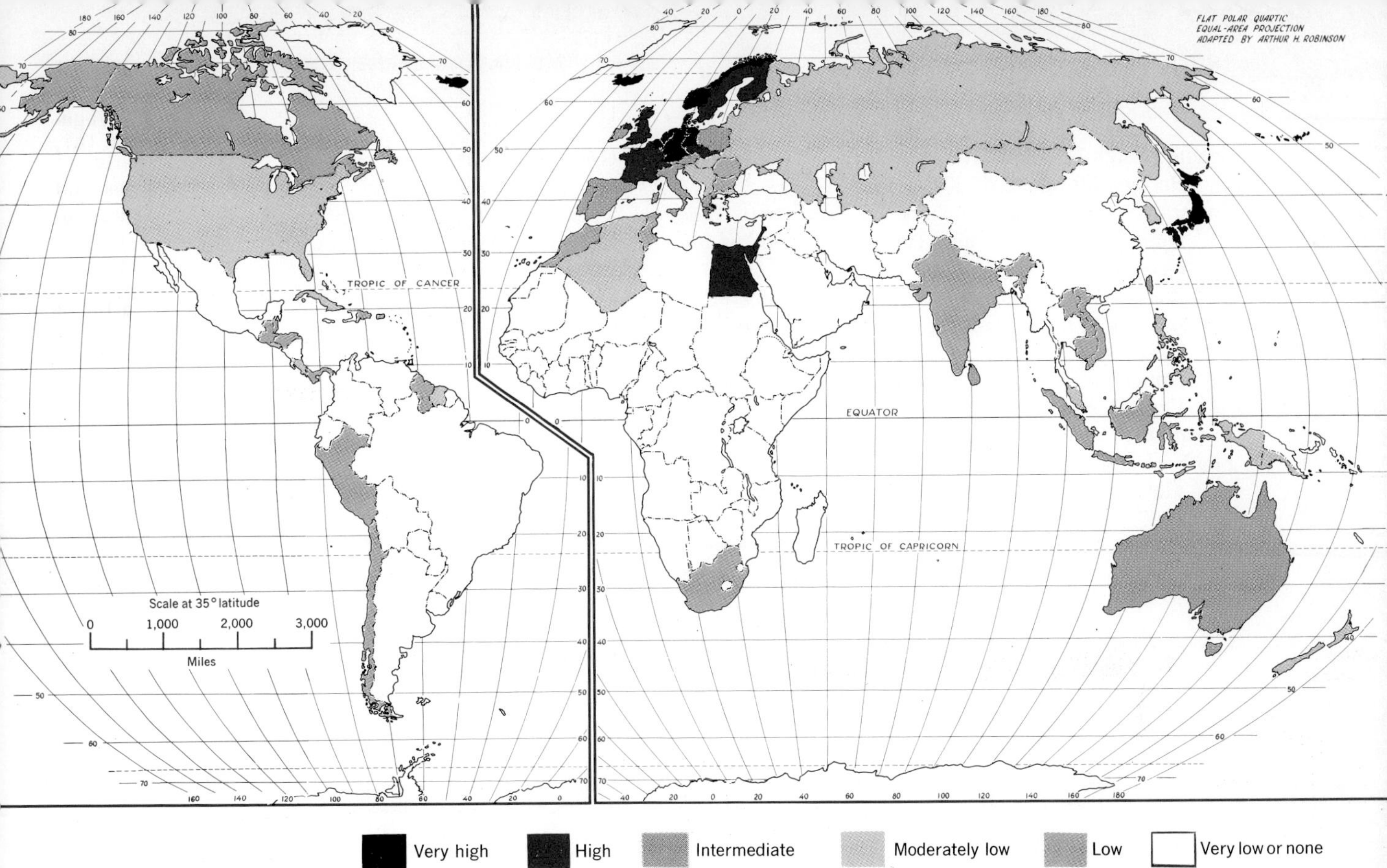

Figure 6.7 ***World pattern of intensity of fertilizer application.*** *Entire nations are classified according to the intensity of their application of commercial fertilizer per unit of agricultural land. Northwestern Europe and Japan are the leaders. Although it uses much fertilizer, the United States does not rank among the world leaders on a per-acre basis. (After Ursula Ewald,* Recent Developments of the World Fertiliser Market: A Statistical Analysis, *Kiel, Institut fuer Weltwirtschaft, 1957)*

ulations increase. As on land, the tiniest forms are microscopic and unicellular, often indistinguishable from their botanical counterparts. More than on land, these small forms constitute the food supply for many larger forms of life which man exploits. Of the more than forty thousand known categories of fish, over one thousand have been designated as commercial.

REFERENCES

Albrecht, William A.: "Soil Fertility and Biotic Geography," *Geographical Review,* **47**:86–105, 1957.

Aschmann, Homer: "The Evolution of a Wild Landscape and Its Persistence in Southern California," *Annals of the Association of American Geographers,* **49** (3, part 2): 34–56, 1959.

Barnes, Carleton P.: "The Geographic Study of Soils," in Preston E. James and Clarence F. Jones (eds.), *American Geography: Inventory and Prospect,* Syracuse University Press for the Association of American Geographers, Syracuse, N. Y., 1954, pp. 383–394.

Bennett, Hugh H.: "Soil Erosion in Spain," *Geographical Review,* **50:**59–72, 1960.

Carter, George F., and Robert L. Pendleton: "The Humid Soil: Process and Time," *Geographical Review,* **46:**488–509, 1956.

Dansereau, Pierre: *Biogeography: An Ecological Perspective,* The Ronald Press Company, New York, 1957.

De Laubenfels, David J.: "The Status of 'Conifers' in Vegetational Classification," *Annals of the Association of American Geographers,* **47:**145–149, 1957.

Finch, Vernor C., et al.: *Elements of Geography,* McGraw-Hill Book Company, Inc., New York, 1957. (Especially chaps. 20–22.)

Grass, Yearbook of Agriculture, 1948, U.S. Department of Agriculture, 1948.

Küchler, A. W.: "Classification and Purpose in Vegetation Maps," *Geographical Review,* **46:**155–187, 1956.

———: "Plant Geography," in Preston E. James and Clarence F. Jones (eds.), *American Geography: Inventory and Prospect,* Syracuse University Press for the Association of American Geographers, Syracuse, N. Y., 1954, pp. 429–440.

Trees, Yearbook of Agriculture, 1949, U.S. Department of Agriculture, 1949.

PART THREE WORLD PATTERNS OF PRODUCTION AND EXCHANGE

Economic geography becomes most complex when it is studied with respect to all of the world's societies, large and small, advanced and primitive, and to the inevitable relationships among those societies—relationships that are evidenced by the numerous transport and communication routes, global and local, of the land, sea, and air.

INTRODUCTION, PAGE 11

7 WORLD PATTERNS OF PRODUCTION

MOST COMMODITIES THAT ARE CONSUMED MUST BE FIRST PRODUCED BY NATURE or man. As indicated in this book's introduction, much production results from six occupations of which five—agriculture, grazing, forest-products industries, fishing and hunting, and minerals extraction—involve direct exploitation of nature by man. Manufacturing is unique in that it depends chiefly upon the other five occupations, notably agriculture and minerals extraction, to supply most of its basic raw materials. However, a few but an increasing number of manufactured products, e.g., chemicals, are made synthetically, and are only slightly reliant on the other five productive occupations.

Throughout most of this chapter, the focus of our attention will be upon the location of these six occupations, and some of their subdivisions, upon the earth's surface. An important prerequisite to such an assessment, however, involves numbers: how many people are at work in this world, and of that total how many are engaged in each of the productive occupations and in the service occupations? Although complete, fully reliable data are not as yet forthcoming, an approximation is shown in Table 7.1. Agriculture is the mainstay of population support, accounting for over one-half of all working persons. Manufacturing and handicraft activities are second, ranking far ahead of the last four, each of which accounts for about 1 per cent or less of the world's labor force.

AGRICULTURE

Agriculture has been the bulwark of population support throughout recorded time, and not until the Industrial Revolution has it given way to manufacturing and some of the service occupations. Because industrialism is still an embryo in much of the world, agriculture dominates even the current scene. Evaluated in terms of labor force, its dominance is now restricted to countries which are considered underdeveloped. In terms of the amount of land utilized, however, the dominance of agriculture is unchallenged throughout

TABLE 7.1

*Allocation of the world's labor force**

Productive occupations	*Per cent*
Agriculture and grazing†	53.5
Manufacturing and handicrafts	18.0
Minerals extraction and quarrying	1.1
Fishing and hunting	0.5
Forest-products industries	0.5
All other occupations	26.4
Total	100.0

* The world's labor force is here considered to amount to 40 per cent of its population.

† Data on grazing are not separated from those on agriculture in source materials; however, it seems unlikely that the grazing labor force amounts to more than 1 per cent of the world's total labor force.

SOURCE: Computed from information in W. S. Woytinsky and E. S. Woytinsky, *World Population and Production,* The Twentieth Century Fund, Inc., New York, 1953, pp. 364–365, 724–725; *Yearbook of Labor Statistics,* International Labor Office, Geneva, 1954; *The State of Food and Agriculture, 1958,* United Nations Food and Agriculture Organization, Rome, 1958, p. 171. There is, of course, an overlap among occupations; many persons engaged in part-time manufacturing or handicrafts, for example, are also engaged in part-time farming. Compensation for this overlap has been made in the table, so that two part-time handicraft workers are considered as one full-time, etc.

the world, except by grazing. Between 7 and 10 per cent of the earth's total land surface, excluding Antarctica, is cultivated. In physical area, this amount ranges from 2½ to over 3 billion acres (computations vary)—an amount so large that, if it were evenly divided among the world's people, every man, woman, and child could lay claim to about 1 acre of cultivated land. An additional amount of untilled land—between 2½ and 5 billion acres—is in permanent meadows and pastures that are used partially for agriculture and partially for grazing. Thus an average of somewhat over 2 acres of cropland and permanent pasture is available to each one of us.

AGRICULTURAL TYPES AND REGIONS

The portion of the earth's surface devoted to agriculture has been subdivided into a number of regions based on types of practice. One such classification is shown in Fig. 7.1. It involves mainly three criteria: (1) the degree of commercialization, or tendency to exchange finished products; (2) the type of crop or combination of crops and animals; and (3) the intensity of land use. Eight types and their regional expressions are to be considered here: (1) primitive-subsistence agriculture, shifting and sedentary; (2) intensive-subsistence agriculture; (3) plantation agriculture; (4) mediterranean agriculture; (5) commercial grain farming; (6) commercial crop and livestock farming; (7) commercial dairy farming; and (8) commercial gardening and fruit culture.

Primitive-subsistence agriculture, shifting and sedentary

The criterion characterizing this type of agriculture is that it is primarily a rather crude production for subsistence, and few of its harvested crops enter either the domestic or world markets.

World Distribution. Primitive-subsistence agriculture is found extensively throughout the tropical and some of the subtropical portions of all landforms in the low latitudes. As a general classification, it encompasses more of the earth's surface than does any other agricultural type. In terms of land actually cultivated, however, it is comparatively unimportant; only a small fraction of the world's tilled land is situated in areas of primitive-subsistence agriculture.

Natural Environmental and Cultural Associations. This type of agriculture is found mainly in tropical rain-forest climate along with tropical rain-forest vegetation on red and yellow soils. It extends especially into the tropical savanna climate, along with associated tropical savanna vegetational and soil types. Notably in Latin America, it reaches also

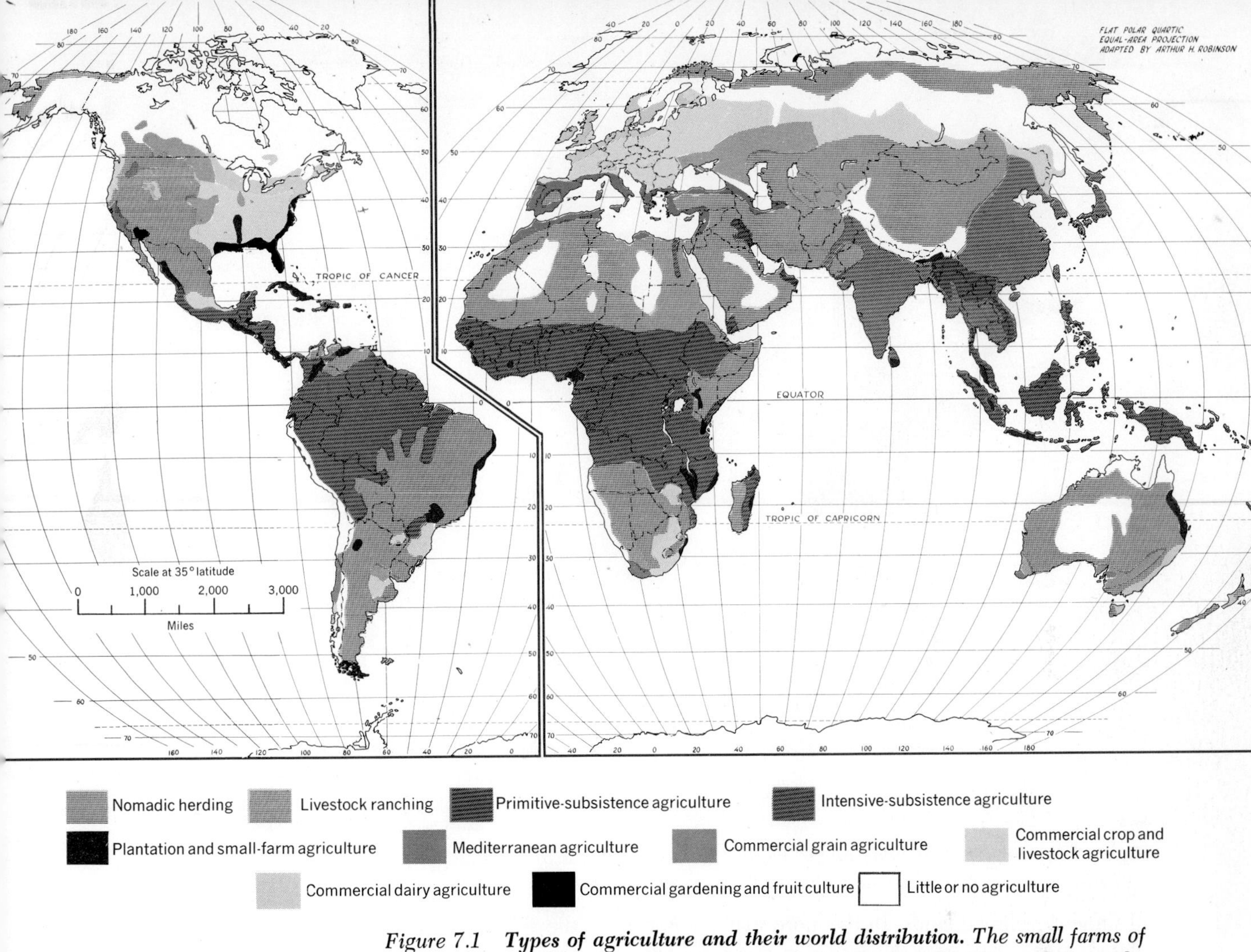

Figure 7.1 ***Types of agriculture and their world distribution.*** *The small farms of plantation and small-farm agriculture usually are plots tilled by workers on the edges or commercially unused sections of the plantations. In a few places, however, the small farms are independent from plantations. In Costa Rica, for example, there are many small farms and almost no plantations.*

into undifferentiated highland climate, and in Africa into low-latitude semiarid as well as undifferentiated highland climates. It is found in all categories of landforms, although best developed where well-drained, flat land exists. Its growing season is free of frost except in higher elevations (Figs. 7.1, 7.2, and 5.1).

Inasmuch as this type of agriculture is so widely distributed, it necessarily involves many societies of differing cultures. In both hemispheres, these societies tend to be small and aloof from more intricate civilizations as well as from each other. Many are tribally organized. Most of the waking hours of individuals are spent in livelihood activities, of which agriculture is the most complex; other activities include crude forest-products industries, hunting, fishing, and grazing.

Association with Populations. The occupance of regions of subsistence agriculture is prevailingly sparse and rural. It contains small pockets, however, of rather heavy population density, usually in coastal locations and in some mountain and upland valleys. Some of these pockets are experiencing a rather marked population growth that is coincident with, and a part of, the general population growth

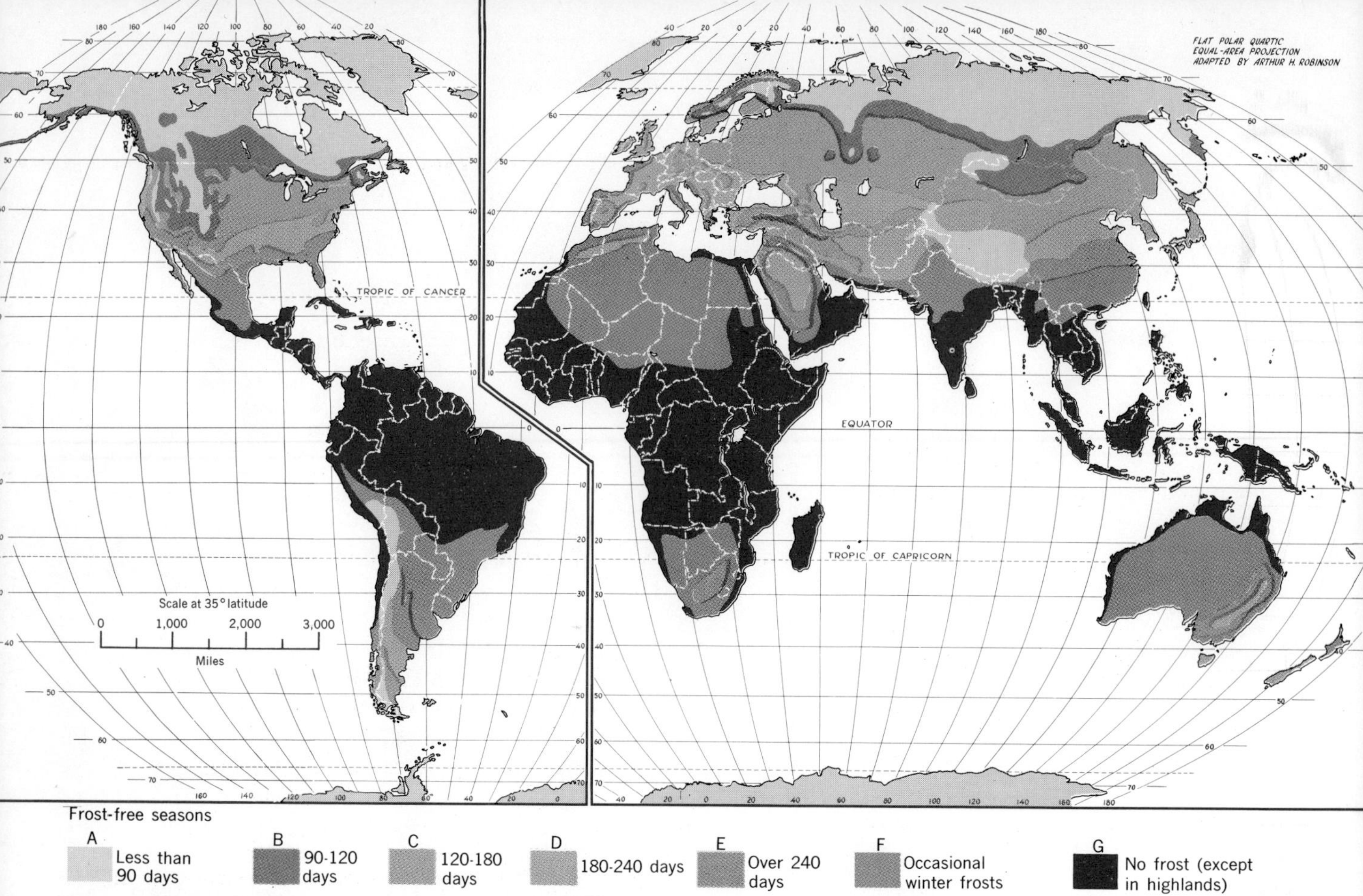

Figure 7.2 ***Frost-free periods of the world. At current levels of technology, agriculture is not practical where the frost-free period is less than 90 days.***

of underdeveloped lands. In the more sparsely populated areas, the growth does not seem so pronounced, although information on some of these areas is not always complete. Country-to-city migration is also apparent, chiefly in the same small nodal areas of dense population pressure.

Production. As implied in its title, this is a hand-to-mouth, simple agriculture. The tools range in complexity from a stick in a human hand to an animal-drawn plow. In very elementary cultures, planting is done in existing forest clearings, usually by gouging holes in the ground with a stick and inserting seeds among endemic shorter types of vegetation. In some areas the taller trees are burned or hacked away in small clearings; these are abandoned when the soil has become depleted after only a few years' use, and the cultivators move to new clearings and new homes. In yet other areas, the fields are permanently cleared but rotated, so that one field may lie fallow for a year or two. In still other areas, the fields are planted and harvested continuously, but their yields remain low. Fertilization in the modern sense is rare throughout regions of this type of agriculture, and market exchange is usually limited to small amounts of produce exchanged in local bazaars. Only a trickle of their products reaches the world markets. In a few places, usually under foreign encouragement, some crops are planted for commercial harvest. These include palm trees planted for their coconuts or palm oil, and cacao trees which yield cocoa. However, most crops are consumed domestically, including the harvests from such well-known plants as corn (or maize), sorghums, dry (or upland) rice, cassava (or manioc), beans, peas, peanuts, and varieties of squash and melons. Animals, found principally among the more culturally advanced of the small but numerous societies in regions of subsistence agriculture, are mostly sheep, goats, and cattle, and are located in semiarid lands rather than forests. The uplands and mountains, particularly in Latin America, are the habitat of the llama and alpaca as well as more familiar species.

Association with Political Units and Economies. Only a few political units are essentially encompassed by regions of primitive-subsistence agriculture. The most conspicuous examples are the former Belgian Congo, Gabon, Congo (French), the Central African Republic, Nigeria, Ghana, and Liberia in Africa; the three Guianas in South America; and Malaya in southeastern Asia. Portions of Brazil, Ethiopia, Indonesia, and still other countries extend into this type of agricultural region.

Whether in the Western or Eastern Hemisphere, the political units dominated by primitive-subsistence agriculture tend to be underdeveloped, with technical advancement more or less limited to the plantations, mining enterprises, and cities where European influence has been pronounced. In addition, many of these countries with subsistence agriculture are political and/or economic dependencies of more powerful foreign economies.

Intensive-subsistence agriculture

This classification, like the one discussed immediately above, is based chiefly on the comparatively small exchange of finished products, which tend to be fashioned at home mainly for home consumption. As implied by its title, intensive-subsistence differs from primitive-subsistence agriculture principally in the intensity of its land use—in the necessity to utilize all possible land for agricultural purposes and to wring the maximum yield from every piece of land. Yet the methods of these regions, surprisingly, are frequently crude and the yields as low as those of regions considered more primitive.

World Distribution. Intensive-subsistence agriculture is concentrated in eastern and southern Asia, where it covers practically all cultivated land. These include India, Communist China, Japan, Pakistan, Burma, Thailand, Cambodia, North Vietnam, South Vietnam, and South Korea. A few comparatively tiny representations of this type of land use are found elsewhere, primarily in the Eastern Hemisphere; the most conspicuous is the Nile River delta of Egypt.

Unlike primitive-subsistence agriculture, the regions of intensive-subsistence agriculture include large amounts of land actually cultivated. India alone contains nearly one-sixth of the world's total cultivated land, and Communist China an additional one-twelfth. The amount held by other nations in this category is much smaller, but aggregately worthy of note. All in all, intensive-subsistence regions cover about 30 per cent of the world's cultivated land.

Natural Environmental and Cultural Associations. This type of agriculture (concentrated in southeastern Asia) is best developed under tropical and subtropical climates, where the growing seasons are long. Smaller appendages extend northward from these locations along the Pacific coast to northern Communist China, Korea, and Japan. Intensive-subsistence agriculture is carried on in tropical rainforest, tropical savanna, humid subtropical, and humid continental climates, together with their associated vegetational and soil types. Nearly all these regions are influenced by the Asian monsoons and hence experience rather pronounced summer-rain–winter-drought precipitation conditions (although the winters are moist in some sections, particularly southern Communist China and Japan). Occasionally a moisture deficiency occurs in summer, especially in northern Communist China and in India, causing crop failure and famine. Because of the high population pressures, all usable land is cultivated, regardless of landform.

Not all climates of southern and eastern Asia favor this agriculture. The regions of intensive-subsistence agriculture are bordered on the Asian interior by territory that is either too high or too dry to permit this type of land use at current technological levels (Fig. 5.1).

Cultural as well as natural patterns are considerations especially important to this type of agriculture. The various natural conditions where intensive-subsistence agriculture occurs are roughly duplicated elsewhere—for example, along the southern, eastern, and northern sections of North America. However, intensive-subsistence agriculture is not found conspicuously in the North American counterparts of the Asian climates. The reasons for this, while partially attributable to the much lighter population pressure in North America compared to southeastern Asia, appear also to be partially cultural. Thus, comparing agriculture in eastern Asia to that in eastern North America we find striking examples of similar natural conditions that have been used very differently under the guiding rules and laws of differing cultures.

Association with Populations. Approximately one-half of the world's people live in the regions of intensive-subsistence agriculture. The heavily populated effective areas of Communist China, India, Japan, and Pakistan, as well as of smaller nations, are farmed by intensive-subsistence practices.

Production. The emphasis here is upon food, which is produced most efficiently by raising crops that man can consume directly. Where animals are present, they tend to be used for draft purposes, or are scavengers, or are homeless "mavericks" protected by religious beliefs. The crops are mainly grains and vegetables. Paddy rice predominates in most areas where it can be grown, and these areas extend discontinuously from central and southern Japan and Korea equatorward to the warmest margins of regions of intensive-subsistence agriculture. In places where fields cannot be flooded dry, or upland, rice is grown. The significance of rice to regions of this type of agriculture is apparent in the fact that about 85 per cent of all the world's rice is produced here. As will be demonstrated in greater detail in a later chapter, most of the world's international trade in rice is in reality a coastwise movement along eastern and southern Asia. Wheat, corn, barley, sorghum, millet, and some oats tend to be grown actively where rice does not thrive, their areas of growth overlapping somewhat with those of rice. Nongrain crops include soybeans (mainly in northern Communist China and all of Korea); peanuts (in southern India and northern Communist China); sugar cane (in India, southern Communist China, Pakistan); sesame seed, rape seed, tobacco, tea, many garden vegetables, and some fruits.

These regions also grow fibers, notably cotton (in western India, northeastern Communist China, upper West Pakistan, and the Nile flood plain and delta of Egypt); jute (in the Ganges-Brahmaputra delta of East Pakistan and India); silk (in central and southern Japan; coastal and central Communist China); and hemp (in northern Communist China and southern Japan). These regions dominate the world exports of jute and silk, and also contribute other fibers (on a smaller scale) to world markets.

Animals and poultry tend to be distributed unevenly in accordance with cultural (usually religious) belief as well as economic utility. Swine and poultry abound as scavengers in Communist China but are virtually nonexistent in India and in areas dominated by the Moslem faith. India probably contains more cattle than any other nation; estimates place the total at between one-fifth and one-third of that of the entire world. Except for draft purposes, however, most of these animals are of little use to man but are protected from slaughter by religious beliefs and social mores. Sheep and goats are found in significant numbers in the regions of intensive-subsistence agriculture, most prominently in India.

In non-Communist lands, holdings tend to be small, seldom exceeding 5 acres per farm owner, and generally of even lesser size. The poorer families, especially the landless workers, have benefited during this century from a number of land-reform programs, wherein efforts are made to bring more land into production and to redistribute some land heretofore controlled by large landowners, many of them absentee landlords. Because of the heavy populations, however, it does not seem that such measures will permanently solve the problem of small holdings.

The ownership of land in most Communist countries is being assumed by the national governments, although a form of token redistribution among the landless sometimes precedes this appropriation. The actual working of the land tends to be done mainly by groups of farm families organized into collectives; with the size of holding allocated to each collective varying in accordance with land productivity and with the amount of land generally available. Whether this type of agricultural organization will result in generally higher yields remains yet to be demonstrated. It does not appear likely, however, that any type of organization will alleviate completely the heavy man-land ratio of these regions.

Not only are the holdings small, but yields are low (with Japan a major exception). Wheat yields in India are only 10 bushels per acre and in Communist China only 16 bushels per acre, as compared with 18 bushels per acre in the United States and 35 bushels per acre in intensively farmed France. Yields of other crops tend also to be low. One of the main reasons for this appears to be the continued adherence to outmoded agricultural methods. For example, few commercial fertilizers are applied, and many of the animal manures are used for fuel rather than for fertilizer. A marked increase in crop yields of these areas could be effected by applying techniques and materials that have been developed and discovered elsewhere, and some of the foreign-aid programs of the United States, the United Nations, and other nations and organizations involve some efforts toward this objective. The question arises, however, as to whether any yield increases resulting from use of advanced techniques might provide only temporary relief in any event since population in these regions keeps burgeoning with each succeeding year.

Association with Political Units and Economies. Nearly all countries characterized by subsistence agriculture are politically sovereign, and most received their independence only after the Second World War. (Japan stands out in many ways as an exception.) Their economies tend to be underdeveloped and exhibit a low propensity to exchange. Because of their heavy population pressures, however, their aggregate market potential is high (Table 3.1).

Plantation agriculture

For want of better nomenclature, the term *plantation* is used in this book to denote sizable tracts of agricultural land owned by private individuals or corporations, and operated directly or indirectly by a centralized management. Some degree of specialization in both labor and harvested crops usually exists, and most of the crops are sold in the world markets. The labor tends to be done by either hired workers or tenants. Agricultural methods and tools tend to be more technically advanced than in most smaller farming operations. The classification of regions of plantation agriculture is based, therefore, upon the size of holding, the mode of ownership, the mode of operation, and the degree of commercialization.

World Distribution. The majority of the world's plantation regions are situated in the low latitudes, and only a few are located poleward of the Tropic of Cancer or the Tropic of Capricorn. Notably in the southeastern United States, however, this type of agriculture extends conspicuously but erratically as far north as lat 35°. Like primitive-subsistence farming, plantation agriculture is found in both hemispheres; indeed, plantation districts frequently appear on a map as islands of intense commercial activity surrounded by great areas of subsistence agriculture.

Natural Environmental and Cultural Associations. Most plantations are situated within tropical savanna, humid subtropical, or tropical rain-forest climates and their associated vegetation and soils. Where certain crops require year-long cool temperatures, the intermediate and lower reaches of undifferentiated highland climates are also utilized. Flat, fertile, well-drained land, at the varying elevations needed to grow crop specialties, is preferred by plantation owners and managers.

Culturally, the plantation is a European product—although, paradoxically, few plantations exist in Europe today. In areas where Europeans have migrated in substantial numbers, plantations can be considered as a part of present-day domestic cultural patterns. This is generally true of plantations in the United States, Latin America, and Australia. Notably in Africa and southeastern Asia, however, the plantations represent injections of European culture into indigenous ways of life. In some areas, such as United Fruit Company's enterprises in Caribbean America, the plantations represent an injection of one type of Europeanized culture into another.

Association with Population. Unlike the two forms of subsistence agriculture discussed previously, plantation districts do not occupy large portions of the earth's land surface. Instead, they appear as rather small but distinctive splotches, surrounded by other types of livelihood (Fig. 7.1). Plantation agriculture, therefore, does not provide livelihood for people distributed over wide areas, as do primitive-subsistence and intensive-subsistence agricultures.

More often than not, plantation districts coincide with areas of moderate or even heavy population density. To some extent, the plantations create such population clusters, since they provide employment for many workers who live on or in the vicinity of the plantations. Yet in some instances it appears quite likely that such population clusters would exist even if there were no plantations, for all forms of agriculture are oriented to good land.

Production. Plantation agriculture is mainly a commercial venture initiated by individual owners and operators. Usually, it involves the growth of commodities for sale in markets where those commodities cannot be grown because of adverse climatic and/or other natural environmental features. Sugar, cotton, bananas, coffee, rubber, copra, tobacco, and tea head the list of such commodities; some items of lesser significance are rice, cinchona, sisal, henequen, hemp, peanuts, palm oil and kernels, cacao, gutta percha, and the once-prized spices. Of the eight leaders, four are tree crops.

The plantations are usually owned by Europeans or descendants of Europeans, who may or may not reside on the plantations or even in the country where the plantations are situated. They are usually managed by Europeans or highly trusted non-Europeans (often partly European in extraction), and most of the labor is non-European. European or Europeanized control over management is retained where (1) rigid time schedules of production have to be met, (2) complex farming practices and tools are utilized, and/or (3) heavy financial investment is necessary. Nearly all plantations must contend with at least one of these specifications.

Plantation laborers usually are hired help or tenant farmers. Where there is hired help, management tends to be more centralized, since control over laborers is direct. Where the tenant system dominates, decisions as to specific land use are sometimes left to the tenant, as long as these decisions do not alter the general directives of the landowner. Control by the landowner is often maintained not only through leasing arrangements but also through ownership of harvesting machinery or preliminary-milling equipment.

The mechanization of agriculture has influenced plantations, although the nature and extent vary with the crops produced and with the attitudes and financial reserves of the owners. The major effects are the reduction of the degree of dependence on human labor, and the possible enlargement of operating units. The planting and cultivating operations usually are more easily mechanized than is harvesting. Most plantations have been slow to mechanize, partly because of the very cheap labor already at their disposal.

Association with Political Units and Economies. Plantations, especially those in the low latitudes, tend to be located in underdeveloped economies (compare Figs. 7.1 and 1.4). In Latin America and southeastern Asia, most of the political units that are associated with such factors are independent, and several in Africa are either currently self-governing or are about to become so. Most of the Latin American political units have been sovereign for over a century, but most of the Asian and African units are just beginning to assume the responsibilities of self-government. The emotions involved in the struggles for independence may affect plantation agriculture adversely in Asia and Africa, and the question of whether, and in what form, plantations will survive has not yet been answered. Notably in southeastern Asia, plantations are being broken up into subsistence tracts.

The current distribution of ownership or control of plantations is suggested by the patterns of political affiliation and money blocs (compare Figs. 7.1, 1.5, and page 12). Thus, the agricultural operations controlled by the United Kingdom are located primarily in the sterling bloc and in the British Commonwealth. Foreign enterprises of other European nations are also located mainly in the political or economic affiliates of those nations. The United States has focused especially on Caribbean America, an area within the dollar bloc.

Mediterranean agriculture

Areas dominated by mediterranean climate have evolved a rather distinctive mode of land use. This classification, the only one to be designated on the basis of its associated climate, is in reality a classification mainly on the basis of land utilization.

World Distribution. Like its associated climate, mediterranean agriculture is found on continental western fringes generally between lat 30–40° N and S. It is most extensive along the arable margins of the Mediterranean Sea, which is the "western fringe" of the Eurasian-African land mass, and is found also in southwestern United States, central Chile, the southernmost tip of Africa, and the western fringes of Australia.

Natural Environmental and Cultural Associations. The mediterranean climate throughout the world tends to be near low or high mountains. Since the seasonal distribution of precipitation in this climate is that of winter moisture and summer deficiency, the uplands and mountains play a role in land use by capturing much of the winter snow and not releasing it as running water until the following summer, at which time it is most welcome for irrigation purposes.

Although these regions contain populations that are native or of native-European mixture, they are for the most part dominated by European cultures. Only in parts of the Middle East do non-European peoples tend to be in control of political units and economies; and even here, chiefly because of the petroleum riches being extracted by European and United States interests and because of its strategic contiguity with the iron curtain, European influence (including some from the Soviet Union) is felt.

Association with Populations. It has been suggested that the garden of Eden may have existed in this type of climate. If so, it is not surprising that the garden was attractive to man. Throughout the world, mediterranean climate tends to overlie small but rather dense population clusters which border the sea on one side and extend up the uplands and mountains on the other. In the United States, pronounced migrations to this climate from other parts of the nation have occurred during and since the last war, and if the present trend continues, California may well become the most populous state in the nation.

Production. Mediterranean agriculture reflects mediterranean climate. Generally found in this type of agricultural region are (1) crops which yield early in the season, having reached maturity through utilization of winter and early spring precipitation; (2) crops which withstand the dry summers without requiring irrigation; and (3) crops which benefit from irrigation water created by melting snow in nearby mountains, or from water that has been delayed in its initial flow by the vegetation in the catchment basins of these highlands. Grains, notably wheat, dominate the first category; three crops—olives, dates, and cork oak—together with some drought-resistant vines, prevail in the second; and a wide variety of garden vegetables and fruits make up the third. The intensity of land use and the allocation of land among the three categories vary not only with such natural environmental conditions as amount and annual distribution of precipitation, but also with such economic factors as size and accessibility of domestic and foreign markets. In the Northern Hemisphere, the mediterranean climate regions supply fruit and vegetables to thickly settled manufacturing regions located within a feasible range of transportation. In the Southern Hemisphere, where populations are more sparse and accessible markets correspondingly smaller, less land is devoted to truck gardening.

In addition to crops, most mediterranean landscapes contain animals. More often than not, the animals are subordinate in significance to crops. Beef and beef-dairy cattle are present especially in Chile, California, and parts of southern Europe. Sheep and goats are the most numerous around the Mediterranean Sea and in Australia and Africa. Swine are found chiefly in southern Europe.

Association with Political Units and Economies. Mediterranean agriculture is found almost entirely in political units that are independent and in economies at a high or moderate level of technical advancement (compare Figs. 7.1 and 1.4). Only northern Africa and the Middle East exhibit the unstable conditions which characterize underdeveloped lands.

Commercial grain farming

This type of agricultural region is distinguished mainly by the type of crop produced and by the degree to which that crop enters into commercial markets, usually world markets. The comparatively few sizable regions engaging in this type of agriculture tend to specialize in the production of one particular grain crop, growing it almost entirely for commercial markets.

World Distribution. Regions of commercial grain farming are prominent in the middle latitudes of central and western North America and of central Asia, and appear in patches in the middle latitudes of South America and Australia (Fig. 7.1).

Natural Environmental and Cultural Associations. Most commercial grain farming is found in semiarid climate and its associated vegetational and soil types, although such farming extends into peripheral climates and conditions. In Argentina and Uruguay commercial grain farming takes place almost completely in humid subtropical climate. As with farm land generally, flat land is desired; but since these crops are raised almost entirely without irrigation, other land can be used. In the Palouse country of eastern Washington, for example, rather sharply undulating hills are used.

If one assumes that the Soviet Union has now "Europeanized" Soviet Middle Asia, it can be stated that all areas of commercial grain farming are associated with the European cultural heritage. However, no sizable areas of commercial grain farming are found in Europe itself, except in European Russia.

Association with Populations. Commercial grain farming involves the utilization of machines, much land, and few people. Consequently, it is usually found where populations tend to be sparse, except in such areas as effective Argentina, effective Uruguay, and the effective area of the Soviet Union, where commercial grain farming overlaps other productive activities, particularly manufacturing (compare Fig. 7.1 and page 13).

Production. Like plantations, commercial grain farms are large, financed by high capital investment, specialized as to crops produced, and centrally managed.

In non-Communist countries, commercial grain farms tend to differ from plantations chiefly in that (1) their land valuation per acre tends to be lower than that of plantations, and so cultivation on grain farms is designed to achieve a high yield per worker, with only secondary emphasis placed upon yield per acre; (2) their yield per worker is maximized through the use of machines; and (3) they are usually owner-operated, and most of the labor is supplied by members of the owner's family or a few hired hands.

Communist nations have no plantations as such, so comparison between their commercial grain farms and plantations is not possible. Commercial grain farming in Communist nations is mostly restricted to the Soviet Union, where it is conducted primarily on collective farms.

Wheat is outstanding among crops grown in commercial grain farming regions. Corn, oats, and barley are noteworthy. Since the crops from commercial grain farms are raised mainly for sale, the few animals maintained on such farms are used chiefly for draft purposes. It seems likely that the number of animals will dwindle as use of machines increases.

Association with Political Units and Economies. The technically advanced economies with commercial grain farms can be divided into two categories: (1) those in which grain is a major component of exports and hence vital to the country's commercial life and (2) those in which grain as an export crop is not so predominant, because of (*a*) a major domestic demand for it and (*b*) competition from other types of farming. Canada, Australia, and Argentina are leading examples of the first category. Large in physical area, containing climates well suited to growing grain, and yet small in aggregate population, these countries depend on grain as an export. The United States and the Soviet Union are the main examples of the second category. Their large domestic populations consume much of the grain directly or indirectly, and hence exports of the grain, while large, are not so vital to their economic well-being as is true of Canada, Australia, and Argentina.

Commercial crop and livestock farming

This type of agricultural region is defined principally on the basis of the variety, intermixture, and commercial nature of its crop and animal products.

World Distribution. Commercial crop and livestock farming is found almost entirely in the middle latitudes. Nearly all nations with commercial crop and livestock farming are technically advanced, and most are situated in North America or Eurasia.

Natural Environmental and Cultural Associations. The climates most frequently associated with crop and livestock farming are the humid continental warm-summer, humid continental cool-summer, marine, humid subtropical, and subarctic. The core climates of the group with respect to specific regions of crop and livestock farming tend to be the humid continental warm-summer and marine, and the others tend to be peripheral.

The main cultural influences affecting crop and livestock farming, like those of plantation agriculture, mediterranean agriculture, and commercial grain farming, have been derived, sometimes with modifications, from Europe.

Production. This is an agriculture with diversification, rotation-of-crops, and high yield. Methods and tools used in these regions are among the most advanced of all agricultural regions, and efforts are made to achieve both a high yield per person and a high yield per acre, particularly in Europe. Such achievement means use of commercial fertilizers as well as animal manures, careful rotation of crops and pastures, wise use of animals, and use of modern machinery. Crops include the grains (corn, wheat, oats, rye, barley); root crops (potatoes, sugar beets, garden vegetables); fruits (apples, peaches, pears, etc.); vines (particularly in Europe); fibers (notably flax); and diverse other crops (alfalfa, clover, rape seed, linseed, buckwheat, etc.). Animals are raised as well (particularly swine, beef and dairy cattle, sheep). This is a commercially oriented production with some subsistence characteristics showing through the commercial veneer. A farmer in such regions usually sells most of his crops and/or animals, but not too many of these enter into the world markets; nearly all are in heavy domestic demand.

Associations with Political Units and Economies. We have noted that this type of agriculture prevails in technically advanced nations and is most widespread in the Northern Hemisphere. The Soviet Union, the United States, and Western Europe each contain large representations, with smaller portions

A small farm in the hills of Boone County, West Virginia. Economists of the technically advanced United States consider this size of farm and type of diversified, somewhat hand-to-mouth farming to be submarginal and unable to compete with larger farms using more scientific practices. Farmers in many underdeveloped countries would consider this place a luxury beyond belief.

found in Canada, Mexico, Brazil, Argentina, the Union of South Africa, the Rhodesias, and the far northeast of Communist China.

Commercial dairy farming

This is a relatively intensive type of agriculture usually found in places where many crops will not mature fully but will mature enough for dairy feed. Climates associated with this agriculture are the cooler portions of humid continental, marine, or undifferentiated highland climates. Since milk and milk products are the chief items for sale, many places of production lie close to the markets. The area of dairy farming in North America is within and generally north from the continent's cluster of manufacturing cities; the two areas in Europe are on either side of Europe's manufacturing districts; and the area in Australia is around and between the major cities. Some dairying, as in much of New Zealand and part of Australia, produces more than local markets can consume, and hence much butter, cheese, etc., are made specifically for more distant markets. Thus, dairy farming is a technically advanced occupation producing for markets where high levels of living prevail. Except in Europe, most commerce in milk and milk products is domestic. In Europe, however, such commerce is more international in character, chiefly because a number of small nations comprise the areas of supply and demand.

Commercial gardening and fruit culture

This is an intensive type of farming, utilizing advanced methods and tools for growing high-value produce for sale chiefly in urban markets located within a feasible transportation range. The produce consists of a wide range of truck-garden vegetables and middle-latitude as well as low-latitude fruits. Such agriculture is most conspicuous along the fringes of the Atlantic Ocean and Gulf of Mexico in the United States, and is found elsewhere in places too small to appear satisfactorily on a global map. These smaller places, too, are generally accessible to urban markets, and are located mostly in Europe, Argentina, and Australia. Commercial gardening and fruit culture are found mainly in technically advanced economies rooted in European civilizations, and their location as well as their extensiveness tend to be closely associated with markets; the natural environment is a secondary consideration. Indeed, many such tracts, well located to markets, often receive much attention and financial investment toward overcoming adverse natural environmental features. Specific techniques include the use of greenhouses, the supplying of plant nutrients by chemical means, and the use of irrigating water in humid as well as dry climates to overcome any temporary moisture deficiency.

Technically advanced and underdeveloped conditions

Of the eight agricultural types discussed, the first two prevail in underdeveloped economies and the last five in technically advanced economies. (Fig. 7.1 and Fig. 1.4). One, plantation agriculture, occurs chiefly in underdeveloped areas, but is to a great extent a transplant of technically advanced conditions which affect only the plantation districts and not surrounding native economies. Most plantations depend upon international not domestic markets. Six types of farming associated with technical advance account for the majority of agricultural commodities entering into international trade.

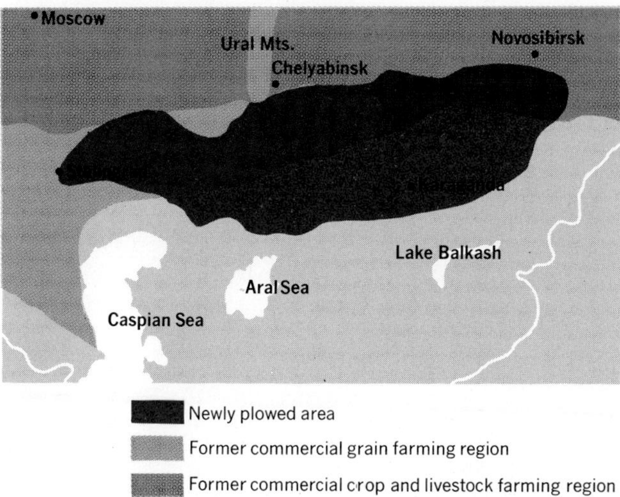

Figure 7.3 ***Newly plowed land in the virgin- and idle-lands project of the Soviet Union.*** *The map shows only the territory of most active plowing. Other territory in both European Russia and Soviet Middle Asia also was plowed, especially along the irrigated margins of mountains fringing Soviet Middle Asia. Not all plowing of virgin and idle lands took place in previously uncultivated territory. There is a definite overlap of the virgin and idle lands project into the regions of both commercial grain farming and commercial crop and livestock farming, the patterns of which are shown in the map. Plowing in these areas was chiefly of idle rather than virgin land.*

Trends in agricultural land use

The major trends in agricultural land use involve both the amount of land cultivated and the productivity per acre and per worker. During the last two decades, the amount of land under cultivation has been increased by about 165 million acres—less than 7 per cent of the 1936 acreage. Over one-half of this increase took place in the Soviet Union after the Second World War; some 93 million acres of land, much of it on the drier margins of that nation's commercial-grain-farming region, were plowed up (Fig. 7.3). Some new land was added in Communist China, India, and the smaller nations of Asia; some 75 million acres were added to cropland in these areas. About 7 million acres were

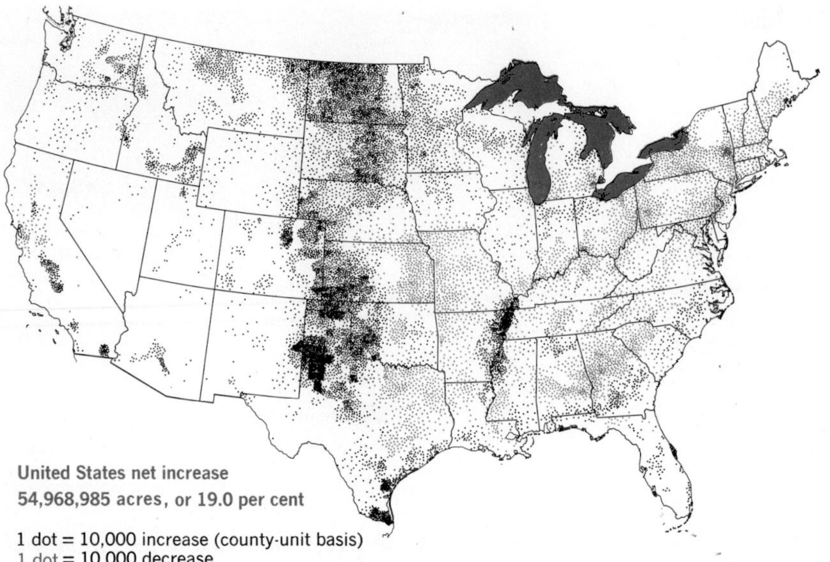

Figure 7.4 ***Changes in cropland harvested in the United States between 1899 and 1949.*** *Great Plains land was plowed and land in the East and South was returned to forest.*

added in Africa, 6 million in Latin America, and 3 million in Europe. In the United States, some 20 million acres were *withdrawn* from production, at least temporarily, because of surpluses of wheat, cotton, and other crops. (This figure represents a *net* decrease; actually there have been some additions, but not enough to compensate for the withdrawals.) Most of this land is in United States commercial grain farming and commercial crop and livestock farming regions (Figs. 7.4, 7.5, and 7.6).

World productivity per acre increased between 1936 and 1958—wheat, from 14.5 to 17.3 bushels per acre; rice, from 16.7 to 17 bushels; corn, from 21.4 to 30 bushels; beans, from 610 to 621 pounds; soybeans, from 16 to 19 bushels; cotton, from 195 to 266 pounds; and tobacco, from 877 to 918 pounds. Increases were particularly marked in technically advanced countries, where use of new types of

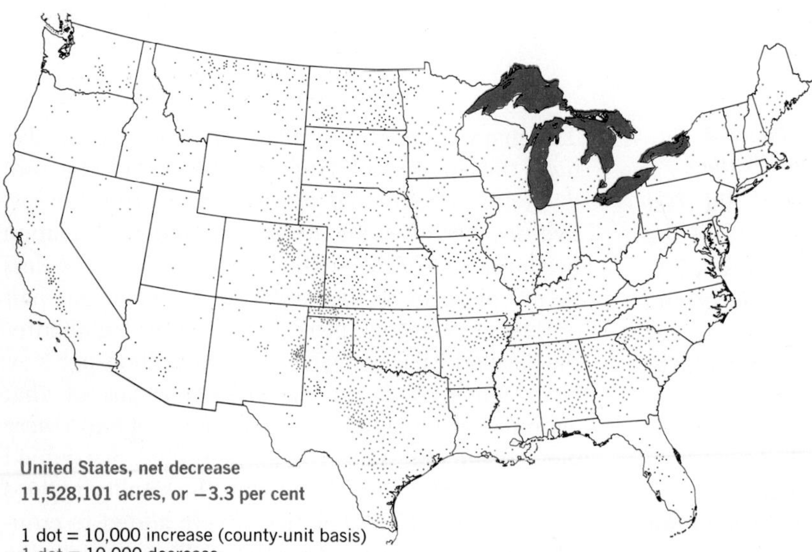

Figure 7.5 ***Changes in cropland harvest in the United States between 1949 and 1954.*** *Heaviest withdrawals were in the South and parts of the Great Plains. Why the reverse trend in the Great Plains from that in Fig. 7.4? (U.S. Bureau of the Census)*

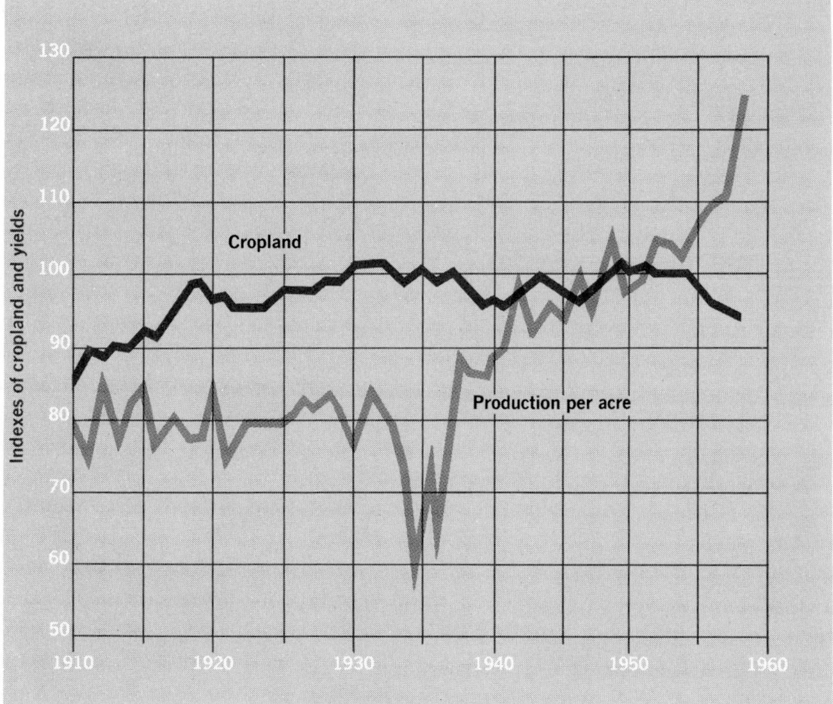

Figure 7.6 ***Trends in the amount of cropland harvested and yield per acre in the United States, in per cent of 1947–1949 conditions.*** *Cropland has decreased in amount, notably since the mid-1950s, but yield per acre has risen sharply. (After* The Chemical Industry Facts Book, *1960–1961, p. 71)*

seed and fertilizers is more or less commonplace. These practices plus mechanization also have meant higher yields per worker in technically advanced countries. Some underdeveloped economies are beginning to improve their farming methods, however, with results already beginning to become apparent. The increase of production in Communist countries, whether technically advanced or underdeveloped, is even more pronounced.

MANUFACTURING

Although commonplace in most technically advanced nations, the manufacturing plant is a comparatively recent innovation to underdeveloped lands—so recent, in fact, that many such lands have yet to experience it other than as a novelty. Indeed, when one remembers that the steam engine, which stimulated the Industrial Revolution, came into being less than two centuries ago, he realizes that the factory is a comparatively recent innovation to the entire world. In its short span of existence, however, the factory and the factory system have radically altered economies. This change is perhaps most dramatically expressed in terms of value of product: according to conservative estimates, manufacturing is accountable for commodities valued aggregately at about twice the output of agriculture, and over five times that of minerals extraction activities. In terms of employment (where handicraft industries are included), manufacturing still lags behind agriculture, employing about 18 per cent of all workers; but it is far ahead of the other occupations (Table 7.1), and is growing rapidly. In terms of amount of area occupied, it is rather inconspicuous; however, one of the outstanding characteristics of modern manufacturing is its extremely high output per acre of occupied land.

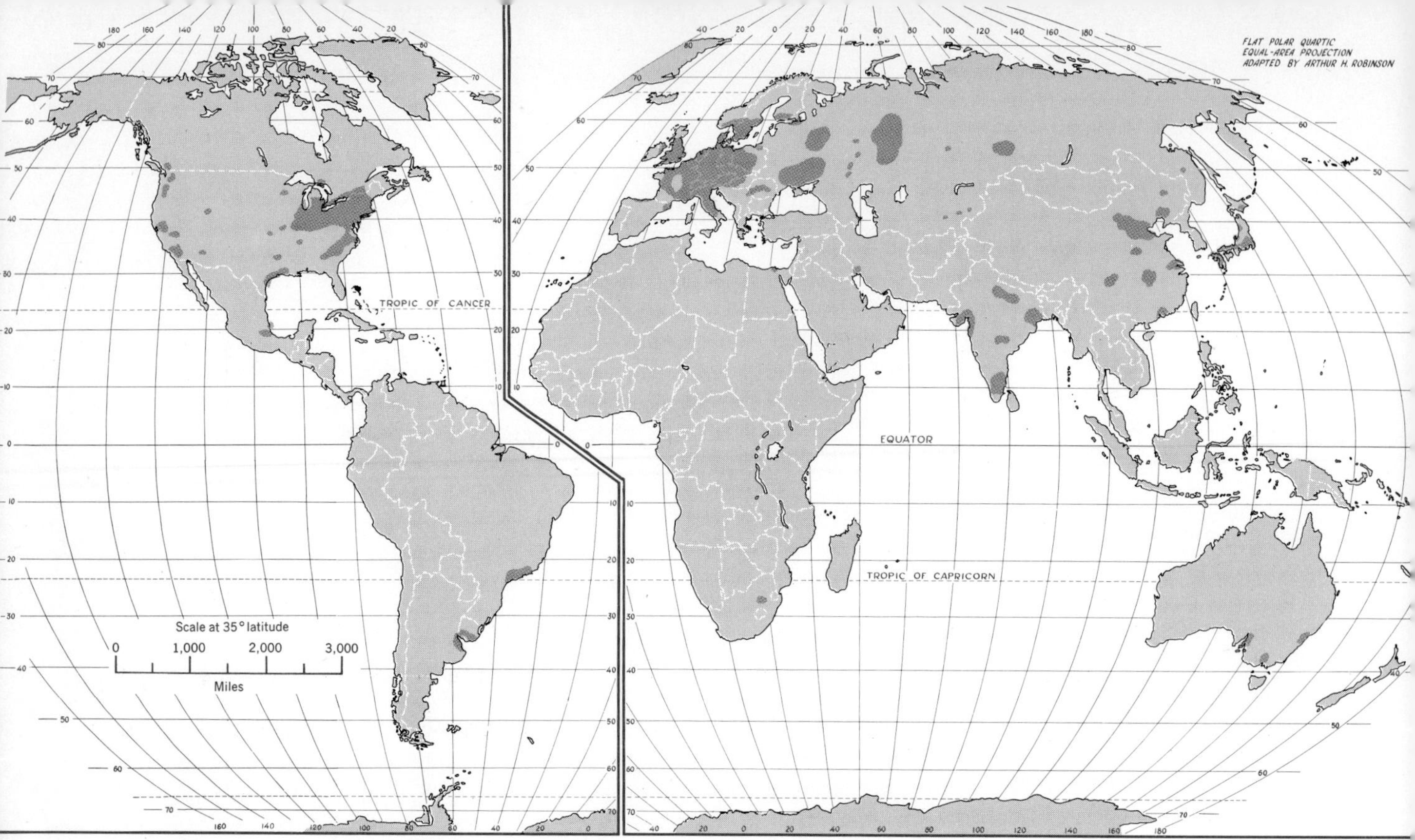

Figure 7.7 ***World distribution of manufacturing*** *(generalized). Each of these manufacturing regions or areas contains land used for agriculture or other nonmanufacturing purposes. However, as time passes and cities and manufacturing plants become larger and more numerous, much more of this rural land will be occupied by urban and manufacturing facilities.*

MANUFACTURING AREAS

In the world as a whole, four areas of manufacturing and numerous smaller, outlying clusters are generally recognized (Fig. 7.7). Two of these areas have become congealed into rather distinctive regions of manufacturing, and the other two represent somewhat arbitrary classifications of more dispersed locations. The four areas are (1) the manufacturing region of Europe; (2) the manufacturing region of east central North America; (3) the manufacturing of the Soviet Union; and (4) the manufacturing of eastern and southern Asia. The reader will note that each area cores a densely populated section of the world. Smaller manufacturing clusters and places are located in each of these major areas as well as in outlying countries, such as Australia, the Union of South Africa, Argentina, Brazil, Mexico, Venezuela, and Chile.

Europe

The boundary of the European manufacturing belt extends from Glasgow in the Scottish lowlands northeastward to Stockholm and Helsinki, southwestward along the border of the Soviet Union to Warsaw in Poland, southwestward to Budapest in Hungary, northwestward to Vienna in Austria, southward to Naples in Italy, northwestward to Marseilles, Toulouse, and Bordeaux in France, and thence to Cardiff, Dublin, Belfast, and Glasgow. Within this broad region are some districts of heavier intensity that concentrate in particular places and some districts that are separated by open countryside. Beyond, in such locations as northern Spain and Portugal, central and eastern Romania, and eastern Bulgaria, are small and dynamic manufacturing activities, usually located in isolated cities.

This region is the cradle area of the factory. Although ravaged by war, it remains today among the most productive of all manufacturing regions. Its production, however, cannot be ascribed to any single economy, because a variety of nations lie wholly or partially within it. Since the Second World War, the disruptive effect of conflicting ideologies has been added to that of nationalism, and the iron curtain tends to separate the tier of countries in eastern Europe from the rest.

North America

The periphery of the North American manufacturing region connects the major cities of Boston, New York, Philadelphia, Baltimore, Durham, Charlotte (North Carolina), Columbia (South Carolina), Augusta, Birmingham, Chattanooga, Louisville, St. Louis, Peoria, Chicago, Milwaukee, Detroit, Toronto, Montreal, Quebec, and, coming full circle, Boston (Figs. 7.7 and 7.8). The belt includes all points on this line and, as in Europe, embraces open countrysides as well as districts of intense concentration. Particularly during and since the last war, manufacturing has become much more important in the Gulf South and the Far West, both of which lie outside the region itself. Only the United States and Canada share this manufacturing.

Soviet Union

Manufacturing in the Soviet Union is an admixture of the old and new to a degree not experienced elsewhere. Five major districts predominate; three have roots in pre-Soviet history and two are largely products of the Communist regime. The older districts include the Ukrainian industrial district, north of the Black Sea; the Moscow industrial district, focused on the nation's capital city; and the Leningrad industrial district consisting chiefly of the city itself. Farther east are the Urals industrial district, given only passing attention in czarist times, and the Kuznets industrial district, entirely a Soviet creation. Isolated production centers of note are situated particularly along the Volga River, in oases of Soviet central Asia, and at key points on the Trans-Siberian Railway.

Eastern and southern Asia

Factories in eastern and southern Asia are especially concentrated in Japan, Communist China, and India (Fig. 7.7). Except in Japan, few manufacturing districts as such can be said to exist, and even these are small in comparison with districts in Europe or North America. Instead, manufacturing in eastern and southern Asia is focused in single cities. There are indications, however, that more complex districts are evolving in Communist China and India.

Comparative significance

What is the contribution of each of these manufacturing areas to the total of world manufacturing? Our answer will vary with our yardstick. We shall consider three criteria: (1) size of total labor force, and its allocation to specific commodities; (2) value of production; and (3) volume of energy consumption.

Labor Force. Using labor-force statistics to make this kind of comparison is somewhat misleading since these statistics include *both* handicraft and manufacturing workers, and the former account for an estimated one-half of the total. Eastern and southern Asia, where handicraft workers are especially numerous, is responsible for over one-third of all manufacturing employment. European manufacturing accounts for nearly another one-third, that of the Soviet Union for about one-sixth, and that of North America for slightly less than one-sixth.

What is this labor force producing? For the world as a whole, an estimated 12 per cent is engaged in the output of food, beverages, and tobacco; 32 per cent in textiles and clothing; 22 per cent in metals, machinery, transportation equipment, etc.; and 34 per cent in other commodities. Each of the four major manufacturing areas has a similar per-

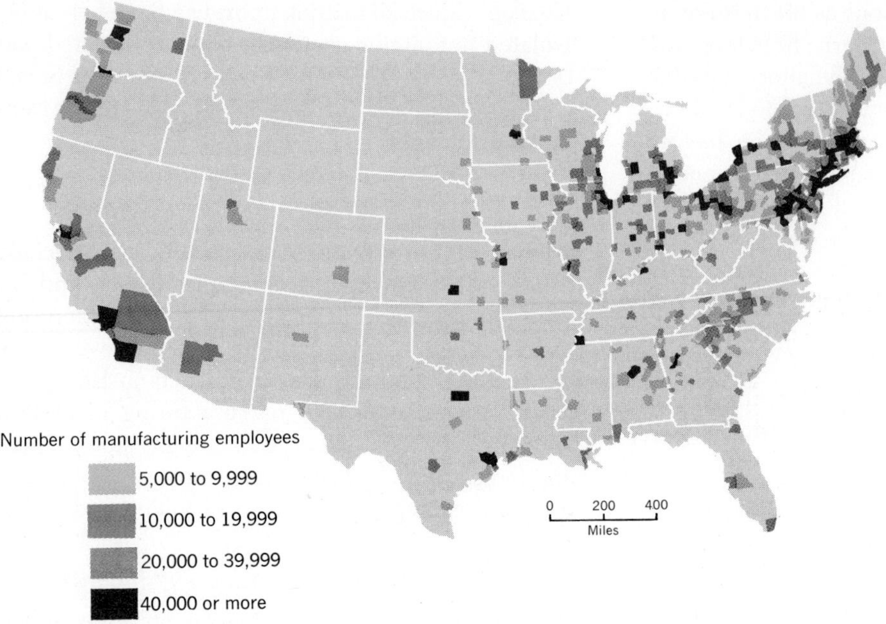

Figure 7.8 ***Distribution of manufacturing in the United States,*** *in terms of number of manufacturing employees per county. The manufacturing belt of the East and Piedmont South is clearly visible, as are the growing districts of the Pacific West and Gulf South. The large size of the areas in California and some other states is a distortion owing to the large size of the counties. (After a map by the U.S. Bureau of the Census)*

centage of its labor force in food and associated industries and in miscellaneous industries, but not in the other two categories. The three most technically advanced areas—North America, Europe, and the Soviet Union—allocate only about 20 per cent of their respective labor forces to textiles and clothing, and nearly 35 per cent to metals, machinery, and transportation equipment. In contrast, eastern and southern Asia allocates about 40 per cent of its manufacturing labor force to textiles and clothing, and only about 10 per cent to the metals and related industries. However, Japan, Communist China, and India are currently stressing metals, and it is probable that a higher percentage of the labor force of this part of the world will be devoted to such manufacturing in the future.

Volume of Production. Measured by value, the volume of the world's manufacturing output is concentrated in North America, Europe, and the Soviet Union. By recent estimate, North America accounts for nearly 40 per cent of all the world's manufactured goods (including the output from handicrafts), Europe almost 30 per cent, and the Soviet Union slightly under 20 per cent. The goods manufactured have been discussed in the foregoing account of labor-force allocation.

Energy. When the world's manufacturing areas are assessed in terms of nonhuman energy consumed, their order of significance is strikingly similar to that of industrial output. Manufacturing in North America accounts for nearly 45 per cent of all nonhuman energy consumed in the world's manufacturing; in Europe, nearly 30 per cent; and in the Soviet Union, about 15 per cent.

Trends

The world's manufacturing is experiencing certain trends, some of which are general and some of which are apparent only in specific manufacturing areas.

General. Perhaps the most significant trend in manufacturing is its sharp increase; it more than doubled in the 1937–1947 decade (when measured in currency, with no allowance for inflation), and has continued to rise at a higher rate. A second general trend has been the constant increase in factories at the expense of handicraft industries, even when measured by labor force. Still a third trend, particularly apparent in North America, Europe, and the Soviet Union, has been the automation of industry—the substitution, in many sectors of manufacturing, of automatic or quasi-automatic machinery and apparatus for human labor.

In North America. Trends which are more or less unique to each manufacturing area have also been noted. In North America, perhaps the most significant of such trends (other than automation, which is more advanced in this region than in any other) have been: (1) the rise of certain industries at the relative expense of others; (2) the relatively rapid growth of the manufacturing belt—notably its western half—compared to the growth of manufacturing elsewhere in the continent; and (3) the heightened dependence, especially of the United States, on foreign supply sources of raw materials and energy.

In brief, industries producing chemicals, machinery, transportation equipment, metals, instruments, etc., have risen sharply in proportionate significance to the food, textile, apparel, lumber, and other industries; these last, once paramount and still important, have not increased as rapidly.

In regional growth, essentially all manufacturing districts, large and small, have expanded during the century. In the early part of the century, the manufacturing belt reigned more or less supreme, and other parts of the nation were definitely subordinate to it. (The southward migration of the cotton textile industry, discussed in Chapter 33, was a marked exception to this trend.) Within that belt, the western portion gained at the relative expense, and sometimes the absolute expense, of the east. During and since the Second World War, however, manufacturing has expanded in volume in other parts of the country—especially in the Pacific, Gulf, and Piedmont states (Figs. 7.9, 7.10, and 7.11).

The United States economy, particularly, is more and more dependent upon foreign mineral sources. Many of this country's highest-quality ores are completely or nearly consumed, and the United States must now choose whether to exploit ores of intermediate or low quality, or import high-quality materials. Both alternatives are being practiced. The country is importing larger amounts of iron, copper, lead, zinc, aluminum, and other metals (in each case, largely as ore or concentrates), as well as petroleum. Some of these, especially petroleum, exist in substantial amounts domestically, and the use of foreign sources is a result of policy rather than need.

In Europe. Probably the most impressive trend in Europe, other than its rapid postwar recovery in manufacturing activity, is the successful achievement of a measure of economic unification. The manufacturing of Europe is divided among more than twenty large and small nations. Wiser Europeans have realized that in the twentieth century only unified giants of production can enter successfully into manufacturing competition. Consequently, a movement was activated soon after the last war to reduce the restrictive effects of national boundary lines upon the movement of goods, money, and people. Among the most successful of the initial plans was the European Coal and Steel Community, initiated in 1952. Members are France, West Germany, Italy, the Netherlands, Belgium, and Luxembourg. This plan sought, successfully, to increase cooperation among the six nations for a limited objective—the production and exchange of coal, steel, and related raw materials. Unlike other schemes not as successful, the Coal and Steel Community has an *international* administering body with jurisdiction over national governments in matters relating to the production of coal and steel commodities, with a source of revenue more or less independent of national government action. The community was successful enough that a European common market (the European Economic Community) and an atomic energy program (the European Community of Atomic Energy), composed of the same nations and with similar administrative arrangements, were brought into being in 1957. Indeed, it is possible that even larger areas of cooperation, including nearly all non-Communist countries in Europe may evolve. Although the exact nature and extent of an international union hangs in the balance of current decision, Europe appears to be moving toward a measure of unprecedented

Figure 7.9 ***Expenditure for new manufacturing plants and equipment in the United States from 1951 to 1957, in billions of dollars. Measured in this way, the western part of the manufacturing belt is growing the most rapidly.*** *(After* Area Development Bulletin, *U.S. Office of Area Development)*

cooperation—at least in manufacturing and transportation. Similar trends in agriculture are not yet very evident.

In the Soviet Union. The Soviet Union has been characterized by a rapid increase in over-all manufacture, particularly in the production of metals and

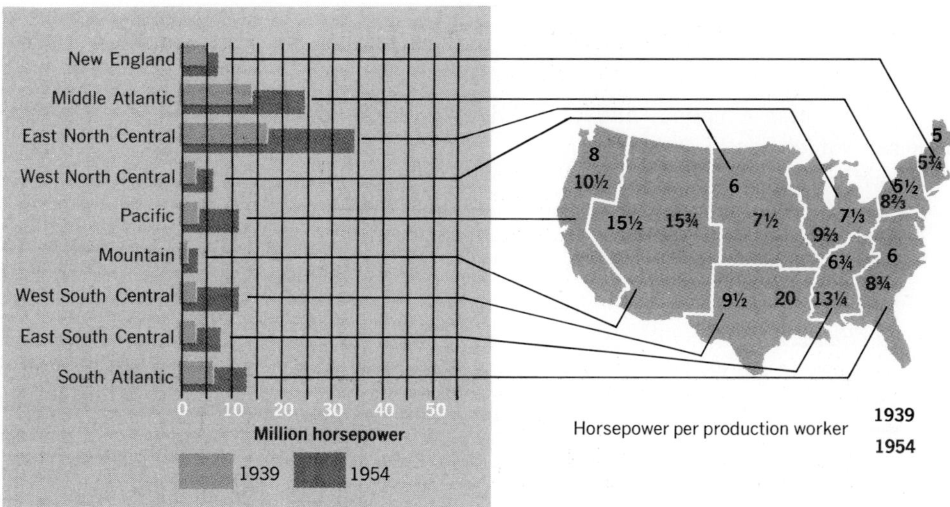

Figure 7.10 ***Changes in horsepower capacity of factory equipment in the United States between 1939 and 1954.*** *As in Fig. 7.9, the highest increase is in the manufacturing belt, notably its western section. However, the Pacific, Gulf, and southern Piedmont sections are expanding. How do you account for the very sharp increase in horsepower per production worker in the Gulf states? (After* Area Development Bulletin, *U.S. Office of Area Development)*

associated goods. Steel output, for example, has expanded almost fifteen times since the First Five-Year Plan was initiated in 1928, and the Soviet Union is now second only to the United States in steel production. Another unique feature to Soviet manufacturing has been the planned development of new manufacturing areas—first the Urals district, then the Kuznets district, and currently the

Figure 7.11 ***Changes in manufacturing employment within the United States from 1899 to 1955.*** *The graph allocates percentages of national employment to each section for the years shown. Measured by labor force, our manufacturing appears to be shifting westward and southward. The Pacific West is growing the most rapidly. However, many of the new industries there are not so highly automated as industries of the manufacturing belt and the South, and actual growth of manufacturing there is not quite so fast as this map suggests. Compare with Figs. 7.9 and 7.10. (After* Area Development Bulletin, *U.S. Office of Area Development)*

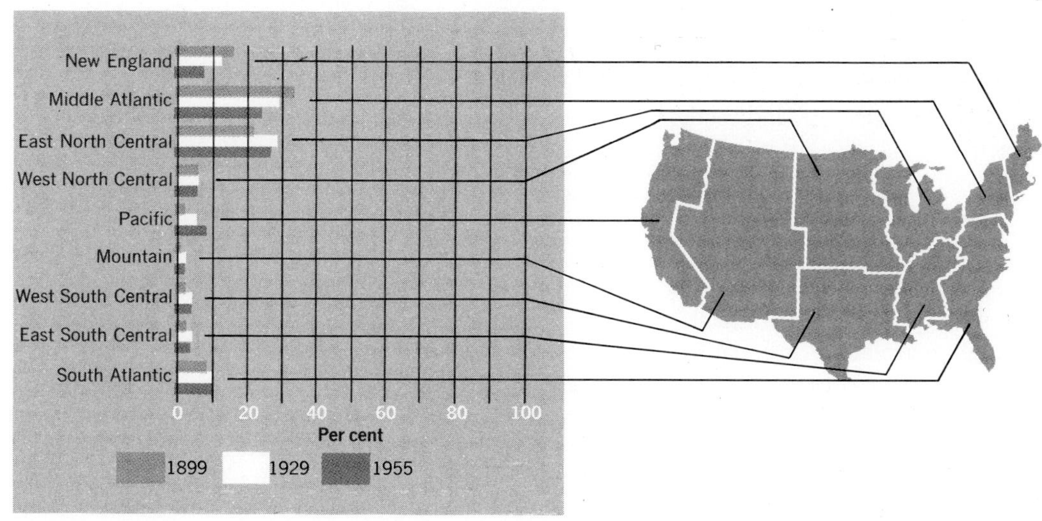

Irkutsk (Lake Baikal) district, as well as smaller clusters. The purpose of such development appears largely to be to increase the manufacturing output of the nation, and to provide "islands" of self-sufficiency in as many parts as possible of that vast country, so that the amount of freight hauled over the railroads—which, of all transportation media in the Soviet Union, necessarily carry the most freight—can be minimized.

In Eastern and Southern Asia. In eastern and southern Asia, there has been a resurgence in Japanese manufacturing, despite the loss of much of the Asian market and despite the decline in such Japanese prewar specialties as silk, which lost a competitive battle to nylon and rayon in the world (chiefly United States) markets. In Communist China and India the trend is toward more manufacturing, although the necessary factories and tools have been slow to appear. Each country has a Five-Year Plan for achieving certain objectives in manufacturing as well as in other areas of endeavor. That of Communist China is modeled rather closely after that of the Soviet Union, including marked emphasis upon the manufacturing of steel rather than food and textiles, and the use of police force and other coercive measures to assure that such emphasis will be maintained. India's Five-Year Plan, while providing for the increase in heavy industries, has been oriented more toward the production and processing of agricultural goods than has been true of the Communist programs, and it is not noteworthily buttressed by police and other coercive power.

THE LESSER PRODUCTIVE OCCUPATIONS

MINERALS EXTRACTION

Whether viewed in terms of labor force (Table 7.1) or area of land occupied, the extraction of minerals is not so directly important in most economies as is agriculture or manufacturing. The value of its annual output, however, is appreciable, and the implications of that output are even more significant, because most of the world's inanimate energy and a sizable portion of its raw materials for manufacture are made available, directly or indirectly, through minerals extraction.

Commodities extracted

Although the total list of extracted commodities is long—at least 200 minerals are now being extracted for commercial purposes—only a few are paramount. Most important are coal, petroleum, and natural gas, the fuels and lubricants so vital to mechanized production. Measured by value, these are responsible for about three-fifths of all mined and quarried commodities. Of the minerals to be used other than for the production of energy, the metals and nonmetals are of about equal importance. Dominant among the metals (exclusive of the precious metals) are iron, manganese, copper, aluminum, zinc, lead, and chromium. Rather surprisingly, the leading commodities among the nonenergy, nonmetal products are such common materials as stone, clay, and sand, as well as such products as phosphate, potash, salt, gypsum, and asbestos.

Association with economies

Without the extraction of minerals on a grand scale, this Industrial Age could never have evolved, for minerals are vital ingredients of mechanized production. Effective mineral extraction, therefore, is almost entirely a function of technically advanced nations (Figs. 1.4 and 4.5). Once these nations have depleted their domestic resources, they begin exploitation in other, usually underdeveloped, countries. With certain exceptions, such as the important investment by the United States in the petroleum of the Middle East, there is a tendency for the technically advanced countries to focus attention upon areas where their own political and economic influence is pronounced. Among specific commodities currently sought rather urgently by these nations are petroleum and a variety of metallic ores, including that of uranium, the source of nuclear energy.

The underdeveloped countries, lacking know-how and capital, traditionally have agreed to the sale of their minerals to the technically advanced countries. Today, however, some of the governments of these underdeveloped countries, fired by an ardent nationalism and benefiting from their strategic position in the cold-war struggle, are giving serious attention to the development of more of their own means of minerals extraction, with the products of that extraction to be used for domestic consumption.

FISHING AND HUNTING

Hunting as a livelihood industry supports so few people that only passing reference need be given it in a book concerned with the global aspects of economic geography. Commercial fishing is much more significant; and yet even this industry, supporting probably about ½ per cent of the world's labor force, is a minor productive occupation in comparison with such giants as agriculture and manufacturing.

World distribution

In the broadest sense, the term *fishing* refers to the taking of all marine zoological life—life ranging in size and distribution from microscopic plankton found along inland waterways and in the open seas to the mighty ocean-dwelling mammal, the whale. In practice, about seven-eighths of all commercial fishing, measured by volume of catch, is done in the open oceans, and the remainder is done on water bodies and waterways on the earth's land surface. Four major ocean fishing areas—three of them immediately offshore from major clusters of world population—are generally recognized. These are the shallow seas offshore from eastern and southern Asia, northwestern Europe, eastern and southern Anglo-America, and western Anglo-America (Fig. 4.1). All, it will be noted, are in the Northern Hemisphere.

Association with economies

Fishing is unusual in that it is actively associated with economies ranging from those which are very high in technical development to those which are markedly underdeveloped. In terms of labor-force allocation, eastern and southern Asia in general and Japan in particular are very prominent: about two-thirds of the world's labor force in commercial fishing is found in eastern and southern Asia, with over one-fifth in Japan alone. Europe, by this criterion, is second with about 15 per cent of the world's fishermen, and Anglo-America and the Soviet Union each account for approximately 7 per cent.

Somewhat more than one-third of the world's fish catch is landed in eastern and southern Asia. Europe accounts for about one-fourth, North America for over 15 per cent, and the Soviet Union for nearly 10 per cent. The difference between the output per worker of technically advanced and underdeveloped countries is not so pronounced as is true of manufacturing or agriculture. This is due partially to the fact that the Industrial Age is only now catching up with the fishing industry. Especially since the last war, the floating cannery, a large ship from which the fish are not only caught but on which they are also processed in essentially one continuous operation, is coming into some use. Japan has shown particular interest in adoption of this modern means of commercial fishing.

FOREST-PRODUCTS INDUSTRIES

Accounting for less than 1 per cent of the world's labor force, forest-products industries involve the exploitation of trees that have not been planted by man. Although wood is their primary product, forest-products industries are responsible for a long list of materials, including maple sirup, naval stores, cork, tanning materials, rubber, camphor, quinine, and various assortments of nuts and gums.

Exploiting products of forests, these industries exist where accessible forests are to be found. Coniferous softwoods are utilized the most actively, with deciduous and tropical hardwoods of respective secondary and tertiary significance. Large-scale forest utilization is chiefly an occupation of large, young, technically advanced economies. The United States and the Soviet Union each accounts currently for about one-fifth of all wood being cut. Heavily populated Europe utilizes an additional fifth of all exploited wood, and the remainder is consumed by all other political units. The most active areas of exploitation are in humid continental cool-summer, subarctic, marine, and humid subtropical climates.

GRAZING

The number of people who rely entirely upon nature's forage for raising their livestock is very small; usually some form of agriculture tends to overlap grazing activities. Most of the purest forms of grazing are found in connection with the nomadic herding involving the sparse populations of semiarid Asia and Africa, and of the Eurasian and Anglo-American far north. Census information is meager concerning these itinerant peoples, but their numbers apparently are small. The animals in question range as to type from the reindeer of the far north to the camel, horse, cow, sheep, and goat of the Asian-African dry country and the yak of the more isolated upland regions of Tibet and its peripheries in central Asia. Where communism has been initiated in these lands, attempts have usually been made to transform the migrants into sedentary agriculturalists.

Grazing in the Occidental world—best developed in the semiarid and tropical savanna climates of North America, South America, South Africa, and Australia—tends to be a matter of either enhancing the world's supply of wool or of permitting animals to gain sufficient weight that they can be fattened elsewhere for slaughter. Distinction is usually made between middle-latitude grazing lands, where diseases are comparatively rare, forage is somewhat better, and finished products are of higher quality, and the low-latitude grazing areas, where the natural environment is less conducive to grazing activities. The areas of each form of grazing can be surmised by comparing Figures 7.1 and 5.1. The middle-latitude grazing is most prodigiously developed in semiarid climate, and the low-latitude grazing in tropical savanna climate. In recent years, low-latitude grazing has benefited from the crossbreeding of standard beef varieties with the low-latitude Brahma and Zulu cattle so as to produce types of animals that can withstand the tropical heat and diseases and concomitantly produce a more edible meat.

REFERENCES

Alexander, John W.: "Industrial Expansion in the United States, 1939–1947," *Economic Geography*, **28**:128–142, 1952.

Harris, Chauncy D.: "Agricultural Production in the United States: The Past Fifty Years and the Next," *Geographical Review*, **47**:175–193, 1957.

———: "Growing Food by Decree in Soviet Russia," *Foreign Affairs*, **33**:1–14, 1955.

Haystead, Ladd, and Gilbert C. Fite: *The Agricultural Regions of the United States*, University of Oklahoma Press, Norman, Okla., 1955.

James, Preston E., and Clarence F. Jones (eds.): *American Geography: Inventory and Prospect*, Syracuse University Press for the Association of American Geographers, Syracuse, N. Y., 1954. (Especially chaps. 6, 9, and 10–12.)

Karan, Pradyumna P., and William M. Jenkins, Jr.: "Geography of Manufacturing in India," *Economic Geography*, **35**:269–278, 1959.

Lonsdale, Richard E., and John H. Thompson: "A Map of the U.S.S.R.'s Manufacturing," *Economic Geography*, **36**:36–52, 1960.

Mighell, Ronald L.: *American Agriculture: Its Structure and Place in the Economy*, John Wiley & Sons, Inc., New York, 1955.

Ovdiyenko, I. K.: "The New Geography of Industry in

China," *Soviet Geography: Review and Translation,* **1** (4):63–78, 1960.

Prunty, Merle, Jr.: "The Renaissance of the Southern Plantation," *Geographical Review,* **45:**459–491, 1955.

Rodgers, Allan: "Some Aspects of Industrial Diversification in the United States," *Economic Geography,* **33:**16–30, 1957.

Sauer, Carl O.: *Agricultural Origins and Dispersals,* The American Geographical Society, New York, 1952.

Stamp, L. Dudley: "The Measurement of Land Resources," *Geographical Review,* **48:**1–15, 1958.

Thomas, William L., Jr. (ed.): *Man's Role in Changing the Face of the Earth,* The University of Chicago Press for the Wenner Gren Foundation for Anthropological Research and the National Science Foundation, Chicago, 1956. (Especially pp. 49–69, 487–503, 692–762, and 851–895.)

Thompson, John H., and Michihiro Miyazaki: "A Map of Japan's Manufacturing," *Geographical Review,* **49:**1–17, 1959.

Weaver, John C.: "Changing Patterns of Cropland Use in the Middle West," *Economic Geography,* **30:**1–47, 1954.

8 LOCATIONAL CONSIDERATIONS IN PRODUCTION

IN THE PRECEDING CHAPTER WE HAVE NOTED THE DISTRIBUTION OF THE WORLD'S productive occupations and industries, and have seen that production is erratic in global arrangement, sometimes finding expression in simple, single-occupation economic landscapes, sometimes in landscapes of moderate complexity, and sometimes in very intricate landscapes which reflect the concomitant presence of all six productive occupations. In other words, we have appraised the "Where?" of global production. In this chapter we shall inquire into the "Why?" of that "Where?"—into the considerations involved in selecting the location of any of the productive occupations and industries.

As man's increasing technology enables him to gain additional freedom from the limitations of nature and to decide with comparative independence and assurance where and how he will live, he is necessarily giving an unprecedented measure of attention to the specific location of his activities. The urgency of such action is compounded notably by the marked growth of populations and of cities and towns within a global surface that is fixed in total area. Under these circumstances, considerations of location have reached the stage where they are applied not only to the productive industries with which we are concerned in this chapter but also to other aspects of economies and cultures—indeed, in the final analysis, to entire populations.

Whatever its future implications for other aspects of human existence, location is currently given very active consideration in connection with production. So appraised, it has already become a subject of specialization for both theoretical- and applied-research workers, particularly in this twentieth century of heightened attention to careful selection of locations for productive enterprises. Most theoretical efforts have been directed toward understanding the pertinent locational aspects of manufacturing and agriculture, the foremost of the world's productive industries. On a more applied basis, however, essentially all productive enterprises have been examined with some interest in their location, for each is owned and/or operated by a manager whose welfare is associated directly or indirectly with the success or failure of that particular enterprise—and location is often a vital ingredient of such success or failure.

MAJOR LOCATIONAL CONSIDERATIONS

If the location of production has become a subject of study, what are its primary components? Obviously, four relevant features are the classical factors of production—capital, land, labor, and entrepreneurship. There are also additional considerations, for the *location* of production involves attention to demand as well as to supply—to consumption as well as production. The size and situation of present and future *markets* thus constitute still a fifth factor of consideration in assessing the location of production. The *transportation of commodities* among places of initial obtainment of raw materials and energy, places of production, and places of consumption comprises a sixth factor. Finally, the *government policies* of political units wherein the production is or expects to be located are of increasing significance. It is important to remember that these seven considerations pertain to all the productive occupations, and not merely to agriculture and manufacturing.

Capital

Capital goods include (1) the tools, or instruments, of production (factories, barns, oil derricks, fishing vessels, machinery, hand tools, etc.), together with (2) the temporary inventories of consumer or producer goods that have not yet been consumed. In matters of industrial location, the first is the more important aspect of capital, as it refers to the operational facilities of the six productive industries—the facilities, in other words, which are subject to locational considerations. Capital also includes money as well as goods, but money is very mobile and not subject to the same locational considerations as goods and hence is not of concern to us here.

Land

Land refers to the natural environment, which has been appraised summarily in Chapters 4, 5, and 6. Specific natural features that enter actively into an appraisal of the *general*, or *regional*, location of production are the sources of (1) *raw materials*, (2) *nonhuman energy* (animal and inanimate energy), and (3) *productive agents*. The significance of raw materials and nonhuman energy for all types of production is obvious. Not so easily apparent is the significance of the agents, which enter into the productive processes as aids rather than as either raw materials or energy. By way of illustration, water (in addition to being a raw material and a source of energy) is often used as a productive agent—for example, in the washing of some textile fibers during the early stages of their manufacture. Similarly, soil and climate can be described more accurately as agents, rather than as raw materials, of agricultural production.

Usually subordinate to the above considerations but nevertheless important is still a fourth feature—the specific bit of land, or *site*, upon which a proposed activity is to be located. Obviously, the site requirements of different farms, mines, factories, etc., vary pronouncedly throughout a given country, and even more throughout all of the world's populated land surface.

As will become more evident later in this chapter, the significance of land—of the natural environment—for the location of production ranges from very high to very low. Certain industries are tightly welded to their locations by natural environmental restrictions, whereas others are comparatively free from such restrictions. Where or when the natural environmental limitations are rigid, man can exercise little choice in matters of location, but where or when such limitations become more general, man has increased freedom—and responsibility—in locational decisions.

Labor

Labor involves the application to production of most human effort, both mental and physical. The only notable exception is the labor of entrepreneurship, which we consider here as a separate factor of production. Labor thus includes those productive efforts which do not enter into the realm of policy making. Since it involves most of the world's working population, it is distributed throughout the world somewhat in accordance with that population.

Entrepreneurship

Entrepreneurship is particularly important to industrial location in that it is responsible for policy-making decisions, among which are decisions as to where productive activities are to be placed. Under capitalism, the prime objective of entrepreneurship has been the realization of an early financial profit. Such an objective obviously includes good judgment in matters of location. In contrast, Communist and some other socialist economies do not emphasize the return of profits to individuals or companies and corporations. Instead, at least in theory, they emphasize an efficient allocation of natural (and human) resources—an allocation which can be achieved only through careful, long-term planning at highest governmental levels. Such policies may involve deficit spending over substantial periods of time in order to bolster embryonic activities that ultimately may become self-supporting. The question logically arises as to whether location based on the profit motive is similar in pattern to that based on long-term planning. A complete answer will not be attempted here, but the question will be raised with regard to specific commodities later in the book. It would appear, however, that the same basic considerations ultimately apply to both outlooks. In other words, deficit financing of an enterprise cannot continue indefinitely, so that an eventual profit —by whatever term it is labeled—will be necessary. However, deficit financing does allow the possibility of taking greater immediate risks than does the system of early profit return, and to this extent the associated locational patterns may differ.

Markets

The crudest of subsistence economies need not involve markets, inasmuch as each person is more or less his own consumer as well as producer, and his market is himself. If we multiply the one person, however, by the millions now living even in single metropolitan areas, we multiply the market accordingly. Under such crowded conditions, production is no longer wholly subsistence in character, even in the more underdeveloped economies. Instead, it is specialized, and it becomes more so as technical levels of economies increase. The focalization of consumption and concomitant focalization and specialization of production raise questions of fixed markets, without which modern exchange is impossible. These, in turn, raise further questions concerning the location of productive enterprises relative to such markets. If an enterprise is to yield a profit, where is its most advantageous location regarding markets as well as the traditional factors of production? Or, from the viewpoint of the planned economy, if an undertaking is to mesh smoothly with the remainder of an economy, where can it be located most advantageously relative to markets and the traditional factors of production?

Transportation

The transfer of a commodity from one place to another requires an expenditure of energy that ultimately is reflected in financial cost—whether in so simple a form as the wages of a human porter or so complex a form as the expenses of developing and operating a nuclear-powered ocean vessel. Such costs are reflected in the exchange values of commodities. In recent years, the term *transport inputs* has been used to designate the energy expended in so moving commodities or people.[1]

Government policy

All governments and all levels of government are vitally concerned with production and exchange of

[1] Technically, transport inputs are calculated by multiplying the total weight of commodities by the distance of movement (where goods are involved), or by multiplying the total number of passengers by distance of movement (where people are involved). Some specialists in location would include transport inputs with the traditional four factors of production. See especially Edward L. Ullman and Walter Isard, *Toward a More Analytical Economic Geography: The Analysis of Flow Phenomena*, Harvard University Press, Cambridge, Mass., 1951; Walter Isard, *Location and Space-economy*, Massachusetts Institute of Technology, Cambridge, Mass., and John Wiley & Sons, Inc., New York, 1956.

commodities. In Communist and some other socialist economies, that concern is so tightly welded with direction that entrepreneurship and government policy can be considered as synonymous. Where economies are not state-owned, government policies usually are distinct from, but frequently very influential over, decisions by private entrepreneurs. These controls may take the form of restrictive laws upheld by specific agencies, or tariffs, or subsidies, or still others. Some such policies, perhaps set forth by one agency, may foster the clustering of certain types of economic activity, whereas other policies, sometimes fostered by another agency, may encourage the dispersal of the same activity. The unhappy entrepreneur thus may well be caught up in a squeeze play that is not at all of his making or to his liking. Governmental policy may be restrictive in form, or it may be an inducement for cooperation, such as a subsidy or other type of financial reward.

LOCATION AND THE PRODUCTIVE OCCUPATIONS

Although all the traditional factors of production, plus markets, transportation, and government policy, are to be given consideration in appraising the locational aspects of the six productive occupations, they do not assume consistent significance when applied to each occupation. Instead, each occupation—and often various components thereof—possesses its own specific locational requirements. Sometimes these requirements are imposed by nature: all the lesser productive occupations—minerals extraction, fishing and hunting, forest-products industries, and grazing—are necessarily located at sites where raw materials occur naturally; the very existence of such occupations depends upon exploiting resources in their natural habitats, and man's choice of location involves only which sites to exploit. In agriculture and manufacturing (especially the latter), however, nature's limitations are not quite so rigid, and man exercises more freedom of choice in locating these industries. Wherever he enjoys such freedom, he gives *comparative costs* serious consideration in the making of his locational decisions, for his stimulus to production tends to be the maximization of profit. Such costs may be divided further into *procurement*, *processing*, and *distribution* costs—of costs for obtaining the necessary ingredients, of combining them, and of making them available for consumption. The first and last of these involve costs of transportation.[2] We have noted that in rigidly planned economies maximization of profits is not a major objective. Even so, careful attention is given to comparative costs in making decisions of location.

In this section we shall examine some general orientation considerations relating to each of the productive occupations before proceeding in the next section into a review of some specific location theories. The order of discussion will be that of the preceding chapter—agriculture, manufacturing, and the lesser occupations of minerals extraction, fishing and hunting, forest-products industries, and grazing.

Agriculture

Three aspects of agriculture are particularly important to an understanding of its current location: (1) it requires comparatively large amounts of permanently used ground for efficient production; (2) as a general occupation, it is somewhat restricted in location by a number of natural environmental features; and (3) it is partially subsistence and partially commercial in nature, with locational considerations meriting particular attention where commercialism is very evident or predominant. It is further affected by a fourth aspect —government policy—that is generally of a quasi-political nature and hence less susceptible to logical analysis.

Areal Dispersedness. Certainly in comparison to manufacturing or minerals extraction, agriculture requires an extensive area of land surface for its production. As shown in Figure 7.1, it encompasses a substantial part of the earth's entire surface. Even individual production units (farms, etc.) are much

[2] See especially E. M. Hoover, *The Location of Economic Activity*, McGraw-Hill Book Company, Inc., New York, 1948.

The outer limits to grazing are set to some degree by nature—by the outer limits to which forage plants will grow. Within these limits, the location of grazing is not tightly fixed in either technically advanced or underdeveloped economies, although ranchers in technically advanced economies are very much aware of location of markets. In some countries the concept of private property, delimited by the barbed-wire fence, adds further limitations to specific producers. These cattle are being moved in the Gallatin River valley of south central Montana. (U.S. Department of Agriculture)

larger than their counterparts in manufacturing. Consequently, considerations involving agricultural production must necessarily involve sizable areas. In addition, more attention can be given to the global location of the subordinate aspects of agriculture than of other productive activities. It has been possible on Figure 7.1, for example, to distinguish eight categories of agricultural land use, and to map each successfully on a world map. By way of comparison, entire manufacturing plants are only a series of scattered points on the same map, with the size of each point exaggerated beyond reality to make it visible to the reader.

Significance of the Natural Environment. Among the six productive occupations, agriculture represents an intermediate stage of man's independence of nature. It is not so rigidly oriented to nature as are the four lesser productive occupations, which must be carried on at the precise source of raw materials. On the other hand, it is not so unhindered by nature as are many components of manufacturing, for which the natural environment constitutes only a secondary consideration in matters of location. The limitations placed upon agriculture by nature are not so apparent in the obtainment of raw materials (seeds, shoots, etc., containing the potential of crop and animal growth), or labor, or nonhuman energy, or entrepreneurship, because these are all quite mobile. The critical agents of agricultural production, however—notably climates and soils—do involve certain restrictions upon agricultural location. Of these, climate is the more important, for man has not yet been able to overcome completely certain absolute minimum temperature and moisture requirements of most domesticated animals and plants. The site requirements, too, are significant; agriculture seldom thrives away from level, well-drained land.

Partial Orientation to Markets. Areas of subsistence agriculture tend to involve more or less spontaneous local use of natural conditions by inhabitants. In areas of commercial or commercial-subsistence agriculture, however, strategically located markets tend to affect the uses of the land, particularly in that they provide for areas of whole or partial crop or animal specialization. How this is done is explained more thoroughly in a later section of this chapter, where the von Thuenen locational theory is examined. At this point in our discussion, it is sufficient to understand that transportation costs from the farm to the market are especially significant.

Agricultural Location and Government Policy. Since the food supply of the Soviet Union is rather low, the government of that nation decreed the plowing up of over 90 million acres of virgin and idle land situated in dust-bowl conditions—and it was done. Being glutted with certain foods and other crops, the government of the United States purchased, from its voting farmers, the release of 20 million acres from domestic production—and it was done (although, by concentrating upon higher output per acre, the ingenious American farmer has kept total production high). These are two examples of the effects of diametrically opposed government policies upon the uses of agricultural land. Other policies too—tariffs, sponsorship of agricultural colleges and technical institutes, initiation of official agricultural agents to instruct in better techniques of farming, development of entire river basins, etc.—all influence the manner and degree of efficiency with which agricultural land is used. Too numerous to explain in detail here, these will be introduced selectively in later chapters devoted to the production, exchange, and consumption of specific agricultural commodities.

Manufacturing

Manufacturing tends to be the least susceptible of all industries to nature's vicissitudes and the most responsive to human locational decisions, because it involves merely the further processing of materials made available from one of the other five productive industries (except in such comparatively rare instances as the taking of nitrogen from the air—instances wherein it provides its own raw materials). As stated earlier, considerations of cost—of procurement, processing, and distribution costs—are particularly relevant in the location of manufacturing.

At this stage in our discussion, it is worthwhile

This land is being used for mineral extraction and agriculture. The location of the oil well is fixed rather closely by the place of oil occurrence in the ground. Mining, like manufacturing, is punctiform *—limited to tiny sites per producing unit. Man's choice in petroleum extraction involves which of several probable sites to exploit. Agricultural enterprises usually occupy much more territory than mining and are not so restricted by nature. Within a broad range of natural environmental limitations, there are several alternative uses for most agricultural land. That shown here could well be devoted to entirely different crops if market conditions change. Here an oil well is "coming in" in the heart of a wheat field near Edmonton, Alberta, Canada. (George Hunter, Toronto)*

also to note that manufacturing differs from the other five productive industries especially in that it may be a large-scale multistage operation, with raw materials often being converted into finished materials by advancement from one manufacturing stage to another. The several stages of manufacture, and the factories in which they are housed, may be located close together or separated by thousands of miles.

Freight Rates and the Orientation of Manufacturing. Since they are the principal ingredients of both procurement and distribution costs, transportation costs are vital considerations in the location of all productive industries, but especially of manufacturing. Transportation costs, to shippers, depend upon *freight rates*—upon intricate systems of arriving at shipping charges. These rates, having evolved over long periods of time, are very complex and are under various jurisdictions. Usually some regulatory governmental agency has control over the domestic rates of a country, whereas oceanic rates are commonly arrived at through shipping conferences—periodic meetings of representatives of all interested carriers. Such rates are detailed enough in total structure to have constituted quite justifiably the entire subject matter of books larger than this one. We have the space only to overview some of their more salient features that apply to the location of manufacturing, as follows:

1. Charges for generating and terminating traffic—terminal charges incurred at the freight yards, stations, and warehouses—usually represent very significant costs of shipment. Generally, such charges are lower in dynamic, large traffic centers handling much cargo. Because of this feature and because of the reduction in per unit freighting costs where large, continuous traffic flows are involved, the shipment costs along routes of heavy traffic are often lower than between a major and an outlying terminal, or between two outlying terminals.

2. Sometimes, in order to equalize the opportunity for competition among the various traffic centers, freight rates are adjusted rather arbitrarily by regulatory bodies. As a result, rates from a common trade area to a moderately active terminal city are made lower than to a very dynamic terminus. The shipper thus can choose between paying a slightly lower rate for slower movement of his goods and paying a higher rate which assures him of more rapid service.

3. In some instances, rates are established by zones rather than on a uniform basis throughout a political unit, and the zone rates are not always similar. In the United States, for example, the class rates in Western and Southern Freight-rate Territories were generally higher than in the Eastern Territory for many years (Fig. 8.1).

4. Moreover, rates do not always vary proportionately with distance, even within a single zone. Instead, they are sometimes arranged on a grouping basis. Thus, for illustration, two small towns, one 10 miles closer than the other to a traffic-generating or -terminating center, may be grouped into a single freight-rate classification regarding that center and hence may ship goods to, or receive goods from, that center at precisely the same rate.

5. Considerations such as value (implied in the stage of manufacture), weight, and bulk of commodities enter actively into freight-rate computations.

6. It is a common practice, notably among railroads in the United States, to permit in-transit freight-rate privileges, wherein a raw material destined for a given market can be halted and processed at any feasible point along the route and then reshipped at the original through rate, provided no back haul is involved. Because rates on raw materials are generally lower than those on finished products, in-transit privileges may result in marked savings for some manufacturers.

7. Competition among the different types of carriers, and among the different firms or other organizations of any single type, is always a major consideration in setting freight rates.

8. The size of shipment also is important, especially from the standpoint of the individual shipper. In railway movement, for example, carload rates are cheaper than less-than-carload rates for individual shipments, because the latter involve placing sev-

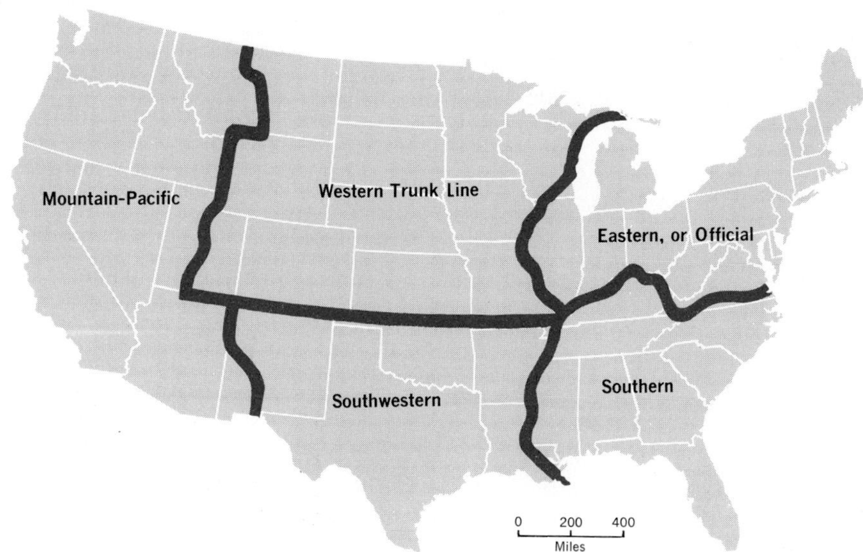

Figure 8.1 ***Railway freight-rate territories of the United States.*** *Western Territory includes the three subdivisions of Western Trunk Line, Southwestern, and Mountain Pacific. The manufacturing belt lies chiefly in Eastern, or Official, Territory. For years, rates differed markedly among these territories, but now they are somewhat equalized.*

eral different shipments into a single freight car—an operation involving extra handling and recording costs.

Although all these features are given careful attention by those responsible for locating manufacturing plants, the magnetism of commercial cities is outstandingly important. Because freight costs between dynamic centers of traffic generation and termination often are lower than those to, or between, smaller towns, manufacturers are prone to take advantage of such economies. The result is a tendency for manufacturing to concentrate in the vicinities of these large *break-of-bulk* cities—noticeably, during recent years, in the suburbs of such cities. Often such cities are, in turn, components of major manufacturing clusters or districts, and the freight-rate advantage is only one added attraction to location there.

Orientation Tendencies of Manufacturing. TOWARD RAW MATERIALS. Some manufacturing tends to be situated near raw materials. This is particularly true of industries or stages of industries either which result in a pronounced decrease in the bulk or the weight of raw materials or which enable the preservation of otherwise perishable commodities. Were they located elsewhere, either procurement would be impossible because of spoilage, or its costs would be excessively high because of the large amounts of worthless materials being transported. The milling and sometimes the smelting of low-grade ores, the sawing of lumber, the ginning of cotton, the extraction of sugar from both beets and cane, and the canning of many varieties of fruits and vegetables are good examples of such industries. Orientation to raw materials may or may not be associated with the fact that raw materials constitute significant percentages of the value of finished products (Table 8.1).

TOWARD ENERGY. In the early stages of the Industrial Revolution, coal was the major source of inanimate power. Man's ability to process his raw materials was then comparatively inefficient (with a high ratio of energy to raw materials required), and it was cheaper to move the raw materials to the energy. The better coal deposits thus marked many sites of intensive manufacturing. This was especially true of heavy industry in Europe and in Europeanized sections of the globe. Today, however, with the increase in the efficiency of processing and the concomitant increase in the mobility of power—including the substitution of liquid and

TABLE 8.1

Labor and raw materials expressed as a percentage of the value of shipments in the United States, 1954

Industry	*Labor (wages)*	*Materials (costs)*
Blast furnaces (iron)	6	77
Cigarettes	6	59
Petroleum products	7	84
Flour and meal	7	83
Meat	10	86
Sulfuric acid	12	53
Distilled liquor, except brandy	13	50
Beet sugar	14	67
Canned fruits and vegetables	16	62
Wood pulp	16	55
Hydraulic cement	21	35
Woolen and worsted fabrics	24	65
Electrical appliances	25	47
Cotton broad-woven fabrics	28	60
Sawmill and planing-mill products	28	54
Women's and misses dresses	29	55
Machine tools	38	31
Ship building and repairing	47	36

SOURCE: Computed from *United States Census of Manufactures, 1954.*

gaseous fuels for coal in many areas—manufacturing tends to be less power-oriented than in the past. Nevertheless, the sites of most industrial districts remain near the coal seams that once were vital, and still are important, to their continued operation. A few industries are power-oriented even today. For example, the electrolytic processes in refining aluminum require very large amounts of electricity that cannot be stored effectively or transported efficiently beyond a range of 500 miles from its source. Hence they locate near power sites.

TOWARD LABOR. The world's handicraft industries, carried on mainly in households, are rather pronouncedly labor-oriented. In the past and, to a degree, in the present, some manufacturing of technically advanced societies must give labor serious consideration. Indeed the migration of much of the United States cotton-textile industry from New England to the Piedmont South, about which we shall have more to say in Chapter 33, appears to have been appreciably a search for cheaper labor. Some factories, requiring only a minimum of skills (such as small textile plants and shoe plants) tend to locate where a surplus of female labor might exist—in some mining areas, for example, where family incomes are low and work for the normal breadwinner is uncertain. Certain other firms making diverse products appear to have moved to areas of moderate urbanization, where labor unions are not so powerful as they are in the larger cities.

Modern manufacturing, however, appears to be decreasingly labor-oriented. This is due appreciably to the growing mobility of labor, which may migrate long distances in response to both seasonal and permanent offers of employment. It is due also to the automation, or quasi automation, of some industrial plants. Although labor is a major factor for certain industries, labor is on the whole less costly to manufacturing than are raw materials (Table 8.1).

TOWARD MARKETS. Agglomerations of people, especially urban dwellers, signify markets. Historically, past and present capital cities of many European nations, attracting populations to serve their governmental and other service functions, have been excellent examples of such markets, stimulating local manufacturing even though other manufacturing requisites might not be at hand. Most of the present-day or one-time European capitals—London, Paris, Berlin, Vienna, Warsaw, Moscow, and Leningrad, to name a few—have thriving diversified manufacturing that is, or once was, in large measure oriented toward markets. In this Industrial Age, with the earth's rapidly growing populations migrating to the cities in higher and higher numbers, urban markets are becoming more important.

Certain types of manufacturing, designed particularly to provide daily consumer necessities, are present in so many of the earth's cities and towns—particularly those of Europe and of Europeanized regions—that they have come to be known as *ubiquitous industries.* These process the milk and

Manufacturing may be oriented physically to raw materials. Some of the raw materials for this petrochemical plant near Edmonton come from nearby petroleum tanks and refineries. (Province of Alberta)

its products, bake the bread, and—in this twentieth century—prepare the soft drinks for local populations. They are invariably market-oriented.

Where stages of manufacture exist, or where one industry uses the by-products of another, the location of such industries in proximity may result in a saving of transportation costs—a saving that is often all the more pronounced if the end-product market is also in proximity. Many agglomerated industries, therefore, are located in areas of dense urban populations—in consumer market areas. Since the end products of manufacture are of relatively high value and since they often require extraordinarily large amounts of space in shipment because of their unwieldy shapes, they may command high freight rates when transported over long distances. A tendency therefore exists for the final stages of multistage manufacturing to be oriented to the market areas, just as the early stages are somewhat oriented toward raw materials. Much of the agglomerated manufacturing in market regions is thus comprised of plants devoted to the later stages of processing.

MARKETS, RAW MATERIALS, ENERGY, LABOR, PEOPLE. As societies and economies become increasingly clustered in districts of high densities of habitation and land use, it becomes correspondingly difficult to distinguish one specific orientation of a manufacturing plant or industry. If present in areas of large populations, such an enterprise is assured a market for its consumer goods and many of its producer goods. Increasingly, with the reuse of various commodities (such as wastepaper that is manufactured into newsprint and other low-grade papers and into cardboard; new and old scrap iron, copper, lead, aluminum, and other metals which are remelted into raw-material form), many of the raw materials now come from these heavily populated clusters—from areas once regarded wholly as markets. Energy, increasingly mobile, may be obtained from firms in the market areas—firms which act also to supply the fuel needs of resident populations. Labor too may be obtained from these populations. In short, much modern manufacturing appears to be oriented to urban areas of dense population, rather than to any one of the specific locational considerations.

FOOTLOOSE INDUSTRIES. For some industries, no specific advantages in procurement, processing, and distribution costs are gained as a result of location near raw materials, energy, labor, or markets. These are usually called *footloose industries.* Often their special position results from the fact that, while their processing makes full use of raw materials initially present in commodities (so that little weight or bulk is lost in manufacture), they can benefit by using the in-transit freight-rate privilege and hence can process their raw materials at any point along the route between the raw materials and the market without incurring increased freight costs. If no other locational factor is worthy of serious attention, they tend to locate with respect to terminal facilities, and hence are found frequently in break-of-bulk centers.

Government Policy and the Location of Manufacturing. NATIONAL GOVERNMENTS. Government policy is not an insignificant consideration in the location of manufacturing. It is more potent in countries where national governments own or closely control the factors of production—indeed, it is absolute in Communist nations—but nowhere can it be overlooked. In recent years, national governments have discouraged undue concentration of manufacturing, chiefly because of beliefs that (1) clustered manufacturing makes excellent wartime targets and (2) concentrated economic and political power tends to result in excessive regional contrasts in domestic economic development—tends, in other words, to produce domestic "technically advanced" and "underdeveloped" regions.

STATE AND LOCAL GOVERNMENTS. State and local government policy is sometimes made known in the manner described above for national government policy. More often, however, it is to be found in such forms as taxation, local planning, public utilities, and industrial areas already equipped with certain facilities.

Water and the Location of Manufacturing. Water is no longer abundant in most manufacturing areas—even those in the more moist climates. The large and multiplying needs for industrial uses, for the burgeoning populations, for agriculture, for hydroelectric power creation, and for still other purposes in complex modern societies has come to mean that water is a serious consideration with respect to plant location. Unfortunately, man must plan in terms of a minimum rather than an average supply in appraising water requirements, for water must be available in quantities sufficient to sustain human activity over periods of deficiency or drought. Until new sources, such as inexpensive water from the seas and oceans, are made available, this problem will increase in severity. Doubtless we shall store and recirculate more water in the future than we now do. (Present and future uses of water in the United States are graphed in Fig. 5.2.)

The lesser productive occupations

As stated previously, the lesser productive occupations involve industries which must necessarily locate where raw materials occur. The choice in location, therefore, involves chiefly the selection of natural deposits which can be exploited in view of the current objectives of entrepreneurship—whether those of financial profit (as in most nations), or of developing new industrial regions of a planned economy (as in some Communist and other nations). The question becomes particularly acute, by way of illustration, with the depletion of high-grade reserves of well-located materials which have been exploited over a substantial period of time and which have attracted substantial quantities of expensive capital equipment. If the total reserves of recoverable resources are still high, despite the fact that the highest-quality materials are nearly gone, should additional capital equipment be brought in to exploit these materials of intermediate quality, or should exploitation operations be transferred to untapped, high-quality reserves located elsewhere?

SOME LOCATIONAL THEORIES AND CONCEPTS

Economic activities are always in intricate association with nature, and are almost always the current expression of very slow developmental processes involving long periods of time. They contain, therefore, a host of variables; and any attempt to hypothesize their respective locations is necessarily somewhat theoretical. Nevertheless, some theories and concepts have been conceived that are of service to us.

The von Thuenen theory

The basis for much of today's work in location, notably agricultural location, was contributed over a century ago by J. H. von Thuenen.[3] Much of this theory resulted from his curiosity concerning the influence of market price and transport cost upon ground rent, and ultimately upon land uses which would yield the highest rent and hence the most profit. Since agriculture was a paramount productive occupation in the city-states occupying what is now much of Germany, the question was addressed chiefly to the use of agricultural land.

The Theory. Von Thuenen assumed an isolated state comprised solely of a large town situated in the center of a uniformly fertile plain, and possessing only overland (horse-and-wagon) transportation connections to that plain. The plain was cultivated all around the town and for some distance away, but at a certain circular outer line cultivation ceased and wilderness prevailed, despite the uniform fertility of the plain. The town depended upon the plain for its supply of produce and, in turn, supplied the plain with its needs and wants.

By isolating the state, von Thuenen excluded international trade and other external influences. By assuming uniform natural conditions, he brought under control, for this study, significant differences in nature. Yet the resulting land use was not calculated to be uniform; instead, it took expression in a series of concentric circles of varying radii, with the town acting as their common center (Fig. 8.2). Within each circle was raised the crop or crop-and-animal combination that yielded the highest land rent (market price, less the cost of transport to market; costs of production did not have to be deducted because they were theoretically uniform throughout the plain). Perishable commodities (fresh milk, truck-garden products, and vegetables) requiring quick as well as inexpensive transportation were nearest the town. Beyond was timber, a necessity to the townspeople, and yet a commodity that weighed so much that high transport costs would price it too high if it were not close by. Still farther out were systems of crop rotation common in Germany, with grain playing a major role. Finally, near the outer margins, were animal specialties involving preserved products (butter, cheese, etc.), many of which needed to be reduced sharply in weight or volume before the long and arduous shipment into the town. The edge of cultivated land marked the outer limit of all acreage that needed to be cultivated in order to supply the total population—both country and town—of the isolated state.

Implications of the Theory. The significant implications of von Thuenen's work are that, given his assumptions, the rent from land is largely a matter of *market price less the cost of transportation.* Since, in most areas of the world, entrepreneurs want to maximize their profits, they naturally plant crops which they feel will yield the highest rent. As a result, there is some difference in the types of crops grown, in the systems and techniques of their growth, and in the intensity of land use.

[3] J. H. von Thuenen, *Der isolierte Staat in Beziehung auf Landwirtschaft und Nationoloekonomie,* Friedrich Perthes, Hamburg, Germany, 1826.

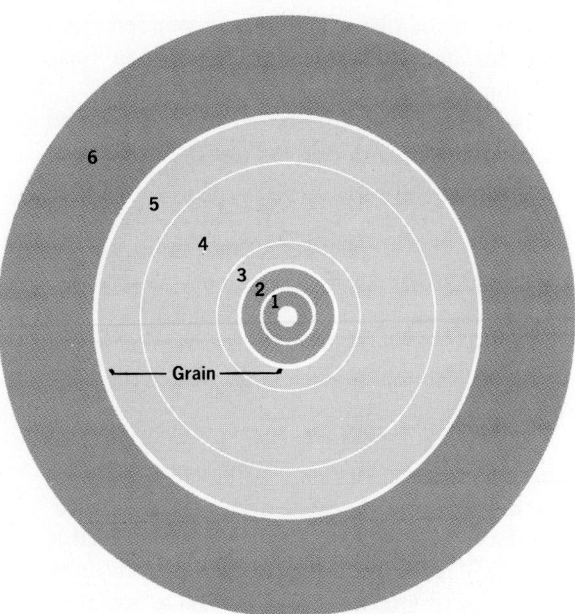

Figure 8.2 **The von Thuenen circles.** *The white dot in the center is the city. Circle 1 encloses a district of intensive dairying (fluid milk) and truck gardening. Circle 2 contains wood-cutting industries, necessarily close to market because a high demand exists within the city for wood and because slow and costly animals and wagons were the chief forms of land transportation in the prerailway time of von Thuenen. Circles 3, 4, and 5 surround crop-rotation systems, each of which involves grain. Intensity of land use within these circles decreases with increased distance from the central city. Circle 6 encloses a very extensive type of stock raising, with emphasis upon wool, butter, cheese, etc.—products which can be preserved for long periods of time and which can stand the cost of a long haul to market. Beyond is uncultivated land that is capable of cultivation if necessary.*

When we remove the assumptions from von Thuenen's theory and consider further the effects upon his rings of modern, efficient transportation, we begin to question its applicability—certainly to the modern world. Nevertheless, we do see today many truck gardens near big cities (although they sometimes suffer in competition with specialty truck-garden areas in more favorable climates—areas reaching their markets with very efficient transportation media); we do see a tendency for countrysides near favored transportation routes to be farmed intensively (witness the location of many plantations on seacoasts); we do see the world's fluid-milk dairy-farming districts located immediately beside the world's major markets for such milk (Fig. 7.1 and page 13); we do see dairy farming specializing in butter, cheese, etc., situated in the comparatively inaccessible upper Alps, and beef industries specializing in canned beef, soup, etc., situated in inaccessible places such as the savanna grasslands of Venezuela and Argentina. Some measure of verification of von Thuenen's conclusions are visible, even today, in the world's agricultural landscapes.

The Weber theory of industrial location

Von Thuenen's work stimulated other efforts, most of which were directed toward an understanding of the locational aspects of manufacturing. Among such efforts was the work of another German economist, Alfred Weber, who published his best-known book in 1909.[4]

The Theory. Although concerned in passing with the location of all economic activities, Weber directed his main attention to manufacturing. Assuming (1) an inelastic demand for products, (2) a single country whose population was endowed with a common cultural heritage, including stage of economic development, (3) fixed locations and sizes of individual places of consumption, (4) given locations of raw materials, and (5) a given dispersal of labor whose supply was not limited and whose costs varied from place to place, Weber attempted to rationalize the forces that would be ultimately responsible for the location of a manufacturing plant on a specific site. These forces he reasoned to be (1) regional and (2) local (agglomerative and

[4] Alfred Weber, *Ueber den Standort der Industrien*, Tuebingen, 1909, translated by Carl J. Friedrich as *Alfred Weber's Theory of the Location of Industries*, University of Chicago Press, Chicago, 1928.

deglomerative). The most important of the regional forces was the cost of transportation, which ought to be minimized with respect to raw material and energy resources, as well as with respect to markets. The sites of each of these three features usually outlined a triangle, each point of which was conceived to exert a force equal to its approximate share of the end-product cost, and the place of optimum location of a specific plant was the point at which all the forces neutralized each other (Fig. 8.3). Once established, this optimum general location had to be adjusted further to allow for inequalities in labor costs, the second component of the regional forces affecting manufacturing location. The regional location, in turn, was subject to still further adjustment because of local forces of agglomeration and deglomeration. Agglomeration was the clustering together of factories because of such mutual advantages as using each other's products. Deglomeration was the scattering of factories because of such disadvantages of agglomeration as high rent.

Implications of the Theory. Weber's ideas are now regarded chiefly as historical milestones, some of which have become foundations upon which more refined concepts are constructed. Although there are some who take exception to both his procedure and his conclusions, there are few who will not admit that he contributed significantly to location theory, notably to emphasizing the importance of transportation costs to locating single factories.

Later concepts

These initial inquiries into location theory were largely by German scholars, and their work, while very important, was necessarily a form of pioneering—a foundation for later efforts. Von Thuenen's results were particularly relevant with respect to the competition for land by various agricultural crops and systems, and Weber's contributions were effective in achieving a better insight into considerations involved in the location of individual manufacturing plants. However, they and their contemporaries were inheritors of a common culture, and their

The question asked by von Thuenen is, "To what degree do transport costs to and from the city influence land use in the surrounding countryside?" Edmonton, Canada, and a part of its surrounding territory. (Photographic Survey Corporation, Ltd., Toronto)

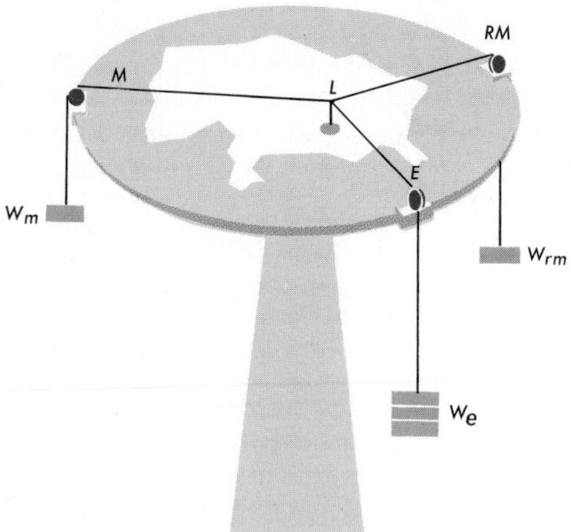

W = Weight of transported materials
M = Location of markets for plant's products
RM = Location of raw materials going into plant's products
E = Location of energy for plant
L = Location of point of minimum transportation costs

Figure 8.3 ***Weber's theory of location for individual plants.*** *The plant's regional location is at the point of minimum transport costs. (After Carl H. Cotterill,* Industrial Plant Location: Its Application to Zinc Smelting, *American Zinc, Lead, and Smelting Company, St. Louis, 1950, Fig. IV-1, p. 67)*

theories were constructed in the light of that culture. Questions inevitably arose, not only concerning the applicability of their work to areas beyond Germany, but also to its relevance to the location of all economic activities, and to the competition in some areas among such activities for all available land.

During this century, curiosity has been whetted in other nations, notably the United States and Sweden.[5] The resulting works are based largely on the earlier German work, and although the weaknesses of that work have been probed, no single, comprehensive, new theory which might act as a full substitute has yet appeared. This is due in no small measure to the intricacy of the subject matter, particularly to the almost infinite number of variables encountered in studying even one of its many ramifications. Among the aspects of location theory now under study are: (1) locational considerations involving entire regions as well as single factories; (2) the forces exerted by central places, notably metropolitan areas, cities, and towns, both in attracting economic activity to their specific sites and in affecting the type of land use in countrysides and communities beyond those sites; and (3) the relationships between freight rates and actual distance in an assessment of transportation costs and associated "pull" of centrally located places. Interest in these and related questions is definitely on the rise, and more and more articles and books are focused upon them. Indeed, a new field of regional science has appeared. Most of the work now being done in this field involves the creation of hypothetical models, based upon mathematical probability, and the comparison of existing conditions with such models in an attempt to derive some viable laws of spatial interaction.

[5] In addition to the previously cited works of Hoover, Isard, and Ullman, see especially August Loesch, *The Economics of Location,* Yale University Press, New Haven, Conn., 1954; and Tord Palander, *Beiträge zur Standortstheorie,* Almqvist & Wiksells Boktryckeri-A.-B., Uppsala, Sweden, 1935.

REFERENCES

Alexander, John W., et al.: "Freight Rates: Selected Aspects of Uniform and Nodal Regions," *Economic Geography,* **34**:1–18, 1958.

Berry, Brian J. L., and William L. Garrison: "The Functional Bases of the Central Place Hierarchy," *Economic Geography,* **34**:145–154, 1958.

Dunn, Edgar S., Jr.: *The Location of Agricultural Production,* University of Florida Press, Gainesville, Fla., 1954.

Friedrich, Carl J.: *Alfred Weber's Theory of the Location of Industries,* University of Chicago Press, Chicago, 1928.

Fulton, Maurice: "Plant Location, 1965," *Harvard Business Review,* **33** (2):40–50, 1955.

Grotewald, Andreas: "Von Thünen in Retrospect," *Economic Geography,* **35:**346–355, 1959.

Harris, Chauncy D.: "The Market Factor in the Localization of Industry in the United States," *Annals of the Association of American Geographers,* **44:**315–348, 1954.

Hoover, E. M.: *The Location of Economic Activity,* McGraw-Hill Book Company, Inc., New York, 1948.

Isard, Walter: *Location and Space-economy,* Massachusetts Institute of Technology, Cambridge, Mass., and John Wiley & Sons, Inc., New York, 1956.

Loesch, August: *The Economics of Location,* Yale University Press, New Haven, Conn., 1954.

McCarty, H. H.: "An Approach to a Theory of Economic Geography," *Economic Geography,* **30:**95–101, 1954.

Melamid, Alexander: "Economic Aspects of Industrial Dispersal," *Social Research,* **23:**310–322, 1956.

Nicholson, R. J.: "The Regional Location of Industry: An Empirical Study Based on the Regional Tables of the 1948 Census of Production," *The Economic Journal,* **66:**467–481, 1956.

North, Douglas C.: "Location Theory and Regional Economic Growth," *Journal of Political Economy,* **63:**243–258, 1955.

Palander, Tord: *Beiträge zur Standortstheorie,* Almqvist & Wiksells Boktryckeri–A.–B., Uppsala, Sweden, 1935.

Pant, Y. P.: "Dynamics of Industrial Location in India," *Modern Review,* **96:**402–404, 1954.

Perloff, Harvey S., et al.: *Regions, Resources, and Economic Growth,* The Johns Hopkins Press for Resources for the Future, Inc., Baltimore, 1960.

Renner, George T.: "Geography of Industrial Localization," *Economic Geography,* **23:**165–187, 1947.

9 WORLD PATTERNS OF TRANSPORTATION

TODAY'S VOLUME OF CONSUMPTION AND PRODUCTION WOULD HAVE BEEN IMPOSSIBLE without large-scale transportation and communication. Particularly vital is commodity movement, which is as important to the functioning of the world's economies as is the flow of blood through the human body. Communication and the transportation of people are of interest to us usually when and if they somehow affect commodity flow. The significance of transportation has been suggested and implied throughout this book, and has been emphasized in the preceding chapter, where transport costs were stated to be of critical importance to the location and continued operation of many types of productive industries. In this chapter we shall focus attention upon the actual media of transportation, the better to understand the commodity movement which is discussed in the chapter to follow.

The media under consideration are ocean vessels; lake vessels; inland-waterway, coastwise, and intercoastal craft; railway trains; motor trucks; pipelines; airways; and the more elementary transportation forms involving direct human and/or animal effort, whether in drayage or actual carrying. Of these, the ocean vessel and the railway train are the leading carriers. The former is probably responsible for over one-half, and the latter for over one-third, of the ton-mileage (weight multiplied by distance) of all the world's freight,[1] with the inland-waterway craft, motor truck, and pipeline of more than noteworthy significance. In terms of tonnage alone, however, the railroad train is the world's prime mover, carrying an estimated two-thirds or more of the weight of all cargoes.

Among specific nations for which data are compiled, the railroad is consistently important, and the other carriers vary in significance with individual cases. An appreciable range of choice among carriers is available to shippers in most technically advanced nations, where transportation facilities and networks are at their peak of development. This is particularly true in Western Europe and the United States, Canada, and the Soviet Union. The effective areas of most nations are characterized by relatively intensive development of transportation facilities.

[1] Carl Pirath, *Die Grundlagen der Verkehrswirtschaft*, Springer-Verlag, Vienna, 1949, p. 95.

WATER TRANSPORTATION

Water not only supports the weight of its carriers but also is relatively frictionless. Moreover, its routes usually need little, if any, artificial maintenance. Transportation media utilizing water thus are comparatively inexpensive to operate, particularly when heavy, bulky merchandise is the cargo. By way of illustration, the costs of shipping bulk commodities in vessels restricted to the Great Lakes of North America are calculated to be as low as $\frac{1}{10}$ of 1 cent per ton-mile; for ocean vessels, $\frac{1}{5}$ of 1 cent per ton-mile; for pipelines, about $\frac{3}{10}$ of 1 cent per ton-mile; for inland waterway and coasting craft, $\frac{3}{10}$ of 1 cent per ton-mile; for railway trains, 1–2 cents per ton-mile; for trucks, at least 5 cents per ton-mile; for aircraft, at least 16 cents per ton-mile; for an animal and wagon or cart, about 30 cents per ton-mile; and for a human porter, as high as $1 per ton-mile. (These quotations are generalized averages.)

Although an economical means of transportation, the water carrier also is comparatively slow and hence tends to specialize in liquid or solid bulk cargoes and other merchandise for which rapid delivery is not a must. This is particularly true of inland-waterway and coasting craft, which are in constant competition with the faster overland media that are particularly attractive to shippers of perishable commodities and package cargo. Ocean-crossing vessels, on the other hand, are free from such competition and hence haul appreciably larger quantities of semifinished and finished commodities. All water craft are also in competition with the embryonically developed air-freighting services, but the volume of commerce handled by the latter is as yet very small.

TRANSOCEAN SHIPPING

The carriers

The world's merchant fleet involves nearly forty thousand vessels which are larger than 100 gross registered tons,[2] and these aggregate a grand total of over 118 million gross registered tons. More than 60 per cent of these are no larger than 2,000 gross registered tons each, and as a rule do not venture out into the open seas. Another 30 per cent are registered at between 2,000 and 8,000 gross tons, and only 10 per cent are in the class of distinctively large ships, which range between 8,000 and 83,000 gross registered tons. Some tankers with deadweight capacities of over 100,000 metric tons now are operating, and even larger ones are under construction. It is perhaps needless to add that ships of intermediate and large tonnage categories are the leading transoceanic carriers.

Approximately two-thirds of all merchant ships of 1,000 gross registered tons or over are all-purpose freighters, another one-sixth are tankers, and the remainder are combination passenger and cargo vessels. The freighters are somewhat smaller in size than either the tankers or the combined-purpose ships. The extensive use of tankers and combined-purpose ships is a comparatively recent innovation, and hence these tend to be larger than the single-purpose freighters, some of which are quite old. Indeed, many older vessels are used only when shipping is active, and are kept in "moth balls" at other times.

[2] Ship tonnages are variously designated as follows: *gross tonnage*, used in official registries of ownership, signifies the total capacity of a ship measured in per ton units of 100 cubic feet, less certain authorized deductions; *net tonnage*, used to admit and clear ships in harbors and to assess dues, etc., involves the same measuring unit as gross tonnage but provides also for the subtraction of space occupied by quarters for the captain, crew, passengers etc., and thus depicts the actual carrying capacity of a ship; *measurement tonnage*, used to assign space to shippers, is arrived at in a manner generally like that used in reaching net tonnage, except that the measuring unit is 40 cubic feet; *displacement tonnage*, expressed in either long tons (2,240 pounds) or metric tons (2,205 pounds), refers to the weight of water which a vessel displaces and may pertain to an unloaded ship plus weight of crew (displacement light) or a fully loaded ship, including fuel (displacement loaded); *deadweight tonnage* designates the cargo-carrying capacity of a ship and is expressed in either long or metric tons.

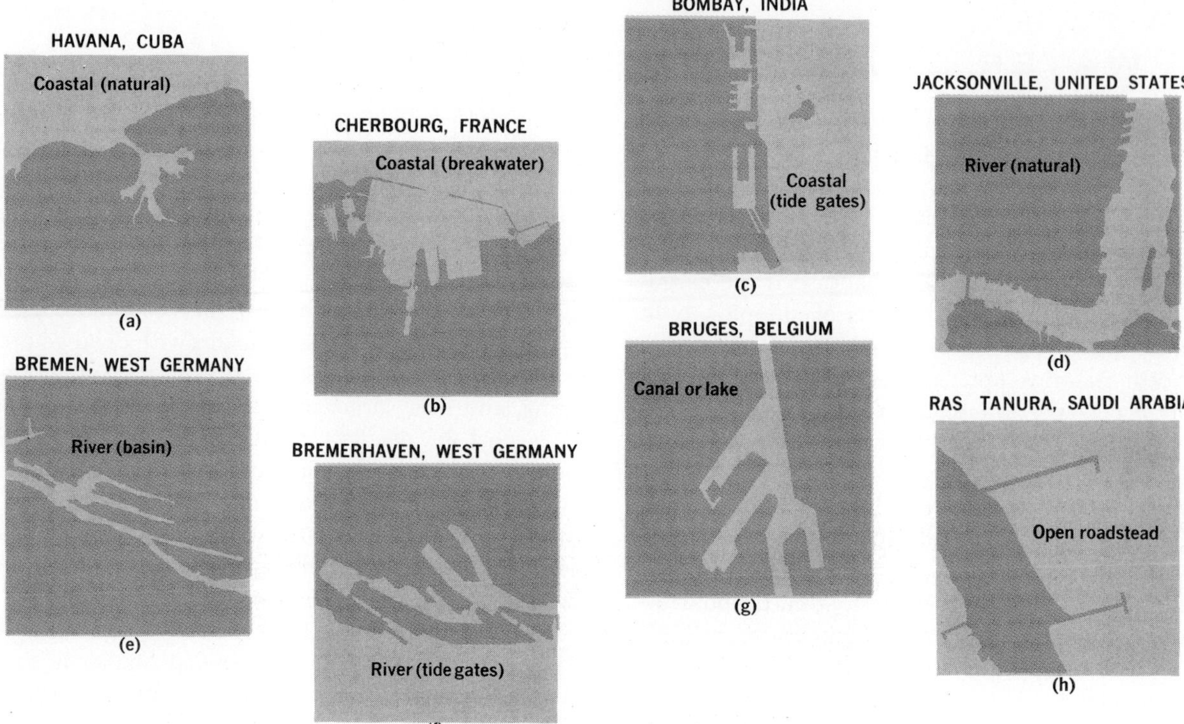

Figure 9.1 **Harbor types.** *A natural coastal harbor is sheltered from wind and open water by virtue of location on a shore-line indentation. A breakwater coastal harbor lies behind a man-made breakwater that provides shelter from wind and open water. The water in a tide-gate coastal harbor is kept at a constant level by locks, regardless of rise and fall of tides. A natural river harbor is like a natural coastal harbor except that it is located on a river; its port facilities, however, frequently are parallel to the waterway on which it lies. In a river-basin harbor, slips for vessels are dug into the river's banks or flood plain, usually obliquely or at a right angle to the trend of the river. A tide-gate river harbor is like a tide-gate coastal harbor except that it is located on a river. A canal or lake harbor usually is artificial rather than natural, and may be connected to open water by an artificial waterway. The facilities of an open-roadstead port reach into the water as jetties; under these circumstances, a natural harbor can scarcely be said to exist, and cargo may be carried between ship and shore in small boats. (After drawings in* World Port Index, *U.S. Government Printing Office, Washington, D.C., 1953)*

The terminals

Ships load and unload at *ports,* wherein are found the necessary facilities for such operations. Although only a few ports forward and receive most of the world's commerce, many exist; a recent government document lists and describes some 6,312 ports accessible to ocean-going ships.[3] Port facilities necessarily include, of course, some means of accepting the cargo which a ship's gear, if need be, can put over the side of the ship. The simplest "ports" possess small-boat service to and from the

[3] *World Port Index,* U.S. Government Printing Office, Washington, D. C., 1953.

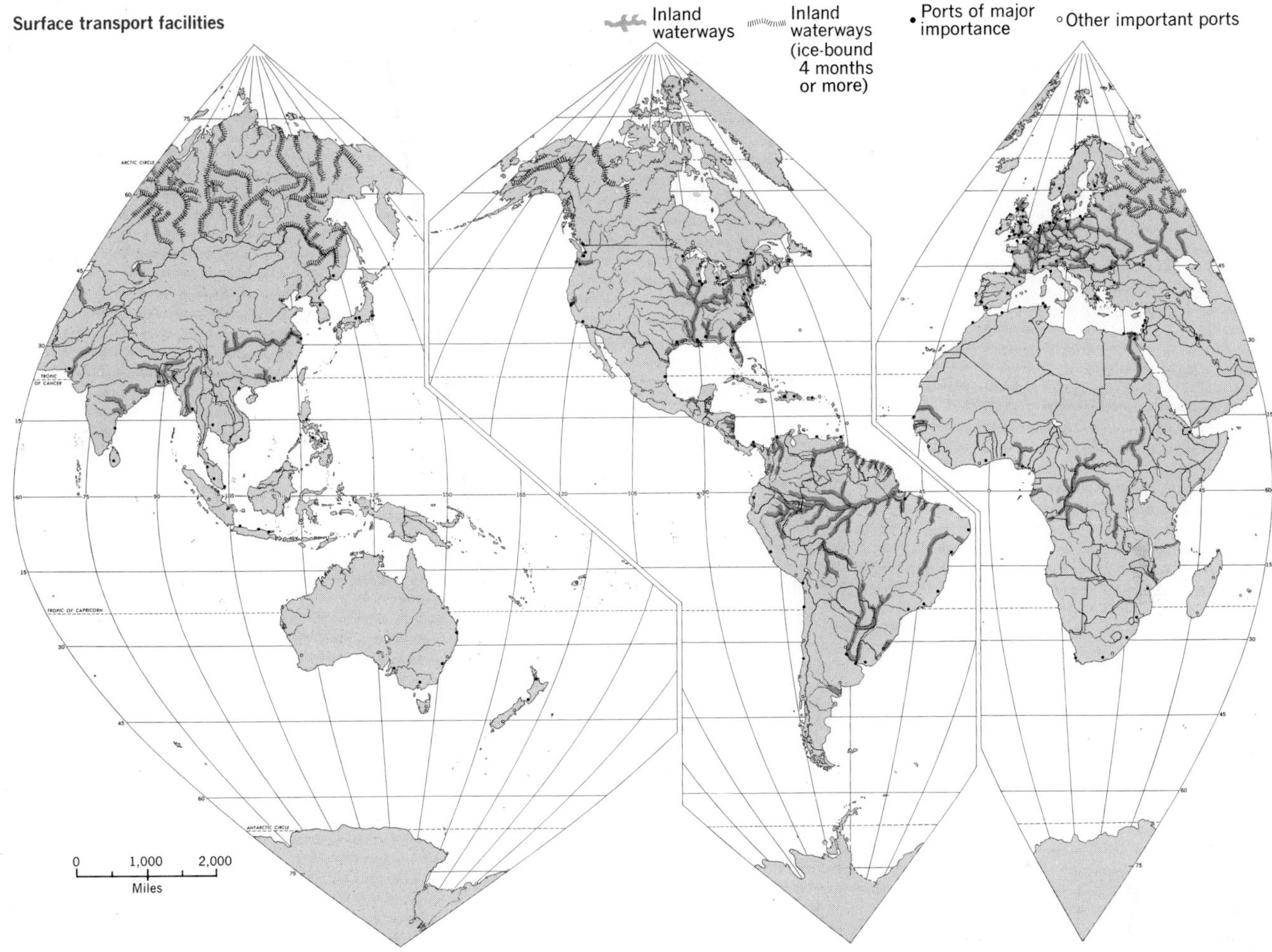

Figure 9.2 ***The world's leading ports, and inland water routes.***

ship and precious little else. From this crude stage of development, the world's port facilities range upward in completeness and complexity, until ultimately they entail the intricate systems of piers, wharves, sheds, warehouses, tank farms, grain elevators, dry docks, dolphins for midstream tie-up, fixed and floating cranes, towage, lighterage, and stevedoring arrangements, ship repairing and chandlering services, and the associated constant activities of a leading seaport.

Most ports are located in *natural harbors,* which are the crucial places along coast lines where natural conditions favor the putting in of water craft. A coastal indentation that combines ice-free, naturally deep water, with freedom from obstructions and protection from extremes of weather is considered to be an excellent site for harbor development. An additional amenity is the contiguous presence of an inland waterway or lowland overland route by which a hinterland can be easily reached. The port-harbor types of the world have been classified as natural coastal, breakwater coastal, tide-gate coastal, natural river, artificial river, tide-gate river, canal or lake, and open roadstead, as is shown in Figure 9.1. Obviously, their specific port-harbor associations vary, but their function is

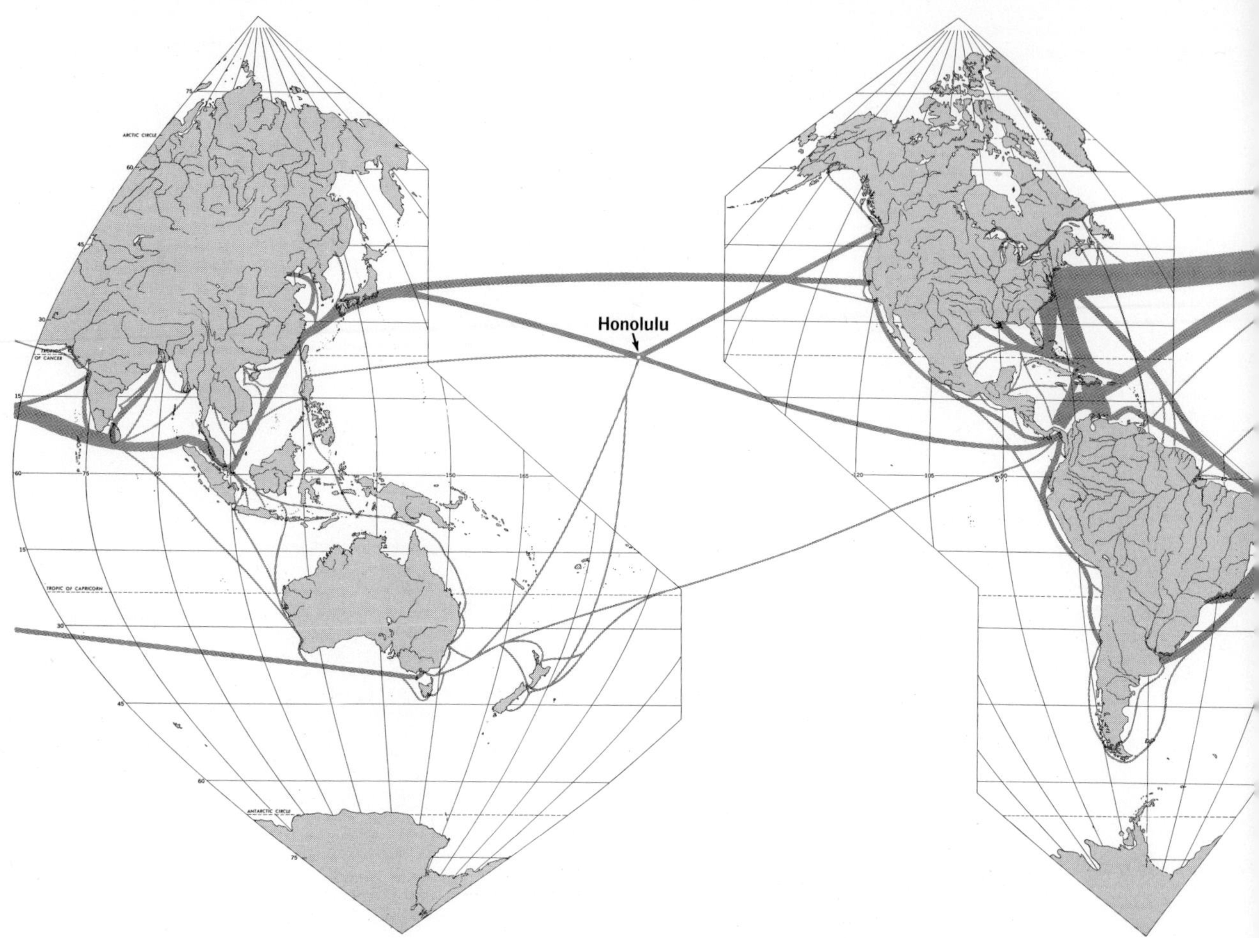

Figure 9.2 (continued) ***The world's leading sea lanes.*** *(All information, Encyclopaedia Britannica)*

inevitably the movement, with or without accompanying storage, of cargo.

Despite the spate of seaports, most of the world's commerce is transited through only a comparatively small number of major terminals. The reader will note a distinctive tendency toward the clustering of such terminals along the coasts of technically advanced nations (compare Figs. 9.2 and 1.4). The seaports of underdeveloped nations, in contrast, are much more markedly separated from each other, with each one serving its own, rather conspicuous hinterland. In many cases, an underdeveloped nation possesses only one port, and the nation becomes the hinterland.

The routes

Although the potentialities for roaming are vast, the world's ocean shipping follows rather well-defined channels. Most operate regularly between leading ports, having been attracted there by the active demand or supply conditions of the hinterlands of those ports. Where possible, they follow the *great circle route*—the shortest distance between two points on the earth's surface—deviating from this route only where markets or natural conditions necessitate their doing so (Fig. 9.2). The resultant traffic lanes can be grouped in five broad and overlapping patterns: (1) the North Atlantic

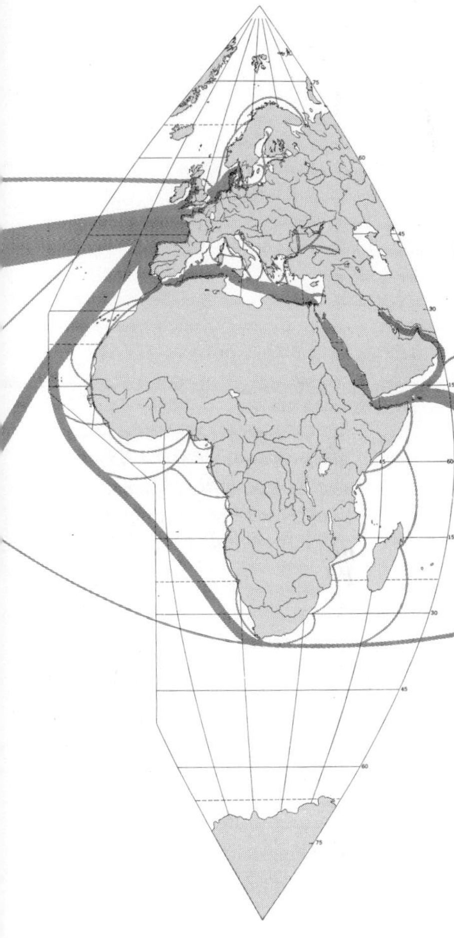

routes, which extend between the dynamic manufacturing and commercial regions of Anglo-America and Europe; (2) the inter-American routes, which connect the United States, Canada, and Alaska with each other and with Latin American nations, notably those of Caribbean America; (3) the Latin American–European routes, which are especially pronounced between southern Latin America and Europe; (4) the European-African-Asian routes which, separating at Gibraltar, serve not only the Mediterranean Sea, the Indian Ocean, the China Sea, the Sea of Japan, and the Pacific Ocean, but also reach ports along the western, southern, and eastern coasts of Africa; and (5) the Pacific Ocean routes from Asia and Oceania to the Americas. Complemented by smaller trading routes which cross the Pacific Ocean and which fill other interstices of the over-all pattern, these routes basically connect the technically advanced areas of Europe and North America with each other and with outlying underdeveloped lands as well as with outlying technically advanced areas (study carefully Fig. 9.2). Most of these routes benefit substantially from man-made or man-improved waterways: the North Atlantic routes now project into the Great Lakes via the improved St. Lawrence Seaway, and the Panama and Suez Canals are crucial foci, respectively, of the inter-American and European-African-Asian routes.

Ownership and operational policies

The world's merchant fleet essentially is owned by governments, corporations and companies, other institutions, or individual citizens, of technically advanced nations. This ownership may or may not be reflected in flag registration, because some shipowners prefer to register their vessels under flags of nations other than the ones of which they are citizens. Currently, about 21 per cent of all gross registered tonnage of merchant vessels is under the flag of the United States, 16 per cent under that of the United Kingdom, 10 per cent under that of Liberia, and over 8 per cent under that of Norway. Much of the remainder is registered under the flags of Japan, Italy, Panama, France, the Netherlands, West Germany, Sweden, the Soviet Union, and Denmark. All but Liberia and Panama are technically advanced, and the high figures in these countries result from the fact that they permit ship-owning citizens of other nations to take advantage of certain exemptions and inducements of their laws by registering under their flags.

When examined by schedules of operation, the world's nonmilitary freight-carrying fleets may be subdivided into *liners, tramps,* and *private carriers.* Liners maintain regularly scheduled service for passengers, passengers and cargo, and cargo only. They are particularly numerous on the North Atlantic trade routes but also offer direct service to nearly every active seaport, with transshipment to smaller

Ocean vessels entering the Côte Ste. Catherine Lock of the St. Lawrence Seaway near Montreal (National Film Board of Canada).

coastwise vessels of goods destined for smaller ports. They usually are the largest and fastest civilian ships in existence and, when carrying merchandise, tend to haul the more expensive goods which can stand their higher freighting charges and which are attracted to their faster service.

Tramp ships do not maintain regular schedules and carry whatever cargo is available at any port of call—usually bulk freight that is low in value. Compared with liners they tend to be older, smaller, more uncertain in schedule, and willing to carry almost any legitimate cargo if time is not a decisive factor as to when that cargo should arrive.

A black-and-white distinction between tramp and liner shipping is perhaps somewhat misleading, for some companies keep their ships of intermediate age, size, and speed on a stand-by basis, sometimes using them in liner services and sometimes sending them out on tramping junkets.

Private carriers are used primarily by large manufacturing concerns to deliver raw materials, fuel, or finished products. They are particularly numerous in association with corporations and companies of the United States that refine petroleum or produce industrial metals. Many are tankers.

Trends

A century ago nearly all of the world's ships were sailing craft. Then came the steamship, which for over fifty years burned coal and now largely consumes fuel oil from petroleum. It is augmented today by the internal combustion engine, which also burns petroleum products. Indeed, the majority of new vessels have internal combustion engines. The fuel of tomorrow, already well past the initial stages of experimentation, is nuclear power. The increasing efficiency of fuel consumption will aid both liner and tramp shipping to the extent that longer uninterrupted hauls of heavier loads will be possible and few delays will be attributable to the putting in of a vessel to a port for refueling. Concomitantly, this same increase in efficiency will mean a decline in much of the bulk-cargo traffic, for the fuels being delivered to strategically located refueling points—the fuels which may be replaced by long-lasting, mobile nuclear power sources—constitute significant quantities of such traffic.

As stated previously, ships are increasing in size and versatility of use. Both the tanker, a semihollow liquid carrier, and the combination pas-

A "sausage" made of woven nylon skin used experimentally to carry petroleum products between the United Kingdom and the Netherlands (British Information Services).

senger-cargo vessel are comparatively new to the world's merchant marine. Tankers are particularly effective cargo carriers, for their cargoes can be pumped mechanically off and on the ship and can automatically fill every cubic inch of the hold without human aid. Consequently, tankers carry not only petroleum but also other materials which can be reduced to liquids, like latex and sulfur, and goods normally canned or bottled, like fruit juices or wines. Even the surface tanker, however, may soon become obsolescent. Now under consideration is a nuclear-powered submarine tanker which has a cargo capacity as high as 100,000 deadweight tons and which skims along at 35 knots (nautical miles) per hour immediately beneath the oceanic surfaces, thus avoiding the stormy buffeting absorbed by surface carriers. Also receiving attention is the idea of the coastwise hauling of liquid materials by placing them in large, plastic "goatskins" and pulling them with tugboats.

The trends in operational policies are toward more regularly scheduled liner service, with special attention to combined passenger-freight vessels, whether such vessels are tankers or dry-cargo carriers. Another trend is toward diversification of ownership; at the turn of the century, the Union Jack of the United Kingdom flew over approximately one-half of the tonnage of the world's merchant fleet. Today, even though dominated by relatively few nations, that fleet is of much more varied nationality, Scandinavian Europe and the Soviet Union having emerged into notable prominence. Even some of the underdeveloped nations are planning to increase their fleets, and there are possibilities that the diversity of flag registration may become even more pronounced than it is now.

The harbor and port at Duluth-Superior, which until the opening of the Great Lakes–St. Lawrence Seaway was almost wholly a lake port. In the middleground are docks for the loading of iron ore upon lake vessels, and in the background are facilities for the storing and loading of grain. (Standard Oil Company of New Jersey)

INLAND-WATERWAY AND COASTAL SHIPPING

The carriers

Except for lake vessels, inland-waterway craft are quite small. They are seldom able to carry more than 3,000 deadweight tons. Most carry even less. Notably in North America and in some areas of northwestern Europe, the actual carriers are shallow draft barges laced together, either in single-file arrangement or in pairs, and towed by tugboats. Indeed, when timber is moved, the barges are often dispensed with, and the tugs merely pull the log cargo made up into large rafts. Inland-waterway or coastal craft seldom draw more than 6 or 7 feet of water, and hence generally do not require channels deeper than 9 feet. In contrast, most lake carriers are larger, sometimes carrying more than 20,000 deadweight tons. Those of the Great Lakes of North America were until recently built to specifications necessitating a 20-foot channel depth; but, with the deepening of those channels to 27 feet as a part of the program of the Great Lakes–St. Lawrence Seaway, ships drawing 25 feet of water may pass through them with ease.

The terminals

Inland-waterway and coastal carriers specialize in bulk freight, and their terminal facilities reflect such specialization. More often than not, those facilities are incorporated into the over-all structure of a major port, where inland and coastwise carriers meet with transocean shipping for transshipment purposes. Where such terminals are not combined with active seaport facilities, as was true along the western margin of Lake Superior before the advent of the Great Lakes–St. Lawrence Seaway, they are predominantly geared to bulk transfer and hence are dominated by gravity chutes, loading shovels, grain elevators, pumping gear, and other trappings for loading and unloading such merchandise.

The routes

In the world patterns of inland and coastal shipping, the technically advanced lands are once again very conspicuous (Fig. 9.2). The routes in Europe are both very numerous and very actively used. The routes of the United States (Alaska excepted) and of European Russia are moderately numerous and moderately utilized. The routes of eastern and southern Asia are moderately numerous but very actively used. The routes of the very high and very low latitudes are used lightly except in eastern and southern Asia. Of all continents only Australia is without inland routes.

Operation

Inland-waterway operation is perhaps best understood when studied regionally, for the commerce involved is mainly domestic or regional. We are concerned here chiefly with the activities of North America, Western Europe, the Soviet Union and Eastern Europe, southeastern Asia, South America, Africa, and Australia.

North America. Three categories of inland and coastal shipping are particularly discernible in North America, the first two involving ocean-going vessels: (1) Great Lakes–St. Lawrence shipping; (2) coastwise and intercoastal ocean-going traffic; and (3) inland and intracoastal movements.

The Great Lakes–St. Lawrence shipping lanes account for about one-half of the water-borne domestic transportation (measured in ton-miles) of the United States, and essentially all the coastwise shipping of Canada, as well as international movements between the two countries and the flow of merchandise to and from overseas. The lakes and river are maintained naturally except in a very few constricted places but are frozen for at least four months of each year. The primary cargo movement is of southbound iron ore and limestone, northbound coal, and eastbound grain and petroleum products, with general cargo constituting a poor fifth in tonnage.

The worth of this system has been enhanced recently by the completion of the Great Lakes–St. Lawrence Seaway under the joint auspices and control of Canada and the United States (Fig. 9.3). Constructed as a multipurpose project involving objectives of power creation, flood control, and recreation as well as navigation, the seaway marks man's most recent successful attempt at landform incision, joining such previously completed canals as Suez, Panama, and Kiel, and numerous smaller cuts. For the United States, the seaway means easy access to needed iron ores, many of which originate in Labrador and are being placed on lake-type vessels at the port of Seven Islands in Canada. For Canada, it means comparatively unimpeded shipping along

Figure 9.3 ***The Great Lakes-St. Lawrence Seaway.*** *The main map shows only the St. Lawrence River, the navigable channel of which has been constructed and is maintained by both the United States and Canada. The inset shows the entire Great Lakes-St. Lawrence Seaway. Except for the Welland Canal between Lakes Erie and Ontario, the small segments connecting the Great Lakes have been deepened and are maintained by the United States alone. The channel depth of the entire seaway is 27 feet. At Montreal the water is deeper. More than three-fourths of the world's merchant shipping can move up the seaway as far as Chicago or Duluth. The remaining one-fourth involves vessels too large for the seaway.*

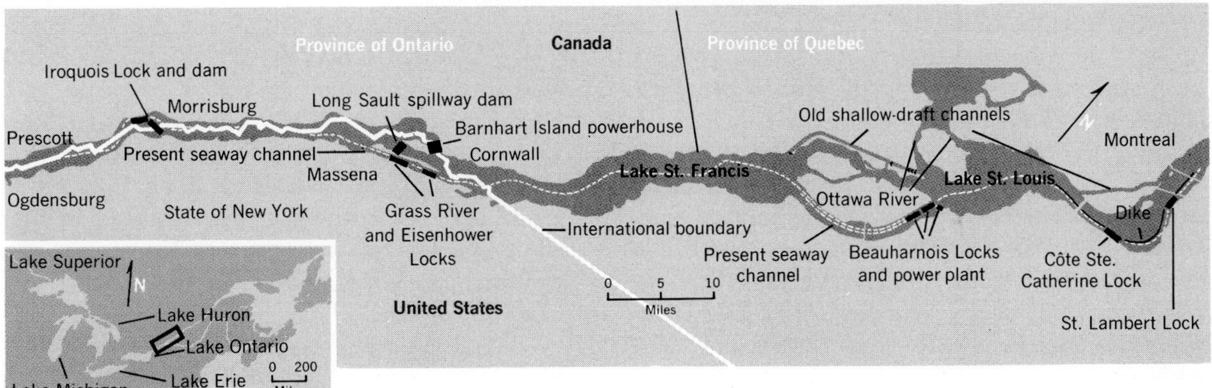

the southern margin of that nation's effective territory.

The coastwise and intercoastal ocean-going commerce is found mainly along the Atlantic and Gulf Coasts of the United States, and involves primarily the movement of petroleum from the seaports of Texas and Louisiana, and of Appalachian coal transshipped at Hampton Roads and smaller eastern ports to the fuel-hungry and populous Northeastern states. Along the Pacific Coast, petroleum from southern California to the far Northwest of the United States comprises a movement of secondary significance. Finally, a decreasing quantity of bulk goods moves between the two coasts via the Panama Canal.

The active inland and intracoastal shipping lanes, usually no more than 9 feet deep and dominated by smaller craft, are also situated chiefly within the United States (Fig. 9.2). The major traffic is along such waterways as the Mississippi, the Illinois (plus its connections to Chicago), the Ohio, and the Tennessee Rivers, and along the Gulf Intracoastal Waterway from Mobile to Corpus Christi and Houston. Petroleum and coal are overwhelmingly predominant among the freighted commodities. Petroleum products are also important along the New York State Barge Canal, along with some grain.

Western Europe. The European coastline is largely submergent, so that the oceans and seas have encroached upon the land, and the resultant large and small peninsulas and indentations are conducive to coastwise shipping. Such sizable and relatively constant rivers as the Rhine, the Danube, and the Elbe Rivers, interconnected and augumented by lesser rivers and by a series of canals, add to the possibilities of such shipping. Much of the commerce of Europe, therefore, is water-borne—the coastwise cargoes in small craft of 3,000 deadweight tons or less, the river and canal cargoes in units of progressively shallower draft and carrying capacity as the upstream segments of waterways are approached. Many of the river boats as well as ocean vessels are individually owned carriers, which along some routes are more prevalent than barges. Specific freight includes coal, iron ore, petroleum, grain, sand and gravel, fertilizers, and other bulk freight as well as a very limited amount of package cargo.

The Soviet Union and Eastern Europe. The iron curtain, imperfectly formed but confined to Russia before the last war, now orients much of the commerce of eastern Europe toward the Soviet Union. Its presence has meant a rearrangement of most of the traffic lanes of the northern portion of eastern Europe, which before the last war looked appreciably to such westward-trending arteries as the Elbe River, the Mittelland Canal, and complementary overland routes for trade outlets. The effects of the iron curtain have not been quite so drastic in south central Europe, which traditionally has looked eastward toward the Black Sea via the Danube River route, but even here some change of orientation has occurred.

The inland waterways of the Soviet Union proper, although fewer than those in Western Europe, usually are quite long. The interconnected system involving the Volga and Don Rivers and Lakes Ladoga and Onega is of outstanding significance, for it allows water craft to reach the White, Baltic, Black, or Caspian Seas from any point along its length, including the capital city of Moscow. The final splice within this system was added with the completion of the Volga-Don Canal in 1952, thus providing for interchange between the Volga River–Caspian Sea routes and those of the Don River, Black Sea, and associated waterways. The lion's share, possibly as much as 85 per cent, of the river commerce of the Soviet Union travels over this system—including the 50 per cent of the nation's total which moves over the Volga River alone—with most of the remainder accounted for by the northward-flowing rivers of European and Asian Russia. The commerce is comprised largely of timber in the far north, and coal, petroleum, grain, iron ore, and fish in the central and southern regions. Essentially all rivers are frozen in winter for at least four months, and those in the far north for a much longer time.

Coastwise commerce is limited chiefly to the Black and Caspian Seas and to the summer runs

Transshipment between coastwise vessel and inland-waterway barge at Amsterdam (Pan American World Airways).

along the fringes of the Soviet Arctic. Intercoastal shipping is of little importance, partially because of the distance involved. Such shipping is virtually overseas commerce; the distance from Odessa to Vladivostok via the Suez Canal is almost as great as that between the same two ports via the Panama Canal!

The Outlying Areas. The small-craft shipping of much of southeastern Asia, Latin America, Africa, and Australia is very much a matter of coastwise vessel movement. Such activity is pronounced within the island nations of Japan, the Philippines, and Indonesia, and is equally or even more active along the rim of Asia's mainland from Communist China to West Pakistan. It is definitely reduced in intensity, although very much present, along the coasts of continents in the southern hemisphere.

The inland-waterway movement, while less conspicuous than coastwise shipping, is evident. Ocean vessels of intermediate size reach Hankow on the Yangtze River of Communist China, and much smaller shipping continues upstream to Chungking. Small native craft shuttle between Rangoon and Mandalay on the Irrawaddy River of Burma. Similar navigation occurs on a number of natural waterways of this general portion of Asia and in Africa, the more actively used being the lower Ganges and Brahmaputra, the Mahanadi, the Kistna, the Cauvery Rivers of India; the Indus of West Pakistan; segments of the Nile in Egypt and Sudan; and of the Congo, the Niger, and smaller rivers of Africa. In South America, the most frequently utilized waterways are the Magdalena, the lower Orinoco, the main stream and several tributaries of the Amazon, and the lower Parana-Paraguay-Plata. Navigation is interrupted by rapids on some rivers, notably those in Africa and the Magdalena River in South America.

Ownership and trends

Most inland-waterway and coastwise commerce is transported by craft belonging to the country wherein the goods are being moved. In Communist nations, its capital equipment, like that of all other transportation and production, is essentially state-owned. In the United States, it is essentially all privately owned. In the remaining areas the ownership varies, with a tendency for predominance of state ownership in many European political units and in the more technically advanced of the underdeveloped nations.

Over the past quarter century, the amount of inland-waterway and coastwise shipping has not increased in general proportion to the increase in the world's productivity nor that of transoceanic commerce. This is partially because the pipeline, a strong competitor of the small water carrier, has come to be a significant mover of liquid and gaseous materials. Also important has been changing technology, especially the substitution of petroleum for coal in many areas, and the resultant decline in coal as a predominant item in domestic and coastwise commerce.

OVERLAND TRANSPORTATION

THE RAILWAYS

A century and a half ago the railway was virtually unknown. A century ago it had established itself as a major carrier. Today, although having suffered in competition with other carriers, notably the truck and the pipeline, it remains the world's prime mover of commodity tonnages.

Railway-car ferries in the port of New York carrying freight cars from one part of the port to another. Most operations like this one are intraharbor, although car ferries connect the United States with Cuba. (Standard Oil Company of New Jersey)

The carriers

At mid-century, there were recorded in the entire world over 200,000 locomotives, approximately 400,000 passenger cars, and between 6½ and 7 million freight cars.[4] Most of the locomotives were steam-driven, but diesel and electric motors were very much in evidence. Diesel motors had gained almost complete supremacy in the United States and appreciable recognition in Canada, Sweden, and other nations. Electric motors had been used particularly in Switzerland, Sweden, Italy, the Netherlands, Norway, and Austria, and to a noteworthy degree in Japan, Brazil, and the Soviet Union. Freight cars, particularly numerous in technically advanced nations, vary among nations as to size and load carried: the typical freight-car shipment in the United States and Canada ranges from 25 to 40 tons; in the United Kingdom the average shipment is 7 tons; in Denmark, 10 tons; in France, 14 tons; in Portugal, 7 tons.

The terminals

Trains, like ships, are loaded and unloaded, and therefore many of their individual terminals are more or less miniature versions of those in seaports. Their terminal facilities are not usually so concentrated as those of seaports, however, because the freight cars can be shunted more effectively than

[4] W. S. Woytinsky and E. S. Woytinsky, *World Commerce and Governments,* The Twentieth Century Fund, Inc., New York, 1955, p. 357.

ships to individual warehouses. Unlike vessels, trains are made up of a series of individual carrying units and must be broken up periodically so that the freight-car components can be forwarded to new trains or sidings. At critical junctions, usually key cities, *classification yards* exist for the purpose of breaking and reforming trains. Once found close to civic centers, these facilities are now being constructed predominantly in suburbs, often at the crossings of main lines entering urbanized areas and belt lines which, circling those areas, provide railway facilities to manufacturing plants and other industries that have shifted to the suburbs. This is particularly true in the United States.

The Conway Classification Yard of the Pennsylvania Railroad near Pittsburgh, Pennsylvania. Trains approaching over one of the few lines at this end of the yard are broken up, car by car, and the separate cars sent to newly forming trains on one of the many tracks in the distance. Modern classification yards have a hump, or hill, at the point where the few tracks are to be seen. A switch engine pushes a newly arrived train over this hump, and the various cars are cut loose at the top of the hump. They then roll by gravity to designated tracks. (Pennsylvania Railroad)

The routes

The world's railways are as unevenly distributed as the levels of its technical advancement and its populations. Tightly woven networks exist in the most active and populous areas of North America and Europe, and each sends tentacles in all directions toward either the oceans or empty countrysides. Away from these nodes, railway development has been much more erratic (Fig. 9.4).

North America. The United States and the effective territory of Canada are so thoroughly crisscrossed with railway lines that only the most isolated outreaches are beyond easy accessibility (Fig. 9.4). These two nations rank first and third, respectively, among all nations when appraised by trackage, with the more than 220,000 miles of main lines in the United States amounting to more than four times that of Canada (and nearly three times that of the second-ranking Soviet Union). But even such dense networks do not reveal the intensity of traffic they make possible, for many lines are double-tracked and/or equipped with centralized traffic-control systems for maximizing the use of individual tracks by dispatching trains accurately. The outlying areas of North America—Alaska, northern Canada, the intermontane west of Canada and the United States, and Caribbean America—are places of isolated lines rather than networks, and the monotonous regularity of such lines is broken only by an occasional junction point or an even more infrequent node marking the presence of a population cluster and productive industry.

Western Europe. The network of rail lines in northwestern Europe is even more closely woven

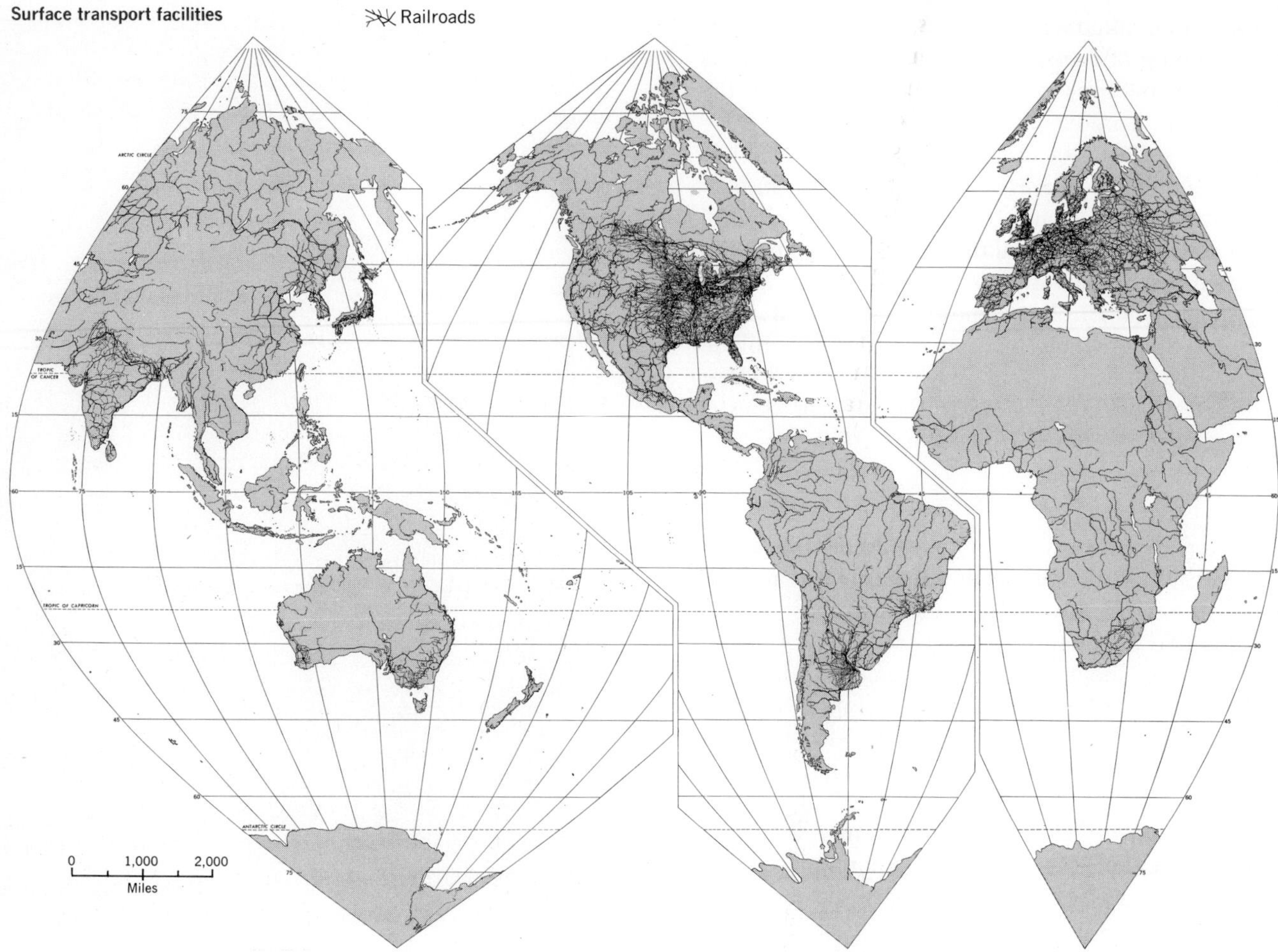

Figure 9.4 ***The world's railroad lines.*** *The network in Communist China and Asian Russia now is denser than the map indicates. (Encyclopaedia Britannica)*

in its densely settled core districts than is true in most corresponding core districts of North America, for in Europe the motor vehicle and the pipeline, while active, do not offer the degree of competition to railways that is found in the United States and Canada. From those densely tracked districts, the European lines extend toward the Arctic north, the Soviet Union, and the Mediterranean Sea.

The Soviet Union and Eastern Europe. The Soviet satellite countries along Russia's western perimeter represent transitions from the northwestern European network to the less dense but extensive system of the Soviet Union. The three most industrially advanced of these—East Germany, Poland, and Czechoslovakia—contain much more trackage than do their more rural southern neighbors; but in all these countries, as in the Soviet Union, the railway is the foremost freight carrier.

Most railways in the Soviet Union are west of the Ural Mountains. From this area of concentration, tracks stretch as individual lines or as a series of lines toward the north, south, and particularly the Asian east. Here, in the rapidly developing portion of the effective territory of the Soviet Union, new tracks are being constructed among the Urals and Kuznets industrial districts, the new Karaganda coal fields, the newly developing Irkutsk industrial district, and the agricultural oases and cities along the southern fringe of Soviet Middle Asia. Probably the best-known of the many Russian railroads is the Trans-Siberian, winding for over 5,000 miles from Moscow to Vladivostok on the Pacific coast. Along this and parallel routes, the Soviet Union's effective area is slowly being extended eastward.

Other Areas of the World. Railway development in places other than the three most technically advanced areas reflects closely the past influence of Europe. In Latin America, the Union of South Africa, and Australia, the railroads were direct cultural implants by Europeans or their descendants. In India, where an effective network exists, and in most of Africa and much of southeastern Asia, where the lines are more sporadic and tend to serve key seaports, the railroads quite often have been constructed in an earlier time by the colonialist nations (and hence are excellent evidence that the impact of colonialism upon areas where it now prevails or once prevailed is certainly not entirely disadvantageous). Japan industrialized and constructed its railways only after quasi-enforced contact with the Occidental World in the form of Admiral Perry's heralded visit there, a visit preceded by some prior liaison with the island nation by Dutch traders. China's early railroads were built chiefly by European capital, and many of the later ones, notably in Manchuria, by Japan when under Japanese control. Korea's numerous railroads also were largely constructed by the Japanese. Turkey's railroads were initiated through the efforts and financial backing of German, French, and British firms, as were others in the Middle East and czarist Russia. The direct and indirect influence of Europe upon the world is probably in no way more effectively, thoroughly, and clearly attested than in the current pattern of the railway lines.

Among outlying nations, the technically advanced but commercially oriented countries display route patterns suggesting commodity movement between ocean port and hinterland. Argentina, the Union of South Africa, and Australia are striking examples (Fig. 9.4). Interestingly, the underdeveloped areas evidence generally similar route patterns—but the individual lines, often constructed by foreign interests for exploitation and homeward shipment of mineral or agricultural resources, are fewer in number. Only in Japan, India, and Korea do nationwide networks prevail in these outlying areas, and these owe their existence to conditions indicated earlier in this chapter.

New Railway Lines. The world as a whole appears to be experiencing a slight retrenchment in total railway lines, with the more than 776,000 miles of 1930 having been reduced to about 768,000 miles in 1950.[5] Most of this retrenchment involves feeder lines of technically advanced lands such as the United States—lines which are suffering in competition with motor vehicles and other forms of transport. Notably in the Communist nations, however, the railroad trackage is increasing. Besides new lines in the Soviet Union and in some of its European neighbors, railways are being added in Communist China and peripheral Asian nations. Particular emphasis is being placed upon establishing better overland connections between the Soviet Union and Communist China, the two giants among Communist nations. Not long ago, a line was completed from the north plain of Communist China through Ulan Bator in Mongolia to the Trans-Siberian junction city of Ulan-Ude. The most important line is in construction from that same plain across the Gobi Desert to the city of Alma-Ata in Soviet Middle Asia. Planned long before the Communist coup in China but pushed vigorously by the new government, this route is intended to give coastal Communist China more effective control over the distant northwest as well as to provide liaison with her northern and western neighbors.

The Critical Importance of Gauge. Because the world's railway lines have "growed" like Topsy, their specifications differ. One of the most critical of such specifications is gauge—the distance between

[5] W. S. Woytinsky and E. S. Woytinsky, *World Commerce and Governments,* The Twentieth Century Fund, Inc., New York, 1955, p. 341.

These truck trailers are brought for short distances to railway terminals by the truck tractors to which they are attached on the highway. They then are loaded on flat cars such as this one for longer hauls. Several varieties of this method now are being used in North America and Europe (General American Transportation Corporation).

the rails. Where tracks of differing gauges meet, usually at political borders, entire trainloads of merchandise must be transferred, for the simple reason that the rolling stock of one gauge cannot be accommodated by the track of a different gauge. Occasionally, but not often, a third rail is added to a railway bed so that trains of at least two gauges can utilize the same route.

There are many gauges, but the most common are *standard* (4 feet, 8½ inches); *broad* (at least 5 feet, and in some cases, wider); and *narrow* (comprising many different gauges, the most common being meter gauge, which is 3 feet, 3⅛ inches, and a gauge in most former British colonies of 3 feet 6 inches).

Most of North America—notably the United States, Canada, Mexico, and Cuba—is dominated by the standard gauge, with car ferries making the mainland-island connections. The same gauge is found in most of Western Europe, except in Spain and Portugal, where the gauge is 5 feet 6½ inches; in Ireland, where it is 5 feet 3 inches, and in the Austrian Alps, where a narrow as well as a standard gauge is extensively employed. The broad gauge of 5 feet is accepted throughout the Soviet Union, but not in many of its neighbors.

In the outlying areas, however, the gauges are much more varied. That of Argentina is mainly broad (5 feet 6 inches), but some of the trackage is also meter. In Brazil, Chile, Ecuador, Bolivia, and the southern sections of Caribbean America the gauge is meter, and in Peru and Uruguay it is mostly standard. In Egypt, Morocco, and the Asian nations of the Middle East the gauge is principally standard, as it is in Communist China and Korea. In central and southern Africa it is chiefly narrow (3 feet 6 inches). In India it is partly broad (5 feet 6 inches), partly narrow, partly meter. Along the Asian rim from Burma to Japan it is mainly meter (except, of course, for Communist China). In Australia it is broad (5 feet 3 inches), standard, and narrow, and in New Zealand it is narrow.

The most persistent uniformity of gauge and the highest measure of railroading versatility are found, with some exceptions, in the most technically advanced nations. Perhaps one day we shall have a plan farsighted enough to provide for complete uniformity of gauge throughout the land areas of the world.

Operational policies, ownership, and trends

Despite the extensiveness of its trackage, the railroad train is mainly a short-haul carrier when compared with the ocean vessel. In large nations like the Soviet Union, Canada, and the United States, its average haul is only 400 miles, and in the small countries of northwestern Europe only 75 to 150 miles. The operational policies and trends vary with ownership. Government-owned railroads predominate in all Communist nations; nearly all of Europe; most of southeastern Asia, Australia, and New Zealand; and in such separated countries as the Union of South Africa, Morocco, Algeria, Tunisia, Argentina, Colombia, and Mexico, and in the state of Alaska. Government ownership is present but not always predominant in Canada, Brazil, Chile, Portugal, Switzerland, and Greece. Among the tech-

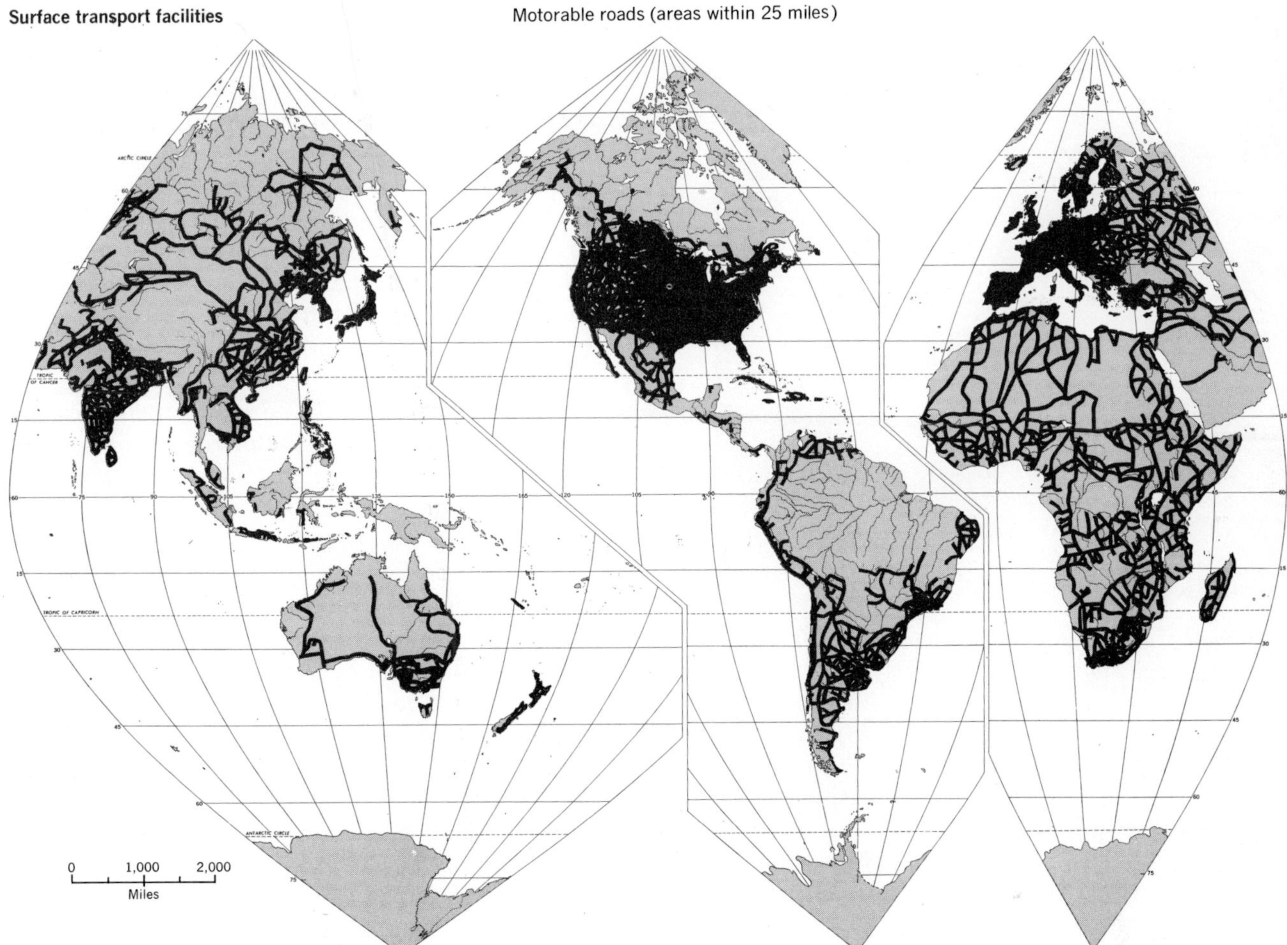

Figure 9.5 ***The world's motorable roads*** *(Encyclopaedia Britannica).*

nically advanced lands, only in the United States are essentially all lines privately owned.

In most of the world's political units the railroad train is an important carrier of passengers as well as freight, and hence the lines assume a multiuse status. However, in much of Europe, in Canada, and particularly in the United States, the automobile accounts for a substantial share of the passenger traffic—in the United States for nearly 90 per cent of all its nonlocal passenger miles. Moreover, in these same nations the motor truck and the pipeline are offering new and serious competition in freight commerce. Therefore, the most notable trends in over-all policies of railway freight haulage are apparent in the United States, where the railway companies are encountering increasing competition from other media and where many private lines are attempting to remain competitive by (1) relinquishing uneconomical feeder lines that carry both passengers and freight; (2) operating subsidiary trucking companies, the trucks replacing rail runs in certain areas and being hauled on flat cars ("piggyback") in joint rail-highway operations; (3) charging slightly lower rates; and (4) abandoning passenger service. Despite all these operational changes, however, the future of railroads in the United States—particularly of the short-haul railroads in Eastern or Trunk Line Territory that

Laying a 34-inch pipeline between Alberta and Winnipeg (Trans-Canada Pipe Lines, Ltd.).

now cope with still added competition from ships on the Great Lakes–St. Lawrence Seaway—does not appear to offer promise of continued overwhelming dominance in freight movement. Less than one-half of the domestic intercity freight of the United States now is carried by rail. As recently as 1928, nearly four-fifths moved by rail.

In contrast, the government-owned railroads of the world will probably continue into the foreseeable future at their present or even higher relative positions. Since they are subsidized, they will carry what needs to be carried—people, package freight, bulk goods—where other carriers are not more effective. This is especially true of the planned economies in the Communist countries.

THE HIGHWAYS

Except in some underdeveloped countries, the motor vehicle is a vital necessity for the local deliveries in most cities and towns, and during the past quarter century it has begun to compete actively for intercity freight (Fig. 9.5). In the United States, for example, nearly 20 per cent of the ton-mile freight movement is by truck. In Europe the figure is not so high, but the truck has won a following there too, notably during and since the aftermath of the last war, at which time many army vehicles were converted to civilian use to carry the merchandise which could not be hauled by the damaged railroads and other carriers. Even in the Soviet Union, where the construction of motor vehicles and roads has not been emphasized as much as railways, the truck accounts for nearly 4 per cent of the ton-mileage of all freight.

It appears, therefore, that throughout the world and particularly in non-Communist, technically advanced lands the motor truck will become a serious competitor for the high-value, low-bulk type of commerce that moves between, as well as within, urban units.

THE PIPELINES

Pipelines serve: (1) to transport liquids and gases the entire distance from the sources of raw materials to markets; (2) to carry liquids from the sources of raw materials to ports of shipment; and (3) to carry liquids from receiving ports to ultimate markets. At present, they are used overwhelmingly to transfer petroleum and its products and natural gas but offer promise of conveying diverse other materials that are liquefied or can be carried in suspension. Currently, pipelines range downward from 36 inches in diameter. Once constructed, they are comparatively simple to maintain—indeed, are quasi-automatic in operation.

Pipeline networks are well developed in the United States and more than noteworthy in the Middle East, the Soviet Union, Canada, and Venezuela. In the United States, where they had been well established by the outbreak of the last war and received much more attention during that war when many coastwise tankers were sunk by German submarines, they are now responsible for about 18 per cent of the ton-mileage of all freight. Among the other areas with pipelines, the Soviet Union is like the United States in that its network is chiefly one of internal development. The Middle East and Venezuela are important areas of pipeline move-

A lull in transportation at Marin, Venezuela. On a unit basis, this type of transport is the most costly of all. (Standard Oil Company of New Jersey)

ment from supply sources to seaports, and Canada is both an area of internal supply (from the Mountain West to the Great Lakes) and of seaports to markets (via the lines from Portland, Maine).

PACK ANIMALS, PORTERS, AND DRAYAGE

In the most technically advanced nations, the draft animal is rapidly disappearing, and the human porter is all but unknown. (Reasonable facsimiles of the human porter are to be seen, paradoxically, in such busy places as the garment district of New York City where, in the heart of Manhattan island, they unconcernedly push rackloads of dresses down streets already choked with automobile traffic!) In many underdeveloped economies, however, as well as in some economies that are quite accomplished technically, the horse and wagon, the ox and cart, the dog team, the pack animal—horse, yak, camel, alpaca, llama, even the sheep and goat—are still actively employed in transportation. It has been estimated, for example, that in the Communist China of today human porters are probably second only to water transportation as movers of freight *on a volume basis.*[6] Thus, although information concerning them is meager and although they are a part of the passing scene, such animate forms as these are not to be overlooked in the total evaluation of transportation.

[6] Rhoads Murphey, "China's Transport Problem, and Communist Planning," *Economic Geography,* 32:19, 1956.

AIR TRANSPORTATION

The airplane, fast achieving supremacy in the domestic passenger traffic of technically advanced lands as well as in world travel, is as yet comparatively unimportant as a carrier of freight. Being forced to expend its energy to remain aloft as well as to achieve thrust, the plane is as yet no match in economy for the self-floating ship or the rail-bound train. In technically advanced countries, it performs the vital service of carrying many of the mails and of hurrying critically needed specialties to their destinations. In the outlying areas, especially those otherwise isolated or nearly isolated from civilization, it carries more generalized types of cargo—but for a price.

TRANSPORTATION AND LIVELIHOOD

Until now we have considered transportation chiefly with respect to its contribution to economic activity by providing for the flow of commerce between places of activity. In doing this, transportation also performs another important service to economies—that of livelihood. It is probable that as much as 5 per cent of the world's labor force is engaged in transportation activities. As might be anticipated, there are more such workers in technically advanced nations and in those underdeveloped lands where something of commercial value is being exploited than in quasi-dormant subsistence economies.

REFERENCES

Jefferson, Mark: "The Civilizing Rails," *Economic Geography,* **4:**217–231, 1928.

Lloyd's Register of Shipping, 1954–1955, 2 vols., London, 1954.

Mayer, Harold M.: *The Port of Chicago and the St. Lawrence Seaway,* University of Chicago Department of Geography Research Paper 49, Chicago, 1957.

Mikesell, Marvin W.: "Market Centers of Northeastern Spain," *Geographical Review,* **50:**247–251, 1960.

Murphey, Rhoads: "China's Transport Problem and Communist Planning," *Economic Geography,* **32:** 17–28, 1956.

Patton, Donald: "The Traffic Pattern on American Inland Waterways," *Economic Geography,* **32:**29–37, 1956.

Thomas, Benjamin J.: "Trade Routes of Algeria and the Sahara," *University of California Publications in Geography,* **8** (3):165–288, 1957.

Thomas, William L., Jr. (ed.): *Man's Role in Changing the Face of the Earth,* University of Chicago Press for the Wenner Gren Foundation for Anthropological Research and the National Science Foundation, Chicago, 1956. (Especially pp. 862–880.)

Ullman, Edward L.: "The Railroad Pattern of the United States," *Geographical Review,* **39:**242–256, 1949.

———: "Trade Centers and Tributary Areas of the Philippines," *Geographical Review,* **50:**203–218, 1960.

Wiens, Herold J.: "Riverine and Coastal Junks in China's Commerce," *Economic Geography,* **31:** 248–264, 1955.

World Railways, 1954–1955, Sampson Low, Marston and Co., Ltd., London, 1955.

Woytinsky, W. S., and E. S. Woytinsky: *World Commerce and Governments,* The Twentieth Century Fund, Inc., New York, 1955. (Especially chaps. 7–11.)

10 WORLD PATTERNS OF TRADE

TRANSPORTATION MAKES POSSIBLE THE MOVEMENT OF GOODS AMONG NATIONS; it is the means to an objective. Trade *is* the movement of those same goods; it is an objective. Yet, in a sense, trade is also a means—a way of satisfying as many as possible of man's almost insatiable desires for a variety of economic goods.

Trade exists either because localized demand for materials exceeds (or is expected to exceed) the possibilities of its localized supply or because the supply exceeds the demand. This demand-supply imbalance, in turn, may be due to differences among human beings, or among their cultures, or among the particular features of their natural environment. For example, insulin is purchased by a person with diabetes because it is a bodily necessity; here the demand is due to a unique human deficiency. Rice is a staple among foods and an imported commodity in most of the larger nations of the Far East; here the demand is in large measure cultural—the result of a developed taste for this particular food. It may well be in part natural, for rice grows well in this area of the world. The Asian trade in rice is due to an excess of demand over supply in the importing nations. This excess is partly ascribable to essentially human factors—to the high natural increases in those nations—but is due also to cultural and natural factors, for man has not yet utilized nature efficiently enough in this part of the world to produce rice in quantities that are adequate for domestic consumption—and who is to say whether the limitations to his production are entirely natural, or cultural, or human? Certainly higher yields per acre and per person could be achieved with known methods that are used elsewhere, but how can these be purchased or otherwise made available? And even if they were utilized to the utmost, would the production yet be adequate, especially when the high natural increases in population are considered?

If enough space were available, we could add many other examples to those of the rice and of the insulin, and we should arrive eventually at the same impasse in our efforts to seek a precise cause of trade. Suffice it to say that the very many and pronounced differences among human beings, their cultures, and their respective shares of the earth's natural features appear to be indirectly responsible for trade. The direct cause was stated in the last paragraph: the excesses of localized demand (desire plus purchasing power) over localized supply of, or of supply over demand for, the commodities traded. These excesses, it should be emphasized, have deep roots in the past.

The resulting commerce may be considered at several levels of classification: First, there is trade between individuals; this is too detailed and each transaction too trivial to be of much service to our examination. Second, there is exchange of goods between market centers and their trading areas and between ports and their hinterlands; this is of appreciable interest to us. Finally, there is trade among nations, and this is of decided interest to us. All three levels, but particularly the last two, are best developed and organized in technically advanced nations, and the generalizations below are applicable only loosely to underdeveloped nations. The appropriateness of their application increases with degree of technical advancement.

MARKET CENTERS AND TRADING AREAS; PORTS AND HINTERLANDS

Almost all urbanized settlements are trading centers for their resident populations and for the people living in adjacent countrysides. Of course, they usually contain other activities, like manufacturing, which are important to their welfare but which need not be emphasized in this discussion of trade. In a few places of specialized effort, such as political capitals, resorts, and mining and university towns, the trade may be restricted essentially to the population of the urbanized settlement itself; but exceptions like these are rare. Generally, each urban settlement, large or small, has its own trading area which is a composite of all of the trading territories served by individual firms located in that settlement.

HIERARCHICAL ARRANGEMENT

The size, distinguishing features, and complexity of each trading area tend to vary in accordance with the size of the market center with which it shares an interdependence. Moreover, the trading centers and areas are in a recognizable hierarchical order, with the territory of each included also with that of the larger units. Thus the market and supply areas of hamlets are encompassed by those of villages; of villages by those of small towns; of small towns by those of large towns; of large towns by those of cities; of cities by those of metropolises (Fig. 10.1).[1] In practice, the hierarchy cannot always be readily distinguished, but its presence is very real. A major reason for its existence is that all goods and services are not available from all sizes of settlements, and persons seeking a particular type of good or service necessarily will go to the urbanized unit where it can be had. In other words, nearly every settlement in the hierarchy offers all the goods and services obtainable from all settlements of a lower level, plus certain specialties that cannot be found in those smaller settlements.

Villages and hamlets

These smallest of market centers, often as much rural as urban, are the most numerous, and their trading areas are correspondingly the smallest. Usually they offer only retail trade, and this only in the most regularly consumed commodities—groceries, gasoline, drugs, commonplace hardware, etc. Often these are all sold from the same store. Nearly all retail services are absent, and the existing few are frequently carried on in private dwellings. The fa-

[1] The terms *village, town, city,* etc., are used here to designate increasing size and complexity of urbanized settlements, and not to refer to their political organization or administration. Rural villages of certain cultures are chiefly residential, and do not fit easily into the above classification.

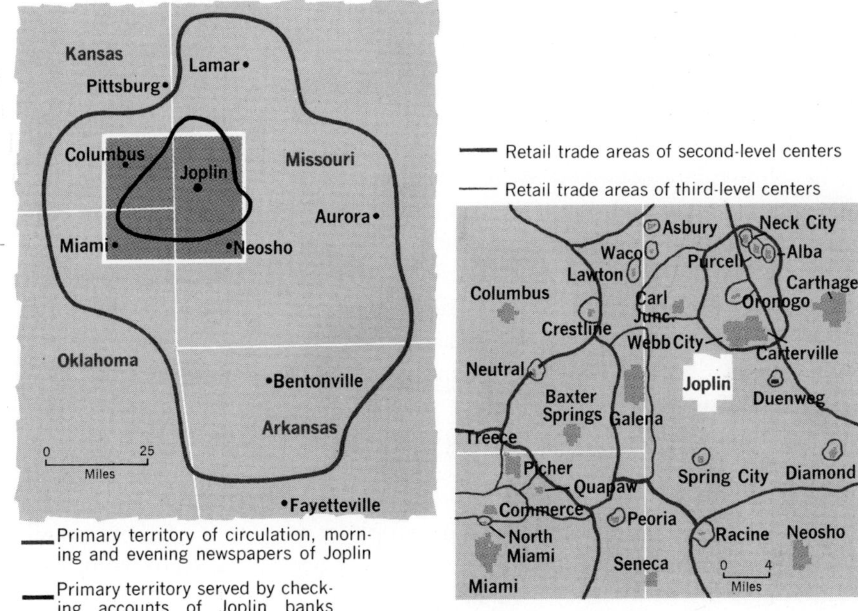

Figure 10.1 ***The hierarchy of market centers and retail-trade areas in the vicinity of Joplin, Missouri.*** *Trade areas are not sharply bounded, as the classifications might imply, but merge almost indefinably into one another as a result of the different sizes of trading territories of the various firms in a trading center. Joplin, with a population of 40,000, offers a rather wide variety of retail goods and services, competing with other cities of similar or larger size, such as Kansas City, Wichita, Tulsa, and nearby Springfield. However, some highly specialized services not available at Joplin may be available in a larger center like Kansas City. The small-scale view shows two delimitations of Joplin's retail-trade area—one measured conservatively on the basis of residence of customers with checking accounts in Joplin banks, and the other measured liberally on the basis of territory served by Joplin's morning and evening newspapers. The boundaries of retail-trade territories of most other Joplin firms lie between these two extremes. The large-scale view shows Joplin's immediate vicinity and includes all urban units which compete with Joplin for some retail trade. They all lie within the territory usually considered to be Joplin's retail-trade area. The boundaries to their trading areas are drawn on the basis of interviews with merchants in each center. The larger towns—Columbus, Pittsburg, Baxter Springs, Miami, Neosho, Carthage, and Webb City-Carterville—range in population from 3,000 to 20,000. These are considered here to be at the second hierarchal level, offering a variety of goods and services that is substantial but not so wide nor so specialized as is found in Joplin. Their trading areas are shown by heavy lines. The many smaller settlements are here considered to be at the third hierarchal level. They sell groceries, gasoline, and other day-to-day consumer goods.*

cilities for accommodating surplus goods from the surrounding countrysides are equally parsimonious, for markets in such small settlements cannot compete satisfactorily with those of towns that almost always are not far away. Villages and hamlets are thus essentially market centers of convenience upon which nearby residents can depend for life's daily necessities.

Towns

In addition to the simple retailing services operating in competition with those of the villages and hamlets, the towns offer more highly specialized retailing possibilities as well as the more elementary types of wholesaling outlets and certain professional and trade services. Thus it is possible not only to obtain a wider selection of food, gasoline, drugs, hardware, etc., but also to "shop around" among the small but numerous clothing and shoe stores, ten-cent stores, appliance stores, bakeries, automobile dealers, farm-machinery distributors, and a variety of other outlets. Not infrequently (notably in the United States) coast-to-coast retail organizations are represented, but, except for food supermarkets, their stores are usually rather modest. The wholesale firms tend to be those servicing the numerous retail outlets of the nearby villages and rural routes, with petroleum products and groceries among the leading commodities so handled. Service firms specializing in cleaning, laundering, shoe repairing, automobile repairing, etc., are well represented in towns, as are the legal and medical professions.

Towns are often market as well as supply centers. Official or unofficial market places usually are set aside in towns for exchange of fresh produce from the country, and some of the retail establishments also purchase such produce for local resale. In areas of grain production, grain elevators are frequently the tallest structures in the town's skyline, except, perhaps, for the stilt-foundationed water tanks. Flour mills, hay mills, sugar refineries, canneries, milk-processing plants, and stockyards are still other marketing outlets found in towns of varying size.

Cities and metropolitan areas

The largest urbanized settlements, like the intermediate and the smallest, dominate the retail trade of their respective adjacent countrysides; but, unlike the smallest and in a manner only suggested by settlements of intermediate size and activity, they are influential in trade that is removed—sometimes far removed—from their actual locations. These largest urban agglomerations are the places to go for commodities that simply cannot be obtained otherwise, as well as for a much wider selection of the more ubiquitous goods. These commodities are dispensed sometimes from huge establishments like Macy's and Gimbels, sometimes from offices like those in the Empire State Building, sometimes from a rolltop desk along the waterfront.

The retail influence of urban agglomerations is very real, but wholesaling activities are the functions which truly extend the over-all impact of the larger urban units to other parts of a country and to other countries. Reaching beyond the retail-trade areas of these units are wholesale territories—first, contiguous areas which are consistently dominated by the urban units which core them, and, secondly, "twilight zones" of competition between the wholesale territories of two or more cities or metropolises. Beyond these "twilight zones" the impact of the largest urban units is reduced to tentacles which, reaching to almost every settlement—perhaps in the form of branch stores or regional headquarters, or traveling salesmen—are constant reminders of the presence and prestige of the world's largest urban agglomerations.

Other equally dynamic ties act to gather in surplus commodities from different portions of a given country or from different countries so that they can be made available for redistribution. The market-center–trading-area bonds between these largest of urban units and their outlying associates thus make possible reciprocity of impact, whether outlying associates be in adjacent, continuous retail- and wholesale-trade territories or in the form of individual contacts from positions well beyond the outer margins of those territories.

Ports and hinterlands

Merged into, and yet distinguishable from, the market-center–trading-area relationships are connections between ports and *hinterlands*. A hinterland differs from a trading area in being oriented to the incoming and outgoing foreign and coastwise shipping of a port, rather than to the retail-wholesale features of an urbanized settlement. Of course, many ports are also market centers and possess both trading areas and hinterlands, although the two usually do not precisely overlap. The ports in question may be water ports or airports but almost invariably are the former and in most cases are seaports.

Continuous and Discontinuous Hinterlands. Just as trade centers have their contiguous trading areas and their more distant, less distinctive trading ter-

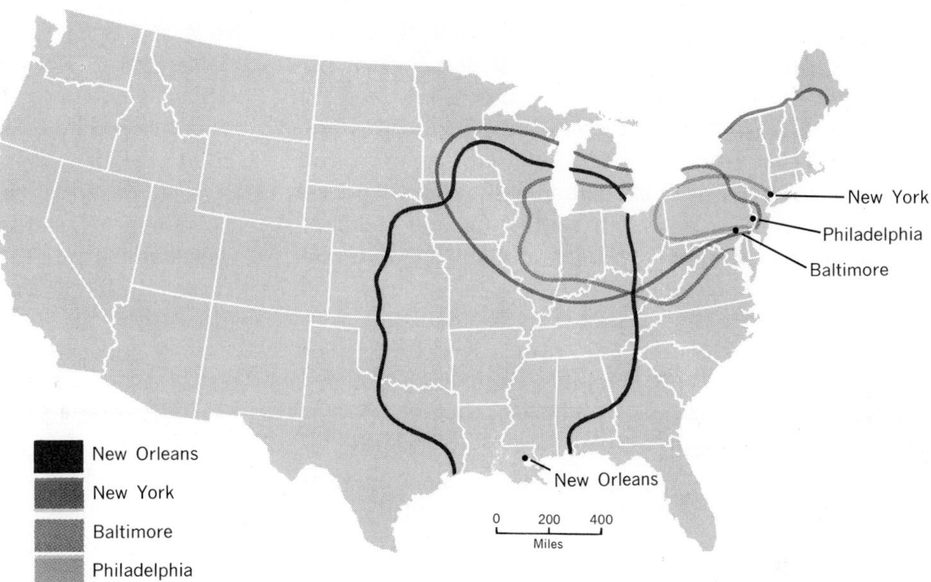

Figure 10.2 ***Export-cargo hinterlands of New York, Philadelphia, Baltimore, and New Orleans.*** *Note the active competition among three of the four ports for commerce originating in the western half of the manufacturing belt. (After Donald J. Patton, "General Cargo Hinterlands of New York, Philadelphia, Baltimore, and New Orleans,"* Annals of the Association of American Geographers, *48: 436–455, 1958)*

ritories, so do seaports lay claim to *continuous* and *discontinuous* hinterlands. The former are more or less generally recognized as being clearly oriented to their adjacent seaports. The latter are the more nebulous areas, beyond all continuous hinterlands, to which no seaport can lay exclusive claim and in which all vie for commerce. Discontinuous hinterlands are found more often in large nations: the Middle West of the United States (Fig. 10.2), the Urals region and the eastern portion of the effective territory of the Soviet Union, the central portion of the peninsula of India. Some examples may be found also in nations of intermediate size: in prewar Germany and postwar West Germany, the discontinuous hinterland was (and is) the southernmost reaches of the country, north of the Alps; in France, it lies just to the southeast of Paris; in Sweden, it is in the heart of that country's effective territory. For the commerce of these uncommitted, nebulously delimited discontinuous hinterlands the major seaports are always in particularly active competition.

Effects of Political Boundaries. Unless a nation is landlocked, it usually prefers to ship and receive cargoes via its own ports, and not infrequently political influence is exerted toward this objective. This influence sometimes results in arbitrarily adjusted freight rates, sometimes in specific permissive or prohibitive regulations, and sometimes takes still other forms. The net effect, however, is that boundaries between nations tend also to be the boundaries of the continuous hinterlands and the contiguous trading areas of seaports and market centers. Being more nebulous, the discontinuous hinterlands cross national boundaries more easily. The political boundaries of lower-level units of government—states, provinces, counties, etc.—do not appear to be reflected so strongly in the seaport-hinterland relationships, although some degree of political influence is discernible even here.

FUNCTIONAL ORGANIZATION

The foreign and domestic trade of nations is thus not a uniform flow from or to a countryside but is channeled into specific trading territories with connections to and from market centers and seaports. Each center, together with its outlying territory and its connecting transportation and communication, may be conceived as a *unit of organization.* This is a term used in geography and in some related fields to refer to the manner in which societies are *functionally organized*—to the arrangements they have established for accomplishing their objectives. Every unit of organization consists of a focal point where the critical decisions are made and most of the critical processes carried on. The focal point cannot live satisfactorily in isolation, however, but must have an interassociation with some type of outlying area with which continuous and intimate contact is provided by lines and media of transportation and communication.

A unit of organization may be small or large and need not be economic: it may be a farm, with the farmstead the focal point and the fields the outlying territory; it may be a church, with the building the focal point and the residential pattern of membership the outlying area; it may be a political unit, with the capital the focal point and the unit itself the outlying territory. It is nowhere better expressed, however, than in the previously described relationships between market centers and seaports and their respective trading territories. The trade of nations is thus functionally organized and can best be viewed as an erratic, throbbing movement constantly being filtered through the world's focal points to and from its outlying areas. These focal points, in turn, are not uniformly spaced but are primarily the unevenly distributed clusters and isolated positions of the world's large seaports and other cities, towns, villages, and even hamlets, most of which are situated in those dynamic, active portions of nations previously designated in this book as effective areas.

INTERNATIONAL TRADE

International trade is also functionally organized, with its focal points being the world's technically advanced nations, notably the effective areas of northwestern Europe and east central Anglo-America, as well as lesser areas of consumption and production. It thus exhibits a pattern that should not be new to the readers of this book: marked activity is found in the more dynamic portions of technically advanced nations, while the outlying countries participate more or less in direct proportion to their propensities to exchange and/or their population pressures.

A market in a technically advanced economy: the Winnipeg Grain Exchange (National Film Board of Canada).

ROLES OF SELECTED NATIONS

The United States

In 1940, the United States surpassed the United Kingdom in total value of trade and since then has pushed onward to an extent unappreciated by the majority of its citizens. Today the country is Gargantuan in world commerce, accounting for over one-seventh of all imports and over one-fifth of all exports (Fig. 10.3). And yet, despite this commanding position, the United States economy is almost independent of foreign trade, which amounts to less than 10 per cent of its national income. By way of comparison, the value of foreign trade of many European nations amounts to 20 to 65 per cent of their respective national incomes. Furthermore, increases in United States production have outdis-

A market in an underdeveloped economy: the Sunday market in Cuzco, Peru (Standard Oil Company of New Jersey).

tanced those in trade, despite the country's commanding position in the world markets, so that it is actually less dependent upon trade than it was a century ago. Thus the United States is in the paradoxical situation of being a giant among commercial colleagues yet oriented almost wholly toward a very active domestic consumption. Small wonder that every statement and action of the country is weighed with utmost gravity by other non-Communist nations, nearly all of which are either oriented toward, or even seriously dependent upon, the world's markets. Small wonder, too, that such statements and actions are given equally serious consideration by the Communist nations, for no less an authority than Karl Marx forecast over a century ago the eventual decline of capitalism

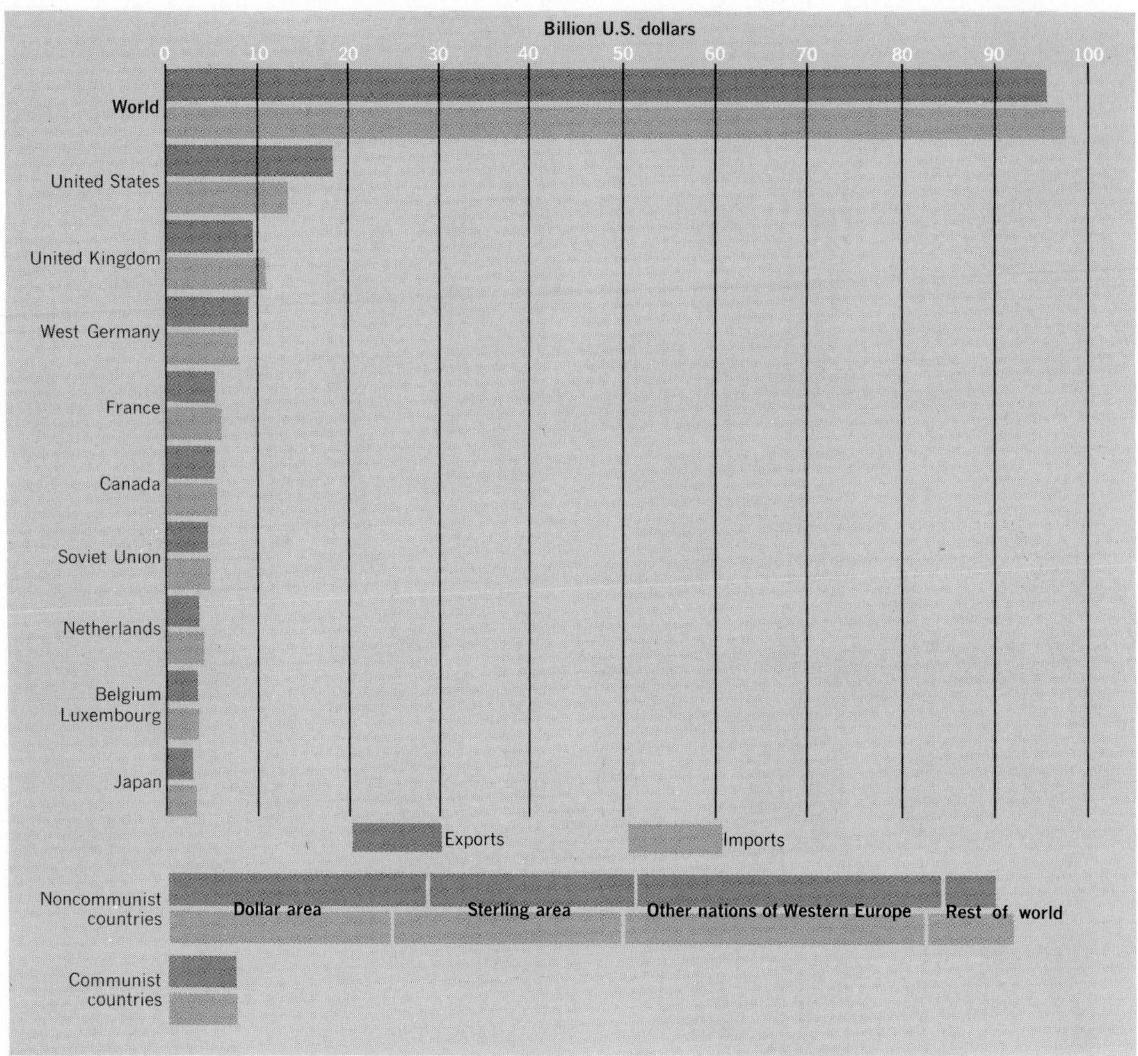

Figure 10.3 ***Exports and imports of the world, of the leading trading nations, of non-Communist and Communist blocs, and of the leading money areas or blocs.*** *The difference in totals between world exports and imports is due to different ways of keeping records in various countries.*

because of recurring financial depressions, and stated further that the United States was to be the last bulwark of capitalism. The concern of the free world's trading nations is not abated by the international-trade record of the United States, which has been rather sporadic in world-market associations, sometimes becoming quite active and sometimes returning to a policy of quasi isolation. Most of this concern now appears to be without good foundation, however, as the United States now is reaching out quite actively into other areas for raw materials and fuels.

Imports. Canada is the leading and one of the most consistent trading partners of the United States, accounting for about one-fifth of both its imports and exports (Fig. 10.4). Newsprint, timber, increasing amounts of iron ore, nickel, meat, fish, and grain are among the leaders in a long list of imported commodities. No other single nation is as consistent a supplier as is Canada, although the United Kingdom, Mexico, Japan, Cuba, Venezuela, West Germany, and Italy each contribute between 3 and 8 per cent of the total. Western Europe supplies manufactured products. Latin America, notably the dollar bloc, supplies petroleum and products of tropical agriculture.

Exports. Of the materials going from the United States to its largest individual customer, Canada, semifinished and finished iron and steel goods, including motors and machinery, are of major importance, with coal and petroleum not far behind. In addition, a wide variety of materials, mostly in some stage of manufacture, are forwarded. Otherwise, the pattern of trading partners is not markedly unlike that of imports. Manufactured commodities comprise almost two-thirds of the value of these exports, with no other classification of pronounced secondary importance.

Nations in the dollar bloc

As was suggested in the preceding paragraphs, the United States carries on an active trade with the dollar bloc (Fig. 10.4), but is not necessarily oriented toward that bloc. In contrast, the nations usually considered to be a part of the dollar bloc are very much dependent for their markets upon the United States. This one country accounts for over 70 per cent of the value of Canada's imports and 60 per cent of the value of her exports; 80 per cent and 70 per cent, respectively, of those of Mexico; 74 and 71 per cent, of Honduras; 64 and 81 per cent, of Colombia; 67 and 30 per cent, of Venezuela; 72 and 58 per cent, of Haiti. The trade of North America and Caribbean America, certainly, is focused upon the United States.

The United Kingdom

Long the leader in world trade, the United Kingdom since 1940 has been second only to the United States and now accounts for approximately one-tenth of the value of the world's imports and exports (Fig. 10.5). This cradle nation of the Industrial Revolution has come to be the very symbol of a manufacturing based largely upon local fuels and know-how and foreign raw materials and markets.

Imports. Being an old hand at world trade, the United Kingdom has commercial ties to many lands, both near and far. Because these are so numerous and quasi-nebulous—resembling somewhat the discontinuous hinterlands of seaports—they can be categorized only generally. So categorized, they include the sterling bloc, which accounts for approximately 40 per cent of the nation's imports; Western Europe, which is responsible for about 26 per cent; and the Western Hemisphere, which supplies most of the remainder. No single nation is outstanding, although the United States, Canada, and Australia are noteworthy, each forwarding 10 per cent or less of all imports. Over one-third of such imports to this agriculturally deficient nation is comprised of food, and well over another one-third of raw materials for manufacture.

Exports. The sterling bloc receives nearly one-half of all British exports, Western Europe nearly 30 per cent, and the Western Hemisphere about 20 per cent. As is true of imports, no single nation enjoys the favorable trade position with the United Kingdom that Canada occupies with respect to the United States; in other words, no single nation generally receives more than 10 per cent of the outgoing materials from the United Kingdom, although Australia, the Union of South Africa, Canada, and the United States are leading market areas. The commodity export lists are completely dominated by manufactured goods, especially those involving metals.

Nations in the sterling bloc

Despite the apparent solidarity of the sterling bloc in comparison with other currency areas, the United Kingdom does not dominate the trade with individual nations in this bloc to the extent that the United States is uncontested in the dollar bloc. An examination of the world's trading nations reveals

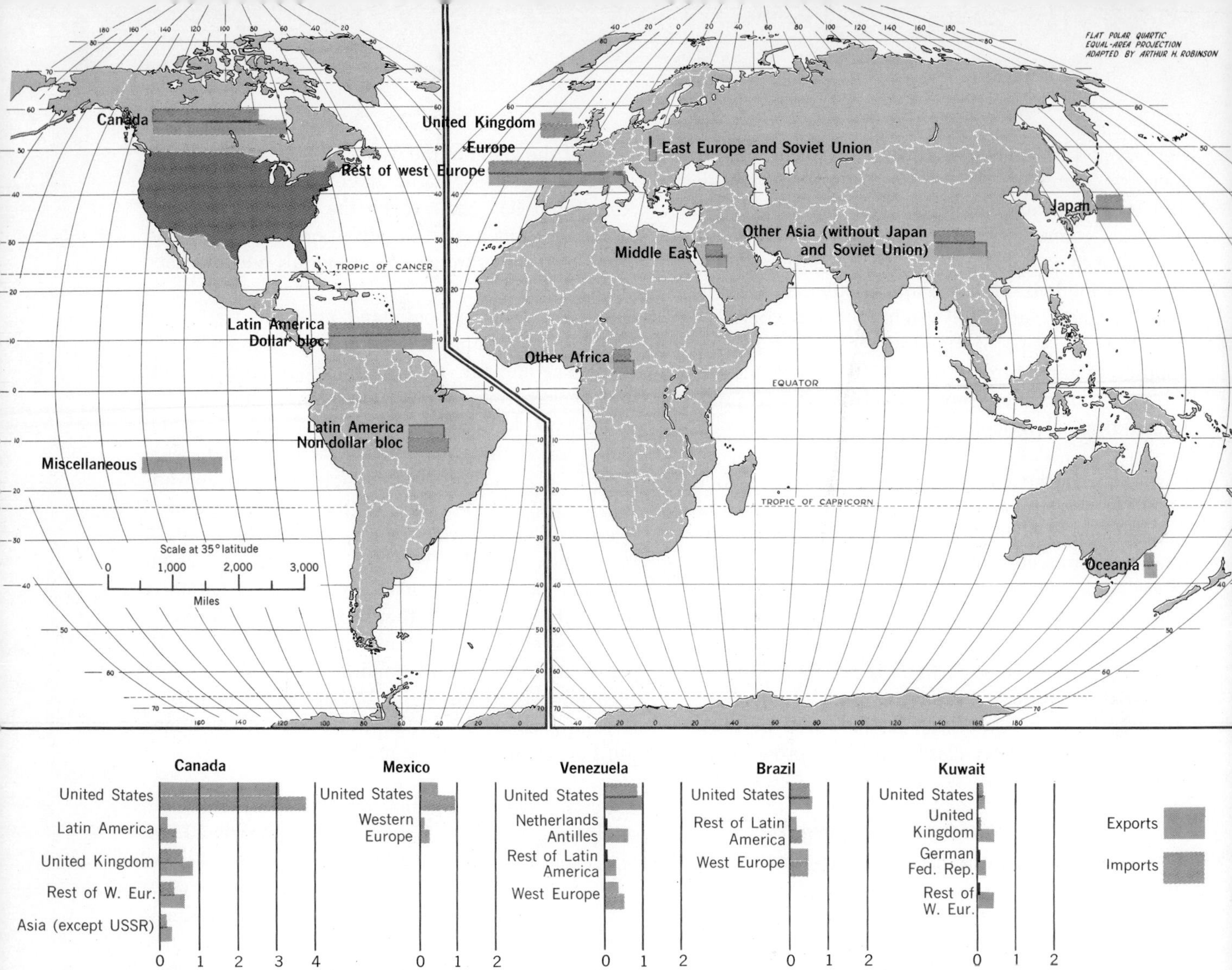

Figure 10.4 ***Exports and imports of the United States and of some of the leading countries and groups of countries with which the United States trades.*** *The map shows trade of the United States, and the graphs beneath show trade of some important trading partners. According to the map, the United States exports some 3.7 billion dollars of goods to Canada and imports some 3 billion dollars of goods from Canada. The graph for Canada, of course, indicates the reverse of these figures. However, the graphs are drawn from statistical reports, and they may vary slightly from the data on the map because of discrepancies in reports from different countries. The miscellaneous bar on the map refers to economic and military aid.*

that the United Kingdom is still clearly and consistently predominant in the trade of nearly all its overseas territories that are still ruled from London, as well as that of such British Commonwealth nations as Australia, New Zealand, Ceylon, India, Pakistan, and Canada (p. 12). A substantial portion of British trade with sterling-bloc members is not on such an assured basis, however, but involves

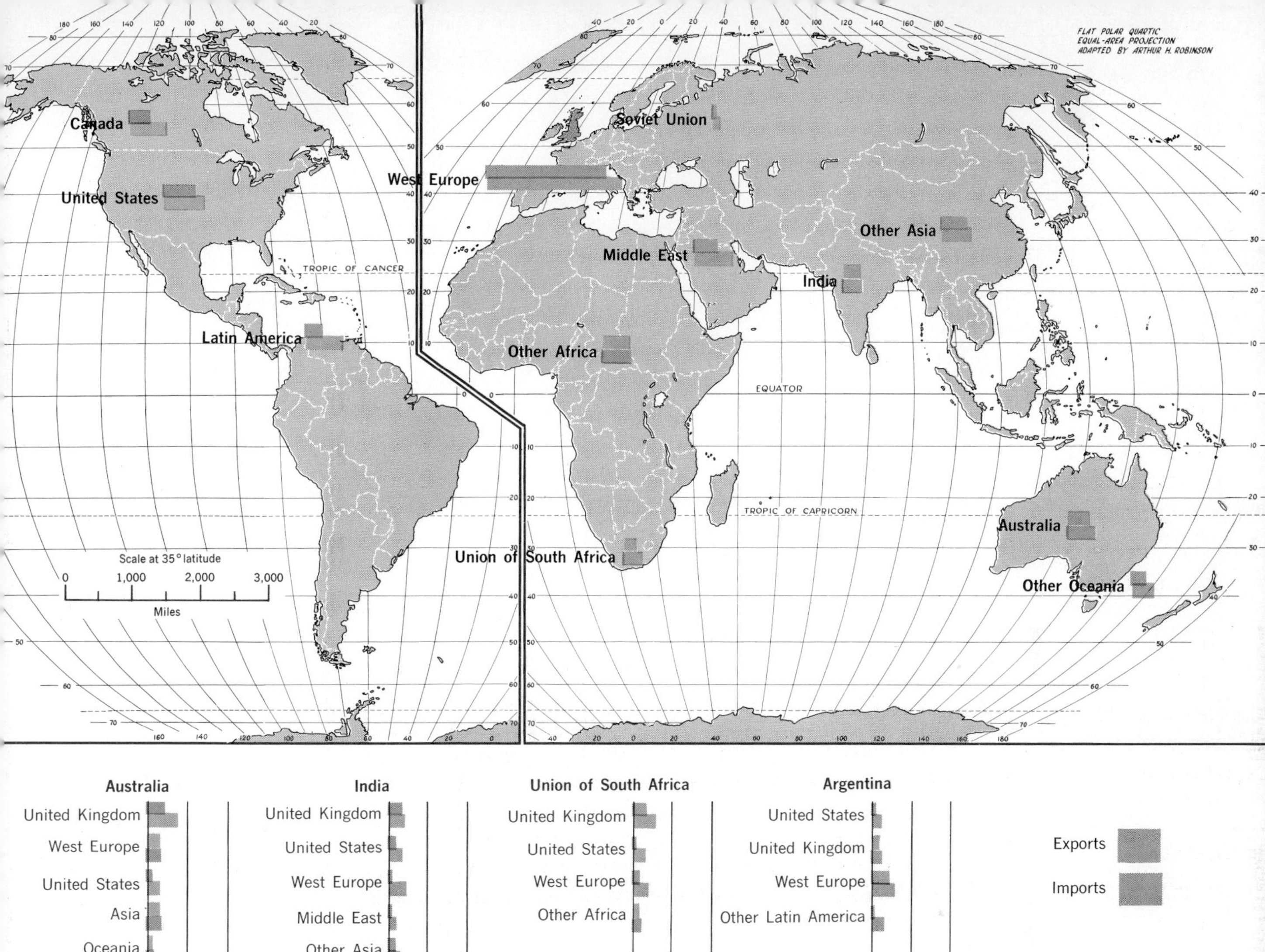

Figure 10.5 ***Exports and imports of the United Kingdom and of some of that country's leading trading partners.*** *Trade with Eastern Europe is too small to be mapped accurately. For further explanation, see Fig. 10.4.*

constant and intense competition with other active manufacturing and commercial nations. Moreover, as the tide of nationalism continues to sweep the once-colonial portions of the world, there is every indication that such competition will continue. The current trade of some nations within both the British Commonwealth and the sterling bloc is indicative: of India's exports and imports, about one-fifth involve the United Kingdom and one-sixth the United States, with West Germany and Japan becoming more active in competition; Burma's trade is with neighboring non-Communist Asian nations as well as the United Kingdom; Pakistan's commerce is with India, Japan, West Germany, Italy, the United States, and still other nations.

Other nations with overseas affiliations

Most of the continental European nations with overseas affiliations have financial and political arrangements not unlike those between the United

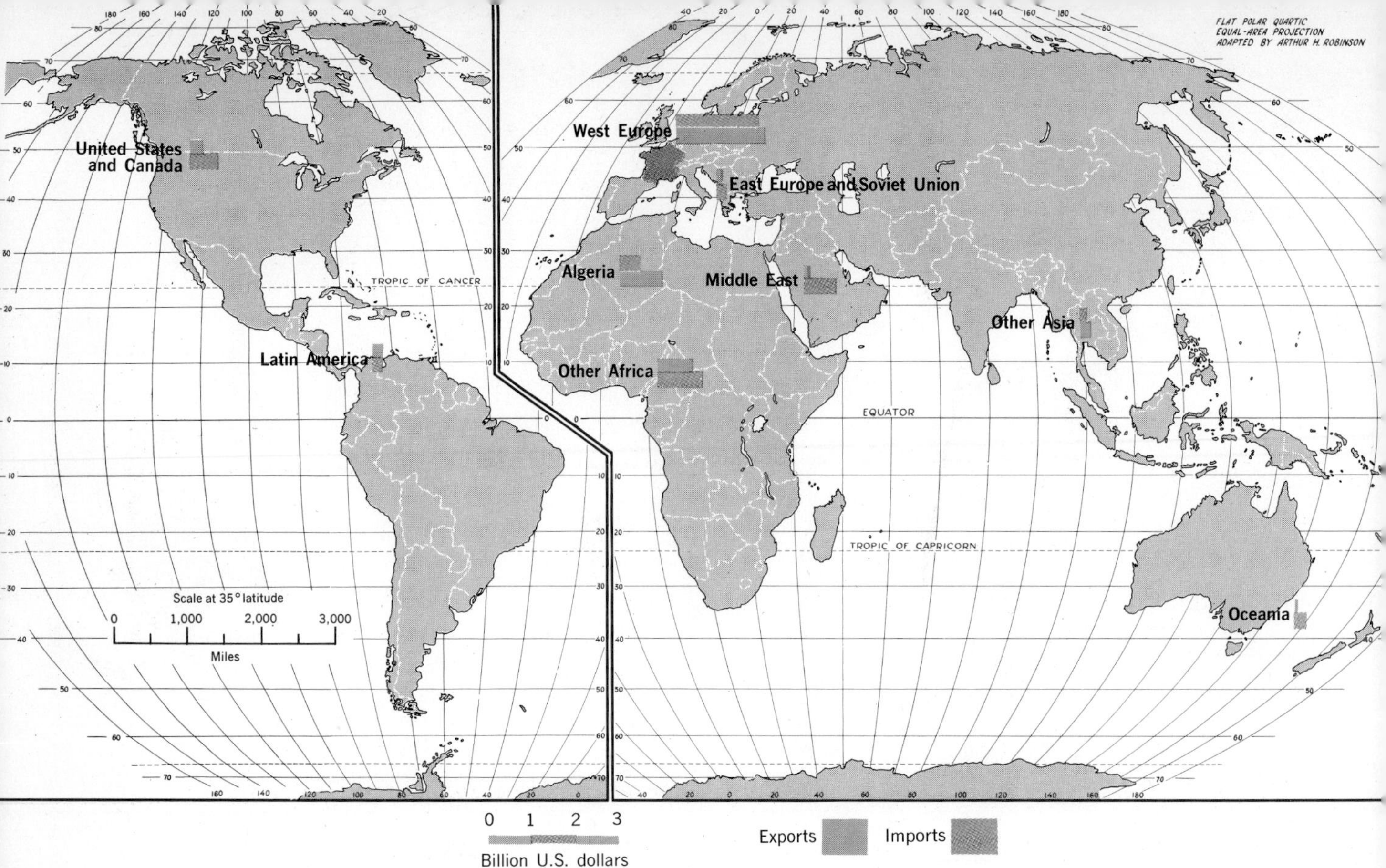

Figure 10.6 ***Exports and imports of France.***

Kingdom and its political British Commonwealth and its economic sterling bloc. France, Portugal, the Netherlands, and Spain are the most conspicuous of such nations, and their commercial ties to their affiliated countries and dependencies vary: about 25 per cent of French imports and 35 per cent of the country's exports are with overseas affiliates (Fig. 10.6); Portugal, which has not yet experienced active expressions for political separation, relies upon her overseas colonies for about 15 per cent of her imports and over 25 per cent of her exports. The Netherlands, left after the last war with only a few shreds of once sizable overseas holdings, scarcely records an overseas trade with affiliated countries. This is true also of Spain, whose waning status as a colonialist nation declined to near-impotency in the Spanish-American War. Anticipating continued decline of their overseas trade, several European nations are seriously considering closer cooperation or even unification, as described in Chapter 7.

The orientation of the overseas affiliations to the economies of their European affiliates also varies, in so far as can be ascertained from existing records. Areas under the French flag appear to be particularly active in commerce with the mother country. The remaining ties, involving chiefly subsistence economies, are more nebulous.

Uncommitted nations

In both the technically advanced and underdeveloped portions of the world are nations with no specific trading commitments with other nations. These not infrequently contribute to international trade in a manner similar to that of the tramp ship in ocean shipping: they take up the slack and fill the gaps where necessary. This is particularly true of nations which have no specific trade orientation but shift about, year after year, selling where the opportunities are the most inviting. Most such nations are located either beyond the dollar bloc in

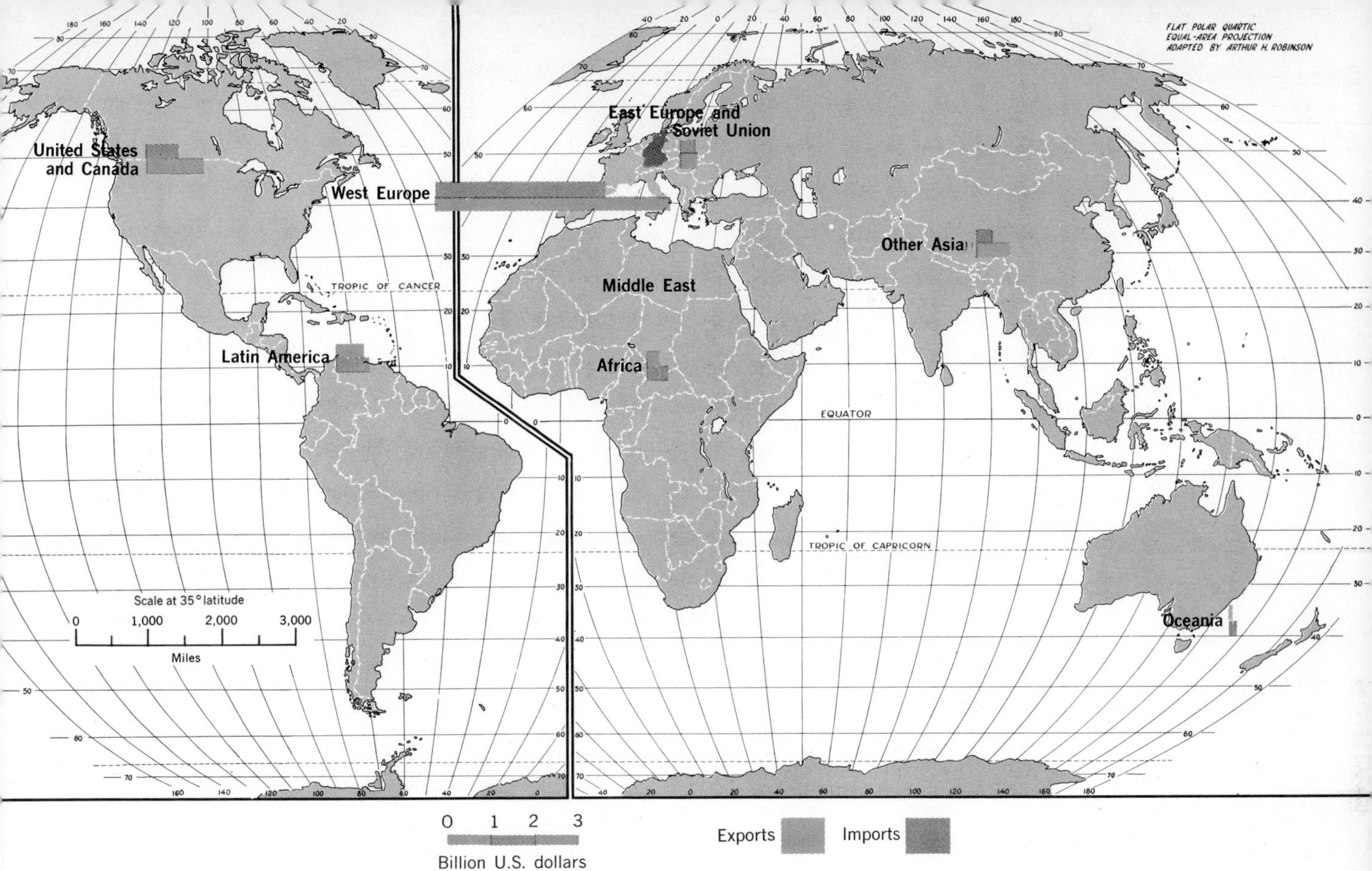

Figure 10.7 Exports and imports of the German Federal Republic.

South America or in Scandinavian, east central, or southern Europe. Argentina, for example, relies upon neighboring Brazil and more distant northwestern Europe and the United States for most of its incoming manufactured and other goods and its outgoing agricultural, mineral, and miscellaneous other commodities, but its record of selection among these nations is not consistent. Brazil, Chile, Bolivia, Ecuador, Peru, and Uruguay, although oriented decidedly to the economy of the United States, are yet more independent economically of that nation than are the dollar-bloc countries. Paraguay trades mostly with its South American neighbors.

The nations of Europe without overseas associations tend to act also as world market "equalizers" (Fig. 10.7). Most of these nations predominantly buy from and sell to their immediate neighbors or the United States and Canada, but they are not committed among these or other nations. Japan also is an "equalizer" (Fig. 10.8).

Communist nations

Although information concerning the trade of Communist nations is not complete, most of their production appears to be for domestic consumption. Such trade as does exist is chiefly with other Communist countries, particularly between the Soviet Union and its neighbors to the west and south (Fig. 10.9). Among exports from the Soviet Union are nonferrous metals (notably manganese), timber, grain, cotton, and some industrial machinery and supplies. Imports to the Soviet Union include various finished goods, notably from the factories of East Germany, Czechoslovakia, and Poland; timber from neutral Finland, and tin and rubber from Communist China and other nations of southern Asia. Communist China's imports are chiefly machinery to equip its new factories, and its exports are largely agricultural and mineral products. North Korea has a surplus of a few minerals but a dearth

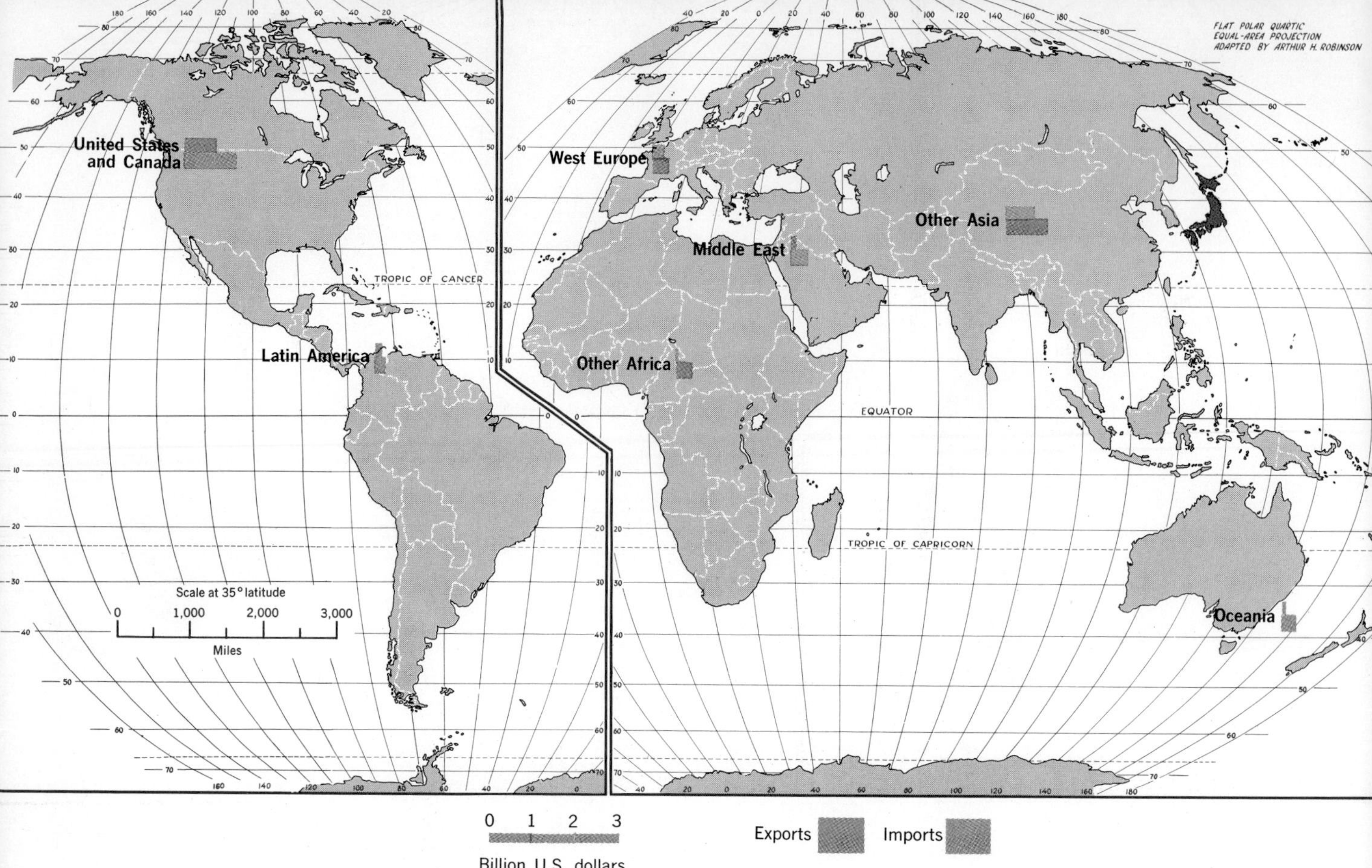

Figure 10.8 ***Exports and imports of Japan.***

of agricultural produce, whereas North Vietnam offers limited quantities of both minerals and agricultural commodities. In Eastern Europe, the northern nations are more technically advanced and highly industrialized than their southern neighbors, and respective exports and imports reflect this.

TARIFFS AND RELATED CONTROLS

We have noted previously that trade arises from differences among people, their cultures, and their natural conditions, and that it is partially channeled into its present paths by such features as domestic and overseas investment of capital, transportation costs, and the ownership of transportation media. Yet other influences upon the volume and direction of world trade are exerted through such devices as *quotas, exchange controls, compensations, tariffs,* and *trade agreements.* The first may involve specific limitations by governments with respect to both the amounts of designated commodities which can be legally imported or exported and the nations to or from which they can be shipped. The next two are more indirect: exchange controls are tools through which is made known the unwillingness of a country to accept, or permit its merchants to accept, more than specified amounts of the currency of other nations. Compensations, in contrast, are subsidy arrangements for the encouragement or discouragement of certain trade by governments making such aid available. Except during times of emergency and other extraordinary times, however, the aggregate effect of these tools of trade control is not so pronounced as that of tariffs, which are assessments levied by governments upon commodities entering or leaving their areas of jurisdiction,[2]

[2] More specifically, the word *tariff* refers to schedules of specific duties, and the word *customs* to the total import assessments. However, we are using the word *tariff* as synonymous with *customs* in accordance with increasingly common practice.

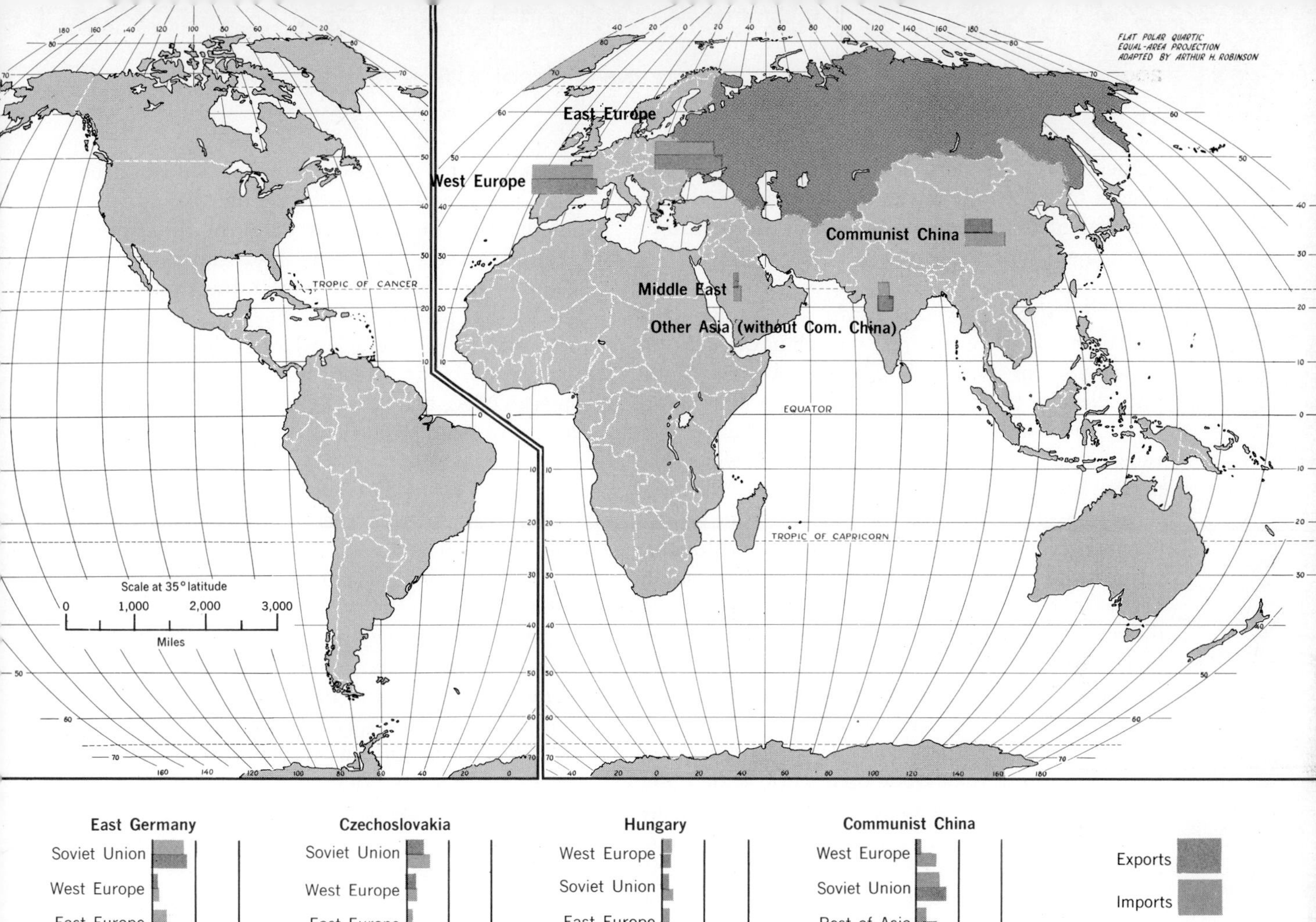

Figure 10.9 ***Exports and imports of the Soviet Union and some of its leading trading partners.*** *For detailed explanation, see Fig. 10.4.*

and of trade agreements, which are designed for purposes suggested in their title. All these various means of channeling trade overlap in actual practice, but we shall be particularly interested in the last two.

Tariff classification

Tariffs may be considered from several points of view. When weighed as to purpose, they are divisible into *protective* and *revenue* classifications, the former designed to protect a home industry from foreign competition and the latter to yield taxes to the government responsible for the tariff. Applied to commodity movement, tariffs are either *import* or *export* measures—i.e., levied upon either incoming or outgoing merchandise. Considered as to actual duties, tariffs may be *specific,* wherein an exact sum per unit is levied upon the merchandise in question; *ad valorem,* wherein the levy is in terms of per cent of the value of that merchandise; or *compound,* wherein some type of combination of the specific and of the ad valorem duties is employed.

Tariffs and technically advanced non-Communist nations

The tariffs of technically advanced nations outside the iron curtain are essentially all import measures, and their levels have varied with both time and place. They stand today at heights that can best be generalized as more than moderately restrictive. This is true not only of the United States and Canada but of many nations in northwestern Europe and some in outlying areas.

The United States and Canada. Beginning with the time of its inception and climaxing in the Hawley-Smoot Tariff of 1930, the United States formalized a tariff policy which, while fluctuating, trended toward increasingly high protective barriers. During the past quarter century, however, the nation has reversed that trend; whereas the total duty collections amounted to nearly 20 per cent of all imports and almost 60 per cent of all dutiable imports in 1932, they now amount to approximately 5 per cent of all imports and 12 per cent of all dutiable imports.[3] These figures evidence a decline in United States tariffs that is not generally known. Indeed, tariffs of that country rank beneath those of most other leading commercial nations, including many Western European countries which long have been advocating freer trade on a world-wide basis. The existing measures, some of them still high, are applicable chiefly to foreign products which might compete with domestic manufacturing and agriculture. In some cases the tariff decline represents an apparent rather than a real concession, inasmuch as quotas and/or other control measures have been substituted to check the inward flow of undesired goods.

Canada, occupying a pivot position in world trade by maintaining membership in both the British Commonwealth and the dollar bloc, nevertheless maintains tariffs as high as those of the country's southern neighbor.

Northwestern Europe. The tariff policies of Western Europe vary among the several nations involved, with the lowest duties prevailing in the north, intermediate rates in the latitudinal center, and the highest measures in the south. As is true in the United States, these measures reflect domestic production, and they tend to be highest upon manufactured commodities in the industrial north, and upon harvested produce in the agricultural south. This suggests that many of these are protective measures for home industries, but a sizable number—probably more than in the United States—are also for purposes of revenue. Commodities taxed for revenue purposes are largely luxury items and "necessities" for which there is not an absolute need: coffee, tea, tobacco, wines and liquors, sugar, and petroleum products.

Outlying Technically Advanced Nations. The tariff policies of outlying technically advanced nations differ pronouncedly. In Argentina, tariffs are quite high, accounting for as much as 40 per cent of the total revenue to the national government. As might be anticipated, they are highest on agricultural and industrial materials competing with products of home industry, and of intermediate levels or essentially absent where relating to needed raw materials or products not in competition with domestic production. Chile also derives a sizable revenue from tariffs, but many of these are export measures assessed on outgoing copper, iron, and other minerals as well as on imports. The same generalization can be made of Venezuela, with petroleum and iron being particularly subject to export assessments. In contrast, Australia and the Union of South Africa tend to follow more moderate tariff policies and also to work closely with the member nations of the sterling bloc and the British Commonwealth.

Tariffs and underdeveloped nations

The trade of most underdeveloped nations is rather light, and many of their governments are relatively youthful, having gained independence only recently. Consequently, tariff policies are frequently not yet discernible. Such tariffs as do exist are chiefly revenue measures assessed against outgoing mineral and agricultural products purchased by foreigners, and upon imported luxuries. In Latin America, where independence is not a recent innovation, such duties are often responsible for 25 to 50 per cent of all revenues to the levying governments.

[3] W. S. Woytinsky, and E. S. Woytinsky, *World Commerce and Governments*, The Twentieth Century Fund, Inc., New York, 1955, pp. 262–264.

Tariffs and Communist nations

Trade is a monopoly of national governments in Communist nations. Tariffs therefore do not assume the importance here that they do in other areas of the world. In certain of the more active trading countries where adjustments must be made between world market price and domestic price of specified commodities, a form of tariff is employed. Measures like quotas also are used occasionally.

Trade agreements

Traditional Agreements. Trade agreements traditionally have been more or less documented "gentlemen's agreements" executed bilaterally, with each interested nation entering into a number of such relationships with different nations as partners. Almost invariably they involve mutually satisfactory policy deviations on the part of each contracting nation—deviations which are in effect concessions granted to the other nation or nations participating in the proceedings of a given agreement. Where negotiated under the protective umbrella of an affiliation like a currency bloc or a loose political confederation, they usually have been completed and executed with maximum ease and finesse. However, they have been employed as well where no such affiliations are involved. More recently, they have come increasingly to entail several nations, as is evidenced particularly by the General Agreement on Tariffs and Trade.

The General Agreement on Tariffs and Trade (GATT). Immediately after the last war an international trade confederation came into being largely as a result of efforts by the United States. GATT, as it has come to be known, is a loose contractual arrangement with no governing body but with a membership of thirty-five nations which aggregately are responsible for over 80 per cent of all international trade. This membership includes Australia, Austria, Belgium, Brazil, Burma, Canada, Ceylon, Chile, Cuba, Czechoslovakia, Denmark, the Dominican Republic, West Germany, Finland, France, Greece, Haiti, India, Indonesia, Italy, Japan, Liberia, Luxembourg, the Netherlands, New Zealand, Nicaragua, Norway, Pakistan, Peru, Southern Rhodesia, Sweden, Turkey, the Union of South Africa, the United Kingdom, and the United States.

The primary purpose of GATT is to promote conferences which might result in the reduction of tariffs or other import restrictions, in the facilitation of payments, and in the settling of complaints. Initially many of the conferences were bilateral but recently have come to involve several nations. Although too young to be examined critically, GATT does appear to be augmenting a trend toward more extensive and unhindered trade—a trend which commenced shortly after the Depression of the 1930s.

Other Agreements. Although GATT contains a membership reaching to most parts of the world, it is by no means the only such agreement in the world. In Chapter 7 we noted some of Western Europe's trade agreements, notably the Coal and Steel Community and the European Economic Community, both of which involve West Germany, France, the Netherlands, Belgium, Luxembourg, and Italy. Another such group in Europe is the Outer Seven, made up of the United Kingdom, Austria, Denmark, Norway, Portugal, Sweden, and Switzerland. This group is much less cohesive than the European Economic Community, and some experts question whether it is accomplishing any real purpose. Unlike the European Economic Community, the Outer Seven does not aspire to a common market surrounded by a common tariff wall. Instead, each member nation retains its own tariffs but makes certain exceptions to other members, so that a series of "gentlemen's agreements" replaces coordinated policy. Still another European-centered organization including tariff reduction among its objectives is the Organization for European Economic Cooperation (OEEC). It contains the thirteen nations already mentioned, plus Greece, Turkey, Spain, Ireland, and Iceland. This group now is being enlarged into a transatlantic organization called the Organization for Economic Cooperation and Development (OECD). It includes the eighteen European nations already mentioned, plus the United States and Canada. Its objectives are primarily the stimulation of world trade, partly through aid to underdeveloped economies and partly through other measures. Still other regional organizations include tariff reduction among their objectives. As might be expected, the most active and powerful members of such organizations usually are technically advanced.

THE FUTURE OF INTERNATIONAL TRADE

We are concerned here with the immediate future of international trade, the indices of which are now within view. Among such indices, both the *status quo* and the new must be considered.

The status quo

Over one-half of the value of all international commerce is made up of semifinished and finished goods, about one-fourth of agricultural foodstuffs and beverage commodities, and the remainder of crude materials, including fuels. This trade is oriented sharply toward the United States and the United Kingdom, which two nations account for well over one-fourth of the world's total international commerce. Together with the four next most active trading nations—West Germany, France, Canada, and the Netherlands—they account for nearly one-half of all such commerce.[4] As has been stated previously, these world leaders also are the nodal points concerning outlying areas of political and economic affiliation. The dollar bloc dominated by the United States accounts for about one-fourth of all trade, and the sterling bloc of the United Kingdom for nearly an additional one-fourth. The *status quo* is thus one of pronounced domination by a very few technically advanced nations of all world trade.

The challenge

The challenge to this traditionally evolved state of affairs is essentially twofold and involves: (1) the rising economic productivity and influence of some Communist nations and (2) the increasing measure of economic and political independence on the part of underdeveloped nations.

Potential Competition from Communist Nations. Notably since the death of Stalin, the Communist nations have begun to emerge from behind the iron curtain. In the realm of economics, they not only have offered limited technical assistance and loans to certain underdeveloped nations but have established a few trading relationships. At present, it appears that their economies are sufficiently embryonic in development that they will not offer a truly serious challenge to the *status quo* in the immediate future. It should be remembered, however, that essentially all Communist nations are areas of a chronic food shortage which becomes catastrophic during times of famine—more often than not, when the summer monsoons of Asia do not bring their usual moisture of that continent. To date, the various plans and other efforts have not been sufficient to overcome the pronounced and stubborn natural limitations to the agriculture of Communist nations, and agricultural output has not reached the planned specifications. In contrast, the build-up of manufacturing and mining facilities has been quite rapid, and usually in accordance with the various plans. Therefore it is logical to expect that the Soviet Union in particular might attempt to follow the time-honored footsteps of the United Kingdom and embark upon a policy of exchanging finished products and surplus minerals in the world markets for agricultural products, and thus hope to realize a twofold objective of satisfying home demand for such products and concomitantly gaining economic and political friendships abroad.

Increasing Independence of Underdeveloped Nations. The second aspect of the challenge to the *status quo* in foreign trade is more widespread in global distribution and less centrally organized than is the Communist movement. This is the expressed determination of many underdeveloped nations to attain an increased measure of economic self-sufficiency. Emphasis to date has been upon the

[4] However, the Soviet Union is rapidly becoming more active in trade, and in some years now replaces the Netherlands in sixth place (Fig. 10.3).

production of foods, fibers, and a small number of metals, chiefly iron and steel products.

The ultimate effect of such limited industrialization in underdeveloped lands is as yet a matter of argument. One school of thought maintains that this trend will mean a loss of markets and raw materials to nations now industrialized, whereas a second maintains that it will mean an increase in over-all standard of living as well as production—of demand as well as supply—and that the underdeveloped nations will assume roles regarding currently industrialized nations that are not dissimilar from the roles these nations currently enjoy with respect to each other. In other words, instead of a decline of factory output, the total world demand will be enlarged enough so that trade between nations will be even greater than it is now, and so that each nation will tend to market its specialties on an international basis.

TRADE AND LIVELIHOOD

Trade, like transportation, not only provides liaison among regions but also makes it possible for people to earn a living. It accounts for possibly as much as 10 per cent of the world's labor force and as much as 15 to 18 per cent in the most active commercial nations. It thus supports far more people than does any of the world's lesser productive occupations of minerals extraction, fishing, forest-products industries, and grazing, and is responsible for over one-half as many working personnel as there are in manufacturing.

REFERENCES

Alexander, John: "International Trade: Selected Types of World Regions," *Economic Geography*, **36:**95–115, 1960.

Berry, Brian J. L.: "The Impact of Expanding Metropolitan Communities upon the Central Place Hierarchy," *Annals of the Association of American Geographers*, **50:**112–116, 1960.

Grotewald, Andreas, and Lois Grotewald: "Some Geographic Aspects of International Trade," *Economic Geography*, **33:**257–266, 1957.

Hance, William A., and Irene S. Van Dongen: "Beira, Mozambique Gateway to Central Africa," *Annals of the Association of American Geographers*, **47:** 307–335, 1957.

———, and ———: "Dar Es Salaam, The Port and its Tributary Area," *Annals of the Association of American Geographers*, **48:**419–435, 1958.

Isaacs, Asher: *International Trade, Tariff and Commercial Policies.* Richard D. Irwin, Inc., Homewood, Ill., 1948. (Especially chaps. 14 and 18–25.)

MacDougall, Donald, and Rosemary Hutt: "Imperial Preference," *Economic Journal*, **64:**233–257, 1954.

Maze, Frederick: "The Chinese Maritime Customs Service: Brief Synopsis of Its Genesis and Development," *Far Eastern Economic Review*, **15:**330–335, 1953.

Meyer, F. V.: "Complementarity and the Lowering of Tariffs," *American Economic Review*, **46:**323–335, 1956.

Patton, Donald J.: "General Cargo Hinterlands of New York, Philadelphia, Baltimore and New Orleans," *Annals of the Association of American Geographers*, **48:**436–455, 1958.

"Tariff System in Japan," *Trade and Industry of Japan*, May, 1955, pp. 74–77.

Thoman, Richard S.: *Free Ports and Foreign-Trade Zones*, Cornell Maritime Press, Cambridge, Md., 1956.

Ullman, Edward L.: *American Commodity Flow*, University of Washington Press, Seattle, 1957.

Woytinsky, W. S., and E. S. Woytinsky: *World Commerce and Governments*, The Twentieth Century Fund, Inc., New York, 1955. (Especially chaps. 1–6.)

PART FOUR THE SOURCES AND APPLICATION OF ENERGY

Man looks to nature not only for raw materials and agents of production but also for most of the energy without which the Industrial Revolution would have been impossible. INTRODUCTION, PAGE 16

11 THE SIGNIFICANCE OF ENERGY

TECHNICALLY ADVANCED NATIONS ARE FAIRLY BURSTING WITH ENERGY, WITHOUT which their existence as such would be impossible. We simply push a button, and there it is—in factories, in homes, in transportation and communication equipment. Of course, much planning, past and present, and large-scale implementation of those plans are needed to make energy so readily available. Generations born to these conditions can realize only with some effort the amount of time once necessary to do life's simple chores under less favorable circumstances. Cutting the wood for the kitchen range and the pot-bellied stove in the living room (the bedrooms being unheated), pumping the water or drawing it from an open well by hand for human and animal use, hauling produce to town and groceries home by slow team and wagon—these activities were time-consuming. However, they were only prerequisites to the real work of the day—the dawn-to-daylight work in the fields with either animals or hand tools, or in the small artisan shops from which our gigantic factories have evolved. Most people in underdeveloped economies and some in technically advanced ones still live under such conditions.

Intensive use of inanimate energy has increased hand in hand with the rise of manufacturing—and with good reason, for both are direct outgrowths of the Industrial Revolution of previous centuries. However, we now are living in a century in which other productive occupations—and many of the service occupations also—are consumers of inanimate energy on an important and expanding scale. Similarly with use of energy by economies: once inanimate energy was considered almost the property of technically advanced economies, but now more and more underdeveloped economies are coming to appreciate its significance. Non-Communist and Communist nations have shown a keen appreciation of inanimate energy. Indeed, non-Communist nations of Western Europe and its offshoots first demonstrated its significance. Communist nations have emphasized it in their planned development. Because inanimate energy is so increasingly vital to so many different sectors of an economy as well as to so many different types of economy and so many specific economies, it is accorded a special section in this book.

In certain arid areas of the world the camel has not as yet been replaced as a means of locomotion. In other areas the rocket has sent a man whizzing around the earth in less than two hours. (British Information Services)

CONSUMPTION

Total consumption and uses

A recent survey by the United Nations indicates that the total world consumption of energy amounts to the equivalent of nearly 3,700 million metric tons of coal and that it is increasing at the rate of 4 per cent per year.[1] More than one-half of this energy is believed to be used in manufacturing, one-fifth in transportation, one-fifth in domestic heating, and the remainder in all other uses.

[1] *World Energy Supplies, 1955–1958,* United Nations Statistical Office, New York, 1960, p. 7.

National consumption

About four-fifths of all energy is consumed within technically advanced nations, and only about one-fifth within underdeveloped economies. The United States accounts for 36 per cent of the grand total; the Soviet Union, for 16 per cent; the United Kingdom, for 7 per cent; and West Germany, for 6 per cent (Fig. 11.1). Western Europe, including the United Kingdom and West Germany, consumes 20 per cent and eastern Europe about 7 per cent; nearly all European consumption occurs in the technically advanced countries. Japan, Canada, Argentina, Chile, Uruguay, the Union of South Africa, Australia, and New Zealand together use up an additional 7 per cent. Of the pronouncedly underdeveloped economies, Communist China probably leads. Reported data indicate that India is probably second, with 1.5 per cent of the world total.

Approximately 70 per cent of all energy consumption takes place within non-Communist nations, and the remainder within the Communist bloc. Russia alone accounts for over one-half of consumption by Communist nations.

Per capita consumption

The consumption of energy per inhabitant, shown in Figure 11.2, further emphasizes the overwhelming dominance of technically advanced nations, especially the United States and Europe. Besides the United States, individual nations of prominence include Canada, the United Kingdom, East Germany, Kuwait, and Czechoslovakia. Most of the remaining nations of northwestern Europe are high per capita consumers, as are the Soviet Union, Venezuela, the Union of South Africa, Australia, and New Zealand.

PRODUCTION

Man's ascendance from the animal level and the significance of inanimate energy to that ascendance is a familiar story, and therefore we shall content ourselves with the outline presented in Table 11.1. Note that before A.D. 1200 man's progress in obtaining inanimate energy is reckoned in millenniums,

In technically advanced countries energy is produced chiefly by inanimate means. This is a control board in a petroleum refinery. The man watches instruments; the apparatus does the work. (Standard Oil Company of New Jersey)

In underdeveloped countries the chief source of energy is still animate. In India these oxen move forward to raise a container of water, then back up to lower the container for another load. (Government of India Press Information Bureau)

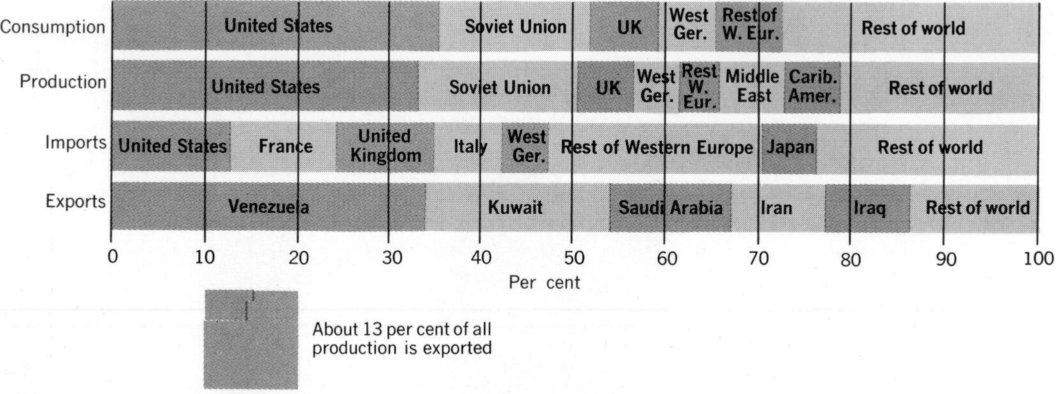

Figure 11.1 ***Consumption, production, import, and export of inanimate energy.*** *Note the dominance of technically advanced lands in consumption, production, and imports, and of technically underdeveloped lands in exports. The exports largely involve petroleum moving from the Middle East and Venezuela to Europe and the United States.*

TABLE 11.1

The chronicle of inanimate energy

Source of inanimate energy	*Approximate time of earliest specified use*	*Specified use*
Wood	Prehistoric	Domestic cooking and space heating; perhaps handicrafts.
Wood	Early historic	Handicrafts.
Wind	Early historic	Transportation.
Water	Perhaps early historic; certainly in classical antiquity	Handicrafts and crude mills.
Coal	Early thirteenth century	Space heating and domestic cooking.
Coal	Early eighteenth century	Steam engines for factories; coke for metal working.
Coal	Early nineteenth century	Steam engines for transportation.
Petroleum	Late nineteenth and early twentieth centuries	Space heating and lighting; domestic cooking; motors for transportation.
Electricity	Late nineteenth and early twentieth centuries	Motors for factory machines and transportation.*
Coal, petroleum wood, natural gas	Early twentieth century	Electricity generation in thermoelectric units.
Water	Early twentieth century	Electricity generation.
Electricity	Early twentieth century	Metal processing; space heating and lighting; domestic cooking.
Natural gas	Early twentieth century	Space heating; domestic cooking.
Nuclear energy	Middle twentieth century	Electricity generation and specialized uses.

* Experimentally.

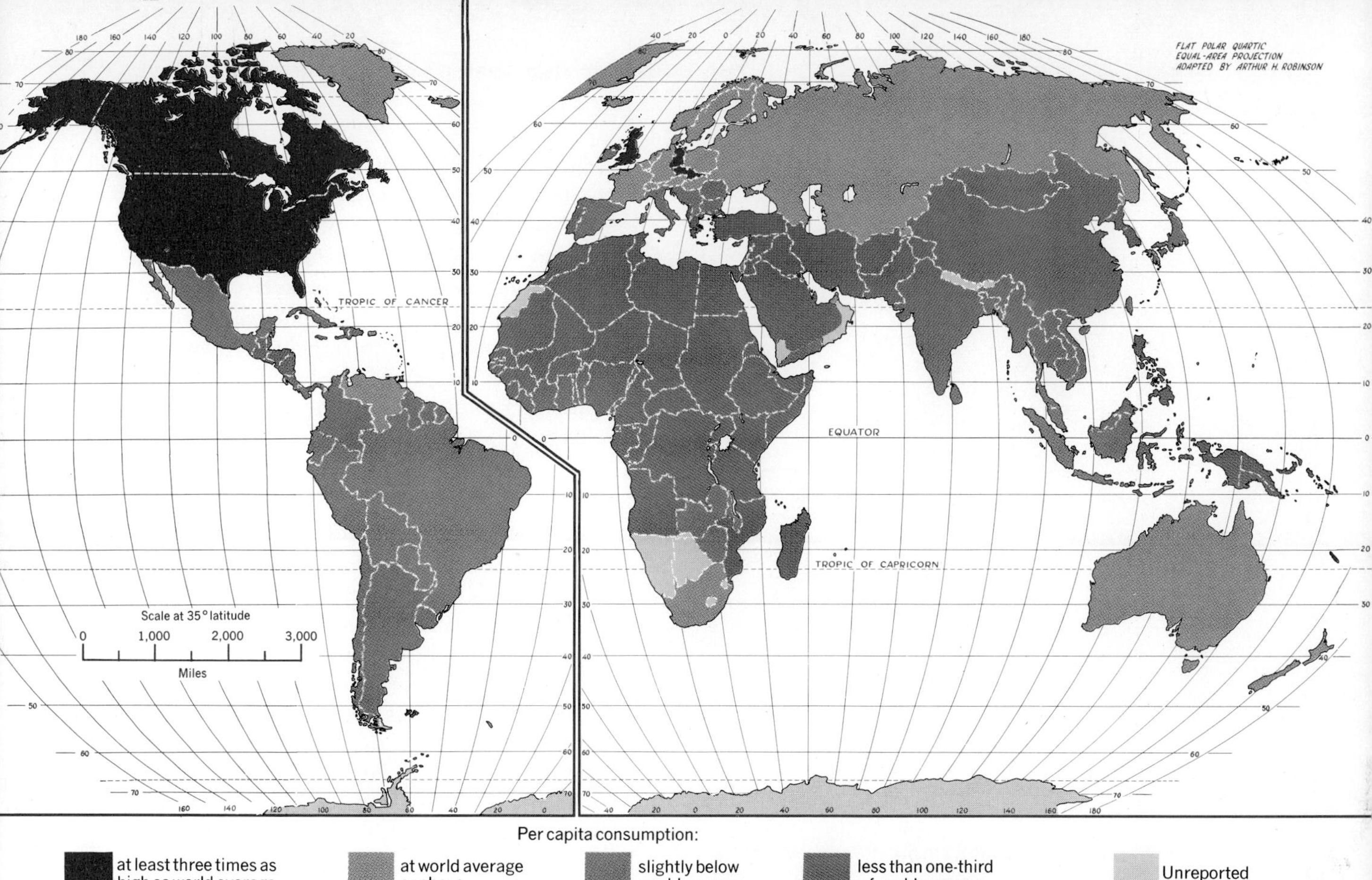

Figure 11.2 ***Per capita consumption of inanimate energy.*** *The rate in the United States is nearly seven times the world average, and in Canada nearly four times that average. Tiny, underdeveloped Kuwait is also among the leaders. Why? The reported per capita consumption in East Germany was only slightly higher than that reported for West Germany; the difference was sufficient to place it in a higher category, but some experts believe the East German statistics are exaggerated.*

between A.D. 1200 and 1800 in centuries, and since A.D. 1800 in fractions of centuries. Viewed in such a perspective, man's progress toward this particular objective appears on the threshold of a level of fruition that taxes our imagination. Here is an excellent illustration of the debt owed by current generations to those who have lived and worked and thought in times past.

Changes in energy sources for the United States are graphed in Figure 11.3. During the past century, this country has experienced two parallel trends—from wood to coal before 1900, and from coal to petroleum and natural gas since. Meanwhile, energy consumed has increased dramatically.

Current production

Nearly all energy comes from inanimate sources, and the remainder from human and animal muscles. Over one-half of the inanimate energy is derived from coal and coke, nearly one-third from petroleum, about one-seventh from natural gas, and a very small portion from hydroelectricity (Fig. 11.4). The sources for individual nations are seldom so diversified. Most of the leading manufacturing countries of Europe depend chiefly upon coal and coke. In Scandinavia and the high mountains of south central Europe, hydroelectric power is very important. In Italy, natural gas is the primary

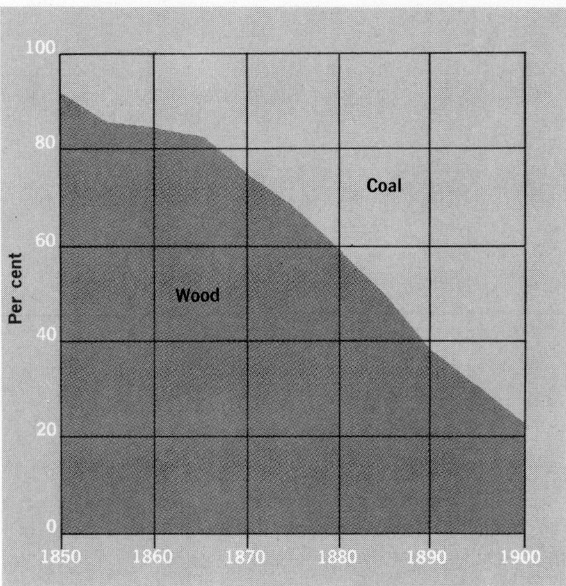

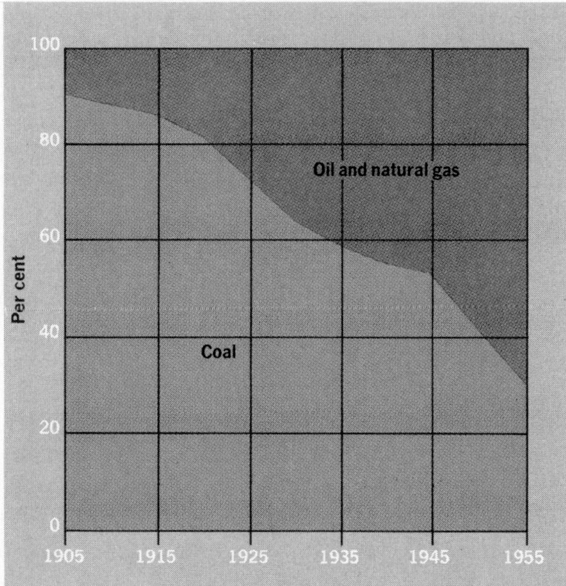

Figure 11.3 ***A century of change in prime sources of energy in the United States.*** *At all times, small amounts of energy came from sources not shown. (After* Annual Report, *Resources for the Future, Inc., 1957, pp. 28–29)*

source, with hydroelectricity second. Countries of eastern and southern Asia also depend largely upon coal, as do the Union of South Africa and Australia. In the Middle East, petroleum is essentially the sole source of energy, and it is very important in Caribbean America. The diversification in world energy sources is due largely to diversification in the United States and the Soviet Union, which two nations produce over one-half of all inanimate energy.

Irreplaceable and recurring sources

The common sources of inanimate energy—coal, petroleum, natural gas, and their associated materials—are of mineral origin. So is nuclear energy—as long as it comes from a natural element. These, supplying nearly all inanimate energy, are irreplaceable, i.e., used up with use. Although the extent of their reserves is not yet known and although existing estimates are constantly reevaluated as machinery and techniques become more efficient, definite limits to the reserves obviously must exist.

Recurring sources of energy—animate energy, wood, water, wind, and direct solar energy—can be replaced or recycled, or come from almost inexhaustible reservoirs, so that their reserves can be considered virtually limitless. With an increasingly technological world dependent so emphatically upon energy output, the time may well come when these sources will receive more attention than they now do.

TRADE AND TRANSPORTATION OF ENERGY

Transporting and storing most sources of inanimate energy are comparatively easy operations. Coal is easily stored—indeed, does not require protected storage. Furthermore, it lends itself to transfer by all surface carriers but pipelines and has been moved experimentally, as powder suspended in liquid, through these. However, it is bulky and heavy, especially when considered in terms of heat value per unit; when coal is being transported, only moderate amounts of actual energy are being moved. Petroleum and natural gas are more efficient in heat value and lend themselves to all types of surface transportation. However, they require carefully sealed, rather expensive storage tanks and/or underground facilities. Electricity, however, cannot be stored efficiently and cannot be transferred economically beyond 500 miles at existing cost-price ratios. Furthermore, it requires its own custom-built transport medium, the power line. Nuclear energy offers special promise in transportation. Containing tremendous amounts of energy per unit of weight, this source is very mobile and probably will become more so.

The transfer of most energy is a domestic operation. However, about 13 per cent of the world's total production is exported (Fig. 11.1). Such exports are comprised almost entirely of petroleum moving out of the Middle East and Caribbean America to technically advanced nations whose voracious consuming capacities exceed their own high rates of production. The United States, Western Europe, and Japan are the primary areas of energy receipt.

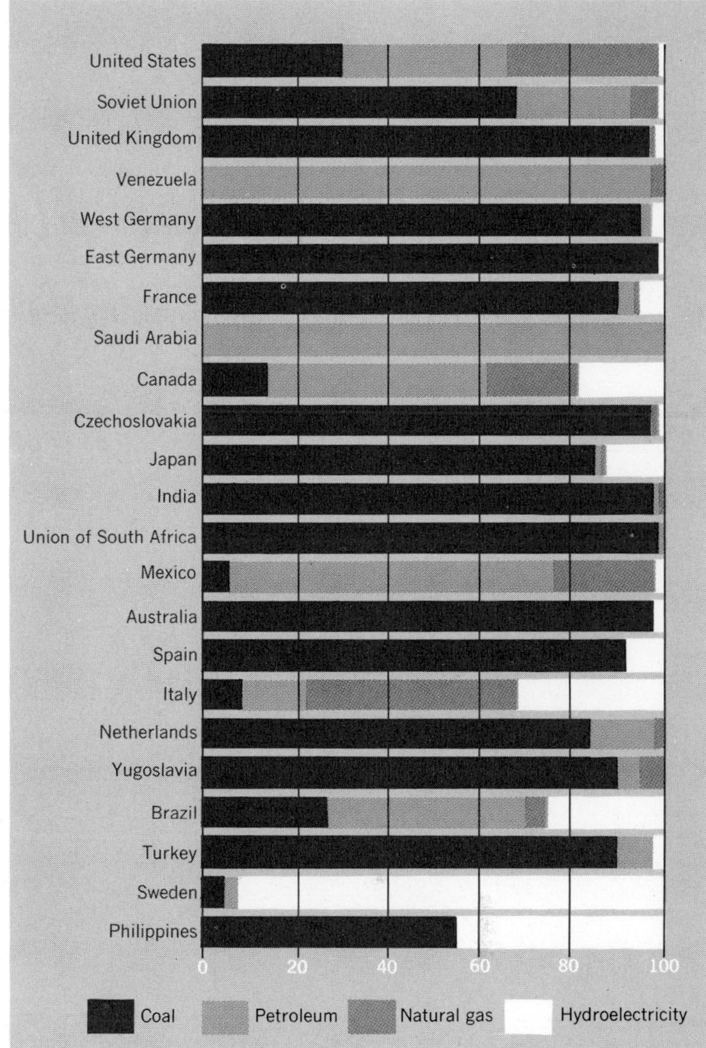

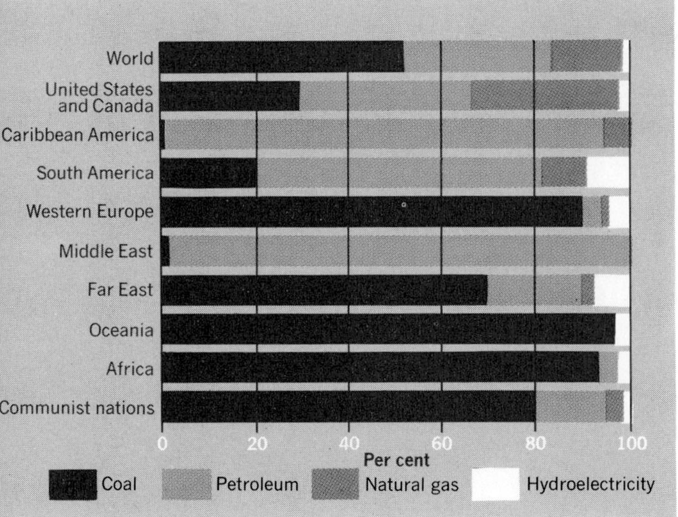

Figure 11.4 **Coal, petroleum, natural gas, and hydroelectricity as sources of inanimate energy for the world and selected regions and for selected nations.** *The arrangement above is by declining rank in production. Note that the graphs show consumption only of hydroelectric energy, not of all electrical energy. Much thermoelectric energy is obtained by burning coal, petroleum, or some other fuel. About 7 per cent of the world's inanimate energy comes from all electrical energy combined.*

REFERENCES

Cottrell, W. Frederick: *Energy and Society,* McGraw-Hill Book Company, Inc., New York, 1955.

Energy Resources of the World, U.S. Department of State, 1949.

Resources for Freedom: vol. 3, *The Outlook for Energy Sources,* President's Materials Policy Commission, 1952.

Schurr, Sam H., and Bruce C. Netschert: *Energy in the American Economy, 1850–1975,* The Johns Hopkins Press for Resources for the Future, Inc., Baltimore, 1960.

Thirring, Hans: *Power Production,* George G. Harrap & Co., Ltd., London, 1956. (Especially chap. 2 and summary.)

World Energy Supplies 1955–1958, United Nations Statistical Office, New York, 1960.

12 ENERGY FROM COAL

A CENTURY AGO, COAL WAS THE DIRECT OR INDIRECT SOURCE OF MOST OF THE world's inanimate energy. Now it supplies only about one-half of such energy. Yet the volume of its extraction is currently at an unprecedentedly high level, and there are indications that in the coming decades it might regain at least a part of its once-paramount world position.

NATURAL OCCURRENCE

Coal as a substance

Composition. Coal is made up of varying amounts of carbon, hydrogen, oxygen, nitrogen, and impurities. Some of its carbon remains solid when heated, and some gasifies, together with other gaseous elements. These gaseous materials are called *volatile matter,* which ignites easily but does not burn so continuously or smokelessly as does the fixed carbon. Moisture and incombustible ash, also present in most coal, are usually liabilities rather than assets to its usefulness. *Coke* is made from coal by heating and distilling it to drive off volatile matter and other impurities, so that a residue of solid, fixed carbon remains. Coke is used chiefly to smelt iron ore. The volatile matter of coal once was wasted, but now largely is conserved and subsequently utilized.

Classification. Coal is divided into several categories and subcategories on the basis of the heating value of its carbon. The resulting ranks range in ascending order of fixed carbon content from *lignite* through stages of *bituminous coal* to *anthracite* (Fig. 12.1). Coal of the lowest rank is brown and is high in ash and moisture content; in the other ranks the carbon is increasingly predominant.

Organic matter insufficiently decomposed and carbonized to qualify as coal is called *peat.*

Derivation. As was stated in Chapter 4, coal is preponderantly an organically derived sedimentary rock, although anthracite is often rather highly metamorphosed. Most geologists now subscribe to the theory that vegetation once luxuriant, from large trees to smaller plants, was submerged in swamps and other brackish waters and subsequently covered by other, usually

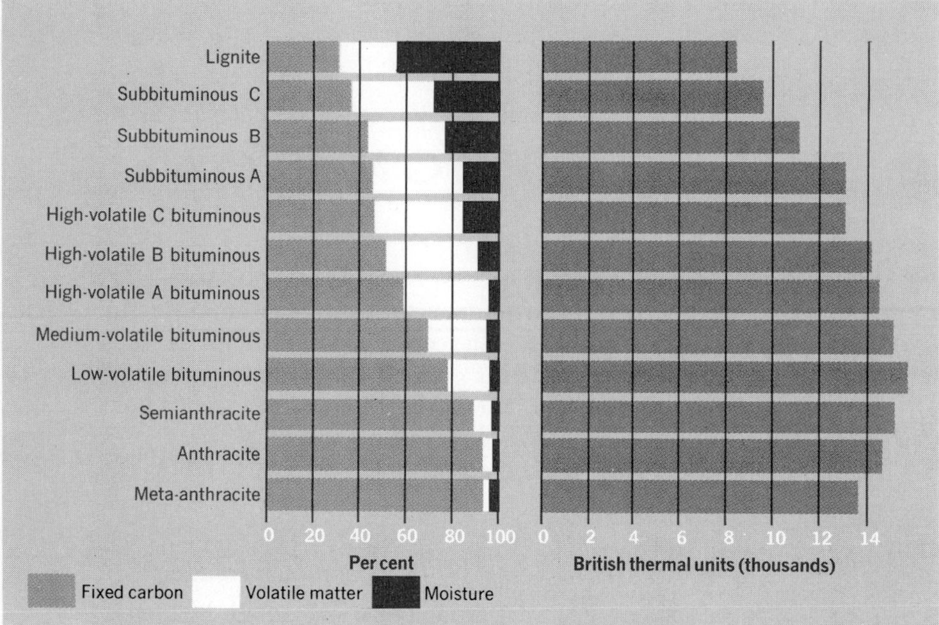

Figure 12.1 **Ranks of coal.** *The right-hand graph shows heat values in British thermal units per pound, and the left-hand graph indicates the amounts of fixed carbon, volatile matter, and moisture in each rank (assuming no ash content).* (After U.S. Geological Survey Professional Paper 100, *Washington, D.C.)*

nonorganic sediments. The initial accumulations were chiefly organic muck which eventually congealed into peat. In time an overburden of sedimentary beds resulted in compaction of these peaty materials, often to such an extent that initial thicknesses of more than 10 feet were compressed into coal beds of 1 foot or even less. If the deposition of overburden was accompanied or followed by crustal movement, the beds were often compacted even further.

Although peat is still being formed in some of the middle-latitude and high-latitude climates, most of the world's coal has resulted from sporadic rather than persistent developmental processes. Indeed, the most intensively exploited fields were formed during two successive periods of geologic history believed to have begun over 250 million years ago. Some coal has been accumulated in later periods of geologic time, but most of this is made up of low rank bituminous coal and lignite. The rate of replenishment of coal is so slow that it definitely may be regarded as an irreplaceable resource.

Reserves. Three highly significant generalizations can be made of the world's coal reserves: (1) they are primarily bituminous, (2) they are extensive, and (3) they are unevenly distributed among nations. As is indicated in Table 12.1, about four-fifths of known world reserves are anthracite and bituminous materials. Since the total reserves of anthracite are very small, the figure refers essentially to bituminous coals, many of which are of coking quality. The total coal and lignite reserves of at least 5 trillion tons[2] are sufficient to last for more than two thousand years at the current rate of extraction, which now is over 2½ billion metric tons per year. Over one-third of the total coal and lignite reserves are situated in the United States, nearly one-fourth in the Soviet Union, and possibly as much as one-fifth in Communist China. No other single nation is generally credited with more than 7 per cent of the world's reserves, although non-Communist European nations aggregately account for over 10 per cent of the total figure.

[2] Of course, while reliable, this is only *one* estimate; and, in matters as complex as this, other estimates by equally competent experts may be at variance with these figures. The generalizations among estimates, however, tend to agree, and differences are usually in degree rather than kind.

TABLE 12.1

World coal reserves, in millions of metric tons

Region and country	Anthracite, bituminous, and subbituminous coal	Lignite and brown coal	Total	Per cent of world total
Anglo-America				
United States	1,325,564	495,265	1,820,829	36.4
Canada	65,053	24,592	89,645	1.8
Total	1,390,617	519,857	1,910,474	38.2
Soviet Union	998,000	202,000	1,200,000	24.0
Asia				
Communist China	1,011,000	600	1,011,600	20.2
India	62,143	2,833	64,976	1.3
Japan	16,218	473	16,691	0.3
Others	7,214	349	7,563	0.2
Total	1,096,575	4,255	1,100,830	22.0
Europe				
Germany*	279,516	56,758	336,274	6.7
United Kingdom	172,200	n†	172,200	3.4
Poland	80,000	18	80,018	1.6
Czechoslovakia	6,450	12,500	18,950	0.4
France	11,224	125	11,349	0.2
Portugal	6,036	4,200	10,236	0.2
Others	16,619	14,289	30,908	0.6
Total	572,045	87,890	659,935	13.1
Africa				
Union of South Africa	68,014	0	68,014	1.4
Others	1,720	210	1,930	n
Total	69,734	210	69,944	1.4
Oceania				
Australia	13,900	39,200	53,100	1.1
Others	57	489	546	n
Total	13,957	39,689	53,646	1.1
Latin America				
Colombia	10,000	0	10,000	0.2
Chile	2,116	n	2,116	n
Others	1,617	4	1,621	n
Total	13,733	4	13,737	0.2
World total	4,154,661	853,905	5,008,566	100.0

* Most of the bituminous and anthracite coal is in West Germany, and most of the lignite is in East Germany.
† Negligible.
SOURCE: *Coal Resources of the United States,* United States Geological Survey Circular 293, 1953, p. 40.

Natural occurrence and economic geography

Like all commodities, coal is of maximum significance to economic geography when considered with respect to its existing or potential capacity to satisfy certain economic needs and wants. This capacity, in turn, depends largely upon the feasibility, under existing or potential cost-price ratios, of (1) extracting the coal and (2) transporting it to market. Natural conditions which notably affect the feasibility of extraction are the types of coal sought, the manner of its present-day occurrence, and the associated natural features which might aid or hinder extraction. The conditions affecting transportation are chiefly the location of deposits with respect to existing or potential markets; secondary considerations are the associated natural features which might aid or hinder such transportation.

Feasibility of Extraction. TYPES OF COAL SOUGHT. Lignites, with their comparatively low carbon content and relatively high proportion of unwanted ash and moisture, are generally utilized only where the cost of obtaining other fuels is prohibitively high. The lower ranks of bituminous coals are almost in the lignite category of demand and are bypassed unless their extraction becomes absolutely necessary. Anthracite, once in appreciable demand as a household fuel in the United States and some few other nations, has suffered during the past half century in competition with fuel oil and natural gas. The better-quality bituminous coals, which have the highest Btu content of all coal (Fig. 12.1) and which coke to maximum satisfaction, are the most highly prized. Other factors being equal, the world demand is greatest for the high-quality bituminous coal, with less demand for intermediate ranks of bituminous material and least for low-rank bituminous, lignite, and anthracite reserves.

MODE OF OCCURRENCE. Since coal is a sedimentary rock, it has been deposited in *seams* which, although sometimes folded or fractured, are more continuous than are accumulations of most materials that have been deposited or reworked by underground water. These seams may range in thickness from a mere trace to over 100 feet but usually are from 1 to 12 feet thick. Some seams may be very extensive horizontally—the Pittsburgh seam, for example, underlies a surface of more than 14,000 square miles—whereas others extend for a few square feet or even less. More often than not several seams, interspersed with other sedimentary beds, exist at levels ranging from actual outcrops to depths so low that as yet they have not been carefully estimated. Coals of bituminous and lower rank tend to be less disturbed stratigraphically than are anthracitic and related materials, the quasi-metamorphosed deposits of which are often found as unevenly compressed folds and other structural deformations.

MINING TECHNIQUES. Most coal mining takes place at depths of 1,500 feet or less beneath the land surface, although mines of more than 4,000 feet in depth are worked. Nearly all mining fields are in reality composites of individual seams existing at different levels. Specific extraction is done by shaft-and-tunnel, slope, drift, open-pit and auger methods, and experiments are now being conducted in underground gasification and hydraulic mining. The first involves the sinking of vertical shafts from the land surface and the opening of tunnels from these shafts along the exploited seams. The slope method generally resembles the shaft-and-tunnel method, except that a sloping rather than a vertical entrance provides access to the coal. The drift mining is to be seen in areas where coal beds outcrop either on level surfaces or along stream valleys, etc., and differs from the first two only in that the preliminary sinking of a shaft or opening of a slope is unnecessary. Open-pit mining, sometimes called strip mining, or stripping, entails the removal, usually by mechanized equipment, of unwanted surface materials overlying shallow seams and the direct exploitation of the unearthed coal. Auger mining, a comparatively recent innovation, involves the gouging of coal seams with giant mechanized augers. It may be carried on either above or below ground level. Still in the laboratory and pilot-plant stages are the gasification of underground coal and the subsequent collection of the gas for later use. A sixth technique, called hydraulic mining, now is being used especially in the Soviet Union. It involves the washing down of coal faces with powerful jetstreams of water.

NATURAL CONDITIONS ASSOCIATED WITH EXTRACTION. We have discussed previously the critical importance of rock structure to coal mining. Besides the structural arrangement of the coal and its adjacent beds, however, there are other natural features which usually affect coal extraction. Three of the most relevant of these are: (1) rigidity of the coal and its proximate materials, (2) elevation and slope conditions, and (3) the presence of water in excessive quantities. The rigidity of coal affects the ease of its removal regardless of method; the rigidity of adjacent materials is important to the ease of lifting the overburden in open-pit mining; and the rigidity of both the coal and the nearby beds is significant in the stability of shafts and tunnels in underground mining. Elevation and associated slope conditions are especially important to underground mining, for somehow the loosened materials must be brought to the land surface—sometimes a costly operation. Water, although a necessary agent to some types of mining, is a serious deterrent to such extraction when present in excessively large amounts within or near the mined strata, and one of the most serious and persistent problems in both underground and surface coal mining in some areas is controlling inundation.

Climate is a natural feature that also affects mining, particularly the open-pit mining of the middle and high latitudes, where such operations may be discontinued for the winter months. Areas subject to continuously heavy precipitation, notably to sudden, torrential storms, are in constant danger of inundation of their mines.

Feasibility of Transportation. Abstract statements concerning the feasibility of coal transportation are of little value, and therefore a more detailed treatment of this subject will be postponed until specific regions are discussed later in this chapter. Suffice it to say here that usable but unexploited reserves are usually found in places which are too far from mass markets, too inaccessible because of rugged terrain, and/or too inaccessible because of harsh climates, to warrant their current exploitation.

These are some aspects of the mechanized mining of coal: Above, a modern underground auger, from which the mined coal is taken to ground level by conveyor belts. Below, open-pit mining, or stripping. Usually two machines are in operation—a large one to remove the overburden which tends to be present in far greater amounts than coal, and a smaller one to remove and load the coal. Some of these machines are big enough to hold an entire automobile in their loading buckets. (Peabody Coal Company)

WORLD CONSUMPTION, PRODUCTION, AND TRADE

Each year over 2½ billion tons of coal are extracted and consumed. Despite coal's significance as a commercial source of energy, it does not enter very actively into international trade, because the major consuming nations draw heavily from their own reserves (Fig. 12.2). Only about 6 per cent of all mined coal is exported. Such commerce as does exist is surprisingly diverse in global extent. Among the more conspicuous trade flows are those from the United States to Canada, amounting to over 10 per cent of all internationally traded coal, and from the United States and lesser suppliers to West Germany, France, and Italy, each of which accepts upward or downward of 10 per cent of all coal entering world markets.

Some nations—notably Belgium and to a lesser degree West Germany, the Netherlands, and France—are active in the reexport of coal, although the total amount so traded is comparatively small. West Germany, interestingly, both imports and exports sizable quantities of coal, but not much of these are actually reexports. Instead, United States coal is imported and German coal exported. Coal bunkering (storing at key ports and railway terminals for refueling), a leading activity in the heyday of the coal-fired steamship, now is comparatively modest.

Until recently, there was no noteworthy coal trade among Communist nations, since nearly all the more active Communist economies are quite well endowed naturally with coal deposits. However, both Poland and the Soviet Union recently have emerged as coal exporters of more than passing significance, and coal-deficient East Germany is an importer of some consequence. Most of this coal trade is among the Communist nations, but some passes through the iron curtain, particularly in Europe.

On the whole the world coal output now is slowly rising. International trade in coal fluctuates from year to year, but generally is not rising so fast as production.

COAL AND THE ECONOMIES OF INDIVIDUAL NATIONS

On the world scene, coal production is experiencing unusual change. In the United States and Western Europe, it is declining relatively in competition with petroleum products, natural gas, and in some cases hydroelectricity. In other parts of the world, however, its output is on the rise. This is especially true of such underdeveloped but expanding economies as Communist China and India. Indeed, the output of Communist China, included in the "miscellaneous" category only a few years ago, now reportedly is behind only that of the Soviet Union and the United States. However, because Communist nations have been known to exaggerate their output in their embryonic years, we shall appraise that output somewhat more cautiously than we would under other circumstances.

The Soviet Union

The Soviet Union is a nation in which the production of both coal and peat is expanding rapidly, the output of coal having increased seventeenfold and peat more than ninefold since 1928, the year of initiation of the five-year plans. The current coal output of the Soviet Union exceeds that of the United States and probably will continue to do so, partially because the United States has turned to other sources of fuel to keep much of its economy active. Slightly under one-third of the Soviet Union's coal output is lignite, and most of the remainder is bituminous coal.

Consumption. Coal and lignite supply over 65 per cent of the inanimate energy used in the Soviet Union. Demand for it stems mainly from the manufacturing industries, particularly the iron and steel plants, as well as from households and transportation media. Inasmuch as most of the population and associated industries are in European Russia and most of the more inexpensively mined coal is in Asian Russia, a regional consumption-production imbalance that now is only embryonic may assume serious proportions as the economy matures.

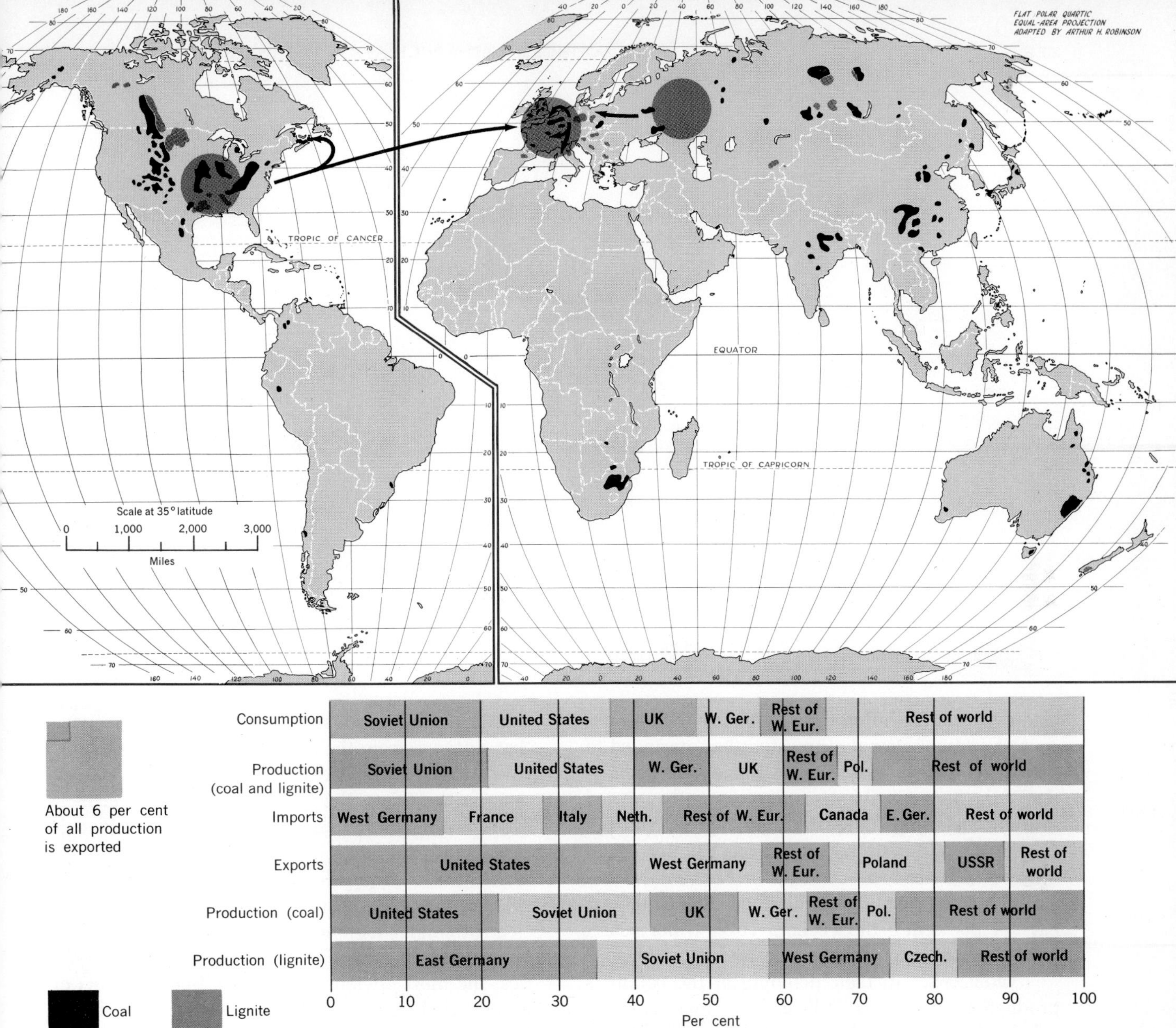

Figure 12.2 **Consumption, production, import, and export of coal, including lignite.** *Now that coal has largely given way to petroleum products as a fuel in ocean shipping, the volume of its world trade has declined sharply. Communist China appears to be increasing its coal output very rapidly, and preliminary reports indicate that it may rank in output behind only the Soviet Union and the United States. Circles show places of heavy consumption.*

Production and Transportation. COAL FIELDS. The coal fields of European Russia were rather well known during czarist times, whereas those east of the Ural Mountains have largely been developed and, in some cases, discovered, since the 1917 revolution. The old Donets field, situated to the north of the Black Sea, was the primary source of domestic coal in czarist and postrevolutionary days, accounting as late as 1928 for nearly 80 per cent of the Russian annual output (Fig. 12.3). It is still the

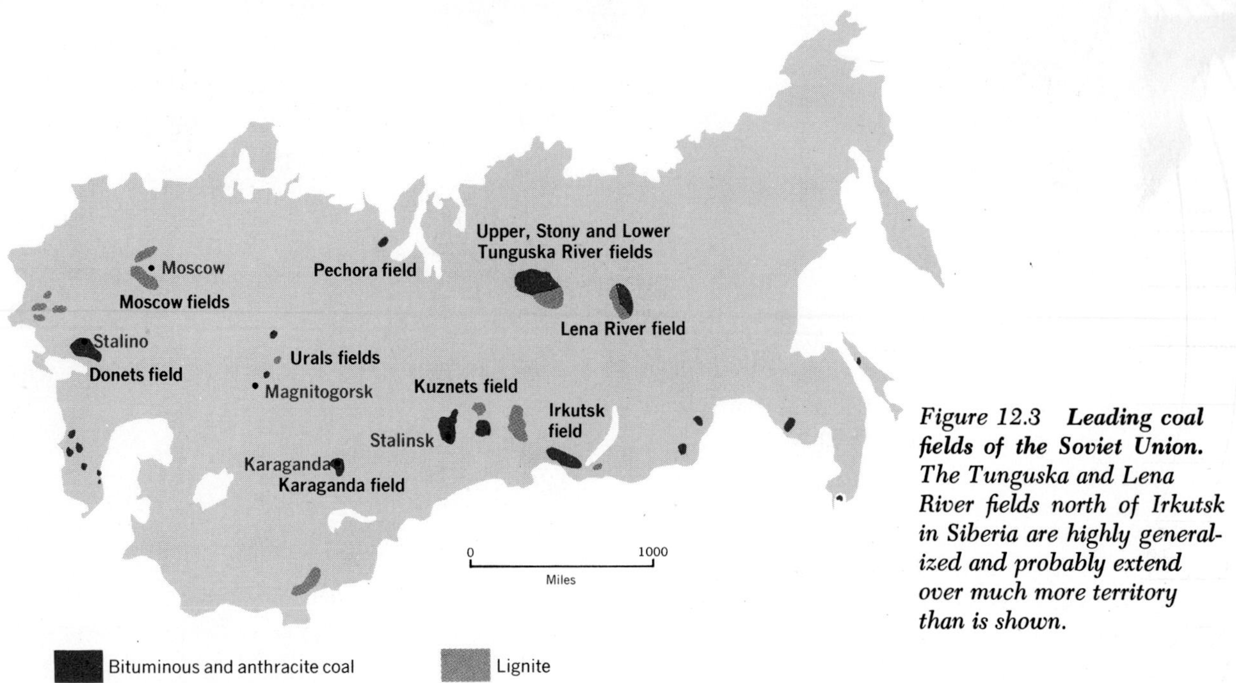

Figure 12.3 ***Leading coal fields of the Soviet Union.*** *The Tunguska and Lena River fields north of Irkutsk in Siberia are highly generalized and probably extend over much more territory than is shown.*

leading producer but now supplies less than 40 per cent of a total national output that has expanded to over seventeen times its 1928 volume. The remainder of the Soviet coal now comes from rather varied sources, including the Asian Kuznets field (15 per cent of the nation's total), the Urals (12 per cent), Moscow (10 per cent), Irkutsk (7 per cent), Karaganda (6 per cent), the scattered fields to the far east (4 per cent), the Pechora (over 3 per cent), as well as lesser sources.[3]

PROBLEMS. In their planning of the country's production of coal as well as other materials, the rulers of the Soviet Union cannot overlook cost-price ratios, although short-run attention to them is not so pronounced as in the Western World. The costs in this case are in large measure those of transportation; for, as has been stated, the comparatively expensive railways haul most of the freight of the Soviet Union, thereby connecting fields that are thousands of miles apart. For example, the Kuznets field is well over 1,000 miles from the Urals industrial region, and over twice that distance from the Donets basin and from Moscow (Fig. 12.3). The developing Irkutsk field is even farther from Europe—some 800 miles farther. Transporting coal these great distances by land is costly, and the Soviet planners have tried to minimize such costs by developing industrial areas as close as possible to the sources of their energy.

Although theoretically sound, this thinking has been partially altered in the light of certain realities, the most obvious of which is that the costs of mining coal vary sharply among the leading fields. For example, the cost of extracting 1 metric ton of coal in the Donets is approximately 93 rubles; in the Kuznets, about 63 rubles; in Karaganda, 47 rubles.[4] Although there are significant differences in the quality of coal extracted, the relatively high cost of mining in the deep, rather steeply inclining, and often folded fields of the Donets is a marked

[3] Promyshlennost S.S.S.R., *Statisticheskii Sbornik,* 1957, p. 142.

[4] V. F. Vasiutin, *Razmeshchenie Proizvoditel'nykh Sil S.S.S.R. v Shestoi Piatiletke.* One ruble equaled 25 cents in United States currency at the official rate of exchange at the time of this writing.

factor in the relative (but not absolute) decline of that producing field.

TYPES OF COAL. Of the coal produced in the Soviet Union, a surprisingly large amount—about 17 per cent—is anthracite, mined chiefly in the Donets and the Kuznets fields. It is used largely for space heating. Some 55 per cent is bituminous coal, and the remaining 28 per cent is lignite. The bituminous ranks are mined in almost every field of the Soviet Union, whereas the poorer brown coal is obtained especially in the vicinity of Moscow.

MINING METHODS AND EFFICIENCY. Except for auger mining, the standard underground and open-pit techniques are employed in the Soviet Union. Open-pit mining, supplying nearly 18 per cent of all production, is found especially in the Asian fields. Still another technique, hydraulic mining, reportedly has been introduced into the Donets, Kuznets, and Karaganda fields, and is now estimated to be producing at least 4 million tons annually. This method involves the use of water jets to cut and float the coal in a manner not unlike the hydraulic mining for precious metals employed in other areas of the world. Its efficiency is said to be such that between 5 and 6 metric tons of coal are produced per man-shift—an average below the 8 tons per man-shift in the coal-mining industry of the United States but over three times the 1.6 tons per man-shift now characteristic of the Soviet Union and the most efficient mining nations of Western Europe.

Reserves. The known reserves of coal in the Soviet Union exceed those of any other nation but the United States. They are found chiefly in Asia, the Kuznets field accounting for nearly one-fourth of the total, and the nebulous, rather indefinitely known beds in the vicinity of the Upper, Stony, and Lower Tunguska Rivers and the Lena River comprising an additional one-fourth. Far below these in volume is the Donets field (with about 6 per cent of the nation's coal), the Irkutsk field (with another 6 per cent), the Karaganda field (with nearly 4 per cent), as well as lesser deposits, the more significant of which are at widely separated places in Asian Russia.

The United States

The United States annually consumes approximately one-sixth of the world's coal output, produces a surplus that varies with economic conditions but usually ranges between 5 and 10 per cent of its annual production, and sends that surplus mainly to Canada and Western Europe. Although outstanding in world competition, that production is only about five-sixths of the volume once attained during peak output periods of the two world wars. Domestic reserves, and internal productive capacity as well, are extensive, and consequently the United States investment overseas in coal production is very, very moderate. Indeed, the current limitations upon home production are those of demand rather than of existing or potential supply.

Consumption. The nearly 400 million metric tons of coal consumed each year in the United States is essentially all bituminous coal. Two major demand sources exist for this coal, and each accounts for over one-fourth of the annual consumption: (1) rapidly growing thermoelectric plants—utilizing coal to heat water to run giant turbines which, in turn, energize huge electric generators—have become unusually efficient in recent years and are the newest source of major demand; (2) the traditional coking facilities of the iron and steel industry have retained their long-held outstanding status as coal consumers. The remaining one-half of the demand for coal is shared on a much smaller individual scale by manufacturing plants and domestic households using the substance chiefly for space heating; by railroad trains; by steam vessels; and by other diverse consuming media. It is perhaps needless to add that the shift from coal to petroleum products and natural gas for many transportation and space-heating purposes has meant a serious decline in coal consumption—a decline now being offset partially by the rising purchases of the thermoelectric industries.

Production. Bituminous-coal and anthracite fields of the United States include the *Appalachian field,* the *Eastern Interior field,* the *Western Interior field,*

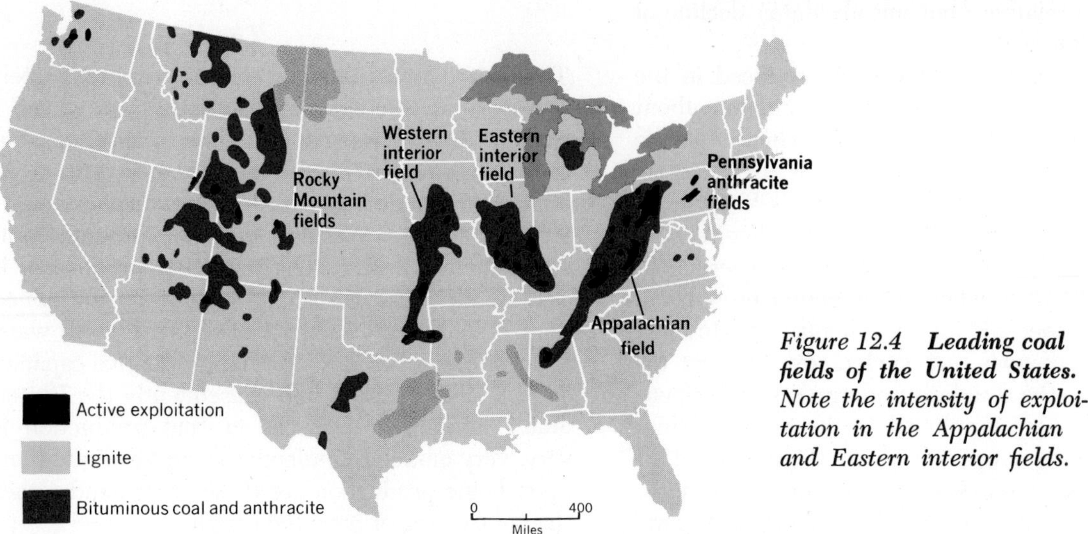

Figure 12.4 **Leading coal fields of the United States.** *Note the intensity of exploitation in the Appalachian and Eastern interior fields.*

and the *Rocky Mountain field,* as well as less extensive deposits (Fig. 12.4). A general tendency exists for the rank of the bituminous coals in these deposits to decrease progressively from east to west.

In addition to the black coals, rather continuous lignite fields underlie the northern Great Plains, being situated notably in North Dakota and to a lesser degree in South Dakota and Montana. Discontinuous reserves also exist in a broad area stretching from the lower Rio Grande River in Texas to western Tennessee and southwestern Alabama (Fig. 12.4).

THE APPALACHIAN FIELD. Nearly three-fourths of all bituminous coal and essentially all the anthracite of the United States are obtained from the Appalachian field, one of the most favorably and extensively endowed coal fields in the entire world.

The bituminous-coal beds are remarkably undisturbed geologically from Kentucky and West Virginia northward to Pennsylvania, although they have undergone appreciable faulting and folding to the south. Most range in thickness from 1 to 9 feet, although some exploited by open-pit methods may be thinner. They are surprisingly continuous; in western Pennsylvania, the famous Pittsburgh seam, more or less uninterrupted in the vicinity and to the south of the city after which it is named, long provided the state's bituminous-coal production and even now accounts for over 40 per cent of that output.[5] The depth of exploited seams in the northern portion of the Appalachian field is seldom in excess of 1,000 feet, and not infrequently ranges from 200 to 500 feet. In the southern Appalachians, coal is mined at generally similar or slightly lower depths, but it is in thinner, less continuous seams and hence is not so readily extracted.

Thus the rock structure of the Appalachian field, particularly of the northern two-thirds of that field, could scarcely have lent itself more completely to modern mechanized mining if it had been drawn and constructed to human specifications. Its comparative stability, combined with the exploitability of so many of its seams, is almost a silent invitation to the machines which are now commonplace in both underground and surface mining, and which account for about 90 per cent of the actual cutting of the coal mined underground and essentially all of the removal of that mined by open-pit

[5] For an informative account of selected geographic aspects of coal mining in western Pennsylvania, see George F. Deasy and Phyllis R. Griess, "Some New Maps of the Underground Bituminous Coal Mining Industry of Pennsylvania," *Annals of the Association of American Geographers,* **47**:336–349, 1957; *ibid.*, "Geographical Significance of Recent Changes in Mining in the Bituminous Coal Fields of Pennsylvania," *Economic Geography,* **33**:283–298, 1957.

and auger methods. A better harmony of exploitation between nature and man would be difficult to find.

The actual exploitation is very erratic in distribution. West Virginia (which originates nearly one-third of all bituminous coal produced in the United States) and Pennsylvania (which accounts for more than one-fifth) are the outstanding leaders in both the Appalachian field and the nation. States producing less include Kentucky (encompassing portions of both the Appalachian and Eastern Interior fields), Ohio, Virginia, Alabama and most of the adjoining states possessing some share of Appalachian coal.

The reserves of bituminous coal in the Appalachian field make up more than 20 per cent of the nation's total known supply of all coal, including lignite.

The anthracite deposits are situated in the folded and faulted structures of the ridges and valleys of eastern Pennsylvania and, in lesser degree, western Virginia. Nearly 95 per cent of the nation's reserves are in the Pennsylvania locations, and at current rates of extraction these should last for more than eight centuries.

THE EASTERN INTERIOR FIELD. Most of the coal mined in the United States but not in the Appalachian field is extracted in the Eastern Interior field, which originates over 15 per cent of the nation's total annual production. Illinois, Kentucky, and Indiana are the primary states involved. The field itself underlies terrain that is more or less undulating except where the beds of the Ohio River and its tributaries have become rather sharply incised. Exploited seams range in depth from essentially nothing to 1,000 feet or even more. Rather paradoxically, mining has shifted southward during the past century, with more coal exploited in southern Illinois than in the upper portions of the state. This shift is due partially to the quality of the coal, which does not coke satisfactorily, and must be mixed with Appalachian coal for most steelmaking purposes. The northern markets of Great Lakes iron and steel centers are thus not so attractive as they otherwise would be.

Although Illinois contains more high-quality bituminous coal than any other state in the United States, the known coal supply of the Eastern Interior field amounts only to about 10 per cent of all known national reserves.

THE WESTERN INTERIOR FIELD. The coal measures of this field outcrop along the southern, western, and northern margins of the Ozarks Mountains, dipping in their respective directions away from that upland area. Missouri, Oklahoma, Kansas, Iowa, and Arkansas are the primary producing states. The individual beds are thinner and of a poorer quality than those of the two fields previously discussed, and their reserves are about equal to those of the Eastern Interior field—in other words, about 10 per cent of the nation's total. A very small portion of anthracite is present in Arkansas, but the remainder is bituminous coal. Most of the exploited seams are at or near the series of coal outcrops, and coal-mining sites thus form an irregular arc pattern to the south, west, and north of the Ozarks.

THE ROCKY MOUNTAIN FIELD. Except for the anthracite deposits, the three fields previously discussed are more or less in horizontal arrangement, and the beds are thus generalized as being relatively continuous. The Rocky Mountain field, however, is in reality a series of fragments of once continuous seams that have become fractured and torn in the processes of mountain building. Encompassing portions of Colorado, New Mexico, Arizona, Utah, Wyoming, Montana, and Idaho, this field is the largest of all the bituminous coal fields of the United States with respect to its total physical area; but because of its fragmented nature, it is not actually so extensive as is suggested by that area. Nevertheless, it does contain the largest reserves of bituminous coal in the nation, although much is of subbituminous rank. Well over one-fourth of the coal reserves of the United States is found here, about three-fifths of it being low-rank bituminous material. In addition, a small reserve of anthracite occurs in western Colorado, and a trace in northern New Mexico. The bituminous-coal seams are to be found at varied depths because of the deformation of the sedimentary beds of which they are a part, and range from vertical to horizontal positions.

Their depths exceed in several places the cutoff limits of 4,000 feet sometimes used in estimating reserves. Utah, Wyoming, Colorado, and Montana are the major producing states.

LESSER BITUMINOUS-COAL FIELDS. Michigan contains a small coal supply known as the Northern field, Texas has a somewhat larger deposit in its Southwestern field, and Washington possesses a still larger but nevertheless comparatively moderate reserve sometimes designated as the Pacific field. None of these, however, is of much more than local significance in both production and reserves.

LIGNITE FIELDS. The world's largest known deposits of lignite are situated at shallow depths in North Dakota, Montana, and South Dakota, and amount to approximately one-fourth of the coal and lignite reserves of the United States (Fig. 12.4). By far the largest portion of these reserves lies in North Dakota. A second, less continuous, and much smaller field extends across the Mississippi River from southeastern Texas. Despite such ample reserves, however, lignite production in this country is very small, being unable to compete commercially with the output of better-located, higher-quality bituminous coals.

UNITED STATES MINING COMPANIES AND METHODS. Although coal mining in the United States, like most other industries, is experiencing tendencies toward centralization, such tendencies are not so pronounced as in some other industries. To be sure, there are large companies engaged in coal extraction; but they are not the focally organized giants of production such as are found, for example, in copper mining, petroleum recovery, iron and steel manufacture, and automobile fabrication. Some coal mines are owned or otherwise controlled by producers of industrial metals.

With respect to mining methods, there are now nearly ten thousand coal mines (*mines*, not *companies*) now in operation. Some 3½ per cent of these produce nearly 45 per cent of all coal and mainly are controlled by companies of appreciable financial standing.

Underground mines account for essentially three-fourths of all extracted coal and strip mines for almost all of the remainder. Strip mines, scarcely in existence before the First World War, increased both absolutely and proportionately until the end of the Second World War and since that time have more or less leveled off in both numbers and output. The relative efficiency of strip mining over underground methods with respect to the business of removing coal from the ground has been proved; what has not been demonstrated to universal satisfaction in many areas is that the overburden removed for stripping purposes can (or will) be replaced fully so that portions of the nation do not become "rural slums."

Yields from auger mining as yet are far less than 1 per cent of the total, but this method offers future promise, if only because of its efficiency: one man mines slightly more than 7 short tons of coal per day in underground mines, almost 18 tons per day in strip mines, and over 25 tons daily with auger equipment.

Transportation. Coal today has an unprecedented orientation toward producer-goods industries. The decline in demand for coal as an agent of household heating has removed a partial orientation toward direct consumption, and although its influence is still felt by individual human beings, its current movement from mine to market is chiefly toward industries rather than toward populations. The direction of movement is still toward the heavily populated sections of the country, which are also the leading areas of manufacturing (Fig. 12.5).

SIGNIFICANCE OF THE RAILROADS. Although it has declined slightly in relative position over the past quarter century, the railroad is a primary coal-hauling medium, accounting for about 75 per cent of all mined coal; about 12 per cent is carried by water craft, 10 per cent by truck, and the remainder used at the mines (Fig. 12.6).[6] The railroad is more vital to shipments in the Western Interior and Rocky Mountain fields, where the long distances to

[6] It should be remembered, however, that these figures apply to freight loaded at the mines and that not all such coal moves to its ultimate destination via the medium into which it is initially placed.

Figure 12.5 ***Coke-making plants in the United States.*** *The plants are called ovens. The hollow circles show location of* beehive *ovens—crude contraptions usually made of brick in which coal is distilled inefficiently into coke, with all of the volatile matter lost to the atmosphere. These are found chiefly in western Pennsylvania and Virginia. They are small, hiring only a few workers. The solid dots and brown squares show by-product coke ovens, which not only are more efficient converters of coal into coke but also conserve volatile matter for other uses. Very many of the newer, larger by-product ovens are located away from the coal fields and near iron and steel industries along the southern shores of the Great Lakes. Some of these are integrated directly into the iron and steel plants.*

extensive markets discourages the use of the motor truck and the near-absence of water routes essentially precludes movement by barge. Nevertheless, most of the railway traffic in coal is in the East, as Table 12.2 suggests.

TRAFFIC FLOW. Inasmuch as the Appalachian field accounts for about three-fourths of the coal extracted within the United States, a correspondingly outstanding share of all of this country's coal traffic originates there. Nearly all coal mined in West Virginia, the leading state of production, is forwarded to other areas—either down to the eastern seacoast (chiefly to Hampton Roads) for coastwise shipment or export, or northwest via the

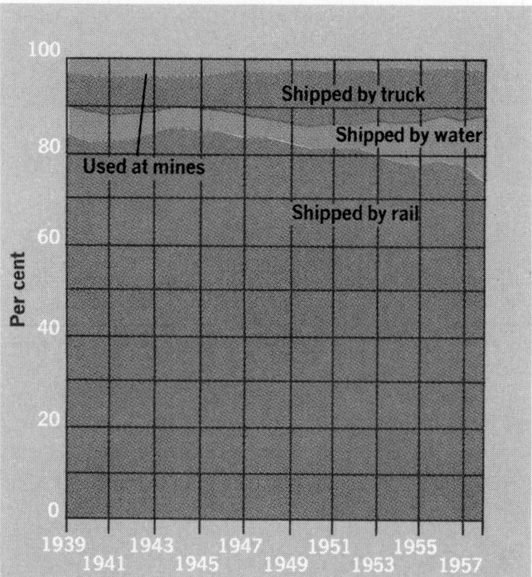

Figure 12.6 **Movement of bituminous coal and lignite to final destination in the United States.** *Shipments by water have been increasing at the relative expense of both truck and rail, especially since 1955. Why? (After Bruce C. Netschert,* The Future Supply of Energy Resources, *reprint no. 14, Resources for the Future, Inc., p. 37)*

Kanawha River valley and lesser river valleys to the western half of the manufacturing belt or perhaps on to Canada via Toledo and smaller shipping centers. In contrast, much of the Pennsylvania coal—between 30 and 40 per cent—is used locally, an approximately equal amount being shipped to the highly urbanized eastern portion of the manufacturing belt, and the remainder forwarded to and beyond the Great Lakes. An estimated one-tenth of all United States coal production is transshipped along the Atlantic Coast to water carriers for coastwise shipment or export, and another one-tenth is similarly transshipped along the shores of the Great Lakes.

From the other major mining areas, surpluses over domestic demand tend to move to the manufacturing belt, or if those areas are located in the western portion of the Rocky Mountain field, toward the Pacific Coast.

SIGNIFICANCE OF FREIGHT RATES. The importance of freight rates to coal transportation by rail in the United States has been excellently summarized by Walter H. Voskuil:[7]

> It frequently costs the coal industry as much to move coal to market as it does to mine the coal, sometimes more. . . .
>
> Railways, in making freight rates for coal, group points of origin or destination, or both. Generally all mines in one group have the same rate to common destinations. The base rate is usually that of the group closest to a particular market, with more distant mines having a differential above the base rate, that is, the more distant mines pay less per mile than the closer mines. The differentials permit mines in each district to obtain a share of their logical markets. Group boundaries are occasionally changed, but comparatively few alterations have been made in the group differentials in the past 30 years. The changes that have been made were to remove either undue preference or undue prejudice . . . .
>
> Because freight rates comprise such a large proportion of the delivered coal, rate adjustments have important effects on the economical location of mines. The rate structure has developed from competitive pressures without following any carefully planned long-range principle. Outstanding features of the structure are (1) wide blanketing of rates for both origins and destinations; (2) differentials between competing groups of producing centers; and (3) a relatively high level of rates on short hauls.
>
> There is a marked disregard of distance in both the blanketed and the differential rates. Some hauls in Ohio are twice as long as others for the same rate. To both the tidewater and the lake-cargo markets, the Middle Appalachian field has lower rates relative to distance than has the Northern Appalachian field, and these rates have caused marked shifts in shipments to tidewater and lake markets.

TRUCK AND WATER CARRIERS. The truck is of rising importance to the transportation of coal in the United States, serving especially in two capacities: (1) as a very short-haul go-between connecting mines with railroad sidings (wherein its volume of cargo movement, about 6 per cent of the nation's total, is usually subsumed under the 75 per cent of

[7] Walter H. Voskuil, *Minerals in World Industry,* McGraw-Hill Book Company, Inc., New York, 1955, pp. 105–107.

all coal that travels by rail, since most of the ton-mileage involved is rail movement) and (2) as a carrier to final destination, in which classification it accounts for about 10 per cent of all coal loadings at the nation's mines. In this second capacity the truck has found particular favor in situations where the total distance is not over 400 miles, for on such short hauls the truck can compete in freight rates with rail traffic and offer the additional convenience of delivery to the doorstep of the purchaser.

Water movement has increased in recent years. The direct loading from mines to water craft takes place chiefly along the short but busy Monongahela River above Pittsburgh, and secondarily along the other tributaries as well as the main artery of the Ohio River. The Mississippi and Tombigbee Rivers, together with subsidiary streams situated near coal fields and/or markets, also are busy. In addition, as has been stated, coal forms a significant cargo in both Great Lakes and Atlantic Coast shipping, although it has been carried overland initially from the mines to these coasts.

TABLE 12.2

Freight cars loaded with coal in 1956

Railroad line	*Number of cars*
Chesapeake and Ohio	1,004,728
Baltimore and Ohio	778,068
Norfolk and Western	772,102
Louisville and Nashville	634,142
Pennsylvania	556,726
Illinois Central	546,811
New York Central	404,647
Virginian	279,198
Monongahela	157,697
Nickel Plate	142,121
Clinchfield	104,493
Western Maryland	98,999
Chicago and Eastern Illinois	71,116
Pittsburgh and Lake Erie	37,654

SOURCE: *Railway Age,* July 22, 1957, p. 22.

West Germany

Prewar Germany contained approximately 7 per cent of the world's estimated coal reserves (Table 12.1). Of the bituminous and higher ranks, the outstanding majority were in the western portion of the country. Indeed, nearly 90 per cent of the strictly bituminous coals were in the Ruhr field, with most of the remainder in the Aachen field, the Saar field, and, to the east, the Silesian field. Very extensive deposits of lignite, amounting to nearly one-fifth of the country's total reserves, were situated in eastern Germany southwest of Berlin, near the Ruhr field in Westphalia, and in other, more scattered fields.

The dismemberment of Germany during the aftermath of the last war involved also the fragmentation of the country's coal reserves. The Silesian field, previously shared by Germany, Poland, and Czechoslovakia, was allocated to the two latter countries. The Saxony lignite deposits were included with territory that initially was occupied by the Soviet Union and subsequently became East Germany. All the western fields, including the mighty Ruhr, were a part of territory initially occupied by the non-Communist victors, and eventually all were absorbed into West Germany, which now controls the lion's share of the coal production in what was Germany a quarter of a century ago.

Consumption. To a degree almost without parallel, manufacturing and allied industries make demands upon coal in West Germany. They consume approximately 56 per cent of all inanimate energy, of which 95 per cent is supplied by coal. By way of comparison, in the United Kingdom about 46 per cent of such energy is consumed by manufacturing and associated industries; in France, about 40 per cent; and in Italy, 34 per cent. Household heating and overland transportation also consume considerable energy in West Germany. In all these outlets, however, imported petroleum and/or its products are gaining at the relative expense of coal.

Production. Essentially paralyzed and a marked liability immediately after the Second World War, coal mining in West Germany quickly was reactivated, and its output now is exceeded in the world

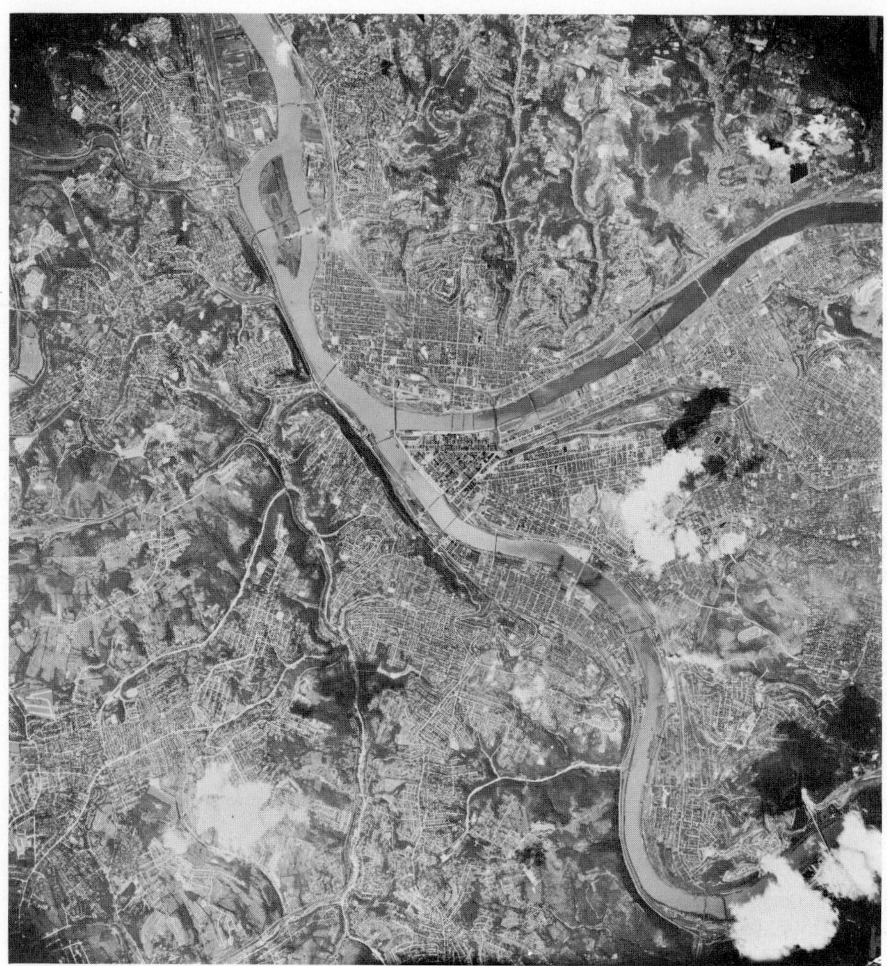

Pittsburgh—where the Allegheny River (upper right) and the Monongahela River (lower right) meet to form the Ohio River (upper left). The name has come to be symbolic of coal mining as well as iron and steel manufacture. Most mining occurs to the south and east of the city. Coal traffic on the Monongahela and Ohio Rivers is high; on the Allegheny River, low. (U.S. Air Force)

only by those of the Soviet Union and the United States (and possibly Communist China). This output of nearly 220 million metric tons involves bituminous coal and anthracite as well as lignite. In terms of tonnage, the bituminous coal comprises about 55 per cent, the lignite 40 per cent, and the anthracite 5 per cent of the nation's total.

THE RUHR. Basically, the mining of bituminous and anthracite coal in West Germany is confined closely to the Ruhr district, which produces about 90 per cent of the country's coal. This patch of ground, scarcely more than 10 miles in north-south extent and not more than 40 miles from east to west, has been a major source of German economic effort in times of both peace and war (Fig. 12.7). The underlying coal deposits are one of the world's most concentrated, with at least 130 seams existing at depths ranging from surface outcrops to more than 9,000 feet.[8] The rocks have been folded and faulted, with the intensity that is more severe at lower depths. Coals range from semianthracite, found deep in the earth, to bituminous at the higher levels. Medium-volatile coking coals tend to overlie the anthracitic materials, with high-volatile bituminous coals—excellent for space heating and transportation as well as for such purposes as the production of synthetic gasoline—at the shallower levels.

[8] See especially Chauncy D. Harris, "The Ruhr Coal-mining District," *Geographical Review*, 36:194–221, 1946.

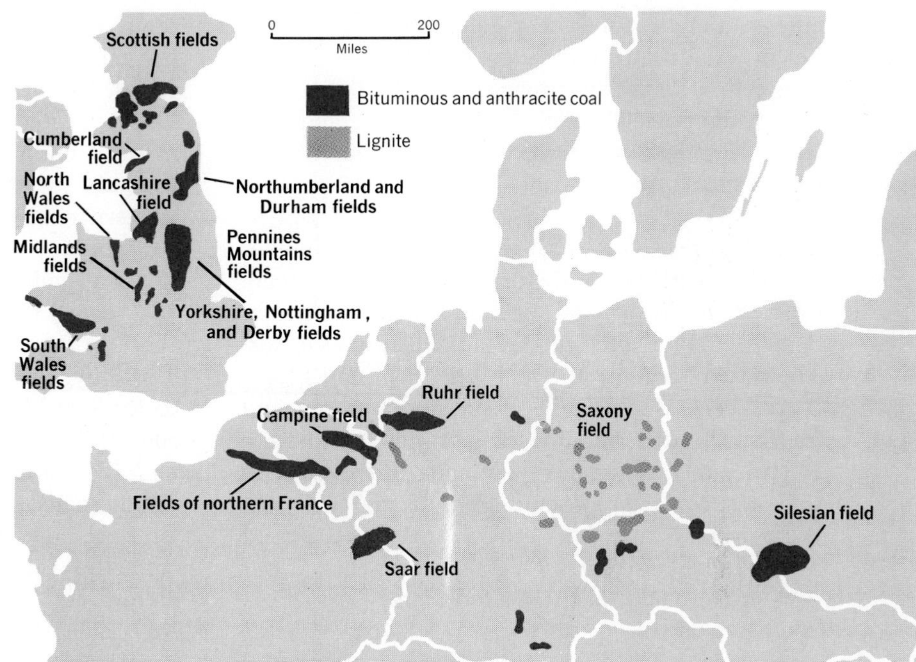

Figure 12.7 ***Leading coal fields of Europe.*** *Note the large reserves of lignite in East Germany. The Aachen field is here shown as an extension of the Campine field into West Germany.*

LESSER BITUMINOUS-COAL FIELDS. The Saar field, almost entirely underlain with coal deposits that extend across the political boundary line into France, and the Aachen field, which reaches discontinuously across the borders of Belgium and France, supply most of the high-quality West German coals not mined in the Ruhr district.

LIGNITE FIELDS. Despite losses of very productive lignite fields now in East Germany, West Germany currently produces nearly 100 million metric tons of lignite annually, largely from deposits near the Ruhr in Westphalia and from scattered fields in the central part of the country and along its eastern margin. This is used chiefly for space heating and generation of electricity.

Transportation. The active coal fields of West Germany are situated in the approximate latitudinal center of a nation that is not large, and consequently the maximum length of coal haul does not often exceed 400 miles, and the average is much shorter. Moreover, the Ruhr and some of the lesser fields are on water routes reaching both inland and to the sea. Unlike the Soviet Union, and to a lesser degree, the United States, West Germany is not faced with serious problems of excessive distances in transportation. Water, railroad, and truck media are all used actively in this nation, where heavy industry and associated populations are concentrated on the coal fields and in the seaports but where industries and populations of moderate intensity are surprisingly uniform in distribution.

The United Kingdom

Since the dawn of the Industrial Age, the United Kingdom has been a major world producer of coal. Today, like most of Western Europe, the nation is still very much dependent upon the black fuel, which furnishes more than nine-tenths of its energy requirements. Production, however, has declined to approximately 75 per cent of the 1913 output, the highest in the country's history. Exports, once amounting to over 33 per cent of all production, have decreased to a small figure that is almost canceled by imports. Reserves are estimated to be sufficient for the next two centuries, but they are becoming more costly and difficult to exploit. Labor has decreased in supply. Alternative sources of energy, notably nuclear potentialities, are being given serious attention. Nevertheless, the United Kingdom is currently surpassed only by the United States, the Soviet Union, West Germany, and possibly Communist China in the total volume of coal extraction.

Consumption. Now that the exports of bunker coal have withered to the degree that they scarcely exist, the major demand for British coal comes from domestic manufacturing and individual households. These two account for over 40 per cent and nearly 20 per cent, respectively, of the domestic demand for British coal, with the coal-gas plants, thermoelectric units, and railways ranging downward in their respective proportions from 12 to 7 per cent of the total. Nearly 7 per cent of British coal is used at the mines, in contrast with the less than 3 per cent so consumed in the United States.

Production. British coal extraction is from a series of fields which are variously categorized but which we shall classify as those of: (1) the Scottish lowlands, (2) the Pennine uplands, and (3) the peninsula of Wales.

THE SCOTTISH LOWLANDS. Occupying a structural and topographic trough that may be the floor of a rift valley, the coals of the Scottish lowlands extend with occasional interruption from coast to coast and reach under ocean waters beyond each of the two terminal cities of Glasgow and Edinburgh (Fig. 12.7). Although some of the coal outcrops, most is underground. A small amount is anthracite, but most is of a noncoking, easily combustible bituminous rank. The Scottish sources currently account for slightly more than one-tenth of all British production.[9]

THE PENNINE UPLANDS. The several fields buttressing the Pennine uplands are chiefly the remnant limbs of a domal structure from which the apex has been removed by erosion. Consequently they dip away irregularly to the east, south, and west from the core of the Pennine uplands. The seams generally reach downward at rather sharp angles, and the mining, which has been in progress for centuries, has necessarily deepened as the coal faces have retreated. Indeed, the average level of mining in the United Kingdom is over 1,200 feet beneath the land surface, and some of the mines along the western margin of the Pennines exceed depths of 4,000 feet.

Five mining fields are usually recognized as comprising the Pennines complex. They are: (1) the Northumberland and Durham, and (2) the Yorkshire, Derbyshire, and Nottinghamshire fields to the east; (3) the West Midland field along the southwest; (4) the North Wales and Lancashire, and (5) the Cumberland fields to the west. All in all, these account for over three-fourths of the British coal output, with well over one-third coming from the Yorkshire, Derbyshire, and Nottinghamshire fields. The quality ranges from excellent coking grades to the more prevalent grades that are satisfactory for purposes other than coking.

THE PENINSULA OF WALES. This field once supplied much of the British coal that was shipped to bunkers and ultimately to the holds of many ships in the world's merchant fleet. Even today it accounts for more of such exports than does any other field. Complex in structure, grading downward from anthracite and excellent bituminous coal, and ranging from surface outcrops to over 4,000 feet in depth, these coals comprise somewhat more than one-tenth of the annual British output.

MINOR RESERVES. Beneath the famed white cliffs of Dover is yet another coal field which is very much subordinate, in respect to both production and reserves. In the vicinity of Bristol are the Bristol and Somerset and Forest of Dean fields, which are also minor in reserves and output.

MINING METHODS AND PRODUCTIVITY. There were nearly thirteen hundred active coal mines in the United Kingdom in 1955. Most of these were underground; only about 5 per cent of the over-all production is from open-pit mines. The average productivity per worker is low, ranging up to 1.6 metric tons per man-shift, in contrast to the approximately 8 metric tons per man-shift achieved in the highly mechanized coal industry of the United

[9] See especially Trevor M. Thomas, "Recent Trends and Developments in the British Coal Mining Industry," *Economic Geography*, 34:19–41, 1958.

States. Because of the unusual depths and the discontinuous structural arrangements of many British deposits, mechanization is difficult to apply there. By and large, the best seams have already been taken up, and the beds now being extracted are frequently and increasingly interlaced with foreign matter that must be removed before utilization.

ADMINISTRATION AND PLANS. The British coal-mining industry was nationalized in 1947 and now is administered by a public corporation responsible to Parliament. Most of the mines are actually operated by this corporation, known as the National Coal Board. Although productivity has increased during the past decade, the new administrators continue to be beset with the almost insolvable problems with which their predecessors were confronted.

Three essential ingredients of financial profit are adequate raw materials, capital goods, and labor supply. The United Kingdom is currently giving attention to all three.

In the matter of reserves, one of the most pressing problems is selective utilization. It is estimated that the United Kingdom has a probable minimum of 172.2 billion tons of coal, of which over 43 billion tons are recoverable under current cost-price conditions—enough, as we have stated, to last for two centuries at the present rate of extraction. About three-fifths of these currently recoverable deposits appear to lie in the Pennines complex, and the remaining two-fifths is almost equally divided between the Scottish lowlands and the peninsula of Wales. Unfortunately, however, some of the coals that are needed the most urgently are also the costliest to mine. Although the National Coal Board is operating "in the black" financially, most of the individual mining fields are not; and it is only the very profitable returns from the Yorkshire, Derbyshire, and Nottinghamshire enterprises that now enable the National Coal Board to show a profit from their coal mining operation.[10]

The discarding of obsolete mines, notably small ones, and the reequipping of those offering the highest production potential are primary objectives in offsetting the deficiencies caused by inadequate capital goods. In addition, some new mines are to be opened. Particular attention is being given to larger units.

The labor shortage is being met partially through the installation of more efficient machinery and the initiation of more efficient methods, and partially through a planned discouragement of further departures from the mines by working personnel. The coal-mining labor force, which declined by over one-third to its 1947 level of 700,000, has remained more or less constant since that time. It has been estimated that almost 90 per cent of this labor force will be needed to achieve the planned output of 240 million tons per year.[11]

Transportation and Trade. British industries developed over most of the country's workable coal deposits, and attracted populations thereto. Thus, except for the London vicinity, most of the highly industrialized and populated districts of the United Kingdom are locally supplied with much of the coal they consume. Because of the small size and island nature of the nation, such transportation as must be accomplished, whether by water or land, is no serious problem.

Exports of coal are chiefly to coal-hungry neighboring nations—Denmark, Ireland, Sweden, France. Imports are from the United States and Western European nations with coal surpluses.

East Germany

East Germany now produces nearly 95 per cent as much coal and lignite as does its western counterpart, and thereby the country has achieved a rank in world production just beneath that of the United Kingdom. Nearly all of this is lignite from the Saxony deposits and is used especially for the generation of electricity and for space heating. Much bituminous coal must still be imported.

Communist China

Since 1955 the coal production in Communist China reportedly has more than tripled, and the goals of the current plan are such that the nation might well

[10] *Ibid.*, pp. 28–29.

[11] *Ibid.*, p. 35.

be one of the leading contenders within a few years. (Their own reports place them third among world producers now.) The reserves are vast (Table 12.1) and are comparatively accessible. Although Manchuria is currently the major area of exploitation, much attention is now being given to the extensive deposits situated along the southward-flowing Yellow River immediately upstream of the flood plain of that waterway. Most of Communist China's coal deposits that are known to be extensive are in the northeastern portion of the country, and these deposits offer promise of continuing into the immediate future their current predominance in production. In all probability, however, a regional economic development not unlike that being carried out in the Soviet Union will take place if more extensive reserves of coal can be discovered and/or exploited to the south and west. Preliminary reports suggest that this is already under way.

The rest of the world

The six leading nations are responsible for about 75 per cent of the world's coal output, and the rest of the world for the remaining 25 per cent. Of this latter group, which includes at least 57 political units, no single country offers serious competition to any one of the leaders. Non-Communist countries of note include France, Japan, India, Belgium, the Union of South Africa, Australia, and Canada. Communist nations of moderate production are Poland and Czechoslovakia (Fig. 12.2).

THE OUTLOOK

Despite relative losses during the past century in competition with other fuels, coal is now being produced and consumed in the world on an unprecedented scale. This upward trend has been due mainly to (1) the initiation of more dynamic economies and concomitant coal consumption in the Communist bloc; (2) the moderate increase in absolute demand for coal in most non-Communist technically advanced nations, even those which have come to depend partially upon other sources of energy; (3) the embryonic but rising demand for coal on the part of some non-Communist underdeveloped nations.

Between 1950 and 1959, the world production of coal increased by some 735 million metric tons. Over one-half of this increase was accounted for by the Soviet Union and Communist China, and over 60 per cent by the Communist bloc. There is every indication that this rate of increase will continue into the next decade, as coal is the one source of energy present in large known quantities in several Communist nations.

Most of the growth in coal production not attributable to Communist efforts has been due to the postwar reactivation of war-damaged technically advanced nations. This is particularly true in Western Europe; here the Coal and Steel Community has stimulated the output and exchange of this commodity by essentially abolishing all tariffs on coal among West Germany, France, Belgium, the Netherlands, Luxembourg, and Italy—the six participating nations. Most of the increase has been in West Germany. (Indeed, the two nations now comprising what remains of prewar Germany jointly produce appreciably more coal than was mined at any time of Nazi control.) In the United States, where coal output declined temporarily after 1947, the demand has again become reactivated because of new uses of the material as a fuel and a raw material. In outlying technically advanced lands, especially Japan, Australia, and the Union of South Africa, the output has either increased moderately or remained more or less stable.

The small amount of increase attributable to non-Communist underdeveloped lands has been in India, Turkey, the Central African Federation, and a few nations of Latin America.

The outlook for coal consumption, therefore, is toward an increase, notably in the Communist bloc. Regardless of location, this consumption will be supplied mainly through production from domestic sources, as it is now. Such commerce as exists will be mainly a flow from nations of vast reserves and existing or potential productive capacity—in other words, from the United States, and perhaps the Soviet Union and Communist China.

REFERENCES

Averitt, Paul, et al.: *Coal Resources of the United States,* United States Geological Survey Circular 293, 1953.

Bateman, Alan M.: *Economic Mineral Deposits,* John Wiley & Sons, Inc., New York, and Chapman & Hall, Ltd., London, 1950. (Especially pp. 634–651.)

Deasy, George F., and Phyllis R. Griess: "Geographical Significance of Recent Changes in Mining in the Bituminous Coal Fields of Pennsylvania," *Economic Geography,* **33:**283–298, 1957.

——— and ———: "Some New Maps of the Underground Bituminous Coal Mining Industry of Pennsylvania." *Annals of the Association of American Geographers,* **47:**336–349, 1957.

Francis, Wilfrid: *Coal,* Edward Arnold & Co., London, 1954.

Harris, Chauncy D.: "The Ruhr Coal-mining District," *Geographical Review,* **36:**194–221, 1946.

Murphy, Raymond E., and Hugh E. Spittal: "Movements in the Center of Coal Mining in the Appalachian Plateaus," *Geographical Review,* **35:**624–633, 1945.

Pounds, Norman J. G.: *The Ruhr,* Indiana University Press, Bloomington, Ind., 1952.

Thomas, Trevor M.: "Recent Trends and Developments in the British Coal Mining Industry," *Economic Geography,* **34:**19–41, 1958.

Voskuil, Walter H.: *Minerals in World Industry,* McGraw-Hill Book Company, Inc., New York, 1955. (Especially chaps. 8–11.)

Woytinsky, W. S., and E. S. Woytinsky: *World Population and Production,* The Twentieth Century Fund, Inc., New York, 1953. (Especially chap. 23.)

13 ENERGY FROM PETROLEUM AND NATURAL GAS

COAL MADE POSSIBLE THE INITIATION OF THE INDUSTRIAL AGE ON AN IMPRESSIVE scale. Petroleum and natural gas, acting in some cases as competitors and in others as complementing agents to coal, have brought about today's great range of realized industrial potentialities. Bulky, heavy, and greasily dirty, coal has found its most widespread application in large structures and machines which, if they are at all mobile, move only slowly. Petroleum and natural gas and their products, on the other hand, not only contain more energy per unit of weight[1] but can be applied with equally satisfactory results to something as tiny as a model airplane (or, on a more practical basis, a lawn mower or an outboard motor), or to something as fast as an airplane, as large as an ocean vessel, as stationary as a factory, as personal as an automobile. Moreover, being nonsolids, they can be extracted and transported rather easily.

It is this versatility of application combined with thermal efficiency and facility of extraction and transfer that has been largely responsible for the rapid ascendance of petroleum and natural gas, particularly the former, into the primary ranks of energy-source materials.

The role of petroleum in the world's economic affairs is such that it provides an exceptionally good case study illustrating the generalizations in previous chapters of this book: (1) it occurs in association with varying natural conditions, some of them favorable and some unfavorable to its development; (2) most of its current consumption and the facilities of production are traceable to, and controlled by, technically advanced nations; (3) in the non-Communist world, exploitation is largely by sizable, privately owned corporations, whereas in Communist nations ownership and operation is by the state; (4) appreciable investment, chiefly from non-Communist, technically advanced areas, has found its way to certain

[1] About 19,000 Btu per pound, compared with 15,000, more or less, for coal, 11,760 for grain alcohol, 7,500 for wood.

petroleum-rich underdeveloped lands; and (5) political and economic nationalism is an active force in petroleum recovery.

NATURAL OCCURRENCE

Petroleum and natural gas as substances

Petroleum and natural gas are composed of varying mixtures of the elements carbon and hydrogen, plus certain minor additional elements. Whether, in a specific instance, the materials in question occur as gases, liquids, or waxy solids depends largely upon the carbon-hydrogen ratio. The term *petroleum* is usually applied only to the liquid materials, some of which contain gases and solids in solution or suspension, and these may be light, medium, or heavy. When the lighter oils are distilled or evaporated, either naturally or by man, the residue is usually a compound of hydrocarbons known as *paraffin*. Further distillation often results in another hydrocarbon arrangement called *asphalt*. Petroleum with a predominantly paraffin base tends to be lighter in color and vaporizes at a lower temperature than does that which is primarily asphaltic. These terms, as many readers are aware, are retained throughout the industry, being applied often at service stations where motor oil is purchased. Still other oils are of *mixed base*, containing both paraffin and asphalt.

Derivation. Like coal, petroleum and natural gas are generally believed to have been derived from organic sources and occur today in complexes of sedimentary beds. The details of their origin, however, are somewhat different from that of coal.

Petroleum and Natural Gas as Migrant Materials. In truth, we are not absolutely certain of the origin of petroleum and natural gas to the extent of our certainty about the origin of coal. This is largely because petroleum and natural gas have not always existed in, or necessarily near, the places where they now are found but have moved slowly, as millenniums of time have passed, through porous rocks from their nebulous places of origin to the traps where they are now gathered. If we knew more about those places of origin, we could be more specific in theorizing the derivation of the materials which have migrated from them.

The Declining Concept of Inorganic Origin. It was once felt that petroleum may have originated wholly from chemical reactions within the upper rocks of the earth's crust, with such reactions possibly intensified by volcanism and/or by the action of underground water. Most available evidence, however, does not support this view.

The Concept of Organic Origin. It now appears that petroleum and natural gas may well have been created through the chemical alteration of plant and animal life, especially plankton[2] that were once buried in deep muck underlying brackish waters. When the muck was covered by other sediment, it was compressed. Eventually, in partial response to the compressive forces, the droplets of petroleum moved away, activated either by the natural gas that had formed in the initial stages of alteration or by water. If nearby rock beds were sufficiently porous, the hydrocarbons entered them and traveled through them until encountering some sort of impenetrable barrier to migration. If overlying rocks and underlying materials were likewise impenetrable, the petroleum and gas gathered within the pores of the rock through which it had traveled —awaiting, as it were, exploitation by man.

Characteristics of Traps. Places of accumulation of petroleum and natural gas are usually referred to as *traps*. Essentially all these are found in sedimentary rocks, and hence the association of petroleum and natural-gas extraction with such strata (Fig. 13.1). They may occur at any depth at which the sedimentary rocks are found. Oil has been discovered at depths exceeding 20,000 feet from the land surface of the drilling vicinity, but nearly all current production is at depths from 1,000 to 15,000 feet. Usually the gas migrates to the highest levels in the trap, with the petroleum at a level lower.

[2] See Chap. 6.

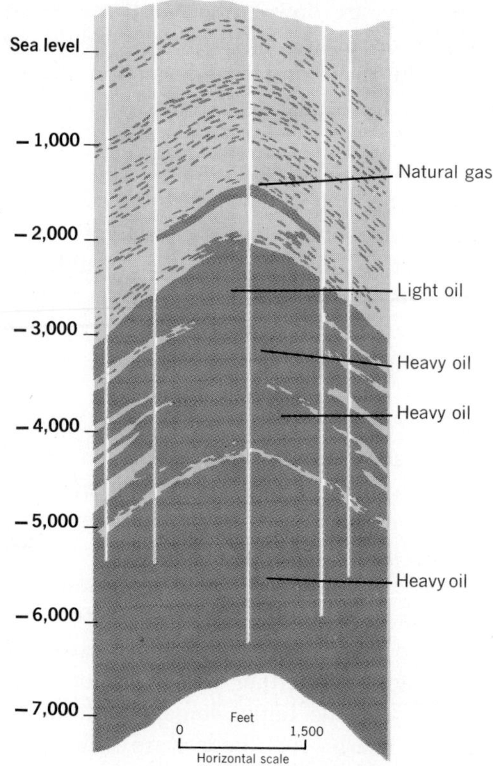

Figure 13.1 ***Petroleum and natural gas in an anticlinal formation near Los Angeles.*** *This is an unusually rich deposit. Anticlines are only one of a number of traps in which underground petroleum and natural gas accumulate. The two here are seen in the same trap, with the gas above the petroleum. This is typical where petroleum and natural gas occur together, but they do not always do so. (After drawing by Decius reproduced by Powers, AIME, as shown in Alan M. Batemen,* Economic Mineral Deposits, *John Wiley & Sons, Inc., New York, 1950, p. 664)*

Potential and existing reserves

Petroleum. Inasmuch as petroleum is a liquid migrant that has accumulated rather haphazardly, the areas of its occurrence and the amount of its reserves cannot be determined with the same degree of reliability that accompanies estimates of a solid, sedimentary material like coal. Instead, its potentialities are expressed in terms of *sedimentary basins* of possible accumulation, and its reserves in terms of *petroliferous areas* of known occurrence.

SEDIMENTARY BASINS. The peculiarities of petroleum formation more or less have restricted its global extent to places of rather deep accumulation of quasi-disturbed sedimentary rocks. Certain types of landforms and rock structures, therefore, can be expected to be nonpetroliferous: youthful mountains and igneous shields, for example, are usually without substantial petroleum. Thus, on a map of sedimentary basins (Fig. 13.2), most of the world's high mountains and its shields of surfacing igneous materials are considered to be nonpetroliferous.

Considered by continent, the world's sedimentary basins are the most widespread in Asia, North America, tropical South America, with Europe, Africa, and Australia not so well endowed.

Considered by nation, the Soviet Union and the United States, in that order, encompass the most extensive sedimentary basins (but not necessarily *proved* reserves). Brazil, Canada, and Communist China also offer possibilities.

PETROLIFEROUS AREAS. Proved reserves of petroleum are shown in Table 13.1. These, like the sedimentary basins of which they are a part, are erratic in distribution, and the amounts of their actual reserves cannot be detected or even inferred on maps of their global extent (compare Table 13.1 with Fig. 13.2). Furthermore, the known reserves of any commodity actually are to be viewed only as working inventories at a certain time under given assumptions—and this is particularly true of petroleum, the search for which is continuous and active. The known reserves of one year may vary appreciably from those of another with the development of a single major field or series of fields.

Having taken due caution, we can now note that the nations around the Persian Gulf in the Middle East aggregately control the most extensive known reserves in the world. Of other nations, the United States and the Soviet Union are the leaders, and Venezuela is more than noteworthy.

ADEQUACY. Unlike those of coal, known reserves of petroleum are sufficient to last for less than half a century at the current consumption and production rate—and that rate has more than

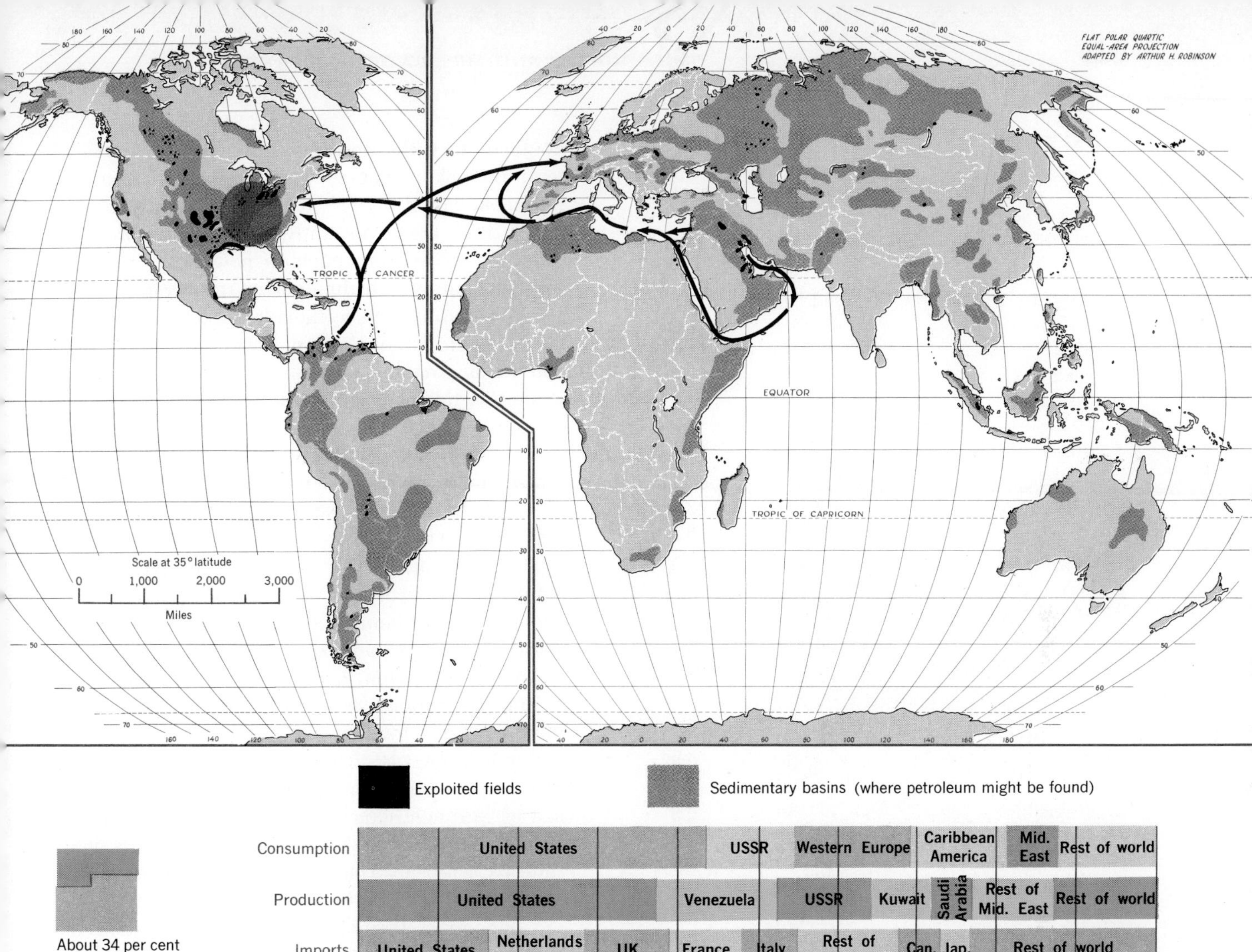

Figure 13.2 ***Sedimentary basins, fields of exploitation, and the consumption, production, import, and export of crude petroleum.*** *The Great Plains of North America and analogous landforms in South America appear to offer excellent possibilities for future petroleum extraction. Europe has few fields and dim prospects. Much of the Soviet Union may be underlain by petroleum. By far the largest known reserves are in the Middle East. Eastern Europe and southern Asia (exclusive of the Middle East), much of Africa south of the Sahara, and nearly all of Australia are believed not to be highly petroliferous. (After Wallace E. Pratt, and Dorothy Good,* World Geography of Petroleum, *Princeton University Press for the American Geographical Society, 1950, inset opp. p. 14)*

TABLE 13.1

World oil reserves in 1959

Region and country	*Million barrels*	*Per cent of world total*
Asia		
Kuwait	62,000	20.9
Saudi Arabia	50,000	16.8
Iran	35,000	11.8
Iraq	25,000	8.4
Neutral zone	6,500	2.2
Qatar	2,500	0.8
Other Middle East	365	0.1
Total Middle East	181,365	61.0
East Indies	9,530	3.2
Other Far East	645	0.2
Total Asia	191,540	64.4
Anglo-America		
United States	38,240	12.9
Canada	4,000	1.4
Total	42,240	14.3
Latin America		
Venezuela	18,000	6.1
Mexico	2,500	0.8
Argentina	2,000	0.7
Colombia	750	0.3
Trinidad	425	0.1
Peru	325	0.1
Other Latin America	435	0.1
Total	24,435	8.2
Africa		
Algeria (including Sahara)	5,000	1.7
Other Africa	2,275	0.8
Total	7,275	2.5
Western Europe	1,565	0.5
Total non-Communist countries	267,055	89.9
Communist countries		
Soviet Union	28,000	9.4
Eastern Europe and Communist China	2,135	0.7
Total	30,135	10.1
World total	297,190	100.0

SOURCE: Data for United States, American Petroleum Institute; for Canada, Canadian Petroleum Association; for others, *Oil and Gas Journal.*

doubled since the Second World War. The short-term outlook is not so gloomy as the foregoing statement would suggest, however, as new pools are being discovered constantly, and much more efficient use of existing pools is now being realized through improved techniques of recovery, refining, and consumption. Nevertheless, the long-range outlook for petroleum is not so promising as for coal; and within the life span of some of the younger readers of this book, the time may well come when substitute sources of petroleum (such as oil shale), or sources of energy other than petroleum, will be utilized more generally.

DISTRIBUTION AMONG TECHNICALLY ADVANCED AND UNDERDEVELOPED NATIONS. One of the most significant geographical aspects concerning current petroleum reserves is that they are primarily in underdeveloped lands. A probable 75 per cent of all known petroleum, and approximately 80 per cent of known petroleum in non-Communist nations, is in underdeveloped countries! The Middle East alone accounts for about 70 per cent of the non-Communist petroleum reserves. The tiny sheikdom of Kuwait, 8,000 square miles in area (about the size of Massachusetts) contains the largest known reserves of all nations, including the mighty United States! Caribbean America and, in lesser measure, the Far East are also important supply areas.

In contrast, the technically advanced nations of Western Europe, nearly all of them looking to petroleum for more and more of their energy, are essentially without reserves, as is Japan and the technically advanced nations of the Southern Hemisphere. Only the United States, the Soviet Union, and Canada of the technically advanced group possess reserves of significance.

DISTRIBUTION BETWEEN THE NON-COMMUNIST AND COMMUNIST BLOCS. In all probability, the bloc of Communist nations possesses over 10 per cent of the world's known petroleum reserves, nearly all of which are in the Soviet Union. This is one very important reason why the Middle East, with its very large reserves and its location so close to the Soviet Union, is an object of grave concern by nations on either side of the iron curtain.

Whether Communist China will come into a

noteworthy position is not currently known; the nation has rather extensive sedimentary beds (Fig. 13.2) which may or may not yield results in the intensive exploration to which they are now being subjected. Other Asian Communist nations are essentially without petroleum. In Europe, Rumania has long been a producer and Hungary is also active, but the resources of both countries appear limited. The other Communist nations of Europe, although underlain rather extensively with sedimentary beds, offer little probability of active yields.

Natural Gas. Petroleum may or may not be associated in occurrence with natural gas, a source of energy that is fast gaining its own reputation, particularly in the United States. Although occurring chiefly in gaseous form, this commodity is consumed as a liquid if the hydrocarbons involved can be made to turn into a light gasoline during the refining process.

No reliable world estimates of the extent of natural-gas reserves have yet been assembled. The United States is the only nation making extensive use of this commodity, being responsible for over 70 per cent of world consumption. Estimates indicate that nearly 212 trillion cubic feet of gas and over 5 billion barrels of liquid natural gas are known to exist on the mainland portion of the country. Reduced to a common denominator and compared with petroleum, these amount to an equivalent of over 40 billion barrels of petroleum—an excess of nearly 2 billion barrels over the actual petroleum reserves of the United States.

Other nations of known reserves include the Soviet Union, Canada, Venezuela, Mexico, Italy, Indonesia and Brunei.

Additional Materials. The petroleum and natural-gas deposits which man is currently utilizing so intensively represent the final products of long chemical and physical change wrought by nature on the raw materials of these substances. Man also has access to other materials that yield crude oil, but with these he must do more of the actual work of concentration than needed with petroleum or natural gas. These sources are *oil shale* and *tar sands.*

OIL SHALE. As suggested by its title, oil shale was once mud and/or clay impregnated with organic remains. As was true in the formation of petroleum, these deposits congealed and were compressed with the passage of time and the addition of overlying beds, but the organic matter largely remained as a part of the newly formed shales. It is in this form that oil shale is mined and processed, with the ultimate yields including not only oil but also gas and fixed carbon. The volume of return is low in comparison with the cost of mining and processing, but potentialities appear quite good for further improvement of technology.

The United States has been particularly well endowed with this natural resource, and Sweden, the Soviet Union, Communist China, and Australia to a noteworthy degree.

TAR SANDS. In the vicinity of Canada's Athabaska River, east of the Rockies, is a series of sandy deposits impregnated with organic matter at varying stages of transition into petroleum, including some reserves of the end product. Estimates do not agree as to the total amount of these reserves, but it is not inconsiderable. Like the oil shale, they are more costly to process than petroleum and natural gas and furthermore are comparatively removed from markets. Therefore, they await future development.

Reserves Compared. The world's reserves of petroleum and natural gas are usually given more serious attention than the other petroliferous possibilities, chiefly because of the relatively advanced technology and high efficiency now characterizing their use. Their total known reserves, however, are low when compared with output—not enough to last for another half century at current production rates. There is every indication that more will be available as a result of future drilling, improvement in refining, etc., but no guarantee exists of an assured long-term supply. Oil shales and tar sands, on the other hand, are estimated to be comparatively extensive. The state of Colorado alone is believed to contain two-thirds as much petroleum in oil shales as the entire world contains in liquid form, and an even larger amount of petroleum may be included in the tar sands along Canada's Athabaska River.[3] Inasmuch as additional deposits of both oil shale and tar sands exist in places other than these leading deposits, it is apparent that the world faces no immediate shortage of petroleum. The outlook for individual nations, however, varies sharply with their respective natural endowments and stages of technological development.

Associated natural conditions

Rock Structure. Since petroleum and natural gas are nonsolids extracted by means of gear lowered from the land surface of drilling areas, the natural conditions associated with their obtainment differ from those associated with coal and other solids. In brief, the major problems of underground mining do not exist, because the shafts, slopes, drifts, and tunnels are unnecessary. Nor are there the disadvantages of open-pit mining. Of course, the rock structure is nevertheless important, especially in connection with the formation and present-day orientation of the previously described traps where petroleum and natural gas accumulate, and the difficulties subsequently encountered by man in locating these traps.

Uneven Distribution of Known Reserves. Certainly of equal significance to the task of recovering petroleum and natural gas, however, is the comparatively limited amount and very uneven distribution of their reserves. More specifically, the technically advanced lands which do not possess much petroleum and natural gas within their own political boundaries extract these products in foreign lands, often under natural conditions that are not at all favorable. Thus it is that the world's most extensive reserves, those of the Middle East, are situated in dry climates that for centuries have been unattractive to civilizations. Nevertheless they are being developed very rapidly despite generally unfavorable local natural conditions. Similarly, the climates and related conditions of Caribbean America and the Far East are not the most desirable in the world, and yet exploitation continues.

Continental Shelves. Like coal, petroleum and natural gas sometimes are exploited in the continental shelves which extend under the seas. Unlike the mining of such coal, however, which begins on dry land and follows seams down under the sea and therefore is more or less similar to drift mining on land, the extraction of petroleum along such shelves involves the sinking of vertical shafts from either floating or anchored gear overlying the water above. Needless to say, this often adds appreciable expense to the task of exploration and recovery.

Distance. If position in space is a natural factor, then the unusually long distances separating some areas of production and consumption are a natural handicap. Thousands of miles lie between the producing fields in the Far East, the Middle East, and Caribbean America, for example, and some of their markets. Fortunately, in each case such distance mainly involves easily traversed water; all these production sites are within comparatively close reach of oceans and seas. Overland handling by quasi-automatic pipelines and by tank cars, tank trucks, and other equipment is also, in the main, rather unhindered.

Natural Assets. We have suggested a few of the natural hindrances with which man must sometimes cope in the extraction of petroleum. It would be misleading, however, to consider nature as entirely in opposition to human effort. The precise assets, like the liabilities, cannot be easily generalized but become quickly apparent in the examination of any given site. For example, we shall see shortly that the major petroleum fields of the United States are located in eastern Texas and neighboring states. Here the depths of occurrence are not excessive, the terrain is comparatively even, the climate and associated conditions are not seriously adverse. Petroleum can be not only extracted with relative ease from such fields but can be transported with facility to places of consumption.

[3] Estimates by the U.S. Bureau of Mines, as reported in W. S. Woytinsky, and E. S. Woytinsky, *World Population and Production,* The Twentieth Century Fund, Inc., New York, 1953, pp. 891–893.

Although oil and water may not mix in the realm of physical science, they do mix in the realm of the economic geographer. Without water to provide cheap transportation, much of the world's heavy international commerce in petroleum and its products probably would not be possible. The photograph shows shallow water at Lake Maracaibo in Venezuela. Several wells like these now are offshore from southern and southwestern United States. (Standard Oil Company of New Jersey)

CONSUMPTION

Petroleum

At the beginning of the Second World War, approximately 2 billion barrels of petroleum were being consumed annually throughout the world. When that war ended, the figure had been increased to 3 billion barrels. Now it stands at over 7 billion barrels.

At the beginning of the Second World War, about three-fifths of all consumed petroleum was used up within the United States. When the war ended, that fraction was slightly higher. Now less than one-half of the world consumption of crude petroleum is allocable to the United States (Fig. 13.2).

The preceding two paragraphs suggest some very important trends concerning the use of petroleum, as well as of competitive fuels. A giant of energy consumption, the United States also has

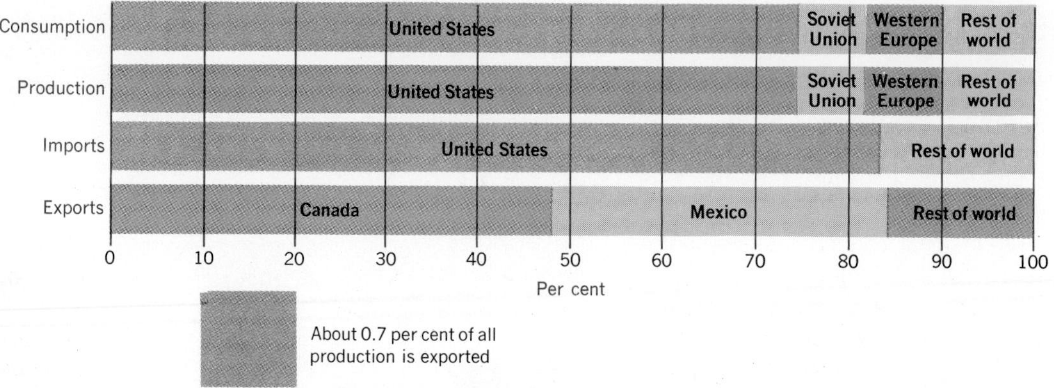

Figure 13.3 ***Consumption, production, import, and export of natural and manufactured gas.*** *Manufactured gas includes that from gas works, refineries, and other sources, but especially from coke ovens.*

been a pioneer in the development of technology for petroleum discovery and exploitation. Generalizations concerning the significance of petroleum as a world-wide source of energy tend to obscure the fundamental truth that most of the energy that has been released from petroleum has been consumed within the United States, which, it will be remembered, annually uses up about one-third of all the world's energy. The comparatively rapid twentieth-century shift to petroleum thus has been carried out primarily within the United States, the economy of which is so large that the shift is reflected pronouncedly in statistics of world consumption. The pioneering spirit and the powerful impact of such actions by the United States can scarcely be overstated.

However, as is evidenced by the declining proportionate consumption on the part of the United States in a rapidly rising world consumption of petroleum, other technically advanced nations have taken note of the advantages of petroleum over other sources of energy and are now following the lead of the United States in its use. The Soviet Union, which now consumes a probable 10 per cent of the world's petroleum, and Western Europe, which accounts for almost 15 per cent, are the most active in this respect. (Fig. 13.2). Caribbean America and the Middle East also appear to rank high as consumers, but actually most of their "consumption" is merely refining for export.

Natural gas

Well-endowed with domestic supplies of natural gas, the United States has currently assumed an impressive lead in the production and consumption of this commodity. As previously explained, nearly 75 per cent of the world consumption of this commodity (plus manufactured gas) is accounted for by the United States, about 75 per cent being used up by industry and the remainder by households (Fig. 13.3). As is true of petroleum, other countries are consuming more natural gas than they once did; but only those with rather good domestic natural supplies offer promise of really expanded activity under existing technology. Ranking well behind the United States are the Soviet Union (8 per cent of the world's total consumption) and Western Europe (also about 8 per cent; see Fig. 13.3).

PRODUCTION

The annual world production of petroleum and natural gas can be said to be approximately equal to the consumption.

The United States

Although declining proportionately, the United States has no peer in either the extraction or the refining of petroleum. In either category, this country accounts for at least 40 per cent of the world total (Fig. 13.2).

Major Areas of Crude Extraction. The extraction of petroleum, unlike that of coal, is carried out predominantly in the south central and southwestern portions of the country. Texas alone accounts for nearly 35 per cent of the nation's crude petroleum, and, in combination with California and Louisiana, this state produces more than one-half of the nation's total. Even the states of moderate production—Oklahoma, Kansas, Illinois, Wyoming, New Mexico—are in the middle western or arid western portion of the country. Nor does there appear to be any major changes in the immediate future: Texas contains over 50 per cent, California about 13 per cent, Louisiana approximately 10 per cent, and Oklahoma over 7 per cent of the nation's known reserves. Some of the Gulf and California deposits are in the offshore continental shelves.[4]

Major Areas of Natural-gas Extraction. Approximately 70 per cent of the natural-gas extraction in the United States occurs in wells where essentially no petroleum exists. However, the general areas of intensive extraction are usually not far from places of petroleum occurrence. Texas and Louisiana are outstanding in both production and reserves, while Oklahoma, New Mexico, California, and Kansas may be accorded honorable mention.

Technology of Refining. Refining is a semiautomatic, almost endless process which, although involving several stages, tends to take place at a single site. Older, more elementary methods of distillation have been replaced by more advanced methods which permit not only the recovery of the desired products but also their recovery (within limits) in desired percentages of the finished products. Moreover, essentially all of the crude petroleum ultimately is utilized, and there is little waste. Labor, constituting less than 6 per cent of the value of the finished product, is used to turn the few switches, guard the grounds, etc.

The significance of these qualities of technology to economic geography is at least twofold: (1) because the efficiency of that technology permits only negligible waste, it is as economical to ship crude petroleum as it is to ship finished products, and hence refineries tend to be located near either markets or raw materials; (2) the small size of the labor force associated with the industry signifies that it is a minor source of livelihood employment and that relatively few settlements and only sparse populations will be directly dependent upon it.

Major Areas of Refinery Production. The United States boasts more than half of the world's approximately seven hundred refineries and an equal proportion of all refining capacity. About 95 per cent of the raw materials is comprised of crude petroleum, and the rest is liquid natural gas. Of the commodities emerging from such production, approximately 44 per cent is gasoline, 38 per cent fuel oil, and the remainder diversified products which number in the thousands.

The largest refinery output is located along the Gulf Coast (Figs. 13.4 and 13.5). The California region, where heavy production and consumption

[4] Offshore from California and from Texas, Louisiana, and, in lesser measure, neighboring states are substantial petroleum reserves that have accumulated in the rock structure of what are now continental shelves. For years there has been disagreement between these states and the Federal government concerning ownership of this oil. A major step toward giving the states control of this land was taken in 1953 with the passage of the United States Continental Shelf Lands Act, giving the jurisdiction to the states within their "traditional and historic boundaries." Now the question has arisen as to how far seaward such boundaries extend. The Federal government maintains that they do not reach beyond 3 miles from the shore line—the traditional limit of coastal waters claimed by this country. The states claim territory beyond this limit, however—Louisiana claiming submerged land as far as 30 miles from the shore line. Recent Supreme Court rulings have reinforced the Federal government's claim to land beyond the 3-mile limit in California, Alabama, Louisiana, and Mississippi but have awarded to Florida and Texas title to lands reaching to 10.5 miles from the shore line. Such differential treatment results largely from varying interpretations of the phrase "traditional and historic boundaries." The entire matter probably is not yet resolved, and congressional action may be attempted.

Raw-material-oriented industry: petroleum refining near Texas City, Texas (U.S. Bureau of Reclamation).

coincide, as well as the Atlantic Coast, where markets predominate, also are very important. Much of the remainder is to be seen along the Great Plains section of the Texas-Kansas-Oklahoma areas of production. In addition to their heavy yields from crude petroleum, none of these areas is without some evidence of the refining of liquid natural gas. As might be anticipated, however, it is Texas and Louisiana which predominate in the production of this commodity.

Administration. The recovery and refining of petroleum in the United States is essentially a responsibility of private enterprise acting under government control. Although at one time single individuals played dominant roles in these operations, they have been largely replaced by giant corporations, many of which are rather tenuously interassociated through controlling ownership of stock and other means. The significance of these corporations to the economy of the country is suggested by the fact that seventeen of them, engaged in the extraction, transportation, and/or refining of petroleum, are included in a list of the 100 leading corporations in the United States when ranked by volume of sales! Indeed, two are among the five uppermost of such companies, six are among the top fifteen, and eleven among the leading fifty. As will be explained in further detail later in this chapter, not all the current operations of these corporations are confined to the United States; and yet most such companies have grown to their present positions mainly because of their domestic activities, upon which they are still dependent for a sizable share of their over-all output and sales.

The Middle East

Although the petroleum wealth of the Middle East has been suspected for some time and initial extraction was begun at about the turn of the twentieth century, full knowledge of the immensity of reserves and full-scale exploitation of those reserves are developments that have come about since the Second World War.

Extraction. Over one-fifth of the world's extracted petroleum comes from these very sizable fields in the Middle East. The speed with which some of these fields have been developed in recent years is illustrated in the fact that production increased by approximately 50 per cent from 1950 to 1954. Three political units are leading producers: Saudi Arabia, Kuwait, and Iraq. A fourth, Iran, also was until recently a primary source, but production there has never fully recovered from the strife of 1951 and the resultant nationalization of much of the industry. Saudi Arabia and Kuwait each account for almost a third of total production, with most of the remainder allocable to Iraq.

The fields tend to be in two clusters (Fig. 13.6). The largest fringes the southwestern, western, and northern portions of the Persian Gulf, whereas the lesser one is almost entirely in Iraq, not far from the Tigris River valley in the upper portion of the country.

Refining. In contrast to the United States, the Middle East contains approximately fifteen refineries which aggregately amount to about 7 per cent

Figure 13.4 **Distribution of petroleum refineries in the United States.** *Note the clustering near raw materials or markets.*

of all refining capacity. In short, most of the petroleum that is extracted in the Middle East is shipped in crude form to refineries located near the markets.

Ownership and Administration. The petroleum belongs to the nations within whose boundaries it occurs; but these, being economically underdeveloped, have leased out sizable tracts to firms from overseas—chiefly to private companies of the United States, as well as to companies in the United Kingdom, France, and the Netherlands. United States interests now control an estimated 58 per cent of all reserves; British firms, over 28 per cent; and the French, over 5 per cent. Almost invariably

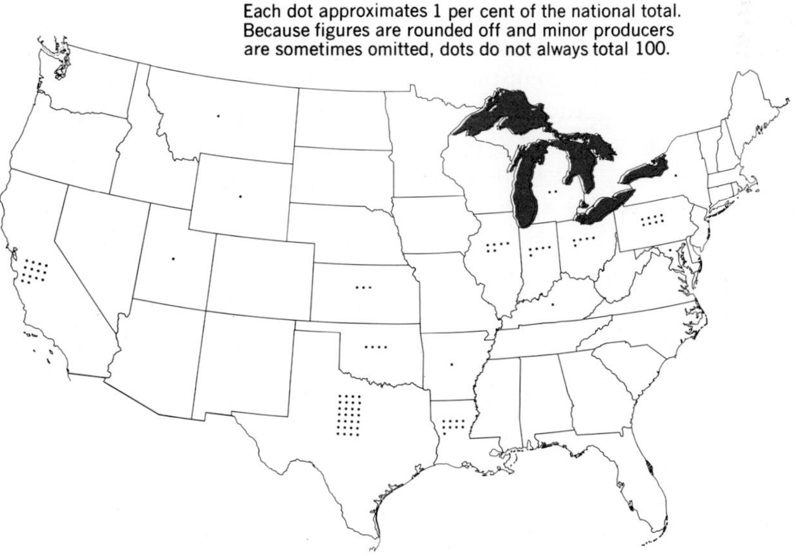

Figure 13.5 **Value of shipments from petroleum refineries in the United States.** *The output of New Jersey, an important refining state, was not included in the reported data. Also unreported was the production in the Southeast and in some single states elsewhere. All in all, the Middle Atlantic and New England states refine nearly 16 per cent of the nation's petroleum. How does this compare with the volume in Texas and Louisiana?*

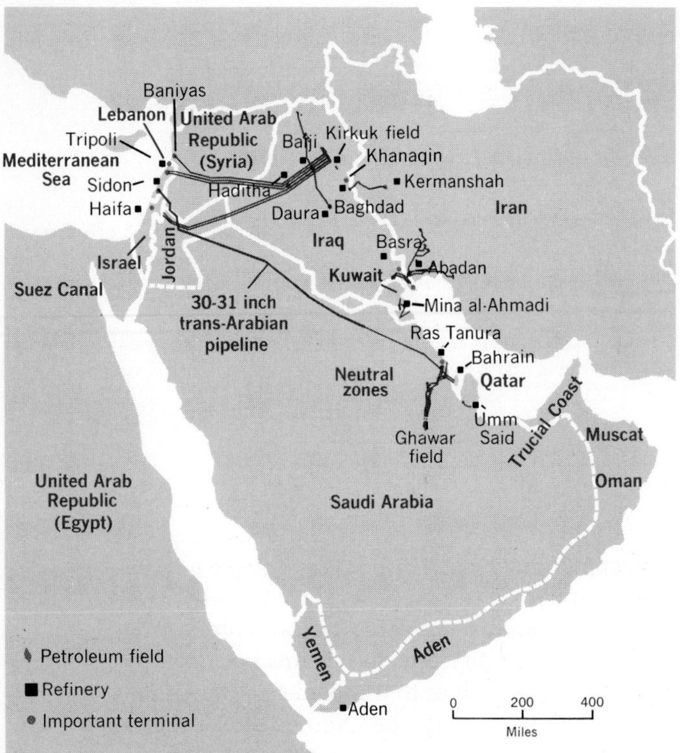

Figure 13.6 ***Petroleum fields, refineries, and pipelines of the Middle East.*** *Why do the pipelines terminate north of the Suez Canal in the Mediterranean Sea?*

the existing concessions are valid until about the year 2000, and the countries possessing the petroleum realize approximately one-half of the net profits of the companies operating the concessions.

The United States companies have been especially active to the southwest of the Persian Gulf and hold almost all the concessions in Saudi Arabia, the Neutral Zone, and the island of Bahrein. In addition, American firms control 50 per cent of the concessions in Kuwait, 40 per cent of those in Iran, and nearly 25 per cent of those in Iraq and Qatar.

British investment has been particularly heavy in Kuwait (50 per cent of all concessions), Iran (40 per cent), Iraq and Qatar (over 25 per cent each). The French have been active in Iraq and Qatar (almost 25 per cent of petroleum investment within each political unit), as well as Iran (6 per cent). Dutch interest has been mainly in Iran, Iraq, and Qatar (with ownership of less than 25 per cent).

Venezuela

Second among individual producing nations, Venezuela currently accounts for about 15 per cent of the world's total petroleum output. The leading fields are in and along the margins of Lake Maracaibo, and to the east near the mouth of the Orinoco River. Nowhere is production far from the sea, and this is fortunate, for most of the petroleum is exported. Both crude petroleum and refined products are shipped, the latter having been processed either in one of the several refineries within or near the fields of extraction or in one of the few but large refineries on the nearby Dutch-owned islands of Aruba and Curaçao in the Netherlands Antilles (Fig. 13.2).

Companies from the United States, the United Kingdom, and the Netherlands are represented in the country, with nearly three-fourths of both reserves and output controlled by firms in the United States.

The Soviet Union

Ranking close to Venezuela in output is the Soviet Union, the production of which has risen more than sevenfold since 1928 and nearly threefold since 1950. Here, in contrast to fields previously discussed, the facilities of production are state-owned.

For a number of years the leading producing field has been at Baku, near the point of entry of the Caucasus Mountains into the Caspian Sea. It was this field which was the major domestic supplier of the war effort against the invading Germans. A second very important producing area had begun to be developed even before the advent of that war, however, and it has been given even more attention since the war's end. Known as the Second Baku, this source area really is a series of fields situated to the southwest of the Ural Mountains along the Volga River. The rapid increases in Soviet petroleum production are due mainly to activity in this area, the output of which increased more than tenfold in the decade after the Second World War and which now accounts for as much as three-fifths of all petroleum recovered in the Soviet Union. The Baku field accounts for an additional one-sixth, and the remaining sources are small and scattered, with the island of Sakhalin of noteworthy importance.

Lesser nations

The remaining 13 per cent of the world's petroleum comes from a number of political units, of which Canada, Mexico, Indonesia, Rumania, and Colombia are among the more outstanding. With certain exceptions, the exploitation in non-Communist nations is by firms of the United States, the United Kingdom, the Netherlands, and France. Those in Rumania and other Communist nations are under the direct administration of their respective national governments after the manner exemplified by the Soviet Union.

TRADE AND TRANSPORTATION

Domestic movement

The movement of petroleum from places of production to those of consumption is largely domestic. More than three-fifths of all crude petroleum and refined products does not cross the political boundaries of the country of origin. A very few nations account for most of such internal trade; the United States and, in much lesser measure, the Soviet Union, are the leaders.

The transfer of natural gas is almost entirely a domestic service, confined even more closely to the economies of a very few nations than the commerce in petroleum.

The United States. COMMERCE. With its sizable land area, its rather generous endowment of natural reserves, and its well-organized system of production acting in response to a whetted domestic demand, the United States accounts for the lion's share of all intranational shipments. The primary movement is from Texas, Louisiana, and regionally neighboring states to the heavily populated manufacturing belt of the Northeast—in other words, from the major areas of production to outstanding areas of consumption. A secondary traffic pattern is from the same area of origin to consumers on the periphery of the manufacturing belt in the South, Middle West, and far North. A third movement is from southern California on the West Coast to points in the Pacific Northwest. A fourth is intercoastal—either via the Panama Canal or overland transport.

TRANSPORTATION MEDIA. Approximately 70 per cent of the petroleum and essentially all the natural gas extracted in the United States moves by pipeline to refineries. Virtual networks of petroleum and natural-gas pipelines serve almost every area of the United States where the demand is upward from moderate. There is now a coast-to-coast reach of natural-gas pipelines, and the petroleum pipelines are nearly as extensive. Individual lines in the United States range in diameter from 6 to 34 inches. Probably the best-known of the individual lines are the Big Inch (24 inches in diameter) and the Little Inch (20 inches), which reach from eastern Texas to the seaboard portion of the manufacturing belt. Built during the last war to carry petroleum and petroleum products otherwise delayed because of the toll taken on the coastwise tanker fleet by German submarines, these now carry natural gas. Among the newest major connections is a 30-inch line stretching from the coastal portion of the Rio Grande River to the New York vicinity some 1,840 miles away.

The pattern of pipeline distribution in the United States reflects the relative significance of this medium of transportation with respect to the commodities being forwarded. The natural-gas lines, carrying essentially all of this commodity, extend directly from areas of production to those of consumption, with their routes sometimes actually paralleling coast lines. Petroleum pipelines are also oriented directly to market areas, particularly where no outstanding competition exists with water transportation. Near the coasts, however—particularly in the Gulf South—these lines reach from the oil fields to the sea, thus facilitating some coastwise tanker movement.

The 30 per cent of domestic petroleum commerce not attributable to pipelines is accounted for by water craft, railway tank cars, and tank trucks, the last two tending to be short-haul carriers. Most of the water movement is by coastwise tanker, although some barge freighting occurs. The primary direction of such movement is from the Gulf South to the shores of the Middle Atlantic states. Ownership and/or control of tank trucks and railway tank cars, like that of pipelines, is chiefly vested in the producing companies. In contrast, nearly all the petroleum-carrying water craft are owned by firms engaged in public conveyance.

Other Nations. A small but increasing amount of domestic commerce in natural gas and an appreciable and increasing amount of domestic commerce in petroleum is found in nations other than the United States. Such commerce tends to move from places of production to those of consumption via the transportation media prevailing in the respective nations. Pipelines, financed mainly by foreign technically advanced nations, are prime movers of petroleum in the Middle East and Caribbean America (especially Venezuela). Diversely financed, they are important in Canada. Financed by the state, they are prominent in the Soviet Union, Rumania, and outlying nations most of which are in the Communist bloc. Movement by railway tank car and water craft is also important in the Soviet Union. Western Europe handles petroleum by water craft, railway tank cars, and tank trucks as well as a few pipelines. Production and/or consumption in the remaining lands, many of which are underdeveloped and essentially without demand for such products, is often near the coast line, and the resultant trade is chiefly international rather than domestic.

International movement

Although well below the volume of domestic commerce, international trade in petroleum is by no means insignificant, exceeding by more than 50 per cent the total analogous traffic in coal (measured by weight). Indeed, over one-third of the world's petroleum output is exported (Fig. 13.2). This global circulation pattern is rather simple in its major outlines: prevailing shipments from the Middle East and Caribbean America move to Western Europe and Anglo-America, and small but numerous trade flows connect countries in South America, the Far East, Oceania, and Africa to these two mammoth producing regions as well as to lesser fields.

Perhaps it is needless to state that there is an overwhelming influence from technically advanced nations upon the current global pattern of trade in petroleum. These are the nations in which internal demand exceeds domestic supply—even in the well-endowed United States—and to these nations comes most internationally traded petroleum. Furthermore, the foreign investment from such nations is heavy; for example, nearly one-third of the direct foreign investment of the United States is in foreign petroleum. A few corporations are of outstanding significance: the Royal Dutch Shell Corporation (comprised of approximately five hundred companies and headquartered in the United Kingdom and the Netherlands) accounts for 14 per cent of the petroleum output of the non-Communist world, and the Standard Oil Company of New Jersey (headquartered in the United States) is responsible for an even higher figure.

The petroleum and/or its refined products are forwarded to temporary or ultimate destinations chiefly in tankers registered under the flags of a very few technically advanced nations, notably the United States, the United Kingdom, and Norway. Upon arrival these varied products are subject to tariffs and other taxes and restrictions that differ widely from nation to nation but are rather severe in much of Europe, particularly West Germany and the United Kingdom. The tariff on imported petroleum is not so high in the United States, but the volume of imports tends to be regulated by other means.

Political and economic arrangements

The exploitation of a resource invariably involves a host of legal, political, and economic arrangements which are usually compounded if such exploitation is undertaken in a foreign land. An excellent overview of some of these has been written in the *World Petroleum Report:*[5]

Oil Laws.

There are four major legal systems governing oil development and production throughout the world. The first of these is the system found in the United States and Canada, under which the oil industry has been developed by a very large number of operators, both large and small. In the United States there are extensive private rights to the subsoil, whereas in Canada such rights are primarily the property of the government. However, this has not prevented a similar pattern of development, particularly since both countries employ a distinctive method of financial encouragement to supply the very large sums necessary, viz., the depletion allowance and the expensing privileges. Both systems employ conservation and prorationing;[6] these are not generally found outside the USA and Canada. And both grant relatively small parcels of land for exploration and development to any one company or individual.

Another unique feature of the North American system is the duration of the production phase, which both in Canada and the United States lasts so long as production in commercial amounts continues; whereas in other countries it is granted only for a specified period. The regulations governing methods used in drilling and production, and for the prevention of waste, also are more highly developed than in any other area.

A second system for the regulation of oil exploration and development is complete or partial nationalization of the industry, such as is found in Mexico, Argentina, Brazil, Chile, the communist countries, and in some other countries in less complete form. Without exception, the demands for capital essential to a rapid growth of the oil industry have exceeded the amounts at the disposal of these countries which have nationalized oil, and they have fallen behind. Some, such as Mexico, have succeeded in building a sizable industry, but all have fallen behind normal expectations and needs. Inadequate capital structure has been aggravated by political considerations, as in Mexico—where the artificially low internal price structure has held down the rate of capital formation, and has prevented adequate investment.

A third system is that found in the major producing countries of the Middle East. These countries have no mining nor oil laws. They are characterized by large concessions which have been concluded, for very long periods, between the oil companies concerned and the local rulers. Generally, these contracts are based on the 50–50 profit sharing concept which originated in Venezuela. However, there are important differences between the various countries of the Middle East because some of them provide for division before foreign taxes, and some after. In addition, there are substantial differences in the method of calculation of the value of production. These differences have tended to iron themselves out, since all the concessions contain a clause stating that any more favorable conditions given to another Middle Eastern country must also be extended to the concessionary country. Furthermore, several of the countries have concluded agreements between themselves for the exchange of information on the details of concession arrangements.

The fourth major system is that found in the majority of South American countries; and it has been adopted, with substantial changes, in many other countries. This is the regulation of oil exploration and production by means of a single petroleum law (sometimes contained as part of the general mining law) which reserves subsoil rights to the nation but grants rights for their development to private enterprises composed either of foreign or local capital.

In recent years an increasing number of countries has adopted this system. They include most of the Central American and Caribbean countries, Guatemala being an example; some countries of Africa, such as Libya and Egypt; Middle Eastern countries, including Turkey, Israel and, to a modified degree, Syria; and countries of the Far East, such as Pakistan and the various states of Australia. Modification of the general mining law is generally used in Europe—as in France, Italy, and Spain—rather than a separate petroleum law.

Most of these laws divide operations into two phases, viz., exploration and exploitation. During the exploration period the duration of the concession initially is about three to five years, with provisions for extensions based on minimum expenditures and sometimes on drilling by the concessionaire. In the case of France, the extension is proportional to the investment; in most other countries extensions are granted if a minimum level has been reached. The concession area is unlimited only in France. In other countries, explora-

[5] *World Petroleum Report*, Mona Palmer Publishing Company, New York, 1957, pp. 16, 19, 22. By permission of the publisher.

[6] Note by the author of the text: These are technical terms referring to enforced curtailment by governments of excessive extraction.

tion areas are small compared with holdings in the major Middle Eastern producing countries, and a limit on the number of concessions per company is enforced. Many laws have eased provisions in areas difficult of access, as in the less accessible areas of Colombia or in the Montaña region of Peru where area limitations are more liberal.

An essential feature of the exploration phase is the guaranteed right of the exploration concessionaire to an exploitation concession covering any discovery he may make. This is essential in view of the large initial investment which is necessary to discover production.

During the exploitation phase, the concessionaire is often subject to the 50–50 profits' sharing arrangement. This originally was designed for such countries as Venezuela, where production has been established for more than a quarter century. It is an advanced concept in the petroleum law of a country which has not had established production, but is contained nevertheless in many of the recently-enacted laws. Generally, the division is accomplished by an income tax which is levied after previous taxes and authorized deductions have been taken from gross income. It absorbs remaining income to accomplish an equal division between company and government. Some countries (not including Venezuela) grant depletion allowances which reduce the impact of this provision—although in some countries, such as Libya, it does not take effect until a certain minimum production level has been achieved.

Extensions of the exploitation period—which generally runs from 30 to 50 years—are usually given subject to the "terms and conditions then in force." Often there is a prohibition against changes in important concession provisions during the life of the concession.

The area covered by the exploitation concession is generally in the neighborhood of one-half the exploration area. The selection of this one-half is left in part to the concessionaire; the remainder reverts to the government, which sometimes establishes "reserves" and regrants the area subject to competitive bidding therefor.

Royalty rates on production vary widely—from unspecified rates in countries such as Switzerland to 12½ per cent in the United States, 16⅔ per cent in Venezuela, and up to 25 per cent in Egypt. Many royalty rates vary with the distance of production sites from nearest marine terminal, as in Colombia and Argentina. Some vary with production rates, usually increasing as production rises.

An initial tax is levied on both exploration and exploitation concessions, and an annual surface tax is generally payable—with suitable guarantees against damage to be posted. Often the surface taxes are deductible from royalties paid during development.

An important aspect pertaining both to exploration and exploitation phases is the obligatory employment and training of nationals of the country in which operations take place. This requirement is found in many countries, and obliges the concessionaire's employment of a certain percentage of nationals in the labor force (usually 75 per cent or more). Often there are certain social welfare obligations—including housing, medical care, etc.

A final series of important provisions are those relating to the transfer of concession rights and the right of voluntary surrender. Generally, concessionaires are given the right to surrender all or part of their concession area, provided concession obligations have been met. Transfer of rights is generally subject to government approval, which is forthcoming only if the transferee meets specified minimum qualifications, and if the transfer does not increase his areas already held to more than the maximums specified in the law.

National Factors.

The attitude of the various governments toward participation of private capital, foreign and domestic, in their local oil industry has undergone a significant change since the end of World War II.

Workable petroleum laws have been passed in Israel, Guatemala, Turkey, Pakistan, Canada, Panama, Bolivia, Libya, Egypt, the Philippines, Peru, Honduras, Iran (where the consortium was worked out after nationalization), and Sicily.

Countries wherein a workable law and/or concession arrangements have been maintained or improved include Venezuela, Colombia, France, England, The Netherlands, Spain (which in 1952 gave a substantial concession contract to an American company, overcoming previous limitations on foreign ownership), Australia, New Guinea, Papua, Switzerland, Iraq, Kuwait, Saudi Arabia, Kuwait–Saudi Arabia Neutral Zone, and the Trucial Coast (including Muscat and Oman).

No major producing countries have joined permanently the ranks of the nationalized countries since the end of World War II. Indonesia still permits substantial private operations on areas held before the war, although Shell's producing properties have not yet been returned (a new law is now being drafted after extensive consultation with various other governments, such as that of Venezuela). Iran, after a brief experiment with nationalization, has returned much of her area to the consortium. Established monopolies in Argentina, Mexico, Brazil, and Chile have remained nationalized—although Argentina and Chile may soon relax their hold. Egypt, however, recently nationalized oil holdings by French and British interests.

Monopolies remain in Afghanistan, the communist countries, and in India—where the government has expressed its determination to take over the industry. Italy has retained its hold over the Po valley, but permits exploration by private enterprises throughout the remainder of peninsular Italy. In Syria a workable law is overshadowed by restrictive ownership requirements.

The trend toward increased governmental participation has continued—with new arrangements in Pakistan, India, Burma, and France indicative of the tendency. Many petroleum laws and concession arrangements—such as the petroleum law of Peru, which provides for offering of 30% of stock of exploring companies to Peruvian citizens, and the obligation in Saudi Arabia to offer 20 per cent of stock in newly formed companies—call for increased governmental participation.

The quotation above treats only a few of the almost endless number of human interrelationships involved in the field of economic geography.

OUTLOOK

In much of the world and notably in technically advanced lands, the consumption of petroleum and natural gas is increasing rather rapidly, despite the comparatively small volume of known reserves. The short-term outlook is toward a continuation of this trend, with technology and efficient management used increasingly to get maximum yields from existing resources and with more efforts by technically advanced nations to develop oil fields wherever such development is feasible. Because the probability of truly extensive reserves is slight, however, the long-term outlook is a gradual veering toward other sources of energy, including that old stand-by, coal, and such new additions and possibilities as atomic and solar energy. In consumption, it is probable that the technically advanced countries will continue to dominate with respect to both petroleum and natural gas, both of which are so adaptable to the intricate and complex machinery of such countries.

REFERENCES

Alderfer, E. B., and H. E. Michl: *Economics of American Industry,* McGraw-Hill Book Company, Inc., New York, 1957. (Especially chap. 16.)

Hager, Dorsey: *Practical Oil Geology,* McGraw-Hill Book Company, Inc., New York, 1951.

Isard, Walter, and Eugene W. Schooler: *Locational Factors in the Petrochemical Industry with Special Reference to Future Expansion in the Arkansas-White-Red River Basins,* U.S. Office of Area Development, 1955.

Melamid, Alexander: "Geographical Distribution of Petroleum Refining Capacities: A Study of the European Refining Program," *Economic Geography,* **31:**168–178, 1955.

Netschert, Bruce C.: *The Future Supply of Oil and Gas,* Johns Hopkins Press for Resources for the Future, Inc., Baltimore, 1958.

Parsons, James J.: "The Geography of Natural Gas in the United States," *Economic Geography,* **26:**162–178, 1950.

Pratt, Wallace E., and Dorothy Good: *World Geography of Petroleum,* Princeton University Press for the American Geographical Society of New York, Princeton, N.J., 1950.

Resources for Freedom: vol. 3, *The Outlook for Energy Sources,* President's Materials Policy Commission, 1952. (Especially pp. 2–21.)

Spangler, Miller B.: *New Technology and the Supply of Petroleum,* University of Chicago Press, Chicago, 1956.

World Petroleum Report, Mona Palmer Publishing Company, New York, 1957.

Woytinsky, W. S., and E. S. Woytinsky: *World Population and Production,* The Twentieth Century Fund, Inc., New York, 1953. (Especially chap. 24.)

14 ELECTRIC AND NUCLEAR ENERGY

COAL, PETROLEUM, AND THEIR ASSOCIATED NATURAL MATERIALS ARE SPECIFICS in the natural environment, and it is not surprising that man came to know them with the passing of time; for these existed, often actually outcropping or seeping at landform surfaces, long before man began to walk the earth. Human beings, since they are creatures of curiosity, had opportunity to become familiar with such materials not only through sight but also through touch, taste, and smell.

Electricity and nuclear power, however, are more elusive. To be sure, electricity long has flashed rather crudely across the sky in the form of lightning; but a flash is scarcely sufficient time for serious study of an object, and lightning somehow does not lend itself to capture and subsequent laboratory observation. These energy forms—nuclear power especially—have been realized more through man's reliance upon his reasoning facilities than through his use of the senses. Small wonder that they have come to be known so recently! Indeed, as one scans the timetable of energy utilization (Table 11.1), he wonders why it was that electric power came into use at about the same time as petroleum.

ELECTRICITY

It is more accurate to think of electricity as a form rather than a source of energy because, unlike the fuels and nuclear sources, it is not taken directly from nature but is derived essentially from man-made generators. These, in turn, are activated by energy in a different form. Over two-thirds of all electric energy comes from generators that are driven by turbines powered chiefly by (1) steam which has been heated by coal, petroleum products, natural gas, or less common sources, including atomic energy, or by (2) internal combustion engines powered by gasoline, etc. (Fig. 14.1). Such energy is called *fuel-generated,* or *thermoelectric,* energy. Nearly one-third is obtained from generators driven by turbines powered by running water. This is called *hydroelectric* energy. Finally, a very small amount of electricity is secured from wind chargers, solar chargers, etc.

Thus, in the chapters on coal and petroleum, we have been giving at least partial attention, frequently by implication, to the production of electric energy, and we shall be thinking partially of electricity generation when we discuss atomic power later in this chapter. Among the sources of electric energy not given special attention elsewhere in this book are the hydroelectric sources, which currently account for at least 2 per cent[1] of world output.

CONSUMPTION

Electric energy is not easily stored in large quantities, and hence the amount of its annual consumption is essentially that of production minus losses; this is truer of electric energy than of most other forms of energy.

The world

The annual consumption of all electric energy amounts to about 7 per cent of the consumption of energy from all sources[2] (Fig. 11.4). Most of this is used by manufacturing industries, which account for between 50 and 90 per cent of electricity consumption in the majority of countries where it is used at all. Within the category of manufacturing, electricity is utilized chiefly to drive motors and secondarily to heat electric furnaces, maintain electrolytic cells,[3] and light factories. Transportation, commercial, and household activities are also important consumers of electricity, yet the last-named reaches its peak significance in technically advanced nations.

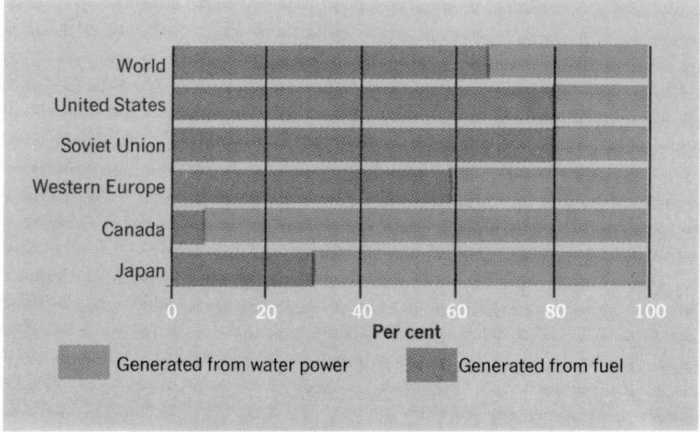

Figure 14.1 ***Electricity generated from water power compared with electricity generated from fuel in selected countries and areas.*** *Percentages in the United States and the Soviet Union are about the same. Why is hydroelectric energy so important in Canada and Japan?*

Individual nations

The consumption of electricity, like that of coal, petroleum, and natural gas, reflects the overwhelming dominance of a very few technically advanced nations in world economic affairs. The United States is responsible for using up nearly two-fifths of the world's electric energy, the Soviet Union for one-

---

[1] Because energy comes in so many forms, reducing all of them to a common denominator is always tricky. The percentage above, taken from the United Nations publication *World Energy Supplies, 1955–1958,* differs sharply from an earlier report by that same organization *(World Energy Supplies, 1951–1954),* which allocates 8 per cent of all energy to electricity. The cause: differences in assumed ratios to the common denominator.

[2] However, it should be kept in mind that about two-thirds of this electricity was obtained from fuel-generated units consuming coal, petroleum, and natural gas, which are the actual sources of thermoelectric electricity.

[3] This terminology is doubtless familiar to the reader except possibly the electrolytic processes. One of the peculiar functions performed by electricity is the end processing of certain materials. The most common process is *electrolysis,* the passing of an electric current through a weak acid into which certain smelted or concentrated metals have been submerged. Under the stimulus of the current, the metals disassociate themselves from their matrixes and attach themselves in almost a pure state to electric terminals that are also submerged in the bath. This and other electric processes use up much electricity, as is suggested by the following annotation of kilowatthours consumed per ton of finished product: titanium, 40,000; aluminum, 18,000; electrolytic magnesium, 16,000; electrolytic manganese, 10,200; 70 per cent ferrotungsten, 7,600; sodium chlorate, 5,200; rayon, 5,200; phosphoric acid, 3,900; electrolytic zinc, 3,400; chlorine, 3,000: (Data from *Resources of Freedom,* vol. 3, *The Outlook for Energy Sources,* President's Materials Policy Commission, 1952, p. 34.) Managers of plants producing these and similarly derived commodities must always give the cost of power very careful consideration and often must locate their facilities in the vicinity of electricity production.

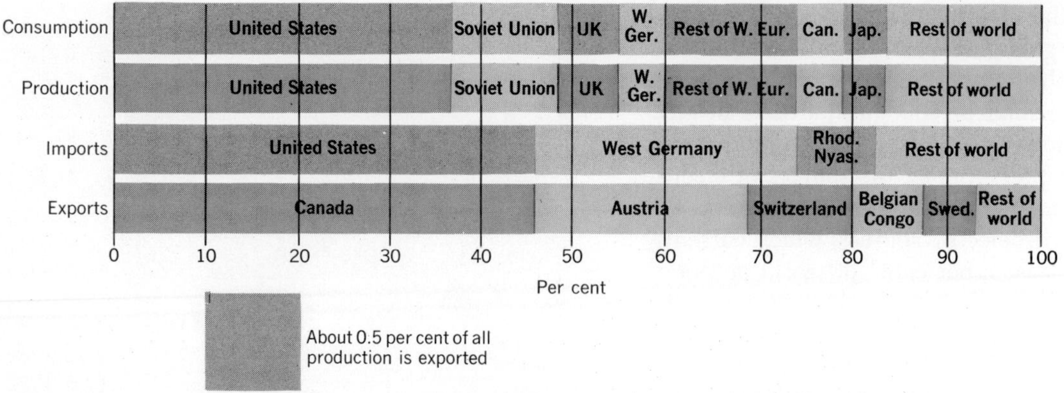

Figure 14.2 ***Consumption, production, import, and export of electricity.*** *Only a tiny amount enters international trade. To what areas does Canada export electricity? Austria? Switzerland? The former Belgian Congo?*

eighth, and Western Europe for one-fourth. No single nation of this last group accounts for more than 6 per cent of the world total, but the United Kingdom, West Germany, and France are predominant. Some additional countries also are significant, the most outstanding being Canada and Japan (Fig. 14.2 and Table 14.1). All in all, eight nations—the United States, the Soviet Union, the United Kingdom, Canada, West Germany, Japan, France, and Italy—consume over three-fourths of the world's electric energy.

PRODUCTION AND TRADE

Inasmuch as electricity cannot be transmitted economically beyond an absolute range of 500 miles and an optimum distance of 300 miles from its point of origin, and cannot be stored satisfactorily, it does not enter actively into international trade, and only in a few areas is its long-distance transmission of more than passing significance.[4] Slightly more than ½ per cent of all electricity enters into international trade, and this is chiefly (1) a series of give-and-take exchanges among the small, dynamic nations of Western Europe, and (2) a unilateral movement from Canada to the United States.

The United States

The commercial production of electricity in the United States began essentially at the turn of the century and quickly expanded into a major industry involving an interesting variety of administrative organizations—private firms acting as public utilities, private firms producing for their own manufacturing purposes, cooperatives, and levels of government ranging from the municipal to Federal. The rate of its increase in output has been almost as marked as its administration has been complex: 6 billion kilowatthours were produced in 1902, 388.7 billion in 1950, and 797.4 billion in 1959, and an estimated 1,400 billion will be generated in 1975![5]

Thermoelectric Units. Even at the outset, thermoelectric units outproduced hydroelectric plants in the United States by a ratio of at least 2:1—a ratio that increased over the years to 3:1 at mid-century, and is expected to reach 4:1 by 1975, despite the

[4] Wherever networks of power facilities exist, however, it is possible for a producing unit or region to aid an area beyond the 500-mile range if cooperation is achieved among the administering organizations. This is done by having a unit or region of electricity surplus divert that extra amount to neighboring facilities; these, in turn, divert their newly acquired surplus to their neighbors, and ultimately the region of power shortage is thus reached.

[5] *Resources for Freedom, op. cit.*, pp. 32, 36, for figures on initial, 1950, and future production; mimeographed report from the Federal Power Commission for 1959 production.

innovation of the Tennessee Valley Authority and other river-basin-development programs. As explained in previous chapters, coal has been the main fuel for thermoelectric, or fuel-generated, power units, and its relative position is strengthening rather than lessening: in 1950 it was responsible for nearly one-half of the nation's total electricity, with petroleum products and natural gas sharing an additional one-fourth, and hydroelectric power supplying the final one-fourth. Furthermore, the President's Materials Policy Commission has estimated that by 1975 coal will supply about three-fifths of an electrical output which will have more than tripled its 1950 level. Petroleum products and natural gas will each supply one-tenth, and hydroelectric power the remaining one-fifth.

Thermoelectric plants tend to be located at the point of maximum profit. In some areas it is cheaper to transport electricity via transmission line than it is to forward a fuel via any one of several carriers, and hence the power stations are located near the source of the fuel. Under different circumstances, however, the conditions are reversed, and the stations are located near the primary markets rather than near fuel sources. In practice, most of the thermoelectric units tend to be near markets, their distribution corresponding remarkably with the location of the manufacturing belt and major urban areas—the major places of consumption.

Thermoelectric units possess two really major advantages over hydroelectric plants: (1) mobility and (2) low initial costs. The first point we have described in the paragraph above; they need not be located at a given site but can be located at the point of maximum financial return or other advantage. The second point is appreciated with the realization that the initial costs of a thermoelectric unit are chiefly those of the generator, the turbine, the structure in which to house them, and the arrangement for the storage and application of their fuel. In contrast, the initial costs of a hydroelectric plant usually involve the construction of a major dam—safe not only for the electric plant but also for people and property hundreds of miles away. The lake behind the dam will frequently inundate hundreds of thousands of acres of ground and associated settlements—even cities—and the purchase of such land is costly. This, in addition to generators, turbines, rectifiers, etc.!

TABLE 14.1

World electric power: fifteen countries with greatest installed capacity

Country	*Installed capacity 1,000 kw*	
	1948	*1959*
United States	69,615	174,998
Soviet Union	18,000	59,140
United Kingdom	13,300	33,820
West Germany	6,175	24,850
Canada	9,404	23,333
Japan	10,061	21,573
France	10,910	20,650
Italy	6,190	15,700
Communist China	na*	9,500
Sweden	3,780	8,388
East Germany	4,500	7,100
Spain	1,738	6,546
Poland	na	6,098
Norway	3,000	5,911
Australia	2,280	5,470
World total†	193,012	499,465

* Not available.
† The fifteen leading producers accounted for nearly 85 per cent of the world's installed capacity in 1959.
SOURCE: Federal Power Commission.

Until recently, however, hydroelectric plants were considered to be somewhat more economical over a period of years than most thermoelectric plants. Once the dam is built and the reservoir formed, most additional expense involves maintenance. Nature provides the power. Yet, notably since the last war, thermoelectric units are becoming increasingly efficient and inexpensive to operate since much larger generators are now being employed. The resultant electrical output exceeds appreciably the amount of additional fuel required.

In the United States, thermoelectric units have been used particularly by private firms, which control nearly 90 per cent of this country's fuel-generated energy output. Most of these firms are public utilities, but a minority are companies and corporations producing to meet their own needs.

Hydroelectric Units. Unlike their thermoelectric counterparts, hydroelectric-power units must be located where moving water is to be had—preferably water in an assured, uniform supply over rapids or falls high enough so that substantial natural force is available to turn the turbines. Essentially this means rivers and streams, although the idea of harnessing some tides has been given serious consideration. In distribution, therefore, hydroelectric units are located closer to river drainage basins than to markets, the optimum sites being favorable in respect to both these features.

The significance of climate in the generation of hydroelectric power is pronounced. Optimum climates provide sufficiently continuous moisture to assure a constant power output and yet are not so cold that severe winter freezing ensues. The moist, rather moderate climates of the eastern half of the United States (humid subtropical, humid continental warm-summer and cool-summer), and that of much of the Pacific Northwest (marine) are notably conducive to hydroelectric-power generation, as are the conditions on the high (chiefly western) slopes of the Sierra Nevada, Cascade, and Rocky Mountains.

Landforms and drainage, acting in coordination with climates, are also important to the generation of hydroelectric power. Landforms not only provide the elevation which is so vital to the building up of water pressure for subsequent activating of the turbines but also contain the sites—some good, some intermediate, some bad—for dam construction. A choice site should have a firm rock base, should be narrow enough so that a dam is feasible, and should be so located that a reservoir can form without the inundation of an excessive amount of countryside.

Drainage tends to be a direct response to precipitation except where natural or man-made reservoirs exist, where winter freezing temporarily paralyzes water flow, or where the summertime melting of winter-deposited snow and ice stimulates delayed stream activity. Ideal drainage conditions for hydroelectric generation involve waterways that are of uniform flow. This is accomplished when, as does the St. Lawrence River, a waterway drains a sizable lake or inland sea and hence flows evenly despite fluctuations in precipitation.

Unlike thermoelectric units, hydroelectric plants and their associated dams cannot stand alone satisfactorily in the landscape—unaffected by, and unaffecting, surrounding features. For dams impound and conserve water that is of increasingly short supply; they provide for the inundation of heretofore useful land by reservoirs which, in turn, often become focal points for recreationists and other interested people and groups; they affect navigable channels and sometimes interfere with fishing runs—in short, their presence in an area means the alteration of the character of the countryside into which they have been injected. They are key factors in the wise use of any river drainage basin.

Partially because of their many-sided ramifications, hydroelectric plants tend to be of greater interest to governments than do fuel-generated units. In the United States, the Federal government owns nearly 50 per cent, and lower levels of government over 5 per cent, of all hydroelectric capacity. Federal-government ownership or control tends to be asserted through three administrative channels: (1) in the Tennessee River valley, the Tennessee Valley Authority, a public corporation has jurisdiction over aspects of the valley involving electric-power production, flood control, navigation, irrigation, and recreation; (2) along rivers and streams where navigation is the major objective, the Corps of Engineers of the Department of Defense is responsible for building and maintaining Federal dams; (3) in areas where irrigation and other land-reclamation projects are paramount, the Bureau of Reclamation of the Department of the Interior is responsible for the Federal dams and associated measures. Not infrequently, these two last agencies are both active along a single river, the Corps of Engineers along the trunk section and the Bureau of Reclamation along the upper tributaries. Although not all Federal dams are large, most of the very large dams in the United States are Federal dams. Included in this group are such familiar giants as Grand Coulee, Hoover, McNary, Bonneville, Oahe, Wilson, Garrison, and Shasta.

Private enterprise in hydroelectric power, although secondary to government, is not insignificant, for it owns about 40 per cent of all hydroelectric capacity. Private firms serving as public utilities are paramount, accounting for over 35 per cent of the national production, leaving less than 5 per cent to companies generating for their own consumption. By and large, their dams are smaller and are situated more markedly in the Eastern portion of the country than is true of government-owned projects. Thus they are near markets and concomitantly are located on good production sites.

The remaining 5 per cent of United States hydroelectric production is accounted for by cooperatives, public power districts, and facilities owned by the various states.

Interlocking Circuits among Thermoelectric and Hydroelectric Units. Like most human creations, specific thermoelectric and hydroelectric units are not completely dependable. Fuel shortages or mechanical failures may disrupt the output of thermoelectric units, and water shortages or mechanical failures may do the same for hydroelectric units. These units, therefore, are usually interconnected in a series of transmission lines, so that all basic electricity requirements can be met, even during times of emergency, and so that maximum advantage can be taken of optimum operating conditions. During times of high water, for example, it might be more advantageous to run the hydroelectric units at their peak loads, and rest the fuel-generated units. Conversely, the latter are ready for action in case of drought, etc.

Thermoelectric and Hydroelectric Potential. The potential for thermoelectric production is basically without limit, for all that is vital for such production is water and a source of heat. Presumably, even if the very extensive reserves of coal known to exist in the United States should be used up (after some thousands of years at our present rate of use!), endless solar energy could be adapted for this purpose.

Hydroelectric power, however, is limited to the number of available sites and the capacity of the turbines and associated generators that can be mounted on each site. It is estimated that approximately one-fifth of the potential hydroelectric capacity of the United States has been developed, and this has been done mostly in the Southeastern and Middle Atlantic states. Among individual states, tiny Rhode Island and Delaware are making almost full use of their potential, and the Piedmont states of North Carolina, South Carolina, and Alabama have reached about one-half of their estimated capacities. Tennessee is not quite three-fifths developed, despite the fact that it cores the famed Tennessee Valley Authority. Most of the Great Lakes states have realized about one-third of their rather niggardly potential. Among the Western states, where most of the nation's potential exists, only Nevada has been developed to a high stage. It is

The Grand Coulee Dam is the largest single hydroelectric unit in the United States. It has an installed capacity of 1,974,000 kilowatts. Second in the nation is Hoover Dam, with 1,250,000 kilowatts. Dams like this one are very costly to build, but not too costly to maintain. (U.S. Bureau of Reclamation)

here, in the Far West and the Mountain West, that most of the nation's future hydroelectric power will be created, for these two areas aggregately boast nearly 60 per cent of the nation's estimated total potential.

The Soviet Union

Although comparatively modest, the production of electricity in the Soviet Union is somewhat analogous to the generation of electric power in the United States. In both countries, primary reliance is placed upon thermoelectric units, which tend to be clustered in areas of heavy population pressure and manufacturing activity. In both countries, coal is the chief fuel in thermoelectric production. In both countries, some coal fields are located in or near the centers of consumption, so that the fuel-generated units can be oriented simultaneously to fuels and markets. In both countries, hydroelectric power has been given more than passing attention, but appreciable potential remains—chiefly in countrysides of relatively sparse population somewhat removed from the main centers of consumption. And in both countries, the output of electricity has increased almost phenomenally since the turn of the century, and especially since mid-century.

The most striking difference between the electrical output of the two countries is to be found not so much in geographical patterns of distribution as in administration: in contrast to the predominance of private enterprise in the United States, state ownership and control prevails in the Soviet Union, and electricity generation is only one component in the comprehensive planning of that country.

Thermoelectric Units. In the coal-rich Ukraine and Moscow regions, fuel-generated units are especially numerous and active. The lignites of the Moscow region can be used almost as efficiently as the better-quality Donets coals—for their sole purpose is essentially to heat water—and both regions are hence outstanding producers. Additional units are to be found in the Urals, Kuznets, Irkutsk, and adjacent places of consumption, including Vladivostok on the Pacific Coast. Although these major producers more or less outline the over-all distribution pattern of thermoelectric units, many smaller generating stations are present in lesser cities and towns as a result of the Soviet policy of rendering each of its economic regions as independent economically as possible so that the burden of transportation is minimized. Currently, thermoelectric units account for about 80 per cent and hydroelectric plants 20 per cent of Russia's total electrical output. Fuels include not only coal but also wood waste and other products, peat, petroleum, and natural gas.

Hydroelectric Power. Most of the 30 billion kilowatthours of hydroelectric power generated in the Soviet Union in 1956[6] was from dams along the Volga, Dnieper, and Kama Rivers. The potential in European Russia, however, is not overly impressive, amounting to not more than 6 times the developed power, assuming average river flow.

It is in Asian Russia that the remarkable potential exists—so remarkable, in fact, that the Soviet Union is exceeded among political units only by the former Belgian Congo in estimated total hydroelectric potential. Nearly one-eighth of the world total is credited to the Soviet Union, which possesses more than twice the potential of the United States. Most of this is in the highlands, plateaus, and mountains east of the Yenisei River and along the mountains constituting the southern border of Soviet Central Asia.

One of the most outstanding hydroelectric possibilities, smaller than the Great Lakes–St. Lawrence system but otherwise somewhat analogous to it, is Lake Baikal and its associated waterways. This deepest of world lakes, almost 5,000 feet in depth, is fed principally by the Selenga River and drained mainly by the Angara River. A constant water supply is thus assured on the Angara for hydroelectric-power generation.

In addition to distance from market, most of the places of potential hydroelectric-power production in the Soviet Union are faced with a rather

[6] The United States produced 122 billion kilowatthours of hydroelectric power in the same year.

serious difficulty in their adverse climates (subarctic, humid continental cool- and warm-summer, tundra). These are not only extremely frigid during the winter months but in some areas exhibit a tendency toward erratic seasonal precipitation, with the wet-summer–dry-winter monsoon conditions that prevail over eastern and southern Asia apparent even in some outer fringes of these northerly reaches. In the interior, continental-type climates tend also to be wetter in summer than in winter. River flow is affected accordingly.

Electricity and the Seven-Year Plan. The objectives of the current Seven-Year Plan call for the generation of 510 billion kilowatthours of electricity annually by 1965, as compared with 42.2 billion produced in 1945, 91.2 billion in 1950, and 233 billion in 1958. Both the thermoelectric and hydroelectric units are being given attention. Inasmuch as manufacturing, transportation, and commercial activities consume almost 90 per cent of all Soviet electric power, the initiation of new activities is not to occur until sufficient energy exists for their successful operation. Otherwise a demand surplus might develop. Energy, including electric energy, is thus a pivotal consideration in Soviet economic planning.

Western Europe

The very pronounced rate of recent increase in electricity generation in the United States and the Soviet Union has been matched by that in Western Europe, the output of which will soon amount to twice its 1950 level. As stated previously, the United Kingdom, West Germany, France, and Italy are the leading nations. Whether the output is from thermoelectric or hydroelectric sources depends largely upon the presence or absence of fuels and/or natural conditions conducive to water-power utilization (Fig. 14.1). Accordingly, the Netherlands depends entirely upon thermoelectric units and Norway almost entirely upon hydroelectric units; the remaining countries may be ranked at levels somewhere between these two extremes. Of the leaders, the United Kingdom depends upon thermoelectric units for 97 per cent of electrical output, West Germany for 84 per cent, France for 51 per cent, and Italy for 20 per cent, the remainder being supplied by hydroelectric sources. For all of non-Communist Europe, about three-fifths of the electricity comes from fuel-generated units and the remainder from water power. Households account for a generally higher percentage of total consumption than in the Soviet Union, but not so high as in the United States.

Canada

Canada's production of electricity has also mushroomed during the latter portion of this century. Nearly 95 per cent of this is hydroelectric power, obtained chiefly along the northern margins of the Great Lakes–St. Lawrence system and in the Pacific west. The completion of the Great Lakes–St. Lawrence Seaway, the hydroelectric costs, profits, and administration of which are shared by the province of Ontario and the state of New York, has added to this output.

Japan

Japan's tiny rivers and rivulets, bursting over short trajectories to the sea, are not the most ideal for the smooth functioning of hydroelectric units. The monsoon climate, which makes for seasonal rainfall, is of no help. Yet some rivers drain lakes of generally small but varying size and have a quasi-assured flow. All in all, various waterways supply nearly 70 per cent of the total electricity of Japan, a country which, in turn, accounts for nearly two-thirds of the entire Asian electrical production, excluding that of the Soviet Union (Fig. 14.1). The three southern islands contain most of the sites for both hydroelectric and thermoelectric units.

Communist nations

Only about 20 per cent of the world's electric energy is generated by Communist nations, and approximately three-fourths of this amount is attributable to the Soviet Union. Among the lesser nations, East Germany, Czechoslovakia, and Communist China are the leaders. Except in North Korea and Yugoslavia, thermoelectric units are the mainstays of production.

Outlying nations

We have emphasized to this point in the chapter the dynamic manufacturing nations in Anglo-America, Europe, the Soviet Union, and some of their immediate neighbors. Countries which are removed from these core areas, whether they are technically advanced or underdeveloped, send forth only modest contributions to the world supply of electric power. The reader has probably correctly anticipated that Australia, the Union of South Africa, and Brazil are foremost among these outlying nations, and that the remaining countries, most of them underdeveloped, do not presently produce much electric energy.

POLICIES

Like petroleum, most electric energy is produced with capital equipment belonging to technically advanced nations. Unlike petroleum, most such energy is produced within the domestic confines of those nations. Foreign investment, overseas transportation media and costs, tariffs, etc., are considerations which, if they enter at all into the electrical production scene, do so very moderately. Home production is an outstanding administrative policy in the generation of electricity.

A second policy is that of government control and/or ownership. Even in the United States, the production of electric energy is a governmental responsibility to a much higher degree than is the output of coal, petroleum, or natural gas. In most other countries, essentially all generating plants are government-owned, and the trend is toward more, rather than less, of this type of ownership.

A third policy is in reality two policies, divided by the iron curtain: in the Communist orbit, the lion's share of electrical production is utilized by manufacturing, transportation, and commerce. In much of the non-Communist world, notably in the technically advanced nations, a relatively higher percentage is made available to individuals and households.

POTENTIAL

If most of the world's developed electricity is in technically advanced lands, the potential—certainly for hydroelectricity—is elsewhere. The combination of rainy climates (especially tropical rain-forest) with landforms of at least moderate height (especially in central Africa) renders many underdeveloped countries potentially rich in this source of power. Africa alone possesses an estimated 40 per cent of the world total potential, with Asia accounting for nearly 23 per cent, North America for 13 per cent, Europe for nearly 11 per cent, South America for over 10 per cent, and Oceania for about 3 per cent.

Nearly one-fifth of the world's potential lies in rainy, rather high-standing landforms of the former Belgian Congo, and almost all the neighbors of that country are also well provided with possibilities. Eastern and southern Asia and Latin America also have possibilities. The difficulty is chiefly lack of demand, which is desire plus purchasing power. The markets of technically advanced lands are too far removed—much beyond the 500-mile limit—for sales there, and most native populations simply cannot afford the luxury, either as individuals or as groups acting through their governments, of electrical consumption. With increasing nationalistic tendencies in many of these countries, however, it is probable that more of this potential will be realized before the turn of the next century.

NUCLEAR ENERGY

On December 2, 1942, beneath some of the stands in an unused football stadium at the University of Chicago, history's first successfully controlled nuclear fission—release of energy from an atomic nucleus—was achieved after many years of international cooperation and experimentation. One of several wartime projects, this reaction found its first major application in a military use—the produc-

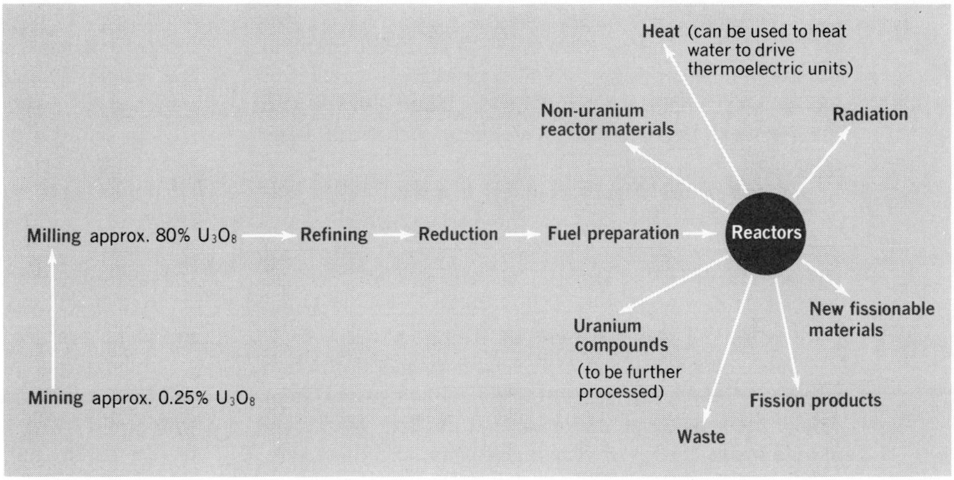

Figure 14.3 ***The chain of operations in obtaining energy and materials through fission*** *(after* Atomic Energy Facts, *Atomic Energy Commission, Washington, D.C., 1957, opp. p. iv).*

tion of a bomb. But its significance for peacetime purposes is also pronounced—so much so that its discovery has been termed the most striking technical advance since the discovery of fire.

OVERVIEW OF FISSION

Basic concepts

Nuclear energy results from a conversion of matter into energy. The matter thus far found to be sufficiently instable for such conversion consists of uranium (uranium 235 and uranium 233) and plutonium (plutonium 239).[7] The first of these, uranium 235, occurs naturally, and the other two are derived by man from natural elements. The uranium 233 comes chiefly from thorium 232, and plutonium 239 comes chiefly from uranium 238. When the reaction of these fissionable materials occurs under certain circumstances without retardation, the atomic bomb is achieved. Although man has designed some means of slowing the reaction, he has not yet gone beyond rather cumbersome techniques and thus has not yet been able to utilize handily the energy released from controlled nuclear fission. This does not mean that he has been unable to use nuclear energy but that he has not been able to make much use of it directly except for purposes of destruction. What he has done has been to use the energy generated by controlled fission to heat water into steam which, in turn, activates thermoelectric units in the traditional manner. It is in this indirect utilization that atomic power is currently finding its most pronounced technical application as a source of energy.[8] Energy resulting from nuclear fission can be used also to heat factories and households and for other heating purposes.

Appraisal by the Atomic Energy Commission

The United States Atomic Energy Commission recently has summarized atomic energy utilization as follows:[9]

> The accompanying chart [Fig. 14.3] pictures the chain of industrial operations involved in supplying the uranium fuel and special materials needed by the atomic industry and illustrates the broad fields of application for reactors and their products.

[7] The numbers in parentheses following the names of the elements indicate the different numbers of neutrons in the nuclei of specific elements. See especially B. C. Netschert, and S. H. Shurr, *Atomic Energy Applications with Special Reference to Underdeveloped Countries,* Johns Hopkins Press for Resources for the Future, Inc., Baltimore, 1957, p. 1.

[8] We are speaking here of the usefulness of radioactive materials as a source of *energy* and hence mention only in passing their usefulness in measuring, in medicine, in food preservation, etc.

[9] *Atomic Energy Facts,* United States Atomic Energy Commission, 1957, pp. iv–v.

The chart begins with *mining*. The western part of the United States, with more than 1,000 uranium mines, has become the nation's primary source of this increasingly important ore. Canada, South Africa and the [former] Belgian Congo continue to furnish large quantities.

A ton of ore usually contains less than 10 pounds of "U-three-O-eight" (U_3O_8), the oxide in which uranium content is generally expressed. Average content of United States ore is about 5 pounds per ton or 0.25 percent U_3O_8. *Milling* near the mine yields a concentrate averaging about 80 percent U_3O_8.

This concentrate is converted into metal through a series of chemical and metallurgical processing steps called feed material operations. It is first *refined* to orange oxide (UO_3) of very high purity, and this oxide, in turn, is converted to *green salt* (UF_4).

Then two paths are followed—one for the production of normal uranium metal and the other for production of enriched metal containing more of the fissionable "235" isotope than occurs in nature. For the production of normal metal, the green salt (UF_4) is reduced to metal and cast into ingots which can then be fabricated into fuel elements for reactors. Three large Government-owned feed materials centers for these operations are to be augmented by a fourth which will be built and operated privately to supply materials for which the Government has contracted.

To produce enriched uranium metal, the green salt (UF_4) is converted by *fluorination* to uranium hexafluoride (UF_6) which becomes feed to the Commission's large *gaseous diffusion* plants. By tapping the line at different places, uranium hexafluoride of almost any desired degree of enrichment can be drawn off. The uranium in this gas is *reduced* to metal for the fabrication of enriched fuel elements or is made into other forms of fuel for *reactors*.

Thus far much of the output of the diffusion plants has been enriched uranium for weapons. Likewise, most of the natural uranium metal has been fabricated into fuel elements for reactors that produce plutonium for weapons.

The fuel elements of all *reactors* must be removed when only a small part of their uranium has been consumed. After "cooling" to reduce its extremely high radioactivity, irradiated fuel goes to a chemical *separations* plant where plutonium and the unused uranium are recovered. The separated uranium has a lower isotopic enrichment than the original fuel elements because of uranium 235 burn-up in the reactor. This partially depleted uranium in various *uranium compounds* is returned to the process stream for reuse. Usually it is fed to a *gaseous diffusion* plant for enrichment, but if the uranium 235 content is sufficient it might be returned directly.

In addition to the fuels, other special *reactor materials* have been developed. For example, the metals, zirconium and beryllium, and heavy water, formerly laboratory curiosities, are now produced in quantity at a small fraction of their former cost. Graphite of "laboratory purity" is now a production item.

All reactors produce *heat, radiation* and *fission products.*

The large quantities of highly radioactive fission product *wastes* from separations plants are concentrated and stored. Some radioisotopes, useful in industry, research, and medicine, are recovered from the mixed, "gross" fission products, but by and large, the utilization and disposition of these wastes constitute a challenging problem to scientists and engineers.

Of the several forms of *radiation* generated by reactors, neutron radiation is of chief value. Research reactors are designed especially for the utilization of neutrons in different kinds of research. Neutrons are also used to produce most radioisotopes by the irradiation of the proper target materials.

In production reactors, neutrons produce the *new fissionable material,* plutonium, from the fertile material, uranium 238. Indeed, any reactor can produce some plutonium if its fuel contains uranium 238. Similarly, uranium 233 can be produced from thorium. Plutonium, thus far used mostly for weapons, and uranium 233 are also potential reactor fuels.

Power reactors are designed to utilize reactor *heat* at as high temperatures as possible for good power plant efficiency. The Government is developing power reactors for the propulsion of submarines, ships and aircraft and for small portable military power plants. Government and industry are cooperating in the development of central station electric power plant reactors.

The use of reactors for space and process heating, that is, for warming buildings and for chemical and metallurgical processing, is being investigated.

NUCLEAR ENERGY AND ECONOMIC GEOGRAPHY

Significant assets of nuclear energy

The advent of nuclear energy is especially significant to the economic geographer in that such energy is: (1) a source heretofore unknown and

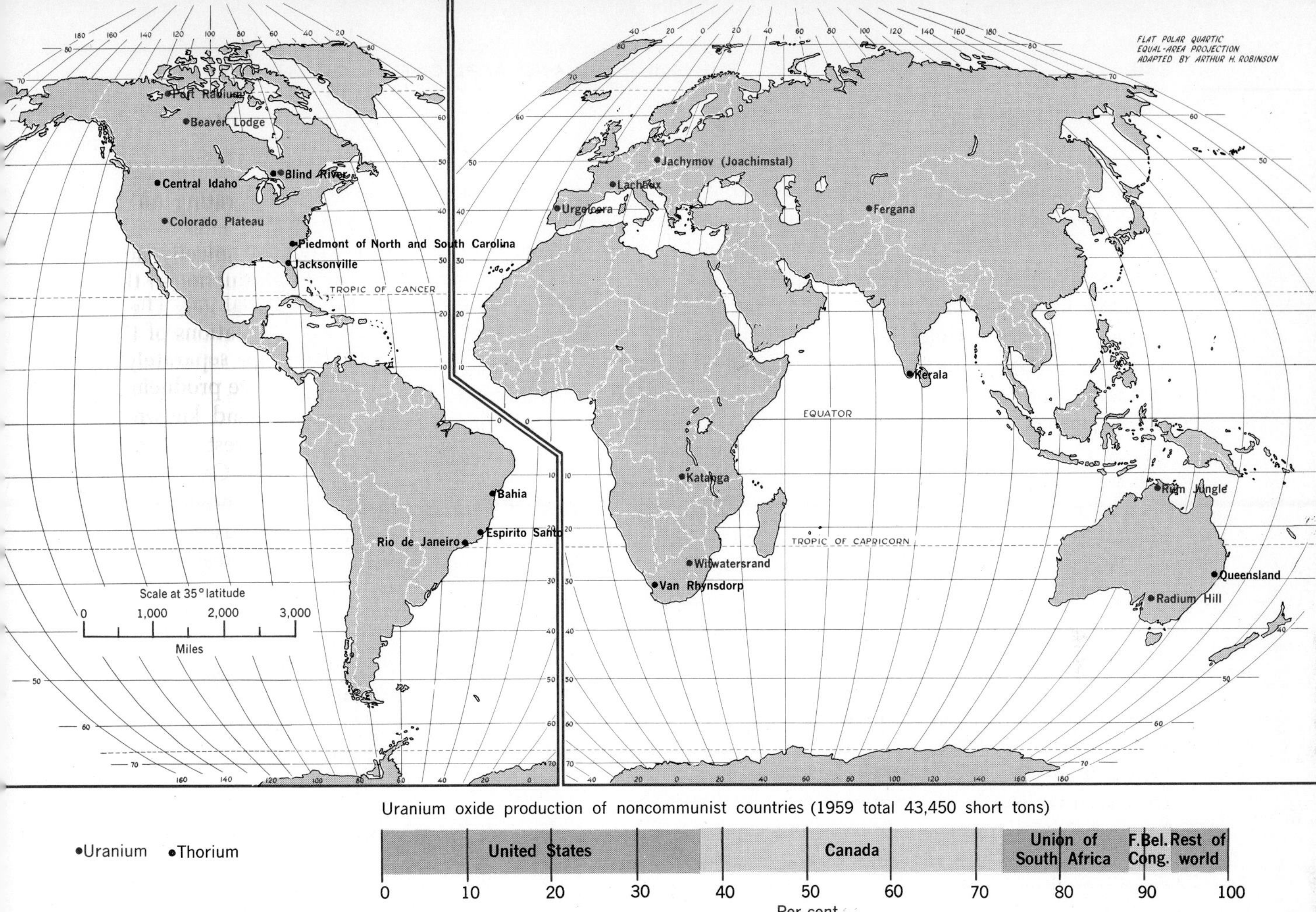

Figure 14.4 ***World production of uranium and thorium. The United States and Canada dominate the non-Communist uranium output.***

unused, (2) apparently rather extensive in natural reserves, (3) highly mobile, (4) applicable not only to actual production but also to transportation, space heating, and other economic activities, and (5) rapidly moving from the laboratory stages to those of economic and other application.

Distribution of Reserves. We have discussed at an earlier place in this chapter the first point listed above—the uniqueness of nuclear energy—and hence shall pass on quickly to natural reserves. Uranium exists in sizable exploitable quantities on both sides of the iron curtain, and thorium in the non-Communist nations. The exact amounts and the ratio of these to rate of exploitation have not been generally revealed.

The leading uranium deposits of the non-Communist world are in the Great Bear–Great Slave Lakes vicinity and at Blind River north of Lake Huron in Canada, at scattered sites but chiefly in western Colorado and eastern Utah and northwestern New Mexico in the United States, at Katanga in the former Belgian Congo, at Witwatersrand in the Union of South Africa, and at the Rum Jungle and Radium Hill sites in Australia (Fig. 14.4). Communist deposits are mainly at Jachymov (Joachimstal) in Czechoslovakia and at Fergana and other sites in the Soviet Union.

Thorium deposits are known to exist chiefly in the northwestern and southeastern parts of the United States, along the southeastern coast of Brazil, at van Rhynsdorp in the Union of South

Africa, at Kerala on the southern tip of India, and at Queensland in eastern Australia. No sizable quantities have been reported in Communist countries.

Mobility. Although careful precaution must be taken to avoid radioactive contamination, nuclear energy is highly mobile. Energy from fission is 3 million times that obtained from burning an equivalent weight of coal.[10] The resultant lowering of fuel transportation costs is self-evident. Those nations and other organizations which heretofore have been either essentially without inanimate energy because of poor natural endowment and/or high transportation costs, or have been forced to pay such costs to keep an economy in motion, can now avail themselves of this new form of energy—if its production becomes sufficiently economical to justify its common use.

Applicability. We have mentioned the use of fission-generated heat to create electricity. Such heat can also be used for space heating if certain technicalities can be overcome. It can also be used for transportation—especially large units such as ships and submarines. Indeed, atomic-driven ocean vessels and submarines are already in use. Applicability to overland and air-transportation media involves smaller transporting units, to which the sources of nuclear energy, as yet cumbersome, are not easily adapted. Moreover, aircraft must use the energy for lift as well as thrust, and heavy, bulky equipment does not lift readily. There also are possibilities for energy from fusion rather than fission.

Stages of Development. Although some attention has been given to the use of nuclear energy for direct transportation and space heating, most of the leading nations are now concentrating on the use of it to generate electricity. The most pronounced interest has been shown by technically advanced nations deficient in domestic production of the fossil fuels—petroleum, coal, and natural gas. The United Kingdom and the six European nations of the Coal and Steel Community (the latter separately organized into an analogous cooperative producing group containing the same members and known as Euratom) have shown keen interest, as have the United States, the Soviet Union, Canada, Sweden, and some additional technically advanced nations as well as underdeveloped countries. In all probability, nuclear sources will be responsible for a noteworthy share of the world's inanimate energy by 1975.

[10] Walter Isard and Vincent Whitney, *Atomic Power,* McGraw-Hill Book Company, Inc., The Blakiston Division, New York, 1952.

Significant liabilities of nuclear energy

Of the several liabilities and difficulties in man's use of nuclear energy, two are paramount: (1) cost and (2) danger of contamination.

Cost. As yet, the production of nuclear energy is more costly than the obtainment of energy from the fossil fuels and running water. There is evidence, however, that in a very few years such cost differentials will narrow or even disappear, so this liability is only temporary.

Danger of Contamination. When fission occurs, a residue remains. Parts of this residue can be used for additional purposes, but some is radioactive waste. How to dispose of this waste—which will increase in amount as nuclear energy becomes more abundant—is a serious problem which cannot be solved permanently by the present methods of burial in the ground or the open seas. Moreover, in the event of a crash involving nuclear-driven transportation media, rather extensive, sometimes heavily populated areas might be subject to contamination.

THE OUTLOOK FOR ELECTRIC AND NUCLEAR ENERGY

Both electric and nuclear energy, often in conjunction, will increase with the passing of time. The long-range view evidences a proportionate as well as absolute increase. Because of their high cost and complexity, however, it is likely that they will continue to be closely associated with technically advanced nations and to be initiated on an impressive scale elsewhere only with appreciable financial and scientific aid from those nations. The enormous hydroelectric potential in certain underdeveloped countries, coupled with their need for general improvement, indicates that these political units may look more to hydroelectric power, developed on a river-basin plan like the Tennessee Valley Authority of the United States, rather than to nuclear sources.

REFERENCES

Atomic Energy Facts, United States Atomic Energy Commission, 1957.

Boehm, E. A.: "Ownership and Control of the Electricity Supply Industry in Australia," *Economic Record,* **32:**257–272, 1956.

British Information Services: *Nuclear Energy in Britain,* Cox and Sharland, Ltd., London, 1959.

Dean, Gordon: *Report on the Atom,* Alfred A. Knopf, Inc., New York, 1957.

"Electric Power," *News from Behind the Iron Curtain,* September, 1956.

The Electric Power Situation in Europe, United Nations Economic Commission for Europe, New York, 1957.

Estall, R. C.: "The Problem of Power in the United Kingdom," *Economic Geography,* **34:**80–89, 1958.

Isard, Walter, and Vincent Whitney: *Atomic Power,* McGraw-Hill Book Company, Inc., The Blakiston Division, New York, 1952.

Knorr, Klaus E.: *Euratom and American Policy,* Princeton University Press, Princeton, N.J., 1956.

Lapp, Ralph E.: *Atoms and People,* Harper & Brothers, New York, 1956.

Mann, Martin: *Peacetime Uses of Atomic Energy,* The Studio Publications, Inc., New York, 1957.

Mason, Edward S., et al.: *Energy Requirements and Economic Growth,* Washington National Planning Association, Washington, D.C., 1955.

Netschert, B. C., and S. H. Shurr: *Atomic Energy Application with Reference to Underdeveloped Countries,* Johns Hopkins Press for Resources for the Future, Inc., Baltimore, 1957.

Raitt, W. Lindsay: "The Changing Pattern of Norwegian Hydroelectric Development," *Economic Geography,* **34:**127–144, 1958.

World Power Data, United States Federal Power Commission. (Mimeographed annually.)

15 NONFOSSILIFEROUS ORGANIC ENERGY

BEFORE MAN WAS ABLE TO SECURE LARGE AMOUNTS OF ENERGY FROM COAL AND subsequently discovered sources, he relied upon nonfossiliferous, organic materials to supply most of his comparatively modest energy needs (Table 11.1). These sources were primarily wood, human beings, animals, and peat.

Now that the Industrial Age has come to technically advanced economies and is being initiated in a preliminary way into some quasi-developed and underdeveloped economies, the nonfossiliferous organic sources have assumed a more moderate position in the world pattern of energy procurement, aggregately supplying an estimated 20 per cent or less of all obtained energy.[1] Fuel wood probably accounts for nearly 50 per cent of energy credited to nonfossiliferous organic sources, with human beings responsible for nearly 30 per cent, animals approximately 17 per cent, and peat the remaining 3 per cent.

The wood and peat have been and are used in large measure for space heating and cooking, and the animate energy chiefly for production and transportation. Because of this rather sharp utilizational division, we shall discuss wood, peat, and animate energy in that order.

WOOD

Over 40 per cent of all of the world's timber cut is used for fuel wood, most of which is burned directly but a very minor portion of which—approximately one-fifteenth—is converted into charcoal prior to utilization (Fig. 15.1). Hardwood is by far the most significant fuel wood, its annual harvest amounting to about three-fourths of the world's total fuel wood, including essentially all of that converted into charcoal. Indeed, almost 80 per cent of all hardwood is used for fuel. In contrast, only about one-fifth of all softwood is used as fuel, and it supplies the remaining one-fourth of the 22 billion cubic feet of all wood converted annually into energy.

[1] See especially W. S. Woytinsky and E. S. Woytinsky, *World Population and Production,* The Twentieth Century Fund, Inc., New York, 1953, pp. 930–931.

World distribution

Since wood is a forest product, the leading nations of its production and reserves are, of course, those with substantial forest acreage. Thus we have occasion once again to refer to the map of the distribution of world vegetation (Fig. 6.1). In the low latitudes, it will be noted, there are substantial reserves of broadleaf evergreens, most of which are hardwoods. In the high latitudes (particularly in the Northern Hemisphere) and in the high altitudes are very sizable timber stands of primarily coniferous softwoods. With certain exceptions, these two very extensive timber areas either are essentially untouched or are permitted to replenish the annual withdrawal by natural means; neither has been seriously encroached upon by agriculture.

In the subtropics and intermediate latitudes are (or were) timber stands which tend to be deciduous hardwood in the cooler climates and coniferous softwoods in well-drained countrysides of certain subtropic climates. These are, and in some areas have been for centuries, in competition with agriculture; and the extensiveness of their current stands depends largely upon their ability to withstand that competition under the particular set of natural, cultural, and human conditions in which they happen to be located.

It is probably unnecessary to state that, in considering national holdings of these various forests, large nations located in areas where forests remain contain the most sizable timber reserves.

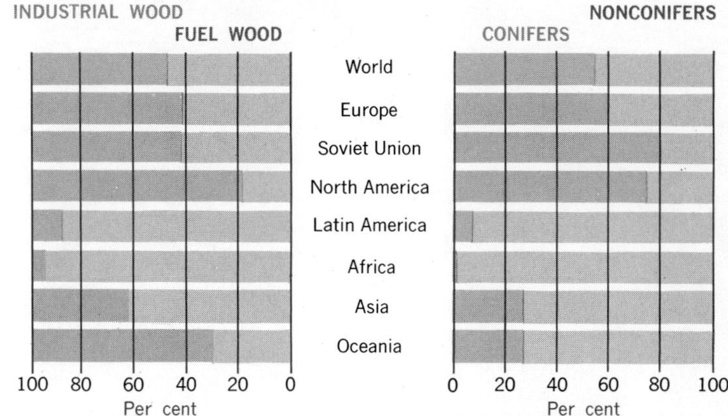

Figure 15.1 ***Sources and utilization of timber in the world and its major divisions.*** *Nearly 60 per cent of the world's timber harvest comes from conifers, and the remainder comes from nonconifers. Well over 40 per cent of all wood is used for fuel, and the remainder is used for industrial purposes. Note the high percentage of fuel wood in total consumption of continents dominated by underdeveloped economies. (After* World Forest Resources, 1955, *FAO, p. 15)*

Leading nations of production and consumption

The seven leading nations of fuel wood production are shown in Table 15.1. Presumably they consume all of their production and export essentially none. Five are classified in this book as technically advanced, and two as underdeveloped. The Soviet Union is the leader, with Brazil firmly in second place. The technically advanced Soviet Union uses about 40 per cent of its annual timber cut for fuel wood, and underdeveloped Brazil almost 90 per cent. The United States is third, although it uses only 15 per cent of its timber cut for fuel wood. It is probable that many nations, especially underdeveloped nations, produce and consume more fuel wood than current records indicate.

TABLE 15.1

Leading nations of fuel wood production

Nation	*Per cent of world total*
Soviet Union*	18
Brazil	14
United States*	9
Indonesia	8
France*	4
Japan*	4
Finland*	2
All others	41

* Technically advanced.
SOURCE: Computed from *Yearbook of Forest Products Statistics, 1957*, FAO, Rome, 1957, pp. 26–31.

The importance of wood as a fuel should not be underestimated—in technically advanced as well as underdeveloped economies. Here wood is being cut for fuel and mine pitprops in the Thetford Chase State Forest of the United Kingdom. (British Information Services)

PEAT

In Chapter 12 we defined peat as organic matter insufficiently decomposed and carbonized to qualify as coal. Although not fossiliferous, it is sufficiently carbonized to be able to burn when it is dried and, preferably, pressed into briquettes. It has also been gasified at its source, and the gas transmitted by pipeline.

Between 50 and 60 million tons of peat are exploited each year, and over four-fifths of this world total is accounted for by the Soviet Union. There the material is used to heat steam for thermoelectric generating stations as well as for space heat-

Peat is used primarily in the Soviet Union. It is used moderately in the rest of Europe, and very little elsewhere. Here blocks of peat are being cut and stacked in a bog in eastern Canada, one of the few in North America. (Capital Press, Ottawa)

ing. The importance attached to peat within the economy of that nation is evidenced in the reported tenfold increase in its production there between 1928, the year the Five-Year Plans were initiated, and 1955. Although most of the nation's sizable reserves are in the high latitudes, many of these are permanently saturated with moisture and hence are difficult to exploit. Most of the actual recovery is from lesser reserves found in slightly lower latitudes in an area extending southward from Leningrad to Kiev, and eastward past Novosibirsk.

Ireland, with an annual production amounting to less than 8 per cent that of the Soviet Union, is second among world nations in peat utilization, with West Germany, Denmark, East Germany, the Netherlands, and South Korea also noteworthy.

HUMAN ENERGY

At the dawn of civilization man, like the other animals, relied wholly upon his own muscles for performing work. Rather surprisingly in this twentieth century that has become symbolic of the Industrial Age, a probable one-half of the world's labor force still relies chiefly upon human muscular energy to perform work. The reader has doubtless anticipated correctly that most of these people are in the very heavily populated, underdeveloped lands—whether in such gigantic nations as Communist China or India, or in nations of intermediate size, such as Indonesia, or in small nations, such as Haiti. Human muscular energy assumes particular prominence where the population pressure is so high that essentially all arable land must be devoted directly to sustaining human life. Under these conditions, animals tend to become a luxury.

ANIMAL ENERGY

Like human muscular energy, animal energy is especially important in Asia (excluding the Soviet Union), Latin America, and Africa. Nearly one-third of all energy from work animals is concentrated in Asia, and about one-fourth in Latin America. Africa, which does not utilize much energy, accounts for an additional one-tenth—an amount equal to the respective animal-energy outputs of Anglo-America and the Soviet Union but exceeded by that of Europe. Thus the consumption of such energy is highest in certain underdeveloped economies, intermediate in certain technically advanced economies, and lowest in yet other underdeveloped economies. In the United States, reliance upon animal energy is rapidly decreasing (Fig. 15.2).

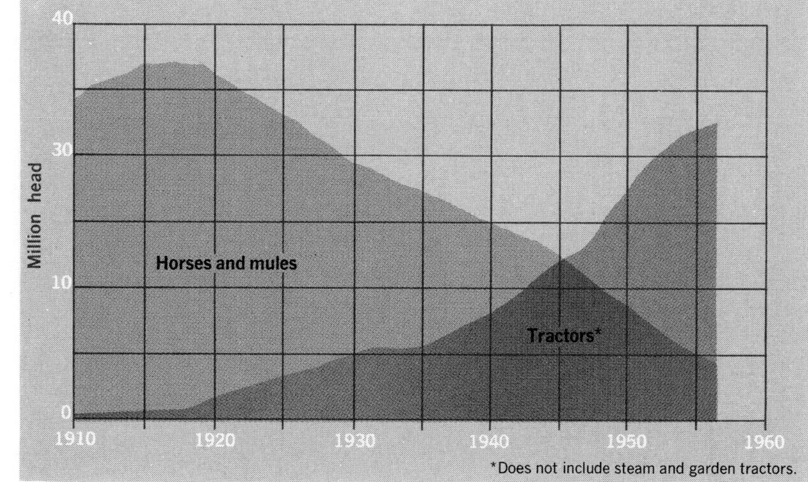

Figure 15.2 **Number of horses and mules compared with number of tractors on farms in the United States** *for the years shown (U.S. Bureau of the Census).*

PART FIVE THE ROLES OF SELECTED COMMODITIES

To satisfy his material needs and wants, man consumes.
To consume, he must first produce. INTRODUCTION, PAGE 3

16 AGRICULTURE AS AN ECONOMIC ACTIVITY

MAN FIRST DOMESTICATED PLANTS AND SOME ANIMALS LONG BEFORE HE LEARNED to write; yet, even in this twentieth century of supertechnology founded upon not only the written word but also highly complex mathematical equations, he still relies heavily upon agriculture. The role of this industry in the functioning of economies can be likened to that of the foot soldier in military operations: each has been subjected to periodic reassessment with changing times and administrators, but neither has been dispensed with entirely. One day, perhaps, there may be a "brave new world" in which living things or facsimiles thereof spring fully grown from test tubes, but that day is beyond the immediate future.

CONSUMPTION

Most agricultural products are consumer rather than producer goods and hence are of direct concern to individuals. In technically underdeveloped nations, notably those with large populations, agricultural products are in such demand that shortages are matters of almost constant concern. Furthermore, the residents of underdeveloped nations tend to spend higher percentages of their real incomes on food and clothing, both of which stem largely from agricultural production (Fig. 3.1). Even so, their diets too often are not balanced and do not contain what is considered to be a minimum calorie content for normal living (Fig. 3.2). In contrast, agricultural commodities are usually available in adequate supply in most technically advanced nations, although some have to be imported. Particularly in the United States, serious problems of surpluses have arisen during the twentieth century (Fig. 16.1). Thus we see the polar positions of some technically underdeveloped and some technically advanced nations—positions involving underproduction on the one hand and underconsumption on the other. The solution would appear to be obvious: send the surpluses to areas of deficiency. But real and apparent obstacles intercede—obstacles such as political and economic self-interest, differences in cultural tastes, government policy, balances of payments, and costs of transportation.

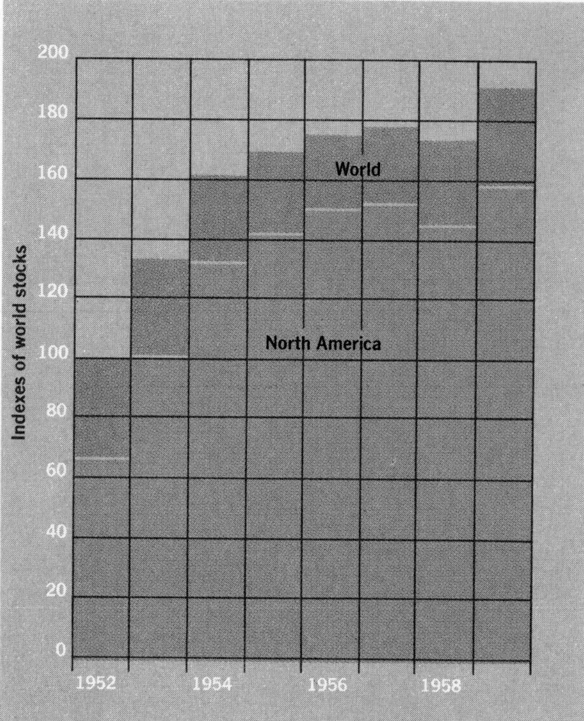

Figure 16.1 ***Trends in the stockpiling of agricultural products in North America and the rest of the world.*** *Stockpiles of 1952 are at a base index number of 100. Leading commodities involved are corn, wheat, and other grain, various dairy products, sugar, coffee, tobacco and cotton, and natural rubber. (After* State of Food and Agriculture, 1959, *FAO, p. 26)*

PRODUCTION

Predominance of agriculture as a livelihood occupation

Despite the rising significance of manufacturing and of the service occupations, agriculture is still overwhelmingly ahead of all others as a source of livelihood, accounting for over one-half of the world's labor force (Table 7.1 and Fig. 16.2).

Technically advanced and underdeveloped economies

Viewed globally, agriculture is carried on with the aid of both very primitive and very advanced methods and tools, and its practice reflects in the world of today what must amount to almost the total range of the occupation's past developmental stages in the most advanced economies. In some places, agricultural methods are so crude as to be scarcely worthy of the term. In other places they are so highly mechanized and specialized that they take on the general appearance of a modern factory system.

We have noted that one means of distinguishing technically advanced from technically underdeveloped economies involves the percentages of respective labor forces in agriculture, with the higher percentages reflecting underdevelopment (Fig. 1.4). As a general rule, nations with over one-half of their labor forces in agriculture also utilize rather inefficient methods and equipment, so that yields per person and, to a degree, per acre are comparatively low (Figs. 16.3 and 6.6). In most such nations, there is substantial evidence that agriculture will continue to be a mainstay of economic support. In contrast, many technically advanced nations are witnessing rather sharp declines in the agricultural components of their labor forces, and they are relying upon increasing efficiency per man-hour to maintain or even raise output (Figs. 16.3 and 16.4).

Land use

Agriculture requires sizable surface areas per unit of production. In practice, the sizes of farming units vary appreciably in accordance with population pressures, cultures, natural environmental conditions, national policies, etc. Nevertheless, all agriculture spreads itself over countrysides so that large sections of the earth's surface can be mapped as devoted to this one industry. Manufacturing, in contrast, is punctiform, and any world map depicting manufacturing places is likely to have such places exaggerated in size so that they will be visible.

Moreover, agricultural land use can be classified and subclassified rather clearly, with the subdivisional patterns retaining their identity on a world map. One such classification is shown in Figure 7.1 and described on pages 124 to 135.

Natural environmental limitations

Although the natural environment is no longer believed to "determine" types of human activity, it does set limits at a given time to certain aspects of such activity. For example, there are specific latitudes and altitudes at which crops cannot be made to grow with commercial success. Of course, today's limits may not exist tomorrow, at which time some of the world's cultures may have been advanced in this respect; but for the here and now, they do exist. Moreover, within this broad area where agriculture may be carried on are more restricted zones pertaining to individual plants and animals. Coffee is a low-latitude product, and bananas do not do well poleward of the subtropics. Nations located in the upper-middle or high latitudes thus must import such commodities, for they cannot grow them at home. Upon this fundamental truth rests the interesting fact that a nation like the United States, troubled with agricultural surpluses, nevertheless imports substantial quantities of agricultural commodities.

Not infrequently, nations craving certain agricultural commodities but lacking the natural environmental conditions for their growth invest in other countries where such production is possible. In many cases, such investment is made in underdeveloped countries by technically advanced nations, and "pockets" of technical advance thus appear in otherwise economically backward landscapes. Occasionally, such pockets are financed by domestic capital of underdeveloped countries and do not represent foreign investment or control.

Human choice

Within the very wide range of possible growth areas of almost every crop and animal, there are only a few places where production of each actually occurs. In examining specific commodities, which we shall do in the chapters to follow, we shall find that the total areas of actual production seldom amount to as much as one-fifth of the areas where natural features are not serious obstacles to such production. Why are the producing sites located

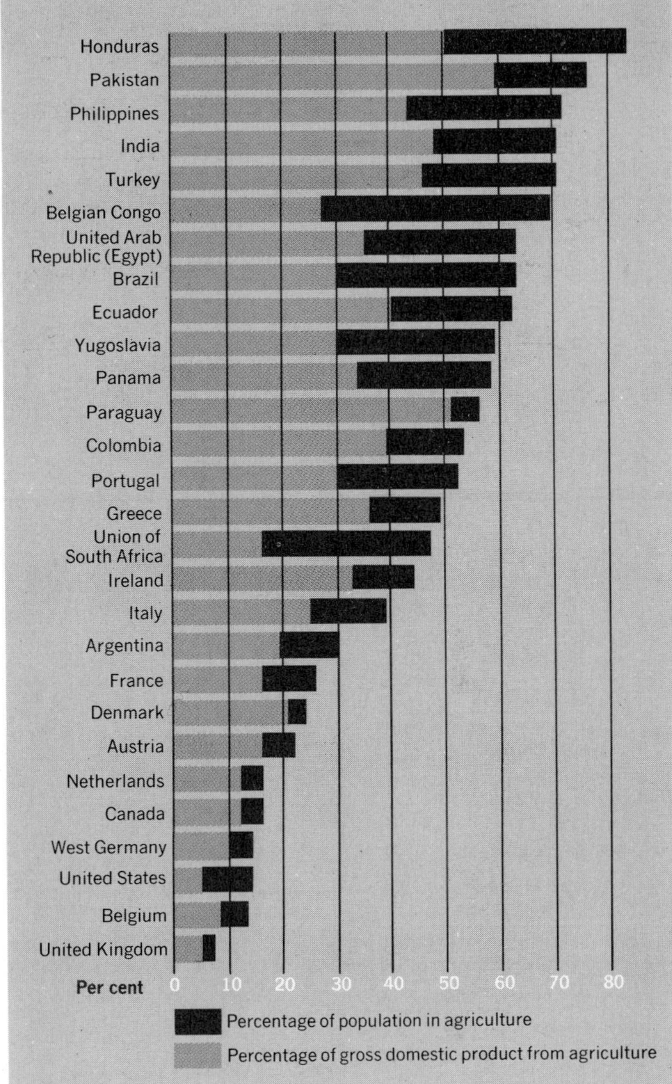

Figure 16.2 ***Per cent of population in agriculture and of gross domestic product derived from agriculture in selected nations.*** *The total bar lengths (gray plus brown) show population in agriculture. For every nation shown, labor force in agriculture exceeds gross domestic product from agriculture—that is, a higher percentage of the labor force is engaged in agriculture than that occupation yields in financial returns to the economy. Other sources must be yielding more revenue, yet hiring fewer workers. In technically advanced economies, both the labor-force and gross-domestic-product percentages for agriculture are low. Why?*

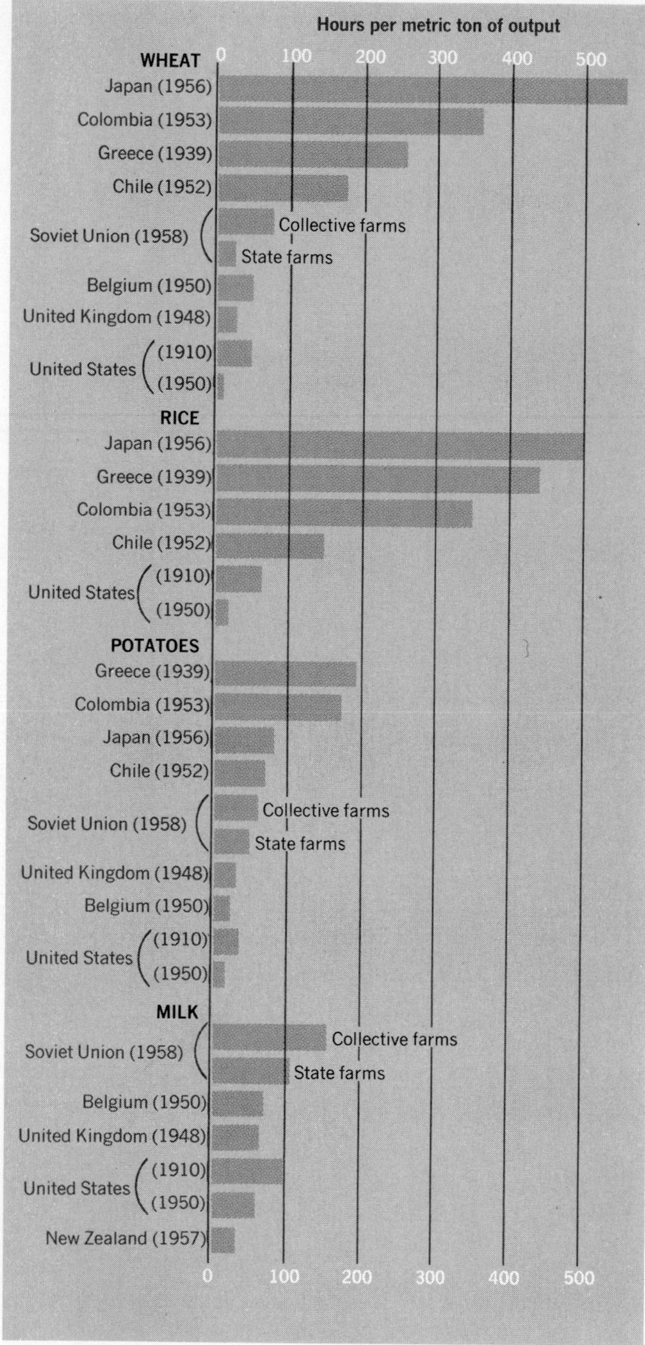

Figure 16.3 ***Per capita productivity in the output of selected agricultural commodities.*** *The graph shows hours of labor expended in producing specified commodities in specified countries at specified times. (After* State of Food and Agriculture, 1959, *FAO, p. 96)*

where they are? The answer involves that elusive and somewhat nebulous characteristic, human choice. Man selects his places of production. Some of his selections may appear to be very rational to an economic geographer—i.e., they may be based upon careful computations of economic costs and returns. This is particularly true of large-scale operations in both technically advanced and underdeveloped countries. Whether owned publicly or privately, such operations tend to be located on the basis of careful study. It is not so true of many

Figure 16.4 ***Levels of per capita agricultural productivity in selected non-Communist areas and the non-Communist world.*** *(World average as used here refers to the non-Communist realm.) The graph was constructed by using index numbers based on money value. The 1952–1957 output for all non-Communist countries equals 100. The very high position of Oceania is due partly to the presence there of large farming units operated by small labor forces. The same can be said for North America. (After* State of Food and Agriculture, 1959, *FAO, p. 17)*

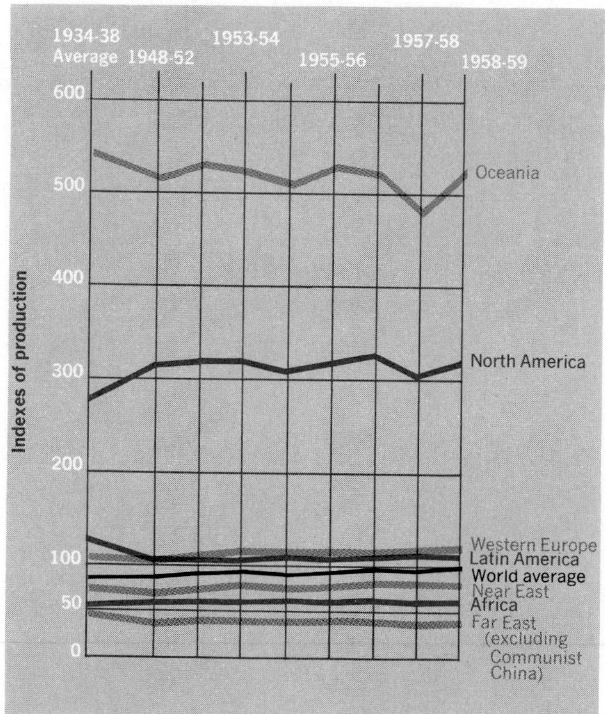

Certainly one key to higher agricultural yields in underdeveloped economies is fertilizer. India does not have nearly enough commercial fertilizer—indeed, not even enough animal manure, for this is used largely for fuel. These farm people are trampling a variety of decaying organic material, mostly vegetable matter, into the waterlogged soil. This practice is better than adding no fertilizer at all, but it is inadequate. (International Cooperation Administration)

smaller-scale, family-type operations, and of some large-scale ones as well, in both underdeveloped and technically advanced countries. Historical inheritance and tradition, emotional ties, and still other considerations that are not wholly or even partially economic may be involved in locational decisions affecting such operations.

Briefly, therefore, we can anticipate in the chapters to follow: (1) broad areas of potential growth of crops and animals, the extent of such areas increasing as man acquires more knowledge with which to push back nature's hindrances and limitations, and (2) more restricted places of actual production, the location of such places attributable largely to human choice from the wide range proffered by nature.

COMMERCE

The world's rapidly growing urban areas are the major focal points for domestic agricultural commerce. At the international level, technically advanced nations are the leading exporters, even though agricultural commodities comprise much

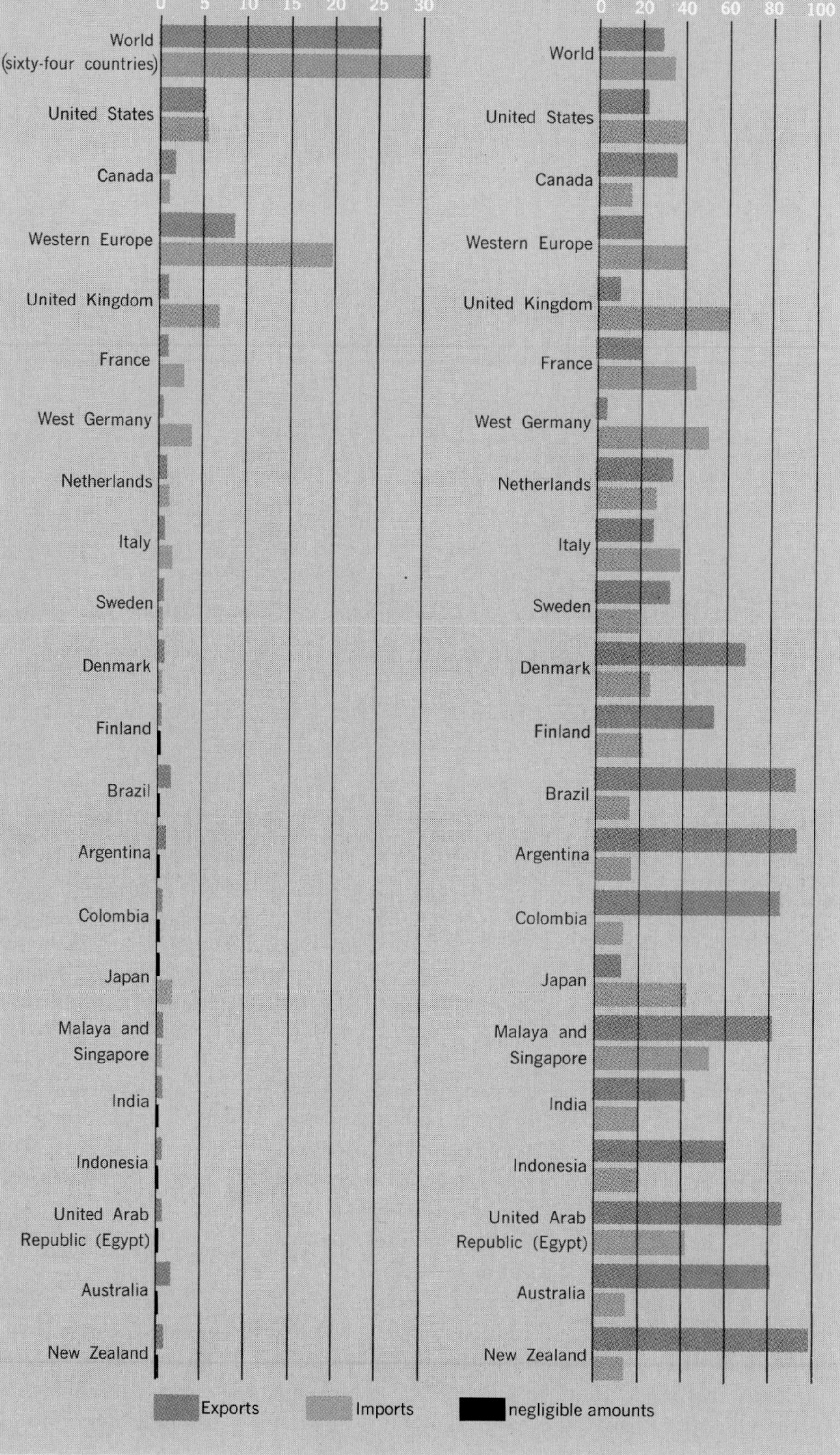

Figure 16.5 **Agricultural commerce in the total commerce of selected nations.** *The left-hand graph shows the value of agricultural and forest-products exports and imports of sixty-four non-Communist countries, and of selected nations. The right-hand graph shows, for each country and for all sixty-four countries, the per cent of total exports and imports accounted for by products of agriculture and forests. For example, about 5 billion dollars in agricultural and forest-products exports are shipped from the United States. This amounts to slightly over 20 per cent of the value of all United States exports.*

smaller percentages of their exports than of exports from most underdeveloped nations (Fig. 16.5). The United States and Western Europe supply over one-half of most agricultural products not originating behind the iron curtain, and the United States alone nearly one-fifth. Technically advanced countries also are the major importers. The United Kingdom accepts nearly one-fourth of all imports not originating behind the iron curtain, and Western Europe nearly two-thirds. No slouch, the United States accepts about one-sixth of that total. Japan is a noteworthy importer, as are most other nations with large populations in eastern and southern Asia. Wheat and other grains, sugar, bananas, citrus fruit, cotton and other textile raw materials, coffee and other beverage crops, and natural rubber are outstanding in a diverse commerce.

The relatively small percentage of the world's agricultural commerce handled by Communist nations involves chiefly a movement of grain, eggs, and meat from the Soviet Union and the southern countries of eastern Europe and of cotton from the Soviet Union to East Germany, Czechoslovakia, and elsewhere. Communist China is a modest exporter of agricultural commodities, largely to the Soviet Union.

17 AGRICULTURE: WHEAT, RICE, AND CORN

AMONG THE WORLD'S LEADING AGRICULTURAL CROPS ARE WHEAT, RICE, AND CORN, each of which normally provides an annual harvest exceeding 6 billion bushels. In aggregate, these three account for over two-thirds of the world's grain supply. All are used mainly as food, most of the wheat and rice being eaten directly and most of the corn being eaten indirectly as meat. All are dietary mainstays, and their roles in the world's economies are intimately associated with the geographical distribution of the world's inhabitants who consume them.

Historically, wheat and rice long have been critically important to mankind's existence—the former especially in western Asia, Europe, and its colonial offshoots and the latter in eastern and southern Asia. Wheat is believed to have been grown in Neolithic time, and rice is known to have been raised for thousands of years. In contrast, corn was unknown to recorded civilizations until the discovery of the Americas. Originally domesticated by the American Indian, corn soon became a favorite of "higher" cultures.

WHEAT

WHEAT CONSUMPTION

Approximately 7 billion bushels of wheat are now consumed each year, and the amount is rapidly rising. Most is eaten by human beings as bread, pastry, macaroni products, noodles, and dumplings (the last two particularly in eastern and southern Asia and in some countries of southern Europe). Between 5 and 15 per cent of the annual harvest is held over as seed, the exact proportion varying with localities. A comparatively small amount, some of it damaged, is fed to animals. Some wheat is consumed in almost every nation; the leaders are the Soviet Union, Communist China, the United States, India, France, Italy, the United Kingdom, Turkey, and Canada (Fig. 17.1). The first three of these nations account for over one-

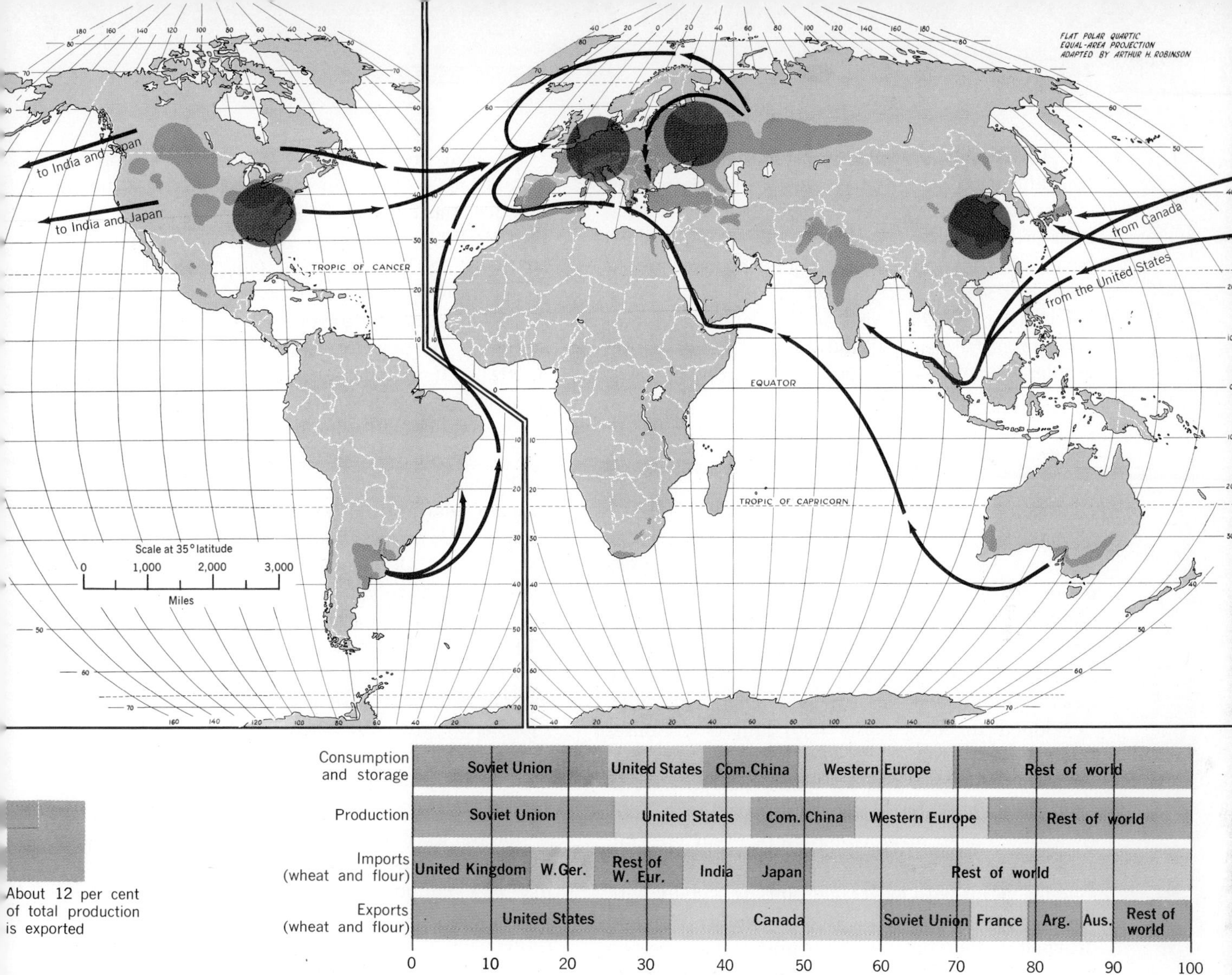

Figure 17.1 **Consumption, production, import, and export of wheat.** *(International trade also includes flour.) Shaded circles show nations or areas of very heavy consumption. The gray shading shows major areas of production. Arrows show only the heaviest international trade.*

half of the world's total, with the Soviet Union currently responsible for almost one-fourth.

The ranking of these nations may reflect high per capita wheat consumption, or it may reflect sheer numbers of people. For example, wheat accounts for less than one-sixth of the per capita calorie intake of Communist China and India, yet because of their very large populations, these nations are among the leaders in aggregate consumption. The Soviet Union, where wheat supplies nearly one-third of the per capita calorie intake, and the United States, where it accounts for about one-fifth, are major world consumers because of both population size and per capita consumption. In contrast, France and Italy contain populations that are only intermediate in size, but each inhabitant receives over one-third his calories from wheat; hence the countries rank fairly high in total consumption.

The trends in wheat consumption are rather constant when measured on a per capita basis. This is particularly true of the technically advanced nations of the occidental world, the leaders of which have used up approximately 2½ bushels per person each year since 1885.[1] For technically underdeveloped nations, marked rises in per capita consumption cannot be expected until the currently pressing problems of excessive population are solved.

WHEAT PRODUCTION

Natural conditions for growth

Climate. Climate tends to set the outer limits to wheat production, the poleward margins having mainly low temperature and short growing season, and the equatorward margins consistently high temperature and humidity. A growing season of at least ninety days is necessary to harvest even the quick-ripening varieties of wheat that have been developed for use in the high latitudes. Consequently, the crop is seldom grown beyond lat 60° N and is restricted by continental position to even lower latitudes in the Southern Hemisphere. At least 9 inches of precipitation per year are considered necessary for wheat growth, although the amount varies with local conditions, especially with the rate of evaporation. Unless water is supplied artificially, therefore, wheat cannot be grown on most deserts and the drier portions of some semiarid country. Precipitation is desirable during the early growth of the plant but a hindrance during the ripening period. Too much moisture causes the spread of destructive diseases and insects, especially when it is accompanied by continuously high temperatures. Wheat therefore does not thrive in the warm, moist climates of the low latitudes, although it is grown there at higher, cooler elevations.

[1] Wilfred Malenbaum, *The World Wheat Economy, 1885–1939*, Harvard University Press, Cambridge, Mass., 1953, pp. 244–245. Of course, there has always been a sizable range of per capita consumption among individual nations. France consumes over 6 bushels per person per year. Some of the Far Eastern nations consume less than one-third of 1 bushel per year.

Wheat growth thus is possible from approximately lat 20–60° N and from lat 20–45° S; but in practice, most wheat is grown in somewhat more restricted territory—from lat 30–55° N and from lat 25–40° S. Even so, the total area of possible wheat growth is very extensive, for it includes key core sections in Asia, North America, and Europe, and large portions of South America, Africa, and Australia. It includes also all or parts of a sizable array of dry, intermediate, and quasi-moist climates of the middle latitudes and subtropics: semiarid, mediterranean, desert (where irrigated), humid continental warm-summer, humid continental cool-summer, marine, and humid subtropical (Fig. 5.1). Despite this wide climatic range, however, nearly two-thirds of all wheat acreage is found where climates are relatively dry (compare Figs. 17.1 and 5.1).

Other Natural Environmental Features. The growth of wheat is affected also by other natural environmental features, particularly landforms and soils. Flat land is the best wheat land, and well-defined slopes are rarely planted to the crop. The world's potential wheat acreage is thus reduced appreciably by extensive areas of mountains and hill country located within the territory where climate permits growth of the plant. (The indirect effect of this high country may be even more significant; for, as was suggested in Chapter 5, mountains and other prominent landforms have a pronounced effect upon climate.)

Some soils also tend to restrict wheat growth. The plant thrives on nature's best soils—the fertile, loamy chestnut and chernozem soils located generally at the zones of transition from the world's semiarid climates to the more humid types. Soils high in clay content can be utilized, as can some of the finer sandy soils. Where the texture is excessively coarse, or the drainage very poor, wheat usually does not grow well.

However, the limitations imposed by soil are not unduly severe. Man has learned much about altering the soil to suit his purposes. For example, the wheat yields per acre in northwestern Europe, where many soils of only moderate natural fertility are carefully tended and artificially fertilized, are among the highest in the world (Fig. 6.6).

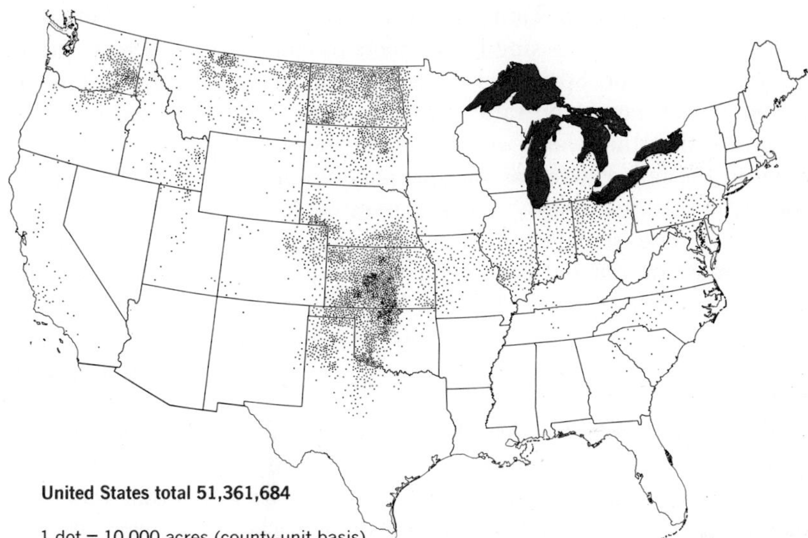

Figure 17.2 **Where wheat is grown in the United States** *(U.S. Bureau of the Census).*

Areas of Potential and Actual Productivity. When the territory occupied by unfavorable landforms and soils is subtracted from the territory of possible wheat growth as delimited climatically, there remains an area of potential appreciably larger than the area actually planted to wheat. Not more than 15 per cent of the land which can grow wheat currently is planted to the crop. The actual limits to wheat production, therefore, are not to be found in the natural environment but in the economies which man has placed thereon. Other crops are grown instead, for reasons suggested in the von Thuenen and subsequent theories (see Chapter 8).

Also important here is a historical consideration. The current areas of wheat specialization, and many other areas where wheat is one of several crops in diversified farming, have not always occupied their present positions and roles. The penetration of settlements with cultures above the aboriginal level into the Americas, Oceania, and much of Africa has taken place comparatively recently. Moreover, such settlement almost invariably has been followed by a time of trial and error in crop growth, until certain crop specialties or combinations have evolved. In the United States, for example, wheat once was grown only in the East and not at all in the West. Indeed, not until this century did much of the present spring and winter wheat belts experience the plow for the first time. As time passed, however, the present patterns took form (Fig. 17.2). These, too, are not necessarily final but may well be altered with changing technology and human conditions.

Categories of wheat

There are many varieties of the wheat plant; nearly two hundred are grown commercially in the United States alone. These have been developed for particular purposes and conditions—quick-maturing varieties for cool lands and some dry lands; drought-resistant varieties for arid and semiarid country; disease-resistant varieties for places where they are most needed. All these special-purpose varieties, as well as those designed for more general uses, have been developed to maximize yields.

Winter and Spring Wheat. Considered by production, wheat frequently is classified as *winter-* and *spring-wheat* types. Planted in the fall, winter wheat lies dormant throughout the winter (or grows, where conditions permit—in mediterranean climate, for example) and shoots up rapidly in the early spring. It ripens in late spring or early summer, having benefited from winter snows and spring rains. In some places, it is pastured for a few weeks during both fall and spring; if not carried to excess, this practice does not harm it but frequently increases the yield by causing more shoots to emerge from a given root. Spring wheat is planted where winter wheat cannot be raised—where winters are so severe that the wheat would die of exposure if sown in the fall. Planted as early as possible in the spring, it matures quickly and is harvested in the middle or late summer. Both winter and spring wheat must be planted each year, for the plant is an annual. Approximately two-thirds of the world wheat acreage is in winter wheat, and the remainder in spring wheat.

Hard and Soft Wheat. Wheat also is classified as *hard* and *soft* types, according to the rigidity of its kernel. Hard wheat, grown chiefly in the world's drier places, is used mainly for bread (and in the Far East, where bread is less common, for noodles, dumplings, etc.). Soft wheat, found especially in the more moist climates of eastern North America and parts of Western Europe, is usually made into pastries.

Leading nations of production

The outstanding nations of production are the leading wheat-consuming countries. The Soviet Union remains in first place, followed by the United States, Communist China, Canada, India, France, Italy, Argentina, Turkey, and Australia (Fig. 17.1).

The Soviet Union. Reportedly having doubled its output of wheat between 1950 and 1959, the Soviet Union now probably leads the world in wheat production, with an annual harvest of over 1.75 billion bushels. Nearly one-third of the country's sown acreage is devoted to wheat. The crop is grown chiefly in association with semiarid climate and chestnut and chernozem soils that dominate a gigantic wedge forming the southern portion of the country's effective area. To an extent, it is found also under the southern fringes of humid continental cool-summer climate, situated to the immediate north of the steppes. The crop's major growth area extends longitudinally for a distance of over 3,000 miles from the rich Ukraine in European Russia around the southern edge of the Ural Mountains to the vicinity of the upper Yenisei River in Asia.

This is an area of crop specialization—of commercial grain farming (Fig. 7.1). Wheat is easily the leading agricultural commodity, accounting for over two-thirds of the weight of all cereals harvested here. Spring wheat predominates, occupying approximately four-fifths of the country's sown wheat acreage. It is grown chiefly in the eastern part of European Russia and in Asian Russia. The comparatively small amount of winter wheat is found chiefly in the Ukraine.

We have spoken previously of the farming system of the Soviet Union, dominated by collectives and containing some state farms. In the commercial-grain-farming area, they are not unlike their counterparts in other parts of the Soviet Union except that they are larger and more completely mechanized. Average yields per acre are still comparatively low—less than 13 bushels for the nation as a whole. Increased use of commercial fertilizers has improved this yield somewhat in recent years, but the basic difficulty is climatic. Precipitation throughout most of the wheat-growing region seldom exceeds 20 inches per year, and becomes progressively less toward the Caspian Sea and Lakes Aral and Balkhash. Moreover, this precipitation is very erratic. In terms of precipitation, the entire southeastern fringe of the country's grain belt resembles somewhat the dust bowl of the United States, although it is located in higher latitudes and correspondingly cooler temperatures than its North American counterpart.

Against this background, it is somewhat surprising that between 1954 and 1956 the Soviet Union plowed up a reported 93 million acres of virgin and idle land located where climatic conditions have been very uncertain (Fig. 7.3). Interestingly, the state farms occupy about 40 per cent of this heretofore virgin and idle land—a much higher percentage than is true of the nation as a whole. A large part of this land has been planted to wheat. Initial yields have been good, and at least temporarily the European Ukraine has lost its supremacy as the leading wheat-producing area of the Soviet Union; the combined yields of old and new wheat land in the eastern part of European Russia and in Asian Russia currently exceed those farther west. It is highly improbable, however, that such large yields can be expected consistently. More likely is the prospect that the Soviet Union soon will have a sizable area upon which to experiment concerning problems of wind erosion and replacement of a natural vegetative cover. The farming here is especially precarious, because average precipitation is very near the minimum necessary for wheat growth and because variations below that average are frequent.

The United States and Canada. As in the Soviet Union, most of the wheat in North America is grown in a system of commercial-grain farming which is associated chiefly with semiarid climate and which extends into humid continental cool-summer and humid continental warm-summer climates (Figs. 17.1 and 5.1). Commercial grain farming in North America, however, is not in one continuous, unbroken area but is fragmented in geographical distribution (Fig. 7.1). Three distinct belts can be recognized: (1) the spring-wheat belt, which extends from the Dakotas of the United States into the Prairie Provinces of Canada; (2) the winter-wheat belt, which covers much of Kansas and reaches into neighboring states; and (3) the Columbia–Snake River Palouse country of eastern Washington and Oregon, where both winter and spring wheat are well represented (Fig. 17.2). In addition to wheat produced in these areas of specialization, a substantial amount is harvested in eastern United States, particularly between the cotton belt and the Great Lakes. In rather sharp contrast to that farther west, this soft-wheat production is not specialized but is meshed into a diversified farming practice (Figs. 17.2 and 7.1).

The United States thus depends upon four major areas of production for its wheat supply. Three of these, accounting for nearly 75 per cent of the annual output, are dominated by commercial-grain-farming practices. Canada, like the Soviet Union, depends almost entirely upon a single commercial-grain-farming region to supply all of its wheat (compare Figs. 17.1 and 7.1).

It should be kept in mind that this is mostly dry-land farming. We have noted that such farming is precarious, especially because of precipitation irregularity. In the winter-wheat belt, for example, the optimum conditions involve slow but continuous rains soon after the autumn planting and winter snows which melt slowly and cooperate with drizzling spring rains to assure a good "start" to the wheat. The spring moisture should continue until the grain has formed and filled, and at that time should be replaced by warm, but not desiccatingly hot, ripening weather. No heavy thunderstorms—above all, none containing hail—should fall and thereby thresh the wheat and break down the stalks so that the grain lies, unharvestable, on the ground. (This last danger has become more pronounced with the substitution of the combine for the older binder and threshing machine. Under the older practice, the wheat could be cut shortly before it was fully ripe. Tied into bundles by the binder, it was placed in shocks that afforded some protection from the elements until threshing time. Now the wheat stands in the field until fully ripe, and is cut and threshed in a single operation. Normally, the newer way is more efficient; but every hour during which a ripe grain of wheat remains unharvested, it is in danger from storms and high winds.)

In practice, the fall rains are often inadequate, the winters "open" (essentially without snow), and the springs dry. It is not uncommon for the winter wheat to die, and for the land to be resown, when winter has passed, to spring wheat, barley, or a quick-ripening grain such as one of the sorghums. Even if a crop "makes" (ripens), it may be destroyed by hail or high winds. Then, too, there is always the danger of locusts, species of which are popularly called grasshoppers, which have plagued man since Biblical times.

The wet and dry years are somewhat cyclic, and this is reflected in the harvest. For example, at the Kansas Agricultural Experiment Station at Colby, the best harvests over a thirty-four-year period ending in 1948 were achieved from 1919 to 1922, 1924 to 1926, 1938 to 1942, and in 1948. In contrast, no yield was forthcoming in 1917, 1933, 1935–1936, and 1940. Allowing the fields to lie fallow (idle but cultivated) every alternate year doubled the yield per acre, resulting in an average

Wheat is harvested with combines in the Prairie Provinces of Canada. The sickles cut the standing wheat (at a high level, so that little straw is taken), and the hoppers collect the threshed grain. Trucks carry the grain from machine to storage bin. The small amount of straw cut with the grain is returned to the field. (National Film Board of Canada)

of 18 bushels as compared to 7.9 bushels when the land was cropped continuously. The absolute range in yield was from zero to 46.3 bushels per acre, the latter being harvested from land which had been allowed to lie fallow during the preceding year.[2]

The commercial grain farms of North America are mainly large individual holdings, and they are becoming larger: in Kansas, the average farm size has increased from 240.7 acres (in 1900) to 370.0 acres (in 1950); in South Dakota, from 362.4 to 674 acres; in Montana, from 885.9 to 1,688.7 acres; in Manitoba, from 274.2 to 338.5 acres; in Saskatchewan, from 285.1 to 550.5 acres. This means fewer farmers, more machinery. Investment in equipment is very high, often going above $20,000 or even to $50,000 per farm. Most owners use their own equipment for plowing, harrowing, and planting, and may or may not own the combines for threshing. However, an increasing amount of the harvest is taken by professionals whose tractors and machinery are usually very modern and capable of making the most of a day's work. These crews commence their summer activity in Texas during May and gradually work their way northward, ending during September in Montana or even farther north. Commercial fertilization is not carried on actively in the wheat belts, although it is receiving increased attention. Nitrogen, particularly, is being added.

Interestingly, the winter-wheat belt is relatively monocultural; i.e., it is utilized appreciably for growing the one crop only. The spring-wheat belt, despite its name, is far less monocultural. Sizable amounts of barley, oats, flax, wild hay, and still other crops are raised here in competition with wheat, which occupies little more than one-half of all cultivated land.

Some wheat also is grown under irrigation and in association with other crops in the commercial-grain areas, although the amount is quite small. Corn, alfalfa, sugar beets, horticultural products, and other crops requiring considerable water are among the leading crops grown in rotation with wheat under irrigation.

The soft wheat of the eastern United States is grown under more intensive farming practices, the holdings being smaller and the per acre application of capital and labor being higher than in the commercial grain belts. Yields usually are above 25 bushels per acre, higher than in the West, but they do not enable these eastern areas to compete successfully in either domestic or world markets. The specialized uses of soft wheat and the higher unit costs of production act to restrict the output. The wheat here is grown in association, and usually in rotation, with legumes (including soybeans) and pasture grasses, as well as corn, oats, barley, tobacco, cotton, and still other crops. It is associated with different crops in various parts of the country.

Communist China and India. The circumstances and problems of wheat growth in Communist China and India are comparatively similar. Both countries rank high among consuming nations. Yet in both nations, domestic production is unable consistently

[2] Edward Higbee, *The American Oasis: The Land and Its Uses*, Alfred A. Knopf, Inc., New York, 1957, p. 130.

In the more humid climates, combines do not work well because the grain does not dry thoroughly before harvest. Here the wheat is cut and tied into bundles with a machine called a binder. It is shocked by hand and later threshed with a threshing machine. This view is in the Scottish Lowlands, near Glasgow. (British Information Services)

to satisfy domestic demand and is not at all able to satisfy actual need. In both countries, production is not a specialized, highly mechanized activity as it is in the Soviet Union, North America, and other areas of commercial grain farming, but it is prevailingly a subsistence type of agriculture (Fig. 7.1). Finally, both are attempting to improve their production, especially through long-range planning at the national level.

Communist China produces an average of over 800 million bushels of wheat each year. Although the crop is rather widespread there, its primary region of growth lies to the north of the Yangtze River, extending to the borders of the Soviet Union and Korea except where such natural environmental features as aridity and mountains restrict crop growth. Approximately the southern half of this region is devoted to winter wheat and the remainder to spring wheat, the line of separation trending southwest from the vicinity of Peking to the upper reaches of the Yellow River on the edge of the Plateau of Tibet. Both the winter and spring wheat are grown in general association with soybeans, corn, barley, a sorghum called *kaoliang,* and millet. In addition, the warmer and more moist portions of the section devoted to winter wheat support some rice and cotton. Particularly where the Yellow Sea exerts a moderating influence on climate, vegetables are grown in both the spring and winter wheat districts.

As it does in the previously discussed commercial-grain-farming areas, climate plays a vital role in production. Again the major difficulties result from erratic precipitation. The average annual amount of moisture appears to be adequate, exceeding 10 inches at inland locations where wheat is grown and increasing to 20 inches or more nearer the Yellow Sea. This, however, is monsoon country, and both temperature and humidity are rather intimately associated with winds that carry moisture from the sea to the land in summer and bring continental aridity toward the sea in winter. When these are functioning in good annual rhythm, precipitation is adequate and the crops come to fruition. But when the dry winter winds remain dominant into the spring and early summer, crops parch and famine results. Traditionally irrigation has been practiced to only a small degree in most of the wheat-growing areas (except the transitional rice-wheat region of the middle and lower Yangtze River valley). However considerable emphasis recently has been placed upon the construction of small reservoirs, wells, and canals. Such improvements, however, provide only a partial cushion against the excesses of climate.

Before the Communist government came to power in 1949, China was a nation of small holdings. In the wheat-growing areas, holdings were larger than in the nation as a whole, averaging between 5 and 8 acres per farming unit, with the higher acreages found generally where the natural environment was more adverse. Farming was intensive in that much labor was applied per acre, but little machinery and few commercial fertilizers were handy. Nevertheless, wheat yields averaged 15 to 17 bushels per acre—higher than the current world average of about 15 bushels per acre.

Since 1949, the Communist government has moved to eliminate the peasant's attachment to his private plots of land. With the establishment of collectives in 1955, largely replaced by communes in 1958, the peasants have been organized into production brigades. The change in policy appears to have increased output per person and per unit of farm land. This has been done largely through intensification of traditional farming practices. Long-range planning, however, calls for new agricultural experiments and the use of modern technology, including mechanization. The plains that comprise much of the wheat-growing areas are ideally suited for many of these projects, and pilot programs now underway have established "high-yield tracts" in which the old field boundaries have been eliminated and the use of agricultural machinery has been introduced on a limited scale.

India's wheat country is located mainly along the central and upper portions of the Ganges River, and scattered acreages are found to the southeast of that waterway. Here, too, are problems of underproduction. Despite the facts that more moisture falls here than in many other wheat-growing areas of the world, that at least one-half of India's wheat land is under irrigation, and that the soils are relatively fertile, yields are generally under 10 bushels per acre and hence among the world's lowest. The uncertainty of monsoon-induced precipitation, which sometimes becomes so deficient that even irrigation water is not to be had, and the inefficiency of many existing agricultural tools and practices are important contributors to such low yields. Double cropping and interculture are common practices where they are feasible. The former consists in growing more than one crop consecutively each year if the growing season is long enough to permit this, and the latter involves the growing of more than one crop in the same field at the same time.

India's First Five-Year Plan, begun in 1952, emphasized increases in foods, fibers, and other agricultural commodities. By 1954–1955, total grain production had increased by at least 20 per cent of the 1950–1951 figure, and its subsequent trends have also been upward. The initiation of improved farming practices, redistribution of holdings to provide more ownership by those tilling the soil, reduction of the number and authority of an excessively large number of middlemen who formerly dealt with the laborers in behalf of the landlords, and reclamation of new land all reportedly have contributed to this increase. Nevertheless, because of the very rapid growth of India's populations, the amount of available land per capita has not increased.

Other Types of Farming and Areas of Production. We have noted three types of farming involving substantial harvests of wheat—commercial grain farming, diversified crop and livestock farming, and intensive-subsistence agriculture (compare Figs. 17.1 and 7.1). If mediterranean agriculture be added, the list will contain essentially all major types of farming where wheat is a leading crop.

Of the remaining areas of wheat production, Europe (excluding the Soviet Union) as a single region is outstanding, with an annual output usually exceeding that of North America. France and Italy are the leading nations, although more than twenty additional European countries also grow the crop. To the north of the European Alpine mountain system, agricultural conditions are somewhat analogous to those of the northeastern United States, although the farms tend to be smaller, less (but increasingly) mechanized, more intensively worked in terms of application of labor and fertilizer, and higher in per acre yields. To the south of the Alpine system, mediterranean climate prevails (a notable exception is the humid subtropical climate of the Po River valley), and farming practices there, while not markedly different from those farther north, have been developed in close harmony with that climate. Of the European producers, France is the sole net exporter of consequence; most do not grow enough wheat for their own needs, and Europe is an outstanding importing continent.

To the east of the Mediterranean Sea, Turkey grows wheat under practices not markedly unlike those of southern Europe, under a mediterranean climate which merges into semiarid toward the center of the peninsula.

In the Southern Hemisphere, Argentina and Australia are important countries of both production and export, utilizing methods and natural environmental conditions generally similar to those of commercial grain farming in North America. In Australia, sheep and sometimes cattle frequently are kept on the same holdings where the wheat is grown, thus lending an aura of livestock raising to an otherwise cash grain system.

WHEAT TRADE AND TRANSPORTATION

Domestic trade

Movement. A comparison of the world's areas of wheat production with its effective areas of heavy population pressure indicates a decided overlap of the two patterns (compare Figs. 17.1 and page 13). In nearly all nations of heavy consumption, the producing regions are either at hand or not very far away, when viewed on a world map. (To be sure, the extremes in distance between points of production and consumption may be appreciable—more than 3,000 miles in the Soviet Union and over 2,000 miles in the United States.) Since only about 12 per cent of all wheat enters into international trade either as a grain or as grain products, the proximity of these places of consumption and production is important. Most wheat moves only a comparatively short distance before being consumed in the country where it was grown.

Transportation Media. The railroad train and the inland and coastal water craft, often with the short-haul aid of the motor truck, transport most of the grain which moves only to domestic markets. To an increasing degree, the truck is also competitive with the traditional long-haul carriers. In North America, the Great Lakes–St. Lawrence system is excellently located for wheat conveyance, as are several of the larger rivers in Europe and the Volga River and associated waterways of the Soviet Union.

By definition, most of the products of intensive-subsistence agriculture in technically underdeveloped countries do not leave the places where they were produced. Those which do leave depend upon animal and human drayage as well as the more advanced water and rail transport.

International trade

Movement. Wheat ranks high in international trade—among the seven leading commodities when assessed by value. This, despite the fact that only about one-eighth of the annual harvest ever leaves the country where it is grown (Fig. 17.1). Over three-fifths of all exports currently are shipped from the United States and Canada. Recently, the Soviet Union has become an exporter, accounting for about one-eighth of the world total. France, Argentina, and Australia also are important. More than one-third of all imports are forwarded to Western Europe, almost one-seventh going to the United Kingdom alone. Japan and India are noteworthy but not large importers, with their significance varying year by year.

TABLE 17.1

International wheat agreement: guaranteed quantities and recorded transactions of wheat and flour (grain equivalent) under terms of the International Wheat Agreement from August to July, 1957–1958 (1,000 bushels)

Signatory country	*Guaranteed quantities**	*Recorded transactions†*						
		United States	*Australia*	*Canada*	*Argentina*	*France*	*Sweden*	*Total*
Importers								
Austria	3,674							
Belgium	16,535	1,829	3	2,337		8		4,177
Bolivia	4,042	694						694
Brazil	7,349							
Costa Rica	1,470	963		462				1,425
Cuba	8,083	7,445		604				8,049
Denmark	1,837	1,221		276				1,497
Dominican Republic	1,286	678		608				1,286
Ecuador	1,837	498		216				714
Egypt	11,023							
El Salvador	919	745		140				885
West Germany	55,116	20,376		25,465		6,830	2,518	55,189
Greece	11,023							
Guatemala	1,653	1,264		398				1,662
Haiti	2,205	1,676		500				2,176
Honduras	919	247		56				303
Iceland	73	21		2				23
India	7,349	7,459						7,459
Indonesia	5,144		2,783					2,783
Ireland	5,512	365	647	1,593				2,605
Israel	8,267	2,378		1,464				3,842
Italy	3,674							
Japan	36,744	20,632	3,082	13,182				36,896
Korea	2,205	204						204
Lebanon	2,756	‡						‡
Liberia	73	49		6				55
Mexico	3,674							
Netherlands	25,721	9,558	83	15,869				25,510

The global pattern of this trade is especially interesting for at least two reasons: First, it is a trade chiefly among technically advanced nations, each of which is essentially autonomous in ownership of the means of wheat production. Thus political and economic domination by one nation over another, although not to be discounted entirely, is not a primary consideration. Second, it is not well developed in Communist nations, which as yet send only small amounts either to each other or to other parts of the world.

What, then, are the primary considerations? The "story of wheat," so often related in nursery-story-like booklets, is in reality a complex narrative deserving far more space than we can give it here. It involves historically developed, very real areas of high demand in the leading importing nations, whose crowded populations have come to appreciate (or at least to demonstrate) that importing wheat from elsewhere is cheaper in the long run than growing it at home, because their time is thereby freed for concentration upon the products

Signatory country	*Guaranteed quantities**	*Recorded transactions†*						
		United States	*Australia*	*Canada*	*Argentina*	*France*	*Sweden*	*Total*
New Zealand	5,879		5,881					5,881
Nicaragua	367	249		100				349
Norway	6,614	1,513		3,448		1,312	202	6,475
Panama	1,102	581		226				807
Peru	7,349	605						605
Philippines	6,063	3,345	454	2,270				6,069
Portugal	5,879	572	32	234		2,133		2,971
Saudi Arabia	3,674	108						108
Spain	4,593							
Switzerland	6,981	336		6,601				6,937
South Africa	5,512							
Vatican City	551	561						561
Venezuela	6,246	4,236		1,991				6,227
Yugoslavia	3,674							
Total	294,647	90,408	12,965	78,048	0	10,283	2,720	194,424
Exporters								
United States	128,493							90,408
Australia	29,432							12,965
Canada	100,089							78,048
Argentina	14,296							0
France	16,082							10,283
Sweden	6,255							2,720
Total	294,647							194,424

* For importing countries, represent quantities which indicated importers were obligated to purchase at minimum prices under the terms of the International Wheat Agreement of 1956; for exporting countries, quantities which the indicated exporters were obligated to sell at maximum prices under the terms of that agreement.

† Represent actually recorded sales by signatory exporting countries to signatory importing countries during August to July, 1957–1958, under the terms of the International Wheat Agreement.

‡ Less than 500 bushels.

SOURCE: *Agricultural Statistics, 1959,* U.S. Department of Agriculture, 1960, p. 9.

which they can produce to best advantage. Similarly, the three major exporting nations, each of which produces most of its wheat in commercial-grain-farming regions where large-scale methods can be utilized, have come to specialize in producing surpluses over their domestic demand.

Government policy plays a subordinate but important role in the patterns of international trade in wheat, a role that may be either positive or negative. Incoming wheat is sometimes considered to be in active competition with domestically grown supplies, and tariffs and other control measures have resulted, as is evidenced by the sizable tariffs on imported wheat in Austria, Italy, and Greece. The United Kingdom admits wheat free of duty but purchases selectively among exporting nations, being careful to maintain good relationships among members of the British Commonwealth. Canada and Australia thus supply most of the imports to this nation. The United States, having established rather rigid quotas on imported wheat, has concomitantly taken the lead in organizing an International Wheat Agreement among buying and selling nations—an agreement guaranteeing to the importing nations that a certain amount of wheat will be available at certain minimum prices, and to the exporting nations that a certain amount of wheat will be sold at certain maximum prices. Signed by twenty-two nations in 1933, the agreement has been renewed periodically, with the number of signatories increasing to forty-eight—forty-two importers and six exporters (Table 17.1). Interestingly, the world's leading importer, the United Kingdom, withdrew from the agreement in 1953 because restrictions were considered excessive.

Unfortunately, however, something is out of kilter. The United States, Canada, Argentina, and Australia are plagued with wheat surpluses which, since 1953, have fluctuated from 30 to over 50 million metric tons and are increasing. Over two-thirds of these surpluses have accumulated in the United States, and over one-fourth in Canada. The governments of some of these nations are attempting to minimize their surpluses by such programs as restrictions of planted acreage but to date have not been very successful. It would appear that government policy will play an even more active future role in the world's wheat economy than in the past.

Transportation Media. In contrast to domestic movement, most international trade in wheat involves ocean paths that sometimes extend more than halfway around the world. By and large, unprocessed wheat tends to make up the cargo; it can be carried without packaging, as a bulk commodity; it contains only a fraction of waste material; and it is comparatively easily handled and preserved. At one time tramp ships were very active in the wheat trade, but liners have come to rely increasingly upon the commodity, both as a "filler" for otherwise incomplete cargoes and as an item of commerce in its own right.

RICE

Like wheat, rice is a dietary mainstay which is consumed primarily in the nations where it is produced. Thus, in a very broad sense, the roles of the two grains in economic geography appear somewhat similar. There is a fundamental distinction between them, however; wheat is predominantly a cereal of technically advanced nations and rice is a staple of technically underdeveloped populations. There are important exceptions to this generalization, but they do not destroy its validity.

RICE CONSUMPTION

The world's annual consumption of rice is now approaching 10 billion bushels, the exact amount fluctuating somewhat with annual productivity.[3] In volume, the consumption of rice exceeds that of wheat. In weight, the consumption is about the same for the two grains, as a bushel of rice weighs 45 pounds whereas a bushel of wheat weighs 60.

Communist China, with over one-third of the world's annual consuming capacity, and India, with over one-fifth, are outstanding sources of demand for the commodity. Of much less significance are Japan, Pakistan, Indonesia, Thailand, Burma, and many others (Fig. 17.3). Per capita as well as aggregate consumption is higher in Asia than elsewhere; an average of nearly 250 pounds is consumed annually per person in Asia (excluding the Soviet Union), as compared with slightly over 40 pounds in Latin America and Oceania, the two areas ranking next.[4]

Seed requirements are less than for wheat, seldom exceeding 5 per cent of the yield. The com-

[3] Most rice is consumed the year it is produced, and no substantial reserves accrue; hence the volume of consumption is rather closely dependent upon annual production.

[4] Because of the heavy populations in southern and eastern Asia, however, the world average for per capita consumption of rice (140.9 pounds) is not far behind the average for wheat (167.6 pounds). The figures are in metric pounds, each of which equals about 1.1 avoirdupois pounds. See: W. S. Woytinsky and E. S. Woytinsky, *World Population and Production,* The Twentieth Century Fund, Inc., New York, 1953, p. 288.

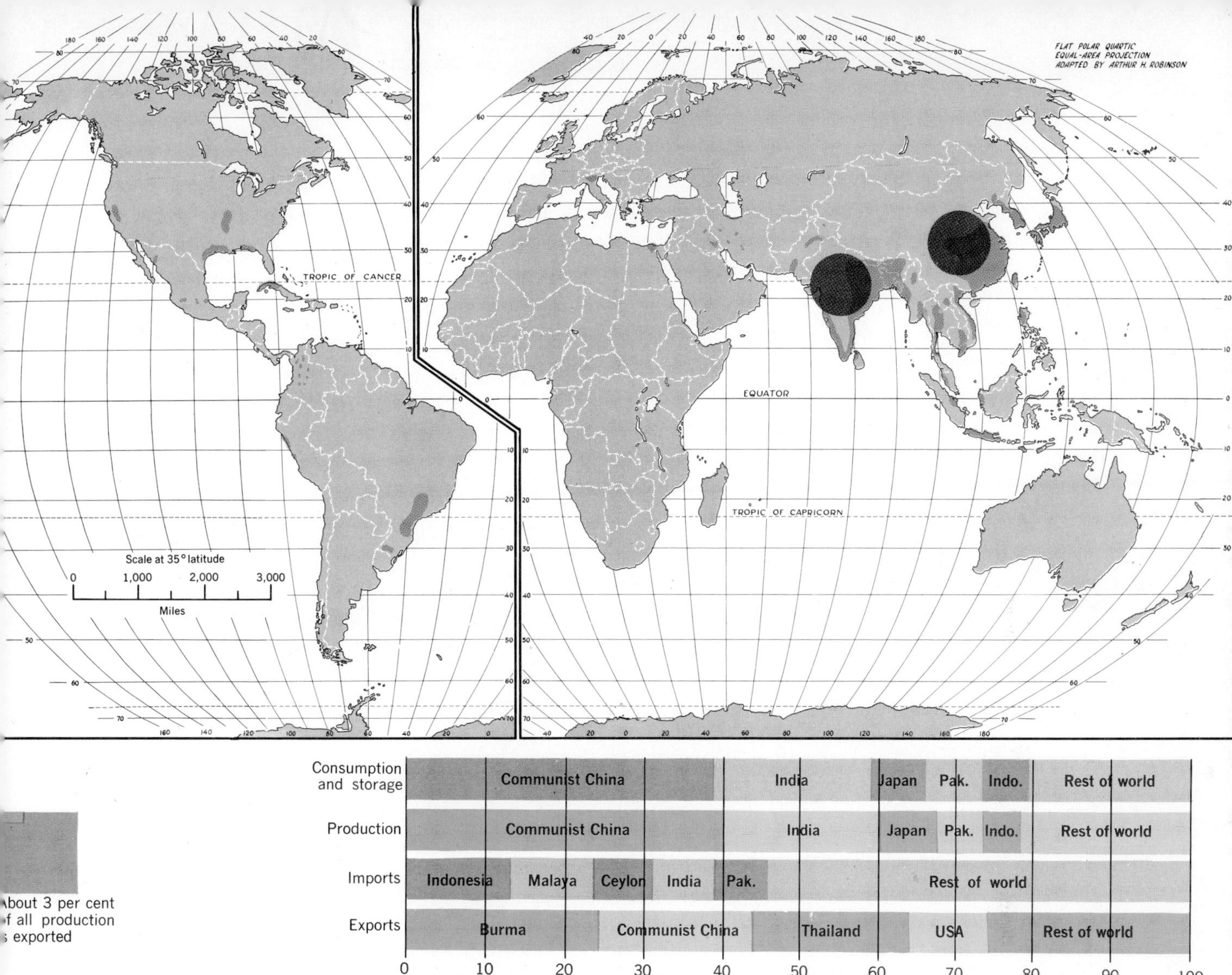

Figure 17.3 ***Consumption, production, import, and export of rice.*** *Shaded circles show nations of very heavy consumption. The gray shading shows major areas of production. During certain years, when famine occurs, India imports much more rice than is shown above. Until recently Japan was a major importer.*

paratively small amount which is fed to animals appears not to exceed the proportion of wheat used for the same purpose.

RICE PRODUCTION

Natural conditions for growth

Climate. Early records suggest that rice was first cultivated in China under subtropical climatic conditions. The plant has adapted easily to the tropics as well as to cooler latitudes. There are very many varieties of rice, and, by making extensive use of them and by assuring an adequate water supply, man has been able to grow rice in most equatorial places, and as far poleward as lat 40° N or S (Fig. 17.3). A minimum growing season of three months with a mean temperature of at least 75° F appears necessary for even the quick-maturing varieties. Hence rice is not generally grown beyond lat 40° N or S, nor at altitudes above 3,000 feet (Fig. 7.2).

Most is grown under humid subtropical, tropical rain-forest, tropical savanna, and mediterranean climates, but rice is also found in semiarid, desert, and humid continental warm-summer climates. Within the very sizable territory where its cultivation is feasible, the plant needs a good supply of water which is often supplied artificially, regardless of climate.

Other Natural Environmental Features. Most rice requires extremely level land for paddies, and can be grown on slopes only after they are terraced. Irregular terrain thus presents a problem to rice culture, but not an insoluble one. Particularly in the Far East, where much labor is expended for each harvested acre, it is not uncommon for slopes to be terraced and placed under cultivation. This is one accomplishment of the intensive-subsistence type of farming that has not been effectively duplicated in the mechanized types of farming in most technically advanced lands.

Soils should be sufficiently heavy to prevent unnecessary percolation and consequent loss of water. Otherwise, rice tolerates appreciably different soil types, but acid and neutral soils appear to yield more satisfactorily than nonacid soils. Artificial fertilization appears to increase the yield, and in parts of the Far East the human waste ("night soil") from the cities and villages is used for this purpose. The result is that fields adjacent to such centers are more productive than those farther away.

Commercial fertilization also is practiced, especially in the United States and Japan, and it is being stressed in the plans of Communist China and India. However, moderate yields can be achieved consistently even without fertilization, as has been done for centuries in some locations of southern and eastern Asia.

Areas of Potential and Actual Productivity. Like wheat, rice occupies only a comparatively small portion of the land where it can be grown. This should not be unexpected in nations which are not major rice consumers, but even in the Far East much more rice could be produced—on many of the jute fields of the lower Ganges and Brahmaputra Rivers in India and East Pakistan, for example. Why is it not grown? The answers appear to lie in cultural taste and hope for economic gain. Other crops are grown instead.

Categories of rice

The thousands of rice varieties are frequently classified in categories of *lowland rice* and *upland rice*. The former includes all rice produced under flooded conditions and the latter all rice grown where such flooding is not feasible, usually at higher elevations. The classification is based upon current agricultural practices rather than upon inherent plant traits, for, genetically, rice is a land plant, a grass. Unlike most land plants, however, it thrives in the flooded paddies where it not only is assured of continuous moisture but also is free from excessive competition with weeds, most of which cannot survive in the paddies.

Some upland rice is found in nearly every rice-growing nation. Incomplete statistics indicate that upland rice occupies less than 10 per cent of all rice land. In Brazil, it occupies nearly four-fifths of the rice land.

Production in the Far East

Leading Nations. To an even greater degree than is true of wheat, rice is grown in the nations where it is consumed. Over 90 per cent of all rice is produced in Asia. Communist China, with 40 per cent of the world's total output, and India, with 20 per cent, are the outstanding single rice-producing nations (Fig. 17.3). Other Asian producers are more numerous than active, lagging far behind these two. Japan, Pakistan, and Indonesia, each responsible for about 6 per cent or less of all rice, are in the forefront of a list of more than 15 nations that are subordinate producers.

Types of Farming and Growing Conditions. The Asian rice crop is grown almost entirely under a system of intensive-subsistence agriculture (compare Figs. 17.3 and 7.1). Yields vary, averaging more than 75 bushels per acre in Japan, 50 in China, 25 in India, and 30 in the world as a whole. (Such yields compare very favorably with world wheat

In eastern and southern Asia, fish are raised in these paddies while the rice is growing (International Cooperation Administration).

yields, which are slightly in excess of 15 bushels per acre; however, it should be remembered that a bushel of rice weighs only three-fourths as much as a bushel of wheat.) Except in Communist China, holdings of actual cropland are very small, not exceeding four acres per household in the major areas of production and often fragmented into tiny plots that are quite removed from each other. Rice occupies nearly one-half of the cultivated land in Japan, over one-third of that in Communist China, and over one-fourth of that in India.

Rice production in eastern and southern Asia

Rice yields are very poor in some underdeveloped areas. They could be improved by such simple techniques as manuring—if the manure were not used for domestic heating and cooking. They could be improved much more with commercial fertilizers and farming methods used in Western Europe and Japan. This is a rice field in India. (International Cooperation Administration)

reflects the changing monsoon winds and associated precipitation there. Where possible, the crop is grown under conditions of some winter precipitation as well as the characteristic summer rainfall and thus does particularly well under tropical rainforest and humid subtropical climates. Even where the winter moisture is deficient or lacking, however, it is a major summer crop, benefiting directly from the water provided by the summer monsoons, aided where necessary by irrigation. Because of the necessity for maximizing output, the techniques of double cropping and interculture are frequently utilized, although the alternative crop (or crops) is not always rice. In the southern sections of Japan, Communist China, and India, two rice harvests per year are realized. Where the growing season will not permit two separate harvests, interculture is practiced; new shoots are inserted between the rows of maturing grain, and planting and harvesting thus overlap. Where even this is not feasible, a quick-maturing winter crop, usually wheat or barley, is grown by either double cropping or interculture.

Planting takes place as early as possible in the spring where frost is the worst hindrance, and at the onset of the rainy season where drought is the primary obstacle. A small amount of rice is seeded directly to the fields, but most is first planted in nursery beds. What happens during and after planting has been described for one major growth area as follows:[5]

[5] John Norman Efferson, *The Production and Marketing of Rice*, Simmons Press, New Orleans, 1952, pp. 191–192. By permission of the author.

In India and Pakistan, as a whole, rice is grown throughout the year with seasonal crops overlapping, making it difficult to establish a definite crop year. Three different crops are produced. (1) The winter crop, sown from May to August and harvested from November to January, (2) the autumn crop, sown in April and May and harvested in September, and (3) the summer crop, sown in January and February and harvested from March to June. The winter crop accounts for 80 percent of the total production of the region, the autumn crop for about 18 percent, and the summer crop for 2 percent. Most of the country depends on natural rainfall for rice irrigation, and the production season is timed according to the coming of the monsoon. In India, in contrast to southeast Asia, the monsoon weather varies from year to year in time and in the amount of rainfall, making rice production more hazardous and causing localized famines from time to time.

About 20 percent of the rice plantings in India and Pakistan are broadcast, and 80 percent are transplanted. Broadcasting results in lower yields than transplanting, but this method necessitates less water for growing plants and for preparing land, and it is used in many regions where irrigation water is a limiting factor. Because of the dry season, no second crops are grown on most of the land in these areas.

The land is prepared for rice in India by plowing with bullock teams of the Brahman type. Although India has a large water buffalo population, these animals are maintained for milk production rather than for work stock. The average labor requirements for growing and harvesting rice amount to 15 man-days and 60 woman-days per acre, or a total of 75 days. The men do the plowing and fitting, and pull up the plants and haul in the crop after harvesting. The women do the setting, weeding, harvesting, and winnowing of the grain after threshing.

Traditionally, in India as well as in most other parts of Asia, only women do the heavy work of transplanting, weeding, and harvesting the rice by hand. According to legend, if men transplant the crop, the plants will fail to tiller and grow; if men weed the crop, the birds will destroy it; and if men harvest the crop, it will decay immediately after the harvest.

Because of water shortages early in the season when the rice plants must be produced, most of the rice nurseries in India are not irrigated. Under the common practice for growing seedbed plants, the seedbed is first covered with a layer of dry grass, leaves, tree limbs, dried cow dung, and all other available inflammable materials; a fire is then set to the mass, and it slowly smolders and burns until converted to ashes. Then the area is lightly plowed, and the seed sown. This ancient practice has its advantages in producing good plants under the existing conditions. It is cheap, since there are no purchased materials; it serves to disinfect the seedbed; and it makes the soil loose and porous, so that the available moisture will be retained and the plants can be pulled up easily without breaking. The rice

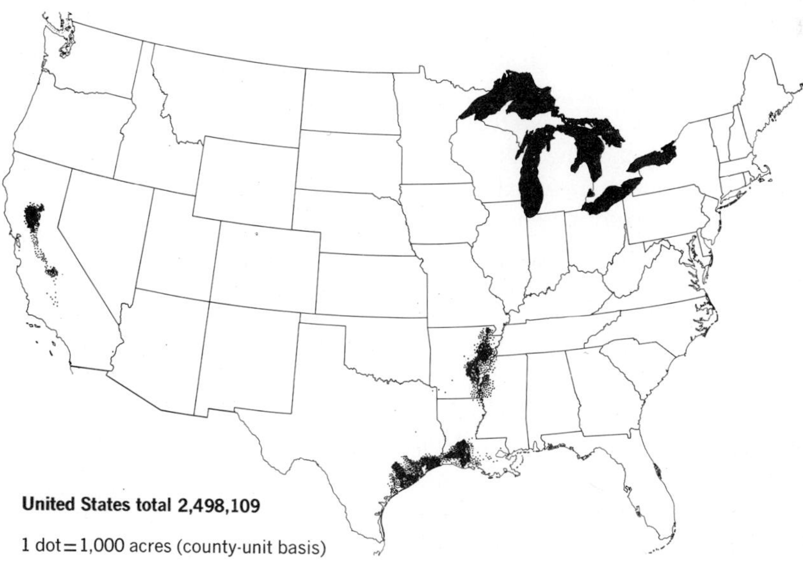

Figure 17.4 ***Where rice is grown in the United States*** *(U.S. Bureau of the Census).*

farmer plants about one acre of nursery plants for each 10 acres of rice. About 40 to 60 pounds of seed per acre of transplanted rice are used by this method as compared with 125 to 150 pounds of seed per acre by the direct broadcast method.

Although allowance should be made for national and local differences, the description above is indicative of the circumstances and conditions under which most lowland rice is grown.

The United States

As yet a comparatively minor rice producer with only slightly more than 1 per cent of the world's annual output, the United States merits particular attention because of its methods, which characteristically involve the maximum use of machines. California, Louisiana, Texas, and Arkansas are the leading producing states, their annual outputs being almost equal (Fig. 17.4). The crop is grown on flat land that is conducive to large-scale, mechanized operations. The dikes around individual "paddies," like the fields themselves, are machine-worked. Commercial fertilizers are used where necessary. Preliminary nursery beds are generally not utilized. Instead, the seed is either planted with grain drills or broadcast from airplanes, the latter method being much faster than the former. Harvesting is now accomplished chiefly with combines, which have been slow to replace binders because of difficulties encountered with a high moisture content in combined rice. This moisture is now removed by mechanical dryers immediately after being taken from the combine, and the difficulties thus have been mainly overcome. Yields per acre currently exceed 60 bushels, approximately twice the average world yield.

RICE TRADE AND TRANSPORTATION

Domestic trade

In the quasi-subsistence conditions under which most rice is consumed and produced, the majority of the annual harvest remains at home. It has been estimated, for example, that nearly 85 per cent of the rice crop in Communist China, and almost 60 per cent of that in India, does not leave the villages where it was produced.[6] The grain which is forwarded into the domestic market usually travels no farther than the nearest large city, making the journey via water craft or cart.

Foreign trade

An even smaller percentage of rice than wheat enters into international trade. If as much as 7 per cent of the annual harvest reaches foreign markets, the volume of such trade may be considered high; more often, the figure ranges between 3 and 4 per cent. Moreover, rice trade is prevailingly not transoceanic but is mainly a coastwise movement essentially devoid of such technical trappings as grain exchanges, with their brokers and clearinghouses, and gigantic ocean steamers, with their complicated shipping lists. Instead, much trade is on an individual basis, the farmer selling to the small merchant, who, utilizing either his own small water craft, or similarly modest means of transport, or that of a professional carrier, forwards the grain to international markets in the nearest large seaport. Increasingly, these negotiations are subject to controls by national governments of the countries wherein they are transacted; indeed, some of those countries are assuming close control over such marketing.

Traditionally, Burma, Thailand, Indochina (now subdivided into North Vietnam, South Vietnam, Cambodia, and Laos), and Korea (now subdivided into North Korea and South Korea) have been the leading nations of rice export. However, the several local conflicts that have erupted in southeastern Asia since the last world war have brought changes. Currently Burma is the only outstanding rice-exporting nation of southeastern Asia. Otherwise, the rice-export patterns of Asia are rather diffuse. In recent years Communist China has sometimes exported large amounts of rice, but as yet no clear indication exists as to whether such exports will become a permanent feature or are merely temporary expressions of a fluctuating gov-

[6] *Ibid.*, pp. 189, 215.

ernment policy. Thailand is also an important exporter.

On the world scene, the United States has moved rapidly to the status of a leading rice-export nation, ranking behind Burma, Communist China, and Thailand (Fig. 17.3). In Europe, Italy has become increasingly active in rice export.

The world pattern of rice imports, again focused on southeastern Asia, likewise is rather diffuse. As with exports, this is due partially to the numerous local conflicts that have broken out since the last war. No single nation dominates the import market, but Indonesia, Malaya, Ceylon, India, and Pakistan are among the leaders.

CORN (MAIZE)

We have noted that, among the world's three leading grains, wheat is oriented particularly to technically advanced nations and rice to technically underdeveloped nations. The orientation of corn is toward a single nation, the United States. All other countries—sparsely or densely populated, dependent or independent, technically underdeveloped or technically advanced—occupy comparatively minor positions (Fig. 17.5).

CORN CONSUMPTION

Well over 6 billion bushels of corn disappear each year. The grain is used for livestock feed, for human food, and for such inedible manufactured products as industrial alcohol. A very small amount—in the United States, less than 1 per cent—is used for seed.

The United States consumes about 50 per cent of the world's corn, nearly 45 per cent being accounted for by the country's livestock industry. No other nation offers more than token competition to this high volume of consumption, although the crop is utilized throughout much of the rest of the world (Fig. 17.5).

CORN PRODUCTION

Natural conditions of growth

Considered with respect to areas of potential growth, corn surpasses either wheat or rice. Some varieties will mature in as few as sixty days and can be grown as far poleward as lat 55° N; others will ripen in dry climates, and still others in very moist climates. Unaided by irrigation, the plant is found in every climatic type except desert, subarctic, and tundra, and under irrigation in all but the last two. Nor are mountains absolutely prohibitive; notably in Latin America, corn is grown at elevations exceeding 12,000 feet, as well as on unterraced slopes. Although sometimes needing fertilization and artificial drainage to provide the best results, soils provide no serious obstacle to corn growth. Optimum soils are the prairie and chernozem types found generally at the drier portions of the world's humid climates.

The United States as outstanding producer

World corn production is dominated by the United States to a degree almost without parallel in the agricultural scene. Of all corn for which statistics are reported—and much probably is not reported—about one-half is grown in this one country (Fig. 17.5).

Conditions of Production. The grain prevails throughout the famed corn belt of the agricultural interior of the United States, its area of growth extending westward into the winter- and spring-wheat belts, southward into the cotton belt, and eastward into diversified farming country (Fig. 17.6). Iowa and Illinois are the two leading states, each accounting for about one-sixth of the nation's corn production. Minnesota, Indiana, Nebraska, Ohio, Missouri, South Dakota, Wisconsin, and Michigan are all important. These ten states account for nearly three-fourths of the nation's corn output.

Natural conditions in the corn belt scarcely could be more favorable for this crop. The climate

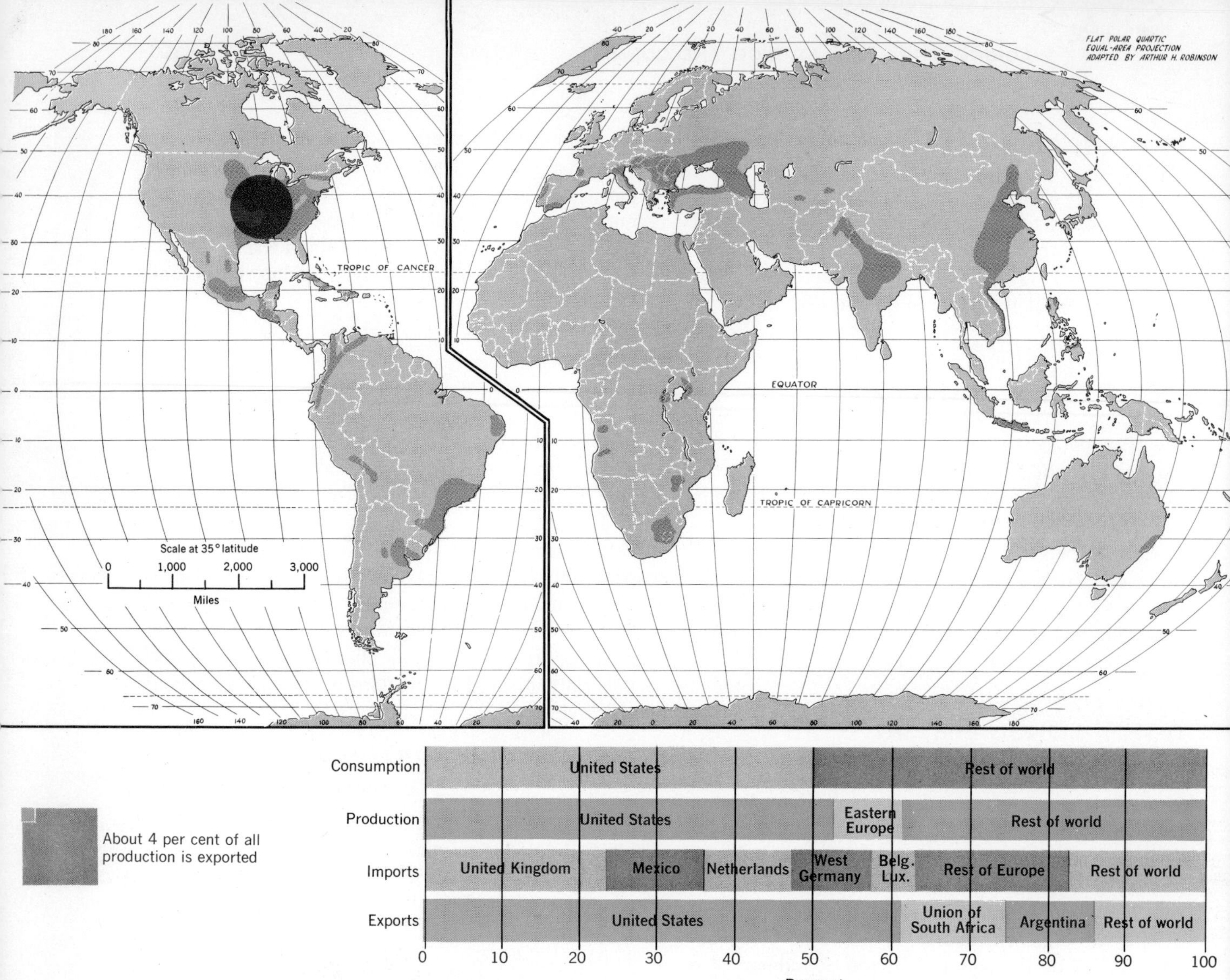

Figure 17.5 ***Consumption, production, import, and export of corn (maize). The United States dominates, using the grain chiefly for animal feed. The circle shows the one country of very heavy consumption. The gray stippling shows areas of production. Not much corn is traded internationally.***

is chiefly humid continental warm-summer, the soils are mainly prairie and chernozem, and the landforms are mostly undulating to flat. Such conditions here differ especially from those of possibly comparable areas elsewhere in that a rather copious, dependable moisture supply occurs in combination with excellent black soils over a sizable piece of territory. Most of the corn belt receives 30 inches or more of precipitation, which is a rather high amount to be associated extensively with the prairie and chernozem soils of this area.

The corn belt is a highly productive, highly mechanized area. Average yields per acre of 68 bushels are achieved in Illinois, 60 in Indiana, 50 or more in Iowa. Mechanization is commonplace; more than four-fifths of all farms report tractors, and

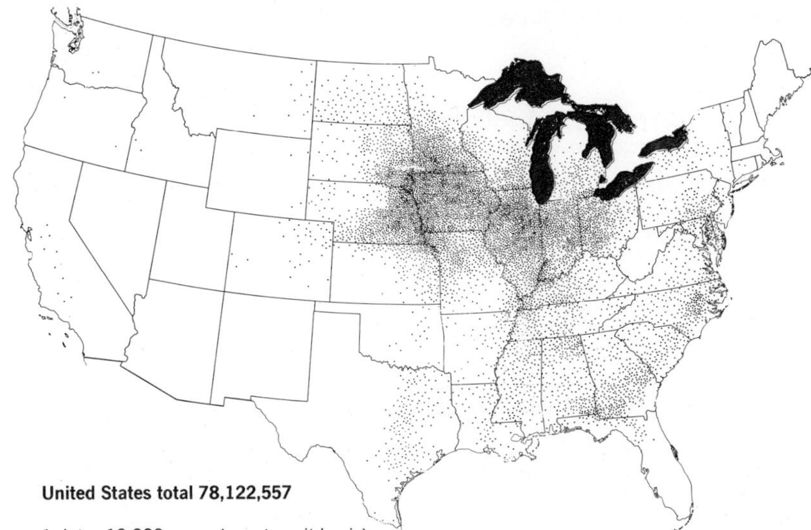

Figure 17.6 ***Where corn is grown in the United States*** *(U.S. Bureau of the Census).*

some report three, four, and even more tractors apiece. More land is cropped than is common throughout the nation, and the value of such land usually exceeds $200 an acre. Unlike the winter-wheat belt, however, the corn belt does not specialize in a single crop. Instead, it possesses a more diversified economic base that includes soybeans, alfalfa, oats, and other crops. Feeding livestock on farms is common. Over 40 per cent of the nation's corn is fed directly to hogs, over 16 per cent to poultry, over 13 per cent to dairy cattle, and about 10 per cent to beef cattle. Within this diversified economy, however, some areas of cash grain, or commercial grain, exist. The largest occupies much of northeastern Illinois, immediately adjacent to Chicago. Here the grain—mostly corn—is sold from the farms where it is grown. Much is purchased by commercial feeders and eventually used as livestock feed. In contrast to other types of farming units, cash-grain farms are increasing in number—notably

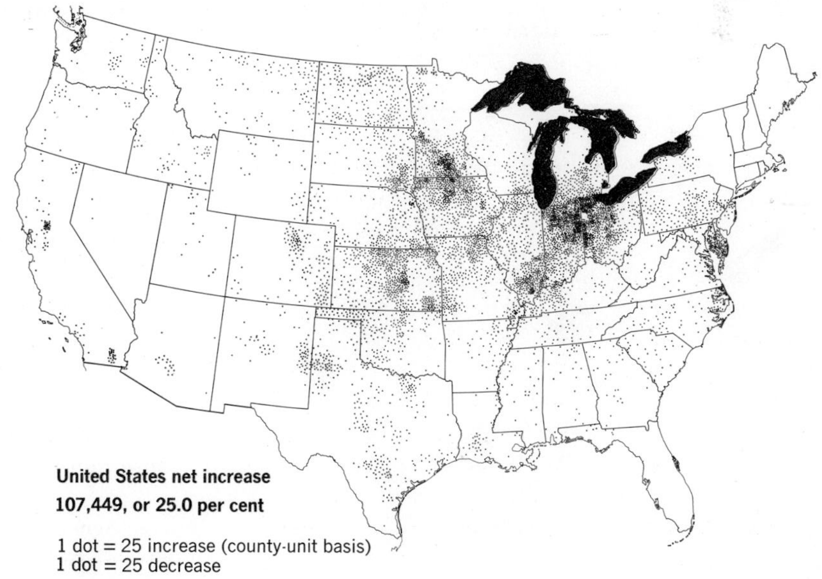

Figure 17.7 ***Increase and decrease of cash-grain farms in the United States from 1949–1954*** *(U.S. Bureau of the Census).*

so in the northwestern and eastern parts of the corn belt (Fig. 17.7).

Production outside the Corn Belt. Beyond the corn belt, the grain is grown chiefly in the South and secondarily in the East and West. In none of these areas is it outstanding. Instead, it is frequently utilized as animal feed on the farms where it is grown. This is especially true of the South, where in many farming operations tractors have not replaced draft animals as rapidly as in the corn belt.

Figure 17.8 ***How double-cross hybrid seed corn is produced.*** *The grandparent ears, of different types, are shown in a row at the top of the picture. The parent ears—first-generation hybrids—are in the center. The second generation, or double-cross, hybrids (from a family "tree" involving four different original types) are at the bottom. (U.S. Department of Agriculture)*

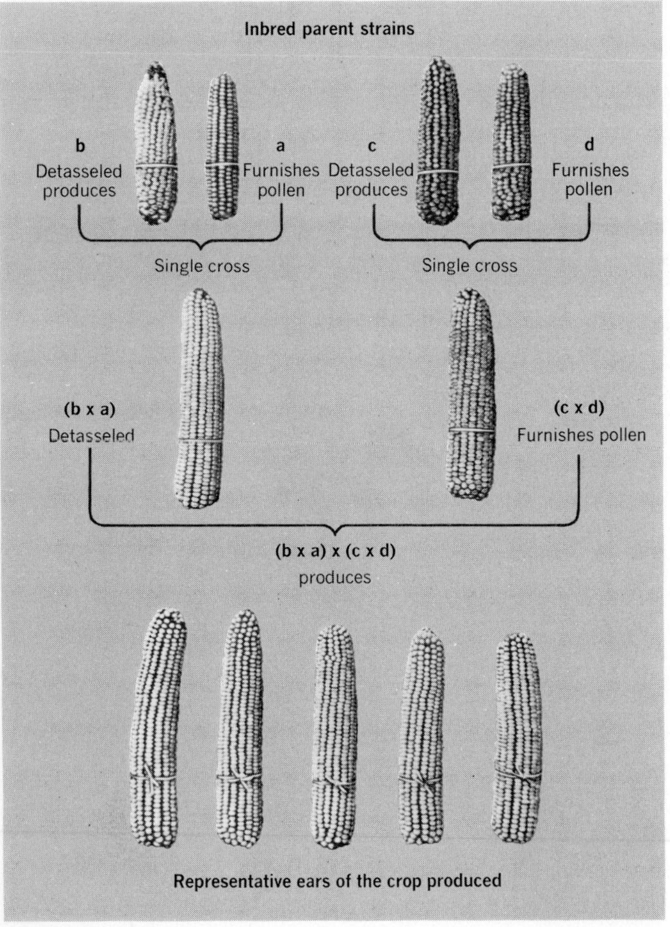

Hybrid Corn. In 1933, the commanding position which the United States long had held in corn production became even more outstanding with the planting of hybrid corn. By 1941, this new type of corn occupied nearly 40 per cent of all corn acreage, and by 1958 nearly 94 per cent. What is hybrid corn? As its name suggests, it is a seed developed from selective crossbreeding of unlike varieties, each of which may have one or more desirable qualities (Fig. 17.8). As a result of its introduction and other technical improvements in corn growing, yields per acre have doubled since the 1930s. In 1958, nearly 52 bushels per acre were recorded for the nation as a whole, whereas in 1932 the yield was only 26.5 bushels per acre. Not only is this new corn yield greater, but the corn grows on a hardier plant which stands more firmly in the fields than do older types and thus lends itself more readily to mechanized harvesting. The nation has reduced its corn acreage by about one-tenth of its 1950–1954 average in order to avoid heavy surpluses. This reduction has not been entirely successful, however, and surpluses have accrued that amount aggregately to about one-fourth of the country's annual harvest.

Production in other parts of the world

We have noted that no nation other than the United States is a major producer of corn. Indeed, this country's output is unmatched even by other continents. Whereas the United States produced nearly 3.8 billion bushels of corn in 1958, Asia (excluding the Soviet Union) recorded an estimated 850 million bushels, Europe (excluding the Soviet Union) 765 million bushels, South America 600 million bushels, and Africa 420 million bushels.[7] The Soviet Union, with 525 million bushels, is now second among national producers and probably will become more important, as it is emphasizing hybrid

[7] *Agricultural Statistics, 1959,* U.S. Department of Agriculture, 1960, p. 32.

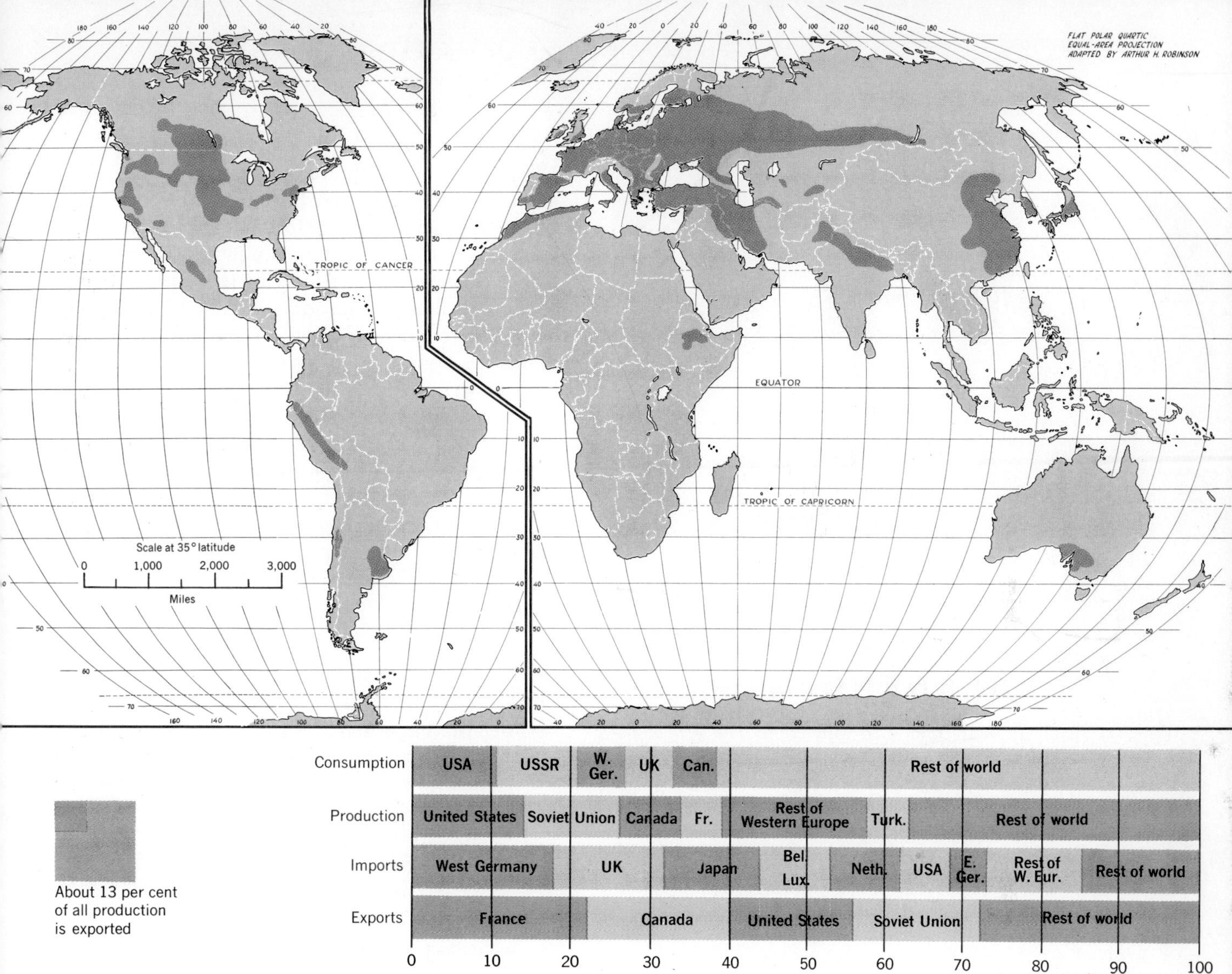

Figure 17.9 ***Consumption, production, import, and export of barley.***

corn in its planned development. Argentina, Mexico, the Union of South Africa, Italy, and India are noteworthy corn producers. Most of the leading producers, it will be noted, are technically advanced.

TRADE IN CORN

No more than 4 per cent of the annual corn harvest enters into international trade, and the trend is erratic (Fig. 17.5). Before the last war, this trade was chiefly a movement from Argentina to the United Kingdom, Belgium, and still other nations of northwestern Europe. Argentina declined as a major exporter during the final years of the Peron regime, and only now is recovering part of that former status. However, the United States now has become more active and currently supplies about three-fourths of all exports—an amount totaling less than one-sixth of all corn now warehoused in the country. The Union of South Africa also has increased its exports, and it now supplies nearly one-seventh of all corn entering world markets. Over two-thirds of all corn moves to Europe, and most of the remainder to either Mexico or Japan.

Hybrid corn (U.S. Department of Agriculture).

Lesser grains

Wheat, rice, and corn are the world leaders among a number of grains that include barley, oats, sorghum, rye, and others. Most are grown in every continent. Of these, barley is now recorded as the leader, having replaced oats in the middle 1900s. It is grown in an amount that ranges each year from one-third to one-half those of the three primary grains. Its consumption, production, and exchange are shown in Fig. 17.9. Like the three primary grains, it is produced chiefly for domestic consumption. Indeed, it frequently is planted as a substitute crop when wheat or corn fails, because it can mature quickly under cool or dry conditions. The remaining grains harvested in comparatively small amounts also are consumed mainly within the countries of their cultivation.

REFERENCES

Callaghan, A. R., and A. J. Millington: *The Wheat Industry in Australia,* Angus and Robertson, Sydney, Australia, 1956.

Efferson, John Norman: *The Production and Marketing of Rice,* Simmons Press, New Orleans, 1952.

Fowke, Vernon C.: *The National Policy and the Wheat Economy,* University of Toronto Press, Toronto, 1957.

Grist, Donald H.: *Rice,* Longmans, Green & Co., Ltd., London, 1953.

Harris, Chauncy D.: "Agricultural Production in the United States: The Past Fifty Years and the Next," *Geographical Review,* **47:**175–193, 1957.

Haystead, Ladd, and Gilbert C. Fite: *The Agricultural Regions of the United States,* University of Oklahoma Press, Norman, Okla., 1955.

Hewes, Leslie, and Arthur C. Schmieding: "Risk in the Central Great Plains," *Geographical Review,* **46:** 375–387, 1956.

Higbee, Edward: *The American Oasis: The Land and Its Uses,* Alfred A. Knopf, Inc., New York, 1957.

Jackson, W. A. Douglas: "Durum Wheat and the Expansion of Dry Farming in the Soviet Union," *Annals of the Association of American Geographers,* **46:**405–410, 1956.

———: "The Virgin and Idle Lands of Western Siberia and Northern Kazakhstan: A Geographical Appraisal," *Geographical Review,* **46:**1–19, 1956.

Kollmorgen, Walter M., and George F. Jenks: "Sidewalk Farming in Toole County, Montana, and Traill County, North Dakota," *Annals of the Association of American Geographers,* **48:**209–231, 1958.

——— and ———: "Suitcase Farming in Sully County, South Dakota," *Annals of the Association of American Geographers,* **48:**27–40, 1958.

Malenbaum, Wilfred: *The World Wheat Economy: 1885–1939,* Harvard University Press, Cambridge, Mass., 1953.

Schonberg, James S.: *The Grain Trade: How It Works,* Exposition Press, New York, 1956.

Spate, O. H. K.: *India and Pakistan: A General and Regional Geography,* Methuen & Co., Ltd., London, and E. P. Dutton & Co., Inc., New York, 1957.

Wallace, Henry A., and William L. Brown: *Corn and Its Early Fathers,* Michigan State College Press, East Lansing, Mich., 1956.

18 AGRICULTURE: SUGAR

SUGAR, LIKE WHEAT AND RICE, IS PRODUCED MAINLY FOR HUMAN CONSUMPTION. Only a comparatively small portion is fed to animals, converted into industrial alcohol, or used in other minor ways. The sugar which is fed to animals usually is in crude molasses or some other residue from processing, and its use is not actually in competition with the use of sugar for human food. Unlike wheat and rice, however, sugar is somewhat of a luxury for which no truly satisfactory substitute exists.

CONSUMPTION

Sugar makes up as much as 15 per cent of the per capita calorie intake of the technically advanced nations which dominate imports. Per capita consumption of sugar is somewhat lower in most technically underdeveloped countries,[1] but its aggregate consumption is frequently high even there because of their large populations.

Annual volume

With allowance for losses in transportation, processing, etc., we can estimate that well over 60 million short tons of sugar are consumed each year. More than seven-eighths is centrifugal, or white, sugar, produced in highly technical processing plants. The remaining one-eighth, lower in sucrose content and usually brown because it contains some molasses, is produced in rather primitive mills. White sugar is consumed almost exclusively within technically advanced nations, and both brown and white sugars are used extensively in many underdeveloped countries. The consumption of brown sugar probably is higher than records indicate because of the uncertainty of census data from many underdeveloped areas.

Leading nations

No nation can be said to monopolize sugar consumption. The United States is the leader, accounting for over 15 per cent of all centrifugal sugar (Fig. 18.1). It is followed by the Soviet Union. The United Kingdom and

[1] Even per capita consumption, however, is sometimes very high in technically underdeveloped countries. Colombia consumes far more sugar per person than most technically advanced countries, and Brazil and Mexico are also important consumers on a per capita basis.

neighboring Western European nations also are active consumers, as is Brazil. India, Communist China, and Pakistan are the principal users of brown sugar, and consume some white sugar as well (Fig. 18.1).

PRODUCTION OF SUGAR CANE

The commercial production of sugar is somewhat unusual in that two wholly different plants are fundamentally involved.[2] Sugar cane, thriving in certain locations of the tropics and subtropics, accounts for about two-thirds of the world's annual yield of both white and brown sugar. The sugar beet, grown in the middle latitudes, is responsible for essentially all of the remaining one-third. Thus the agricultural economies of the low and middle latitudes—economies which often act to complement each other because the one group can grow what the other cannot—are in active competition with respect to sugar production.

Records indicate that cane has been the major source of sugar throughout most of human history. The crop appears to have been developed in Asia, where it has been grown for millenniums. Competition with other sources did not begin until the early part of the nineteenth century, when the beet was introduced into commercial use in Europe. Almost immediately a competition arose, and by the turn of the twentieth century beet sugar accounted for about two-thirds of the world's annual output. During the aftermath of the First World War, however, the positions of the two were reversed, and cane subsequently has continued to supply about two-thirds of the world's demand.

Like wheat, oats, and corn, sugar cane is a grass.[3] Unlike these grains, it is a perennial which sends forth roots for several years if frost or drought does not interfere. It puts down a rather shallow root system that seldom exceeds 16 inches in depth (although some roots have been known to penetrate downward as far as 10 feet), and it grows to heights sometimes exceeding 15 feet. Its sugar content, concentrated in the stalk, ranges from 8 to 20 per cent of its total bulk. The chief by-product involves the stalk's fibers (bagasse) which, although of little agricultural use, are manufactured into insulating board for building construction. Some molasses also is realized.

The crop is associated chiefly with plantation-type farming in the Western Hemisphere and Australia, and with intensive-subsistence farming in Asia and northern Africa (Figs. 18.1 and 7.1).

Natural conditions of growth

From eight to twenty-four months elapse between the sugar-cane planting and harvest, during which time average temperatures must be above 60°F, should be above 70°F, and under optimum conditions would be above 80°F. Growth of the quick-maturing varieties is feasible in places like Louisiana where frost might occur, but most sugar cane is found where no frost is expected. Heavy precipitation is beneficial during the early and intermediate stages of crop growth, but a dry season is desirable before harvest. Consequently, most of the world's sugar cane is grown in tropical savanna climate, or in more moist tropical and subtropical climates which nevertheless contain a season sufficiently dry that a harvest is possible. Also, the crop is grown occasionally under irrigation.

The best land for sugar cane is flat and fertile, with topsoils that retain moisture and subsoils that permit drainage. Since such optimum conditions are rare, most of the world's cane is found on land that is flat or undulating and is well drained. Because of comparatively heavy precipitation, the soils are often rather acid and infertile, and considerable fertilization is necessary for good yields.

The territory where sugar cane can be grown consists of the very sizable portion of the earth between lat 35° N and 35° S, except in mountainous areas, in excessively wet land, and in excessively dry land that is not irrigated. As is true of other crops we have examined previously, the territory of growth potential greatly exceeds the area now

[2] Of course, sugar can be extracted from many plants; we are concerned here with large-scale commercial extraction.

[3] Other common crops which are grasses are barley, rye, millet, and sorghum.

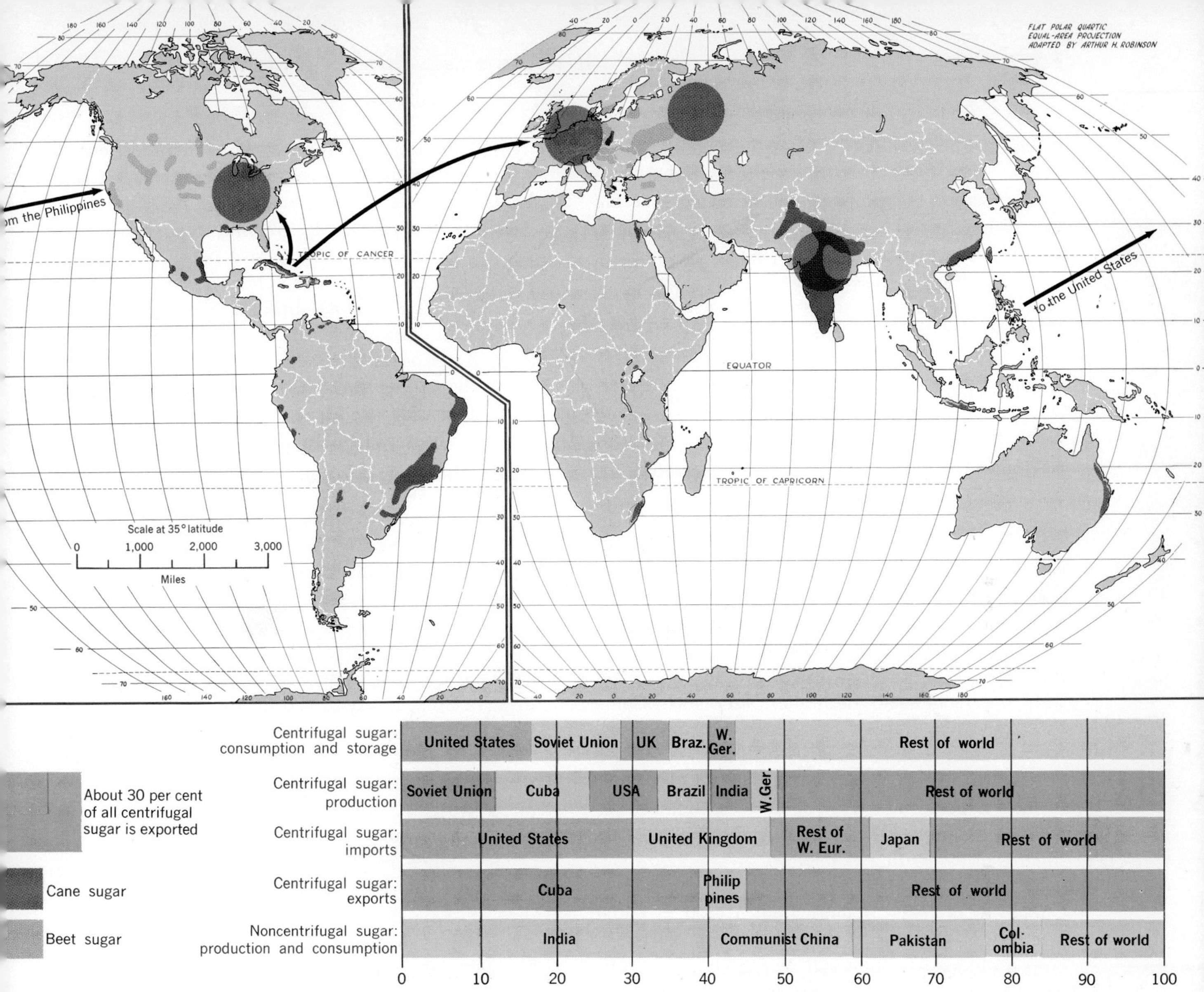

Figure 18.1 ***Consumption, production, import, and export of cane and beet sugar.*** *Centrifugal sugar involves both cane and beets; noncentrifugal sugar involves only cane. Shaded circles show nations or regions of heaviest consumption. The gray stippling shows areas of production. Arrows show direction of heaviest international trade.*

being devoted to sugar cane. The basic limitations to such growth thus appear to lie in human cultures, particularly economies, rather than in nature.

Potentialities for technology

Sugar cane does not lend itself easily to mechanized production. Difficulties are encountered in planting, for sections of the stalk, rather than seed, are placed in the ground, and if the sections are improperly cut or placed, they do not send up healthy shoots. Harvesting and transporting also present problems, as the stalk must be cut at a low level, stripped of its leaves, and yet kept relatively undamaged until it reaches the mill. To date, the production of sugar cane has remained an industry involving much human labor. Nonmechanical technical improvements, such as commercial fertilization, offer more immediate promise than does mechanization. The substitution of tractors for animal power in hauling, etc., also has been demonstrated to be feasible under certain conditions.

Nevertheless, experimentation with, and some application of, machines is found, especially in Australia, Hawaii, and the United States.

Major countries of growth

Cuba is the leader among sugar-cane producers, with India a close second. Each nation produces over 12 per cent of the world's supply, although India's output involves much more brown sugar than the Cuban yield does (Fig. 18.1). Indeed, if complete data were available for India's semisubsistence sugar industry, its output might be shown to exceed Cuba's. Additional political units of importance include Brazil, Communist China, Australia, the Philippines, Mexico, Puerto Rico, Pakistan, the Dominican Republic, Nationalist China, Indonesia, Argentina, and the Union of South Africa. These 14 nations account for about 90 per cent of the world's sugar cane. The United States is not a major producer, even now that Hawaii has become a state; only about 3 per cent of all cane sugar is grown within its territory.

Cuba. Sugar cane is more than a crop in Cuba; it is a symbol of one of the ways of life there. The crop occupies over one-half of the country's cultivated land, and sugar comprises nearly 90 per cent of the value of all exports. It is produced chiefly for foreign markets, and domestic demand accounts for only about 5 per cent of production. Sugar so dominates Cuba's economy that Cuba is self-sufficient in neither food nor the cotton that is basic to textiles in these warm temperatures but depends upon imports for nearly 30 per cent of the food consumed and essentially all of the cotton.

The island, dominated by tropical savanna climate, contains much land conducive to sugar-cane growth. The most intensive cultivation extends from Havana southeastward along both coasts and throughout much of the interior for a distance of over 250 miles. The crop is to be seen almost everywhere, although it is somewhat scarce in the uplands, particularly to the west.

The very favorable growing conditions make possible four or more successive harvests from one planting. Moreover, inasmuch as no frost occurs to force a quick seasonal harvest, the planting and subsequent harvesting can be extended over a substantial period of time, and the periodic glutting of the mills at harvest time is thus minimized. The harvest season usually continues from December until April of the following year. Yields are low—15 to 18 tons of cane per acre, as compared with 60 tons or more per acre in Hawaii and parts of Java. To date, not much capital has been invested in commercial and organic fertilizers. Instead, fields have been taken out of cane when their output has become submarginal.

Once essentially Cuban-owned and concentrated in the vicinity of Havana, the island's sugar-cane industry has undergone rather radical changes in ownership, location, and technology. Prior to the twentieth century, most Cuban sugar was grown under domestic ownership, largely in sizable estates where the land was worked by either tenants or hired workers. Numerous crude grinders for the initial processing were also the property of the estates. Since most of the cane was grown near Havana, expensive overland hauls to the seaport thus were avoided.

The development of the modern sugar mill and the concomitant increase in world demand for sugar altered this agricultural practice. The centrally located sugar mill, or *central,* removed the cane juice far more quickly and efficiently than did the old grinders. Furthermore, a single mill could serve the holdings of an entire vicinity. In a comparatively short time, therefore, the centrals replaced the large estates as foci of economic activity and power. Modern sugar mills, however, are costly as well as efficient, and they quickly attracted foreign capital—especially during the First World War when demand for sugar was high. Investment from the United States and elsewhere in centrals and sugar-cane land has continued to be an important aspect of Cuba's sugar-cane industry. Today, nearly one-fourth of this cane land is owned by firms and individuals of the United States and other countries. Approximately one-half is owned by Cubans, and the remaining one-fourth is under various types of nonspecified ownership. To an even greater degree, mills were built and purchased with this new capital; and of the more than 160 mills now in operation, more than 60 per cent are owned by foreign capital and the remainder by Cubans.[4]

The industry gradually has expanded southeastward from its original location near Havana, and much of the foreign capital is invested in the central and southeastern portion of the island. Although ownership patterns have changed somewhat, over 90 per cent of all Cuban sugar-cane land is still cultivated by tenants, usually under production contracts with the mill owners. The remaining 10 per cent of the sugar-cane acreage belongs to the owners of the centrals. It is usually in the immediate vicinity of the central and worked by hired employees.

The central owners, in turn, are not autonomous but are subjected to rather rigid control by the national government. The output of every single mill is channeled by the government into one of four categories of market: (1) local consumption, (2) exports to the United States, (3) exports to countries other than the United States, and (4) reserves.[5] Since all mills are subject to this close scrutiny, government policy is obviously a very important consideration in assessing the production of sugar in the island. The Cuban government also possesses other regulatory ties to the industry, which is its chief source of trade revenue.

India. Cuba and India, the outstanding sugar-cane-growing nations, are both frequently classified as technically underdeveloped. However, Cuba grows the crop largely for foreign markets, and production there is rather heavily financed and partially controlled from abroad. India, in contrast, utilizes largely domestic methods to produce for a domestic market.

The acreage of sugar-cane land in India, while constituting only slightly over 1 per cent of all cultivated land there, is unequaled in any other nation. Over three-fourths of this land is in and near the central segment of the Ganges River valley to the north, and the remainder is somewhat scattered in the southern peninsula.

Humid subtropical climate with moderately dry winters prevails over the northern growth area. Tropical savanna climate is dominant farther south. Along the southwestern coast is a strip of tropical rain-forest climate in which the winters are also drier than is usually true of this climate type. The dry or semidry season that is necessary for the harvest of sugar cane is thus to be found in all these climate types.

The crop is grown under intensive-subsistence type of agriculture. Yields per acre are low—even beneath those of Cuba. The leanest harvests occur in the north, despite comparatively fertile soils in the Ganges River valley. The very small holdings and inefficient methods there are combined with a climate in which frost sometimes occurs and which is uneven and unpredictable in terms of both

[4] The description of Cuba's situation pertains to conditions there before Fidel Castro came to power. At the time of this writing, events are moving so rapidly both within and outside Cuba that a generalization concerning that country becomes out of date almost before it leaves the author's hand. If the present regime continues in power in Cuba, many changes can be expected. The nationalization of much of the land, centrals, and other holdings heretofore belonging to both foreign and domestic private interests is one probability. Another probability is subsequent redistribution of much of this land among landless or nearly landless peasants. Also a probability is Cuba's looking to markets other than the United States for much of her sugar and other exports. The Soviet Union and Communist China already are making large purchases, despite heavy domestic sugar output in both countries.

Cuba's status, then, can best be described as instable, and can be subjected to more up-to-date generalization only after that instability has given way to a trend that appears definite at least for the years immediately ahead. Because we are not sure whether the economy will return largely to conditions described above or will strike out in wholly new directions, we shall make no attempt at this time to evaluate Cuba's current scene.

[5] Vladimir P. Timoshenko and Boris C. Swerling, *The World's Sugar,* Stanford University Press, Stanford, Calif., 1957, p. 83.

Cutting sugar cane in India. Note the large number of workers and the hand labor involved. (U.S. Department of Agriculture)

temperature and moisture. Yields per acre of 12 tons or less are not uncommon. Farther south, where the tropical climates are more conducive to sugar-cane growth, harvests of 20 to 40 tons per acre are realized. Because of the higher returns here, an increasing proportion of India's sugar cane is being grown in the south. In both the north and south, higher yields are achieved with irrigation.

About three-fifths, or perhaps more, of India's sugar cane is boiled into a sticky, brown mass called *gur*, in which form it is ultimately consumed. The remaining two-fifths is processed initially in modern mills and subsequently forwarded to centrifugal plants to be refined into white sugar. The country appears to be in a stage of transition from gur to centrifugal-sugar production, but the transition is slow. In years when the price of centrifugal sugar is high, the demand for gur quickly increases; and the relative positions of the two types of sugar thus vary rather pronouncedly with their current market prices. The more than 150 centrifugal-sugar mills, owned mostly by private firms or cooperatives, are increasing their output, however, and, despite their rather slow gains, they appear to be moving toward a dominating position. These mills represent technological advancement in India's sugar-cane industry, and their percentage of the country's total product is a rather crude indication of the extent to which that industry has become technically advanced.

India grows enough sugar to satisfy almost all domestic demand. This has not always been true. Prior to 1930, the country was importing approximately 1 million tons of sugar each year. Now, although as much as 200,000 tons may be imported in a year of crop failure due to erratic monsoon conditions, imports are generally insignificant, and occasionally a small export surplus is recorded.

The Five-Year Plans with which the young democracy of India hopes to increase its agricultural output have not as yet placed a more-than-casual interest upon the growth of sugar, which is not considered so essential as certain other food crops.

Brazil. Cuba, India, and Brazil are the "big three" of sugar-cane production, together accounting for nearly one-half of all cane sugar, including gur. Brazil's output is approximately one-half that of either Cuba or India.

Most of the crop is grown along the Atlantic coast or a comparatively short distance inland. To the northeast, an area of heavy concentration is located near the intersection of the coast line and the latitude of 10° S, and, farther south, another is situated at the approximate intersection of that coast and the Tropic of Capricorn (Fig. 18.1). The prevailing climate is tropical savanna, replaced here and there by such tropical rain-forest climate as is not too persistently wet for the harvest period.

Brazilian sugar cane was grown commercially as early as the sixteenth century, and it supplied most of Europe's demand until about 1700. Since that time, competition from other cane-growing areas, notably the West Indies, has become so active that Brazil's efforts have been directed mainly toward the domestic market that subsequently has absorbed most of the output. Traditionally, the low-latitude growth area in the northeastern part of the country has supplied most of the cane. During the 1930s, however, the crop was introduced into the state of São Paulo and adjacent states, and these southerly locations now produce more than one-half of the country's sugar.

The pace of technical advancement of the sugar-cane industry of Brazil appears to be somewhat behind that of Cuba and ahead of that of India. At least one-tenth of the final product is still processed by crude mills into a brown mass not unlike the gur of India. Much of the remaining cane is sent to mills which, although not primitive, are rather small. Almost 70 per cent of Brazil's sugar comes from mills with capacities of less than 1,000 tons of cane per day.[6] These small mills are largely in the older sugar-growing district to the northeast, where farming and processing methods are less advanced technically than in the newer sugar areas to the south.

Government control is quite rigid, and involves taxation as well as regulation. In open domestic competition, the more efficient producers in the São Paulo vicinity might force the withdrawal of northeastern growers from the industry. However, the national government taxes the growers unequally, the producer in the state of São Paulo paying 13 per cent of his production costs in taxes and his counterpart in the northeastern state of Pernambuco paying only 6 per cent.[7] The national government also shields the entire industry from excessive price fluctuations in the world market. In 1957, for example, the domestic prices of Brazilian sugar were appreciably higher than world prices. The Bank of Brazil subsidized the difference between domestic and world market prices in order to stimulate the exports of some 550,000 tons of sugar.[8]

Other countries. Most of the remaining countries noteworthy for sugar-cane growth are technically underdeveloped. In many of these, however, the cane is grown with comparatively advanced tools and methods. The reason is that close political and/or economic liaison has been maintained between these countries and certain technically advanced nations. Thus, the Republic of the Philippines, until recently a dependency of the United States, has benefited appreciably from overseas investment of ideas and capital from the United States. Similarly, India and Pakistan have benefited from former positions in the British Empire and current membership in the British Commonwealth. Indonesia has profited from capital investment and methods once employed there by the Dutch, who are among the world's most experienced cultivators of sugar cane, and although relationships between Indonesia and the Netherlands have recently become strained, a residue of Dutch plantations and methods remains there. Likewise, Taiwan (Nation-

[6] Preston E. James, "Trends in Brazilian Agricultural Development," *Geographical Review,* 43:313–315, 1953.

[7] *Ibid.*

[8] *Foreign Agriculture Circular,* U.S. Department of Agriculture, August 22, 1958, p. 5.

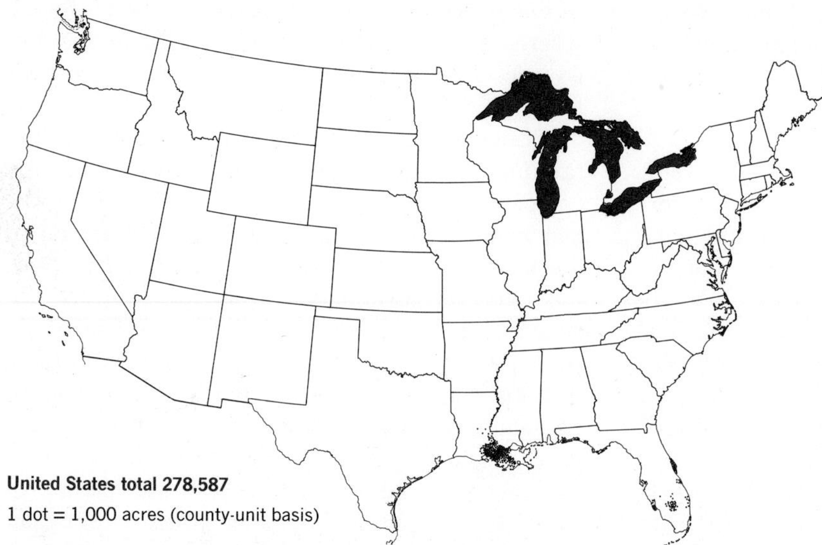

Figure 18.2 ***Where sugar cane is grown in the United States*** *(U.S. Department of Agriculture).*

alist China) profited to an extent by more modern methods introduced there by Japan before that nation was defeated in the Second World War.

A minority of these nations of secondary importance in sugar-cane growth are technically advanced. Australia, Argentina, and the Union of South Africa are the most active, with the United States worthy of mention (Fig. 18.2). Machines tend to replace hand labor in these producing areas. Australia has given particular attention to mechanized planting, and the United States to mechanized harvesting. However, the intricacies of both operations are such that mechanization is slow.

PRODUCTION OF SUGAR BEETS

Like sugar cane, sugar beets are produced chiefly for their sucrose content. The sugar is stored in the root of the plant rather than in the top, which is used mainly for cattle feed. The plant is seeded in early spring of each year, when the frost-free period begins. Usually it is also fertilized commercially at that time. What appears to be an individual seed is actually a small aggregate containing several seeds, and the initial stand of young beets is quite thick. The plants must be blocked (cut away completely for distances of 10 inches or more) and thinned (culled over, usually with human fingers, so that two plants do not grow side by side). When this has been done, individual shoots should be at least 10 inches apart, so that the root system of each can develop properly. The fields frequently are cultivated, and usually are hoed at least twice during the growing period. Harvesting comes in the fall, at which time the green top is removed and the beets are lifted from the ground and taken to the nearest factory or collecting point.

Unlike most commercially grown sugar cane, sugar beets are raised under diversified farming arrangements in rotation with other crops (Figs. 18.1 and 7.1). The two sources of sugar differ also in their by-products. Sugar cane yields only the bagasse and some molasses. Sugar beets yield the tops (the leafy portion of the plants and the caps of the roots) plus pulp (the pithy fibers, etc., of the roots, pulverized and deprived of their sugar content) and some molasses. The tops and pulp of the beets, as well as the molasses of both the cane and the beets, are excellent feed for livestock when used with care.

Sugar beets have been grown commercially for only about a century and a half, having been introduced into France by Napoleon because he was cut off from supplies of cane sugar. The industry wavered temporarily after his defeat but was a going concern by the middle of the nineteenth century.

Mechanized loading of sugar cane in Louisiana. About 200 short tons can be loaded in a 9-hour day. (U.S. Department of Agriculture)

Natural conditions of growth

The sugar beet is a middle-latitude plant and is not grown under tropical or subtropical conditions. A minimum growing season of 150 days is desirable, during which time the average temperatures of the warmest month should be not much above 70°F. The plant is a biennial, but when it is harvested in the fall of each year, its roots are lifted, and so it must be planted again each spring. Precipitation should be plentiful during the first three months of the plant's life but reduced at harvest time to increase the sugar content and facilitate harvesting operations. Because of these exacting moisture requirements, the crop frequently is grown under irrigation. The soils should be fertile but not too firm. A tight soil impedes development of the root, which stores the sugar. This root normally reaches downward about a foot and has auxiliary roots forming a complex system extending as far as 5 feet down and 3 feet horizontally.

Thriving in moderate temperatures, the sugar beet is grown in intermediate to cool climates of the Northern Hemisphere, above lat 35° N. None is produced south of the equator, where low latitudinal positions of the continents essentially preclude it. Most beets are grown under humid continental warm-summer, humid continental cool-summer, marine, and semiarid climates. Irrigation is necessary in the last. As is true of sugar-cane land, the territory of potential growth exceeds greatly the area of planted acreage.

There is essentially no overlap in the growth areas of sugar beets and sugar cane. Instead, those areas more or less fit against each other like pieces in a picture puzzle (Fig. 18.1). Among individual nations, only the United States and Communist China grow both beets and cane in some quantity, and only the United States in sizable acreages.

Potentiality for technology

The planting, cultivating, and lifting of beets have been mechanized operations for some time—first with horse-drawn equipment and later with tractors.

Harvesting sugar beets in Colorado. The beets are discharged in a row at the lower right-hand corner of the photograph, and the tops in a row near the bottom center. Not very long ago, all topping was done by hand-wielded knives. (U.S. Department of Agriculture)

Some success has been achieved with mechanized blocking and even more with mechanized topping, but the thinning operation is still done largely with hand labor. Even this may be discontinued if current experiments in the development of hybrid seed can be put into practice on a large scale. The new seed is a monogerm instead of an aggregate, and it sends up single plants rather than clusters. If monogerm seeds can be planted with almost 100 per cent probability that they will sprout and grow, they may well replace the aggregate type, and thinning will not be so difficult and may even be mechanized. Use of commercial fertilizers long has been a custom in most sugar-beet-growing areas.

Major countries of growth

Approximately three-tenths of the world's beet sugar is produced in the Soviet Union and one-tenth in the United States. West Germany, France, and Italy also are quite active, as are adjacent nations in Western Europe which, as a unit, account for nearly 40 per cent of all beet sugar. Eastern Europe, excluding the Soviet Union, produces an additional 20 per cent.

The Soviet Union. Soviet sugar is grown primarily in the Ukraine, which is responsible for nearly three-fourths of the national supply. Secondary growth areas include the lower Volga River region of eastern European Russia, and irrigated places in Soviet Central Asia. In the Ukraine, chiefly under a humid continental warm-summer climate and a chernozem or related black soil, the crop is grown on both collective and state farms in association with sunflowers, hemp, flax, wheat, and other commodities. Yields average between 6 and 7 tons per acre—about one-half the yield of the United States, and one-third that of Belgium and the Netherlands.

During the last war, the sugar-beet area of the Soviet Union was almost entirely overrun by invading German armies and hence was a gigantic battlefield during both the German advance and retreat. As a result, sugar production in the Soviet Union declined sharply during and after that war and did not recover for several years. Also as a result, more active sugar-beet cultivation was begun in eastern European Russia and in Soviet Central Asia, beyond the reach of the German armies. In the war's aftermath, additional planting occurred farther north in Lithuania, Latvia, and adjacent republics. Except where the crop is grown under irrigation, however, the yields per person and per acre in these areas are not so high as in the Ukraine, to which most of the nation's production has now returned.

Despite the crippling effects of the Second World War, the Soviet Union now produces more sugar beets and more beet sugar than in the interwar years. The current output of sugar is three times the 1943–1949 average, and over 50 per cent above the 1935–1939 average. It appears that the country is approaching self-sufficiency in sugar. Not all of this postwar increase, however, has been due to agricultural practices. The Soviet Union exacted sizable pieces of territory from Poland, Czechoslovakia, and Rumania at the end of the Second World War. Much of this land in Poland and Rumania is excellent for growing sugar beets.

Production appears to be quite advanced technically. Experimental laboratories and farms are responsible for selection and development of new varieties of seed and fertilizers. When past the stages of initial experiment, such varieties are passed on to the state farms for preliminary application and subsequently may be introduced into the collectives. Mechanization of planting, cultivation, and harvesting is extensive, and, as in the United States, efforts are being made to mechanize the remaining operations.

The United States. California produces nearly one-fourth, Colorado nearly one-eighth, and Idaho nearly one-ninth of the total sugar-beet harvest of the United States, with Nebraska, Michigan, Minnesota, Montana, Washington, Oregon, Utah, Wyoming, and North Dakota ranking as significant (Fig. 18.3). The drier western portions of the country (mediterranean, semiarid climates) thus account for the majority of its sugar beets, and the Great Lakes vicinity (humid continental cool-summer, humid continental warm-summer climates) for most of the remainder. Nearly all the western beets are grown under irrigation, and the average yields per acre in these states are nearly twice as high as yields around the Great Lakes.

Inanimate power and machines are utilized to a degree exceeded by no other nation, and all major field operations probably will come to be performed without much hand labor. Characteristically, the improvement of machines is resulting in a progressively decreasing labor force for the industry—a decreasing not only in the number of once vital hand laborers but also of some of the operators of obsolescent machines requiring two or more men for work that now can be accomplished by one. The amount of land devoted to sugar beets on farms also has increased, as has the size of the farms. This change toward larger acreages has been accom-

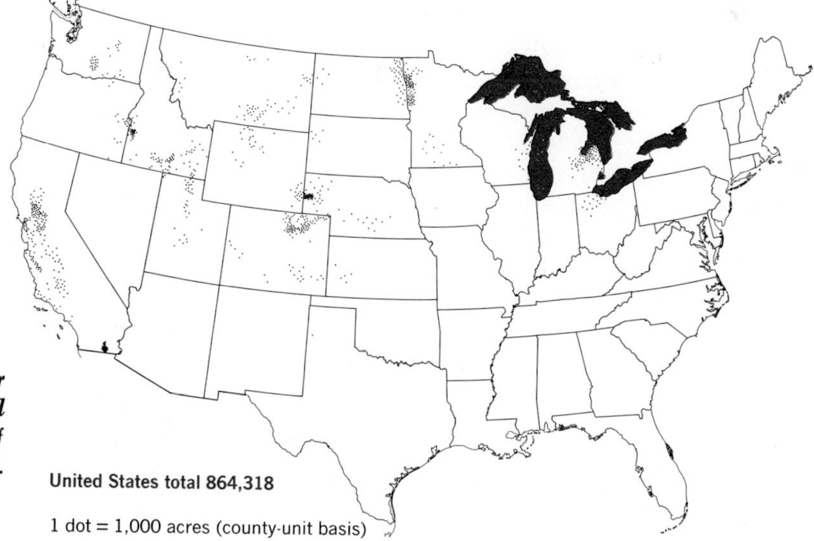

Figure 18.3 ***Where sugar beets are grown in the United States*** *(U.S. Department of Agriculture).*

panied by a gradual westward shift of the industry, especially to California. States in which holdings of suitable land are comparatively large thus appear to be gaining in proportion of national output.[9]

Sugar beets in the United States are grown under close contract arrangements involving the processing companies, the farmers, and usually the spokesmen for the gangs of hired laborers. The contracts stipulate the exact acreages to be grown and the field operations to be performed by the farmers and hired laborers. The beet-field acreages are measured and recorded. If fertilizer is wanted by the farmer, it is available from the company. All in all, these contracts represent an unusually close degree of control over production by the companies. Such control is necessary partially to prevent annual excesses or deficiencies in the amount of sugar beets to be delivered to the factories and partially to aid in fulfilling the quotas of the various sugar acts which have been passed by Congress and which we shall examine more explicitly later in this chapter.

European Nations. We have noted that about three-fifths of all beet sugar is produced in Europe (excluding the Soviet Union). The primary area of such growth extends discontinuously from the Atlantic Ocean to the Ukrainian border of the Soviet Union at lat 40–60° N, with the heaviest densities at about 50° N (Fig. 18.1). Western Europe—notably France, West Germany, and Italy—dominates.

Most of Europe's beet acreage is located north of the Alpine system, where flat-to-undulating land slopes toward the Atlantic Ocean, the North Sea, and the Baltic Sea. Marine climate prevails in the west, and humid continental cool-summer in the east. The largely podzolic and infertile soils are interspersed with a minority of more fertile types, some of them loess-derived, and sugar beets have been attracted particularly to these latter types. Some beets are grown also along the coasts and in river valleys of the mediterranean climate to the south of the Alpine system, as well as in the basins and valleys of the system itself.

[9] Timoshenko and Swerling, *op. cit.*, p. 107.

Commercial sugar-beet production originated in Europe and, protected by substantial tariffs in most countries of growth, has thrived there except when the fields have been ravaged during wartime. The proportion of total cultivated land devoted to sugar beets is quite small, ranging from about 6 per cent in the Netherlands and Belgium to less than 1 per cent in Bulgaria. Particularly in the more technically advanced nations of northwestern Europe, the emphasis is upon high returns per acre. As a result, yields of 18 tons per acre are achieved in Belgium and the Netherlands, and approximately 15 tons per acre in most other nations of northwestern Europe. However, lower returns occur in most countries of southern and eastern Europe, so that the average for the continent (excluding the Soviet Union) is approximately 12 tons per acre—slightly lower than yields in the United States. The high yields in northwestern Europe are appreciably a result of careful, scientific use of commercial and organic fertilizers combined with advanced practices of field cultivation. Mechanization there is also advanced, although many of the tractors and implements are smaller in scale than those of the United States or the Soviet Union. To the south and southeast, agricultural practices tend to be less exact, and mechanization is at a lower stage of development.

TRADE AND TRANSPORTATION

It is interesting to compare the amount of domestic and foreign movement of sugar with, for example, that of wheat and rice, which we examined in the previous chapter. In doing so, we should keep in mind that the world output of sugar is much smaller than that of either wheat or rice: whereas production of white and brown sugar totals 60 million short tons, the harvest of wheat or rice is between three and four times that figure.[10] Thus more wheat and more rice are available for domestic or foreign trade than sugar. By far the largest

[10] The comparison is somewhat misleading in that sugar is a finished product and wheat and rice are essentially raw materials, processed only by threshing.

proportion of each of these two grains—about 90 per cent of the wheat and about 95 per cent of the rice—is consumed domestically. Sugar, while bulking large in domestic commerce, also enters actively into international trade with approximately one-third of its annual harvest entering foreign markets. In terms of tonnage, sugar actually outranks rice and offers marked competition to wheat as an export commodity.

Domestic trade

Essentially all sugar cane and sugar beets are initially processed in the country of production, since both crops are perishables which will spoil quickly after harvest.[11] Hence the traffic between the fields and the raw-material-oriented cane mills and beet factories is almost entirely a short-haul domestic movement involving not more than a few miles where draft animals are used for transport and not more than a few hundred miles where railroads, motor trucks, and other modern media are employed.

Sugar is usually refined before it is consumed. In most beet factories, the process from the raw material to the finished sugar is continuous. Much of the world's cane sugar, however, is refined in market-oriented plants that may be long distances from the crushing mills. Where serving domestic populations, these plants tend to be in the large cities, and the raw sugar usually is forwarded in containers from the mill by rail or truck. Where serving foreign markets, the refineries frequently are located in the consuming nations. The domestic traffic in the country of production for such exported sugar is largely between the mill and the port of export.

International trade

The sugar beet is a more costly source of sugar than is cane, and most countries making use of it have substantial import tariffs or quotas to enable the domestic industry to continue. The quota system of the United States will be discussed later. Tariffs in Europe range as high as 270 per cent of import price and frequently are supplemented by agreements and/or quotas. Nevertheless, international trade in sugar is largely a movement from the low latitudes to the middle latitudes—from underdeveloped to technically advanced nations, most of which are active beet growers. The world markets are dominated by cane sugar, which makes up over 90 per cent of the international trade and nearly all the overseas trade in the product. Exports and imports of beet sugar largely involve continental shipments, either within Europe or between eastern Europe and the Soviet Union.

Leading Nations. Cuba is the outstanding nation of surplus production, being responsible for nearly 40 per cent of all exported sugar. No other single country offers pronounced export competition (Fig. 18.1). The sizable list of additional exporters includes the Republic of the Philippines, Australia, the Dominican Republic, France, Nationalist China, and the United Kingdom.[12]

The outstanding importing countries are the United States and the United Kingdom. The former accepts nearly 30 per cent, the latter about 20 per cent, and both about 50 per cent of all incoming sugar (Fig. 18.1). Japan ranks third, receiving between 8 and 9 per cent. Of the nations which are noteworthy but not leading importers, Canada leads a rather long list that includes numerous European and Asian countries and some on the northwestern rim of Africa as well. Considered regionally, the United States and Canada accept about one-third of all imports, the nations of Europe (almost entirely, of Western Europe) an additional one-third, and the nations of southern and eastern Asia about one-fifth. Africa, the Soviet Union, and Oceania are comparatively minor importers at the present time.

[11] The beets, however, can be stored for a short time before processing, whereas the cane must be milled within a day after the harvest.

[12] These exports generally represent surpluses of domestic production over consumption in all countries listed above except the United Kingdom and France, where they are partially reexports of sugar which have been imported at an earlier time for either refining or storage purposes. Belgium, the Netherlands, and Denmark are also reexporters, but on a smaller scale.

The primary international movement of sugar is thus from a few technically underdeveloped nations[13] of the low latitudes to a few technically advanced nations of the middle latitudes. The secondary movement connects a wide variety of both technically underdeveloped and technically advanced nations. Amidst the complexity of these international trade routes, the dominating positions of the United States and the United Kingdom as importers and of Cuba as an exporter are readily apparent.

Government Policy. Most governments of nations which are affected by the production and consumption of sugar have evidenced a keen and active interest in the role of this commodity in their respective economies. Their interest may take the form of unilateral action or of international agreement, and usually involves both.

Unilateral Action: The United States Sugar Acts. Interesting examples of unilateral action, albeit with consequences far beyond domestic boundaries, are found in the various sugar acts of the United States. The sugar interests of this country have been protected almost continuously by substantial tariffs since 1789. Because domestic growers produce only about 30 per cent of the total amount of sugar consumed in the United States, imports are significant. Prior to 1934, those foreign producers who could compete successfully with domestic producers under the added handicap of the tariff were the major sources of imports. Beginning in 1934, however, a series of sugar acts were passed by Congress, and their primary effect has been the adding of quotas to tariffs—the adding, in other words, of specified amounts to be obtained in specified domestic and foreign producing areas. The imposition of the quotas did not alter drastically the general pattern of international and domestic sugar movement, but it did cause that pattern to crystallize more firmly. Initially, the specifications were in terms of percentages of total domestic consumption, but subsequently they have been expressed in tonnages and thus have become increasingly exact. In other words, specific foreign and domestic growing areas supply specific tonnages of the total amount of sugar consumed in the United States. The respective quotas under the Sugar Act of 1948 as amended in 1956 are given in Table 18.1. The quotas are reestablished yearly.

The quantities and sources of sugar marketed in the United States in 1958 are given in Table 18.2.

The United States thus imports over one-half of all the sugar it consumes. Mainland beet growers produced nearly 25 per cent, and cane growers over 7 per cent, of all sugar consumed in the country in 1958. Approximately one-third was supplied in 1958 by Cuba which, according to the Sugar Act of 1956, has the unusual privilege of supplying a rather small fixed quota plus any amount not forthcoming to the United States markets because of crop failure, etc., in any other areas of production. In 1960, Congress authorized the President to alter Cuba's quota, and essentially no Cuban sugar now reaches the United States.

Other Unilateral Action. The sugar acts and associated tariff of the United States are impressive examples of unilateral action because they are policy components of the world's leading sugar-importing nation, and their provisions affect the welfare of many exporting countries as well as the United States. There are, however, many other examples of such unilateral action, for nearly every major producing nation and several leading consuming nations have taken some formal steps to protect their interests. It was mentioned earlier that nearly every leading non-Communist sugar beet-producing nation on the continent of Europe has enacted substantial import tariffs.[14] Some of the

[13] However, we have noted that, whereas many of these *economies* of low income and living levels may be classified as technically underdeveloped, their *agricultural practices* in the sugar industry may be technically advanced because of past or present contact with technically advanced nations.

[14] The reader will recall that tariffs and other indirect measures for controlling economic action are seldom employed in Communist nations, where the means of production and distribution are state-owned.

governmental policies in Cuba and Brazil also have been noted. These are a few of the many possible additional examples.

International Agreement: The Chadbourne Plan. It has been noted that the sugar acts of the United States have been particularly effective because of that country's status as an importer. It would appear that if any group of nations would be able to control the price and output of sugar, that group would be comprised of importing countries. Certainly the producers—most of all, the surplus producers—cannot hope to control prices; for, except in wartime, the market for sugar is usually a buyer's market. Nevertheless, in 1930 a group of producing nations entered into an agreement involving both government and private adherents for the purpose of limiting the output of sugar and thereby driving up a price which had become comparatively low. Known as the Chadbourne Plan, it attracted the membership of Cuba, Peru, Java, Germany, Belgium, Czechoslovakia, Poland, and Hungary, which aggregately produced more than 40 per cent of the world's sugar in 1930. Initiated at the dawn of the Great Depression, the plan failed. Within five years prices were lower and the world output higher than at the plan's outset, despite the fact that the sugar tonnage of the Chadbourne adherents had been almost halved. Nations which had not signed the agreement had planted sugar.

International Agreement: The Commonwealth Sugar Agreement. The United Kingdom, second only to the United States as a sugar importer, concluded in 1951 and renewed in 1956 a sugar agreement with some producing nations and dependencies in the British Commonwealth, in keeping with a policy of maximizing trade among Commonwealth nations. Under its provisions, the United Kingdom agreed to purchase each year at least 1,500,000 tons of sugar, a figure amounting to almost one-half of the country's imports, from the British Commonwealth at a price which was to be negotiated annually. An additional 800,000 tons would also be purchased, but at prevailing world prices.

TABLE 18.1

Sugar Act of 1948 (as amended in 1956)

Area	Quota, short tons, raw value*
Domestic beet	1,800,000
Domestic cane (excluding Hawaii and Puerto Rico)	500,000
Hawaii	1,052,000
Puerto Rico	1,080,000
Virgin Islands	12,000
Philippines	950,000
Cuba	Small fixed quota plus 96 per cent of remainder of United States requirements†
Other countries	4 per cent of remainder of United States requirements†

* Raw value means the equivalent of 96° sugar as defined in the Sugar Act of 1948.

† However, if domestic requirements should exceed 8,350,000 tons, mainland beet and cane producers have the privilege of supplying 55 per cent of this amount.

TABLE 18.2

Quantities and sources of sugar marketed in the United States in 1958

Area	Amount, short tons, raw value	
Domestic beet	2,240,000	
Domestic cane (excluding Hawaii and Puerto Rico)	681,000	
Hawaii	630,000	
Puerto Rico	823,000	
Virgin Islands	6,000	
Total, domestic sources		4,380,000
Cuba	3,338,000	
Philippines	980,000	
Other countries	378,000	
Total, foreign sources		4,696,000
Grand total		9,076,000

SOURCE: *Agricultural Statistics, 1959,* U.S. Department of Agriculture, 1960, p. 90.

International Agreement: The International Sugar Agreement. Despite the existence of unilateral policies and bloc agreements, the need has been felt for a broad arrangement involving all nations which would join. Accordingly, in 1937 an International Sugar Conference was held, attracting twenty-two members, most of whom were exporting nations. Attempts were made to assign export and import quotas. In 1953, a second and more potent agreement was entered into by sixteen major importing nations and twenty-two exporters, including most of the leaders in production and international trade, and also including the Soviet Union, Czechoslovakia, and Hungary from behind the iron curtain. This was renewed in 1958, effective 1959 to 1963. Its purpose was somewhat similar to the International Wheat Agreement previously discussed—to establish quotas of exports and imports, and to stabilize and equalize prices. It has met with only moderate success, partially because some of its provisions are not closely defined—especially as they pertain to policies of the importing countries.

The free market

From one-tenth to one-fourth of international trade in sugar is conducted in the *free market,* where import and export requirements are not reserved by quota, international agreement, etc.[15] The term is somewhat misleading, for this market is free only in the sense that it is unhindered by restrictions of allocation; import and export duties are still applicable to its sugar. Prices in the free market continuously respond to the supply-demand relationship, and may differ appreciably from the negotiated or otherwise arbitrarily maintained prices which are characteristic of the restricted markets.

Some importing and exporting nations rely entirely upon the free market, but the largest usually do not. The United States normally secures almost none and the United Kingdom less than 10 per cent of their respective imports from the free market. Japan, in contrast, has relied almost entirely upon the free market for sugar imports since losing valuable sugar-producing lands in the last war; and some smaller nations of Europe, notably in Scandinavia, also depend entirely upon the free market. Cuba usually sells over one-third of her exports into the free market, which is also the major outlet for the Dominican Republic, Peru, and numerous other small exporters.

Transportation

International trade in sugar, like that in wheat, mainly involves long transoceanic voyages. Normally the commodity is placed in burlap bags weighing 325 pounds when filled and is shipped as general cargo. During and since the last war, however, sugar has been shipped increasingly as bulk cargo, particularly to the United States and the United Kingdom from Hawaii, the British West Indies, Australia, Brazil, the Dominican Republic, Mauritius, and the Fiji Islands.[16] Progress has been made on the shipment of liquid sugar in tankers.

[15] Other than the very general allocations of the International Sugar Agreement of 1953.

[16] Timoshenko and Swerling, *op. cit.,* pp. 146–147.

REFERENCES

Dyer, Donald R.: "Sugar Regions of Cuba," *Economic Geography,* **32:**177–184, 1956.

Fryer, D. W.: "Recovery of the Sugar Industry in Indonesia," *Economic Geography,* **33:**171–181, 1957.

Hearings before the Senate Committee on Finance, on H.R. 7030, Sugar Act Extension, 84th Cong., 2d Sess., 1956.

James, Preston E.: "Trends in Brazilian Agricultural Development," *Geographical Review,* **43:**301–328, 1953.

Mehta, M. M.: *Structure of Indian Industries,* Popular Book Depot, Bombay, 1955.

Simonett, David S.: "Sugar Production in North Queensland," *Economic Geography,* **30:**223–235, 1954.

Spate, O. H. K.: *India and Pakistan: A General and Regional Geography,* Methuen & Co., Ltd., London, and E. P. Dutton & Co., Inc., New York, 1957.

Timoshenko, Vladimir P., and Boris C. Swerling: *The World's Sugar,* Stanford University Press, Stanford, Calif., 1957.

Williams, Owen: "Sugar Growing and Processing in the Union of South Africa," *Economic Geography,* **35:**356–366, 1959.

Woytinsky, W. S., and E. S. Woytinsky: *World Commerce and Governments,* The Twentieth Century Fund, Inc., New York, 1955. (Especially pp. 133–135, 143, and 265–266.)

——— and ———: *World Population and Production,* The Twentieth Century Fund, Inc., New York, 1953. (Especially pp. 566–574.)

Zimmermann, Erich W.: *World Resources and Industries,* Harper & Brothers, New York, 1951. (Especially chap. 15.)

19 AGRICULTURE: COFFEE, TEA, AND TOBACCO

FROM THE STANDPOINT OF BODILY NEED, COFFEE, TEA, AND TOBACCO ARE luxuries, and many people, perhaps wisely, abstain from their consumption. From the standpoint of economic want and even demand, however, they have become necessities to many rich and poor members of many rich and poor societies. So vital are they considered in everyday living that their availability is a matter of very serious concern, even in wartime. Their highest per capita consumption tends to occur in technically advanced nations (where frequently they are taxed as luxuries), but they are by no means absent from underdeveloped economies.

COFFEE

COFFEE CONSUMPTION

Of the two beverages, coffee is used up in the largest quantities. About 3 million metric tons are consumed annually. Approximately one-half is consumed in the United States and over one-fourth in Western Europe (Fig. 19.1). It is used almost entirely as a beverage, although some experiments have been conducted concerning the feasibility of using the pulp of the coffee bean as a livestock feed. Per capita consumption is highest in Belgium, high in the United States, and varied in most of the other leading nations of consumption. The short-term demand for coffee is comparatively inelastic, and the long-term demand appears to be increasing more or less in proportion to the increase in the world population.

COFFEE PRODUCTION

Coffee is a low-latitude product grown primarily in technically underdeveloped countries largely for export to technically advanced nations. Over 3 million metric tons now are grown each year. The commodity's production and trade exemplify the complementarity of economies in the

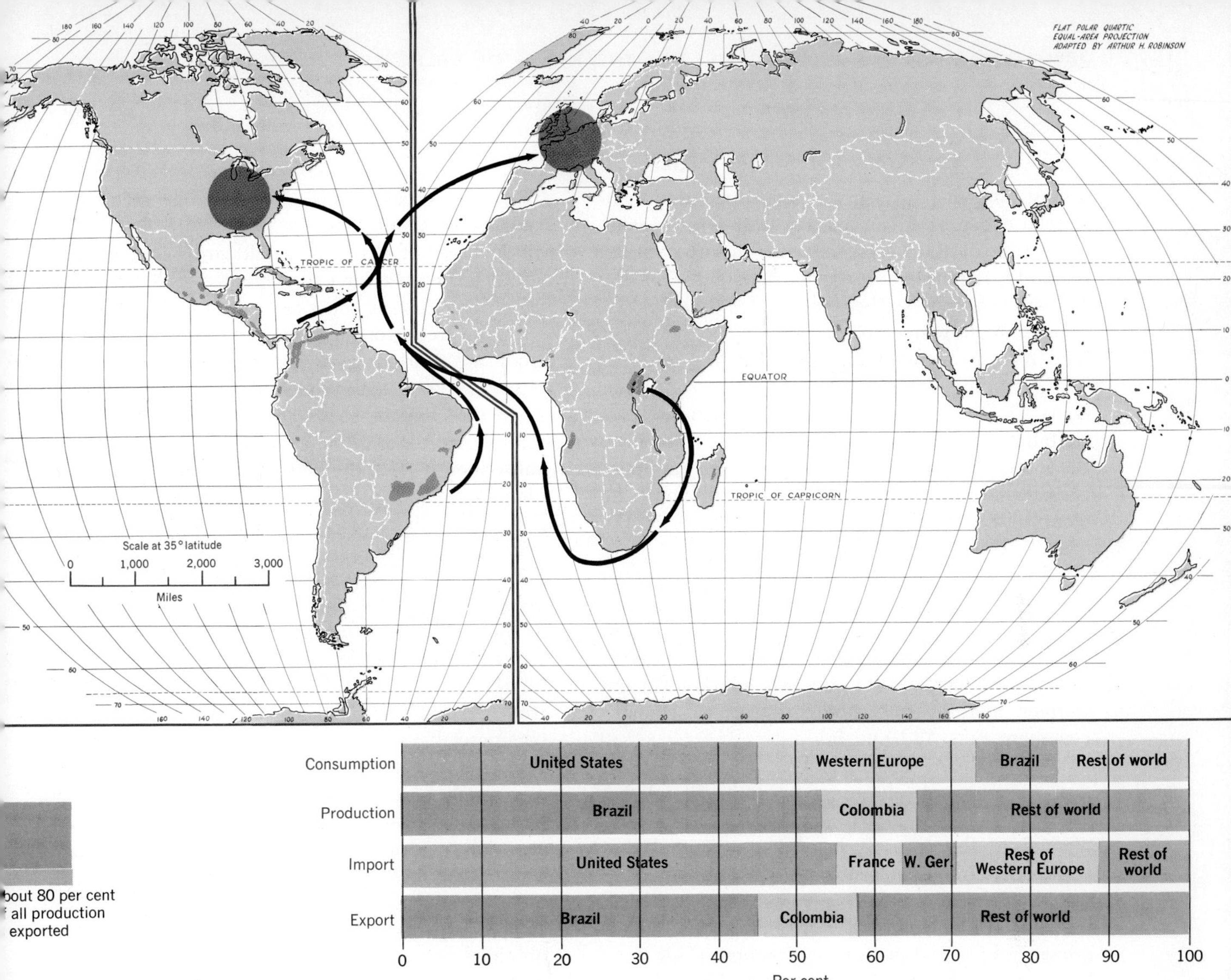

Figure 19.1 ***Consumption, production, import, and export of coffee.*** *Circles show leading nations or regions of very heavy consumption. Gray stippling shows leading areas of production. Note the large amount of coffee entering world markets.*

middle latitudes with those of the low latitudes: because of climatic restrictions, neither the coffee bean nor an acceptable substitute is grown in nations of heaviest consumption, and coffee thereby becomes important in world trade (Fig. 19.1).

Although some coffee is grown on small farms, the crop requires much hand labor and careful management—features suggesting the plantation. A comparison of the world's coffee-growing areas with generalized types of agriculture (Figs. 19.1 and 7.1), documents this suggestion. The natural conditions of coffee growth are somewhat exact, but again the area of potential production greatly exceeds that of existing output. As before, human choice is the deciding criterion in location—this time, however, usually based upon careful cost-price calculations, for coffee is largely a commercial crop sold in the world markets.

Natural conditions of growth

Almost none of the twenty or more species of commercial coffee trees can tolerate frost. This is especially true of the *Coffea arabica,* the one variety probably responsible for over nine-tenths of the world's output.[1] Neither can coffee tolerate extremely high temperatures over long periods of time. Average annual temperatures should be about 68°F, and they should never be below 63°F nor above 77°F. An annual amount of 40 inches of precipitation is necessary for the crop, and from 70 to 100 inches is desirable. As is so often the case with agricultural commodities, the moisture should be plentiful during the developmental stages of the beans and low during the ripening stage.

In practice, most of the world's coffee is grown in uplands of tropical savanna climate, a secondary amount at intermediate elevations of undifferentiated highland climate, and a small remainder in less humid portions of tropical rain-forest and warmer margins of humid subtropical climates (compare Figs. 19.1 and 5.1).

Unlike many agricultural crops, coffee grows well in comparatively rugged terrain. Slopes exceeding 15 or even 20 per cent are not uncommonly planted to the crop. It has been estimated that approximately 60 per cent of Brazil's coffee is produced on slopes of 5 to 15 per cent,[2] and nearly all the coffee of Colombia, El Salvador, and Mexico is grown in hilly and mountainous countrysides.

Much coffee is grown on soils derived from volcanic rocks. Such soils tend to be unusually fertile despite the moist climates in which they frequently occur, for their parent materials contain some replenishments of basic and trace elements. As yet, commercial fertilization is not practiced extensively, although the coffee pulp and other organic debris, including animal manures, frequently are returned to the soil. In addition to their natural fertility, most coffee-growing soils are relatively uncompacted and well drained.

[1] For additional and excellent information on coffee cultivation see V. D. Wickizer, *Coffee, Tea, and Cocoa,* Stanford University Press, Stanford, Calif., 1951, pp. 35–52.

[2] *Ibid.*, p. 44.

Agricultural practices

The coffee cherry forms on trees which usually are kept to maximum heights of 8 to 16 feet under cultivation but normally would grow much taller. Cultivation procedures vary greatly. Although some experimentation is being carried on with the propagation of trees from cuttings and shoots, most of the trees are started from seeds which are planted either directly in the field or in seedbeds. Where sown directly, the seeds are placed in "hills" generally some 10 to 15 feet apart, and the young plants subsequently are thinned so that no more than eight individual plants, and usually fewer, occupy each hill. Where sown in seedbeds, the trees are transplanted within a few months to larger nursery beds and after one or two years are placed in the fields. In contrast to trees grown directly from seed in the fields, these are usually planted singly.

Regardless of planting technique, the trees usually begin to bear within a maximum of five years from the time of initial seeding and become good commercial producers by the time they are eight years old. For the next fifteen to twenty years yields are usually very good, after which time they begin to decline. However, yields for sixty years are not especially uncommon where the soils are favorable. During the best years 1 to 1½ pounds of green coffee beans per tree, and sometimes even more, can be expected. As many as 12 pounds may be obtained from the hills of clustered trees. In most places of growth, harvesting is a selective process in which only fully ripened cherries are individually picked. In Brazil, however, there is usually only one annual harvest, and both green and ripe cherries are taken at that time. After harvest, the beans are extracted from the cherries by one of several methods usually carried out at the agricultural establishment where they are grown, especially if it is a plantation or a large holding. Subsequently, the beans are hulled and graded, sometimes at the places of growth and sometimes in the marketing centers. Ultimately they are forwarded to roasting processers, of which most are located either in receiving seaports of foreign countries or in the larger cities of the countries where the coffee is raised.

An interesting and as yet unresolved difference of opinion exists concerning the need for shade trees rising above the heights of the coffee trees. In many countries, particularly at the lower altitudes, shade trees are employed to protect the coffee trees and their crops from excesses of insolation. In Brazil, however, such protection is usually absent. Apparently, higher-quality coffee may result from artificial shade, but higher yields per acre may be obtained without shade.

In contrast to coffee consumption, the production of coffee varies sharply from year to year. This is due partially to such natural environmental features as occasional frost, cold winds, or drought, and partially to the nature of the coffee tree, which usually does not produce to maximum capacity for two successive years. As a result, the world's coffee output may be higher than the consumption in one year or series of years and lower at other times.

This is part of a coffee fazenda *in Brazil. Note that there are no shade trees here—just rows and rows of coffee trees, neatly separated into fields. (Brazilian Embassy)*

Leading nations of production

Brazil. Still another reason why world coffee production varies so sharply from year to year is that it is dominated by one nation (Fig. 19.1). As long as a century ago, Brazil was growing one-half of all available coffee, and during the intervening years the country sometimes has produced almost three-fourths of the world's annual crop. Now, again responsible for only about one-half of all output, the country still boasts an annual harvest far exceeding that of any other nation. Furthermore, nearly all of Brazil's coffee is grown in a fragmented area encompassing all or parts of the states of São Paulo, Minas Gerais, Paraná, and Espírito Santo (Fig. 19.1). Thus more than 45 per cent of the world's coffee production is subject to the natural environmental vagaries of that area. Small wonder that world production is erratic!

The coffee area is located in the Brazilian highlands which, with exceptions, rise abruptly to general elevations of almost 3,000 feet and to peaks of over 8,000 feet above the narrow coastal plain of the Atlantic Ocean. The divide between interior and coastal drainage is thus comparatively close to the ocean, and the highlands slope prevailingly toward the interior lowlands of South America. Most of the coffee is to be found west of that divide, although some, notably to the northeast of Rio de Janeiro, is on ocean-facing slopes. Brazilian coffee is grown at elevations ranging from 1,200 to 3,000 feet. Nearly all of the coffee area is within a maximum distance of 400 miles from either Santos or Rio de Janeiro, the two main ports of export.

The climate is primarily tropical savanna, which merges into tropical rain-forest climate to the east and into humid subtropical climate to the south (Fig. 5.1). Precipitation ranges from 40 to over 80 inches annually. Frosts and cold winds can be expected in the humid subtropical climate, and an occasional dry spell of serious proportions may be experienced in all places except the southeast. Excellent soils overlie volcanic materials in parts of the state of Paraná and southern São Paulo, but here is also the greatest danger from frost, cold winds, and excessive moisture. Similar volcanic soils are in the north of São Paulo, but in these low latitudes and altitudes the temperatures are consistently too hot. Where possible, however, the coffee is grown on these volcanic soils, which usually are found in places of intensive cultivation. Alter-

These Brazilian men are spreading coffee out to dry. Nature does the work; man just turns the beans over once in a while. (Brazilian Embassy)

native soils are generally much poorer, although they may yield well for the first few years after their initial plowing.

The production unit is chiefly the *fazenda,* a very large plantation under domestic ownership. Foreign capital has played a very small role in the agricultural phases of Brazil's coffee production. Labor on the fazendas is usually supplied by landless tenants, who clear or otherwise prepare the ground and plant both coffee trees and subsistence crops.[3] They exist from the latter until the coffee trees reach bearing age, at which time they move on to clear other ground—ground which may be virgin or may have been cleared several times previously and subsequently allowed to return to pasture and wilderness. The labor of picking, bean extraction, hulling, grading, and transporting is also performed by these workers and their families, using draft animals where feasible. There has been a slight tendency in recent years, particularly since the Depression of the early 1930s, toward the breaking up of some of the fazendas, but as yet it is only a tendency.

Of the problems associated with Brazilian coffee production, the most acute appears to be that of overproduction. It is not just a current problem. As early as the beginning of this century, the output of a burgeoning industry centered in the state of São Paulo had become dangerously high, and low prices threatened. The result was intervention, initially by the state of São Paulo and subsequently by the Federal government. Coffee was purchased, stored, and eventually burned in large quantities in desperate attempts to maintain artificially high prices. The entire program involved a number of valorization schemes, some apparently successful on a short-term basis. Still the world supplies continued to mount, partially because the many Brazilian trees planted at the turn of the century continued to produce and partially because coffee production was introduced or enlarged in other areas of the world—particularly Caribbean America and Africa. When the Depression of the early 1930s

[3] See especially Preston E. James, "Trends in Brazilian Agricultural Development," *Geographical Review,* 43:301–328, 1953.

occurred, more supplies were on hand than were being consumed each year, and coffee destruction became the order of the day. In 1938, more coffee was destroyed than was consumed, and most of this destruction involved Brazilian coffee. Paradoxically, world prices declined during the depression and war years, and did not recover until the removal of price controls in the United States in the late 1940s. Since then prices have pushed upward rather steadily. Meanwhile the number of Brazilian coffee trees has decreased by approximately one-half from the 1933 high of almost 3 billion, and the supply-demand situation in Brazil and in the world has become better balanced. From a maximum of over 28 million bags of coffee in 1930, exportable output in Brazil has declined to approximately 18 million bags in 1958. Government-support prices continue, however, for coffee as well as most other commercial agricultural commodities. The amount of support varies with the grade; payments are high for the better grades and range downward to almost nothing for the lowest grades, most of which are used for fertilizer. With the decline in coffee production has come a trend toward crop diversification; and yet, even today, coffee remains the leader among commercial agricultural crops in Brazil.

Other Countries and Areas. Among other producing nations, only Colombia is in a position to offer very marked competition with Brazil, and this competition is based more upon quality than volume. Whereas nearly all of Brazil's coffee is somewhat harsh in flavor, that from Colombia and a majority of other producing areas is not so harsh and is officially classed as mild. Indeed, the terms *Brazils* and *milds* are often used to classify the types and grades of coffee, which are usually blended in various ways and proportions before entering the consumer markets. Although Colombia's production amounts to less than one-third of Brazil's, its coffee is excellent for blending purposes. In contrast to Brazil, Colombia has increased its output by approximately 25 per cent during the past quarter century. The coffee is grown primarily at elevations of 3,000 to 6,000 feet. A major district of production reaches southward from the vicinity of Medellín along the mountain-bordered Cauca River valley, and a series of smaller districts trends along the eastern cordillera from Nieva through Bogotá to Bucaramanga (Fig. 19.1).

Coffee production is important to most other nations located in, or adjacent to, the Caribbean Sea if local elevations are sufficiently high and other natural environmental conditions are not prohibitively severe. El Salvador, Mexico, and Guatemala are the leaders, but most of the mainland nations are included, as are some island countries. All in all, other nations of Caribbean and Central America account for more coffee than does Colombia.

Elsewhere, coffee is being given particular attention in Africa, where current output is more than three times that of 1935 to 1939. The Ivory Coast, Guinea, the former Belgian Congo, Angola, Uganda, Ethiopia, and Malagasy are the leaders. It would appear that Western Europe will look more and more to Africa for coffee imports. Asiatic production has only recently recovered from a reduction due to struggles for political independence, especially in Indonesia. However, the possibility of its future expansion appears somewhat limited in view of the competition from Latin America and Africa.

COFFEE TRADE AND TRANSPORTATION

Trade

No coffee-producing nation except Brazil contains a population of sizable proportions, and hence most coffee enters into the world markets before being consumed. Indeed, approximately 80 per cent of all coffee is normally exported, although it may be held in storage for some years before this occurs.[4] The primary patterns in this movement are relatively simple—from Brazil, Colombia, and lesser producers in Latin America and Africa to the United States and Western Europe. Although the movement of coffee is chiefly from underdeveloped to technically advanced nations and although the rising produc-

[4] The amount was less, of course, in the years of heavy coffee destruction.

tion in Africa is benefiting by some European capital, the ownership of the means of production is prevailingly domestic. The incoming coffee is subject to no import duties in the United States, but is taxed before entering most European nations at rates ranging up to more than 300 per cent of the dock price. The amounts of these European duties vary not only from nation to nation but also from time to time, and they appear to account appreciably for somewhat erratic patterns of consumption recorded there, particularly since the last war.

It will be noticed that this is almost entirely a trade among non-Communist nations. The division of the world into two ideological blocs has not affected sharply the role of coffee in the world's economies, for Communist nations are mainly consumers of tea rather than coffee and are located generally beyond the latitudes where coffee can be grown effectively on a large scale. Thus they have essentially no influence on either the consumption or the production of the commodity.

Transportation

Most coffee is shipped as beans in jute bags via comparatively short rail hauls to ports of export, and via ocean vessel—usually liners—to ports of import. Since so much coffee enters into international trade, the above generalization can be applied rather extensively. Sailings of ships carrying coffee are regularly posted in the coffee trade journals. The small amount of coffee which is consumed domestically tends to move to the larger cities, of which many are also ports of export; much of this movement is thus similar to the initial movement of coffee destined for markets overseas.

TEA

Tea, like coffee, is mainly a product of technically underdeveloped nations. When sold internationally, it moves principally to technically advanced societies. Its role in the world's economies differs from that of coffee especially in that (1) its volume of consumption (of actual solid matter) is much lower,[5] (2) a substantial part of its consumption occurs in the nations where it is produced, and (3) its primary growth area is not in the Western Hemisphere but in eastern and southern Asia (Fig. 19.2).

TEA CONSUMPTION

Tea is a time-honored beverage, the consumption of which has been recorded in China as early as the third century. Not until the seventeenth century, however, was it introduced commercially to Europe. Imported chiefly by ocean carrier, it replaced coffee as the favorite beverage of the United Kingdom by the beginning of the eighteenth century, and accompanied the British to the outlying Empire. To a lesser degree, it was also accepted on the European mainland. Meanwhile, overland routes from Asia to Europe passed through Russia, and moderate tea drinking became habitual there. Today, the per capita consumption of tea is pronounced within the United Kingdom and some nations of the British Commonwealth, especially Australia and New Zealand. The famed Irish opposition to England did not extend to beverages, and tea has captivated the Emerald Isle to a degree that must be envied by the British.

In total consumption, the United Kingdom again remains supreme, followed by such producing nations as India and Communist China. The United States, Japan, Australia, Canada, Ceylon, and the Soviet Union are also important in aggregate tea consumption.

Like coffee, tea is used almost entirely for human consumption. It is drunk as black, green, or

[5] However, a pound of tea results in approximately 180 to 200 cups of beverage, whereas a pound of coffee yields only 35 to 50 cups. World consumption of the *beverage*, therefore, is higher for tea than for coffee.

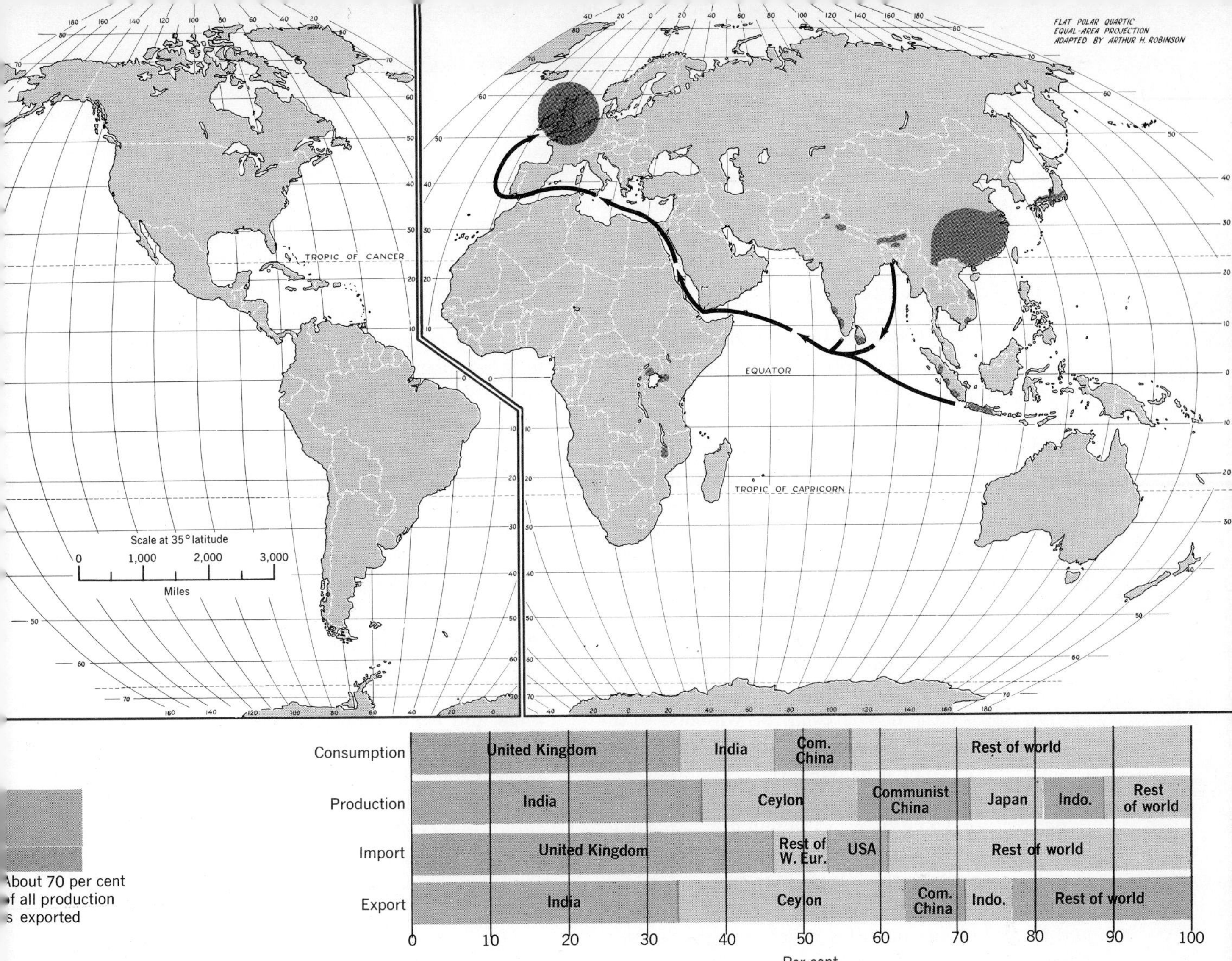

Figure 19.2 ***Consumption, production, import, and export of tea. The circle shows the leading region of very heavy consumption. Gray stippling shows leading areas of production. Data from Communist China are incomplete; more tea probably is consumed there than is recorded. This would mean a lower percentage entering world markets than shown here. The United Kingdom easily leads in reported consumption, even though it must import all the tea it consumes.***

oolong tea; the differences among the categories are due essentially to the extent to which the leaves have been allowed to ferment before processing. To a limited degree, all three types are consumed in almost all nations, and yet specialization is discernible. Black tea, made from leaves that have been allowed to ferment rather thoroughly, is consumed in most technically advanced nations and in several underdeveloped nations where it is grown for export. Green tea comes from leaves which have not been allowed to ferment before processing, and it is consumed largely in Communist China, Japan, and Formosa. Oolong is a specialty made from partially fermented leaves and is consumed in only small amounts, chiefly in technically advanced nations. At least one-third of all consumed tea is probably green tea, and most of the remainder is black.[6]

TEA PRODUCTION

Natural conditions of growth

Climate. Tea requires copious amounts of precipitation, preferably continuous. From 90 to 200 inches is desirable, and a minimum of 60 inches is usually considered necessary; however, particularly in Communist China, some tea is grown where less precipitation occurs. Hailstorms destroy the crop, and planting seldom occurs where these are numerous. The tea tree can survive occasional and moderate frost, but not excessive cold. In practice, most of the world's tea is grown in tropical rain-forest and humid subtropical climates, at elevations up to 7,000 feet in the lower latitudes (Figs. 19.2 and 5.1). The present concentration of tea growing in eastern and southern Asia could be widened to include portions of these climates in other continents if such action were warranted.

Other Natural Conditions. Tea will grow on slopes as well as level land, and in the Far East it is largely relegated to the former by pressure for food crops. The ideal soils should be loose, well drained, and devoid of any qualities which would adversely affect the flavor of the leaf. Sandy loams are among the best. Natural fertility is important but has long been altered in these soils, which have been cultivated for so many centuries, and artificial fertilization is a common practice. Although a variety of insects and diseases are to be coped with, none is extremely serious.

Agricultural practices

The Tree and Its Cultivation. Tea, like coffee, comes from trees which are not allowed to reach their normal heights of 15 to 30 feet but are kept pruned to heights of 2 to 5 feet. The bushlike trees are usually grown under the shade of taller trees; and not infrequently, still a third crop fills such open spaces as remain.

The planting occurs directly from seed in most areas, with the seeds placed either in temporary nursery beds or directly in the fields. Whatever the planting method, the trees ultimately are from 4 to 6 feet apart. From three to eight years is required to bring them to maturity, after which time they are harvested annually between early spring and late fall in northerly latitudes, and continuously in the tropics. In the northern locations, usually no more than three harvests per year are realized, but in the warmer southern climates the trees can be plucked at least every ten days. Depending upon the urgency of market demands, the plucking can be *fine,* wherein only the new, small leaves are taken, or *coarse,* wherein at least one larger leaf and a portion of the stalk are taken. The latter method increases the quantity at the expense of quality.[7] The trees continue to yield for twenty to thirty years and even longer, the length of their specific bearing period varying with natural conditions and agricultural practices.

Plantation Tea. Most of the world's commercially grown black tea is produced on plantations under conditions which have been described as follows:[8]

> That portion of world tea production shipped overseas to Western consuming markets is produced very largely on plantations, gardens, or estates.[9] These plantations are located mainly in certain districts of India, Ceylon, Java, and Sumatra.[10] Although tea is grown

[6] Unfortunately, current data on tea consumption are somewhat incomplete; information from some subsistence production, chiefly of green tea, is lacking.

[7] See especially V. D. Wickizer, *Tea under International Regulation,* Stanford University Press, Stanford, Calif., 1951, pp. 12–23.

[8] Reprinted from *Coffee, Tea, and Cocoa,* by V. D. Wickizer, pp. 178–181, with the permission of the publishers, Stanford University Press. Copyright 1951 by the Board of Trustees of Leland Stanford Junior University.

[9] In North India and Pakistan, plantations are called "gardens" but in South India, Ceylon, and Indonesia they are known as "estates."

[10] Note by the author of the text: However, the recent worsening of relations between Indonesia and the Netherlands, accompanied by an evacuation of Hollanders from Indonesia, has disrupted production in a majority of the estates there. At present, many are occupied by squatters.

throughout the Orient—as far north as Georgia in Transcaucasia (about lat 42° N.) and as far south as Nyasaland (about lat 15° S.)—and is cultivated in South and Central America, the tea output of international significance comes from a few South Asiatic areas not widely separated geographically. The plantations and factories in these regions are part of a business primarily concerned with supplying the Western demand for Eastern tea.

Tea lends itself admirably to the plantation system. Not only is it necessary to employ many workers for tending and harvesting, but every estate has a factory for processing which requires more machinery and skilled supervision than is ordinarily involved in the exploitation of tropical products. Coffee, cocoa, rubber, and some other tropical crops must undergo more or less complicated processing after arriving in the country of consumption. When black tea reaches its ultimate destination, it has only to be blended and packaged for sale. Factory preparation on the estate is of prime importance in the determination of final quality and must therefore be carried on under expert direction. . . .

Tea estates vary in size from 300 to 3,000 acres and larger, with about 500 acres generally considered the *minimum* for economical operation.[11] Factories have tended to increase in size and to manufacture for several estates rather than for one only. These tendencies were apparent in India and Ceylon before the war, and since the war something comparable seems to be going on in Indonesia. Japanese destruction of tea factories in Java and Sumatra drastically reduced their numbers, so that in postwar years the few that were able to operate manufactured for other neighboring estates. Some observers thought it likely that a co-operative system of manufacture would be maintained, "perhaps permanently, so that pre-war individual estate identities may not reappear."[12]

Small companies in India and Ceylon operate relatively few estates, and the large ones many. A system of agents acting for the smaller companies makes possible their survival by obviating the necessity for a full complement of managerial personnel.

"These 'agents' are more properly described as merchant bankers. In many cases the present tea producing companies were established on the initiative of these agents, who had financed the original planters, and they are not only represented on the Boards, but in reality control the companies of which they are nominally the servants. . . ."[13]

Small-scale native production has not been an important factor in the black-tea industry except in Indonesia and Ceylon. Native output is much smaller than suggested by acreage figures because yields are generally lower than for estates. Unlike the rubber industry, where native output grew to be of considerable importance during the interwar period, especially in the Netherlands Indies and British Malaya, commercial tea production remains predominantly a large-scale enterprise. . . .

Manufacturing processes are mechanized to a considerable degree on modern British and Dutch estates, only partly so in Japan, and to a very limited extent in China. In the green-tea countries, of course, the factory is a much less important institution, because the processing involved in the production of unfermented and partially fermented teas is far simpler than in the manufacture of black teas. Partly for this reason, the important producers in the green-tea countries are the smaller farmers rather than the estates. . . .

Except in Indonesia, therefore, the production of black tea from plantations is carried out in essentially the same manner as before the gaining of political independence by the major producing countries. This is especially true in India and Ceylon, where British capital and managership have remained active components of the tea plantations.

Tea on Small Farms and Collectives. In Japan and Nationalist China, tea is grown on small farms, usually on slopes and other places where food crops do not thrive. This is chiefly green tea, produced largely for domestic consumption but also for export. Both black and oolong teas are also produced; and, notably in Nationalist China, oolong tea has become an export specialty. Farming methods in

[11] The range in size of tea gardens is wide; *e.g.*, in India it was from 71 to 5,799 acres in 1942. In Ceylon the *average* size of plantations is about 206 acres, "but the tendency has been to form groups of estates, which function as units, each with one directory and a factory. The area of such a group, however, seldom exceeds 2,500 acres," W. I. Ladejinsky, "Agriculture in Ceylon," *Foreign Agriculture*, January, 1944, VIII, 10.

[12] Gijselman and Steup, "The Batavia Tea Market in 1947," *Economic Review of Indonesia*, Indonesia Department of Economic Affairs, March, 1948, II, 40.

[13] Imperial Economic Committee, *Tea*, p. 24.

both countries are generally not mechanized but otherwise quite modern. Commercial as well as organic fertilization is practiced to maximize yields per acre. Lands are terraced and the plants carefully tended. Such advancement in technique is due in large measure to past and present leadership exercised by the Japanese government, both at home and in possessions held before the last world war—possessions which once included Taiwan, now independent and known as Nationalist China.

Traditionally, the land now governed as Communist China has been a producer of green tea destined principally for the home market. Methods have been wasteful of land, labor, and capital, and the returns have been low. The total amount grown, however, was quite large—at times, perhaps, as much as one-half of the world's green-tea output. Production declined sharply during and after the last world war and subsequent civil war but appears to be increasing once again under the system of commune farming established by the Communist government there.

Leading nations of production

The two leading producing countries, India and Ceylon, utilize plantations to produce black tea, mainly for export. These two are responsible for over one-half of the world's output (Fig. 19.2). Communist China, Japan, Indonesia, Nationalist China, and Pakistan are not insignificant producers. Considerable interest in tea production has been shown recently in Africa, particularly by the British and Portuguese, and Nyasaland, Kenya, and Mozambique are increasingly noteworthy.

TRADE IN TEA

Domestic trade

Tea is light in weight and comparatively small in bulk (particularly when pressed into "bricks") and it can be stored for rather long periods of time. Its domestic trade is appreciably a matter of rather short movement from the countrysides to the closest cities. Human porters, animals, inland water craft, and rails are all utilized. A small amount goes in the reverse direction, particularly to the sparsely populated, high mountain country of Tibet and adjacent areas, where it sometimes serves as currency and more frequently becomes a key ingredient, along with one of several types of milk, in a kind of soup.

International trade

The United Kingdom alone imports nearly one-half of all tea entering the world markets, and affiliated nations of the British Commonwealth account for almost an additional 15 per cent. Thus the British Commonwealth nations import over two-thirds of all tea which crosses political boundary lines. India and Ceylon, in turn, export more than two-thirds of all outgoing tea, so that international trade in tea is largely a matter of movement within the British Commonwealth. We have noted that an appreciable amount of British capital is invested in tea plantations, and this tends to strengthen the ties holding the tea industry largely within the British Commonwealth. Both of the two producing nations, however, have levied export tariffs on the product and benefit appreciably therefrom. No import tariffs have been assessed against tea by the United Kingdom, and only occasional and rather small import tariffs have been levied by other nations of the British Commonwealth.

The United States is the leading non-British Commonwealth importer, accounting for upward of 7 per cent of the total. With essentially no overseas investment in tea plantations, this country purchases almost all its tea on the open markets without commitments. No import tariff is levied.

International trade in tea is subject not only to conditions resulting from British Commonwealth membership of leading producing and consuming nations but also to international agreement. Initiated in 1933, the International Tea Agreement is a pact involving the major countries of tea export—India, Ceylon, Indonesia, and Pakistan. It is a pact among the producers, and not the governments, of those nations, although it makes provisions for compliance with obligations and regulations of those governments. The primary objective of the agreement is the allocation of acreages and exports of tea among the signatory members. It is, therefore, another attempt at regulation by producers; and, in view of the sad ends of so many schemes of this nature, one may well wonder just how long a time will elapse before production in nonsignatory nations begins to offer serious competition.

TOBACCO

Tobacco is a "luxury" that is widely enjoyed. Unlike coffee and tea, it is consumed prevailingly within the nations of its production, and its role in the world's economies involves pronounced consumption as well as production in technically underdeveloped as well as technically advanced nations.

TOBACCO CONSUMPTION

Almost 4 million metric tons of tobacco are consumed each year. Measured in terms of solid matter, this amount is 25 per cent higher than the world's annual consumption of coffee, and about five times that of tea. More than 80 per cent of this consumption involves tobacco grown domestically within more than seventy nations located on all continents but Antarctica. The United States and Communist China are the outstanding consumers, each accounting for about one-fifth of the world's total (Fig. 19.3). India, the Soviet Union, Brazil, and the United Kingdom are also prominent on a long list of active consuming nations. In this group of leaders only the United Kingdom is an outstanding importing as well as consuming nation.

A very small amount of tobacco—usually the waste—is used as a component of insecticides and fertilizers. Most, of course, is smoked, and a fraction is chewed or used as snuff and is thus mainly a consumer commodity; the pattern of its use coincides closely with that of world population distribution.

TOBACCO PRODUCTION

Natural conditions of growth

The climatic limits to tobacco culture are much more indefinite than for most agricultural crops. As a result, the plant is found at latitudes ranging from the equator to almost lat 60° N. A minimum growing season of 120 days is usually necessary, and a longer season is usually desired. Precipitation should be plentiful but not excessive, the exact requirements varying with the rate of evaporation in specific localities. Too little moisture results in low yields and in tobacco which does not burn satisfactorily. Too much moisture results in leaves deficient in certain qualities of aroma and sometimes blemished with fungus growth.

Soil permeability and content are extremely important to tobacco growth. Well-drained soils tend to yield plants with lighter-colored, thinner leaves, and heavy soils tend to send forth plants with darker leaves and a stronger aroma. For some of the lighter-colored tobaccos, used mainly in cigarettes, the soil is regarded as merely a medium through which the plants may be fed by means of commercial fertilizers. Under such conditions, a porous, sandy soil is preferred.

Tobacco may be grown in both level and uneven terrain, and only the very steep slopes may be considered as natural limits to its cultivation. Insects and diseases, while always to be coped with, are not generally prohibitive deterrents to its growth.

Nature thus sets only moderate and changing limits to tobacco culture. The location of the existing production and the type of finished product are matters of human decision to a greater degree than is true of most crops. In practice, however, this has meant government policy as well as decisions by producers, brokers, etc.

Agricultural practices

The Tobacco Plant. Tobacco is obtained from the leaves of *Nicotiana tabacum,* a plant whose origin has been traced to Central and South America. Another species, *Nicotiana rustica,* is indigenous to eastern United States but is now grown mainly in

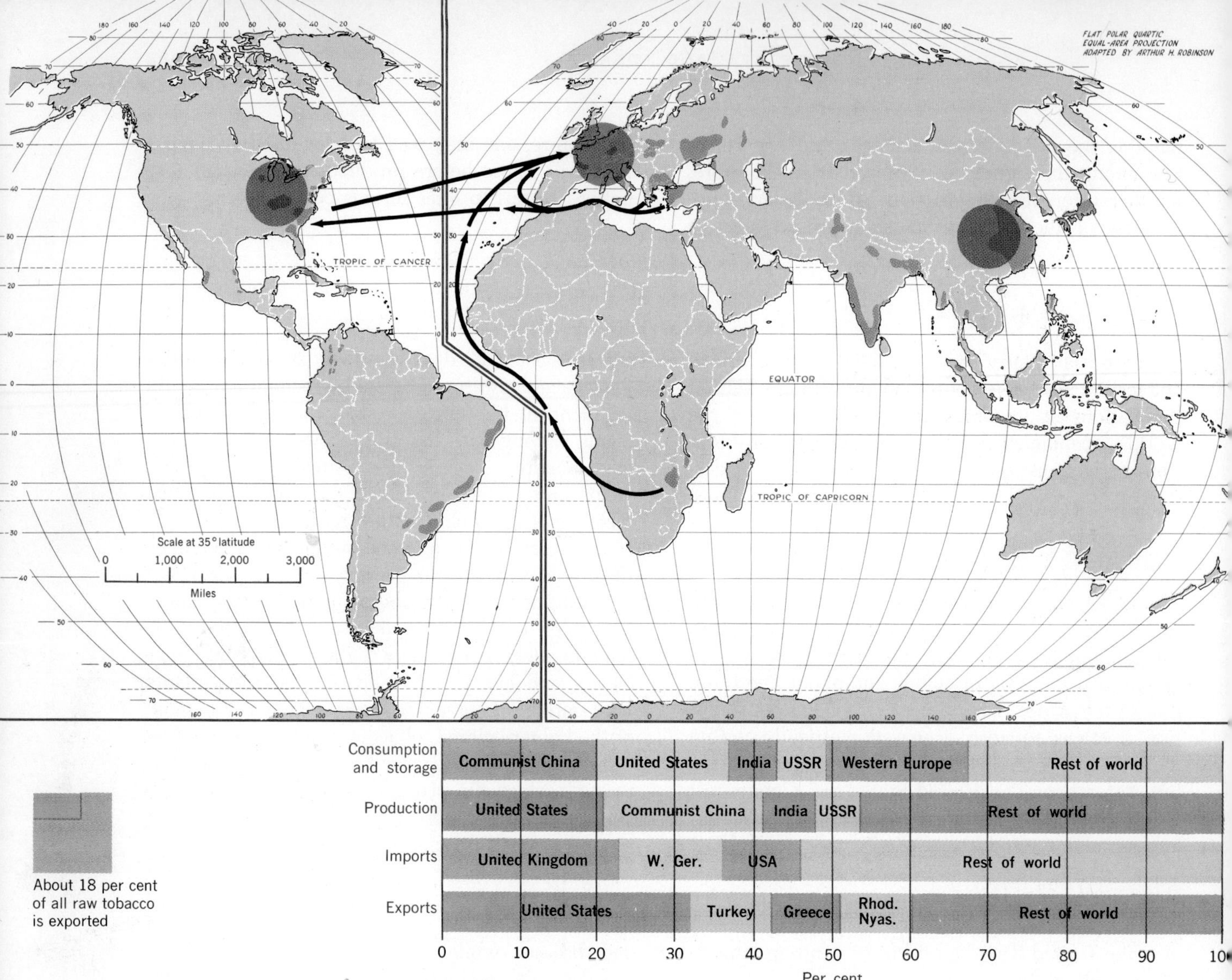

Figure 19.3 ***Consumption, production, import, and export of tobacco.*** *Circles show countries or regions of very heavy consumption. Gray stippling shows areas of production. Why is the percentage of tobacco entering world markets so low?*

parts of Asia and is not a major source of tobacco.[14] The *Nicotiana tabacum* plant is an herb which may attain a height of 10 feet but often is shorter. It is very prolific in production of leaves, some of which are between 1 and 1½ square feet. In terms of effective production, it is an annual, although it often exhibits perennial tendencies.

[14] Wightman W. Garner, *The Production of Tobacco,* McGraw-Hill Book Company, Inc., The Blakiston Division, New York, 1951, pp. 4–9.

Agricultural Practices. Some tobacco is grown on plantations but most is grown on farms of intermediate to small size. The actual fields tend to be very small, for the crop requires a great deal of hand labor. In the United States, for example, nearly three-fourths of all tobacco land is in fields of 15 acres or fewer, and over one-half in fields of 7.5 acres or fewer. These fields are located on farms averaging 100 to 150 acres. In India the fields are much smaller and more fragmented. This was true also of pre-Communist China, but the old fields have been integrated into larger units under the commune system.

Where grown commercially, the plant is first seeded in nursery beds and then transplanted when six to ten weeks old into open fields. Transplanting, although frequently aided by machines, is largely a hand operation. The plants are placed singly in rows 2 to 3 feet apart and the ground around them carefully cultivated. As we have noted previously, commercial fertilizers often are added in amounts designed to obtain certain qualities in the ultimate product. The leaves are ready for harvest some 70 to 130 days after planting. Harvesting involves either cutting the entire stalk or cutting the leaves singly as they mature.

The end qualities of tobacco are determined not only by the varieties cultivated and the techniques of growth, but also by the methods of leaf curing, a process usually carried out on the farms where tobacco is grown. In the United States, some tobacco is allowed to cure in the open air, protected from the elements by ventilated barns. Occasionally, open fires facilitate the operation. Some is cured by fires ignited and burned for several days in barns which, for the most part, are rather tightly closed. In the process, the flavor of the burning wood is imparted to the tobacco as it is being dried. Some is cured by artificial heat passed through the barns in flues and is known as *flue-cured tobacco.* The exact uses for the products of each method vary appreciably in accordance with the varieties of tobacco used and the ultimate requirements of manufacturers. However, air-cured tobacco is used particularly as pipe tobacco and as cigar wrappers, fire-cured tobacco is employed notably as cigar wrappers, and flue-cured tobacco is used especially for filler in cigarettes and cigars as well as for wrappers in cigars.

Leading producing nations

The United States and Communist China each produce about one-fifth of all recorded tobacco. India, the Soviet Union, Japan, Brazil, and Turkey are noteworthy among a host of lesser producers (Fig. 19.3).

Tobacco in the United States. The increasing demands of the cigarette industry for light, flue-cured tobacco have stimulated production in the Piedmont and southeast coast of the Carolinas and Virginia. North Carolina alone accounts for about 45 per cent, and South Carolina and Virginia each for over 8 per cent, of the nation's output (Fig. 19.4). Across the Appalachians is another major tobacco region, centered upon Kentucky and including portions of Tennessee, Indiana, and Ohio. Kentucky produces about 20 per cent of the nation's tobacco, ranking immediately behind North Carolina. The emphasis in this region is upon air-cured tobacco. Farther south, in Florida and Georgia, is a district producing mainly flue-cured tobacco, and to the north are scattered districts in Pennsylvania, Maryland, Connecticut, and lesser states where the method of curing varies rather sharply. Both the southern and the northern districts, however, concentrate upon tobacco to be used as cigar wrapper, binder, and filler.

We have noted that the growing of tobacco in the United States is predominantly an operation involving comparatively small acreages on individual farms and requiring heavy amounts of labor per acre. Since 5 per cent, or less, of the average farm is devoted to tobacco, such farming does not represent specialization in the sense that the winter-wheat belt does but is one aspect of general farming. Alternative crops, many of them grown principally for home consumption, include corn, wheat, and legumes. There is also an appreciable quantity of livestock in the tobacco-growing regions of the United States, kept for both draft purposes and food.

Although the growing of tobacco in a small-scale general-farming system is the prevalent arrangement for production of the crop in the United States, some efforts have been made to utilize larger farming units with their accompanying economies of scale. In the Connecticut River district, average acreages of tobacco fields are much larger than in the South, and the fields are frequently under the control of a corporation. One reason is that comparatively heavy capital investment must be made in tobacco farming in Connecticut, particularly in protection of seedbeds and plants against adverse

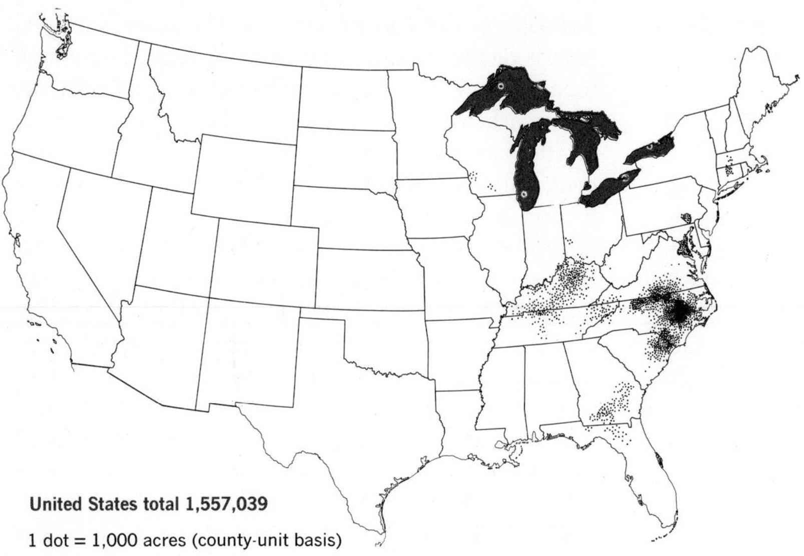

Figure 19.4 ***Where tobacco is grown in the United States*** *(U.S. Bureau of the Census).*

weather conditions and in commercial fertilization. It will be interesting to see whether the trend here is duplicated in the other tobacco-growing areas.

Despite the increase in demand for tobacco, the domestic supply has increased even more rapidly, and today there are surplus stocks amounting to almost 2 million metric tons—more than twice the country's entire production for a single year. Since 1934, government policy has become an important factor in tobacco growth, for, in an attempt to keep the output within limits, the national government has restricted acreages through subsidy arrangements.

Other Producing Nations. Other leading nations of tobacco growth produce chiefly for their home populations, and in none of them is the output as concentrated areally as it is in the United States. Tobacco is grown throughout nearly all of the heavily populated parts of Communist China and India, the nations of second and third rank in world output. The commodity is not high on the priority lists in the planning policies of either nation, and current output of both nations has risen only slightly, if at all, since the middle 1930s. The Soviet Union, also, appears to be producing less tobacco than in the middle 1930s. Most of the remaining areas of production, regardless of world rank, have increased their output during that time. One of the most striking increases has occurred in the Rhodesias and Nyasaland, where the output has quadrupled during the past quarter century.

TOBACCO TRADE

The United States dominates international trade in tobacco, accounting for approximately one-third of all exports and more than one-tenth of all imports (Fig. 19.3).[15] Approximately two-thirds of all imports move to northwestern Europe, with the United Kingdom alone responsible for nearly one-fourth (Fig. 19.3). Among these European nations, import tariffs range from nothing to well over 200 per cent of the dock price of unmanufactured tobacco. The tariff is approximately 60 per cent in the United Kingdom, 123 per cent in West Germany, 212 per cent in Portugal. In contrast, no tariffs on tobacco are levied in France, Italy, and

[15] The surprisingly large volume of imports is due to the need for certain foreign tobaccos for blending purposes. Western Europe also imports and exports rather actively, but this trade is appreciably a reexport business and not chiefly due to the necessity of blending in domestic production.

Sweden. In the United States, the tariff is moderately high, ranging from 33 to 35 per cent.[16]

International trade in tobacco is thus predominantly a movement from a technically advanced nation to other technically advanced nations, all located in the non-Communist sphere of political domination. Overseas investment and international agreements do not play major roles in the production and trade of the commodity. Communist nations, while important in the growth of tobacco, produce chiefly for their domestic markets.

[16] W. S. Woytinsky, and E. S. Woytinsky, *World Commerce and Governments*, The Twentieth Century Fund, Inc., New York, 1955, pp. 280, 288.

REFERENCES

"Annual Coffee Review and Outlook," *Journal of Commerce,* Nov. 23, 1956, pp. 9–13.

"Coffee in Europe—1955," *Tea and Coffee Trade Journal,* December, 1955, pp. 19–22ff.

Garner, Wightman W.: *The Production of Tobacco,* McGraw-Hill Book Company, Inc., The Blakiston Division, New York, 1951.

Harler, C. R.: *The Culture and Marketing of Tea,* Oxford University Press, New York, 1956.

James, Preston E.: *Latin America,* The Odyssey Press, Inc., New York, 1959.

U.S. Department of Agriculture Foreign Agricultural Service: "World Tobacco Analysis," *Consumer Marketing,* February, 1951.

Wickizer, V. D.: *Coffee, Tea, and Cocoa,* Stanford University Press, Stanford, Calif., 1951.

———: *Tea under International Regulation,* Stanford University Press, Stanford, Calif., 1951.

20 AGRICULTURE: PLANT FIBERS

OUR EXAMINATION OF SPECIFIC AGRICULTURAL COMMODITIES THUS FAR HAS been focused upon foods and beverages. In this chapter we shall be concerned with plant fibers, which are the sources of clothing and other woven goods, cordage, and a wide variety of lesser materials. The total list of such fibers is long, and we shall limit our inquiry to the leaders—cotton, jute, and flax. Coincidentally, the selection contains: (1) in cotton, a fiber which is the basic component for most clothing worn throughout the year in the tropics and during warm seasons in higher latitudes and which has many and diverse other uses; (2) in jute, a fiber which is the basic component of tough, inexpensive woven material generally considered too coarse and too cheap for clothing; and (3) in flax, a fiber which is the basic component of some of the finest textiles, used especially for linen sheets, tablecloths, etc. The three thus are produced and consumed for markedly varying reasons, and as a group they illustrate differing aspects of plant-fiber utilization. All have been used for millenniums—the first two notably in India and neighboring places of eastern and southern Asia, and the last in Europe. The Age of Discovery and the Industrial Revolution brought both cotton and jute to Europe and to some of its colonial offshoots, where they were so successful in competition with flax within their respective ranges of application that demand for flax declined. During the last quarter century, nearly all plant fibers have suffered in competition with a newcomer—man-made fibers (rayon, nylon, and related filaments).

COTTON

Cotton is outstanding among vegetable, animal, and synthetic fibers, accounting for approximately one-half of all materials (measured by weight) that are made into cloth.

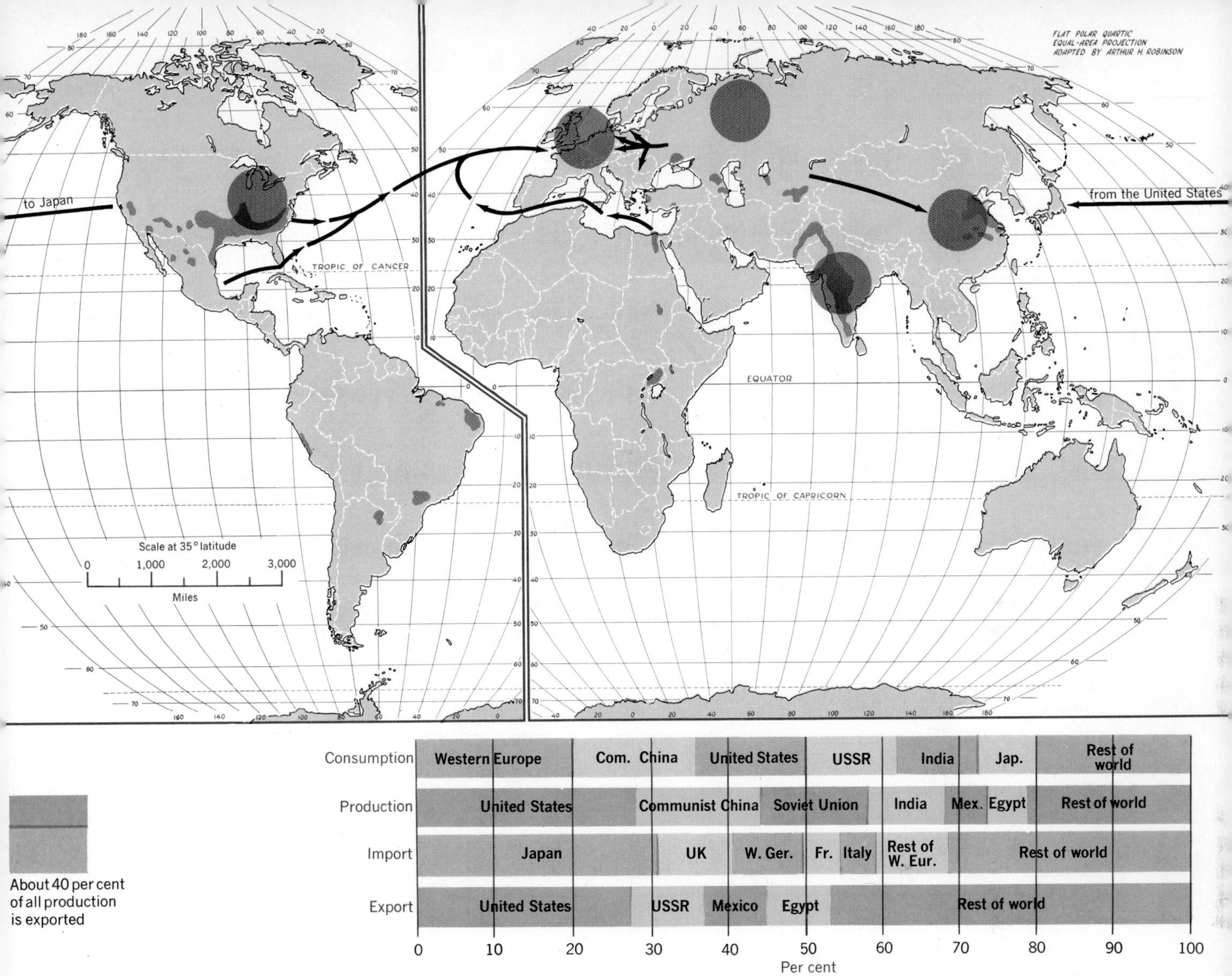

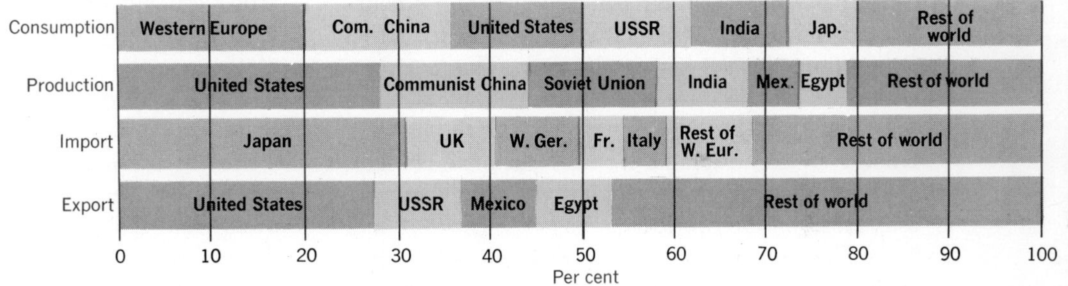

Figure 20.1 ***Consumption, production, import, and export of cotton.*** *Circles show regions and nations of heaviest consumption. Gray stippling shows areas of heaviest production. The sizable world commerce in cotton lies mostly in the Northern Hemisphere. Why?*

COTTON CONSUMPTION

Over 40 million bales of cotton, each weighing about 500 pounds, are consumed every year. This represents a 25 per cent increase over prewar consumption. Approximately 65 per cent occurs in non-Communist nations and 35 per cent in Communist countries. The United States long has been the leader among individual nations and currently is responsible for the utilization of almost 15 per cent of all cotton (Fig. 20.1). Communist China, the Soviet Union, India, and Japan also are major consumers. Recent figures suggest that Communist China's consumption may now exceed that of the United States. Western Europe is very significant as a consuming region, with about one-fifth of the world total.

Nearly 50 per cent of this cotton goes into cloth and another 25 per cent into carpets, curtains, and other household materials. The remainder is used chiefly for industrial purposes, both as a textile and as stuffing, batting, etc. Cotton thus goes primarily into consumer goods, and the volume of its consumption is highest in areas of heavy population. Because they contain so many people, some technically underdeveloped nations are large aggregate consumers of cotton.

COTTON PRODUCTION

Natural conditions of growth

Climate. As produced commercially, cotton requires a growing season of at least 180 days, and preferably of 200 days. During this time, average temperatures should be above 70°F. A minimum precipitation amount of 40 inches and a maximum of 60 inches per year are considered to be optimum unless excessive wetness encourages insect and disease pests. The plant can grow where precipitation is as low as 20 inches annually, but irrigation is required in yet drier climates. The moisture should be comparatively even throughout much of the year but retarded during the fall harvest. Humid subtropical and tropical savanna climates are both conducive to cotton growth, and they contain most of the world's acreage (Figs. 20.1 and 5.1). The small amount which they do not contain is situated mainly in irrigated oases of subtropical and tropical semiarid and desert country. Cotton thus is grown throughout much of the area between lat 50° N and 30° S. It is absent or poorly represented in several technically advanced nations which consume large amounts of the fiber—particularly the countries of Western Europe, Japan, Canada, and Australia. It can be grown in most technically underdeveloped nations and usually is found there, especially if substantial domestic markets are assured by sizable populations in such countries.

Other Natural Features. Cotton grows best on soils which retain moisture at their upper levels and are well drained at lower depths. It favors loams but can do quite well on tighter soils if sufficient moisture is present to prevent excessive compaction around the plant roots. The plant is a notorious soil robber, and both basic and trace elements should be added where the crop is grown in one place for a number of years. Since the reddish, pedalferic soils of both the humid subtropical and the tropical savanna climates tend to be naturally deficient in many of these elements, the maintaining of soil productivity long has been a problem associated with cotton culture. This is one reason why the crop has been concentrated on the richer alluvial soils of river flood plains.

Flat, well-drained land is notably conducive to the growth of the cotton plant. Because of the importance of cotton to many economies, the plant tends to occupy the choice agricultural sites and hence is found on many of the world's flood plains and other alluvial and colluvial areas.

Insect and disease pests can be serious obstacles to a harvest in any single year. It is not uncommon for as much as 20 per cent of a nation's crop, and not unknown for more than one-half of such a crop, to be lost to them. Perhaps the worst of these is the boll weevil, which in 1922 infested almost 85 per cent of the cotton land in the United States—an infestation resulting in production losses from which some of the country's coastal areas have never fully recovered, as cotton growing shifted away from them to places where local climatic conditions were less conducive to the weevil's continued existence. More recently, the advent of improved insecticides and other means of control has meant a decline in the potency of both insects and diseases. They remain serious threats, however, particularly in technically underdeveloped lands which have not always been able to obtain sufficient supplies of modern means of controlling them.

Like most other agricultural commodities, cotton thus can be grown in far greater quantities and on much more land than is now the case. Within the broad limits set by nature—limits which man doubtless could expand appreciably if he chose—man makes the decisions concerning where the cotton is grown, where it is shipped, and where it is consumed.

Agricultural practices

There are several species and a very large number of varieties of the cotton plant. Most of the varieties reach heights of only 2 to 6 feet, but a few, notably in Brazil, are so tall that they are called *tree cotton.* Cotton is predominantly an annual, but some perennial varieties exist, particularly in Peru. The seedbeds are prepared either during the autumn preceding planting or in late winter, for the long growing season requires that the plants get an early start. The cotton seed is planted in rows either with a mechanical drill or by hand, in the latter case being placed in "hills" approximately 8 to 20 inches apart. Subsequently, chopping and thinning operations must be performed, as in sugar-beet culture, so that single plants will be about 1 foot apart. Then comes a period of continuous cultivation—mainly by machine and hoe in technically advanced lands and mainly by hoe in underdeveloped areas. Harvesting, a late fall operation, may involve either taking of all bolls at once or picking them selectively.

The amount of hand labor involved in cotton growth is readily apparent. Only in a few technically advanced nations is the machine making serious inroads upon this dominance of hand labor, but appreciable success has been realized (Fig. 20.2). The major problem, as it is so often in mechanized agriculture, is the necessity for selective operations in thinning and preferably in the harvesting. To date, machines have not demonstrated a capacity to be selective, and this deficiency must be compensated for in mechanized agriculture—through such techniques as planting seeds with sure-fire germinating qualities and refining the various machines so that they can be more selective at all stages of plant growth and harvest.

The length of the staple (fiber) which develops in the cotton boll is an extremely important feature in subsequent manufacturing, because the longer staples form sturdier threads and hence are more highly prized. Cotton therefore is categorized by staple length, a common classification being:

Short staple—less than 1 inch long
Medium staple—1 to 1⅛ inches long
Extra, or long, staple—over 1⅛ inches long

Specific farming practices vary appreciably among the several nations involved, and those of the world's leading nations of production are discussed below.

Leading nations of production

The nations which are outstanding cotton consumers are also outstanding producers, and it is only in nations of intermediate consuming capacity that a marked dependence upon imports begins to be apparent. The ratio of production in non-Communist and Communist nations is approximately the same as of consumption—65:35. The United States definitely is the world leader in production, accounting for 11 to 15 million bales of cotton each year—at least one-fourth of the world output. Its relative share in world production exceeds appreciably that of consumption (Fig. 20.1). Communist China, the Soviet Union, and India also are major producers, and Mexico, a newcomer to the front ranks, is gaining. Egypt, a specialty producer of quality cotton, is more than noteworthy. These six nations account for about four-fifths of the world cotton crop.

The United States. Cotton production in the United States, of course, is largely in the *cotton belt,* which encompasses all or portions of eleven of the fifteen leading states (Fig. 20.3). Within this belt, as well as within the nation, Texas is easily the outstanding producer, being responsible for over one-fourth of the country's cotton. Especially heavy concentrations are found on the relatively moist (for Texas) prairie and chernozem soils near the state's eastern boundary, and on the drier brown steppe soils of the northwest, where irrigation is necessary (Fig. 20.3). California produces nearly one-seventh of the nation's cotton, largely under irrigation on the alluvial and colluvial soils of the upper and central San Joaquin River valley. Output here is on the rise. The Mississippi River flood plain sections of the states of Arkansas and Mississippi also are active producers, as is the central Gila River flood plain of Arizona—the latter under irrigation. Most of the other cotton-growing states are in the area known traditionally as the cotton belt.

The cotton of the Southern states is chiefly of medium staple length, whereas that of the arid West has a slightly longer staple. A comparatively small amount of extra-long-staple cotton is grown in Arizona, Texas, and New Mexico, with a trace in California.

The general conditions of cotton growth in the Southern states are well known. We need not emphasize here the prevalence of the plantation system, utilizing slave labor before the Civil War and the labor of sharecroppers and tenants after that conflict; the traditional importance of an agricultural economy to the South, and of cotton to that economy; the demonstrated tenacity of this agrarian way of life and its persistence with the passing of time.

However, the twentieth century is bringing change to cotton growing in the Southern states and in the nation. This change is especially evident in the shift of growth areas, in the advent of new agricultural practices, and in the decline of total acreage.

CHANGES IN LOCATION. The term *cotton belt* is somewhat of a misnomer; for, to an appreciably greater degree than is true of wheat on the Great Plains, Southern cotton is grown under somewhat diversified farming arrangements involving corn, peanuts, fruit, vegetables, legumes, and still other crops. Nevertheless, a broad area reaching from the Atlantic Ocean to central Texas and from the Gulf of Mexico to the "boot heel" of Missouri is generally designated as the cotton belt. Within this broad area are districts where the crop is grown at an above-average level of intensity (but even here, agriculture is not wholly a one-crop specialty). The most outstanding of these districts are in the black and red prairie soils of Texas and Oklahoma, and the flood plain of the lower Mississippi River (Fig. 20.3). Secondary concentrations are in northeastern Alabama and in the inner coastal-plain portions of Georgia and the Carolinas.

A century ago the cotton-growing areas of the United States were located more solidly within the states bordering and east of the Mississippi River than is true today. Soil erosion and depletion, together with such plagues as that of the boll weevil in the early 1920s, were partially responsible for a decline in parts of the East and South—more specifically, in the Atlantic Coastal Plain, the southern Piedmont, and the well-known belt of black, calcareous soils of central Alabama and northeastern Mississippi. At about the same time, the crop was introduced into north central Texas and southwestern Oklahoma, where the prairie soils were naturally more fertile and the drier climates discouraged the boll weevil.

Locational changes within the United States during the past quarter century have involved both a shift of the industry to focal districts in the Southern states and an initiation of cotton in the

Old and new methods of cotton picking in the United States. On the left, field pickers await the drying of early morning dew before they start the long day's work. On the right, mechanical pickers lumber down the rows of cotton, removing the cotton bolls (and some unwanted debris). Such mechanical pickers now harvest over one-third of the annual cotton crop of the United States (Fig. 20.2). (Standard Oil Company of New Jersey)

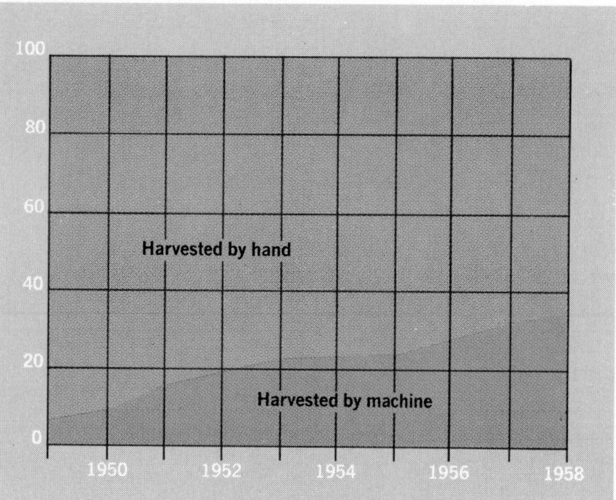

Figure 20.2 ***Trends in methods of harvesting cotton in the United States*** *(after* Textile Organon, *October, 1959, p. 162).*

Western states, notably California and Arizona. The first has been occasioned noteworthily by a planned reduction in the nation's cotton acreage, a reduction about which we shall have more to say later in the chapter. A partial result was that the cotton farmers tended to plant their best land to the crop, and many of those on marginal soils turned to other crops which would not require the application of so much costly commercial fertilizer and labor. The industry thus became increasingly concentrated in the specific districts where it now exists. Meanwhile, cotton production has developed vigorously in the Far West, especially after the Second World War. Here, average yields per acre are sometimes three times as large as in the cotton belt, and increasing enthusiasm for the crop is apparent.

The major locational shifts of cotton agriculture in the United States thus have involved a decline in parts of the cotton belt, a centripetal movement into localized districts of existing production there, and an almost spectacular growth of the activity in the Far West.

What has caused these shifts? The early movement from the East appears to have been due chiefly to the seeking of relief from ravages of the boll weevil and other insects and diseases that do not thrive in the drier climates farther to the west. Also, the weak soils of the East became exhausted under continuous cotton planting at a time when commercial fertilizers were not well understood, so that per acre yield declined there. A third consideration involves the cotton plant itself: varieties of cotton producing the highly prized longer staples can be grown more easily, usually under irrigation, in the less humid climates. Size of holding also is important, especially in this Industrial Age. Although holdings have for a long time been large in much of the South (as will be emphasized later in this chapter), it has been necessary to combine some farms into still larger units to meet the needs of modern mechanized agriculture (Fig. 20.4). In contrast, holdings throughout much of the Great Plains and country still farther west already are large enough for the modern machine. By maximizing economies of scale, Western producing units are able to reduce costs sufficiently to overcome advantages Eastern growers may have in market proximity. This is partially true even of California and Arizona, which as yet have almost no cotton-textile mills and market their cotton in the East and abroad. Subsidization by the Federal government also has been important to the shift of cotton growing, as is explained above.

CHANGES IN AGRICULTURAL PRACTICES. The most significant changes in agricultural practices in cotton growing have been associated with mechanization. The Southern sharecropper in the Mississippi River delta area invests an average of from 109 to 141 hours of labor in each acre of cotton he grows. This is in addition to the work performed by one mule and mule-drawn equipment. In contrast, he need invest an average of only 25 hours of labor in the same acre if he uses a tractor and tractor-drawn equipment.[1] The implications are clear: if certain liabilities can be overcome, the machine will obviate the need for much Southern agricultural labor and concomitantly increase the efficiency of the industry.

[1] J. Allen Tower, "Cotton Change in Alabama, 1879–1946," *Economic Geography*, **26**:6–28, 1950, p. 17.

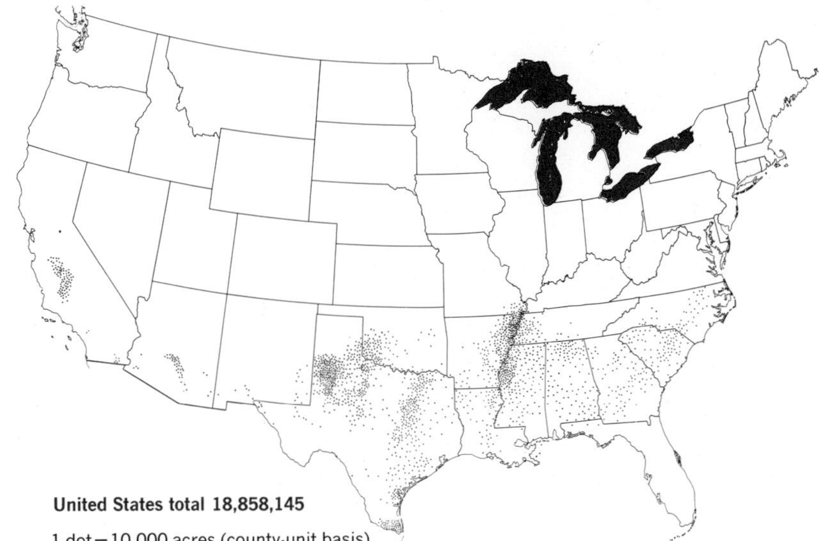

Figure 20.3 **Acreage of cotton harvested in the United States.** *Note the importance of various sections of Texas, of California, and of the Mississippi River flood plain below its confluence with the Ohio River. (U.S. Bureau of the Census)*

Even with its present deficiencies, the machine has altered the occupance of Southern countrysides. Holdings tend to remain large, as they have always been—first with the use of slave labor, subsequently with the use of sharecropper or tenant labor.[2] Under sharecropper and tenant arrangements, however, the actual amount of ground worked by each laborer amounted to 30 to 40 acres, more or less, and there were many such operating units in a single plantation. The coming of the machine has meant a trend toward larger operating units, usually involving whole properties as before the Civil War. The machine, then, has replaced the slave of a century ago in the as yet comparatively small but increasing number of "neoplantations"[3] characterizing the present-day South. To the west, in Texas and Oklahoma and especially in California and adjacent Far Western states, the advent of the machine has been more or less concomitant with the introduction of cotton farming, and these areas have scarcely known the earlier occupance stages which characterized the Deep South.

CHANGE IN ACREAGE. In 1929, there were 43,232,000 acres of cotton harvested in the United States, the average yield per acre being 164.2 pounds. In 1958, there were 11,849,000 acres harvested at an average per acre yield of 466 pounds. The total harvest in 1929 was 14,825,000 bales of cotton; in 1958, 11,512,000 bales.

The figures above summarize a major problem in cotton production in the United States—a rather familiar problem in this nation of plenty and to spare, a paradoxical and somewhat hauntingly tragic problem which cannot be comprehended by inhabitants of many nations where the major efforts are directed toward increasing rather than restricting output. Ours is a problem of cotton overproduction. It has been met, chiefly at the national government level, by policies of subsidized acreage limitation, the ultimate objective being a limitation in output. To an extent, the end objective has been achieved, but not without difficulty; for, having reduced their cotton acreages, the farmers planted their best land to the crop. The Far Western states, with their unusually large yields per acre, benefited particularly. Thus the national yields per acre approximately have doubled since the introduction of the policies of limitation. Annual cotton surpluses

[2] Merle Prunty, Jr., "The Renaissance of the Southern Plantation," *Geographical Review,* **45**:459–491, 1955. In the nine Southeastern states (excluding peninsular Florida), landholdings of 220 acres and larger occupy from 48.6 to 100 per cent of the total farm land in two-fifths of the entire area, and from 61 to 100 per cent of the total farm land in one-fifth of that area.

[3] *Ibid.*

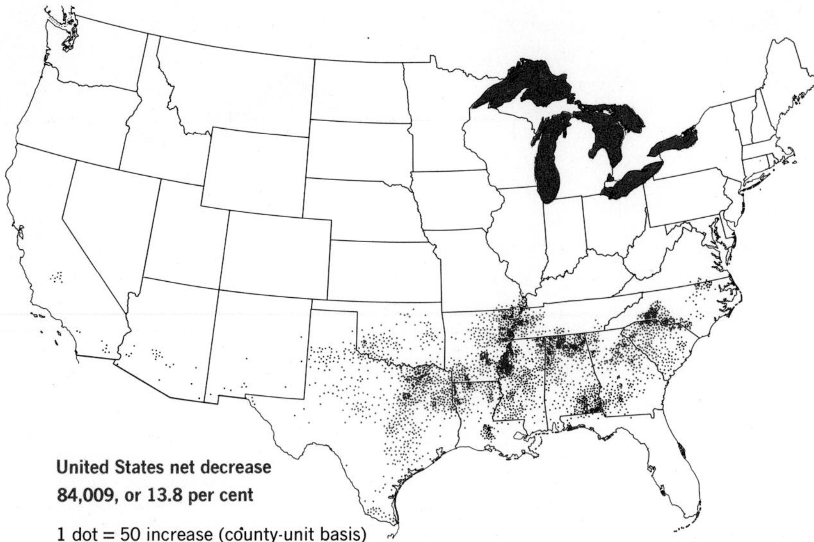

Figure 20.4 ***Change in number of cotton farms of the United States, 1949 to 1954.*** *Note that the map refers to* farms, *not* acreage. *The farms in some of the nation's leading districts of production (Fig. 20.3) obviously are becoming fewer but larger. (U.S. Bureau of the Census)*

have continued to accumulate, both in the United States and abroad, varying appreciably from year to year. In this country total surpluses range from one-half to all of a single year's harvest.

STILL A LEADING INDUSTRY. Despite limitations set by both nature and man, cotton agriculture is still a major industry in the United States, with a cash return amounting to nearly one-seventh of that for all agricultural crops in the nation. Currently, cotton output is valued at almost 2.1 billion dollars, of which 1.9 billion is realized from the sale of the fiber and 0.2 billion from the sale of seed, which is made chiefly into meal and cake for livestock feed. In terms of cash income, it is exceeded only by wheat. In terms of product value, it is also exceeded by corn, much of which is fed to livestock and hence not entered into financial records as cash income.

Communist China. China was an important producer of cotton before the advent of Communism there. In the late 1930s, the country ranked fourth among world producers. Most of the cotton was from short-staple varieties, grown under rather primitive conditions. The primary areas of growth were in the lower deltas of the Yellow and Yangtze Rivers, under humid continental warm-summer and humid subtropical climates. The exact amount of cotton grown each year tended to vary with its price relative to that of food grains, particularly wheat, which was grown in quantity in the same area. Because the climate in this part of China is markedly uneven from year to year with periodic drought, crop failures were not uncommon.

For the first few years after the Communist government came to power, production remained rather low. However, the crop received a high priority in the postrevolutionary planning, and output appears to have increased very rapidly. United Nations sources report a tripling of output between 1949 and 1954, and more than a doubling of the 1954 figure by 1958. The early increases appear to have been due to an expanded acreage, and later ones to increases in yield per acre. About 5 per cent of Communist China's arable land is now planted to cotton. Although some cotton is grown under irrigation in the arid west, no outstandingly new growth areas have been opened up since the revolution. Instead, land was shifted from wheat and other crops to cotton in the traditional growth areas, (and from such crops as rye to wheat in more arid and cool conditions where cotton cannot grow). Increases in yield per acre appear to have been achieved through intensive use of such natural fertilizers as barnyard manures and fish-pond sludge and preliminary use of a small output of commercial fertilizers, through deep plowing with equipment more modern than before the revolution, and through irrigation. The commune system appears to have resulted also in a very intensive use of labor—even more so than before the revolution, for coercion has been added to the traditional stimulus of need.

The Soviet Union. Most of the Soviet Union's cotton is grown under irrigation in Soviet Central Asia (Fig. 20.1). Among the sixteen republics of the Soviet Union, Uzbekistan is outstanding, accounting for over three-fifths of the annual crop. Most of the remainder is grown in adjacent republics, and a minor amount in European Russia.

Before the Communist revolution, the Soviet Union depended upon imports to supply about one-half of all raw cotton entering domestic mills. The same country now ranks third in world output of raw cotton, producing each year over one-half as much as is grown in the United States. Since 1953, it has been an exporter. To do this, production has been increased more than sixfold since 1913.

This has not been an easy accomplishment, for cotton growing in the Soviet Union has met with many of the natural difficulties which have hindered the general output there. Prerevolution harvests of cotton were low, and yields immediately after the revolution were even lower. Initial efforts by the Communist government were directed primarily toward increasing the total crop by increasing acreage—an action later copied by Communist China. By 1931, the amount of land devoted to cotton was more than three times as large as in 1913, but yield per acre had declined to about 60 per cent of the 1913 yield. One reason for the decline in output per acre was that somewhat foolish efforts were made to grow the crop without irrigation in European Russia, particularly the Ukraine and the area north of the Caucasus. By the late 1930s, almost one-fourth of the nation's cotton acreage was located here. Climatic difficulties were among the many encountered—the growing season was too short to assure a reasonable certainty of harvest. A major blow was delivered during the Second World War by invading German armies. However, the government has not given up hope and continues to produce part of its annual cotton crop here and near the Caucasus Mountains to the south. The 1965 target for the current Seven-Year Plan contains a quota of 10.2 per cent for European Russia and 89.8 per cent for Soviet Central Asia. The amount of cotton scheduled for production by 1965 is 5.7 to 6.1 million metric tons (the target is a range rather than a fixed amount)—about twice the current output of the United States.

Not all the difficulties have been natural or caused by war. The initially low yields in Soviet Central Asia were due appreciably to resistance by inhabitants there to the collectivization of their land. Now that this type of resistance has waned and the collective and state farms have replaced private operators, resistance is largely a reluctance to do the large amount of hand labor necessary to grow the crop. In the Soviet Union, as in the United States, the machine has not been able to replace the laborer with complete success, and, in the transition toward mechanization, most work must still be done by hand. Also as in the United States, the sowing operations appear to be largely mechanized; but chopping, cultivation, and harvesting still offer problems to the machine.

Among the cotton varieties, upland types imported from the United States during the nineteenth century are predominant. Most of the cotton yields a staple of medium length, but a small amount of long-staple cotton, not unlike that found in Egypt, is also grown. Commercial fertilizers have been used increasingly, as have crop-rotation schemes, particularly those involving legumes. Recent increases in per acre yields are credited largely to these practices and to careful seed selection.

India and Pakistan. The partition of British India divided not only a sizable political territory but also a rather potent agricultural economy. This is nowhere better realized than in regard to cotton and to jute, discussed later in this chapter.

Cotton production, which may have originated in India, is now carried on primarily in a rather sizable area trending from the southern part of the peninsula to the Indus River of West Pakistan (Fig. 20.1). Associated climates are mainly semi-

A mechanical cotton picker in the Soviet Union (U.S. Department of Agriculture).

arid, desert, and tropical savanna. Most of the cotton is of short and medium staple length in the south, and medium and long staple length in the irrigated places, notably along the Indus River. The shorter-staple varieties predominate.

The partition of India and Pakistan resulted in a division of this land, slightly under four-fifths going to India and the remainder to Pakistan. India's share, while larger, initially involved acreages devoted chiefly to low-yielding short- and medium-staple varieties grown without irrigation. Pakistan received most of the irrigated land, where the high-yielding medium- and long-staple plants are grown. A somewhat diversified cotton economy thus was separated into two relatively specialized areas. Today India ranks fourth among the world's leading cotton-growing nations, and Pakistan ranks seventh (Fig. 20.1). Moreover, the partition awarded most of the existing cotton mills to India, and a once uniform domestic market for cotton thereby was also divided unevenly.

The efforts of the government of postpartition India have been directed at maximizing the domestic cotton production while concomitantly expanding the output of food crops. Therefore, each decision as to whether the cotton harvest can be increased involves careful attention to the possible effect of such expansion upon the output of food. Because of the urgent need to replace domestic sources of cotton that were lost in the partition, the amount of land planted to cotton has risen during the First and Second Five-Year Plans from 10.9 million acres in 1947 to 20.9 million acres in 1958. Total production rose in approximately the same proportion, for per acre yields remained essentially at the low levels of antepartition days (100 pounds or less per acre, as compared with over 400 pounds in the United States). Now, more attention is being given to raising the yields per acre and to growing cotton of a longer staple length. Because of the high cost of commercial fertilizer and the use of a high per cent of all animal manures as fuel, the first of these two objectives will be difficult to attain. Water shortage also will be a liability; only about 4 per cent of India's 20.9 million acres of cotton land is irrigated, despite the fact that natural precipitation throughout much of this land approaches the marginal limit for cotton growth. The second objective—increasing the ratio of medium- and long-staple cotton—is being realized more successfully; well over one-half of the total annual crop is now medium- or long-staple cotton, which is quickly making inroads into the Indian economy under the encouragement of the national government.

Despite production increases, however, India still does not produce quite enough cotton to supply domestic requirements, and the country is a modest importer.

Meanwhile, West Pakistan's cotton output has risen only slightly since partition. Yields per acre here, where irrigation is generally necessary and medium- to long-staple cotton prevails, are almost twice those of India. Customarily a surplus producer, Pakistan has exported decreasing amounts of the commodity as domestic demand has absorbed more and more of the annual harvests. New textile mills have been constructed since partition, and Pakistan's textile plants now receive over five times as much cotton per year as in 1950.

Both India and Pakistan are confronted with serious obstacles in their efforts to stimulate cotton production. Both have adopted the Five-Year-Plan idea to build their economies, including their cotton output. Modern technology is well known to planners at the upper levels of government in both nations, but much remains to be done in transmitting and implementing this knowledge in predominantly agricultural societies where illiteracy is common, where land not infrequently has been subdivided, over centuries of inheriting, into tiny fragments, and where capital for agricultural improvement is scarce and elusive.

Other Nations. Of the many countries producing cotton, the leading four are followed by Mexico, Egypt, Pakistan, and Brazil. Mexico's production is somewhat unique in that it has more than quadrupled during the past quarter century and appears to be climbing still higher. Nearly the entire crop is made up of medium- to long-staple varieties grown under irrigation in scattered districts in the northern half of the country. Associated with the growth of Mexico's *ejidos* (agricultural communities), cotton now accounts for about one-fourth of the country's exports and is the leading export commodity. Pakistan's output was discussed above, with that of India. The long-staple cotton of Egypt's Nile River valley provides from 80 per cent to 90 per cent of that country's export value. The cotton of Brazil is predominantly short-staple, except for small amounts of tree cotton grown in the northeast. Brazil's domestic output supplies most of the country's internal demand, plus an export of large enough amounts so that cotton ranks behind only coffee as an export.

Overview. Because of its critical importance as a consumer commodity, cotton might be expected to be grown in quantities at least equal to population numbers, and to be particularly important to technically underdeveloped nations. During the decade from 1950 to 1960, the world's population grew by slightly more than 12 per cent, whereas its cotton output rose by over 17 per cent. World per capita production thus is on the rise—despite a substantial cut in output of the United States for that decade. However, non-Communist nations other than the United States increased production by only about 25 per cent of their 1950 figures, whereas Communist nations raised production by 60 per cent of their 1950 output. Clearly, the growth of cotton has been emphasized in the planning of the Communist nations—and with success, despite rather severe natural handicaps in both Communist China and the Soviet Union. For such populous but underdeveloped nations as India, where population increase is conspicuously above the world average but cotton output only slightly above it, the situation is sobering.

COTTON TRADE AND TRANSPORTATION

Domestic movement

More than three-fifths of all cotton is consumed domestically. Over nine-tenths of all cotton grown in Communist countries is consumed internally, whereas only slightly more than one-half of the cotton of non-Communist nations is accounted for by domestic markets.

In several of the leading consuming nations, the mills which utilize the raw cotton tend to be located in relative proximity to growing areas. However, major exceptions may be noted in both the United States and the Soviet Union. As discussed in Chapter 33, the cotton-textile manufacturing of the United States largely shifted from New England southward to the Piedmont state of North Carolina and its neighbors. Meanwhile, the primary cotton-growing districts have shifted away from these eastern states to places farther west. A substantial overland haul to market still is necessary in this country. In the Soviet Union, the mills tend to be concentrated in the vicinities of Moscow and Leningrad, which are appreciably removed from the cotton-growing districts in Soviet Middle Asia and southern European Russia. The current Seven-Year-Plan calls for a slight moderation of this inequality; but even if the 1965 target is met, nearly 70 per cent of the country's cotton-textile manufacturing will be in northern European Russia, whereas the cotton-growing districts will remain essentially where they now are. The mills of Communist China and India are in rather close juxtaposition with both raw materials and markets. Domestic movement of their cotton thus is chiefly a short-haul commerce. All the leading countries but the United States depend almost solely upon their railways for this movement, but in the United States the intercity truck and semitrailer are used also.

International trade

The gross pattern of international trade in cotton among non-Communist countries is not complex: surplus cotton moves from the United States and lesser exporting nations primarily to Western Europe and Japan, but also to numerous smaller destinations elsewhere. These last, while not so important individually, are quite numerous. Their over-all significance is documented by the fact that they account for over 30 per cent of all imports.

International trade in raw cotton is thus first and foremost an exchange between technically advanced nations—more specifically, a movement from one technically advanced nation, the United States, where natural environmental conditions are conducive to the growth of cotton, to a number of technically advanced nations where the commodity cannot be raised satisfactorily, if at all (Fig. 20.1). Non-Communist exporting nations other than the United States are for the most part technically underdeveloped. Their aggregate share of world exports, however, is higher than that of the United States, amounting to over one-half of the world total. Many of these nations produce the crop with their own managers, capital, and labor, and they participate in world markets as free agents, comparatively uninfluenced by political and economic affiliations. Cotton is not generally subject to an import tariff,[4] although it is subject to an export tariff in Pakistan and a few other nations.

The small but rising volume of cotton trade in Communist countries is largely a commerce from the Soviet Union to Eastern Europe. In turn, the Soviet Union imports a small amount of cotton, chiefly long-staple types. Most of these imports, however, come from non-Communist Egypt.

[4] There is a rather moderate import tariff on medium- and long-staple cotton in the United States, but essentially none in the leading importing nations of Europe.

JUTE

Jute is one of the most inexpensive of the plant fibers that can be woven. Like cotton, it is believed to be indigenous to India, but, unlike cotton, it continues to be produced almost wholly in the general area of its possible origin.

JUTE CONSUMPTION

The annual world consumption of jute, totaling more than 2 million tons, is exceeded only by that of cotton, which is about four times higher. Too cheap for most clothing other than sackcloth, jute is used principally for burlap bags, rug and carpet backing, upholstery binder, cordage, and similar purposes requiring a tough but inexpensive fiber. It thus provides a transition between the soft and hard fibers, being applied to both woven and non-woven materials.

Although the end products of much jute manufacture are to be found in technically advanced nations, the mills which consume the agricultural crop are chiefly located in India and Pakistan. Over one-half of the annual mill consumption of jute occurs in India, and nearly one-seventh in Pakistan (Fig. 20.5). The remainder is exported to technically advanced countries—chiefly the United Kingdom, France, and West Germany.

JUTE PRODUCTION

Nearly all of the world's jute is grown on the rather extensive delta marking the confluence of the Ganges and Brahmaputra Rivers (Fig. 20.5). Prior to the partition of India and Pakistan, this delta was located in British India. Following that partition, most of it has become the territory of East

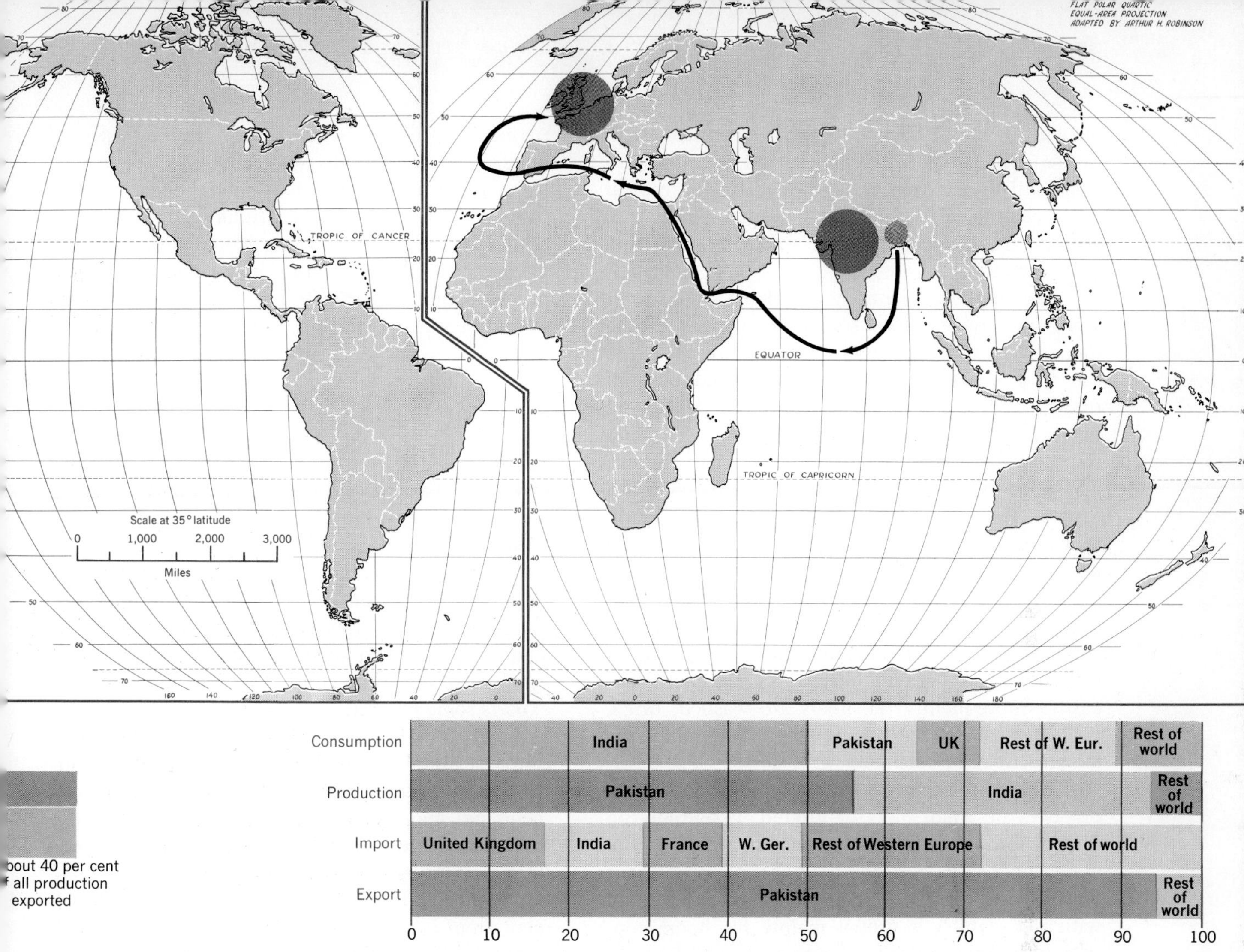

Figure 20.5 ***Consumption, production, import, and export of jute.*** *India is the leading consumer and Pakistan the leading producer. Circles show nations or regions of very heavy consumption, and gray stippling shows the one area of very heavy production.*

Pakistan, with only the western fringes in the new state of India. Conversely, most of the jute mills were in Calcutta and its hinterland to the north and west—in territory that now is a part of India. Since India and Pakistan do not enjoy the best of political and economic relationships, one important result of partition has been the disrupting of what once was a smoothly functioning activity. Pakistan, being loath to ship raw jute to India, is building mills as rapidly as possible. India is equally determined to produce domestically grown jute for her many mills and has utilized some excellent land—which could be planted to food crops—for this purpose. Where once there was a unified and dynamic activity, there are now the embryos of two—neither of which is likely to achieve the stature of their common predecessor.

Jute fibers come from the inner bark (bast) of the jute plant, which reaches heights of 6 to 15 feet and attains a thickness of about ½ inch. The fibers are long, some of them extending the entire length of the plant. Jute thrives under hot, moist conditions and thus is very well adapted to the tropical rainy climate of its major growth area, where it is planted from March to June and harvested from July to October.

The earliest planting and harvesting occur along the lower, more southerly portions of the delta. The seeds are usually broadcast directly into the field. Ideally, the soils there should be well drained, but the plant can grow in fields that are not excessively flooded. Thinning, cultivating, and weeding operations are carried out prior to harvest. The plant is cut by hand after it has reached full growth. Harvesting takes place under moist conditions; for, unlike most agricultural commodities, the desired part of the plant is in the stalk rather than the seeds, blossoms, cherries, or leaves, and ripening is not necessary. After cutting, the stalks are submerged in water and allowed to ret (rot) for a short time so that the fibers can be extracted more easily. Subsequently the fibers are washed, dried, and forwarded to market, usually a city market, via a hierarchy of middlemen.

The crop is grown under native agricultural practices on small plots of ground. Essentially no foreign managership or capital is involved. To the many small farmers in the delta it represents about the only cash crop, and it is always in competition with rice, which is grown mainly for home consumption. Annual floods tend to replenish the soils, notably along the seaward margins of the delta. Artificial fertilizing is uncommon, and commercial fertilizing is essentially absent.

Pakistan now accounts for about 55 per cent of the world's jute output, and India nearly all of the remainder. Brazil, Taiwan, Nepal, Burma, and Communist China are all minor producers. Communist China reportedly has been increasing its output in recent years.

JUTE TRADE AND TRANSPORTATION

Pakistan is the outstanding exporting nation for raw jute. Nearly 60 per cent of the country's annual harvest is shipped overseas, principally to northwestern Europe. An additional 25 per cent crosses the border into India, despite political friction between the two nations. Most is carried by small boat along one of the numerous small streams there. The remainder, amounting to slightly over 15 per cent, is consumed at home. India, meanwhile, also exports some raw jute.

Thus nearly all jute is grown, and about two thirds is initially milled, in two technically underdeveloped countries (Fig. 20.5). Overseas investment and managership are virtually absent in the agricultural production, but much of the mill production is under overseas managership. At one time, jute mill production also involved substantial investment from overseas, but, especially in India, much foreign capital has been supplanted with domestic capital.

FLAX

CONDITIONS OF GROWTH

Flax is an annual which characteristically grows during the warm season in intermediate latitudes and during the cool season in low latitudes. It is a thin-stemmed plant reaching heights of 10 to 40 inches. It is harvested for both its fiber and seed, the former being used mainly as a thread in fine textiles and cordage, and the latter as a source of linseed oil and as a grain for livestock feeding. Like jute, flax is a bast fiber, located in the stalk and extending almost the entire length of the plant. Hence the species most in demand for fiber production tend to be tall and essentially devoid of branches. In contrast, the species yielding oil and grain are usually shorter and contain rather intricate patterns of branches, so that more seeds can form. A rather sharp distinction thus exists between flax species used for fiber and those used for other purposes. There is a tendency for the fiber species to be grown in the cooler climates of the higher intermediate latitudes.

Stalks of flax are fed to the rollers of a breaking machine so that fibers can be removed from the bark of the stems. This is a scene in Northern Ireland. (British Information Services)

CONSUMPTION, PRODUCTION, AND TRADE

Between 600,000 and 800,000 short tons of flax fiber are produced and consumed each year, and the fiber thus ranks immediately beneath cotton and jute when considered by tonnage. Despite its comparatively high position among all fibers, however, it occupies only about one-fourth of all land devoted to flax; the remaining three-fourths is used to produce seed.

The Soviet Union alone accounts for over three-fourths of the world's output of flax grown for fiber, and Poland and Czechoslovakia together grow an additional one-twentieth. Most of the rest is produced in Western Europe.[5] Approximately one-tenth of all production of flax fiber is exported, the commerce being mainly an outflow from Belgium and the Netherlands to other nations of Europe. World consumption, production, and trade in flax thus are functions that are of interest primarily to the technically advanced nations.

[5] In linseed production, however, the Soviet Union ranks appreciably behind the United States, accounting for about 25 per cent of the world's total in comparison to 30 per cent for this country. Argentina, India, and Canada are also important linseed producers.

OTHER PLANT FIBERS

In addition to the three leaders, noteworthy plant fibers on the world scene include hemp, sisal, henequen, and abacá. The first of these, like flax, is grown mainly in the Soviet Union and Europe, and does not enter appreciably into world trade. The others are mainly low-latitude fibers, produced chiefly in technically underdeveloped countries for export to technically advanced nations. Most of the sisal moves from Tanganyika, Indonesia, and Uganda; most of the henequen is forwarded from Mexico; essentially all the abacá originates in the Philippines. World markets for these products lie mainly in the United States, northwestern Europe, and Japan.

REFERENCES

Communist China's Agriculture, U.S. Department of Agriculture Foreign Agriculture Report 115, 1959.

Large, David C.: "Cotton in the San Joachin Valley: A Study of Government in Agriculture," *Geographical Review,* **47**:365–380, 1957.

Prunty, Merle, Jr.: "Recent Quantitative Changes in the Cotton Regions of the Southeastern States," *Economic Geography,* **27**:189–208.

———: "The Renaissance of the Southern Plantation," *Geographical Review,* **45**:459–491, 1955.

Schwartz, Harry: *Russia's Soviet Economy,* Prentice-Hall, Inc., Englewood Cliffs, N.J., 1954. (Especially pp. 366–369.)

Shen, T. H.: *Agricultural Resources of China,* Cornell University Press, Ithaca, N.Y., 1951.

Tower, J. Allen: "Cotton Change in Alabama, 1879–1946," *Economic Geography,* **26**:6–28, 1950.

Volin, Lazar: *A Survey of Soviet Russian Agriculture,* U.S. Government Printing Office, 1951.

———: "The Soviet Union Competes in Cotton," *Foreign Agriculture,* **20** (4):3–5ff, 1956.

Wadia, P. A., and K. T. Merchant: *Our Economic Problem,* Vora and Company, Bombay, 1957. (Especially pp. 186–190 and 458–462.)

Wu, Yuan-Li: *An Economic Survey of Communist China,* Bookman Associates, New York, 1956. (Especially pp. 133–145.)

21 AGRICULTURE AND GRAZING: ANIMAL PRODUCTS

AMONG ECONOMIC ADVANTAGES SUPPLIED TO MAN BY ANIMALS AND FOWL ARE animate energy, milk, meat, eggs, animal fats, and wool. We have noted in Chapter 15 that, although vital to some economies, animal energy supplies no more than 4 per cent of the world's total energy requirements. In a wholly different comparison, we find that the relative importance of specific animal products varies sharply from commodity to commodity (Table 21.1). Milk accounts for about one-fourth of the total tonnage of the world's leading agricultural products, and meat also is among the leaders. In contrast, eggs, animal fats, and wool rank rather low. The world output of animal products has increased, as has that of all leading agricultural commodities (Table 21.1). Except for milk, the production of these animal products has risen faster than that of all leading agricultural products. This increase has been registered especially in technically advanced economies, where the need for it is not so urgent as in technically underdeveloped areas (Fig. 21.1).

We have noted earlier that draft animals are much less efficient than inanimate sources in making energy available. Similarly, animal products generally are less efficient in fulfilling dietary needs and wants than are cereals, sugar, and other plant products. An acre of land will yield only about one-eighth as many calories to the human diet if it grows feed and pasture for beef production as if it grows wheat for direct human consumption. The same acre, if used to produce milk and pork, will supply about one-third as many calories as if planted to wheat. Such commodities as sugar and potatoes are better than wheat in making calories available to man, and a comparison of their respective efficiencies with those of animal products places the latter in an even more unfavorable position. (Of course, man needs a balanced diet as well as a minimum number of calories, but this too can be achieved without animal products if absolutely necessary.)

The presence of large numbers of animals in an economy may or may not signify technical advance. India contains more cattle than any other nation—at least one-sixth of the world total and probably more. Most of the males and some of the cows are used for draft purposes while they are

TECHNICALLY ADVANCED ECONOMIES

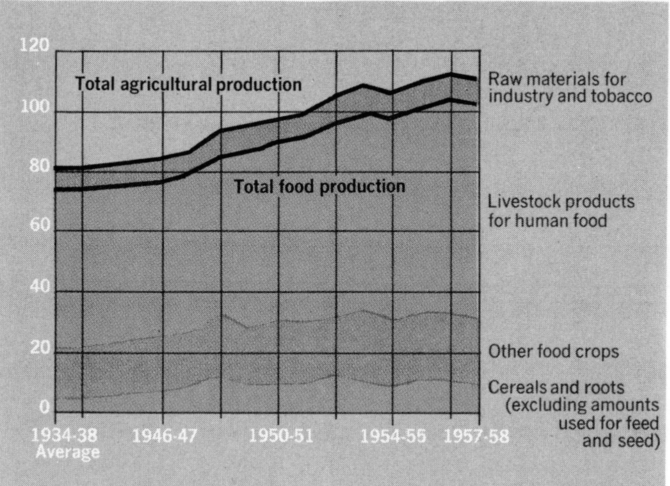

UNDERDEVELOPED ECONOMIES

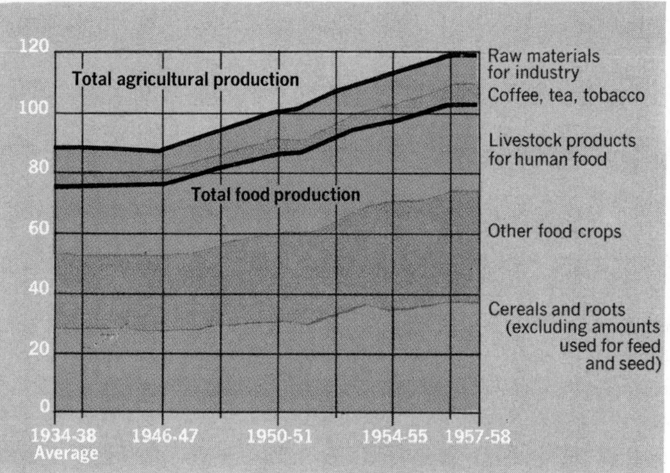

Figure 21.1 ***Trends in the production of food and other agricultural products in technically advanced and underdeveloped economies.*** *In index numbers: total agricultural output in 1948–1953 for all economies = 100. Technically advanced economies are here considered to be in Western Europe, North America, and Oceania. Underdeveloped economies are those of Latin America, non-Communist Asia, and Africa. Communist economies are not included. (After* The State of Food and Agriculture, 1958, *United Nations Food and Agricultural Organization, p. 13)*

TABLE 21.1

Estimated averages of world* production of major agricultural commodities, in millions of metric tons

Commodity	*1934–1938*	*1958–1959*
Milk (including milk products)	193.6	239.5
Corn (maize)	94.1	148.4
Wheat	95.0	138.6
Rice (milled equivalent)	70.2	94.1
Barley	28.5	51.5
Oats	37.5	43.3
Meat†	26.9	39.0
Sugar (centrifugal)	20.0	38.6
Citrus fruit	11.1	19.4
Wine	18.0	20.7
Apples	11.0	18.2
Vegetable oils and oil seeds (oil equivalent)	9.2	15.0
Bananas	8.1	13.0
Eggs	5.82	9.29
Cotton	5.31	6.53
Animal fats	3.01	5.29
Coffee	2.41	3.41
Tobacco	1.96	2.74
Jute	1.95	2.51
Rubber (natural)	0.96	1.99
Wool (greasy basis)	1.51	1.88
Cocoa	0.74	0.86
Tea	0.47	0.75
Total	647.34	914.55

* Excluding Soviet Union, Eastern Europe, and Communist China.

† Beef and veal, mutton and lamb, pork.

SOURCE: *The State of Food and Agriculture, 1959,* United Nations Food and Agricultural Organization, Rome, 1959, p. 171.

physically able to work, but most of the older bullocks and many cows are economic liabilities. The taking of life is contrary to Hindu belief, and the animals continue to multiply. Certain other underdeveloped nations and societies also have sizable animal populations. Communist China possesses a probable one-fourth of the world's swine and at least one-tenth of all chickens. Brazil has almost one-tenth of all swine and one-twelfth of all cattle. In nomadic societies, many of which are located in the dry climates of Asia and Africa and in the high latitudes of Asia, Europe, and North America, animals are vital. Conversely, other technically underdeveloped nations and societies have only small numbers of livestock. Indonesia, Burma, Thailand, and the Philippines are good examples.

The animals of underdeveloped areas tend to be scavengers, since cropland must be used to grow products considered absolutely necessary to human existence. Their products generally are consumed domestically, usually when fresh.

Inanimate power has largely replaced animal muscle as a source of energy in the vanguard nations of technical advancement, and it offers promise of similar replacement in the remaining nations. Hence the animals of such countries are kept mainly and increasingly to supply food, fibers, and leather. In contrast to practices in most technically underdeveloped countries, animal husbandry in technically advanced nations frequently involves the growing of special feed crops and the construction of costly facilities for the care of the animals and their products.

The list of animal products is long. We shall consider here only four: milk, beef, pork (including bacon and ham), and wool.

MILK AND ITS PRODUCTS

CONSUMPTION AND PRODUCTION

Volume and location

The annual production of milk now amounts to about 320 million—nearly one-third of a billion—metric tons.[1] No other of the world's leading agricultural commodities approaches this volume of output, which is about twice that of either wheat or corn, the two leading competitors.

The leading regions of milk production are given in Table 21.2. The dominance of technically advanced lands of the Northern Hemisphere is readily apparent; approximately three-fourths of all production occurs in Europe, Anglo-America, and the Soviet Union. Among single nations, the United States is the leader with about 18 per cent of the world output, followed by the Soviet Union with approximately 17 per cent. The non-Communist nations account for about three-fourths of all milk, and the Communist nations for the remainder.

Most milk and milk products are consumed domestically, and the regions and nations of heaviest consumption tend also to be those of heaviest production. However, specific products vary sharply from country to country. In the United States, about one-half of all milk is consumed fresh, one-fourth made into butter, one-tenth into cheese, and the remainder used variously (Table 21.3). In other leading countries, the amount consumed as fresh

[1] Including Communist nations. Hence this figure differs from that of Table 21.1, where the Communist nations have been omitted.

TABLE 21.2

Leading regions of milk production

Area	*Per cent of world output*
Europe*	37.5
Anglo-America†	20.7
Soviet Union	17.0
Far East	8.4
Latin America	6.2
Near East	4.4
Oceania	3.7
Africa	2.1
Total	100.0

* Including Communist nations in Eastern Europe.
† The United States and Canada.
SOURCE: Computed from *The State of Food and Agriculture, 1958,* United Nations Food and Agriculture Organization, Rome, 1958, pp. 199–214.

milk ranges from 10 to 66 per cent of their respective total production figures. Of the milk products, butter is the leader, but its importance also varies sharply from nation to nation. It uses only 10 per cent of the domestically produced fresh milk of the United Kingdom, relatively the heaviest consumer of fluid milk shown in Table 21.3, but over 70 per cent in New Zealand, a surplus-milk producer which must sell such specialties in the world market—to the United Kingdom and other buyers. The percentages of milk used for other products also are inconsistent in different countries.

Viewed from the perspective of countries rather than commodities, the table offers an interesting bit of evidence concerning the von Thuenen circle theory of land use (Chapter 8). If urbanized Western Europe be considered as his "core city"—i.e., his focal market—then the dairying in such countries as the Netherlands and Denmark would lie within his "inner ring" of fluid-milk production, whereas dairying in such outlying areas as Australia and New Zealand would be in his "outer ring" of cheese and butter production. In the world scene, however, political boundaries, national self-interest, and still other considerations rear their ugly heads and cannot be dismissed by assumption. Such nations as the Netherlands and Denmark are surplus-milk producers, despite sizable domestic markets. They make most of their milk into butter, cheese, and lesser products—as do distant New Zealand and Australia. Thus these four nations, two in von Thuenen's "inner ring" and two in his "outer ring," are among the world's leading exporters of milk products.

Districts, or Belts, of Specialization. Specialization in dairy products tends to occur in places located (1) not far from urban markets and/or (2) in cool climates in which many crops will not mature but will grow well enough to provide forage, hay, and some grain for the dairy animals. As suggested by the von Thuenen theory, location in proximity to market aids in the transfer of the milk to market and at the same time reduces the danger of spoil-

TABLE 21.3

Production and utilization of milk in selected countries, 1958

Country	Total output, billions of pounds	Utilization, per cent of total output					
		Fluid milk	Butter	Cheese	Canned milk	Feed	Other uses
United States	125.2	50	25	10	4	2	9
France	47.0	20	40	19	—	18	3
West Germany	39.4	30	50	5	4	10	1
United Kingdom	25.9	66	10	10	3	7	4
Italy	20.6	28	17	28	n*	27	n
Canada	18.0	37	45	6	5	3	4
Netherlands	13.8	19	33	32	8	5	3
Australia	13.4	23	65	6	—	n	6
New Zealand	11.9	10	71	16	—	2	1
Denmark	11.3	16	60	13	—	5	6
Sweden	8.7	34	49	10	n	5	2
Belgium	8.4	23	64	2	—	8	3
Finland	7.0	41	51	6	—	2	n
Switzerland	6.4	36	23	24	—	15	2
Ireland	6.2	19	63	n	—	13	5
Austria	6.1	40	33	6	n	17	4

* Negligible—i.e., less than 1 per cent.

SOURCE: Computed from *Agricultural Statistics, 1959,* U.S. Department of Agriculture, 1960, p. 388. Minor amounts of goat and/or sheep milk are included in figures for Italy and Switzerland.

age. Location in cool climates makes possible the use of land where a short growing season otherwise would discourage the growing of crops which must ripen before being harvested. Dairy animals readily eat immature grain and silage, and many crops fed to them thus can be gathered before ripening. Also, the grasses and legumes which supply both forage and hay to dairy cattle thrive in cool climates. In addition, cool temperatures facilitate the preservation of milk, which sours quickly in hot climates.[2]

As we have noted in Chapter 7, the actual districts of specialization in dairy products are located in the northeastern United States, northern and Alpine Europe, southeastern Australia (including much of Tasmania), and northern New Zealand.

The dairy belt of the United States is very highly specialized, the herds being comprised almost entirely of cattle breeds developed for their milk-producing qualities. It is located within, and immediately to the north of, the nation's nodal region of urbanization and manufacturing, and thus illustrates well the attraction of both urban markets and cool climates to the dairy industry (Figs. 7.1, 7.8, and 5.1).

Although many European cattle are of dual-purpose breeds developed for producing both meat and milk, there is a marked tendency for specialization in milk animals in the two dairy areas of that continent. Characteristically, the emphasis in northwestern Europe is upon high yields per agricultural unit—in this case, per cow. As a result, the yields per animal in the Netherlands, Belgium, Denmark, Switzerland, West Germany, and the United Kingdom are higher than the national average for dairy cows of the United States, and those from the first three are higher than corresponding yields in this country's leading dairy states.

[2] However, with increasing technical advance, neither locational consideration is as important as formerly. Raising the level of transportation efficiency permits the industry to locate farther from markets and still remain competitive. Using new varieties of quick-maturing crops provides reasonable assurance of harvest in high latitudes. Modern methods of preservation and processing reduce the amount of spoilage due to warm temperatures.

A pipeline runs from the milking parlor to the cooling room of a dairy farm in the United States. Milk flows directly from the cows to the milking machine to this tank, with no human handling. Is automation coming to agriculture? (U.S. Department of Agriculture)

The areas of production in Australia and New Zealand also involve intensive production, but their respective yields of milk per animal are slightly lower than the national average for dairy cows in the United States. Because of the small populations and comparatively light domestic demand for their milk and milk products, these two nations are important exporters.

Production in Nonspecialty Areas. So much has been written and so many photographs have been printed concerning areas specializing in dairy products that it is possible to believe that all of the world's milk and milk products originate in such areas. This is not the case. In the United States, for example, about two-thirds of all milk is produced in the dairy belt and adjoining states—in the territory including and extending eastward from Kansas, Nebraska, and the Dakotas, and reaching northward from the Ohio River and projections from that river (Figs. 21.2 and 21.3). An additional one-fifth is produced in the southeast, including Texas and

Milking time at a collective farm near Tashkent in the Soviet Union (U.S. Department of Agriculture.

Oklahoma, and one-twelfth in the states touching and west of the Rocky Mountains. In Europe, the total milk output in either France or West Germany exceeds appreciably that of the countries located entirely or predominantly in the continent's dairy belts (Table 21.3). The Soviet Union, second only to the United States in world output, has no specific dairy belt (Fig. 7.1).

The production of milk in areas which do not specialize in its output appears to be appreciably a response to local urban markets. Almost every urban unit is supplied with milk from local dairies. Such production is usually integrated into commercial crop and livestock agricultural systems which, in turn, are components of technically advanced economies. This is most evident in those portions of the United States and Europe which lie beyond the respective dairy belts, and in the Soviet Union.

Surplus Production. The increasingly familiar problem of agricultural surpluses in certain technically advanced nations has arisen in connection with milk and its products. As yet, accumulated stocks of butter, cheese, and dried milk are minor in comparison with those of wheat, corn, or even cotton, but they do exist and are becoming more troublesome. Most of the stored merchandise is cheese, the supplies of which in 1958 amounted to some 280,000 metric tons. Substantial amounts of butter (about 190,000 metric tons) and some dried milk (40,999 metric tons) also are stored. Nearly half of the butter has accumulated in Europe and slightly less than one-third in Australia and New Zealand. Most other sizable stocks are in the United States.

Commerce

Domestic. The movement of milk and its products is largely domestic, particularly in large countries where national boundaries do not intersect normal trade routes. The patterns of milk shipment have become sufficiently congealed so that the milksheds from which each major and minor urban unit procures its supply are known. The actual transporting is done largely by tank truck and rail car, refrigerated when necessary, and a daily haul of 200 to 400 miles, or more, is not uncommon. In Europe, with its numerous small countries, the domestic haul generally does not involve long distances. Railway cars are employed to a greater degree in the transfer of milk in Europe than in the United States, but the truck is rapidly gaining favor.

International. Only a tiny fraction of fluid milk and less than one-seventh of all butter and cheese enter into international markets. One might expect that the largest flow of such commerce would focus upon Europe, with its many countries and its array of surpluses and deficiencies. This is correct. At least one-half of all international exports of butter

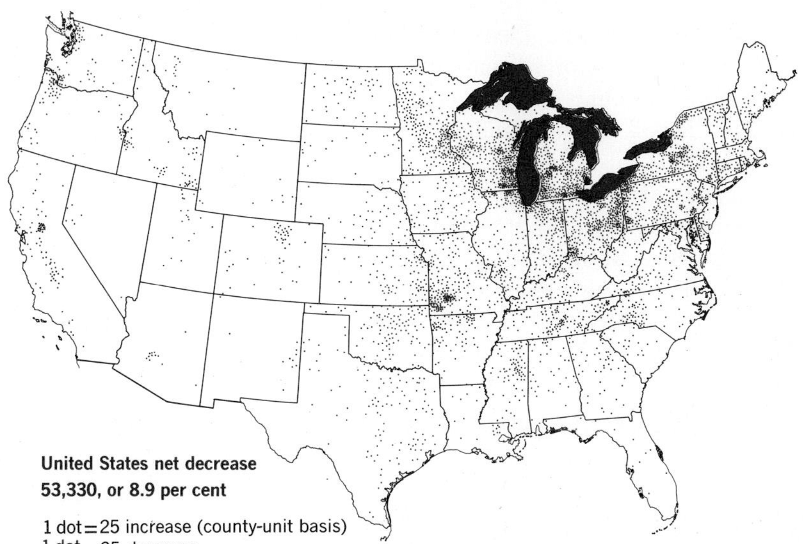

Figure 21.2 ***Increase and decrease in dairy farms of the United States, 1950–1954.*** *There is a marked decline in number of farms, notably in the dairy belt, but total milk yield has risen. How do you account for such trends? (U.S. Bureau of the Census)*

and of canned and powdered milk, and over two-thirds of all exported cheese, originate in Europe. About five-sixths of all butter and four-fifths of all cheese entering into world trade is imported into European countries. Commerce in powdered and canned milk varies somewhat in both volume and direction, sometimes being sent to nations plagued with temporary or chronic famine. Recently, the Far East has accepted nearly one-half of all this processed milk, and Europe somewhat more than one-eighth. Europe is thus outstanding among world regions in the international trade of milk and its products. Most of this commerce is among European countries rather than to and from Europe as a region.

Of individual nations, the United Kingdom is by far the leading importer, accepting as much as three-fourths of all butter and over one-half of all cheese. West Germany, Belgium, Luxembourg, and France (the last receiving butter only) are also

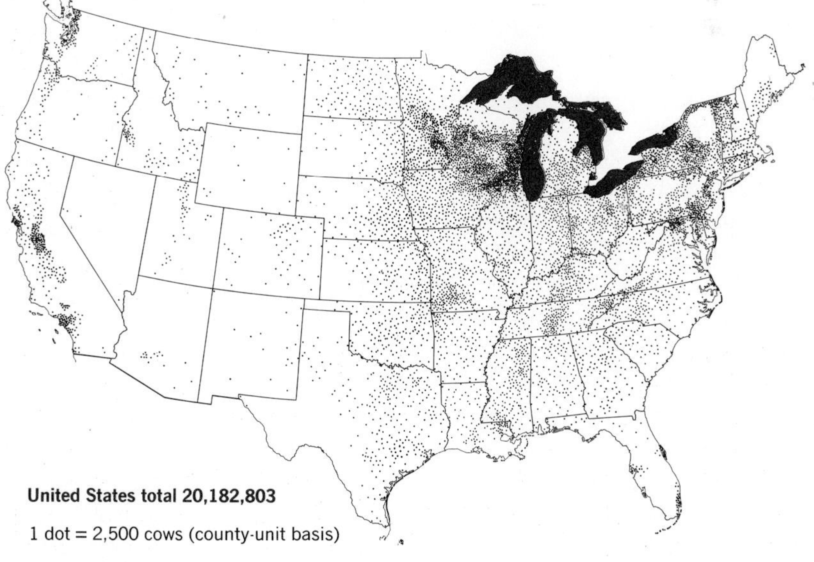

Figure 21.3 ***Milk cows in the United States.*** *There are many in the dairy belt, but many also are in the South and pockets of the West. How would this map compare with a map of human population? (U.S. Bureau of the Census)*

noteworthy importers. Denmark and the Netherlands are the most prominent exporters in Europe, but neither accounts for as much butter or cheese as does far-off New Zealand. Australia and the United States also are among the leaders in the forwarding of these commodities, Australia being particularly active in butter and the United States in cheese. The Netherlands is the dominant shipper of canned and powdered milk, followed by the United States, New Zealand, and Australia. Within the bloc of Communist nations there is essentially no trade in milk or its products at this time.

The dominant flow of milk and its products is thus among non-Communist, technically advanced nations, notably in Europe. Except in West Germany and Portugal, only rather modest import tariffs are maintained on these commodities by the more active trading nations. To a degree, the membership of Australia and New Zealand in the British Commonwealth and the sterling bloc results in a channeling of their exports toward the United Kingdom. By and large, however, world commerce in milk products appears to be more or less a direct response to supply-demand conditions and relatively unaffected by special political and economic arrangements.

BEEF AND VEAL

We have noted previously that animals are raised in both technically advanced and underdeveloped economies, and that records of their existence are not always complete, notably in underdeveloped nations. Available statistical data indicate that of all meat produced and consumed in the world, beef and veal account for about one-half, pork and pork-derived meat for about two-fifths, and mutton, lamb, and goat meat for most of the comparatively small remainder.[3] These data are probably reasonably accurate, especially with respect to beef and veal, which are produced in quantity primarily in technically advanced nations maintaining rather complete records.

BEEF AND VEAL CONSUMPTION

Approximately 25 million metric tons of beef and veal are consumed each year. Most is beef, obtained from sizable animals usually ranging in age from eighteen months to three years at the time of slaughter. Veal, which is the meat of calves usually not over twelve weeks old, is not consumed so actively; in the United States, for example, approximately 9 pounds of beef are consumed for each pound of veal.

Among individual nations, the United States is without serious competition in aggregate consumption, accounting for approximately 30 per cent of all beef and veal. Secondary nations include the Soviet Union, Argentina, Brazil, and some of the more dynamic countries of Western Europe.

Beef and veal are utilized almost entirely as foods, and yet they are relatively inefficient converters of natural environmental nutrients into calories for the human diet. Except in the few and usually small societies practicing nomadic and quasi-nomadic grazing, beef and veal can be considered more or less as luxuries, available in sizable amounts only to economies which can afford them, and their consumption occurs mainly in technically advanced nations. The United States, ranking comparatively high in per capita consumption and extremely high in total consumption, is an excellent example of an economy which can afford them.

However, a number of technically advanced nations of small to intermediate size rank higher than the United States in per capita consumption. Included in this list are Argentina, Uruguay, New Zealand, Australia, Denmark, and Ireland. Each of these contains a rather small population and a cattle industry sufficiently active to enable it to export—in other words, each contains a surplus of domestic supply over demand. A high per capita consumption of beef and veal thus tends to be encouraged in such countries, some of which rank rather low

[3] *Agricultural Statistics, 1959,* U.S. Department of Agriculture, 1960, p. 362.

among technically advanced nations when considered as to level of living. Thus, the consumption of beef and veal, while predominant in technically advanced nations, is not necessarily a close indication of level of living.

BEEF AND VEAL PRODUCTION

Global distribution

The habitat of cattle is extensive, the animals being found in all continents and at latitudes ranging from 60° N to 50° S. With allowance for the unusual situation which we have already noted in India and Pakistan, the world's cattle tend to be concentrated in milder climates—more specifically, in the middle latitudes and at intermediate elevations of the low latitudes. Among climate types, the marine, humid continental warm-summer, humid continental cool-summer, and humid subtropical all contain rather large numbers of cattle. Each of these types, it will be noted, is rather consistently moist, and is capable of growing enough agricultural commodities to support large numbers of both human beings and livestock (compare Figs. 7.1 and 5.1). In contrast, in such climates as semiarid, tropical savanna, or mediterranean, which are either continuously or seasonally dry, generally there are not so many cattle—despite the fact that livestock frequently plays a primary role in the economies with which these climates are associated.

Since international trade in live animals is comparatively light, the primary nations of beef and veal production are those with large cattle populations. There are, of course, exceptions. We have noted, for example, that India realizes only a small percentage of its potential beef production. Also, some dairy areas produce less beef than the size of their cattle populations might indicate. Nevertheless, the world patterns of beef and veal output and of cattle population are reasonably similar.

Leading nations and regions of production

The United States, supplying almost 30 per cent of the world output, has no peers among nations in beef and veal production. Of secondary importance are the Soviet Union and Argentina, each of which accounts for less than one-tenth of the grand total. Brazil, West Germany, France, Australia, the United Kingdom, and Canada are noteworthy producers.

North America, Europe, and Latin America are the leading regions of production, and they aggregately are responsible for about three-fourths of the world total. North America's position is due largely to the high output of the United States, although Canada and Mexico are not unimportant. In contrast, both Europe and Latin America contain several nations which rank above the world average, and their rather high positions as beef- and veal-producing regions are due to the number of nations they contain rather than to the output of any single nation.

The United States. Certainly one of the most remarkable characteristics of beef and veal production in the United States is its growth over the past quarter century. In 1957, the total number of cattle being kept for other than dairy purposes was over twice as large as in 1930, and the production of beef and veal also essentially doubled during the same period.[4] Among reasons for such a dramatic increase are (1) the decline in the number of draft animals and (2) the rise in number and level of living of the American people. The horse-and-mule population of this country is now only about one-fourth as large as it was in 1920, and the substantial amount of cropland released from producing their feed can now be used for other purposes, including beef and veal production. With the rise in the country's level of living and its population has come a growing demand for meat. Thus there has been a growth stimulus from both the supply and the demand sides of the economic equation.

VEAL. From the standpoint of United States production, it is somewhat misleading to classify veal with beef, for a substantial amount of the former comes from dairy herds. Since only a few of the male progeny are kept for breeding purposes, most are either butchered for veal while very young

[4] *Agricultural Statistics, 1957,* U.S. Department of Agriculture, 1958, pp. 376 and 430.

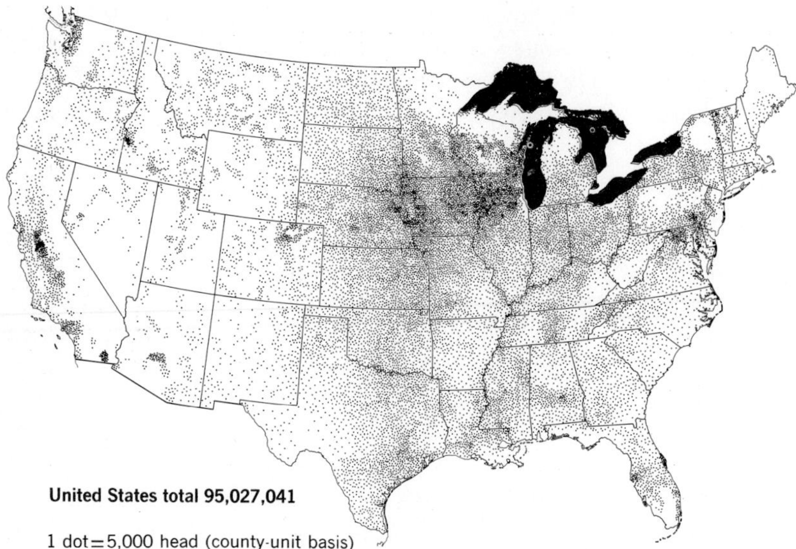

Figure 21.4 ***Distribution of all cattle, both beef and dairy, in the United States.*** *The corn belt leads, but the density is rather heavy throughout much of the nation. Few or no cattle occur in very mountainous, very dry, very cold, and very swampy places. (U.S. Bureau of the Census)*

or fattened for subsequent slaughter. Fattening the somewhat stringy dairy animals, however, is not always economically sound, and much of the nation's veal comes from bull calves born to the dairy herds. The importance of the dairy belt in veal production is suggested by the high-ranking position of Wisconsin, New York, Pennsylvania, and Michigan in the slaughter of calves.

However, the dairy belt is by no means the only source of supply for the nation's veal; Texas ranks immediately behind Wisconsin in calf slaughter, and a number of states in the Central, Far Western, and Southern parts of the country are at least noteworthy suppliers.

BEEF. The trend toward urbanization and specialized employment in the United States has meant an increase in commercial beef production. More and more people are either moving to or being born in the town and city, and they are buying their beef and other meat in packages wrapped neatly in plastic containers. The dominant market, of course, lies in the manufacturing belt, but the Far Western and Southern states are of rising importance.

The immediate sources of supply to the very large slaughter houses are located generally on, or somewhat beyond, the western periphery of the nation's manufacturing belt. Omaha, Chicago, Kansas City, Denver, Fort Worth, Oklahoma City, and St. Joseph (Missouri) are the leading beef-packing centers. Very many small packing plants are clustered within and near the nation's effective areas.

Slaughter cattle reach the nation's large packing houses from farms and feed lots in which livestock raising or fattening are either specialties or one of several interests. They may or may not have been born on the farms from which they are shipped to market. Approximately 58 per cent are estimated to be produced in the Western range, the unirrigated, natural grassland of the nation's seventeen Western states.[5] Most of the remainder are grown on crop and livestock farms of the Middle West, South, and Far West (Fig. 21.4). The animals which are born on the open range usually are transferred to feed lots for fattening at ages ranging from twelve to thirty months. A few, however, are slaughtered while "grass fat"—in other words, when they become as heavy as possible from grazing the range. In either case they are shipped from the grass country. The feed lots which receive most of them are located chiefly within or near the corn belt. There the range cattle often are joined by home-grown herds for a few months of intensive

[5] M. E. Ensminger, *Beef Cattle Husbandry*, Interstate Printers and Publishers, Danville, Ill., 1955, p. 105. This estimate may be high.

feeding before being forwarded to the slaughter houses.

The corn belt long has been the leading region in the fattening of beef, despite the fact that only about 17 per cent of beef cattle nutrition is estimated to be supplied by corn and other concentrates.[6] The roughage which supplies most of the remaining 83 per cent is often made up of corn silage as well as alfalfa, clover, grass hay, and other crops which are easily grown there.

A major, if not more important, factor responsible for the focusing of beef-cattle feed lots upon the corn belt is its location. The open range is to the west, and the city markets are to the east; where better is there a spot for fattening cattle on their way to market? It will be interesting to see whether a similar industry develops on the western side of the open range country as the Pacific Coast markets become larger.

The breeds are increasingly the heavy beef types—Aberdeen Angus, Hereford, the fleshier strains of Shorthorn, etc. In the South, where high temperatures and insects and diseases discourage these breeds, successful efforts have been made to cross them with Zebu and other low-latitude cattle. The result has been a number of distinctly new breeds which produce satisfactory meat and yet are comparatively unaffected by the natural conditions which discourage traditional breeds.

With increasing commercialization of beef production have come larger and more highly mechanized farms and ranches, and a marked decline in their number (Fig. 21.5). This is in keeping with a national trend which we have already noted. However, the livestock industry—whether involving beef cattle, dairy cattle, or swine—is being affected to a degree exceeding the national average. On the whole, only the largest farming units are increasing, regardless of location. Economies of scale are again being demonstrated: the well-financed, mechanized large holding is proving that it can outproduce, unit for unit, the small farmer, and the latter is losing in competition. Interestingly, most of the decreases in number of livestock farms are occurring in the corn belt—where cash-grain farms have *increased* the most rapidly (Fig. 17.7). It would appear that more livestock farmers and diversified farmers now grow grain for sale and that professional feeders buy the grain for their feed lots.

[6] *Ibid.*, p. 177.

The harness registers how many times the animal stretches its neck, lies down, stands up—even the number of times it switches its tail. This time-and-motion study is to produce better beef—and ox-tail soup. (British Information Services)

Other Producing Countries. The United States is so outstanding in commercial beef and veal production that it would be misleading to give any other nation individual treatment. As a group, however, the remaining nations are not inconsequential, for they supply about 70 per cent of the world output.

Among these secondary nations two types of farms are recognizable: (1) those in which the cattle are grown in conjunction with commercial crop and livestock farming, and (2) those in which the animals are raised on livestock ranches and shipped elsewhere for fattening.[7] There is a tendency for

[7] To a degree, both types are also represented in the United States, the first in the humid East and Middle West and the second in the range country of the arid and semiarid West.

Conveyor belts carry cattle feed from the silo to the feeding trough. More and more feed-lot operators in the United States now buy their feed rather than raise it themselves and concentrate their attention wholly upon cattle fattening. (Successful Farming and Century Electric Company)

the first to be oriented toward domestic markets, and for the second to be oriented to both foreign and domestic markets. Most European countries contain good examples of the first type, and Argentina and Australia good examples of the second. Other farming systems, such as are found in the Soviet Union, Brazil, and Canada, do not fit satisfactorily into either category but contain examples of both (Fig. 7.1).

Because of the scarcity of good agricultural land in Europe and because of the inefficiency of animals in transferring calories from nature to the human diet, the best land of Europe is planted largely to crops which can be eaten directly. The cattle are grown and fattened largely on pasture and root crops and their by-products, such as beet pulp, the sugar content of the roots being relied upon to help bring the animals to slaughter condition. Although beef breeds are present, dual-purpose breeds predominate. The meat, while not as fine in quality as that produced by grain and other concentrates used in the United States, is both palatable and nutritious. France, West Germany, and the United Kingdom are the leading European producers. France, Denmark, and Ireland are more than noteworthy exporters.

The beef cattle in Argentina and Australia are grown primarily on sizable holdings located in the immediate hinterlands of seaports which core each country's nodal region of economic activity. In Argentina, this hinterland focuses upon Buenos Aires and nearby cities, and in Australia upon Sidney, Melbourne, and Adelaide. The cattle thus move only short distances from their pastures to the slaughter houses where their carcasses are readied for either domestic or foreign markets. Especially in Argentina, they are fattened for slaughter chiefly on alfalfa and other legumes. While both nations depend mainly upon such cool-latitude beef breeds as Hereford and Angus, each also has a minor, low-latitude beef industry, the meat of which usually is canned for domestic and foreign consumption. As in the South of the United States, the animals raised in hot climates frequently are the result of crossbreeding of imported beef types with native cattle.

The Soviet Union is the only Communist nation with a well-developed commercial cattle industry. Its annual volume of beef production is now second only to that of the United States. Emphasis on beef since the Second World War has been moderate in comparison with that on swine, and output has risen by about 10 per cent of the country's 1951–1955 average. The animals are well distributed throughout the country's effective area of population and economic activity, in apparent conformation with the national policy of maximizing local output of commodities and thereby reducing the volume of internal freight traffic. In the more humid northern portion of that effective area, the cattle are part of a commercial crop-and-livestock-farming system not unlike that of Europe except for the presence in Russia of collective and state farms. In the semiarid land to the south and east, there is a

collectives
rther north
re per ani-
r, much of
the well-
d has been
ng to agri-

estic

estic mar-
and trans-
farming.
ming usu-
ch are the
ucts, and
r of for-
most, the
ast, areas
dominated by livestock ranching tend to be farther from their urban markets, and, especially in such large nations as the United States and Canada, their cattle are shipped to market by truck or rail over appreciable distances. As we have noted, the animals commonly are not shipped all the way at one time but are diverted for a few months to intermediately located feed lots and farms for fattening before being forwarded to the slaughter houses.

Refrigerated trucks, railway cars, and ocean vessels have made possible the relatively easy domestic and international transportation of beef.

International

The low percentage of beef and even lower percentage of live cattle entering into international trade chiefly involve a commerce among technically advanced nations. The major flow is from the Southern to the Northern Hemispheres—from Argentina, Australia, and New Zealand to the United Kingdom and other countries of northwestern Europe, and interestingly, the United States. To an extent, such affiliations as the British Commonwealth and the sterling bloc affect this trade, but such uncommitted countries as Argentina and Uruguay negotiate largely as independents, selling to the highest bidder. Some actual and potential importing nations have restrictive tariffs, quotas, disease and contamination inspections, etc., which reduce the volume of their incoming shipments.

One may well ask what will become of this

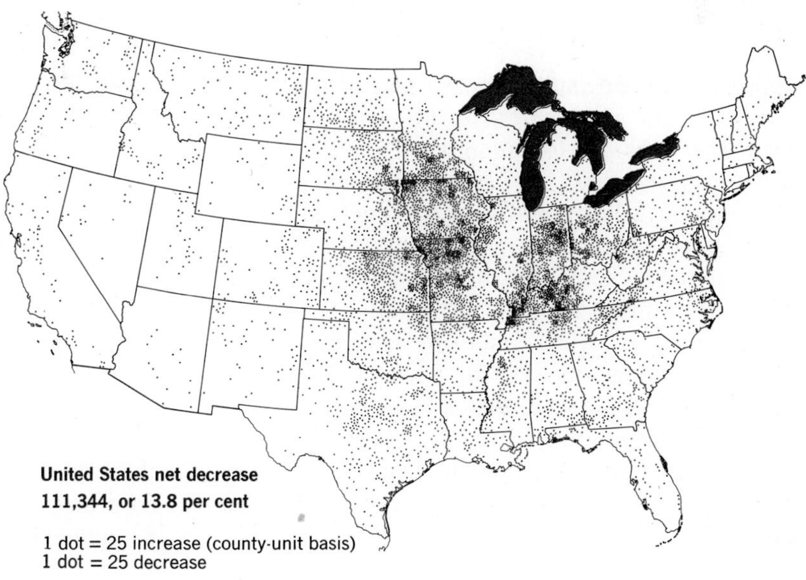

Figure 21.5 ***Increase and decrease in livestock farms of the United States, 1950–1954. There are fewer but larger farms in the traditional livestock-feeding area. Also, some former livestock farms now are cash-grain farms. (U.S. Bureau of the Census)***

trade if and when the European Economic Community and similar plans are fully realized, for these plans envision "Europe for the Europeans"—i.e., the supplying of more European demand for agricultural products from European soil. Where, then, will Argentina and other outlying surplus-producing areas sell their beef? In the United States, itself a heavy producer? In the Soviet Union?

PORK, BACON, AND HAM

Often dismissed as a lowly animal, the hog has found its way into an interesting array of technically advanced and underdeveloped economies. Indeed, except in portions of eastern and southern Asia, the swine population of the world is distributed geographically in a pattern not unlike that of the human population. Not overly handsome and sometimes unaware of life's niceties, this animal is an efficient producer of calories, whether from grain, acorns, skim milk, garbage, or what-have-you. In addition, it reaches slaughter size quickly: usually less than a year is necessary to bring the animals to slaughterable condition. From six to ten pigs make up a litter, and two litters per year are not uncommon. Furthermore, a hog can live in a variety of natural environmental conditions—in the open air where climatic and other excesses are absent or in small and inexpensive shelters.

CONSUMPTION OF PORK AND ITS DERIVED PRODUCTS

Approximately 20 million metric tons of pork, bacon, and ham are reported to be consumed each year. This excludes Communist China, which is a heavy consumer but as yet has not reported its consumption of pork and pork products, although it has reported its swine population. Consumption in Communist China probably exceeds appreciably that of the United States, which is far ahead of any other nation for which data are available. Other prominent nations include the Soviet Union, West Germany, and France. Europe as a region is a major consumer, accounting for nearly one-half of the reported total. Probably one-half of all pork and its products is consumed on each side of the iron curtain.

PRODUCTION AND TRADE OF PORK AND DERIVED MEAT PRODUCTS

Swine are raised largely in the nations where they are consumed, and an even smaller percentage of live animals and meat enters into the world market than is true of beef. Such trade as does occur is primarily in bacon, ham, and salt pork rather than fresh meat and is appreciably a movement within Western Europe. The United Kingdom is unquestionably the leading importing nation, and Denmark, the Netherlands, and Ireland are the major Western European exporters. A secondary movement occurs within the Communist bloc and involves exports from Poland and Communist China to the Soviet Union.

Communist China

The more than one hundred million swine of Communist China are scattered rather generously throughout the lowlands of the east and hill country of the southeast, and clustered in the Szechwan basin to the southwest. Like poultry, which also are scavengers in Communist China, they are present in almost every type of farming area and under varying natural environmental conditions. An increase in their numbers is being encouraged under the Communist regime.

The United States

In sharp contrast to Communist China, the United States treats most of its swine very well during their short stay on this earth, pampering them with corn and other grain, skim milk, alfalfa and other leguminous pasture as well as grass, and even

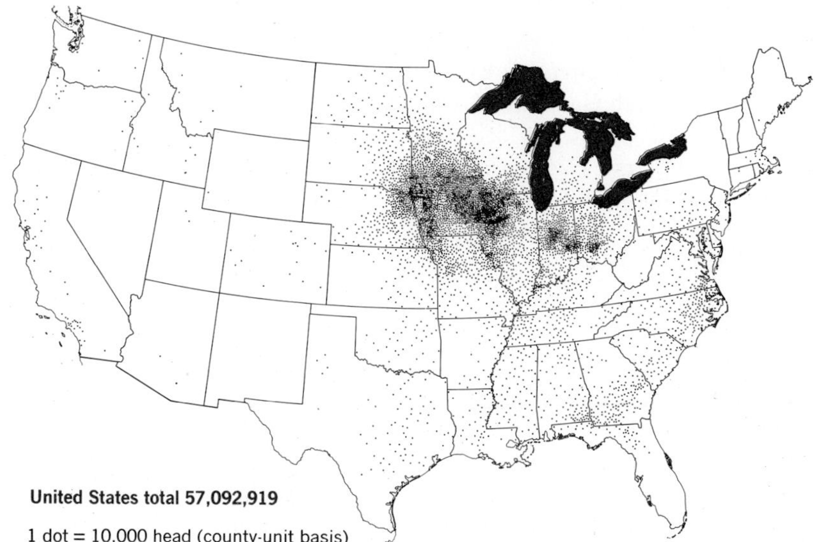

Figure 21.6 ***Distribution of hogs in the United States.*** *There is no mistaking the area of heaviest density. (U.S. Bureau of the Census)*

tempting them with specially prepared concentrates. 'Tis a privilege to be a pig in a technically advanced country! Yet some scavenger aspects remain. A comparatively few swine are raised on garbage, most of which is now cooked to avoid human infection with trichinosis and other diseases traceable through pork to such waste. More are placed in the same feed lots with cattle being fattened for slaughter, and these obtain an appreciable portion of their nourishment from grain and other feed not thoroughly digested by the cattle.[8]

Most of the nation's swine, like most of its beef, are fattened in the corn belt; but, unlike much of the beef, nearly all are born on the farms and feed lots where they are fattened (Fig. 21.6). Iowa alone contains nearly one-fifth of the national total, and Illinois and Indiana jointly contain another one-fifth. Most of the remainder are scattered throughout the southern and eastern portions of the country.

The national volume of pork production has not increased appreciably during the past quarter century in the United States, during which time the output of beef and veal here has nearly doubled. This has been due largely to a heightened demand for beef and veal which an increased level of living has made possible. Production of lard from hogs also is declining relatively, partially because of competition with vegetable oils from soybeans, cottonseed, and other domestic sources.

The number of farms specializing wholly or partly in pork production is decreasing in the United States, whereas the number of cash-grain farms is increasing (Figs. 21.5 and 17.7). This is true especially in the corn belt. The smallest farming units appear to be suffering the greatest number of casualties.

The Soviet Union

Long an important swine producer, the Soviet Union has placed an emphasis upon this commodity since the Second World War, and its annual yield of pork and pork products has risen by nearly 70 per cent of its 1951–1955 average. The over-all pattern of swine growth there coincides closely with the country's effective area. However, the majority of the animals are raised on collective farms in the southern half of the commercial livestock and farming region, chiefly in European Russia but extending around the Urals into Asia. Swine raising also overlaps into the commercial grain region.

[8] This practice, however, is being discouraged somewhat by the fattening of younger cattle which, although they add weight much more rapidly than three-year-olds and four-year-olds, are more efficient in their food digestion. Thus fewer hogs can be fattened in the same feed lots.

Other countries

The swine production of Europe is concentrated notably in West Germany, Poland, and East Germany, where root crops are feed mainstays. The United Kingdom, Czechoslovakia, Hungary, Denmark, and Spain also are important. Indeed, swine are present in impressive numbers throughout most of Europe.

South of the equator, swine are virtually absent in the Eastern Hemisphere. They are present, however, in Latin America—conspicuously so in Brazil, which ranks behind only the three world leaders.

WOOL

Wool[9] long has been a textile mainstay. It remains so in this twentieth century, despite increased utilization of plant fibers and the comparatively recent development of artificial threads. Measured by tonnage, it is now produced and consumed in amounts exceeded among agricultural fibers only by cotton and jute.

WOOL CONSUMPTION

Most wool, unlike cotton, is consumed shortly after production, and essentially no stores are accumulating. The annual consumption thus is equal to that of production, which currently is estimated to be nearly 2 million metric tons, including grease which amounts to over one-third of its total weight (Table 21.1). About seven-tenths of this is used for apparel, knit goods, and blankets, and the remaining three-tenths for carpets and diverse purposes not requiring quality fibers.

Wool consumption is concentrated in the more populous technically advanced lands, which coincidentally are located in climates sufficiently cold to encourage use of warm clothing at least part of the year. Western Europe is the largest regional consumer, using up nearly two-fifths of the annual world production (Fig. 21.7). Among individual nations, the United Kingdom is outstanding, accounting for about one-seventh of the world total. The United States ranks second, with about one-tenth. The Soviet Union is conspicuously in third place and is rapidly rising; between 1950 and 1958, an increase there of 60 per cent has been recorded. Australia, France, West Germany, Japan, Argentina, Italy, and Belgium also are prominent consuming nations. Western Europe consumes over one-third of all wool.

Although both the Soviet Union and Communist China are emphasizing wool, the consumption within the Communist bloc as yet is light in comparison with that elsewhere. Only about one-sixth of all wool is used up behind the iron curtain.

[9] The world annual output of mutton and lamb averages about twice the tonnage and approximately the same value as wool. Mutton and lamb, however, account for less than one-fifth of the world's recorded meat supply, whereas wool is a major fiber. To avoid becoming excessively encyclopedic we shall concentrate upon the fiber and refer only occasionally to the meat.

WOOL PRODUCTION

Natural conditions and agricultural practices

Sheep can graze on pasture where cattle and horses would starve. Their populations therefore encroach upon the world's drier sections to a greater extent than is true of any other domestic animals except goats and camels. Much wool thus is produced in marginal lands of Australia, the Soviet Union, New Zealand, Argentina, the Union of South Africa, the United States, Communist China, Spain, and elsewhere (Fig. 21.7). In most cases these marginal lands are excessively dry, but in some cases they are too wet or too mountainous for other effective uses. Where wool, particularly carpet wool and other inferior grades, is the primary objective, the sheep can be grazed in such pastures throughout most of the year and need be fed, if at all, only

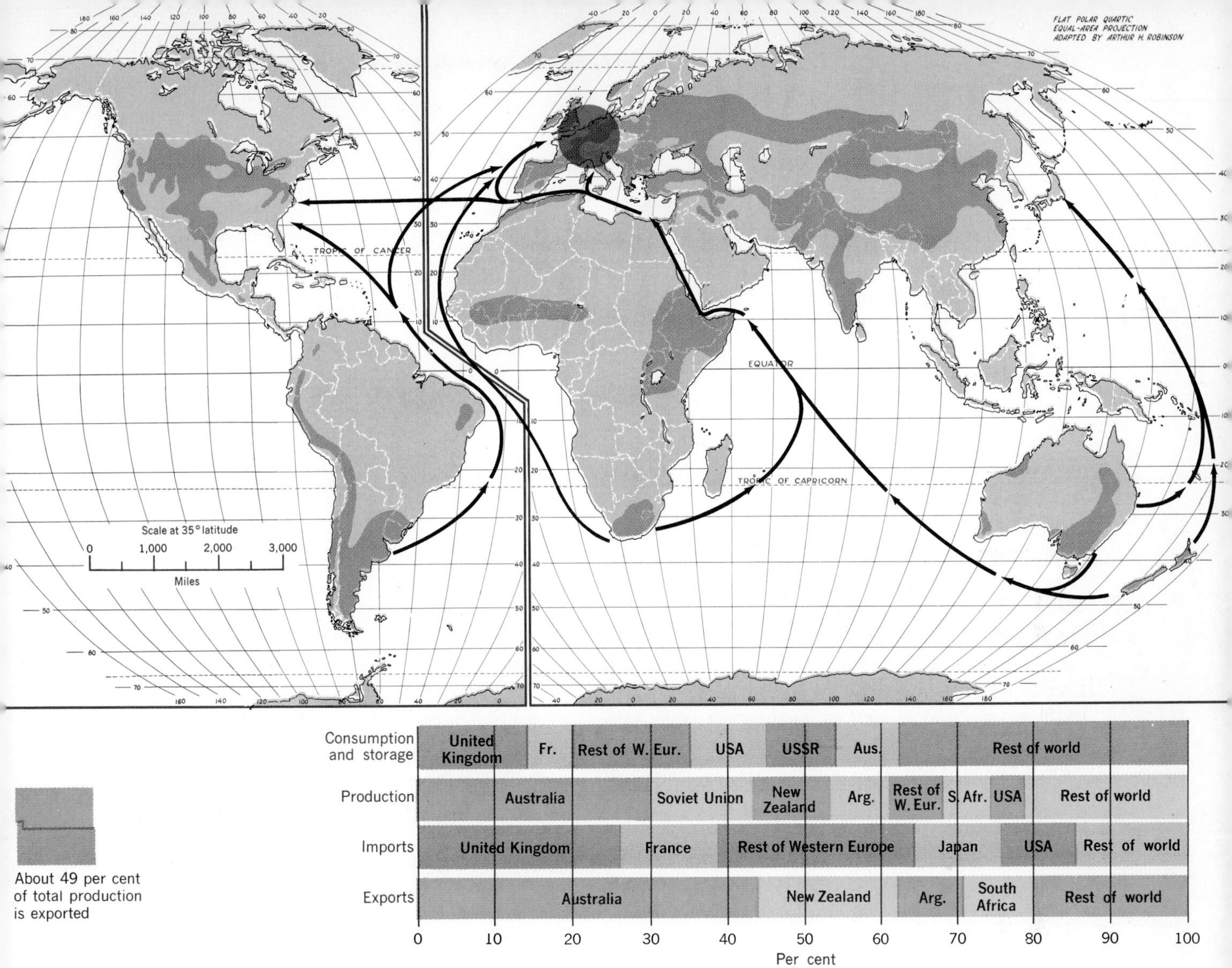

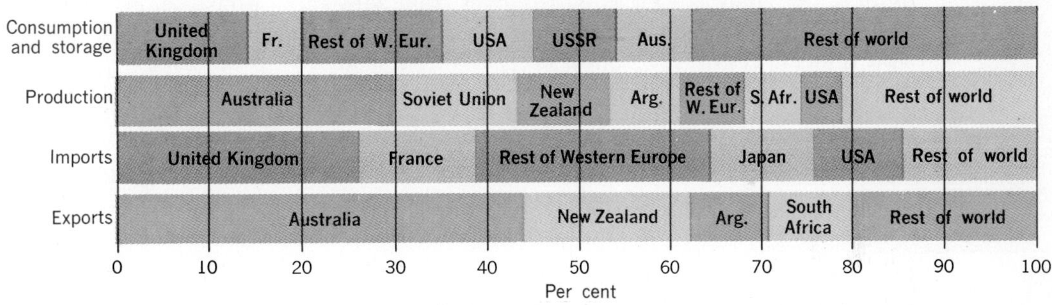

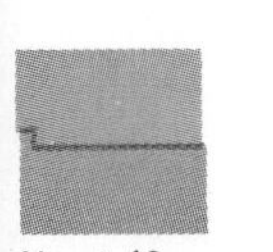

About 49 per cent of total production is exported

Figure 21.7 ***Consumption, production, import, and export of wool.*** *The circle shows the region of very heavy consumption. Should circles have been added for the United States, the Soviet Union, and Australia? The stippling shows the areas where most of the world's sheep are raised. Not all of these are raised for wool; some produce mutton instead. This is especially true of the sheep of the United Kingdom and other parts of northwestern Europe.*

during such times and in such amounts as is necessary to tide them over to the next pasture season. Under such conditions, there is little need for concern about balanced diets, etc., for most of the animals are not going to be fattened and converted into mutton or lamb chops. However, where the better-quality wool, or both meat and wool, are being sought, more attention is given to the conditions under which the animals are grown and fed. This occurs mainly in technically advanced countries, especially in Europe and the eastern United States, where the markets for mutton are close enough to areas of production so that meat as well as wool is an important commodity. It occurs also in some nations which, although shipping their commodities over long distances, have

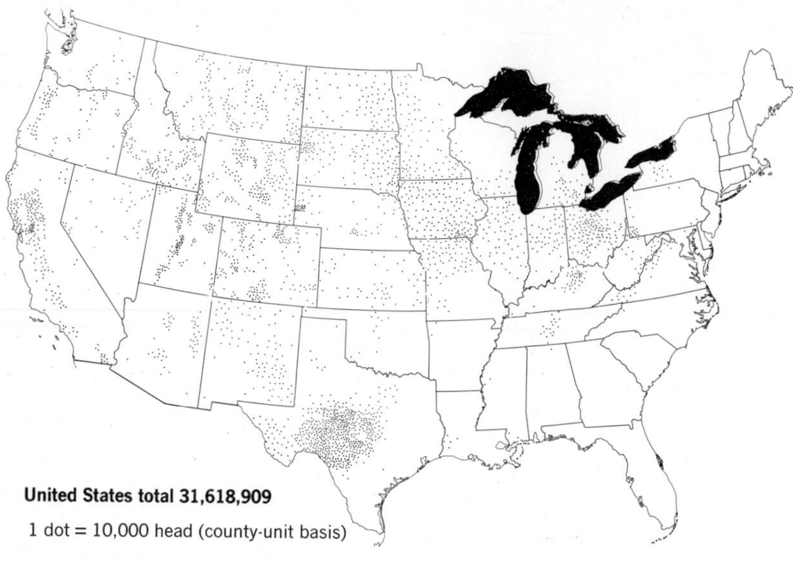

Figure 21.8 ***Where the sheep of the United States are raised.*** *Why the concentration in southwestern Texas? (U.S. Bureau of the Census)*

developed a policy of following careful agricultural practices in order to compete in the world market. For example, an appreciable quantity of mutton and lamb as well as wool moves from Australia and New Zealand to Europe, and as much care is given to the flocks in these two nations as in much of Western Europe.

Nations

Over two-thirds of the world's recorded production of wool comes from sparsely populated nations of the Southern Hemisphere (Fig. 21.7). Australia, with nearly one-third of the world total, is the leader of this group, and New Zealand, Argentina, and the Union of South Africa are very important producers.

Of the remaining one-third, most is produced in nations of its consumption. The Soviet Union, now ranking behind Australia in world output, uses up essentially all of its annual supply. The United States, now producing at less than three-fourths of demonstrated capacity, not only uses up domestic supplies but also imports an even larger amount than is produced at home. Figure 21.8 shows the distribution of sheep in the United States. The nations of Western Europe aggregately produce about one-fourth of their annual voracious consumption.

TRADE IN WOOL

Domestic

Slightly over one-half of all wool is consumed domestically. It is probable that this amount will rise in the immediate future as the output of the Soviet Union and Communist China increases, for both these nations are producing almost entirely for domestic consumption. Except in small countries where men and animals necessarily are crowded together, this trade involves movement, usually by land, over appreciable distances; for, as we have indicated, many sheep are grown in outlying places of marginal productivity that are located even farther from urban agglomerations than are the most extensive types of crop production.

International

World trade in wool is focused sharply upon Western Europe, particularly the United Kingdom, and upon the United States and Japan (Fig. 21.7). Well over two-thirds of this trade moves to Western Europe, over one-fourth going to the United Kingdom alone. Japan and the United States take about one-tenth each. Other importing nations are of much less significance. Australia is easily the leading exporter, followed by New Zealand. These two nations furnish over three-fifths of all exports. Argentina and the Union of South Africa also are important exporters. Wool moves largely from technically advanced economies of the Southern Hemisphere to technically advanced economies of the Northern Hemisphere.

REFERENCES

Calef, Wesley: "The Winter of 1948–49 in the Great Plains," *Annals of the Association of American Geographers,* **40:**267–292, 1950.

Clark, Richard T.: *Production Factors in Range Cattle under Northern Great Plains Conditions,* U.S. Government Printing Office, 1958.

Cooper, M. M.: *Beef Production,* Thomas Nelson & Sons, Ltd., London, 1953.

Critchfield, Howard J.: "The Growth of Pastoralism in Southland, New Zealand," *Economic Geography,* **30:**283–300, 1954.

Davis, Charles M.: "Merino Sheep on the Australian Riverina," *Geographical Review,* **44:**475–494, 1954.

Durand, Loyal, Jr.: "The Migration of Cheese Manufacture in the United States," *Annals of the Association of American Geographers,* **42:**263–282, 1952.

Ensminger, M. E.: *Beef Cattle Husbandry,* Interstate Printers and Publishers, Danville, Ill., 1955.

Henderson, David A.: "'Corn Belt' Cattle Feeding in Eastern Colorado's Irrigated Valleys," *Economic Geography,* **30:**364–372, 1954.

Wallace, William H.: "Railway Traffic and Agriculture in New Zealand," *Economic Geography,* **34:**168–184, 1958.

Weir, Thomas R.: "The Winter Feeding Period in the Southern Interior Plateau of British Columbia," *Annals of the Association of American Geographers,* **44:**194–204, 1954.

22 FOREST-PRODUCTS INDUSTRIES: ROUNDWOOD

WHENEVER AND WHEREVER MAN HAS INHABITED FORESTS, HE HAS FOUND THEM almost indispensable in the obtainment of food, shelter, fuel, and even some types of clothing. His dependence upon them has been exceeded, perhaps, only by his greed; and, as early as 2,500 years ago, practices of controlled forest management were initiated in China to save a declining resource—practices which appear to have ended when the Chou dynasty of that now appreciably deforested land was succeeded by less wise rulers.[1]

Despite human marauding into the choicest stands, however, forests are still very widespread, covering over one-fourth of the earth's land surface (Figs. 22.1 and 6.2).[2] We have noted in Chapter 6 that they reach discontinuously from the equator as far as lat 70° N, and as far south as the tips of nonicebound continents. The acreage of broadleaf forests exceeds that of conifers by an approximate ratio of 2:1. About-two thirds of the world's forests are in sufficiently thick stands and are of sufficiently high quality to be classified as productive. However, nearly one-half of the productive forests occur in isolated places—high mountains, continental interiors, very cold and very hot country, etc.—and hence are classified as inaccessible. Thus only slightly more than one-third of the world's forests are considered to be both productive and accessible at man's current levels of technology. Of these productive, accessible forests, about one-third are coniferous and the remainder are hardwoods. Most of the coniferous forests are in the middle and high latitudes, and most of the hardwood forests are in the low latitudes.[3] When considered in terms of per capita reserves of the major world divisions, the Soviet Union, Latin America, North America, and Oceania are outstanding possessors of accessible forests (Fig. 22.2).

A surprising variety of materials is obtained from trees, the more common being timber, fruits and nuts, vegetable oils, natural rubber, naval

[1] D. Y. Lin, "China," in *A World Geography of Forest Resources,* edited for the American Geographical Society by Stephen Haden-Guest, John K. Wright, and Eileen M. Teclaff, copyright 1956 The Ronald Press Company, New York, p. 693.

[2] Although by no means in virgin stands.

[3] See also W. S. Woytinsky and E. S. Woytinsky, *World Population and Production,* The Twentieth Century Fund, Inc., New York, 1953, p. 693.

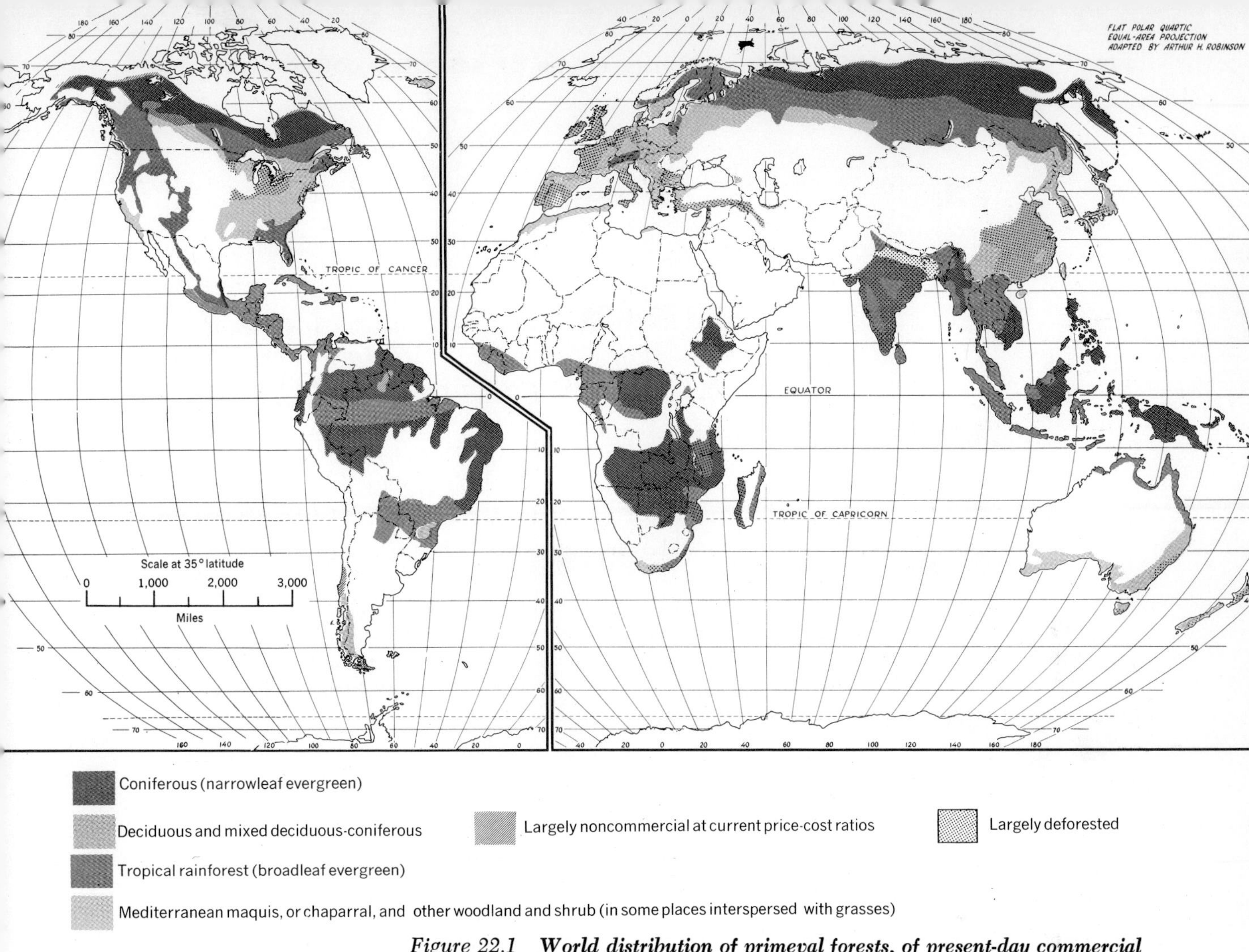

Figure 22.1 ***World distribution of primeval forests, of present-day commercial forests, and of deforestation.***

stores (tar, pitch, turpentine, etc.), cork, tannin extract, camphor, quinine, and sugar.[4] Many of these, however, are domesticated, and their output represents agriculture rather than forest-products industries (see pages 5–9). Among the commodities obtained primarily from forest-products industries, *roundwood* is outstanding. Roundwood is raw timber that as yet has not been cut to dimension timber. It is the product of tree trunks and larger branches from which all small branches have been trimmed.

[4] An excellent and moving appeal for more active development, use, and care of trees has been made by the distinguished geographer J. Russell Smith in *Tree Crops: A Permanent Agriculture,* The Devin-Adair Company, New York, 1950.

CONSUMPTION

Of the world's total annual cut of roundwood, over 700 million cubic meters are estimated to be consumed largely as fuel, and over 900 million as industrial raw materials.[5] Much of the fuel wood is used for cooking, space heating, etc., but most industrial wood is forwarded to sawmills, pulp and paper plants, and fiberboard factories. There is much waste, in both forest and factory.

[5] *The State of Food and Agriculture, 1958,* United Nations Food and Agriculture Organization, Rome, 1958, p. 196. See also Table 22.3 showing production. Keep in mind that almost no roundwood enters into international trade, so that production nearly equals consumption.

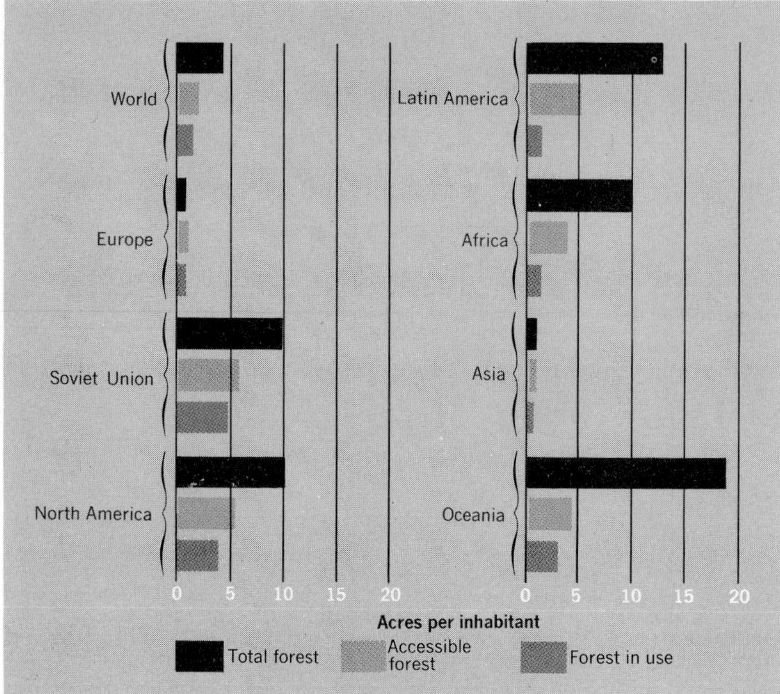

Figure 22.2 ***Acres per inhabitant of total, accessible, and utilized forests for the world and its major divisions.*** *Accessible forest is that which can be reached feasibly by commercial transportation. Why the large difference between total and accessible forests in all major divisions but Europe and Asia (excluding the Soviet Union)? (After* State of Food and Agriculture, 1955, *United Nations Food and Agricultural Organization, p. 6)*

Fuel wood

The Soviet Union and Brazil are the leading recorded users of fuel wood. Nations of secondary importance are Indonesia, the United States, Japan, and France (Table 22.3; the table shows production, which is almost identical with consumption). Technically advanced nations, plus underdeveloped Brazil, Indonesia, and Communist China, thus are at the top of the user list. However, a sizable amount of fuel wood is consumed by the numerous underdeveloped countries, their aggregate share being recorded at over one-half the world total. Their actual share probably is much higher, as the reporting of data is not always too complete in such lands.

Most fuel wood is hardwood, which prevails in the forest of the low latitudes, where the majority of the underdeveloped nations are located. Much is converted into charcoal before being burned. The majority of technically advanced nations that consume fuel wood also obtain it chiefly from their stands of hardwoods.

Industrial wood

Technically advanced nations dominate in the consumption of industrial wood to a far greater degree than they do in fuel-wood use (Table 22.3). The Soviet Union and the United States are far ahead of any others. Canada, Japan, Sweden, and Communist China follow in that order. Europe as a region is important.

Unlike fuel wood, which is used in only one way, industrial wood is used in various ways on the world scene. These are summarized in Table 22.1. Dimension lumber leads, followed by crude timber, pulp and paper, and plywood, fiberboard, etc.

Total consumption

Since less than 2 per cent of the world's roundwood enters into international trade, the leading consuming nations are those that lead in production. These, in turn, are largely nations with extensive forests and sizable populations. The Soviet Union and the United States are easily in the forefront, with the former consuming well over one-fifth, and the latter nearly one-fifth, of the world total (Table 22.3). Brazil is third, and Canada a somewhat surprising fourth.[6] Indonesia, Japan, and Communist China are leading consumers in Asia, ranking ahead of such active countries as Sweden, Finland, and France. Europe as a region is significant, ranking slightly above the United States. The volume of total consumption in most of the world's outlying places is rather light.

Per capita consumption

A classification of roundwood consumption on a per capita, rather than a total, basis results in some interesting shuffles of position (Tables 22.2 and 22.3). Finland is now the leader, followed by Canada, Sweden, Haiti, Bolivia, Uganda, Tanganyika, Norway, Guatemala, and the United States. Here the importance of wood as a fuel to underdeveloped nations becomes clear. Such nations as Haiti, Bolivia, Uganda, Tanganyika, Guatemala, and Panama use it almost exclusively for that purpose.

PRODUCTION

Overlap of forest-products industries and early stages of manufacturing

Forest-products industries are extractive and, with respect to timber, involve only the actual felling of trees. Further work on the felled trees represents early stages of manufacturing. In practice, however, much cut lumber as well as roundwood moves out of forests, and we cannot separate clearly the two activities.

Labor force

Forest-products industries do not provide direct employment for many people. Even when sawmill operators are included, such industries account for only about ½ per cent of the world's total labor force (Table 7.1).

[6] Except for fuel wood, however, we are thinking here of *mill consumption*, of which a substantial share of finished products is exported from Canada and other surplus producers. The figures above refer only to *roundwood*, not its milled products.

TABLE 22.1

Uses of industrial wood

Use	*Per cent of world roundwood cut*
Dimension lumber (boards, etc.)	55
Roundwood cut to lengths but not into boards (pit props, etc.)	20
Pulp and paper	20
Plywood, fiberboard, etc.	5

SOURCE: *The State of Food and Agriculture, 1958*, United Nations Food and Agriculture Organization, Rome, 1958, pp. 170–171.

TABLE 22.2

Leading nations in per capita consumption of roundwood, 1957, in cubic meters of roundwood per person

Nation	*Industrial wood*	*Fuel wood*	*Total roundwood*
World	0.4	0.3	0.7
Finland*	1.0	3.1	4.1
Canada*	2.3	0.5	2.8
Sweden*	1.7	0.8	2.5
Haiti	n	2.3	2.3
Bolivia	†	†	2.3
Uganda	n	2.3	2.3
Tanganyika	n	2.2	2.2
Norway*	1.5	0.6	2.1
Guatemala	0.1	2.0	2.1
United States*	1.7	0.3	2.0
New Zealand*	1.7	0.3	2.0
Australia*	1.3	0.5	1.8
Panama	n	1.8	1.8
Soviet Union*	1.1	0.6	1.7

* Usually considered technically advanced.
† Not available.
n = negligible.
SOURCE: *Yearbook of Forest Products Statistics, 1959*, United Nations Food and Agriculture Organization, Rome, 1959, pp. 116–119. Only actual consumption (excluding waste) is considered.

Natural conditions of growth

We have noted in Chapter 6 the world distribution of forest resources and their association with other natural environmental features, particularly climate (see especially Figs. 6.1 and 5.1, and Table 6.4). It will be noted that the most extensive forest stands are in either the tropics or the high latitudes, where climatic extremes render land undesirable for dense human settlement and yet do not prohibit tree growth.

Leading nations of production

An overview of wood production is shown in Table 22.3. The dominant nations are technically advanced and are located in the Northern Hemisphere. Also included, however, are those underdeveloped nations which on the one hand have sufficiently large populations to create a demand for wood as a fuel and, on the other, have sufficiently large forest reserves to supply that demand. Of the ten leaders, only Brazil, Indonesia, and Communist China are usually classified as underdeveloped. (Communist China's forests, unlike those of the other two leading underdeveloped nations, are small in total reserves. Whether the country can achieve a growth rate to match its current rate of exploitation remains to be seen.)

TABLE 22.3

Leading nations in total production of roundwood, 1958, in millions of cubic meters

Nation or group of nations	*Industrial wood*	*Fuel wood*	*Total roundwood*
Soviet Union*	252.0	124.0	376.0
United States*	242.6	47.3	289.9
Brazil	12.1	90.0	102.1
Canada*	78.5	7.8	86.3
Indonesia†	5.4	70.5	75.9
Japan*	42.8	20.1	62.9
Communist China	31.0	15.5	46.5
Sweden*	35.9	5.5	41.4
Finland*	27.1	13.4	40.5
France*	19.1	18.0	37.1
Europe (excluding Soviet Union)	193.4	101.7	295.1
World total	923.3	708.5	1,631.8

* Usually considered technically advanced.
† 1957 data.
SOURCE: *Yearbook of Forest Products Statistics, 1959*, United Nations Food and Agriculture Organization, Rome, 1959, pp. 4–9. The table shows production, which is almost identical with consumption plus waste.

The Soviet Union. Over four-fifths of the vast forest reserves of the Soviet Union are coniferous, and are found in both European and Asian Russia. Larch, pine, and spruce are the leaders among a wide variety. The few and light stands of deciduous trees are located generally to the south of the conifers (or, in mountainous areas, downslope from them). These are mainly in European Russia, but also are found in scattered districts immediately to the east of the Ural Mountains and in the Far East (Figs. 22.1 and 6.1).

The following discussion, although concerned with aspects of forest-products manufacturing and transportation as well as the forest-products industries themselves, is a vivid account of the role of the tree in the economy of the Soviet Union:[7]

ADMINISTRATIVE CATEGORIES OF FORESTS: RESERVES AND SANCTUARIES. Since 1943 the forests of the U.S.S.R. have been officially divided into three large groups. Group I includes forest preserves, animal sanctuaries, forests surrounding health resorts, forests on blowing soils, forest zones around industrial plants and cities, and shelter belts. In 1953 these forests comprised a total area of 27.2 million hectares[8] and 3.3 billion cubic meters of standing timber, or about 5.5 per cent of the total amount in the country. Cuttings in the forests of this group are confined to thinnings, stand improvements, sanitary cuttings, and removal of overmature and dying trees. Clear-cutting of any kind is strictly forbidden.

PROTECTION FORESTS. Group II includes chiefly forests having a watershed protection value. They are

[7] Raphael Zon, "The Union of Soviet Socialist Republics," in *A World Geography of Forest Resources*, edited for the American Geographical Society by Stephen Haden-Guest, John K. Wright, and Eileen M. Teclaff, copyright 1956 The Ronald Press Company, New York, pp. 409–414.

[8] A hectare equals 2.471 acres, a cubic meter equals 35.2875 cubic feet, and a kilometer equals 0.62 mile.

located principally in the central and western regions of European Russia, cover some 85.4 million hectares, and have a volume of standing timber estimated at 2.9 billion cubic meters, or 5 per cent of the total volume for the country. Except for strips of forests about 7 kilometers wide along the shores of the Volga and its tributaries, in which no cuttings of any kind are allowed (this prohibition has lately been extended to some other rivers), light commercial cuttings are permitted in the forests of this group.

COMMERCIAL FORESTS. Group III includes all other forests. They are the commercial forests of the country, open for economic exploitation, and are found principally in the northern part of European Russia and in Siberia, embracing about 950 million hectares and comprising some 52.5 billion cubic meters or 89.5 per cent of the entire timber stand. In these forests all forms of cutting, including concentrated clear-cuttings, are allowed, the sole provision being that the cutover areas must be regenerated, naturally or artificially, within a specified short time. The volume of cutting is not limited by the annual growth, but is determined by the economic and industrial needs of the country.

THE TIMBER INDUSTRY. In spite of the great forest wealth of the U.S.S.R. and the herculean efforts on the part of the government to foster its development, the timber industry is still yielding only 80 per cent of the country's timber needs. There are frequent timber shortages of one kind or another, and the industry is in a state of chronic crisis. Several factors contribute to this state of affairs.

GROWING DOMESTIC DEMAND FOR FOREST PRODUCTS. The industrialization of the country is making increasingly greater domestic demands upon the products of the forest, and an additional heavy demand is for materials needed in reconstructing the 2¼ million houses destroyed during the war. The timber industry is making strides but is not keeping pace with the more rapidly growing needs. . . .

The rate of growth of the industry may be judged from the available figures of timber consumption. In the 1920's the annual consumption of timber of all kinds was around 200 million cubic meters (including about 11.5 million exported abroad); in the early 1940's it rose to over 300 million, and at present it is estimated to be close to 400 million, of which very little is exported. Paper consumption, which before the war was 293,000 tons a year, has now been increased to about 360,000 tons; although the pulp and paper industry has been growing lately at the rate of about 18 per cent a year, paper consumption is still only one-half that of England and one-fourteenth that of the United States.

THE EASTWARD SHIFT OF THE TIMBER INDUSTRY. In the past most of the sawmills, cellulose and paper plants, and other wood-using industries were located in the southern, western, and interior industrial regions of European Russia. Because of the uneven geographic distribution of the forests in the U.S.S.R., these regions, especially the southern and western, were not well endowed with forests to begin with, and, as a result of prolonged overcutting, what forests there are in them have been nearing exhaustion for many years. Hence, to keep the industries going it has become necessary to bring logs from constantly increasing distances, mostly by rail and partly by water—a very uneconomical operation. Moreover, most of the plants themselves have become obsolete and inefficient.

The need of moving the centers of wood-using industries from this region to northeastern European Russia, the Urals, and Siberia was already recognized in the 1920's and the war [the Second World War] hastened the shift itself. Many of the plants were destroyed by the enemy and will not be restored; others were picked up bodily and hurriedly transferred to the east before the advancing armies.

During the last two decades the efforts of the government have been directed toward tapping the resources of the hitherto poorly developed territories. This has meant building new railroads and connecting the large rivers with canals to transport enormous stocks of mature timber from the north and east to the timber-deficient south. One of the first steps was to connect the Arctic and White Sea ports with Leningrad by rail and canal, and Leningrad with the Volga and Moscow by means of the Volga-Moscow Canal. Three new branch railroads, totaling 2,300 kilometers, were completed in the far north during 1937–42. These run from east to west over a difficult terrain and frozen tundra, connecting up with the main railroads running south from Archangel and Murmansk. The output of the sawmills in Archangel, which in the past was shipped almost entirely abroad, could now be diverted for domestic use in southern and central European Russia. Therefore, timber exports from the ports of Leningrad, Archangel, and Murmansk have become greatly reduced, and the character of the exports is also changing. At the same time, large new inland lumber-processing centers have come into existence, mostly at the intersection of rail lines and rivers; the most notable example is Kotlas, where the North Pechora railroad crosses the Northern Dvina River. Construction in the near future of an additional 3,600 kilometers of railroads through the forested regions of northern European Russia is projected, and a comparable increase for Siberia. At the same time, energetic measures are being taken to improve the water-transportation facilities, which play a very important role, since each year some 61 million cubic meters of timber are floated down the waterways of the U.S.S.R. The extent of these waterways is now some 200,000 kilometers, and extensive river-improvement work is going on continuously to increase it.

In addition to the new railroads and river improvements, several deep canals connecting the main rivers are being dug. Some of these have already been completed, others now under construction are due for completion in the next few years, and still others are only in the blueprint stage. Thus, a great network of canals and railroads will ultimately enable all parts of central and southern European Russia—the Ukraine, the Donets coal region, north Caucasia, and Transcaucasia—to receive the needed supplies of lumber, mining timber, and pulp wood from Karelia and the upper reaches of the Kama, Volga, and Viatka rivers. Within the last twelve years several large cellulose-paper mills, sawmills, and wood chemical plants have been put into operation near the city of Gorki on the Volga, and also on the Kama.

A new industry has recently come into existence in the north: the manufacture of prefabricated houses and standardized constructional parts. The pressure for the construction of new dwellings in the U.S.S.R. is enormous, to restore the one-third of the dwelling area of Soviet cities that was destroyed by the invading armies and to provide new dwellings for the growing population. Rapid erection of houses for the people who lost their homes during the war, as well as for the new towns and cities springing up around industrial centers—especially the mining centers, where, as in Donbas, no timber is available nearby—is an urgent necessity. Prefabricated houses seem to be an answer to the building problem, and the vast forests of the north provide the chief raw materials for the house-building plants. The Five-Year Plan for 1950–55 envisaged the need for the erection and repair of some 3,400,000 dwellings, and there are now more than sixty plants turning out prefabricated houses in the U.S.S.R., some of them producing as many as 7,000 houses per year.

Similar developments are taking place in the Urals and in Asian Russia, especially in the basins of the rivers Ob and Yenisei, which flow through the heart of the enormous Siberian forests. A great deal of logging is being done along the banks of the Siberian rivers. The logs, in huge rafts containing 30,000 cubic meters each, are towed south up the rivers to Krasnoyarsk, Novosirbirsk, Barnaul, and other industrial centers, and, with the opening of the Northern Sea Route for normal transportation, the larger Siberian rivers, which all flow north, are now assuming an increasing inportance for floating logs down toward the Arctic. Along the Arctic coast there have sprung up many sawmill centers. In Igarka, at the head of the estuary of the Yenisei, for instance, large sawmills have been built, rivaling those of Archangel. Igarka is accessible to seagoing vessels, and may eventually become an important port for timber exports to western Europe.

Great stress is laid on the building in the near future of twenty new pulp and paper plants. The pulp and paper industry before the war centered largely in the west and in the Karelian and Leningrad regions—important Soviet battlegrounds in World War II—and, consequently, was greatly crippled. The first large pulp and paper plant in the Far East was erected in 1942 in Komsomolsk on the Amur River. In western Siberia two paper mills were built before the war, one in 1936 at Barnaul on the Ob and another in 1937 at Krasnoyarsk on the Yenisei.

A forest area in eastern Siberia which will no doubt soon become an important center of the timber industry lies on the upper Lena and Angara rivers and their tributaries within the Lake Baikal watershed and not very far north of Irkutsk. It is a part of a much larger area that has been only partially surveyed. Before the war there were a few small factories and shops in this region. The wood consumed, including that used by the river boats and the settlers, amounted to less than 700,000 cubic meters a year. The average density of the population was less than one person per square kilometer. By 1952 the timber output from this area, which contains a total volume of about 550 million cubic meters, had reached several million cubic meters a year. Large sawmills and cellulose, veneer, and wood-distillation plants have been built on the Chuna near the village of Bratsk. Since this vast region is remote from the main wood-using centers of the country, and local needs, because of sparse population, are insignificant, the forest products must be shipped to the industrial centers of western Siberia. To this end, branch railroads are being built from the Trans-Siberian line east to the Lena. After these railroads have been completed, the structural timber will be sent to the poorly wooded regions of northern Siberia, Kazakhstan, and Central Asia, and pit props to the coal basins of Cheremkhovo and Karaganda.

Thus, the timber industry is beginning to take a strong foothold in Siberia in the face of many heavy odds and the necessity of enormous capital investments. Indeed, in the course of the next several years most of the centers of the timber industry of the whole U.S.S.R. will shift from the south, west, and northwest to northeastern European Russia, the Urals, and Siberia. This migration is in many respects analogous to that of the timber industry of the United States during the last half century. In 1899 the states east of the Rockies produced 66 per cent, the south 24 per cent, and the western states 10 per cent of the entire timber output of the country. A half century later the timber production of the eastern states had fallen to about a quarter, that of the South stood at about a quarter (after a sharp decline from 37 per cent in 1919), while that of the western states had risen to nearly one-half the United States total. Although in both cases the problem has been largely one of transportation, the exhaustion of the forests in the older regions of timber exploitation has not been without its effects.

Many difficulties will still have to be overcome before the planned shift can be completed in the U.S.S.R., but it is unmistakably under way. At the beginning of 1953 some 1,720 large timber-producing enterprises had received definite allocations in the new regions of exploitable timber reserves, with a total possible annual cut of 300 million cubic meters over a period of 21 years. It was expected that by the end of 1955 more than seven-tenths of the total annual cut would be concentrated in the north of European Russia, the Urals, Siberia, and the Far East.

EXCESSIVE CONSUMPTION OF FUEL WOOD. While the government is endeavoring to open new territories for forest exploitation in order to meet the growing domestic demand for wood and especially for structural timber, it is also seeking to obtain more useful wood from the trees that are already being cut. The amount of structural timber that has been obtained in the past averaged only about 50 per cent of the volume of the trees, but by better utilization this percentage has now been increased in many places to 65 and 70. The hardwoods, which used to contribute only a small amount of structural timber, are being drawn upon for a larger share of it, up to 10 per cent of the entire output. But, most of all, the government is seeking to reduce the consumption of fuel wood and to substitute other sources of fuel. Wood is still one of the most used fuels in the U.S.S.R. for industrial purposes and especially for heating, although its relative place is diminishing. . . .

The portable sawmill can be moved easily to the timber stands which are its raw materials (U.S. Forest Service).

This young stand of loblolly pine is located near Oxford, Mississippi. The farmer, on the right, found that raising pine was more remunerative than raising cotton. (U.S. Forest Service)

CUT-GROWTH RATES. The trees in the Soviet Union grow very slowly, not infrequently requiring more than a century and a half to attain sawlog size. Despite this, however, and despite the rising demands of the domestic market, the total reserves are so vast that at present its total annual growth is almost twice that of the cut.[9] There is no immediate danger of excessive exploitation.

TRENDS. There is every reason to expect that the Russian people will continue to increase the rate of exploitation of their forests. The major problems appear to be economic rather than natural: the total reserves are more than adequate, but most are located far to the east in Asian Russia, whereas the major areas of demand are, and will continue to be, in European Russia.

The United States. The territory now lying within continental United States is believed once to have contained more than 900 million acres of forest—an amount exceeding the current reserves of all other nations except the Soviet Union and Brazil. With certain exceptions, almost the entire portion of the country east of the Mississippi was forest-covered, as was much of the mountainous and coastal country of the West. Conifers and deciduous trees were to be seen in substantial stands, for this part of the world is in the middle latitudes, where trees of both categories are frequently present and often intermingled (Fig. 6.1).

Approximately one-third of this original forest acreage has been converted to other uses, and some 600 million acres are still in forests. These comprise over 6 per cent of the world total reserves. (The figures here, from the U.S. Department of Agriculture, are more conservative than estimates from the United Nations; see Table 6.1.) Over two-thirds of these reserves are thought to be both productive and accessible. About one-tenth is classified as old-growth saw timber—stands with trees large enough to be made into the finest grades of lumber. The other nine-tenths are made up of second- or later-growth timber—of trees frequently too small for the best lumber, but useful for poorer lumber, pulpwood, mine pit props, and other products.

The actual timber volume of conifers in the nation's currently exploitable forests exceeds that of hardwoods by a ratio slightly in excess of 2:1.[10] Conifers constitute more than 95 per cent of the reserves in the West and Alaska, somewhat less than 50 per cent of the reserves in the South, and slightly over 20 per cent of the reserves in the Northeast (Fig. 22.1). Hardwoods dominate conspicuously in the Northeast and moderately in the South but are insignificant in the West and in Alaska. The Douglas fir, ponderosa and Jeffrey pine, and western hemlock are the leading conifers of the West; the longleaf and slash pine and the shortleaf and loblolly pine are the leading conifers of the South; and varieties of spruce, fir, and pine make up most of the small amount of conifers in the Northeast. Among the hardwoods, the famous maple-birch-beech association is very conspicuous

[9] *Ibid.*, p. 401.

[10] Alaska's coastal forests are included in this estimate.

in the Northeast, with aspen important in the vicinity of Lake Superior. Toward the southern margin of the Great Lakes and New England, the oak-hickory and related hardwoods begin to assume a prominence which continues southward to the boundary of the southern conifers. In the flood plain of the Mississippi River and along certain coastal swamps are the hardwood swamp forests—varieties of gum, cypress, maple, cottonwood, and other trees—which can grow in continuously moist or even flooded terrain.

HISTORICAL TRENDS IN EXPLOITATION. Two interrelated trends are outstanding in the country's record of tree cutting: (1) excessive exploitation and (2) the migration of the industry. The excessive rate at which the United States has used up its forests has been emphasized frequently, and a retelling of the story now may seem unnecessary. Nevertheless, the truth is that we have been wasteful of this precious resource—and even today have not evidenced a fully mature wisdom in its use. Before the turn of the century, our forebears had hacked the forests of New England and the Great Lakes states virtually to pieces.[11] Too often the land they occupied was not diverted to other uses but was abandoned to the elements. Second-growth forests, too many of them scraggly and untended, have usually reappeared on such land, and some subsequently have been harvested.

In the Southern states, exploitation has been nearly as active. Its marks, however, are not so clearly stamped as in the North—appreciably because a southern pine can grow to pulp size in twelve years and to log size in twenty years, thus replacing a previous stand at least three times as fast as in New England.

In the early part of the twentieth century the forest cutters turned their attention to the rich reserves of the West, where exists most of the small percentage of the nation's virgin timber. At the dawn of this century, the West supplied only about

This stand of Southern slash pine, nineteen years old, is in Crisp County, Georgia (U.S. Forest Service).

[11] Northern New England, for example, is striving to seek new activities which will support local cities and towns—and coastal seaports. The forest-products industry there, once the pride of the country, is now comparatively inactive except in the obtainment of pulpwood. The removal of forests was partially for the express purpose of clearing the land for farming, as old newspapers and historical records clearly indicate. Yet the farms, when they came into being, could not compete with the growing agricultural industry of the Middle West, with its fertile black soils and its location squarely in front of the onrush of a then westward-migrating people. Their virgin forests largely removed, their farms unable to compete nationally, the northern New Englanders began to ask, "What is to be done?" The obvious answer was—and is—to give more careful attention to scientific tree growth. But trees grow slowly in New England, reaching log size only after seventy-five years. Thus one generation must plant for another to harvest—initially. Of course, if a sustained-yield practice is followed, the harvest thenceforth will be continuous. But, as yet, the northern New Englander has not seen the wisdom of this action. See Richard S. Thoman, "Portland, Maine: An Economic-Urban Appraisal," *Economic Geography*, **27**:348–367, 1951; and "The Geography of the Portland, Maine, Area," unpublished master's thesis, University of Colorado, Boulder, Colo., 1948.

A stand of mature Douglas fir in Oregon (U.S. Forest Service).

one-tenth of the nation's wood requirements. By mid-century, it was furnishing almost one-half but recently has declined. Fortunately, most of the Western forests have been placed under the protective custody or control of the government, so that their wanton removal has been deterred. Fortunately, too, some of the forest cutters, notably the larger organizations, are achieving increasing efficiency in wood extraction and at the same time are adopting some sustained-yield practices. Such changes in outlook and method resulted appreciably from a conservation movement which became active in the latter part of the last century and has gained momentum in this century. However, much remains to be done in the way of improvement.

CURRENT EXPLOITATION. Aspects of the two past trends in forest exploitation are still with us. True, the industry has curbed its excesses in exploitation, and the annual growth rate for the entire nation, including Alaska, is higher than the annual cut. However, much of the growth is of young, as yet unharvestable, timber, and of hardwoods; in contrast, the heaviest cutting involves the largest trees, many of which are first growth, and also involves softwoods, the total annual harvest of which exceeds that of hardwoods by an approximate ratio of 2:1. When we reach the stage of replenishing the mature conifers as rapidly as we cut them, we shall have arrived, other considerations apart, at a point of wise use of this resource.

The westward movement of timber extraction appears to have ended, and a backwash toward the South and East is now in process. Of sharply rising importance is the South, where softwoods reach both pulp and log size at least three times as fast as in the North and West (Figs. 22.3, 22.4, 22.5, and 22.6). The South now supplies over 45 per cent of the nation's timber (in board feet), compared with 35 per cent from the West, and its share doubtless will increase.

TECHNICAL IMPROVEMENT. Economies of scale are manifesting themselves particularly in the forest-products industry. The chain saw has replaced the axe in the more progressive areas, and both transportation and initial sawing now involve use of inanimate energy and equipment driven by such energy. Output per person is rising, and the labor force consequently is not growing in proportion to the output of wood. Over one-half of the roundwood is used for lumber, the sawmills frequently being either at or near the places where the trees are actually felled (Figs. 22.3 and 22.4). Of the more than sixty thousand sawmills in the United States 2 per cent account for nearly one-half of the total lumber output. Most of these are located in the West, where holdings are large.

OWNERSHIP. Somewhat surprisingly, however, economies of scale may not be realized in this country to their fullest potentialities. The explanation is to be found mainly in the ownership of commercial forest land. About three-fourths of all such land is in private hands, nearly one-fifth is under Federal government ownership or control, and the remainder is under the jurisdiction of state and local governments. Most of the federally owned land is in the West, where it constitutes more than three-fifths of all commercial forest. Most of the privately owned land is in the East and South, the latter being the section toward which the timber industry is now looking increasingly for a future supply. A surprising amount of this privately owned land is in small tracts: farm wood lots, many not over 100 acres in size, aggregately contain more than three-eighths of it, and holdings of fewer than 5,000 acres constitute another three-eighths.[12] It is unfeasible to establish a large sawmill on such holdings unless they are within easy reach of that mill and their lumber can be sold to it. The traditional independence of the American small landowner mitigates against this, and the end result may well be uneconomic in that smaller, less efficient mills and pulp and paper plants, etc., will be utilized.

A partial solution to this dilemma lies in the acquisition of sizable acreages, through either purchase or lease, by large companies and corporations, and the use of such land on a sustained-yield basis. To a degree this is now being initiated—especially in the South, where trees grow rapidly.

Europe. No other nation is a serious rival to either the Soviet Union or the United States in the output of roundwood (Table 22.3). The continent of Europe (exclusive of the Soviet Union), however, is an important producer, offering close competition to the two leading nations. But the forest-products industries of Europe are especially interesting also in that they frequently represent more than mere extraction from nature. Man has lived in Europe for many centuries and, noteworthily in nations of heaviest consumption, has felt the pinch of timber scarcity for at least the last century. Consequently, several European nations are on a sustained-yield basis, importing when it is necessary to satisfy a demand that exceeds domestic supply.

EUROPEAN FORESTS. The land area of Europe, like that of the entire world, is still slightly more than one-fourth in forests. The trees are both coniferous and deciduous, and the two categories are almost equally represented (Fig. 22.1). The former dominate in the high latitudes and in the upper elevations of the intermediate latitudes, whereas the latter are especially conspicuous in the low-lying countrysides of coastal and central Europe.

EUROPEAN OWNERSHIP AND PRODUCTION. Most of the non-Communist European countries contain some forest land which is privately owned and more which is publicly owned. Cutting practices, however, are generally controlled by the respective governments more rigidly than in the United States. In the majority of the Communist nations, the land is publicly owned and is exploited through plans and administrative structures not unlike those of the Soviet Union. Sweden, Finland, France, West Germany, Poland, Yugoslavia, Rumania, Czechoslovakia, and Italy are the leading nations of roundwood output in Europe.

Production Elsewhere. Other nations, or even regions, of outstanding roundwood production are scattered rather widely throughout the world. Some are technically advanced and some are underdeveloped, the latter using a higher percentage of their annual harvests for fuel. Some produce mainly for ultimate export (of finished products, rather than roundwood), and some for the domestic market.

TRADE AND TRANSPORTATION

Domestic

In this chapter we are concerned chiefly with roundwood which has been processed only slightly. Of course, at least preliminary sawing is necessary for further handling after such timber is felled, the

[12] H. R. Josephson and Dwight Hair, "The United States," in American Geographical Society, *A World Geography of Forest Resources,* The Ronald Press Company, New York, 1956, chap. 8, pp. 160–165. Obviously a substantial share of the forests we are describing is in farm wood lots, and the extraction of products from such forests technically is an agricultural activity.

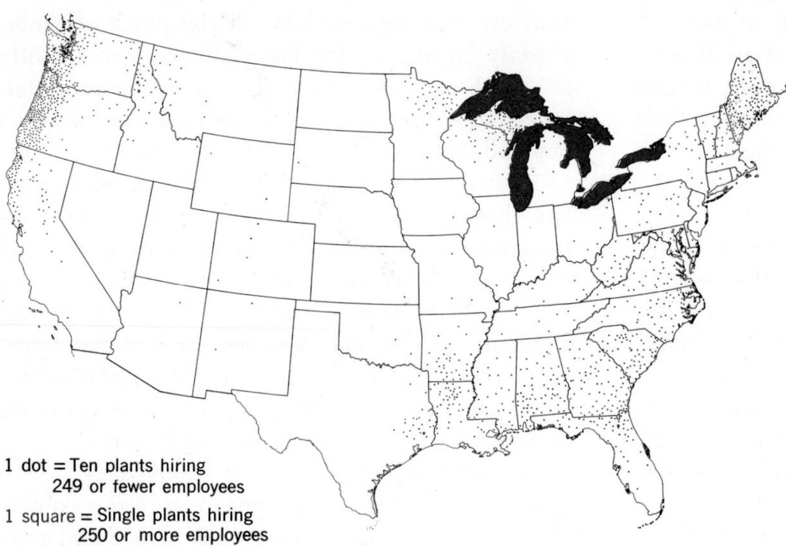

Figure 22.3 ***Distribution of logging camps and contractors in the United States.*** *Most plants are small, but they are numerous.*

usual practice being to cut it into lengths suitable for lumber, pulpwood, mine pit props, etc. The actual movement to the nearest sawmill usually involves very short distances, and that to the nearest pulp mill only moderate distances. The movement is overwhelmingly domestic. Not uncommonly, local rivers are utilized, the logs being floated downstream. When lakes or coastal waters are made use of, the logs are joined to form huge rafts, which are pulled by a small tugboat. Under other conditions, the timber may be hauled by truck or rail.

In technically advanced countries, the transportation of roundwood is becoming increasingly mechanized, even at sites of tree felling. In some technically underdeveloped lands both human labor and that of animals are relied upon—the latter involving elephants, in southeastern Asia, as well as the more familiar draft animals.

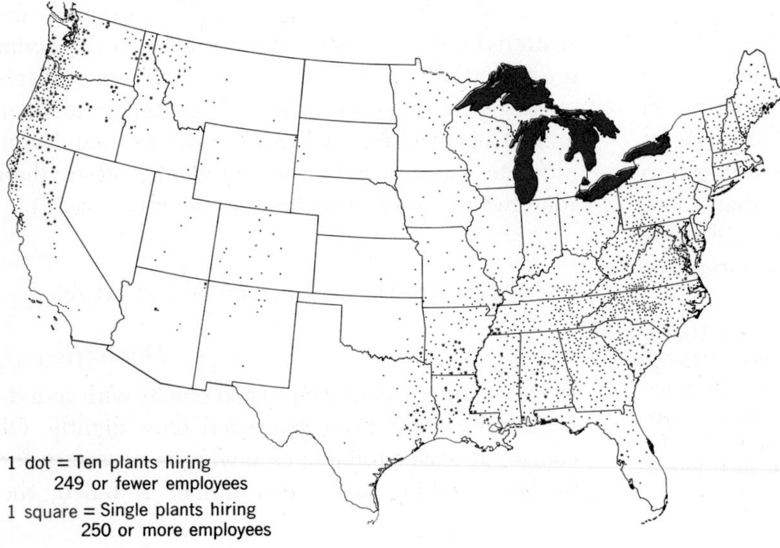

Figure 22.4 ***Distribution of sawmills and planing mills in the United States.*** *These mills accept timber from the logging camps and contractors (Fig. 22.3). There are more large mills than large logging camps and contractors. Also, more of the mills are located in the western half of the manufacturing belt than is true of logging camps and contractors. Why?*

International

We have noted that less than 2 per cent of the world's roundwood enters into international trade. This is mainly in the form of pulpwood, of pit props, or of roundwood destined to become lumber or fuel.

Pulpwood. About one-half of the trade among leading countries involves pulpwood, imported chiefly into the United States from Canada, and into West Germany, Italy, France, the United Kingdom, and other consuming nations of Western Europe from Finland, Sweden, and lesser European supply countries. There is also a noteworthy but erratic trade between Finland and Sweden and a conspicuous movement both to and from France. North America accounts for nearly one-half, and Europe for nearly all of the remainder, of this traffic in pulpwood, most of which comes from coniferous forests.

Pit props. Approximately one-seventh of the trade in crude timber involves pit props, used to strengthen walls and support ceilings in mines. These are shipped almost entirely to the United Kingdom and West Germany from Finland, Sweden, and Portugal. Again, softwoods predominate.

Other roundwood. The remaining international trade in crude timber is largely roundwood destined to be made into lumber, and occasionally into fuel. About three-fourths is hardwood. Nearly one-half of this hardwood moves to Japan, mainly from the Philippines, and most of the rest goes to Europe from scattered sources, many of which are located in the tropics. The much smaller softwood movement is somewhat like that in pulpwood, except that more European countries act as suppliers in that portion of the world and that the roles of the United States and Canada are reversed, the latter being the more active as an importing nation.

Figure 22.5 ***Value of products shipped from logging camps and contractors.*** *Note that the Pacific West and the South dominate. Measured by volume and not value, the South would lead.*

Figure 22.6 ***Value of products from sawmills and planing mills.*** *Again, the Pacific West and South dominate.*

REFERENCES

Coppock, J. T.: "A Decade of Post-war Forestry in Great Britain," *Economic Geography*, **36:**127–138, 1960.

Darby, H. C.: "The Clearing of the English Woodlands," *Geography*, **36** (2):71–83, 1951.

Haden-Guest, Stephen (ed.), et al.: *A World Geography of Forest Resources*, The Ronald Press Company for the American Geographical Society, New York, 1956.

The Nation Looks at Its Resources: Report of the Mid-

Century Conference on Resources for the Future, Resources for the Future, Inc., Washington, D.C., 1954.

Pinchot, Gifford: *Breaking New Ground,* Harcourt, Brace and Company, Inc., New York, 1947.

Shantz, H. L.: "An Estimate of the Shrinkage of Africa's Tropical Forest," *Unasylva,* **2**:66–67, 1948.

Smith, J. Russell: *Tree Crops: A Permanent Agriculture,* The Devin-Adair Company, New York, 1950.

Stanford Research Institute: "America's Demand for Wood—1929–1975," *Forest Products Research Society Journal,* **4**:181–195, 1954.

The State of Food and Agriculture, 1959, United Nations Food and Agriculture Organization, Rome, 1959.

World Forest Resources, United Nations Food and Agriculture Organization, Rome, 1955.

Yearbook of Forest Products Statistics, 1959, United Nations Food and Agriculture Organization, Rome, 1959.

Zon, Raphael, and W. N. Sparhawk: *Forest Resources of the World,* 2 vols., McGraw-Hill Book Company, Inc., New York, 1923.

23 FISHING: ASSORTED PRODUCTS

FISHING AND HUNTING ARE VERY OLD OCCUPATIONS, OLDER THAN AGRICULTURE. They are also unusually difficult, for they are carried on under almost continuous exposure to some of nature's severest elements. Today, they do not provide a livelihood for very many people. Although important to some primitive societies as a means of earning a living, hunting virtually has disappeared throughout most of the world, largely having been replaced by other occupations,[1] and is now engaged in largely as a sport or hobby. Perhaps because man has found no better uses for the places where fishing is carried on, fishing persists as a commercial occupation as well as a sport or hobby. However, it is a minor livelihood activity, accounting for about ½ per cent of the world's labor force (Table 7.1).[2] A supplementary labor force of about equal size processes the catch, keeps the nets and gear in operating condition, etc. So measured, fishing is about equal in importance to forest-products industries and to grazing, and about one-half as important as mining. It does not begin to approach the stature of either agriculture or manufacturing.

CONSUMPTION

Total consumption

Considered by live weight, over 30 million metric tons of fish and fish products of all kinds are caught each year (Fig. 23.1). An estimated one-half of this catch is either discarded or converted into by-products and bait.[3] This means that about 15 million metric tons of fish actually are eaten

[1] Consult the card catalogue in your library under the heading "Hunting," and note the number of entries treating this activity as a sport and the number treating it as an occupation.

[2] This estimate contains a recognition of part-time fishermen. For example, two people who fish for half a year and farm or work in factories for half a year are considered as a single full-time fisherman.

[3] No precise data are yet available concerning the annual volume of fish consumption for the entire world. The above estimate was reached on the basis of several conferences between the author and representatives of the United States Fish and Wildlife Service.

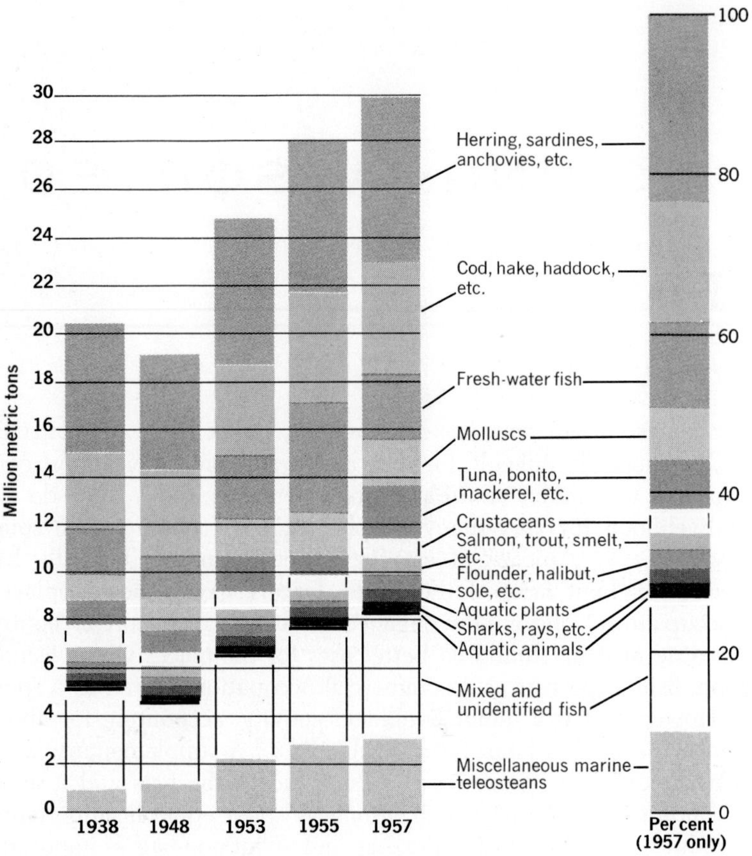

Figure 23.1 ***Kinds of fish taken in the world catch of all marine life*** *(after* Yearbook of Fishery Statistics, 1957, *United Nations Food and Agricultural Organization, pp. xxii–xxiii).*

by human beings annually. A calculated 4.5 million metric tons per year are made into animal and poultry feed, fertilizers, bait, etc. (Fig. 23.2). Thus at least 19.5 million metric tons of fish are estimated to be consumed annually—either as food or as by-products and bait. In all probability even more is utilized—for fertilizer and other inedible materials if not for food.

Comparison with consumption of agricultural products

The actual weight of fish and fish products eaten as food each year is less than 3 per cent of the accumulated total of the world's leading agricultural products. It doubtless ranks much lower in comparison with consumption of all agricultural products, but we do not have the data available for such a comparison. It is less than 9 per cent of the consumption of all milk and milk products. However, it does not compare too unfavorably with the 25 million metric tons of beef and the 20 million metric tons of pork now reported to be produced and eaten annually.[4]

Types of fish consumed

Among the smallest of commercially exploited water life are shrimps and oysters. The largest are whales (which, of course, are mammals). Including and

[4] However, these figures are somewhat biased in favor of meat, for they include the weight of bones which are sold as a part of meat but which are discarded when the meat is eaten. For fish, they include only those very tiny bones, which, for the most part, are eaten; the heads, tails, and larger bones and shells of fish are considered as by-product and discard material and are not included in the 15 million metric tons of fish-derived food estimated to be consumed annually.

between these extremes is a wide variety of genera, species, and subspecies, each with its own size, shape, and physiology.

Fresh-water Fish. Approximately 12 per cent of the world's fish consumption involves fresh-water or fresh-water–salt-water[5] varieties. The carp, eel, perch, catfish, buffalo fish, pike, chub, whitefish, sturgeon, sterlet sturgeon, and salmon are some of the leaders.

Salt-water Varieties. Fish taken from the world's oceans consist of herring, sardines, and related types (which account for nearly 25 per cent of the world's total output and consumption of both fresh- and salt-water fish); cod, haddock, and related types (16 per cent of the world total); crustaceans and mollusks[6] (9 per cent); mackerel, tuna, and related types (6 per cent); and miscellaneous (32 per cent) (see Fig. 23.1).

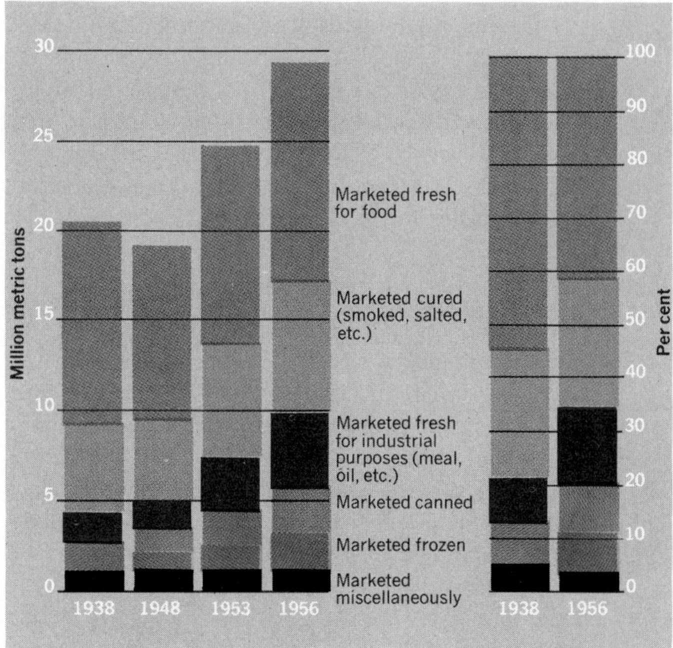

Figure 23.2 ***Disposition of the world's catch of marine life.*** *The tonnages shown include bones and other waste. Note that no fish were frozen in 1938. (After* Yearbook of Fishery Statistics, 1957, *United Nations Food and Agricultural Organization, p. xxv)*

Areas of consumption

Major Areas. The major areas of fish consumption are the world's nodal regions of dense population pressure—especially those which are located near coastlines. This means a focus upon the Northern Hemisphere, where over 94 per cent of the world's total fish catch is marketed. More than one-third is consumed in Asia, over one-fourth in Europe (excluding the Soviet Union), and over one-eighth in the United States and Canada. Japan leads among individual nations with over one-sixth of all fish consumption.

Technically Advanced and Technically Underdeveloped Nations as Consumers. Both technically advanced and underdeveloped nations are consumers of fish. The technically advanced group includes countries in northwestern Europe, in Anglo-America, and in Japan. The underdeveloped group, while conspicuous in southeastern Asia, also includes several countries in Africa, Latin America, and eastern Europe. The technically advanced group consumes at least three-fifths of the world's reported catch.

Types of Fish Consumed and Areas of Consumption. Fresh water fish are particularly important to the human diet in southeastern Asia, and increasingly so in central Africa and in the Soviet Union. They are only moderately popular in North America and Europe.

Mollusks and crustaceans are also consumed to a greater degree in Asia than elsewhere. North America ranks second and Europe a rather poor third. Other areas are of far less significance.

[5] The salmon and related types of fresh-water–salt-water fish begin and end their lives in fresh water. They spend the intervening years in salt water, returning to spawn in the fresh-water streams of their birth. They comprise about 2 per cent of the world's fish catch.

[6] Shellfish are classified into crustaceans and mollusks. The former, including the lobster, shrimp, crab, and many others, are covered with a crustlike skin. The latter—oysters, clams, mussels, snails, and many others—are soft, delicate life forms usually found inside a calcareous shell.

Of the remaining fish—which comprise the bulk of the world's catch—Asia consumes extraordinarily large amounts of mixed and undifferentiated types, as well as substantial tonnages of herring, tuna, and associated varieties. Europe, North America, and the Soviet Union consume less tuna, concentrating instead on herring, cod, and related varieties.

Per capita consumption

One might expect that, in a per capita count, the world's underdeveloped areas would appear as major consumers of fish. This, however, is not generally true. The few underdeveloped nations which rank even among the intermediate group in total consumption are those with large populations. Their per capita consumption is thus low, when measured by existing records. Of course, much of the fishing in some underdeveloped countries is done on a subsistence basis and hence often is not recorded, so that we doubtless do not have a complete view of per capita consumption in all nations. Nevertheless, the leading per capita consuming nations appear to be the technically advanced ones, with Japan leading the list. In Japan, as we have noted, the motive is necessity. To a degree, this is also true in Europe—particularly in southern and eastern Europe. However, religious belief and custom are also important throughout much of Europe and in other areas of the world where Catholicism is an active force. The periodic substitution of fish for meat by Catholic adherents in those areas results in an appreciably larger per capita consumption of fish.

Trends in consumption

In 1938, the world's fish catch slightly exceeded 20 million metric tons, and the amount actually eaten was about 10 million metric tons. Present figures represent almost a 50 per cent increase in fewer than two decades—an increase even more rapid than that of the fast-growing population of the world during the same time period. Per capita consumption of fish obviously is on the rise.

Where have these increases been the most dramatic? If we consider *absolute growth* (1938 output subtracted from 1956 output), we find that the nations and regions of traditionally heavy consumption are outstanding. If, however, we consider *rate of growth* (1938 output subtracted from 1956 output, and the result divided by 1938 output), we find some rather startling shifts of position. Growth rates of South America and Africa rose by over 200 per cent during those nineteen years, and that of the Soviet Union rose by more than 70 per cent. In contrast, growth rates of North America and Asia were up only about 30 per cent, and that of Europe about 45 per cent. Of course, the very high growth rates of South America and Africa are based on a very low rate of 1938 consumption, and their 1956 share of world consumption is still low. However, if trends continue, these two continents will increase their share of the world's markets. Even more striking is the 70 per cent growth rate in the Soviet Union, for this rate is based on a relatively high 1938 output. It would appear that both technically underdeveloped nations and Communist nations will command a larger share of the world's fish markets in the near future than they do now.

PRODUCTION

The annual consumption of fish and fish products approximates the annual catch, and there are virtually no continuously accumulating reserves. International trade, while increasing, is as yet comparatively modest. By and large, therefore, the world's fish catch is landed in the nations where it is utilized.

Natural environmental conditions of production

Fresh Water. Nearly two-thirds of the world's fresh-water fish are taken in eastern and southern Asia (Fig. 23.3). Many of these are raised in shallow ponds, flooded fields, and inlets and are fed artificially. Technically, this type of activity is agriculture rather than fishing, and the natural environment does not play so crucial and direct a role as it would if the fish were forced to fend for themselves. Where fish are not "domesticated" but are

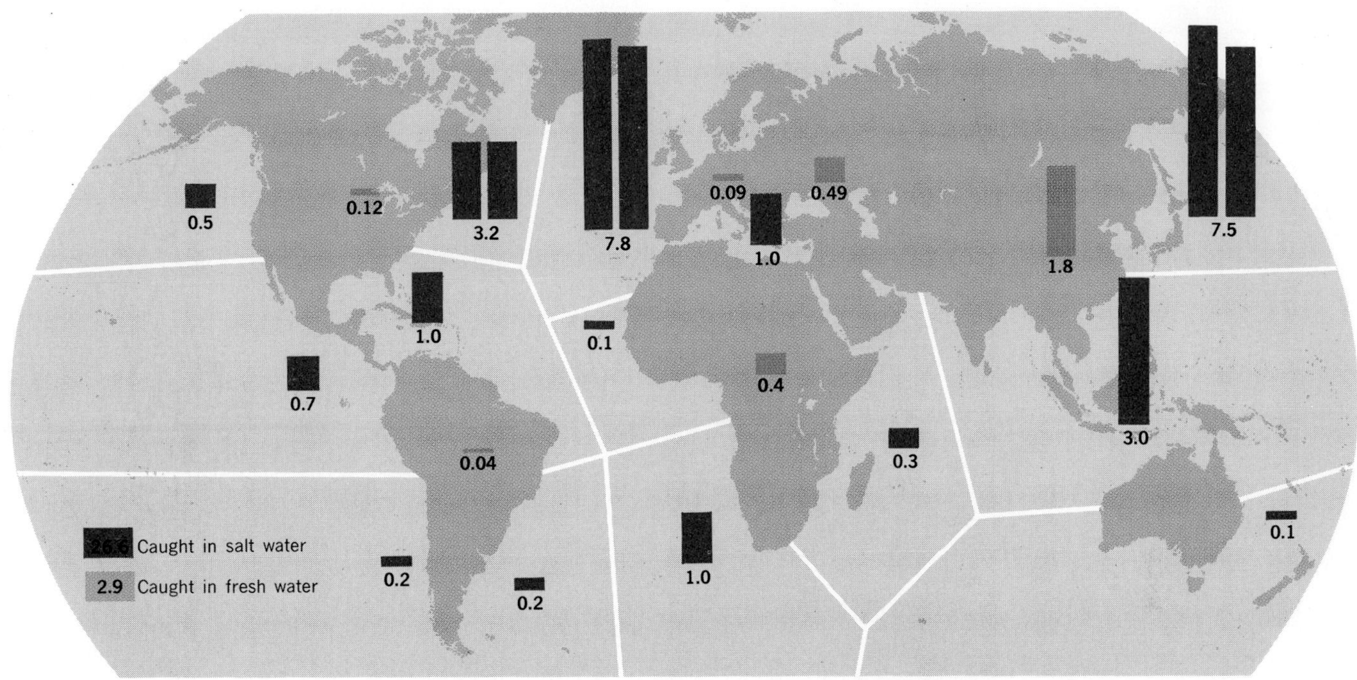

Figure 23.3 ***World catch of all marine life by designated land and water areas.*** *The figures are in millions of metric tons. (After* Yearbook of Fishery Statistics, 1957, *United Nations Food and Agricultural Organization, p. xix)*

caught from waterways and water bodies, the natural environment assumes a more direct and commanding role. It is not, however, excessively restrictive. Fresh-water fish are taken in the tropics, in the middle latitudes, and in the high latitudes. The north-south range of their global distribution is thus as extensive as that of agriculture, and possibly more so.

Specific natural conditions vary, of course, with locality. However, most fresh-water fish are taken in the shallow rivers and streams. Even in larger and deeper water bodies like the Great Lakes, they are caught chiefly in the shallows, where most of their food occurs. The relationship of fresh-water fish to water temperature, food supply, and other relevant natural conditions is not markedly unlike that of maritime fish, which we consider in succeeding paragraphs.

Salt Water. Nearly three-fourths of the earth's surface is covered with water, of which the oceans constitute all but a fraction. Inasmuch as the oceans contain myriads of living organisms, they might be expected to provide man with far more raw materials than they do now. In fact, their potential is still largely unknown. We are certain, however, that the life they contain is very unevenly distributed, both horizontally and vertically. This is true both of *pelagic* life, which tends to inhabit the surface waters, and of *demersal* life, which tends to inhabit the ocean floors, especially in shallow waters.

PLANKTON. Fish, like all organisms, must receive nourishment in order to exist. A clue to their world distribution thus lies in the location of their sources of nourishment. We have noted in Chapter 6 that a basic source is *plankton*—tiny, sometimes microscopic, forms of plant and animal life drifting passively in the water.[7] The animal forms

[7] A few fish feed on higher forms of plant life growing in shallow waters, but their numbers appear to be small.

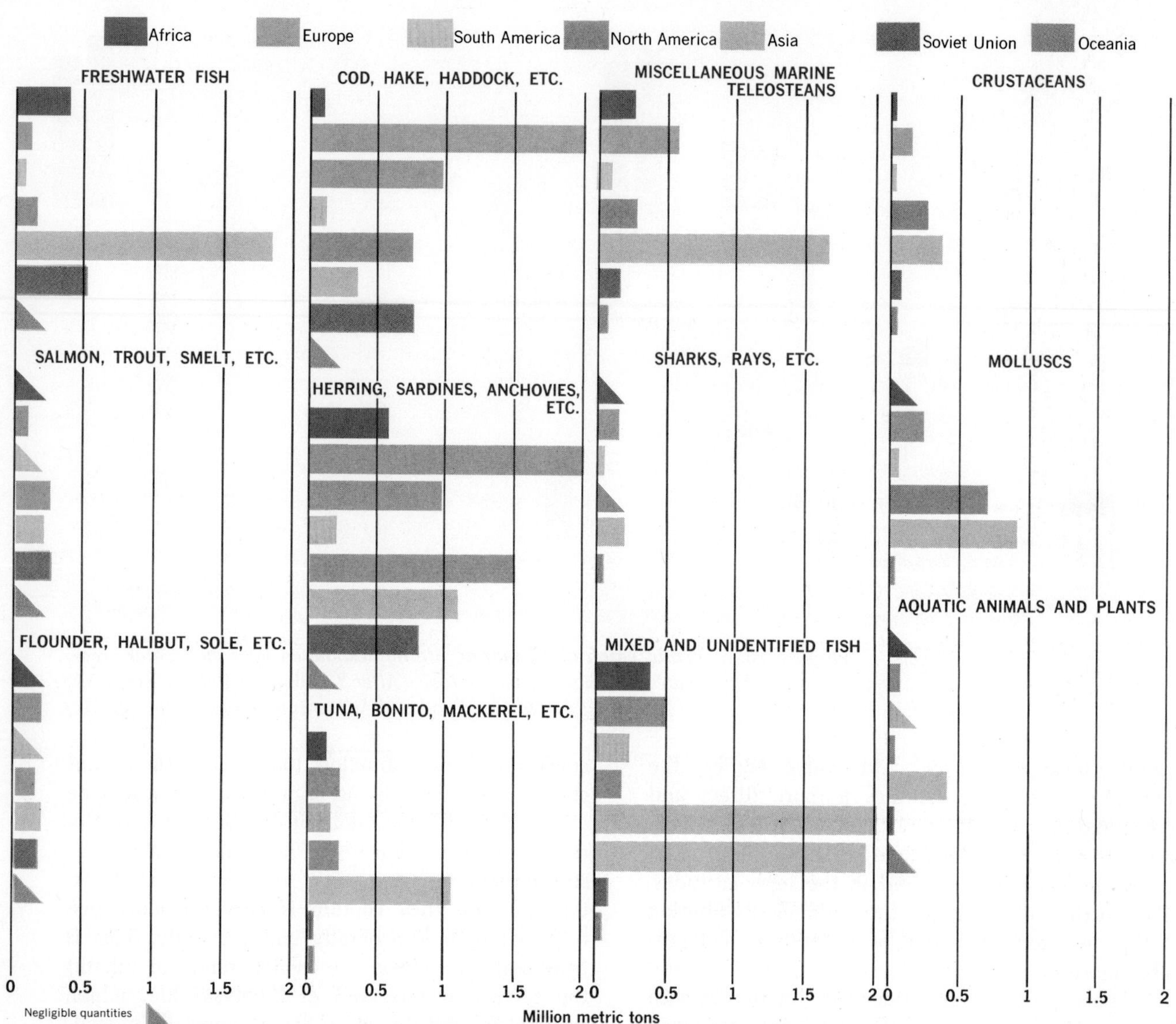

Figure 23.4 ***Kinds of fish taken in different parts of the world*** *(after* Yearbook of Fishery Statistics, 1957, *United Nations Food and Agricultural Organization, p. xxiv).*

of plankton are called *zooplankton,*[8] and the plant forms are called *phytoplankton.* The live forms of the former feed upon the latter, and both are food for small fish, which are eaten by still larger fish, thus creating a *food-supply chain* to the largest forms of oceanic zoological life. Of course, the chain is not always a continuum; some large as well as small fish and sea-dwelling mammals eat the plankton directly,[9] and there are many other excep-

[8] *Zooplankton* is sometimes used to include fish eggs as well as the actual life.

[9] Among these are some whales and sharks.

tional cases. Nevertheless, the supply of plankton—more specifically, of phytoplankton—is a highly critical factor in determining the number of fish which can exist in both oceanic and fresh water. Even more important is the annual rate of phytoplankton *growth,* which acts as a control to the annual fish increase; for obviously no more fish can exist than can be fed. The Malthusian doctrine appears to be appropriate even to fish!

Sunlight and certain nutrient substances and gases are basic requirements to the existence of phytoplankton. Water temperature is also important. Although varying with latitude and season, sunlight tends to penetrate effectively the upper 250 to 300 feet of oceanic waters, and live phytoplankton are not found extensively at lower depths. Nitrates, phosphates, carbon, and other necessary plant nutrients are derived appreciably from decaying plant and animal tissues which sink to lower levels. The phosphates, especially, accumulate there. A portion of these nutrients is brought continuously to the zone of sunlight penetration by upwellings, currents, river and stream discharges (which themselves contain additional nutrients), and other forms of water circulation. Thus they are made available to the phytoplankton. In shallows, such as continental shelves, water movements are especially effective in providing nutrients to the plankton, for the distance of water movement there is not great. The two most necessary gases, carbon dioxide and oxygen, are usually present in the upper water levels and hence available to the phytoplankton. Limitations imposed by temperature, while recognized, are as yet not well known. Temperature differences do not appear to limit commercial fishing excessively as an activity, for fish are caught in latitudes ranging from the tropics to the subpolar areas.

Phytoplankton thus are concentrated especially in shallow waters overlying continental shelves. In addition, they appear to be present but unevenly distributed in the surface waters of oceans, being more numerous where upwellings and ocean currents bring nutrients to the zone of sunlight penetration. The mixing of warm and cold currents adds to the effectiveness of the circulation and to the plankton supply, for each type of current contains its own mixture of nutrients, gases, and other requirements of phytoplankton existence.

The growth of phytoplankton appears to go on at all times of the year but varies in intensity with the season at higher latitudes because of differing rates of efficiency of water penetration by sunlight at different times of the year. During winter the phytoplankton count is low in these latitudes, and the nutrients accumulate. With early spring comes a "burst" of phytoplankton, which thrive on the stored nutrient supply. In late spring the zooplankton and other predators "graze" the phytoplankton excessively, and the numbers of the latter diminish. Nutrients accumulate once again, and coincidentally many of the zooplankton die or are consumed. In the late fall the phytoplankton suddenly become numerous again, although less so than in the preceding spring.

In contrast, tropical phytoplankton appear to experience little, if any, seasonal fluctuation in growth.

Zooplankton exist both with the phytoplankton and at slightly lower depths in the water. In the latter case, they feed from phytoplankton and other residue which have sunk beneath the zone of sunlight penetration.

Despite its seasonal fluctuation at intermediate latitudes, the plankton supply per unit of water appears to be more plentiful there than in the tropics. However, the supply is not uniformly distributed in either intermediate or tropical latitudes. Instead, it is notably abundant over continental shelves and other shallows, in ocean currents, and near upwellings of undersea water. It appears to be most abundant where these features are combined.

PLANKTON, SHOALS, AND FISH. Feeding directly or indirectly upon plankton, the world's salt-water fish are most numerous in the shoals underlain by continental shelves (Figs. 23.3 and 4.1). For many demersal varieties, cod, rosefish, hake, haddock, halibut, flounder, and others,[10] the type of ocean floor is also an important consideration. Most demersal fish feed directly from invertebrates which,

[10] Including the majority of crustaceans and mollusks.

in turn, feed from the food-supply chain leading eventually to plankton. However, most invertebrates shun soft ocean bottoms of mud and muck, choosing instead the harder floors. Hence demersal fish are more numerous where the shoals are made up of hard materials. The pelagic varieties—herring, pilchard, anchovies, menhaden, mackerel, tuna, and others—may migrate much farther from the shallows in their search for food, but even they appear to be in most plentiful supply over or near continental shelves.

On the basis of existing knowledge, therefore, the world's maritime fish are abundant in the vicinities of continental shelves and in the active ocean currents and upwellings, notably where currents of differing temperatures come together. They are most numerous in places satisfying all three of these requirements. Moreover, *schools* of fish tend to occur most often in these last-named places of optimum conditions; here it is possible to drop a net and bring up a catch dominated by a single fish type. In other places the fish appear to be not only reduced in number but also more diversified as to genera, species, etc. Nets dropped here will yield a leaner and more heterogeneous harvest.

Plankton, Fish, and the Human Diet. We have noted in previous chapters that eating meat is a very inefficient method of converting natural foods into human muscular and mental energy. Although as yet we cannot judge accurately the efficiency of using fish toward the same end, we do have some estimates. These indicate that only about 1 ton of fish is produced for every 1,000 tons of plankton made available in the oceans. The loss is due appreciably to inefficiencies in the oceanic food-supply chain. Each fish which eats plankton or another fish utilizes only a part of its food to build flesh. If that fish is consumed by another fish and it, in turn, by another, much food value is lost in converting the plankton at the bottom of the food-supply chain to the fish which man eventually catches and eats. Obviously, it would be far more efficient for man to eat the plankton directly, and

We can glean more fish from the open oceans than we now do, but ultimately we must hatch more of such "crops" as the one shown in this trout hatchery near Lamar, Pennsylvania (U.S. Fish and Wildlife Service).

experiments toward this objective are now being conducted. Doubltess one reason we have not given the matter more serious consideration is that the present inefficiency is not felt as financial loss. Man has essentially no capital investment in the food-supply chain of ocean life and is not so sensitive to losses there as he would be, for example, in agriculture, where he has invested heavily in many parts of the world. Furthermore, the losses which do occur in the ocean are hidden beneath the water surface and thus not so easily appraised as those which are more intimately a part of man's daily living. Nevertheless, the inefficiencies do exist, and only now are we becoming truly aware of them.

The fishing grounds

It is fortunate for man that optimum conditions for maritime fishing are found close to the shore. During the thousands of years when both human minds and fishing craft were unable to cope successfully with the open oceans, man landed substantial quantities of fish from shallow waters near continents. Sizable markets were necessary to accommodate the larger catches, most of which until very recently were sold fresh. The leading fish grounds have developed close to population clusters and even today are located near areas with many inhabitants. The largest catch is taken in the Pacific and Indian Oceans, offshore from eastern Asia (including Siberia) and southern Asia; the next largest in the Atlantic Ocean, offshore from northwestern Europe (including European Russia); and the third and fourth largest, respectively, in the Atlantic and Pacific Oceans off the coasts of the United States and Canada (Figs. 23.3 and 4.1).[11]

Eastern and Southern Asia. The continental shelf of eastern and southern Asia reaches boldly into the Pacific, but only sketchily into the Indian Ocean (Fig. 4.1). To the far north, it merges with the shelf of North America. With decreasing latitude, it narrows along the Kamchatka peninsula and the Sea of Okhotsk of the Soviet Union, and the Sea of Japan adjacent to the Japanese islands. Then it widens suddenly. From Korea to South Vietnam it is well developed, but narrows again at this southeastern corner of the Asia mainland—only to widen once more between that corner and the islands of Indonesia. Over this shelf the warm Japan (Kuroshio) Current trends northward and eastward, moving out to the Pacific at lat 40–50° N. Meanwhile, the cold Ohkotsk (Oyashio) Current, an extension of the even colder Kamchatka Current, flows southwestward from the vicinity of the Bering Sea. The warm and cold waters meet offshore from Honshu, the largest island of Japan. Thus exists the combination of shoals, circulation, and temperature conducive to plankton and fish accumulation. Here are the most actively used of fishing grounds which include the entire shelf.

In contrast, the Monsoon Currents of the Indian Ocean brush past a poorly developed continental shelf offshore from southern Asia (Fig. 4.1). Commercial fishing is much less significant here than in the Pacific.

Northwestern Europe. The North and Baltic Seas and adjacent waters are shallow covers over one of the most widespread and continuous of the world's continental shelves. Furthermore, the more open of these waters are fed by discharges from the North Atlantic Drift, a warm ocean current which has crossed the Atlantic at lower latitudes. Again, a combination of shallow water, circulation, and favorable temperatures makes for concentration of plankton and fish. The North Sea, particularly the Dogger Bank, long has been a favorite fishing ground, and the entire shelf area is well known to fishermen of Europe and the Soviet Union.

The United States and Canada. The most extensive continental-shelf projections of the North American continent are in the high latitudes—in the Bering Sea, the Arctic Ocean, and Hudson Bay

[11] Statistics for fisheries are reported by nation, and the above summaries are based on national groupings. Of course, modern fishing craft range widely and do not always limit their operations to fishing grounds offshore from their native lands. This is notably true of craft searching for pelagic fish, some of which also range rather widely. However, the largest catches of fish of all varieties are made in the continental shelves offshore from the coasts of the active fishing nations.

(Fig. 4.1). None is yet fished extensively, although the first offers more immediate promise than the other two. One must journey southward to intermediate latitudes to find the grounds of highest commercial value. Offshore from Canada's Maritime Provinces and from New England is a series of fishing grounds reaching from Grand Bank near Newfoundland to a shallows near southeastern Massachusetts (Fig. 4.1). To the south the shelf narrows appreciably, and it remains rather narrow around the tip of Florida and into the Gulf of Mexico. The Pacific shelf is more or less a mirror image of that in the Atlantic and the Gulf, being quite narrow as far north as Seattle, Washington, and becoming much wider between Seattle and Alaska.

In the Atlantic, the warm Gulf Stream meets the cold Labrador Current. In the Pacific, the moderately warm North Pacific Drift divides as it strikes North America—to become the cool, southward-flowing California Current and the warm, northward-flowing Alaska Current. The most productive fishing grounds on both sides of North America are found in these places of admixture of warm and cold water over shoals. However, fishing is actively pursued along the western, southern, and eastern margins of the continent.

Other Grounds. We have emphasized the fishing grounds in the Pacific and Atlantic Oceans offshore from Eurasia and North America, which are by far the most important commercially. In many other parts of the world, the continental shelves are too narrow to permit much fishing (Fig. 4.1). Where wide, they often do not benefit from an optimum combination of other natural environmental features conducive to localizing a fish supply.[12] Many are too far from potential markets for any type of fishing except that which uses technically advanced means of fish preservation or processing.

In the open seas, pelagic fish are taken where the more active currents make nutrients available at the upper surface levels. The West Wind Drift of the Southern Hemisphere, flowing almost uninterruptedly around Antarctica, is one of the best plankton providers. Among the sea life attracted are whales, and most of the world's whaling fleet is employed in these waters.

[12] However, our knowledge of marine life, especially that of areas not heavily fished, is as yet not very extensive.

Fishing gear and methods

Man's technology has advanced to the point where he can hurl rockets like giant fireworks into space. He has obtained energy from matter, and is well on the way to standardizing its continuous use from the sun. He flies through the air with a speed and an ease that sometimes must amaze even the birds that were once his models. He has studded portions of the earth with factories, many of them quasi-automatic. He has bred plants and animals into strains to his liking. But when he fishes, either for fun or for real, he usually uses the same old line or net that he has used for thousands of years.

Techniques differ, of course, for taking demersal and pelagic fish types, and sometimes for taking specific species. For freely swimming demersal fish as well as some inhabitants of the floor itself, the line and the trawl are favorites (Fig. 23.5). Some demersals must be lured into traps. A few of the more tenacious varieties must be raked loose by tongs or even by human hands (Fig. 23.5). Most pelagic fish are taken by nets, but some of the larger and stronger are caught with lines or harpoons (Fig. 23.6). Almost every shore adjacent to a fishing ground is the site of fish traps or shore fishing activities which depend upon the high tides, either for bringing fish in or for exposing the burrowing varieties to exploiters during low tides (Fig. 23.7).

The craft and gear which man employs for most fishing are generally small and simple, ranging from the small junks and similarly crude constructions of most technically underdeveloped lands to the larger but still rather unimpressive vessels of most technically advanced nations. Even these larger vessels are seldom longer than 200 feet or wider than 30 feet. Their ratio of power to size is unusually high, especially if they are trawlers and/or are out to sea for long periods of time, because substantial power is needed to drag the heavy trawls across the ocean bottom and to preserve the catch by refrigeration. Crews are small: twenty-five men would be found only on the largest fishing vessels that do not contain processing equipment.

Thus, when he fishes, man uses tools that are surprisingly tiny and crude for this modern age. It is partially for this reason that technically underdeveloped nations compete with some success with more highly developed nations in commercial fishing. All that is needed in the way of capital investment is a boat and a bit of gear, and most individuals—in any type of economy—can somehow acquire these. However, the most modern types of fishing craft and gear are expensive—and this means amounts of capital investment which only large public or private organizations can afford. The fisherman too is well on his way to becoming an "organization man."

This trend is evidenced partially by the current emphasis upon slightly larger fishing craft, notably in technically advanced nations. It is best exemplified, however, in the large floating canneries, introduced before the last war and now in the service of Japan, the Soviet Union, Norway, and other nations. Acting as substitutes for home ports, these vessels are mother ships to sizable fishing fleets. They contain not only storage space for supplies and for processed cargoes but also the machinery and the crews to do the processing. A return to the home port is necessary only after a long time has been spent at sea. The floating cannery now is used actively in the whaling industry of the Southern Hemisphere, particularly by Norway, and in the crab and salmon industry of the North Pacific, especially by Japan and the Soviet Union.

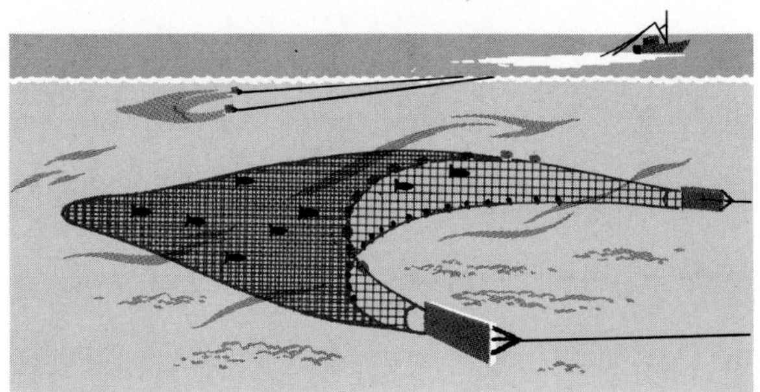

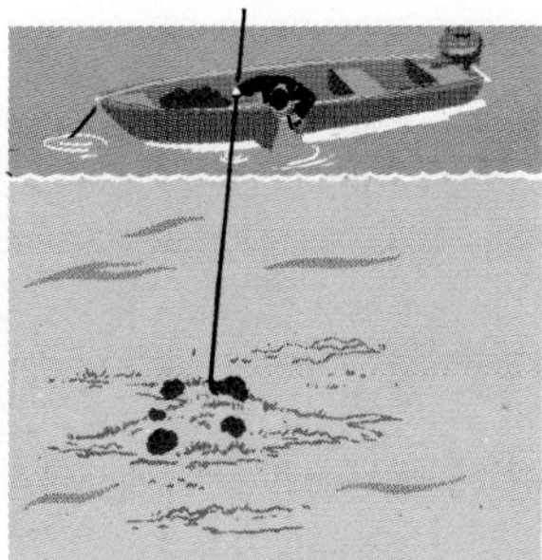

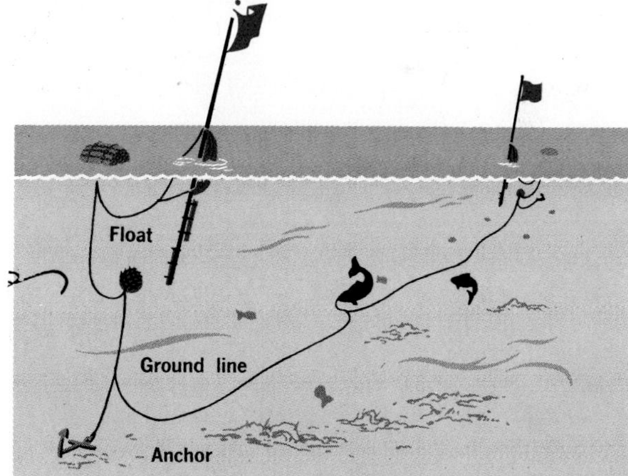

Figure 23.5 **Demersal fishing.** *(1) Trawling the ocean floor; (2) lifting sponges, either by diving or by hooking from a boat; and (3) sinking baited hooks to the ocean floor to catch halibut. Demersal fishing is the taking of marine life from the ocean floor. (After* Commercial Fishing Gear, *U.S. Fish and Wildlife Service Circ. 48)*

Nationalism and fishing

Leading Nations of Production. Nearly three-fifths of the world's fish catch is accounted for by seven nations—Japan, the United States, Communist China, the Soviet Union, Norway, the United Kingdom, and Canada. Japan alone is responsible for over one-sixth of all fish taken. With a burgeoning population and a very limited amount of land upon which to grow food, the country has turned to the oceans with unprecedented aggressiveness. Japanese

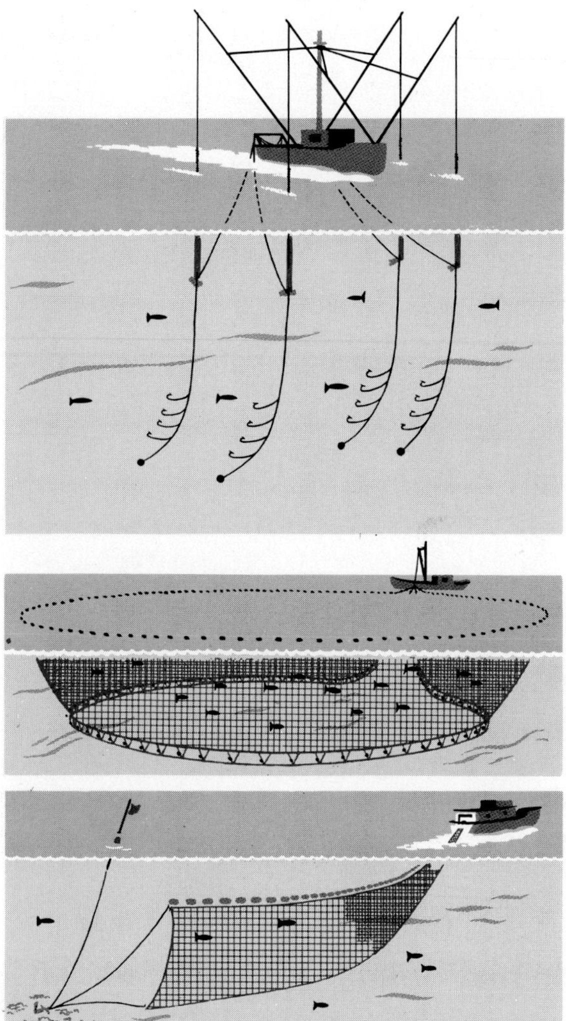

Figure 23.6 **Pelagic fishing.** *(1) Trolling for salmon; (2) purse seining for menhaden; and (3) using gill nets. Pelagic fishing is the taking of marine life from water levels above the ocean floor (cf. Fig. 23.5). The three drawings are self-explanatory except for gill netting; here the fish become entwined by their gills in the net and are taken from the water when the net is withdrawn. (After* Commercial Fishing Gear, *U.S. Fish and Wildlife Service Circ. 48)*

fishing craft range far from the home islands, not infrequently in fleets accompanying a floating cannery. Loss of territory during the last war increased the urgency to obtain food from maritime sources, and by 1958 the country's output was fully one-fourth larger than in 1938. Much of the increase resulted from catching unassorted varieties which had not been taken before the last war. Despite the high man-land ratio in Japan, however, a small portion of the annual catch now is being exported. The Soviet Union and Communist China also are catching many more fish than they did ten years ago. In contrast, the United States has raised its output only slightly above its 1938 level. Most countries of Western Europe have shown modest, if any, increases in their annual production. Some, including the United Kingdom, have declined slightly.

Fish Production and Stage of Economic Advance. Despite their lack of marked growth in output, the world's technically and economically advanced nations are the leading commercial fish producers. Six of the seven leaders, it will be noted, are usually considered to be technically advanced (Table 23.1). All in all, the world's technically advanced nations land approximately three-fifths of its total catch.

Fish Production in Non-Communist and Communist Nations. Non-Communist nations dominate the world's fisheries, accounting for nearly three-fourths of the total reported catch. Only the Soviet Union and Communist China are prominent in Commu-

TABLE 23.1

Leading nations in total catch of fish, 1957

Nation	*Per cent of world tonnage*
Japan*	17.3
United States*	9.7
Communist China	8.6
Soviet Union*	8.5
Norway*	6.7
United Kingdom*	3.8
Canada*	3.6
All others	41.8

* Usually considered technically advanced.
SOURCE: *Yearbook of Fishery Statistics, 1957,* United Nations Food and Agricultural Organization, Rome, 1958, p. xxii.

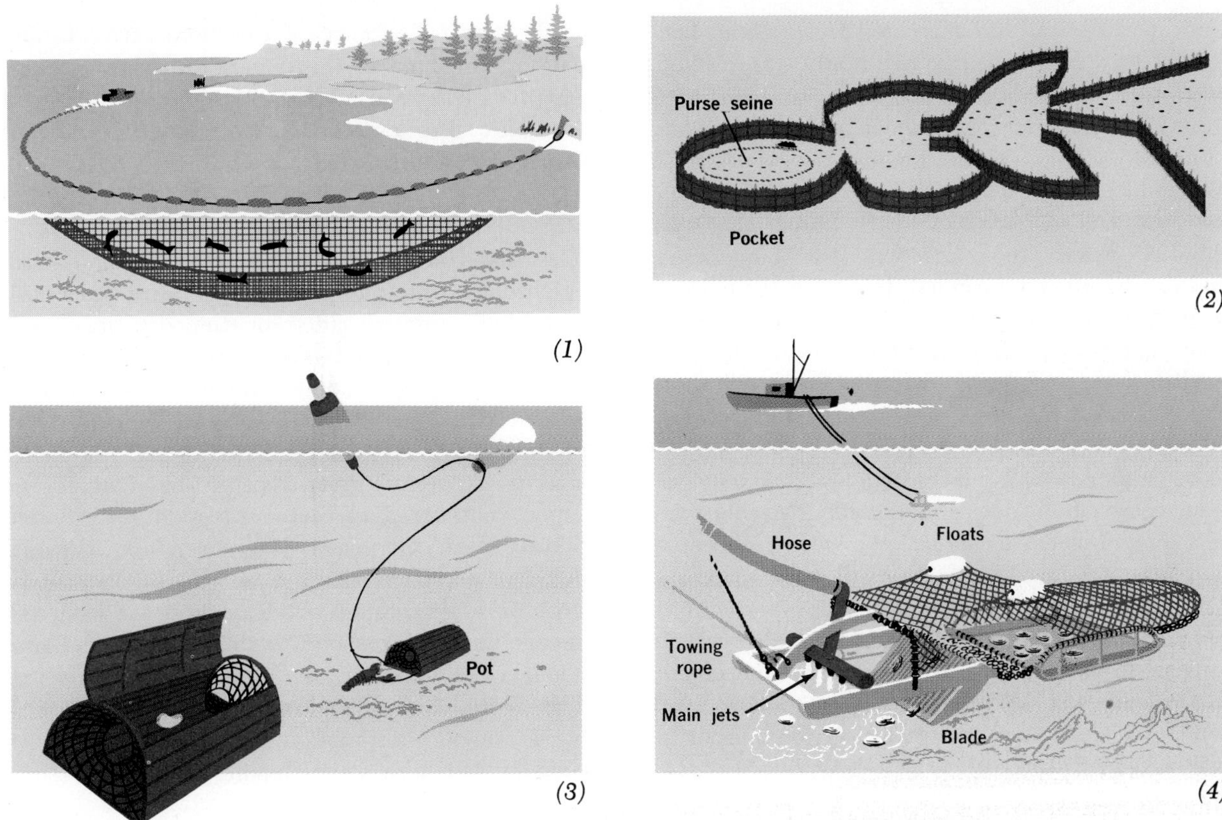

Figure 23.7 ***Fishing near the shore.*** *This involves both pelagic and demersal fishing, but especially the latter. (1) A haul seine; (2) a sardine weir; (3) lobster pots; and (4) a hydraulic surf clam dredge. (After* Commercial Fishing Gear, *U.S. Fish and Wildlife Service Circ. 48)*

nist output, but both of these are among the leaders and both are increasing their production.

Fishing Rights and Territorial Waters. The waters immediately adjacent to a coast are considered to be under the jurisdiction of the nation owning that coast. With respect to fishing, the citizens of that nation usually have exclusive rights. Foreigners are allowed to fish, if at all, only under special license. Beyond, the oceans may be fished without restriction. However, there is no uniform, generally accepted outward limit to territorial waters. The limit specified by most nations is 3 nautical miles, but some claim additional distance for such purposes as fishing and extraction of petroleum. Indeed, some nations claim rights to waters as far as 200 nautical miles from their coasts. As the tempo of fishing activity increases, the ships which range far from their home shores often find themselves in conflict with shore patrols of other nations. To date, attempts at international agreement as to the seaward limit of sovereignty and to fishing rights of foreign vessels within territorial waters have met with something less than success.

TRADE AND TRANSPORTATION

Marketing condition

We have stressed that fish is a perishable which must be either quickly marketed or quickly preserved. As late as 1938, more than one-half of the world's catch was still marketed fresh, about one-fourth was cured, nearly one-tenth was canned, and nearly an additional one-tenth was converted to inedible materials like animal feed and fertilizer (Fig. 23.2). By 1956, the amount consumed fresh was reduced to two-fifths of a world catch which, however, had increased by nearly 50 per cent over the 1938 catch. One-fourth was still being cured, and nearly one-tenth canned. However, the amount being converted to inedible materials increased to about one-sixth of the world total, and almost one-twelfth now was being frozen. Obviously, these new uses and means of preservation signify more versatility in marketing. Fish consumption appears to be gaining favor in places some distance removed from coasts. Both domestic and international markets now involve a higher percentage of entire populations rather than only dwellers on seacoasts. Thus a centuries-old association between fishing grounds and immediately adjacent coastal markets appears to be on the verge of relaxing. Henceforth, the oceans will be of increasing significance as sources of food and raw materials for interior as well as coastal dwellers.

Domestic trade

New techniques of fish preservation are particularly significant in the United States and the Soviet Union, where substantial portions of domestic markets are situated some distance away from ocean coast lines.[13] For most of the more active fishing nations, the haul to the domestic market is short. Japan, northwestern Europe, and India are good examples. The railroad is the primary means of transport to the interior market.

International trade

Less than 10 per cent of the world's annual fish catch enters international markets. Most of the fish so traded is frozen, salted, or canned; a small portion is semiprocessed into fertilizer, oil, or other materials. It is a trade dominated by technically advanced nations. Norway, Canada, Iceland, Denmark, the Netherlands, and the United States are leading exporters. Japan recently has entered the export markets. The United Kingdom, the United States, West Germany, Italy, Belgium, Canada, Sweden, and Denmark are outstanding importers. Both the United States and Canada, it will be noted, engage in some reexport trade, the United States being a net importer, and Canada a net exporter. The United States now imports at least one-third of its annual consumption each year—chiefly from Canada but also from Japan and northwestern Europe.

[13] Of course, the St. Lawrence Seaway in the United States has opened much of that country's interior to ocean shipping, but this development probably will not change the location and organization of the nation's fish-catching and -marketing industry.

REFERENCES

Ackerman, Edward A.: *New England's Fishing Industry,* University of Chicago Press, Chicago, 1941.

Carson, Rachel L.: *The Sea Around Us,* Oxford University Press, New York, 1951.

Gregory, Homer E., and Kathleen Barnes: *North Pacific Fisheries,* American Council Institute of Pacific Relations, New York, 1939.

Hardy, A. C.: *Seafood Ships,* Crosby Lockwood & Son, Ltd., London, 1947.

Marts, M. E., and W. R. D. Sewell: "The Conflict between Fish and Power Resources in the Pacific Northwest," *Annals of the Association of American Geographers,* **50:**42–50, 1960.

Morgan, Robert: *World Sea Fisheries,* Methuen & Co., Ltd., London, 1956.

Rose, John K., "The Margins of the Continents," *Geographical Review,* **49:**275–278, 1959.

Pearcy, G. Etzel: "Geographical Aspects of the Law of the Sea," *Annals of the Association of American Geographers,* **49:**1–23, 1959.

Smith, F. G. Walton, and Henry Chapin: *The Sun, the Sea and Tomorrow,* Charles Scribner's Sons, New York, 1954.

Walford, Lionel A.: *Living Resources of the Sea,* The Ronald Press Company, 1958.

24 MINING AND QUARRYING AS ECONOMIC ACTIVITIES

THE EXTRACTION OF MINERALS AND ROCKS SYMBOLIZES BOTH THE OLD AND THE new in economic geography. On the one hand, this occupation is as ancient as man's use of the materials obtained from it—so ancient, indeed, as to be reflected in the names of such very early time spans in human history as the Old Stone Age and the New Stone Age. On the other hand, a truly dynamic utilization of minerals, and to a lesser degree of rocks, was not initiated until the advent of the Industrial Revolution approximately two hundred years ago. Now, in this twentieth century of unprecedented intensity in economic activity, this utilization has increased to levels which once certainly would have been considered astronomic. Furthermore, there is every reason to predict that future use of both minerals and rocks will be even more intense than the present—not only because economic activity is expanding in nations now considered as technically advanced but also because more and more economically underdeveloped nations are striving toward technical advancement. It is perhaps needless to add that all basic economic functions—consumption, production, and exchange—are involved.

CONSUMPTION

Particular uses

A highly significant consideration in assesssing the consumption of rocks and minerals involves the particular uses for which they are sought. Measured by value, more than three-fifths of all minerals (excluding precious materials) extracted in the world are used to obtain inanimate energy. In the technically advanced United States, this fraction rises to three-fourths. A substantial portion is channeled also into producer goods, for which nearly all basic materials are derived from minerals and rocks. Still a third source of demand, notably for certain rocks, comes from public-interest projects—makers of roads, fills, dams, etc.—which, while very useful to individuals, represent consumer-goods industries only when the term is used in its broadest sense. Only rather modest portions of materials extracted in minerals and rocks thus are converted into such unquestionably consumer goods as automobiles and refrigerators.

Rapid increase

Earlier in this chapter we have suggested that demand for minerals is growing at a surprisingly rapid rate. The suggestion is even more impressive when documented. Measured in mid-twentieth-century dollars, the value of all minerals extracted in the world (excluding such common rocks as sand, gravel, limestone, sandstone, etc.) has risen as shown in Table 24.1. It will be noted that world annual output and associated consumption were very modest during the eighteenth and even the nineteenth centuries, but they have multiplied more than sevenfold since the beginning of the twentieth century and offer promise of an even higher increase.

Dominance of the United States and other technically advanced nations

The close functional association between mineral extraction and factory production has meant a domination of the former by technically advanced nations. During the early stages of the Industrial Revolution, the United Kingdom controlled most of the world's mineral output, although much of that output occurred well beyond the borders of that small island nation. In time, however, the United States came to dominate in mineral output and utilization. In the period after the Second World War, the United States alone consumed about 40 per cent of the world's minerals. Its percentage of production was not quite so high (Table 24.2). During succeeding years, competition from a resurging Western Europe and, slightly later, a rapidly expanding Communist bloc has removed the United States from a position of absolute dominance. However, this country unquestionably remains the key source of demand in the world's mineral market.

Rising importance of Communist nations

The Soviet Union has utilized centralized planning and centralized authority, both augmented by force if necessary, to produce a dynamic economy. Other Communist nations, notably Communist China, are attempting variations of the same course of action. The goals of these nations—certainly that of the Soviet Union—appear to be to maintain unprecedented high rates of growth and thereby expand their economies. They are thinking seriously of active competition with the United States and Western Europe within the next few years and, according to their public announcements, hope to exceed

TABLE 24.1

Increase in world mineral output, 1700–1958, in millions of constant dollars, 1935–1939 average value

Year	*Output*
1700	$ 20.0
1750	35.0
1800	45.0
1850	170.0
1900	2,825.4
1950	12,665.3
1959	21,530.8

SOURCE: For all data except 1959: *Annales des Mines,* November, 1956, p. 42. Data for 1959 approximated by calculating output increases in the five leading minerals. The figures above are in constant dollars, as of the average for 1935–1939. Actual value of the world's 1953 output has been set at 36,488.4 million dollars (*Annales des Mines,* p. 17).

TABLE 24.2

Leading nations of mineral production, 1953

Nation	*Per cent of world mineral output produced*
United States*	34.10
Soviet Union*	12.50
United Kingdom*	5.54
West Germany*	5.22
Venezuela	5.00
Canada*	2.93
France*	2.64
Kuwait	2.31
Saudi Arabia	2.27
Poland*	2.06
All other nations	25.43

* Usually considered technically advanced.

SOURCE: *Annales des Mines,* November, 1956, pp. 16–17.

industrial production of the United States by the 1970s. Whether they can achieve such goals remains to be demonstrated, but they unquestionably will be more active consumers of minerals than they have been in the past.

PRODUCTION

Minerals extraction, quarrying, and livelihood

Minerals extraction and quarrying provide a livelihood for only slightly over 1 per cent of the world's labor force (Table 7.1). Furthermore, it is probable that in the future they will account for an even lower percentage than they now do. No other productive occupation is more thoroughly mechanized and automated, and none offers more promise for the machine. With respect to solids, the bulk handling of much earth will be relied upon increasingly to recover the desired materials. This handling can best be done by machines. With respect to liquids and gases, what man can compete with pumps, pipelines, and continuous flow equipment? The logical conclusion is that mining and quarrying will tend to provide direct livelihood for a smaller and smaller percentage of the world's labor force. This is true in spite of the fact that an increasing amount of mined and quarried products will be moving to the world's factories and to other sources of demand.

Erratic global distribution of minerals and rocks

We have emphasized in Chapter 4 and hence shall note only in passing here that the world's minerals and rocks are very unevenly distributed. This point is especially pertinent regarding minerals, for each has a specialized use for which substitution is difficult if not impossible. Most rocks, when used directly, are used for less sophisticated purposes than minerals, and substitution in their case is usually possible. Minerals, therefore, are important in international trade. Rocks are not, for some form of rock substitute is usually available in the nation of demand.

Fugitive nature of minerals and rocks

An important consideration in the extraction of minerals and rocks is that they are *fugitive* materials—i.e., they are used up with use and cannot begin to be replaced naturally as fast as they are utilized. In this sense, mining and quarrying are without parallel among the productive occupations. None of the others—agriculture, grazing, forest-products industries, and fishing—is so dependent upon fugitive materials. (Manufacturing, of course, cannot be compared here, as it relies mainly upon the five other productive occupations to supply its raw materials and energy.) Careful use of mineral resources, notably those in short world supply, unquestionably should be one of the watchwords of our time.

Adequacy of reserves

Considerations in Appraising Reserves. Because minerals are fugitive materials, it is extremely important to have adequate knowledge of their reserves. Experts responsible for such estimates usually state their findings in terms of *known, indicated,* and *inferred* amounts, either of actual mineral content or of the total volume of ore containing specified percentages of minerals. As the wording indicates, the experts are sure of the amount of known ore, and reasonably certain of the amount of indicated ore. The inferred figure, however, is usually no more than a careful appraisal. More often than not, known ore bodies are considered to involve material in the vicinity where mining is currently being carried on, whereas indicated ore bodies are immediately adjacent to these known ores, and the inferred deposits are located farther away. Of course, this is not always the case. However, we know most about the ores and ore fields which are currently working.

Total Amount of Reserves. If, by their nature, fugitive materials are not being replaced as fast as they are being used, there must be an absolute limit to their reserves. What that limit is, we are not yet sure, for the world as a whole has not yet been faced with the outright shortage of any desired substance. Indeed, our detailed knowledge of the earth's crust beyond a depth of even a very few miles is so scanty that we are not truly certain what may be stored below. However, with increasing world demand upon minerals, there is every probability that much more extensive inquiry will be made during the next half century for fugitive materials. At present, no single nation—not even such global giants as the Soviet Union, Canada, and the United States—contains a full complement of mineral resources. Shortages are remedied through an international trade which, as the best-quality ores in individual nations disappear, is becoming increasingly important. When the world reserves of certain materials become as depleted as those of the largest nations today, man will give much more careful attention to taking stock of what remains.

Impact of technology

The connotations of mineral reserves and of man's technology are so intertwined that consideration of the one without the other would result in a grossly inadequate appraisal. It is through technology that modern man discovers and identifies specific resources, calculates and estimates their reserves, extracts them, and transfers them to market. As his technology improves, so does his position with respect to his mineral resources—until he reaches that absolute mineral resource limit which is not yet known. For as his technology improves, he is able to discover, identify, estimate, extract, and transfer much more efficiently. Sometimes he is able to rework the refuse piles of former mining operations —piles which may have accrued twenty, thirty, or even more years ago—for materials not obtained under those relatively inefficient conditions. Sometimes he is able to substitute minerals in good supply for those which are scarce and thereby maximize the benefit of both. Man's increasing technological efficiency also is very important in yet another sense: a very large share of the world's minerals is in low-grade deposits sometimes containing 1 per cent or even less of the desired materials. Only an extremely apt technology can make their day-to-day exploitation profitable, but once this is possible, may be extensive.

Location of mining activity

We have noted previously that man must mine and quarry where the desired materials occur naturally. Human decision is limited, therefore, to the question, "Which of several natural sites is the most feasible to exploit?" Now that extractable ores tend to be of lower quality than they once were, there is more freedom of human choice, for the simple reason that a number of places usually contain ore of moderate quality whereas only a very few contain premium ore. This has at least two important connotations in economic geography: (1) inasmuch as human decision will play a more significant role in opening new mines, both the pure and applied aspects of location theory will be more significant in determining future mining sites, and (2) the processing of these poor-quality ores—the first stage of manufacturing—necessarily will occur more frequently near the mine than in the past, for who wants to transport over long distances an ore that is largely waste material?

Increasing interdependence among nations

Some scholars have maintained that the Industrial Revolution took hold quickly in the United Kingdom because sizable deposits of coal and some iron and diverse other mineral resources were at hand. Whether or not this is a satisfactory explanation, that nation soon became a major importer of most minerals except coal, for the simple reason that the local supply of most mineral resources except coal became inadequate as the industrial economy expanded. The United States, with a much larger area and resource base, subsequently followed a similar pattern in its economic development. Once reliant upon other countries for only a few minerals like tin and manganese, this nation began in the 1930s to import more and more iron, copper, zinc, lead, aluminum, and other materials, both as ores and as concentrates. (Paradoxically, the economy of the United States was rendering that nation more dependent upon other countries during the very time that isolationism was being stressed, with considerable popular acceptance, by some political

Mining is an ephemeral activity. The ores containing vanadium, silver, and other metals at Cerro de Pasco, shown above, were worked before the coming of the Spanish, and have been worked intermittently since then. Today, the town contains some 20,000 inhabitants. (Standard Oil Company of New Jersey) Central City, Colorado, on the right, is less than a century old but is almost a ghost town; its gold, silver, lead, and other ores are no longer mined (U.S. Forest Service).

leaders.) Most of the Western European nations also have found increasing importation of mineral resources necessary. The Soviet Union, just awakening to its industrial possibilities and containing a large and varied resource base, probably will be more self-sufficient in the immediate future than most nations in high-quality deposits of mineral and rock resources. It will only be a matter of time, however, if present trends continue, until this nation, also, will be faced with decisions as to whether importing an increased array of minerals is more feasible than producing from lower-quality domestic reserves. Interdependence among nations, accompanied by utilization of lower-quality ores, appears almost inevitable in future mineral procurement. Nor will the exchange be restricted to technically advanced nations. Many of the world's minerals lie in underdeveloped nations which, at least currently, lack the means of large scale exploitation. These doubtless will admit money, capital equipment, and technical knowledge from the economically advanced nations and will export most of their extractive yields to such nations—in the immediate future, and probably for some time to come.

25 MINING: INDUSTRIAL MATERIALS NOT USED FOR ENERGY OR IN METALLURGY

NEXT TO SOURCES OF ENERGY, THE MOST VALUABLE GROUP OF MINERALS AND rocks extracted each year is a heterogeneous collection of nonmetallic materials used in equally heterogeneous ways. In the United States, this group accounts for about 20 per cent of the value of all rocks and minerals produced each year (excluding precious materials); fuels are responsible for 70 per cent and metals for only 10 per cent. The use of this heterogeneous group, both per capita and absolute, is heaviest in technically advanced nations, which depend upon domestic reserves as much as possible. As a result, they are not always outstanding commodities in international trade. Furthermore, those which are consumed in largest tonnage tend to be widespread and quasi-ubiquitous in occurrence. In some cases, even domestic movement is limited to short hauls. This is particularly true of the rocks, which are available in some form and composition to many countries and to numerous localities.

Among the rocks in this category are sand and gravel, limestone, sandstone, clay, granite, basalt, slate, and quartzite. Many are used for such everyday purposes as riprap and other fill material necessary for railway and highway beds, river dams and dikes, and diverse kinds of earthen projects. Many are also utilized directly as building materials. A substantial number have several uses (Table 25.1). Limestone, for example, is not only a fill material and a dimension stone but also an agent in iron and steel manufacturing, glass manufacture, leather tanning, water purification, and still other processing. In addition, it is a source of lime in fertilizer, cement, stucco, plaster, whitewash, and numerous lesser products.[1]

Among the leading minerals in this group are phosphate, potash, nitrate, sulfur, gypsum, asbestos, and common salt. Although all occur naturally, some are obtained partially as by-products of mining and

[1] Of course, there are many variations of each rock type, and each tends to have its own purpose.

TABLE 25.1

Procurement and uses of some common nonmetallic rocks and minerals

Rock or mineral	*Method of procurement*	*Use*
Sand and gravel	Quarrying	Cement for road paving, building, etc.; railway beds; highway beds (before paving on better highways, in lieu of paving on secondary roads); glassmaking; filtering of liquids; abrasive agent; diverse other uses
Limestone*	Quarrying	Riprap for fills; railway and highway beds; lime for cement, fertilizer, stucco, plaster, whitewash, other commodities; dimension stone; agent in iron, glass, leather manufacturing; water purification; diverse other uses
Sandstone	Quarrying	Riprap for fills; flagstones for walks; abrasives; dimension stone for building; diverse other uses
Clay	Quarrying	Brick, tile, related building products; refractory linings for industrial furnaces; ceramics; coating and filler for high-grade papers; diverse other uses
Granite	Quarrying	Mainly riprap and dimension stone
Basalt	Quarrying	Mainly riprap
Slate	Quarrying	Roofing, blackboards, insulation, paint filler, diverse other uses
Quartzite	Quarrying	Mainly riprap
Phosphate	Mining†	Mainly fertilizer; many lesser uses such as pharmaceuticals, soft drinks, matches, poultry feed
Potash	Mining‡	Mainly fertilizer; numerous lesser uses such as glass, soap, photographic materials
Nitrate	Mining§	Mainly fertilizer; also used for explosives, rocket propellants, dyes, and other chemicals, as well as an agent of processing in certain foodstuffs
Sulfur	Mining¶	Partially fertilizer, partially numerous products for industry
Gypsum	Mining	Cement, plaster, wallboard tile (especially for building interiors)
Asbestos	Mining	Buildings and other construction requiring resistance to fire
Salt	Mining	Production of various chemicals; livestock raising (as salt licks); water purification; human table use; diverse other uses

* Limestone currently accounts for nearly two-thirds of the weight of all stone quarried in the United States. (Sand and gravel and other uncompacted rocks are not included in this calculation.)

† The element phosphorus in phosphate is also obtained as a by-product of iron-ore smelting, animal slaughtering, and other processing.

‡ The element potassium in potash is also obtained from wood ashes, seaweed, salt brines, and diverse other minor sources.

§ Nitrate is mined chiefly for the element nitrogen. However, most of the world's nitrogen is obtained synthetically in processes which do not involve mining.

¶ Sulfur also is procured in the smelting of iron, copper, zinc, and lead ores, in the distilling of certain coal into coke, and in the refining of certain petroleum and natural gas.

manufacturing operations emphasizing other commodities, and some are secured by still other means. Where obtained from mines, therefore, these materials are frequently in competition with similar commodities derived from other sources. Their uses, like those of the common rocks, usually are numerous and varied, although one or two major uses ordinarily predominate (see Table 25.1).

It is impossible to do justice to all these rocks and minerals in a general textbook, and the selection of a few is necessary. Most of the common rocks, while accounting for large tonnages and value, are obtained primarily through multiplicities of small local operations producing for local markets. In this book, where the viewpoint is chiefly international, we shall concentrate instead upon selected minerals—more specifically, upon phosphate, potash, nitrate, and sulfur. While it is true that in the United States and probably in the world their combined value is much less than that of cement, sand and gravel, and stone, these four minerals are used actively in both agriculture and manufacturing, are at least noteworthy in international trade, and are rapidly rising in significance.

PHOSPHATE

CONSUMPTION

Uses

It has been noted in Chapter 6 that phosphorus is one of the key ingredients of a soil. Man long has sought to replace phosphorus and other soil nutrients lost in crop growth through the spreading of animal manures and, notably in the Far East, of human excrement. While beneficial and still continuing, the manuring practice has not been adequate and, during the past century, has been augmented in technically advanced countries by commercial-fertilizer application. Today in the United Kingdom, for example, animal manures supply somewhat more than one-half of the total nitrogen and potassium, and less than one-third of the phosphorus, applied to the soil annually. The remainder is accounted for by commercial fertilizers. All in all, these fertilizers are sources of demand for nearly 70 per cent of all phosphorus produced in the United States for domestic consumption, with varied industrial commodities accounting for nearly all of the remainder. By way of comparison, almost 80 per cent of all nitrogen and over 90 per cent of all potassium produced in this country go into commercial fertilizers.

Nations of use

The United States is the outstanding consumer of phosphate, followed by the Soviet Union (Fig. 25.1). The two nations jointly are responsible for over one-half of the world consumption, the United States leading by a ratio of slightly more than 3:2. Western European countries utilize nearly all the rest.

Increase in use

Between 1933 and 1959 the consumption of phosphate in the United States increased more than sixfold. In the ten-year period commencing in 1948, world demand also rose sharply, keeping pace with that of the United States. In each case, the increase amounted to about 40 per cent of 1948 consumption.

PRODUCTION

Table 25.2 indicates the world output of the elements phosphorus, potassium, and nitrogen, which are obtained, respectively, from the minerals phosphate, potash, and nitrate. Sources other than minerals exist for each element, and these account for a possible 50 per cent of all phosphorus, only about

TABLE 25.2

World output of phosphorus, potassium, and nitrogen from mineral sources, 1959

Commodity	*Short tons*
Phosphorus (P_2O_5 content) *	10,950,000
Potassium (K_2O content)	9,400,000
Nitrogen (N content) †	315,000

* Phosphoric acid (P_2O_5) content is the author's estimate.
† Output of Chile and Peru.
SOURCE: *Minerals Yearbook.*

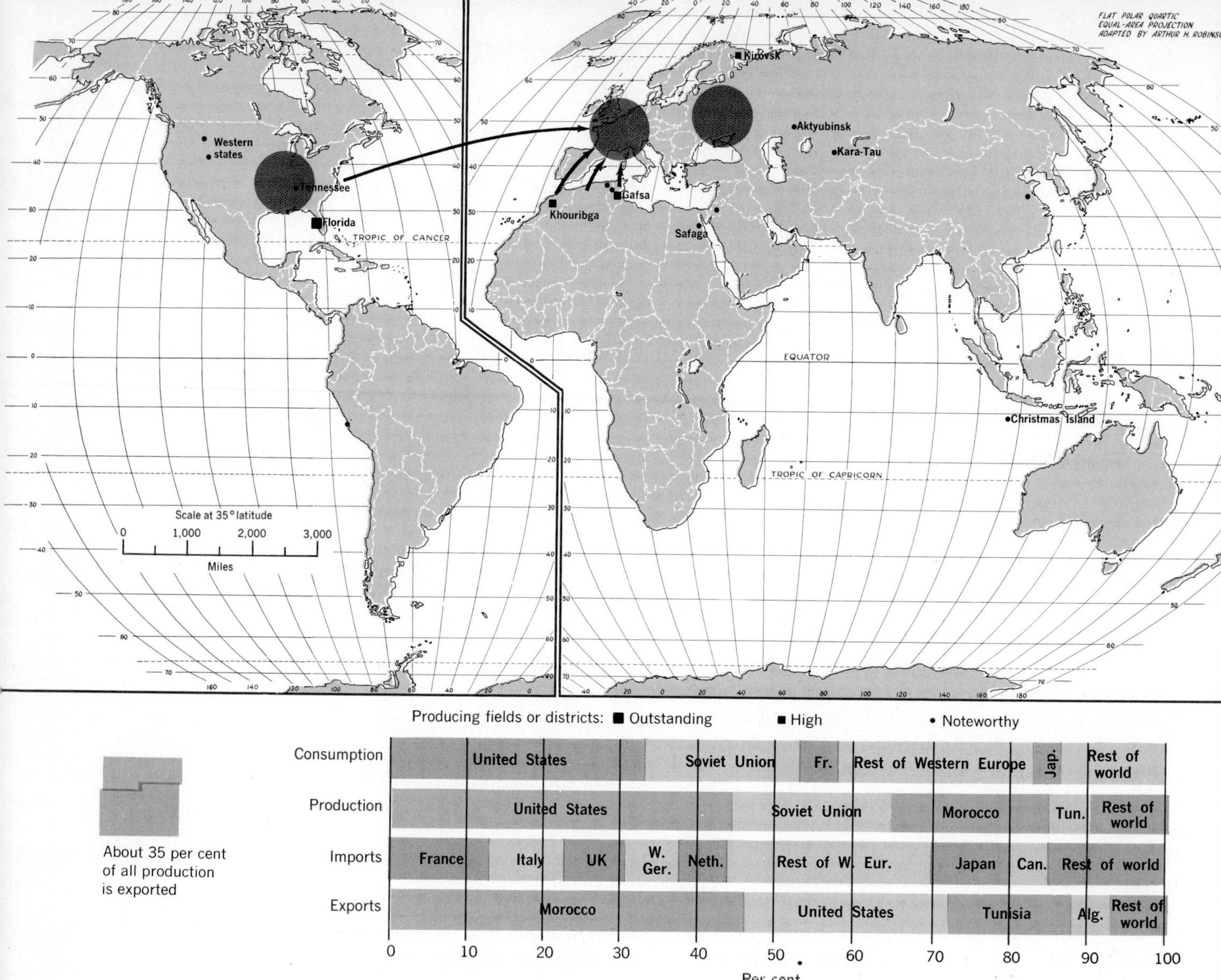

Figure 25.1 ***Consumption, production, import, and export of phosphate rock.*** *Shaded circles show leading nations or regions of consumption. Major producing sites are labeled. Arrows show movement of primary international trade.*

1 per cent of all potassium, and over 97 per cent of all nitrogen (excluding nitrogen from coal).

Phosphorus thus is sought more actively than any other commercial fertilizer. Doubtless this is partially because of the necessity for phosphorus in all forms of life. No plant or animal can exist without it, and it has been called, "the bottleneck of the world's hunger."[2] Given sufficient time, it passes through a cycle not unlike that of water in the well-known hydrologic cycle: originating in igneous rock, some of it eventually becomes transferred to the soil. From here it is absorbed by plants, then by grazing animals, finally by meat-eating and milk-drinking animals. In excrement and decaying bones and flesh it is returned to the land and water—perhaps to enter the soil again immediately and renew the cycle, perhaps to be stored in rock strata for millenniums. That which becomes

[2] *Resources for Freedom,* President's Materials Policy Commission, 1952, vol. 2, p. 156.

sedimentary beds, if it is accessible, may be mined for commercial purposes. In mining the substance, man is thus aiding nature in a process which has been going on for a long, long time.

Natural phosphate occurrence

Natural phosphate is found in both sedimentary and igneous rock, but mostly in the former. Where existing as a sedimentary, the phosphate almost invariably has resulted from one of several processes involving water action. Some occurs as chemically deposited marine phosphate beds. Some is found in phosphatic limestone or marl. Some exists as the result of combinations of the processes responsible for phosphate beds and limestone—combinations in which the phosphates either (1) have replaced pockets of limestone through the action of running water or (2) have been concentrated because running water carried away limestone and other undesirable material. In a few instances, phosphate occurs as *land pebble*—as phosphatic pebbles mixed with other types of gravel. Such phosphate usually has been deposited chemically by water which obtained it from a nearby sedimentary source. A small amount of phosphate is deposited as guano, which is comprised mainly of concentrations of bird or bat droppings. As an igneous material, phosphate occurs rather frequently but usually in small percentages in the mineral apatite. Whatever the source, phosphate is very unevenly distributed, both vertically and horizontally, throughout the world.

The phosphatic content of source materials is usually expressed as *bone phosphate of lime*, or BPL. More accurately, the substance in question is tricalcium phosphate ($Ca_3(PO_4)_2$). To be exploited, a source of phosphate should contain at least 60 per cent BPL, and most commercial deposits contain an even higher percentage.

Adequacy and world distribution of reserves

When measured by present rates of production, the world reserves of phosphate are more than adequate for our times and the foreseeable future. Indeed, a recent estimate places the known commercially exploitable reserves at over 43 billion metric tons. At current phosphate-rock-extraction rates, this is enough to last for at least 2,500 years—and this estimate is thought to be conservative.

Northern Africa, the United States, and the Soviet Union contain most of these deposits (Fig. 25.1). Estimates by different authorities vary rather markedly as to the respective amounts owned by each country, but in all probability Morocco contains more than any other nation, perhaps as much as one-half of the world's total. The United States is well supplied, and the Soviet Union, Tunisia, and Algeria have noteworthy proved reserves.

Production

The United States. The United States is an outstanding producer, as well as consumer, of phosphate. Indeed, it is even more outstanding in production than in consumption, for it is an exporting nation of consequence (Fig. 25.1). Well over one-half the country's rock-phosphate supply is in Idaho, Utah, Montana, Wyoming, and neighboring Western states, and the remainder is chiefly in Florida and, to a very limited degree, Tennessee. The deposits in the West, however, are somewhat inaccessible, both vertically and horizontally. Most are too deep to be mined except with expensive shaft-and-tunnel methods, and are too far from markets and in too rugged a terrain to permit easy overland transportation. Thus, despite their rather high quality, they remain comparatively unexploited.

The Florida deposits, in contrast, are very

Figure 25.2 ***Land-pebble phosphate in Florida*** *(after drawing by Matson, U.S. Geol. Survey, as shown in Alan M. Bateman,* Economic Mineral Deposits, *John Wiley and Sons, Inc., New York, 1950, p. 814).*

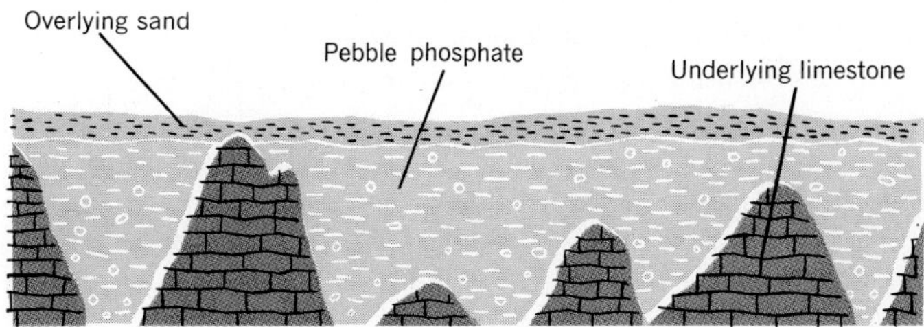

accessible. Nearly all the production is from land pebble, the beds of which are from 2 to 20 feet thick and covered with an overburden generally not exceeding 45 feet in depth (Fig. 25.2). Most are concentrated into a compact area measuring less than 1,000 square miles. As mined, the pebble is from 65 to 75 per cent BPL. Such conditions are almost ideal for highly efficient open-pit mining. Moreover, the deposits are located in the immediate vicinity of the port of Tampa and are not in a disadvantageous position for overland shipment. The quality of the deposits and proximity to both agricultural and manufacturing markets are such that commercial exploitation has encountered no serious obstacles. Furthermore, over three-fourths of Florida's reserves, and over one-fourth of the nation's reserves, are made up of these land-pebble deposits. It would appear that Florida, which now supplies well over 90 per cent of the nation's mined phosphate, will continue to do so for some time.

The remaining 10 per cent of phosphate mined in the United States is obtained in (1) Tennessee and (2) the aforementioned Western states, each category sharing about equally. If trends of the last decade continue, their relative position will remain essentially unchanged.

Meanwhile, the total phosphate output of the nation has risen more than sevenfold since 1933; undoubtedly this rate of growth will continue.

The Soviet Union. Czarist Russia was an importer of phosphate. The present-day Soviet Union produces an estimated 6 million long tons of phosphate rock per year. This amounts to about 40 per cent of the United States production, and nearly 20 per cent of the world total. Currently, the country is a modest exporter.

Nearly three-fourths of the Soviet Union's phosphate is obtained from the mineral apatite, the main reserves of which are near Kirovsk in the Kola Peninsula of northern European Russia (Fig. 25.1). The quality of these deposits is high for apatite but somewhat low in comparison with the best sedimentary deposits. Reserves are relatively large. Sedimentary deposits occur at several sites on the Volga River, at Aktyubinsk southwest of the Urals, and at Kara-Tau in southern Soviet Central Asia. Most of these sites are economically accessible to the country's agricultural and manufacturing markets.

Figure 25.3 ***Phosphate beds in Tunisia and Algeria.*** *Unlike the Florida deposits, these are rather even but warped sedimentary beds, similar to some coal seams (Cf. Fig. 25.2). (After drawing by Cayoux,* Res. Min. France d'Outre-Mer, IV, *Alan M. Bateman,* Economic Mineral Deposits, *John Wiley and Sons, Inc., New York, 1950, p. 817)*

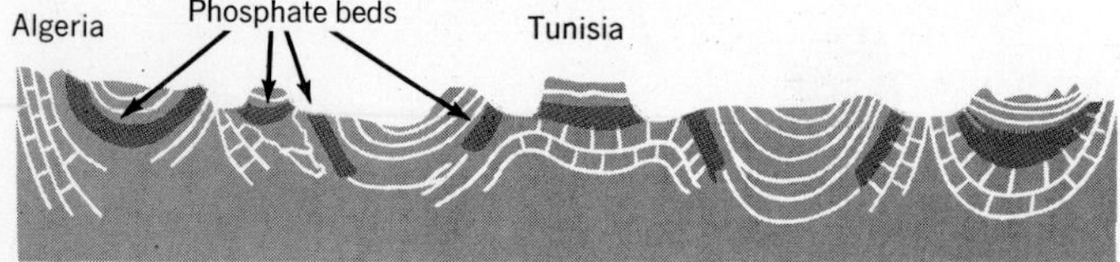

Northern Africa. A distance of nearly 1,000 miles separates the two leading phosphate mining districts of northern Africa. Near Khouribga, some 60 miles inland from the Atlantic seaport of Casablanca in Morocco, are the world's largest deposits. Their quality ranges upward from 70 per cent BPL, and they are easily mined. They currently are responsible for over five-eighths of northern Africa's output, and their rate of increase is higher than elsewhere in the continent.

Far to the east in the vicinity of Gafsa in Tunisia are deposits which also are substantial and economically extractable. Located near the Tunisian-Algerian boundary and extending discontinuously into Algeria, these deposits account for nearly all the non-Moroccan phosphate production in northern Africa (Fig. 25.1). They, too, are easily mined and are located near ocean water; they are served primarily by the Tunisian port of Sfax and lesser ports in Algeria (Fig. 25.3).

A minor producer of phosphate in northern Africa is Egypt, the mines of which are in the vicinity of Safaga on the Red Sea.

Other Producers. The island of Nauru in the Pacific Ocean, a trust territory under the shared administration of Australia, New Zealand, and the United Kingdom, produces slightly over 1 million long tons of phosphate each year. The island is fifth in rank among world producers, being exceeded by the United States, the Soviet Union, Morocco, and Tunisia. Sources of lesser importance include Peru, Christmas Island, Jordan, Makatea, and Ocean Island. Of these, the first two obtain their phosphate almost entirely from guano.

TRADE

Over one-third of all mined phosphate rock enters into international trade. Europe alone of the three large existing market areas is an importer, inasmuch as both the United States and the Soviet Union produce surpluses. With such noteworthy exceptions as Japan and Canada, therefore, world shipments of natural phosphate focus sharply upon Europe, notably Western Europe (Fig. 25.1). North Africa supplies the lion's share of exports. Both political and economic ties are evident in the resulting emphasis in world trade upon shipments from northern Africa to Western Europe. Except for Egypt, the northern African source nations are in the French realm of influence, and their mining activities are financed largely by European capital. Production in Nauru and lesser source areas is likewise dominated from Europe. Essentially no import tariffs are levied on rock phosphate by the leading nations of receipt.

Asia is now entering more actively into world markets as an importing region. Japan has utilized phosphate and other fertilizers for some time, and currently is an important importer (Fig. 25.1). However, both Communist China and India are now awakening to the value of commercial fertilizers—and these two nations jointly contain over one-third of the world's people and nearly one-fourth of all cultivated land.

POTASH

Long prized in the making of soap, matches, pottery, glass, and explosives, as well as in dyeing and leather tanning, potash was secured mainly from wood until the last quarter of the nineteenth century. The wood was burned to ashes in iron pots, and the ashes subsequently leached. The name of the substance has resulted from this manner of its procurement.

With the revolution in agricultural fertilization, potash came into such demand that new methods of obtainment were necessary, and it began to be mined. While not so critical to all plant and animal life as phosphorus, potash is sufficiently necessary to be one of the most actively sold fertilizers.

CONSUMPTION

Over 90 per cent of all potash is destined for commercial-fertilizer production. This cannot be said of any other of the leading minerals going into commercial fertilizers. Like phosphate, potash is utilized largely in technically advanced nations. Inasmuch as it is channeled so predominantly into fertilizers, it tends to be used most actively in countries practicing very intensive agriculture (Figs. 25.4 and 6.7). Europe consumes over one-half of all potash, the United States about one-fourth, the Soviet Union one-eighth, and Japan nearly one-tenth.

The postwar fertilizer demand for the commodity has grown more rapidly than for phosphate, but not so fast as that for nitrogen. The 1955–1956 world consumption of phosphate as a fertilizer was about 126 per cent of that in 1951–1952; of potash, 133 per cent; and of nitrogen, 150 per cent.[3] As is true of phosphate, the Asian portion of the world, notably the Far East, is increasing its rate of consumption of potash more rapidly than any other major area with the possible exception of Oceania. Africa's rate of consumption is also on the rise. The absolute increases in these sections of the world are

[3] Ursula Ewald, *Recent Developments in the World Fertilizer Market: A Statistical Analysis,* Institut fuer Weltwirtschaft, 1957, Kiel, Germany, p. 6.

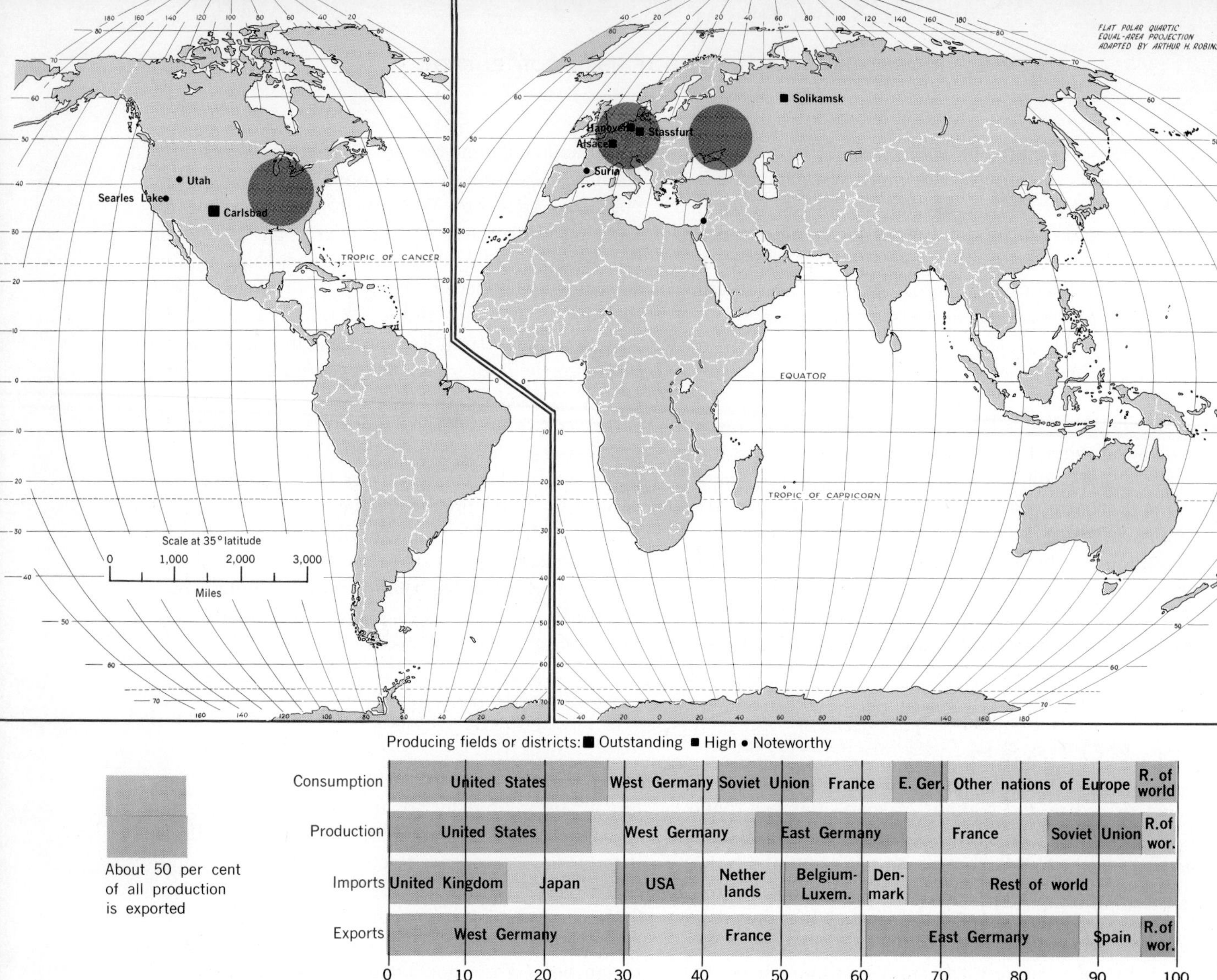

Figure 25.4 ***Consumption, production, import, and export of potash.*** *The circles show leading nations or regions of consumption. Major producing sites are labeled. International trade is chiefly a movement within Western Europe.*

as yet small, but current trends suggest that they too will rise. The rate of potash consumption is also growing in Communist countries, notably the Soviet Union. Western Europe and the United States are still overwhelmingly in the forefront in absolute terms. Because they consume so much, their rate of growth may not seem so marked as the rates of some other areas. However they, also, are using more and more potash (Fig. 25.5). Latin America, somewhat surprisingly, is making use of much less potash and phosphate as fertilizers than either Africa or Asia but does consume appreciable quantities of nitrogen.

PRODUCTION

The annual output of potash, like that of phosphate, is approximately equal to the annual consumption. In each case, working inventories are maintained at only modest size, and there is no reason for them to be raised except in times of emergency. Because potash moves so predominantly into commercial fertilizers (Fig. 25.5), its output is more sensitive to changes in agricultural practices throughout the world than is true of the other leading commodities used in making commercial fertilizers.

Natural occurrence

The mineral potash is closely associated in origin with salt water. It is present in very small quantities in today's oceans, which could become commercial sources if other sources should be depleted. It is mined currently as deposits in beds which have resulted from the evaporation of salt water and as concentrates in brines which have not yet lost all of their water through evaporation. Most comes from the former source and was formed either in sizable areas of marine evaporation or in much smaller terrestrial playa lakes. Despite their origin, the majority of potash reserves are at depths ranging from a few to 3,000 feet.

Adequacy of reserves

Known reserves of potash are sufficient to last for at least 1,000 years, and indicated reserves should last for 4,500 years at current extraction rates. The Soviet Union, West Germany, East Germany, France, Spain, the United States, Poland, and Israel contain most of this supply.

Should the mineral sources become exhausted, an almost endless supply of potash is available in the world's oceans.

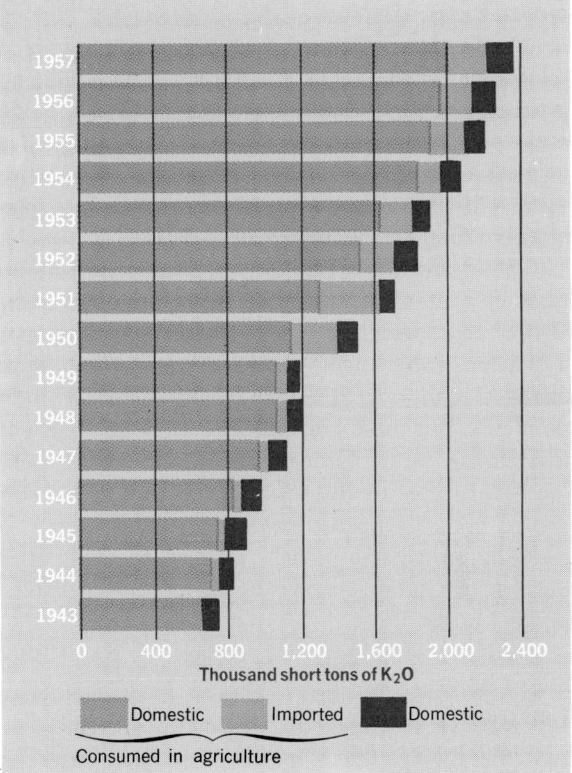

Figure 25.5 ***Use of potash in the United States for years shown.*** *All imported potash and nearly all domestic potash is consumed in agriculture.* (Minerals Yearbook)

Production

We have noted that consumption of potash is most pronounced in technically advanced nations. Nearly all production of the commodity is similarly concentrated. The United States, West Germany, East Germany, France, and the Soviet Union are the leading nations (Fig. 25.4). In this respect, the procuring of potash differs from the obtaining of phosphate, much of which comes from underdeveloped countries of nothern Africa.

The United States. Over one-fourth of all potash is mined in the United States. Production is focused sharply upon the vicinity of Carlsbad, New Mexico, which currently supplies over 90 per cent of the nation's output. Existence of potash in the southeastern corner of the state was revealed in 1925 by oil-well drilling, and the first shipment of crude potash was made in 1931. Although most of the actual mining is still carried on in New Mexico, the reserves reach into much of the Panhandle section of Texas. A broad zone of some 40,000 square miles evidences some potash, and a district of 3,000 square miles definitely contains substantial reserves. Individual beds now being mined range up to 80 feet in thickness and are interspersed with other sedimentaries in a series. The series, in turn, is from 1,000 to 2,600 feet thick, and extends erratically through an even greater vertical distance. The upper levels of potash occur at about 500 feet beneath the land surface, and the lower levels at about 3,500 feet. While the known reserves do not place the United States on a par with the Soviet Union or West Germany, they are enough to last at least a century at current extraction rates. Moreover, it is probable that much more potash is present here than has been proved to date.

Shaft-and-tunnel mining is practiced. The potassium content of salts now being mined is about 18 per cent, which is a slight decline from that of a quarter century ago. At present, six companies are engaged in mining. Some are locally organized independents, but most are branches of national chemical firms. Initial processing operations also are located in the mining area. A semiprocessed substance called *muriate,* as well as other forms of partially processed potash, is forwarded to other parts of the nation—chiefly to the agricultural states of the Middle West.

The remaining potash mined in the United States comes from the brines of Searles Lake in California and sedimentary deposits in Utah.

As in phosphate mining, potash extraction is trending rapidly toward the use of methods and machines which aid the obtainment and procurement of large quantities of intermediate- and low-grade materials. Here as elsewhere in the mining industry, economies of scale are manifesting themselves.

Also as in phosphate mining, the procuring of potash in the United States is largely carried out in one rather small district. To a limited degree for potash, and to a marked degree for phosphate, there are other source materials and areas than the ones being used at this time. However, the commercial advantages of the places and materials of current exploitation for both minerals are such that these places and materials probably will continue to dominate their respective industries for at least the immediately foreseeable future. Thus, despite the alternative possibilities offered by nature in this country, man has seen fit to confine his mining of each substance essentially to a specific district which has pronounced economic advantages.

Europe. About three-fifths of the world's potash is mined in Europe. West Germany, East Germany, and France are by far the leading producers, each contributing in roughly equal amounts to the continent's output. Spain is a minor supplier.

Reserves are more than adequate, especially in

Potash is brought up through a shaft, marked by the tower at the left, and is carried by conveyer directly to the concentration process. Ready for shipment, it is stored in warehouses in the background. This potash mine and concentrating plant is near Carlsbad, New Mexico. Why is the concentration plant located so near the mine? (American Potash Institute)

West and East Germany, where major deposits extend discontinuously from Hanover across the political boundary to Stassfurt. The beds are interwoven with other sedimentaries, as in New Mexico, but are intensively folded and warped. Mining occurs at depths of 1,000 to 3,000 feet in several localized anticlinal upwarps of potassium-impregnated beds that generally lie much lower. The potash content is not high, amounting generally to no more than 10 to 15 per cent. Before the First World War, these reserves supplied nearly all of the world's potash.

French potash is situated primarily in the former province of Alsace, in the Rhine River valley to the country's northeast. Mining depths range from 1,500 to 3,000 feet, and the potassium content of the rocks varies from 15 to 25 per cent.

Both non-Communist and Communist portions of Europe produce as much potash for the world markets as they do for domestic consumption. Most of the potash entering into international trade originates in Europe. Interestingly, most also terminates there.

The Soviet Union. Like that of each of the other leading nations of potash production, the output in the Soviet Union is drawn mainly from a single district—in this case, the Solikamsk vicinity near the upper Kama River and just west of the Urals. These deposits are chiefly of marine origin and occur at depths ranging down to 1,000 feet. They have a potassium content of 20 per cent or less.

Additional reserves are reported near Saratov in European Russia, in Kazakhstan, and in Turkmenia. Late estimates place the total Russian reserves very high.

As in the United States, production of potash began in the Soviet Union in the 1920s and centered in one major site. The Solikamsk vicinity is relatively well located with respect to the agricultural markets of the Soviet Union but not so favorably with respect to seaports that are beginning to export the commodity in very modest amounts. The total output from the Soviet Union currently amounts to about 12 per cent of that of the world.

TRADE

About 50 per cent of all mined potash is sold in world markets. This is largely an international movement between the "have" and "have not" nations of Europe with respect to this commodity. Essentially lacking in potash, the United Kingdom is the world's leading importer, closely followed by Japan. Despite its heavy domestic output, the United States also is an important nation of receipt. The remaining importing nations of prominence are in Western Europe.

More so than is true of phosphate, potash is mined and consumed within technically advanced nations. The not inconsequential exported portion of this commodity represents chiefly an exchange among nations which are economically strong. Some underdeveloped countries, however, are commencing to use potash more actively, and unless they can develop their own sources of supply, they necessarily will import.

NITRATE

Just as the obtaining of phosphate and potash illustrates man's tendency to make economic choices among a limited number of possible mining sites offered by nature, so does the procuring of nitrogen illustrate his capacity to discover alternative sources for commodities in substantial demand but scarce in mineral supply.

BACKGROUND OF CHILEAN NITRATE PRODUCTION

The nation of Chile contains the only known sizable deposits of natural nitrate, which is a source of nitrogen and several materials in lesser demand.

Commercial exploitation of these deposits, commencing in the 1830s, increased gradually but erratically until the 1880s and reached a high point during the First World War. The Chilean government, aware that sources of nitrate were essentially unavailable elsewhere, levied an export tariff amounting at times to approximately one-fourth of the prices charged at receiving ports of importing nations. Moreover, the profits accruing to the Nitrate Producers Association, a monopoly in control of production, not infrequently amounted to an additional 20 per cent of such prices. Although nitrogen began to be obtained in iron- and steel-producing countries as a by-product of coke distillation, the amount so procured was relatively small. The output of Chilean nitrate continued to climb until the climax of the First World War, experiencing only a short recession due to the loss of the German market during the early stages of that conflict—a loss which was quickly offset by increased Allied demand. At this time, over three-fourths of Chile's internal revenue was coming from the export tariff on nitrate.

A nitrate worker in Chile no longer has as much work as he had before the discovery of synthetic nitrate (Hamilton Wright photograph).

Meanwhile, Germany needed nitrogen and was cut off from the Chilean supply. Experiments in securing the element from the air long had been in progress in several nations, and by this time some of these experiments were well past the laboratory stage of development. Given a priority status, the securing of atmospheric nitrogen became a practical reality. Exchange of technical information following the war resulted in the establishment of synthetic-nitrogen plants elsewhere, and in the improvement of techniques. The monopolistic position once held by Chile thus was broken so thoroughly that the country now supplies less than 3 per cent of a world nitrogen output that now exceeds 10 million tons of nitrogen equivalent.

CHILEAN RESERVES AND PRODUCTION

Reserves

The Atacama Desert of northern Chile, one of the world's driest, is a north-south trending valley bordered by coastal ranges on the west and the Andes Mountains on the east. Scattered intermittently along 450 miles of this valley, particularly near the coastal ranges, are deposits of *caliche* covered with overburdens ranging in depth from a few inches to over 40 feet. Translated literally as "a pebble in a brick" or "a flake of lime," *caliche* is made up of sodium nitrate, potassium nitrate, sodium chloride, sodium sulfate, calcium sulfate, and many other materials present in much smaller amounts. The nitrogen content ranges from 5 to 70 per cent, and averages about 25 per cent, or somewhat less. Reserves are substantial, particularly of low-grade materials. They appear to have been concentrated by water evaporation and are of erratic quality and distribution.

Production

Until the past quarter century, production involved much hand labor. The natural conditions, however, favor large-scale mechanization, which has been relied upon increasingly in recent years. Most of the *caliche* is dug with large power shovels and hauled to nearby processing plants on modern railway dump cars—albeit on narrow-gauge tracks. Processing is largely a matter of dissolving the nitrate in water through the use of vats or sprays, subsequently drying the dissolved material, and finally sacking it for shipment to Iquique, Antofagasta, Taltal, and other ports of export. These operations have become increasingly efficient, and some of the most modern yield more than 90 per cent of nitrogen in the rock. *Caliche* with a nitrogen content of 8 per cent or more can now be mined commercially. Sodium nitrate accounts for most of the nitrogen obtained. Among the by-products is iodine, of which the Chilean nitrates constitute an important source.

Since the 1930s, the Chilean government has obtained title to all nitrate properties and regulates production closely. Two major producing companies account for most of the nitrate. Small, independent producers are finding competition excessively keen, and many are closing down operations. Once again, the undeniable cost-price advantages of economies of scale are becoming evident.

Trade

Nearly all Chilean nitrate is exported. The United States, South America, Europe, the Far East, and Oceania are all importers, but only the United States is a major one. Most of the actual and potential importing nations have little or no import tariff on incoming natural nitrate. There is no need for such a tariff: synthetic nitrogen is now selling in the world markets at prices substantially beneath those of nitrogen from Chile, despite recent improvements in the efficiency of recovery and processing of *caliche*. The supply-demand equation for Chilean nitrate has now tipped away from Chile's favor, and that nation, which once commanded almost absolute domination of the world's markets, is now casting about for footholds of survival.

OTHER SOURCES OF MINED NITROGEN

Approximately 80 per cent of the world's nitrogen is extracted directly from the air by manufacturing process,[4] slightly over 17 per cent is produced as a by-product of coking operations, and somewhat under 3 per cent is derived from Chilean nitrates and even less significant sources. Coal is thus a much more important source of mined nitrogen in terms of quantity than is nitrate. The major iron- and steel-producing nations—the United States, the Soviet Union, West Germany, the United Kingdom, France, Japan, and Belgium—rely upon coal for mined nitrogen.

Guano is an organic source of nitrogen and potassium taken from the Peruvian Chincha Islands and from minor scattered sources, including Bat Cave on the southern rim of the Grand Canyon in Arizona.

SULFUR

CONSUMPTION

Uses

More sulfur is produced and consumed each year than either potash or nitrate. It is consumed not so much in the form of raw sulfur as in sulfuric acid, which in many instances is an agent rather than a raw material in a manufacturing process. More than 90 per cent of the sulfur used in the United States, for example, is in the form of sulfuric acid. The utilization of sulfur and sulfuric acid is indicated in Table 25.3. The fertilizer industry is the

[4] And hence will not be treated in this chapter, which emphasizes mining.

TABLE 25.3

Uses of sulfur and sulfuric acid

Use	*Per cent of total used*
Raw sulfur	
Heavy chemicals	50.0
Fertilizer and insecticides	21.0
Pulp and paper	10.0
Paint and varnish	3.6
Explosives	3.0
Dyes and coal-tar products	2.7
Rubber	2.2
Food products	0.2
Miscellaneous	7.3
Total	100.0
Sulfuric acid	
Fertilizer	35.0
Chemicals	21.0
Oil refining	11.0
Rayon and film	6.4
Paints and pigments	6.1
Coal products	6.0
Iron and steel	5.5
Other metallurgical manufacturing	3.2
Explosives	2.0
Textiles	0.8
Miscellaneous	4.0
Total	100.0

SOURCE: Alan M. Bateman, *Economic Mineral Deposits*, John Wiley & Sons, Inc., New York, 1950, p. 788.

prime source of demand for sulfuric acid and an important consumer of raw sulfur.

Nations of use

The sulfur uses shown in Table 25.3 are evidence of the overwhelming importance of technically advanced nations as consumers. The United States is an outstanding consumer, and the Soviet Union and leading nations of Western Europe are more than noteworthy.

MINE PRODUCTION

About 45 per cent of all sulfur comes from iron pyrites and sulfides of nonferrous metals. A small portion is obtained in such operations as the purification of natural gas, refining of petroleum, and burning and distillation of coal. Essentially all the remainder is mined as *native sulfur* in an amount approximately equaling that obtained from pyrites and sulfides. In this chapter, we are concerned only with the native sulfur.

Leading nations and techniques of native-sulfur production

Native sulfur is overwhelmingly a product of North America. The United States, which has been an active producer during much of the present century, alone accounts for over three-fourths of the world total. Mexico, a newcomer with potentialities, provides an additional one-sixth. Japan heads a list of additional but minor producers.

The United States. About three-fourths of all sulfur produced in the United States is native sulfur. This, in turn, comes almost entirely from deposits near the coast lines of Texas and Louisiana. The sulfur occurs in the cap rock of some salt domes which have been upthrust from very great depths; in some instances the depths exceed thousands of feet. It is present in only a few of the numerous domes with which it might be associated. It tends to occur in the lower part of a cavernous limestone at depths ranging generally from 1,000 to 2,000 feet below the land surface. The sulfur zone is vertically and horizontally uneven, and varies from 20 to 350 feet in thickness. The horizontal dimensions of the domes are not inconsequential, ranging from 80 to over 1,000 acres.

Prior to this century, the sulfur was not mined in quantity, because the loose nature of much of the overlying material discouraged shaft-and-tunnel mining. The development of the Frasch process, however, revolutionized sulfur recovery here. Simple in its basic concept, this process involves the pumping of hot water and air directly into the sulfur deposits (Fig. 25.6). The water melts the sulfur, which is forced to the surface by the air. There the sulfur is allowed to resolidify as an essentially pure substance. Thus, in one action, this remarkable process accomplishes what for most minerals would require not only mining but also one or two stages of manufacturing.

Nearly all native sulfur mined in the United States is now Frasch sulfur, of which Texas supplies about three-fifths and Louisiana the remainder. Hard-rock mines in California and other Western states, using traditional shaft-and-tunnel methods, account for a very small amount.

Mexico. World demand for sulfur since the last war has risen so rapidly that it outdistanced its supply by mid-century. Accordingly, special attention has been given to new sources, and Mexico recently has emerged as a major producing nation of raw sulfur. The country now ranks second only to the United States among world producers of native sulfur. Deposits are situated near the eastern coast and are worked almost entirely by the Frasch process. Substantial private investment from the United States has stimulated the development of these deposits.

Lesser Nations. Japan mines some native sulfur on the island of Honshu, chiefly by shaft-and-tunnel means. Sicily, under Italian jurisdiction, has underground deposits which were a prime source of world supply before the activation of the Texas-Louisiana fields and which still produce at least a nominal amount each year. Other production of native sulfur in the world is scattered and relatively minor.

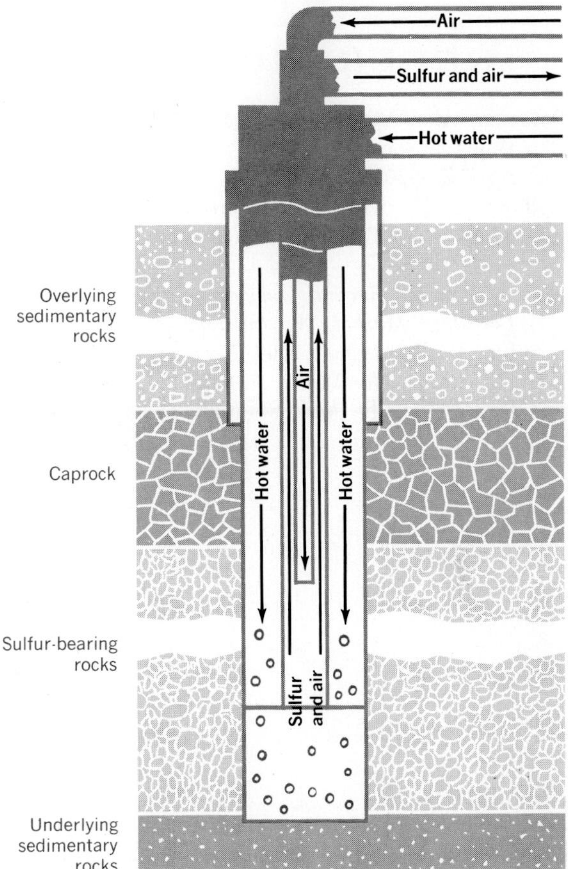

Figure 25.6 ***The Frasch process of sulfur mining.*** *Air and hot water are forced into the sulfur deposits, and melted sulfur and air come to the surface. Sulfur obtained in this way along the Gulf Coast may be as deep as 2,000 feet beneath the surface. (After drawing by Lundy,* Indust. Min. and Rocks, *as reproduced in Alan M. Bateman,* Economic Mineral Deposits, *John Wiley and Sons, Inc., New York, 1950, p. 790)*

TRADE

Statistics treating international trade in sulfur are concerned largely with total quantities, regardless of source. Since native sulfur accounts for less than one-half of the world output, we cannot be absolutely certain of the exact amount of mined sulfur entering world markets. Total sulfur movement, however, suggests the dominance of technically advanced nations as importers. Western Europe is especially active, despite very substantial production there from pyrites and other sources. The United States is a net exporter, although it imports substantial quantities from Mexico and elsewhere. Asia, particularly India, is importing sulfur in increasing quantities. There does not appear to be a very active trade in sulfur among Communist nations.

REFERENCES

Bateman, Alan M.: *Economic Mineral Deposits,* John Wiley & Sons, Inc., New York, 1950. (Especially pp. 749–820.)

Collings, G. H.: *Commercial Fertilizers: Their Sources and Use,* McGraw-Hill Book Company, Inc., New York, 1955.

Ewald, Ursula: *Recent Developments in the World Fertilizer Market: A Statistical Analysis,* Institut fuer Weltwirtschaft, Kiel, Germany, 1957.

Lamer, Mirko: *The World Fertilizer Economy,* Stanford University Press, Stanford, Calif., 1957.

LeBaron, I. M.: "The Phosphate Industry in Florida," *Farm Chemicals,* **120** (8):49–52, 1957.

Pirkle, E. C.: "Economic Considerations of Pebble Phosphate Deposits of Alachua County, Florida," *Economic Geology,* **52**:354–378, 1957.

Woytinsky, W. S., and E. S. Woytinsky: *World Population and Production,* The Twentieth Century Fund, Inc., New York, 1953. (Especially pp. 832–838.)

26 MINING: PRECIOUS MATERIALS

IN THE FUNCTIONING OF THE WORLD'S ECONOMIES, THE FINEST OF PRECIOUS metals and stones enjoy a somewhat unusual status in that most are coveted because of their beauty, permanency, rarity, or other qualities which set them apart from the more common rocks and minerals. Their beauty is such that most were used by man centuries before the Industrial Revolution created an intense interest in mineral procurement. Their permanence is such that known amounts have been preserved for millenniums. Their rarity is such that, even in this twentieth century of large-scale exploitation, their output is reckoned in terms like *fine ounces* and *carats* rather than pounds and tons. Their small bulk and weight, however, should not be taken to indicate that their value also is small: calculated by current United States prices, the combined value of all gold, silver, platinum-group metals, and diamonds produced in 1959 was about 40 per cent of the amount of all iron ore mined in the same year.

Despite their unusual status, precious materials are not used entirely in unusual ways. At least a portion of the annual production of nearly every precious metal or stone either becomes a raw material or processing agent in production or is utilized for some other purpose not markedly unlike that for which more common materials are sought. Indeed, nearly all the platinum-group metals are used industrially, and it is essentially their very high costs which causes them to be grouped with precious materials.

GOLD

UTILIZATION

Manner of use

Gold is the aristocrat of precious metals in the sense that it is used mainly as a foundation for monetary systems. An estimated 90 per cent of new gold either goes into bank reserves or is hoarded, and the remainder, alloyed with copper, silver, nickel, platinum, and other metals, goes into such industrial products as jewelry and watches. Nations in all continents except parts of Asia have tended to favor gold as a foundation for their moneys. The price of gold is set by law and is subject to the vagaries of supply and demand only in so far as these vagaries make an impact upon lawmakers and those who execute laws, allowing some room for maneuver. At various times in history, especially during the heyday of British world supremacy in the latter part of the nineteenth century and the first third of the current century, most of the leading technically advanced nations were on the *gold standard*—i.e., they established a specific and fixed relationship between gold and their own currencies and accepted gold freely in international transactions. Since the 1930s most technically advanced nations have rejected the gold standard for "managed currency" policies in which both the relationship of currency to gold and the volume of gold movement can be regulated more effectively.[1] To a greater extent than in the nineteenth century, the ownership of gold is now in the hands of governments rather than individuals, and its domestic and international movement is closely regulated.

Most of the world's gold thus is laid away by governments as both an actual and psychological security for their monetary systems. Only a small amount goes into industrial use.

[1] However, governments still attempt to maintain a stable and somewhat lasting relationship between gold and currency. Since the United States went off the gold standard in 1934, the price of gold has remained at $35 a fine ounce, despite legal provision for its alteration by the Secretary of the Treasury. Efforts are made to maintain this ratio throughout the world. That these are not always successful is indicated below:

Average price* of "free" gold bars, 1958

City	*Price per fine troy ounce*
Bombay	$57.15
Hong Kong	38.41
Manila	36.35
Paris	36.18
Buenos Aires	36.18
Beirut	35.23
Tangier	35.18

* Prices are quoted at the "free," or black-market, value of the United States dollar in the local markets.
SOURCE: *Minerals Yearbook.*

TABLE 26.1

Gold reserves in non-Communist countries, 1959

Country or organization	*Value in millions of United States dollars*
United States	19,045
United Kingdom	3,072
West Germany	2,879
Switzerland	1,960
France	1,568
Netherlands	1,246
Belgium	1,094
Canada	904
International Monetary Fund	2,562
Other	6,630
Total	40,960

SOURCE: Federal Reserve Bulletin, October, 1960, p. 1204. By August, 1960, the United States reserves were 18,685 million dollars.

Nations of use

Gold stocks in the non-Communist countries as of December, 1959, are shown in Table 26.1. The overwhelming dominance of the United States, with nearly 50 per cent of the total, is striking. However, as late as 1957 that country had nearly 60 per cent of the total. With the economic recovery of Europe, the United States has retreated somewhat from its earlier, even higher level. Also, the Soviet Union is a leading producer of gold, and its reserves, if included, would detract further from the United States dominance.

The United States also is outstanding in gold consumption for industrial purposes, accounting for over one-half of all gold so used. Countries of Western Europe and the Soviet Union account for nearly all of the remainder.

PRODUCTION

Natural occurrence

Although gold at one time occurred entirely in igneous materials, present-day deposits are largely the result of water action. Such reserves may be placer deposits existing along both surface river and stream beds and along former waterways, or they may be subsurface accumulations resulting from the action of underground water. In either case the gold content is usually very low, amounting to no more than 5 fine ounces per ton in even the better-quality ores. Sometimes the gold does not occur alone but in association with other metals and is recovered as a by-product. In the United States, about 60 per cent of the annual gold production now comes from ores containing few, if any, other commercially recoverable metals. One-third of such gold comes from placer deposits and two-thirds from underground sources. Approximately 30 per cent is recovered as a by-product of copper ore, and about 10 per cent as a by-product of lead, zinc, or lead-zinc-copper ores. These by-product sources are almost entirely underground.

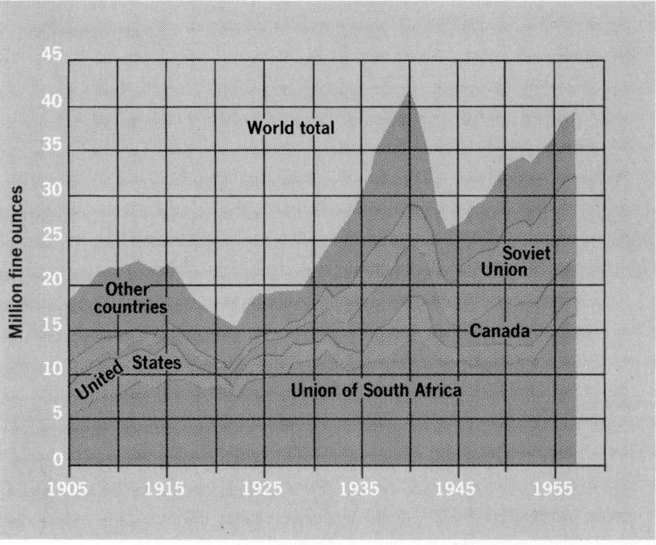

Figure 26.1 ***A half-century of mined-gold output.*** *The trends shown here have continued through 1960, with the Union of South Africa gaining the most rapidly, followed by the Soviet Union.* (Minerals Yearbook)

Leading nations of production

Gold, the saying goes, is where you find it. However, if you own a large ranch, your chances of finding it on your property are substantially better than if you own only a small city lot. The same can be said of nations. Three of the four world leaders in gold production—the Soviet Union, Canada, and the United States—are giants when measured by square miles. However, the Union of South Africa, which is smallest in area among the leading four countries, is also outstandingly foremost in production. It is true that gold is where you find it and that your chances of finding it within your own territory are better if your holdings are large, but you *may* find it on your own property even if you own only a city lot.

The Union of South Africa. Well over 40 per cent of the world's primary gold is produced in the Union of South Africa, and its output is rising (Fig. 26.1). The older producing fields are the Witwatersrand and associated diggings near Johannesburg. West and southwest of these older diggings, but still in Transvaal, are two newer fields, one near the far western Rand and the other near Klerksdorp. About 20 million fine ounces were obtained in 1959 from over 70 million tons of ore mined in the Union of South Africa, the recovery rate averaging approximately 0.28 ounce per ton. In the older fields, some of which have been worked for three-quarters of a century, the diggings are now down to levels of almost 10,000 feet beneath the local surface.

The Soviet Union. Ranking well behind the Union of South Africa but easily ahead of all other competition is the Soviet Union, the average annual production of which has increased from 8.5 million to 10 million fine ounces since the Second World War (Fig. 26.1). Currently, the country supplies an estimated 25 per cent of world output. The main producing fields are far to the east, notably along the upper Lena and Vitim Rivers but also at numerous sites from the Yenisei River eastward. The Ural Mountains and isolated locations in western Siberia are source areas of lesser significance. Both underground and placer deposits are present in the country as a whole.

Canada. Canada's gold is produced in fields situated much more favorably with respect to both domestic and foreign markets than those of the

Soviet Union. Output, amounting to over 10 per cent of the world total, is concentrated in a series of districts which on a large-scale map appear as a single zone lying astride the Ontario-Quebec border, north of the Great Lakes. The former province is the more important, accounting for about 58 per cent of all the Canadian yield. Quebec is responsible for 23 per cent, and the Northwest Territories and British Columbia contribute 8 and 5 per cent, respectively. The Ontario-Quebec deposits are principally underground veins into which the gold has been injected by underground water. One of the longest veins extends nearly 2½ miles. Mining is carried on at depths of 2,000 feet or more. Although the gold occurs with other minerals, notably pyrite, most is not produced as a by-product but is the prime source of attention. Gold now ranks fifth in value among all metallic commodities from Canadian mines.

The United States. Among the leading nations in total gold production, the fourth-ranking United States mines only slightly more than one-tenth of the annual output of that of the Union of South Africa, which is first. Mines of the United States are situated chiefly in the West and far North: South Dakota supplies nearly one-third, Utah over one-fifth, and Alaska approximately one-eighth of the country's annual production, with California, Arizona, Washington, Colorado, and other Western states contributing nearly all of the remainder. The South Dakota gold is mined in the Black Hills, largely in the Homestake Mine. The ore occurs in complex rock structure at depths ranging from a few hundred to over 4,000 feet. It is principally the result of deposition by underground water. Gold is the primary substance sought here, although a very small amount of silver occurs with the gold and is a by-product. The gold content, while low, compares favorably with that of the world's leading producing nation: approximately 0.3 fine troy ounce of the metal is realized from each ton of South Dakota ore, whereas 0.28 fine troy ounce per ton is realized in the Union of South Africa.

Conditions of production differ rather sharply from state to state. In Utah, the gold comes almost entirely from the Bingham area, where it is chiefly a by-product of copper production. In Alaska, as in

Gold mining can be a large-scale operation, as at Yellowknife on the Great Slave Lake of northern Canada. The settlement, water supply, and one underground mine are in the foreground; another underground mine and the concentrating mill are in the background. (George Hunter, Toronto)

In Minas Gerais, Brazil, gold is panned by hand (Brazilian Embassy).

South Dakota, it is the chief metal sought where it is mined, but here it occurs principally as surface and near-surface placer deposits and is obtained largely by dredges working to depths sometimes exceeding 200 feet. In California it is also mined principally from placer deposits, although a noteworthy quantity of underground ore is also mined.

Other Countries. Political units that are lesser producers of gold include Australia, Ghana, Southern Rhodesia, the Philippines, the former Belgian Congo, Colombia, El Salvador, and a host of others. Australia is easily in the forefront of this group, producing nearly 4 per cent of the world's annual yield, chiefly from scattered sites in the west.

Trends. Since the turn of the current century the world's annual gold output has fluctuated between 16 million and 42 million fine ounces (Fig. 26.1). Its general trend has been upward, although it has responded to war periods and, in a lesser degree, to periods of economic depression. Among the four leading producers, only the United States has experienced decline—a decline, it will be noted, which is absolute as well as relative. Each of the other three has achieved substantial gains.

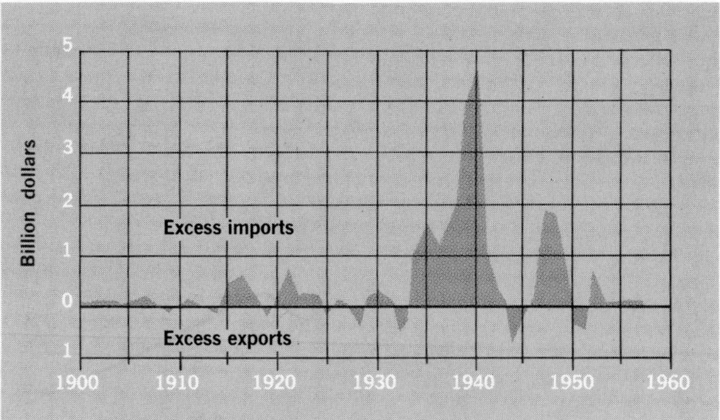

Figure 26.2 ***A half-century of United States export-import policy concerning gold.*** *How do you account for the comparatively few and small periods when this country was a net exporter?* (Minerals Yearbook)

TRADE

The dominance of the United States in world economic affairs is reflected in its commanding position in world gold trade. We have noted that the United States is a comparatively modest producer but that it contains about 50 per cent of the world's stocks of mined gold that have not been used industrially. Figure 26.2 indicates the extent to which the country traditionally has engaged upon a policy of gold import (although that policy has been reversed in the past few years). The United Kingdom and West Germany, having recovered from the Second World War, have accumulated gold reserves exceeding appreciably those of other non-Communist European nations (Table 26.1). This remarkable achievement, however, does not begin to place either country in effective competition with the United States in the world's gold market. Most new gold thus moves from the Union of South Africa and Canada to the United States and Europe. The Soviet Union probably has a noteworthy reserve, but this has been obtained through domestic mining rather than through exchange. Indeed, the Soviet Union sometimes has sold substantial quantities of gold in the past decade. Both international and domestic movement of gold are subject to very close governmental regulation. Indeed, as we have mentioned, present-day ownership of the metal is largely in the hands of governments, whether in non-Communist or Communist countries.

OTHER LEADING PRECIOUS MATERIALS

Precious materials other than gold are used as ingredients and agents of production to a greater extent than gold. They also amount to less in monetary value than gold: the total annual yield of silver, platinum metals, and diamonds amounts to approximately one-half the value of the annual yield of gold.

SILVER

The dominance of gold among the precious metals is in terms of value. In terms of quantity gold is surpassed by silver: between five and six times as much silver is produced each year. But while the market value of gold in the United States is $35 per fine troy ounce, that of silver is approximately 90 cents; hence the difference in total value favors gold.

Consumption

If gold is the prime foundation of monetary systems, silver is their agent at the bazaar. Coins constitute a convenient and easily recognizable small change, and a silver or silver alloy can lend a sense of dignity to a coin without making it unduly expensive. Approximately one-third of the world's annual silver output currently goes into coins. This fraction varies from year to year, and may be as high as one-half or as low as one-fourth. The many industrial and artistic commodities that utilize the remaining annual silver supply, sometimes dipping into silver stocks, include silverware; photographic materials; contacts, wire, and other electrical goods; electroplated products; and dental and medical supplies. The United States is dominant among consuming nations, utilizing nearly one-half of the world's industrial silver and sometimes as much as one-fourth all silver going into coins and bullion. Nearly all remaining demand stems from Western Europe and the Soviet Union.

Production

Like gold, silver is produced mainly in a very few countries. Mexico, the United States, Canada, Peru, and the Soviet Union are the leading producers. Over one-half of the total annual output comes from North America, and nearly two-thirds from the dollar bloc, where there is substantial financial investment from the United States. Only the Soviet Union is outstanding in the Eastern Hemisphere, although Australia deserves at least passing mention. Trends in world output are erratic, and the current yield is only moderately higher than was that in 1900. Peak periods of production occurred before the stock-market crash in 1929 and during the early stages of the Second World War. Neither Mexico nor the United States now mines as much silver as during those two peak periods. Canada and Peru have retained or improved their relative positions, and the Soviet Union has become an increasingly important producer.

Trade

In silver as in gold mining, a high percentage of the product enters international markets. The United States, although a major producer, has followed a policy of silver importation since the early 1930s except during the Second World War. The country's current net annual imports amount to over one-half of all world production, although not all such imports involve newly produced silver. West Germany, the United Kingdom, and other Western European nations are also leading importers of silver.

PLATINUM-GROUP METALS

The platinum-group metals include platinum, palladium, iridium, osmium, rhodium, and ruthenium, all of which tend to occur together in nature. The volume of their output is small: whereas current world production of gold is slightly in excess of 39.6 million fine troy ounces and that of silver is approximately 228.7 million fine ounces, that of the platinum group is approximately 1.2 million fine ounces. The price per ounce varies sharply among the six elements. In the United States, palladium is the cheapest and rhodium the most expensive. The former sells for about $24 and the latter for about $120 per fine ounce. Nearly all sell for more than $75 per fine ounce and thus are at least twice as costly as gold.

Consumption

Despite their high cost, the platinum-group metals are somewhat unusual among precious materials in that they are used almost entirely for industrial purposes. Most are excellent catalytic agents. Platinum and palladium are used in the largest amounts —the platinum notably as a catalytic agent in petroleum refining and other chemical processing, and palladium especially as a raw material for fine electrical parts. Dental and medical, jewelry, and other uses also are significant. The United States consumes about three-fourths of all of the platinum-group metals.

Production and trade

Canada was the outstanding producer of the platinum-group metals until after the Second World War. Since 1950, however, the Union of South Africa has suddenly emerged as the world leader, and now makes available well over one-half of all these metals. South Africa's producing fields involve underground deposits near Bushveld in Transvaal, not far from some of the country's gold-mining activities. However, the ores there contain only small amounts of metals other than platinum, and the two mining industries are essentially independent of each other. Canada's production is concentrated in the Sudbury district, where platinum metals are by-products of underground nickel-copper ores. For a century preceding the First World War Russia was the primary source of platinum metals, for which the Soviet Union now depends chiefly upon placer deposits on both sides of the central Urals.

The United States is the outstanding importing nation of platinum-group metals, and Western Europe imports nearly all of the small remainder. The substantial amounts of these metals originating in the Union of South Africa move largely to the United Kingdom and other Western European nations, where they are refined before being forwarded to the United States or consumed locally. A small amount of refined metals also comes to the United States from the Soviet Union. The very substantial quantities moving from Canada to the United States are also refined rather than crude.

DIAMONDS

Larger, more perfect diamonds become gems, and the smaller, more numerous, but less perfect diamonds, are used for industrial purposes. Measured by value, the world's annual output and consumption of gem diamonds exceeds that of industrial diamonds by an approximate ratio of 4:1. Measured in carats, however, industrial diamonds lead by about the same ratio.

The diamond is made up of the single element carbon that has crystallized under conditions of heat and pressure. It is the hardest natural substance known. Most diamonds have been formed within intrusive igneous materials, but many have been removed by erosional agents and deposited into sedimentary materials. To date the majority of gem diamonds have been found in sedimentary deposits.

Consumption

The uses of gem diamonds are self-evident. Industrial diamonds, once considered so worthless that they sometimes were shipped as vessel ballast in lieu of sand or gravel, are important agents of manufacturing and mining. Because of their hardness, they are excellent surfacing materials for dies, tips for rock drills, and abrasives. *Bort,* or incomplete fragments left over from the recovery of more expensive diamonds, is the name given to much of such industrial material. A black diamond found chiefly in Brazil and known as *carbonado* also is used industrially.

The United States is an outstanding consumer of both gem diamonds and industrial diamonds. The country's demand for gem diamonds does not vary pronouncedly from year to year and currently amounts to about 40 per cent of the world production (Fig. 26.3). Industrial diamonds too are in rather consistent demand in the United States, which ultimately uses an even higher percentage of industrial diamonds than of gem diamonds—well over 60 per cent of world production. A substantial share of both gem diamonds and industrial diamonds is processed in Europe before being forwarded to the United States and elsewhere.

Production and trade

As in mining gold and platinum-group metals, Africa is the leading continent in diamond obtainment. The former Belgian Congo is foremost in industrial-diamond production, supplying nearly three-fourths of the world total. Ghana, the Union of South Africa, and Sierra Leone are secondary industrial-diamond producers, and Angola, Southwest Africa, and Tanganyika are noteworthy. Outside Africa, Brazil and Venezuela are worthy of mention, but their output is generally no higher than that of the lesser African producers. The Soviet Union has announced the discovery of a diamond field in central Siberia that offers promise of at least noteworthy yield, particularly of smaller industrial diamonds. The majority of the world's gem diamonds are taken from the Kimberly area in Cape Province of the Union of South Africa.

Diamond production and sale in non-Communist countries is largely under the control of a single firm, the De Beers Consolidated Mines, Ltd. Chiefly through its marketing outlet, the Diamond

Trading Company (sometimes known as the Diamond Corporation), located in London, De Beers is able to regulate production, price, and volume of trade. The corporation specializes in gem diamonds, which, as we have noted, make up nearly four-fifths of the total value of all diamonds sold each year.

Rough diamonds usually are not processed where they are mined but are forwarded primarily to Western Europe for that purpose. Of the more than twenty thousand diamond cutters and auxiliary workers, over one-half are in Belgium, and the others are in West Germany, the Netherlands, Israel, the United States, and elsewhere. International trade in rough diamonds, especially gem diamonds, thus is essentially a movement from Africa to these processing nations and thence to ultimate markets in the United States and elsewhere. Experiments in making artificial diamonds are now past the laboratory stage, and these may well come into competition with natural diamonds.

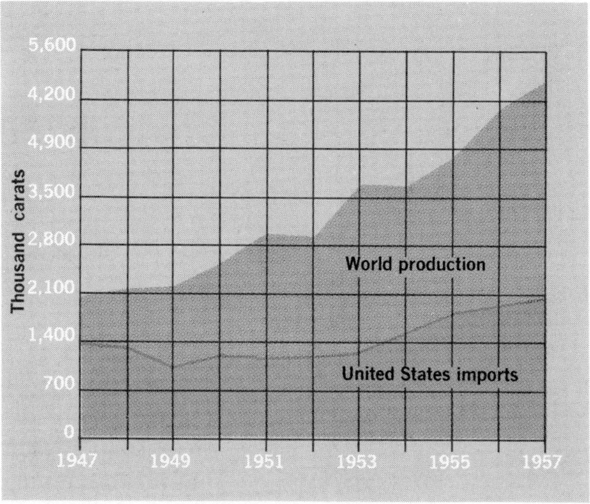

Figure 26.3 ***A half-century record of world production and United States imports of gem diamonds.*** *In 1959 the world output was 5,903,000 carats, of which the United States imported 2,518,419 carats, or slightly over two-fifths.* (Minerals Yearbook)

REFERENCES

"The Diamond Ring," *London Economist,* **185** (5962): 791–793, November 30, 1957.

The Diamond Tool Industry, Industrial Diamond Information Bureau, Berwick-on-Tweed, 1956.

Groseclose, Elgin: "A Look Ahead at Gold and Silver," *Mines Magazine,* **48** (8): 31–37, 1957.

Hahn, Emily: *Diamond,* Weidenfeld and Nicolson, London, 1956.

"International Gold and Dollar Flows," *Federal Reserve Bulletin,* **43**:249–255, March, 1957.

Israel Export Journal, October, 1956. (Special issue covering Ninth Annual Congress of World Federation of Diamond Bourses.)

Leeper, Sir Reginald: "The Development of the Diamond Industry," *Optima,* **7** (3): 125–129, 1957.

Man-made Diamonds, General Electric Company, Research Laboratory, Research Information Services, Schenectady, N.Y., 1955.

Mineral Facts and Problems, U.S. Bureau of Mines, 1960. (Especially pp. 267–282, 347–356, 643–650, and 735–744.)

Voskuil, Walter H.: *Minerals in World Industry,* McGraw-Hill Book Company, Inc., New York, 1955. (Especially chap. 25.)

27 MINING: IRON ORE AND OTHER INDUSTRIAL MATERIALS

THE IMPACT OF THE INDUSTRIAL REVOLUTION UPON AN ECONOMY IS IN NO WAY reflected more directly than in that economy's output and use of iron and steel, copper, aluminum, zinc, lead, tin, manganese, molybdenum, tungsten, nickel, chromium, vanadium, titanium, magnesium, and still other industrial metals. Indeed, some authorities consider per capita production of iron and steel as an important yardstick in measuring the level of an economy's industrial development, for upon such production rest many of the remaining activities of a manufacturing nation. This chapter emphasizes the mining of iron, unquestionably the leader of the group and most basic to manufacturing, and comments selectively upon the remainder.

IRON ORE

CONSUMPTION

Leading nations of consumption

Although the use of iron has been extended in limited degree to the inhabited world, its intensive consumption involves only a relatively few technically advanced nations (Fig. 27.1). Of these, the United States is easily the leader, accounting for one-third of the world total. The Soviet Union is comfortably in second position, followed by West Germany, Communist China, France, and the United Kingdom. World consumption of this commodity thus follows the familiar pattern of dominance by the United States as a nation and of marked activity by Europe as a region, with the Soviet Union and Communist China offering an increased measure of competition to both.

Form of consumption

From the time it is mined, the iron in iron ore passes through several stages of manufacturing before it appears ultimately in either producer or consumer goods. Until the 1940s the places of immediate destination for most of the world's iron ore were the blast and steel furnaces, where the material was consumed much as it came from the mine. This is still true of many

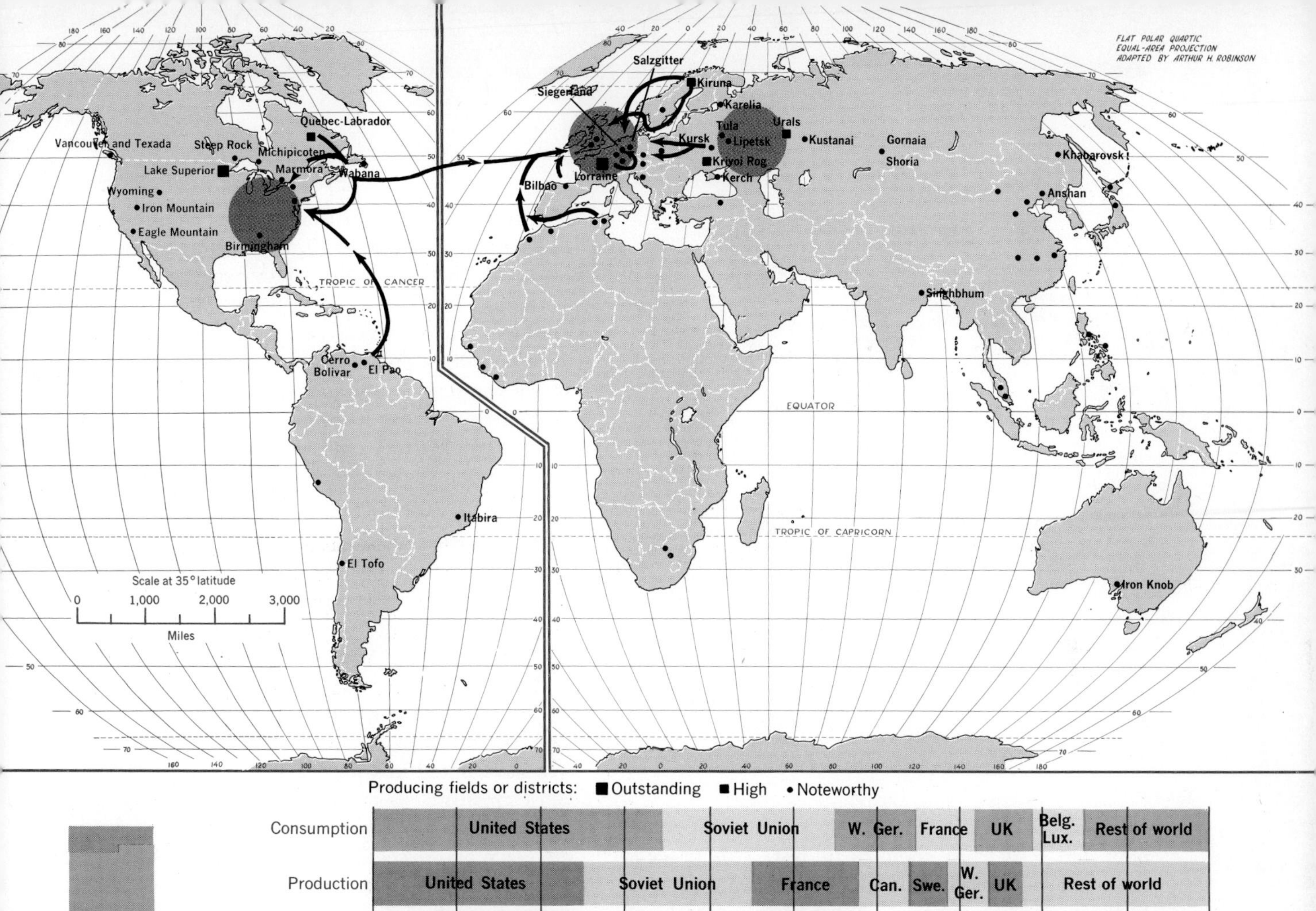

Figure 27.1 ***Consumption, production, import, and export of iron ore.*** *Circles show leading nations or regions of consumption. Leading producing sites are labeled. Arrows show primary international movement. Communist China now reports a consumption exceeding that of France or the United Kingdom. Production there now is said to be higher than in Canada or Sweden, but these reports may be exaggerated.*

of the best ores—those of 51.5 per cent or higher iron content[1]—especially if individual particles comprising those ores are not prevailingly fine. Particularly during and since the Second World War, however, processes of *agglomeration* and *concentration* have come into common use. The first involves the combining of fine particles into lumps, or pellets, which can survive the fiery heat of the blast and steel furnaces—heat which would send

[1] Iron ore of 51.5 per cent or higher iron content and 10 per cent or lower silica content is known in the trade as *direct-shipping ore,* which need not be concentrated before being charged into a blast furnace. It may be agglomerated, however, in order to recover the very fine material.

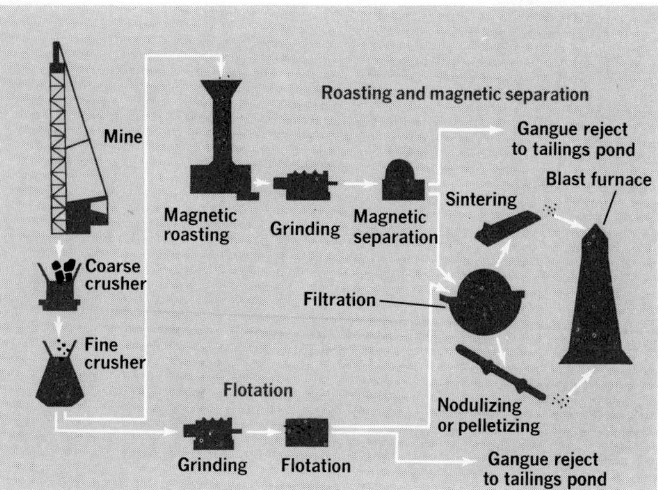

Figure 27.2 ***Two processes of iron-ore beneficiation: roasting and magnetic separation, and flotation.*** *Because they have certain steps in common, these concentration processes are shown here in the same graph; they are, however, two distinct processes.*

many of the original particles up the furnace chimneys and thus cause them to be lost. This process does not necessarily raise the proportion of iron to the total mass of an ore, but it does enable blast furnaces to recover more efficiently the iron which is already present. Concentration, on the other hand, involves the removal of many unwanted materials and the resulting enrichment of the ore before it enters the furnaces. It not only increases the efficiency of furnace operation but also reduces transportation costs from the concentrating plant to the factory. Much of the output of concentrating plants is also agglomerated before being shipped. The term *beneficiation* is being used increasingly to refer to both these processes, although some authorities use it to mean only concentration. Today, a sizable portion of the world's iron ore passes through beneficiation plants before being forwarded to iron and steel mills (Fig. 27.2). In this chapter, where our primary concern is with mining, we shall be especially interested in those beneficiation plants which are located at a short distance from the mines.

Trends in consumption

The current volume of iron-ore consumption is over twice that of 1939, and 70 per cent higher than that of 1949. The outstanding increases have been experienced by the United States and the Soviet Union, each of which has more than doubled its 1939 consumption. Western Europe, partly because it was running in high gear to supply armies in 1939 and partly because it experienced a trying readjustment period after that war, has not increased its consumption so dramatically. Communist China has raised its consumption and output by nearly ten times its 1950 figure within the past decade, if reports from there are accurate.

PRODUCTION AND DOMESTIC TRANSPORTATION

Natural occurrence

We have noted in Chapter 4 that iron is among the most plentiful of substances in the earth's outer crust, comprising over 5 per cent of all leading elements and exceeded only by oxygen, silicon, and aluminum. However, techniques of recovering iron are not so efficient as those for recovering copper, lead, zinc, and some other metals—at least when measured in dollars and cents. An iron content of about 20 per cent is now considered absolute minimum if an iron deposit is to be developed as an ore. In contrast, the metal content of copper need amount only to approximately 1 per cent under certain conditions to be considered commercially exploitable.

Iron-ore Minerals. Of the many iron-bearing minerals, only four contain sufficiently high concentrations of the metal to be considered as substantial commercial sources. These are *magnetite, hematite, limonite* (*göthite*), and *siderite*. Their salient features are outlined in Table 27.1. The first three are by far the leaders in iron content. Magnetite, it will be noted, contains the highest iron percentage. When pure, it is combined with only one other element, oxygen. Hematite also contains only iron and oxygen, with the two elements combined in slightly different proportions from those in magnetite. Limonite contains these same two elements, plus water, and siderite the same two plus carbon. Only in extremely rare situations do any of these minerals occur in the pure state. Usually they are mixed with minor amounts of aluminum, manganese, phosphorus, sulfur, or other elements, and are compounded into a matrix of nonmetallic materials. As found in nature, an ore of 65 per cent iron content is a high-quality ore, and most have 55 per cent or less.

Natural Processes of Iron-ore Concentration. Several quite different natural processes are known to be responsible for raising the iron content of a rock deposit. Some of these processes involve the action of water, either at the surface or underground. By way of illustration, an ore bed may have been laid down as a sedimentary rock and not altered subsequently, so that today it can be mined in much the same general way as a coal seam. Other processes may take place in the absence of water; magmatic materials high in ferrous content may have been brought together by gravity action before they solidified to become part of the igneous rock in which they occur today as an ore. Also, more than one process may have been involved. It is not uncommon for iron-bearing materials, however initially laid down, to have been enriched by selective removal of some of their nonferrous components by the chemical or mechanical action of water. As a result of these and still other processes, iron deposits as found today may be either bedded (stratified) or massive, and may be located either near the surface or at varying levels underground. The shallow ores, if present in substantial amounts, lend themselves excellently to modern large-scale methods and machinery.

Extent and distribution of reserves

We have noted previously that, although there must exist a definite limit to the amount of fugitive minerals, man has not yet been able to find such a limit in the world as a whole for any given material. As his methods and tools improve, he has been

TABLE 27.1
Leading iron-ore minerals

Mineral	*Chemical composition*	*Approximate per cent of iron content when pure**
Magnetite	Fe_3O_4	72
Hematite	Fe_2O_3	70
Limonite (göthite)	$2Fe_2O_3.3H_2O$	60
Siderite	$FeCO_3$	48

* The per cent of iron as found in nature varies markedly; however, the very best ores seldom contain more than 65 per cent.
SOURCE: Calculated from various sources.

able to derive more and more of wanted materials from matrixes once considered worthless. This is particularly true of iron, which, as we have noted, is known to be present in substantial quantities in much of the earth's outer crust. Who is to say how much of this remains to be exploited, since it occurs, albeit in lean proportions, in so many places?

Despite the improbability of arriving at a firm estimate, it is desirable to appraise the iron content of the more obvious concentrations of iron ore. Several such appraisals have been made, and one of the most recent is presented in Table 27.2. The largest reserves indicated in the table, amounting to approximately one-half of the world total iron content, are in the underdeveloped nations of India and Brazil. Both the United States and the Soviet Union are prominent among nations with substantial deposits, as are some of the leading industrial nations of Europe. At the current rate of use, the total reserves shown here are sufficient to last the world for nearly six hundred years. In addition, there exist many deposits of lower-grade materials that as yet have not been classified as ore, because present technology has not been able to render them commercially exploitable. It would appear that the world will not be faced with an iron-ore deficiency in the foreseeable future.

Production in the United States

Although the United States consumes more iron ore than it produces, it is without peer in iron-ore min-

TABLE 27.2

*Estimated world iron-ore reserves, 1959 (in billions of long tons)**

Country	Direct-shipping ore	Ore needing benefi-ciation	Actual iron content
India	21.3	85.0	37.9
Brazil	16.3	36.0	20.9
United States	4.5	60.4	20.1
Soviet Union	33.8	23.9	18.9
Canada	6.6	7.0	5.3
Communist China	4.2	7.0	3.6
France	8.4	—	2.9
Union of South Africa	3.5	—	1.6
Guinea	2.5	—	1.6
Sweden	2.4	—	1.5
Venezuela	2.2	—	1.4
United Kingdom	4.6	—	1.2
Cuba	3.0	—	1.2
Philippines	1.3	—	0.6
Liberia	1.0	—	0.6
Rest of world	11.3	3.5	6.7
Total	126.9	222.8	126.0

* Some world surveys allot very substantial reserves to Southern Rhodesia, but these, like the voluminous deposits (in addition to those shown above) which the Soviet Union claims to possess, have not as yet been fully authenticated. The reader can find much variation from authority to authority concerning iron-ore reserves, partly because of the large amount of iron in the earth's crust in such varying proportions in different places.

SOURCE: Computed from *Mineral Trade Notes,* 49 (2): 18–19 U.S. Bureau of Mines, August, 1959.

ing. The nation's annual output fluctuates markedly, but since the Second World War has ranged above and below 100 million long tons (Fig. 27.3). About one-fourth of the world's iron ore is extracted within the political limits of the United States alone (Fig. 27.1). Over 75 per cent of the country's output comes from the famed Lake Superior ranges, approximately 6 per cent is mined in the Birmingham area of Alabama, and the remainder comes from scattered sites, several of them in the Western states.

The Lake Superior Ranges. The production of iron ore near the western and southern margins of Lake Superior has been the subject of so many articles, both scholarly and popular, that it has by now become almost legendary. Nearly as well known are the six ranges from which nearly all this ore is taken: the renowned Mesabi, and the smaller Marquette, Menominee, Gogebic, Cuyuna, and Vermilion ranges (Fig. 27.4). The output of each is indicated in Table 27.3. The Mesabi, Cuyuna, and Vermilion ranges are situated generally west of Lake Superior, near the lake-head ports of Superior, Duluth, and Two Harbors; the Marquette range is in northern Michigan; and the Gogebic and Menominee ranges are shared by Michigan and Wisconsin. Since 1854, these six ranges have accounted for over 3 billion tons of iron ore, and the Mesabi alone has supplied over 2 billion tons. Hematite is the primary mineral taken from all six ranges, and magnetite ranks second. The former accounts for well over 90 per cent of the Lake Superior ore, and the latter for nearly all of the remainder.

Lake Superior Ores. The ores occur at shallow depths in the Mesabi range, seldom exceeding 200 feet and almost never exceeding 1,000 feet. The width of the mineralized zone here is not generally over 3 miles, but its length is well in excess of 100 miles. The central portion and upper levels of this range once contained relatively high deposits, most of which have been mined. Along the margins and

TABLE 27.3

Iron ore produced in the Lake Superior district, 1959

Producing range	Per cent of total tonnage
Mesabi	83.1
Marquette	5.7
Menominee	4.2
Gogebic	3.5
Cuyuna	2.3
Vermilion	1.2

SOURCE: Calculated from the 1959 report of the American Iron Ore Association, p. 20. The Lake Superior district originated 71,822,894 long tons of crude iron ore, including taconite, in 1959. This figure does not include 866,893 long tons of crude ore originating at Spring Valley in southeastern Minnesota.

beneath this better ore are very substantial reserves of *taconite*, which here is made up of hematite and some magnetite mixed in comparatively lean proportions largely with hard, nonmetallic materials. It is the taconite of this and other Lake Superior ranges which contains the sizable inferred amounts of iron with which the United States is usually credited in international comparisons. Its metal content is low, varying from 20 to 35 per cent, but reserves are substantial, notably at Mesabi.

The better ores of the other five fields, like those at Mesabi, are of direct-shipping quality. Some taconite also occurs at the two ranges in Michigan, where it is known as *jasper*. The Cuyuna ores are somewhat unique in that they contain manganese in amounts approximating 5 per cent of their total bulk. Like those of the Mesabi, these Cuyuna deposits are at comparatively shallow levels, whereas most of the ores in the other ranges are at appreciable depths.

Mining. Open-pit mining predominates in the Mesabi and Cuyuna ranges, and underground mining in the others. Of the nation's 349 currently active iron-ore mines, 179 are located in the Lake Superior region—143 in Minnesota, 33 in Michigan, and 3 in Wisconsin. However, as in most mining operations, the majority of these are comparatively small, producing much fewer than the national average of 500,000 tons of crude ore per unit. A very few mines, each of which produces well over 1 million tons per year, account for most of the ore. This is particularly true in the Mesabi and Cuyuna ranges, where open-pit mines are most numerous.

Beneficiation of Ore Other than Taconite. Commercial beneficiation of ore other than taconite is said to have commenced in Minnesota as early as 1907, and in some Eastern states of the United States at a still earlier time. In 1940, beneficiation was initiated on a general scale in the Lake Superior region as well as in other producing fields in the nation. Minnesota ores, particularly, were subjected to the process; and in 1957, more than one-half of the state's crude iron ore other than taconite was being concentrated before shipment. A smaller portion was agglomerated, but not concentrated. Michigan and Wisconsin, in contrast, have not as yet relied extensively upon the beneficiation of ore other than taconite.

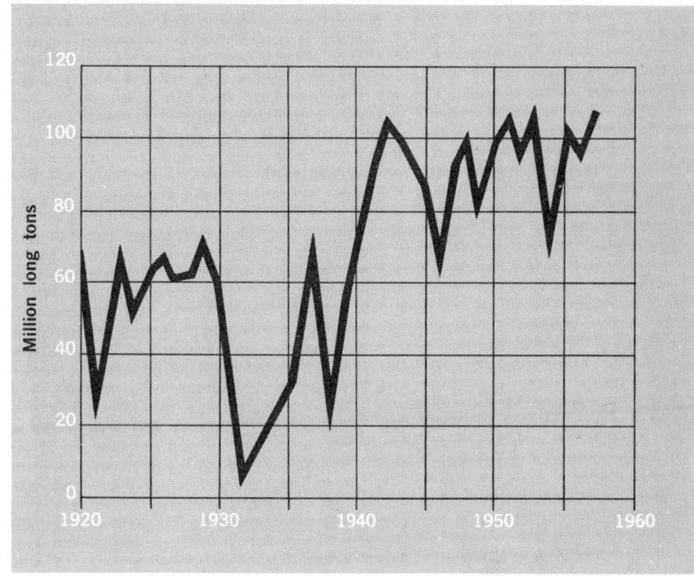

Figure 27.3 ***Production of iron ore in the United States since World War I.*** *Why has output been so erratic?* (Foreign Trade Trends, *American Iron and Steel Institute)*

Figure 27.4 ***The leading iron-ore ranges and lake ports, and other places of interest in the Lake Superior area.***

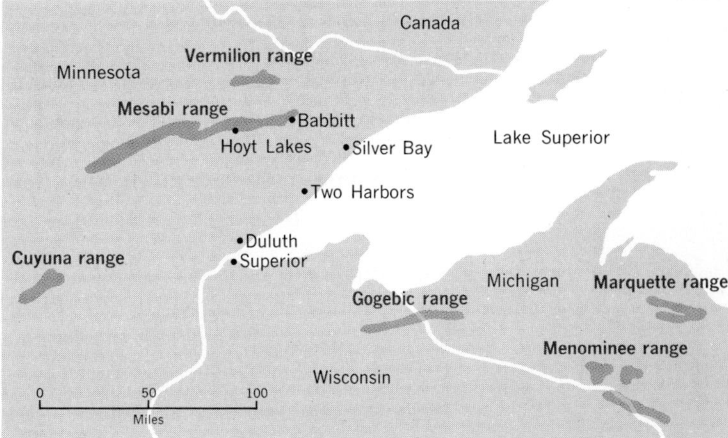

Beneficiation of Taconite. Successful commercial beneficiation of taconite dates back only to the late 1940s, and active processing to the mid-1950s. The process is more complex, partly because taconite is much harder than most other ore, and the wear on the machinery is much faster. Also, it is more difficult to separate the iron from the gangue (unwanted) materials. Most of the serious problems associated with its beneficiation, however, appear to be either solved or within reach of solution. The advent of the process may well mark the dawn of a new era—more accurately, the continuance of an old era—in the Lake Superior mining region. With the depletion of better iron ore there in the face of a rising national demand for iron and steel, serious attention was given to developing iron-ore fields in foreign countries as well as to upgrading some of the remaining Lake Superior deposits. Both movements have acquired momentum. The increasing importation of foreign ores, which we shall discuss in more detail later, is an accomplished fact, and the United States no longer depends almost exclusively upon domestic sources. However, the long-elusive technique of beneficiating domestic taconite is also an accomplished fact, and it would appear that the Lake Superior region will continue to be a vital source area for the nation's iron ore.

Taconite-beneficiation plants are located in the vicinity of the mines chiefly because of the low quality of the ores they treat. In the Lake Superior region, three such plants are now operating on the margins of the Mesabi range, two are active in the Marquette range, one is commencing to function in the Menominee range, and another in the Gogebic range. Concentrated pellets from these plants, accounting in 1956 for only 6 per cent of the tonnage of all ore leaving the Lake Superior region, are expected to amount to 40 per cent of that total by 1966.[2]

Taconite Beneficiation and New Settlements. The beneficiation of taconite is resulting in a mild increase in the populations of some of the mining areas and neighboring countrysides because of new employments which the plants make available. Silver Bay, Babbitt, and Hoyt Lakes are three new communities which are expected to reach populations of 4,000 to 5,000 each. Some of the workers for such plants have come from the mines, where increasing mechanization and more modern methods are resulting in a decrease in the amount of labor needed for each ton of mined ore.[3]

Government Policy. An interesting aspect of the development of the taconite deposits has been the role of government policy—in this case, of the state of Minnesota. Of the several taxes which were assessed against the mining companies of that state, the most severe was an ad valorem tax on exploitable minerals in the ground. This tax discouraged taconite development, because of the very substantial amounts of the substance known to exist. Taconite could not be taxed as long as it was not considered commercially exploitable. Once classified as an ore, however, the taconite reserves would yield tax returns which, because of their large reserves, would be very high—so high that companies interested in exploitation of taconite did not feel they could afford to develop it under existing tax laws. In 1941, the state legislature enacted a new law in which production rather than reserves was taxed, and active commercial development of taconite began immediately.

Transportation of Lake Superior Ores. Nature has favored man not only by concentrating huge amounts of iron ore within the Lake Superior region but also by providing means of cheap transportation to consuming centers. Over 98 per cent of the ore from the Lake Superior region of the United States moves to its ultimate destination over a combination

[2] Clyde F. Kohn and Raymond E. Specht, "The Mining of Taconite, Lake Superior Iron Mining District," *Geographical Review,* 48:528–539, 1958.

[3] In practice, however, only the younger employees tend actually to shift their employment from mine to factory. Miners of forty years and older who have spent most of their productive lives in the mines and know no other trade tend to migrate to other mining areas when there is no longer a local demand for their services. Managers of the new factories customarily bring a cadre of trained employees to the new location and hire younger personnel to fill out their employment lists.

of land and water routes. The lake-head port of Superior forwards well over one-third of this outgoing ore, and Duluth and Two Harbors each account for an additional one-fourth (Fig. 27.4). Escanaba, Silver Bay, Marquette, Ashland, and Taconite Harbor are among the lesser, but noteworthy, iron-ore forwarding ports.

The preference by shippers for the rail-water route is not difficult to understand upon examination of relative transportation costs. Total shipping charges for a ton of iron ore from the Mesabi range to Pittsburgh by rail amount to approximately $7.32, where the rail-water charges are $5.13; from the Mesabi to Chicago, the amounts are $4.27 and $3.01, respectively. Even these figures do not reveal the very low cost of Great Lakes transportation; of the $5.13 total charge per ton for the land-water haul between the Mesabi and Pittsburgh, more than $3 can be assessed to overland hauls (Mesabi to lake ports, about 50 miles, and lower Lake Erie ports to Pittsburgh, about 120 miles), whereas less than $2, including docking charges, is involved in the approximate 1,000-mile haul from the lake-head ports to lower Lake Erie!

The extremes of winter climate represent a natural obstacle which Lake Superior mining and transportation have not yet been able to overcome. From December to March mining is slowed and sometimes stopped altogether, especially in the open pits. Movement by water ceases entirely because of ice. Meanwhile, sufficiently large stocks of ore are accumulated during the summer months at lower Lake Erie and Lake Michigan ports and near the iron and steel plants to permit the latter to continue functioning on a year-round basis.

Mining in Alabama. The forty-seven iron mines in the vicinity of Birmingham, Alabama, produce about 10 million tons of ore, slightly over one-half coming from open-pit operations. The ore here is primarily the result of sedimentary deposition, and most occurs in seams, like coal. The mined product is about 80 per cent hematite, and 20 per cent limonite and other minerals. It is of comparatively low quality (30 to 35 per cent iron content), and contains some phosphorus. However, it also contains enough lime so that much of it is *self-fluxing* (it contains naturally about as much lime as would be added in blast-furnace processing), and it occurs near deposits of coking coal. Thus, the three ingredients most basic to the iron and steel industry—iron, lime, and coal—are found in the same vicinity. Otherwise these inferior ores probably would not be mined. About two-thirds goes to beneficiation plants before being sent to blast furnaces. Most of the Alabama production is forwarded ultimately to Birmingham iron and steel mills, which also receive ore from Georgia and Tennessee, as well as from such foreign sources as Brazil, Canada, Peru, Sweden, Venezuela, India, and South Africa.

Mining Elsewhere in the United States. All other iron-ore mining in the United States accounts for less than 20 per cent of the national output. Individual undertakings are rather widely scattered: Utah is a noteworthy producer, as are the Eastern states of New York, Pennsylvania, and New Jersey, and the Far Western state of California. Georgia also deserves mention, as do Nevada and Wyoming. Much of the production in the Western states is comparatively new and has arisen in response to demand from iron and steel factories established in the West during and since the Second World War to serve regional markets.

Trends in United States Production. In order to meet its expanding economic needs, the United States has relied chiefly upon the mining of larger and larger amounts of domestic iron ore. This has meant the use of methods and machinery which make for economies of scale. Gigantic producing and transporting units have been employed—where possible, in open-pit mines in which they can function to maximum efficiency. Over four-fifths of the nation's iron ore is obtained from such mines. Beneficiation plants are relied on, where necessary, to aid in rendering deposits commercially extractable. About 70 per cent of all crude ore mined in the nation now goes through some sort of beneficiating plant before being forwarded to iron and steel mills, and it may be subjected to even further beneficiation after arrival there. The nation's future would appear to hold increasing importance for these mass-handling techniques, as well as for the leaner ores which they treat.

Production in the Soviet Union

In 1928, when the First Five-Year Plan was initiated in the Soviet Union, that country's total output of iron ore amounted to approximately 6 million tons—slightly more than one-half of the current annual production in the state of Alabama in the United States. Over three-fourths of the 1928 output came from Krivoi Rog and other fields in the Ukraine, just north of the Black Sea (Fig. 27.1). Thirty years later, the country's annual yield of iron ore amounted to over 80 million tons—one-fifth of the world production. The Ukrainian fields continued to lead but supplied only about 55 per cent of the nation's ore. The Urals, which accounted for less than one-sixth of all Soviet iron ore in 1938, were responsible for over 35 per cent in 1958. These two are the outstanding iron-ore mining areas in the Soviet Union, followed by the Kuznets (5 per cent of the nation's total) and scattered sites of lesser significance. From the record as summarized above, two points are clear: (1) the Soviet Union obviously has placed a very high priority on iron-ore mining during the thirty years of scheduled plans, its production having risen more than twelvefold during that time; and (2) some emphasis has also been placed upon deconcentration of the industry, the Urals, Kuznets, and lesser fields to the east having expanded their output at a rate relatively exceeding that of the Ukraine. That the Ukraine still produces over one-half of all Soviet iron ore, however, suggests that even in a Communist state, the advantages of economies of scale are evident—in this case, of maximizing large-scale production at sites of substantial ore supply.

The Ukraine. The primary source area in the Ukraine for iron ore is at Krivoi Rog, where deposits of hematite and some magnetite are mined by underground methods (Fig. 27.1). The iron content averages 50 per cent or somewhat less in a discontinuous belt about 35 miles long and 4 miles wide. Reserves appear to be adequate for current needs, especially of lower-grade ores (35 to 40 per cent iron content). Slightly over one-half of all iron ore mined in the Soviet Union comes from this field. Although captured by the Germans during the Second World War, all the mines were back in full operation within three years after the ending of that conflict. Many which had been destroyed or crippled were reopened with more modern equipment.

A much smaller amount of Ukrainian ore, less than 5 per cent, comes from Kerch, on the eastern tip of the Crimean Peninsula. The ore here is of lower quality (25 to 40 per cent iron content) and contains appreciable quantities of phosphorus, a by-product which, although useful, complicates further processing. The ore occurs at depths ranging generally from 18 to 60 feet below the land surface and is mined almost entirely by open-pit methods and machines. One reason for an even modest production from these low-grade deposits is their coast-line location, from which movement by water is easily accomplished. Reserves, chiefly of limonite, are large but are so poor in quality that Kerch ore is not highly prized in the Soviet Union.

The Urals. No other iron-mining area of the Soviet Union has been brought into productivity more rapidly than has that of the Urals, where annual yields rose from slightly over 1 million tons to nearly 30 million tons between 1938 and 1958. Unlike those of the Ukraine and other parts of European Russia, this producing area and those to the east have been developed almost entirely by the Communist government since the 1917 revolution. Activity in the Urals had become quite pronounced before the Second World War, and it was stimulated by that conflict. The loss of the Ukrainian fields to the Germans meant a pronounced dependence by the Soviet Union upon this Urals area, the only leading domestic producer not then under German control. When peace came, the Urals mining continued to expand. The most active site is at Magnitogorsk (Iron Mountain), where open-pit operations supply over 15 per cent of the nation's iron ore. A district near Nizhni Tagil is second in production, and smaller fields are located at Bakal,

Khalilovo, and several other somewhat scattered sites. Nearly all the Urals mines are on the eastern and southern flanks of the mountains. Much of the ore is magnetite—in some places mixed with several other metals, for the Urals represent a source area for a surprising variety of materials. Although ore that is 60 per cent or higher iron content is present, most of these premium reserves have been mined. Ore grades of 50 per cent iron and lower, some of which not only contain undesirable materials but also must be mined underground, appear to be the major sources of the future.

Other Soviet Iron-ore Production. The Gornaia Shoria field near the Kuznets area of Siberia is currently receiving careful attention by Soviet planners, particularly because it is so near the large coal fields and the growing iron and steel industry there. Its role in the Kuznets operations thus is roughly analogous to that of the iron mines near Birmingham, Alabama. Its reserves, however, are limited, and the Kuznets may be forced to look to fields at Abakan, some 200 miles to the east, to supply iron ore no longer shipped from the Urals (as noted in the discussion below of transportation). There are small producing fields at Tula and Lipetsk near Moscow, at some sites in Karelia near Leningrad, and at deposits in the far east near Khabarovsk.

Soviet Reserves. The Soviet Union claims very large reserves of iron ore—enough, the government maintains, to place that country in the foremost position among all nations. To what degree this claim is justified is not fully known. A very large deposit of comparatively low-grade materials, some of which can be classified as ore, is known to exist in the vicinity of Kursk, south of Moscow. The volume of iron here is sufficient to have long caused compass deviations. Estimates by the Soviet government place these reserves in excess of 200 billion tons—a substantial amount, to put it modestly. It is largely on the basis of these reserves that the Soviet Union claims a paramount position in iron-ore reserves, although reserves at Krivoi Rog, the Urals, and other, more reliable locations are more than adequate for the country's current needs. The major problem to be solved at Kursk, however, is how to extract the iron without excessive costs, for these are important even in government-owned economies. Not only is the iron content low, but also the iron deposits are overlain by several hundred feet of loose, water-soaked sediment and thus do not lend themselves easily to either open-pit or shaft-and-tunnel mining. A newly discovered deposit at Kustanai, east of the Urals, is estimated to contain at least noteworthy reserves of ore, at levels sufficiently shallow to be worked by open-pit methods. On the whole, the iron content of ore in the Soviet Union, like that of the remaining ore in the United States, is not high. In both nations, there are substantial reserves of lower-quality deposits.

Transportation. The Soviet Union has no Great Lakes system connecting its major producing and consuming centers, and the country relies upon its railroads to perform the lion's share of this herculean task. To minimize railroad traffic, efforts are made to render each producing district as self-sufficient as possible. The Ukraine fields now supply most of the blast furnaces in European Russia, except in the Urals, where local ores are available. Most of the Kerch ores either are placed in local blast furnaces or are forwarded by water to the single city of Zhdanov on the northern coast of the Sea of Azov. The Krivoi Rog fields supply nearly all the other markets west of the Urals. At one time the Urals not only took care of local demand but also shipped ore eastward in substantial quantities to the Kuznets area, which had coal but no ore. With the development of the Gornaia Shoria deposits, however, the Kuznets blast furnaces came to depend increasingly upon this local source, which now reportedly furnishes over three-fourths of the iron ore needed in the Kuznets. The expanding output of the Urals is now consumed locally for the most part, with only small amounts going to the Kuznets, to Karaganda, and to European Russia.

Trends. Like the United States, the Soviet Union is rapidly expanding its consumption of iron ore. Also like the United States, the Soviet Union has more than adequate reserves, of which most are of intermediate to low grade. Unlike the United States, the Soviet Union has followed a policy of almost total dependence upon domestic ore and even exports a small amount. This has meant beneficiation, and well over four-fifths of all iron mined in the Soviet Union is first sent to beneficiation plants and then forwarded, as concentrate or agglomerate, to blast and steel furnaces. An even higher percentage will be so treated in the future unless richer ores are discovered or a policy of partial imports is adopted.

Production in Europe

As an area Europe, excluding the Soviet Union, is without equal in the tonnage of iron ore output. About one-third of the world's annual yield is mined there. France, Sweden, West Germany, and the United Kingdom are foremost among a group of twenty-one European producing nations. France and West Germany, it will be noted, are members of the European Coal and Steel Community.

France. France, unquestionably the leader in European iron-ore mining, accounts for about 40 per cent of the total annual output of that region. Over 90 per cent of the country's ore is mined in the northeast, in the province of Lorraine. Here, along either side of the Moselle River in a zone extending from the city of Nancy northward across the political border into Luxembourg, Belgium, and West Germany, are deposits of the famed Minette ore, with its low 30 to 35 per cent iron content. Limonite, hematite, and siderite are all present in this ore in varying quantities, as are some lime, silica, phosphorus, and sulfur. The lime, frequently amounting to 15 to 20 per cent of the matrix, renders much of this ore essentially self-fluxing, but the other materials are not so desirable. Much of the mining is open-pit, especially in the very active area north of Metz. Beneficiation is well past the laboratory stage, but most of the ore is still shipped with an iron content no higher than 35 per cent. About three-fifths of this Minette ore moves to domestic iron and steel mills, and the remainder is exported. Minor production of iron ore occurs at scattered sites to the northwest, east, and south.

Sweden. Second in output among European iron-ore producers is Sweden, the only one of this group that exports most of its ore. Nearly all of this exported ore is mined at Kiruna, north of the Arctic Circle. Here is a sizable ridge, nearly 2 miles long and ⅓ mile wide, composed chiefly of magnetite. The ore is high in quality; 60 or even 70 per cent iron content is not uncommon. In contrast to most iron ore, these deposits appear to have been injected into existing strata as magma, and not to have been altered seriously by water action. Nearby at Luossa is another, smaller ridge which is geologically similar; and at Gallivare, some 50 miles to the south, are still more deposits. Open-pit mines predominate; the Kiruna and the Luossa ridges are worked actively and the Gallivare field slightly. As in open-pit diggings of the northern United States, the Soviet Union, Canada, and still other high-latitude locations, operations are seriously hampered by winter conditions. The long Arctic winter darkness is also a liability in this most northerly of major iron-mining areas, and floodlighting is necessary. Despite its high quality, some of this ore is agglomerated to retain the iron content of its fine particles.

The Kiruna operations are not closely integrated in the Swedish economy except in that they provide substantial revenue. A very small portion of the ore is used domestically, particularly at a small iron-and-steel plant in nearby Lulea. Most, however, is exported through Lulea and through the Norwegian port of Narvik, and it bypasses Sweden on its way to other European nations as well as to destinations farther overseas, including the United States. Meanwhile, the majority of the ore upon which the small Swedish iron and steel industry depends comes from sites farther to the south—sites located in proximity to the manufacturing plants predominating in southern Sweden.

West Germany. Discussions of the iron and steel industry of Europe inevitably focus upon the importance of French and Swedish iron ore, and of coal in the West German Ruhr. Usually overlooked is the highly significant fact that West Germany is no petty extractor of iron ore—that it produces between 30 and 40 per cent of its impressively high demand. This relatively high production has been achieved through efficient exploitation of intermediate- to low-grade deposits of limonite, siderite, and hematite that occur at rather widely separated places in the country. No single field is outstanding; West Germany has no Lorraine or Kiruna. Salzgitter, on the southern margin of the northern plain, is prominent among West Germany's several producers. Its ores of 30 per cent iron content (and 25 per cent silica) are mined by both surface and underground methods. Low-grade deposits at Siegerland and other locations near the Ruhr also are worked actively, as are beds in Bavaria to the south and a few locations to the east.

The United Kingdom. Like West Germany, the United Kingdom has no single iron-ore field of outstanding significance, and yet it manages to produce substantial amounts of iron ore. Most of the country's output comes from sedimentary beds that average less than 30 per cent iron content but are located in eastern England not excessively far from an active market. The mining is largely by open-pit methods, and the product moves almost exclusively to domestic consumers. About 50 per cent of the iron requirements of the United Kingdom are supplied from these sources.

Other European Producers. The four leading nations account for over four-fifths of the European iron-ore output, exclusive of that mined in the Soviet Union. The remaining seventeen mining nations supply one-fifth. Except for tiny Luxembourg, which busily exploits the Minette ores extending across the political boundary line from France, none of these can be said to have a mine or mining field worthy of individual consideration in a world-wide appraisal.

Production in Canada and Venezuela

So far in this discussion we have been concerned with mining, in technically advanced nations, of iron ore which either is moving to domestic markets or is being sold freely in international markets. The capital invested in these enterprises is largely domestic capital, whether stemming from governmental or private sources. In Canada and Venezuela, respectively a technically advanced country and an underdeveloped country,[4] we have examples of ore production for export largely under the stimulus of capital investment from abroad.

Canada. The existence of iron ore has long been known in Canada, but large-scale exploitation has come about only recently. Here is an excellent example of dependence by a technically advanced nation—a nation large in area but small in population and size of economy—upon a more populous and economically stronger neighbor. Some attention by United States concerns was given to Canadian iron-ore fields in the middle 1880s, but when the high-quality reserves of the Lake Superior region of the United States began to be exploited actively, that interest quickly waned. Indeed, Canada soon became dependent upon the output of the Lake Superior ranges for much of its own needs, and by 1924 the mining of Canadian iron ore was almost at a standstill.[5] With the depletion of the better Lake Superior ores in the mid-1950s, however, United States investors evidenced a renewed interest in Canadian ore. By 1957, ten of fourteen companies actively involved in Canadian iron-ore procurement were owned or indirectly controlled by United States interests, and only four were independent of such interests. Over 70 per cent of Canada's total iron-ore production in that year came from the ten United States–controlled companies, and it has been estimated that before 1970 these companies will account for 80 to 90 per cent of Canada's iron-ore production.[6]

[4] Venezuela sometimes is classified as technically advanced, because the revenue from petroleum exploitation there by foreign nations raises the per capita gross national product. However, the level of living, proportion of individual income spent on food, and other population characteristics place it in the underdeveloped category, as far as most of its people are concerned.

[5] Donald Eldon, *American Influence in the Canadian Iron and Steel Industry,* University of Rochester Press, Rochester, N.Y., 1954.

[6] *Mining and Mineral Processing in Canada,* Royal Commission on Canada's Economic Prospects, Ottawa, 1957, p. 64.

Iron ore is mined here by drilling holes, blasting loose the ore, and loading it with power shovels into trucks carrying 22 to 34 tons. This open-pit mine is at Steep Rock, Ontario, Canada. (George Hunter, Toronto)

The outstanding Canadian producing field is its newest, located on the Quebec-Labrador border some 350 miles north of the left bank of the lower St. Lawrence estuary. So new that it has not yet received a generally accepted name, this series of deposits is referred to as Quebec-Labrador, Burnt Creek, Schefferville, and still other names. The Quebec-Labrador field contains very large reserves of direct-shipping ore and has been called by some enthusiasts a "second Mesabi"; but, unlike the original, its ores are more widely dispersed and are rather consistently at shallow levels. Hematite is the primary mineral, and the iron content of measured ores is at least 51 per cent or higher—the minimum specification for direct-shipping ore. Winter weather slows all operations here, as in other high-latitude locations. A railroad has been constructed from here to a new seaport at Seven Islands (more accurately, Sept Îles), which is rapidly becoming one of Canada's leading tonnage ports. The total freight charges from the Quebec-Labrador mines to Cleveland are more than twice those from the Mesabi to the same port,[7] but most of these Canadian ores do not as yet need to be beneficiated, and their total processing costs thus are not so high as many obtained at the Lake Superior region. Additional Canadian iron-ore mining occurs at Steep Rock, northwest of Lake Superior; Wabana, Newfoundland; Michipicoten and Marmora, Ontario; and Vancouver and Texada Islands, off the Pacific coast in British Columbia. United States control over Canadian mining is focused chiefly upon the Quebec-Labrador and Steep Rock fields.

Canada consumes less than 8 per cent of the

[7] Donald Kerr, "The Geography of the Canadian Iron and Steel Industry," *Economic Geography*, **35**:151–163, 1959, pp. 158–159.

iron ore it mines. Nearly 75 per cent goes to the United States, and the remainder to Europe.

Venezuela. Even more rapidly than Canada, Venezuela has emerged as a major iron-ore producer. In 1950 the country was the source of only about 1 million tons of ore. Seven years later, with an output exceeding 15 million tons, it ranked eighth in the world. Two United States corporations, Bethlehem Steel and United States Steel, have provided the capital and entrepreneurship for nearly all of this ore recovery. The mining fields of both firms are in the lower Orinoco River valley. Bethlehem Steel's open-pit mines are at El Pao, from which the ore is shipped by truck and rail to a company-maintained port at San Félix. Here it is placed on light vessels which carry it downstream and along the coast to Puerto de Hierro, located on a Venezuelan promontory near the island of Trinidad. At that port it is transshipped to ocean vessels bound for the Sparrows Point iron-and-steel plant at Baltimore, Maryland. The United States Steel Corporation applies similar methods and machinery to its open-pit operations at Cerro Bolívar, some 150 miles to the west of El Pao. Its river port is Puerto Ordaz, slightly upstream from Bethlehem's San Félix. A channel 26 feet deep at low water along the Orinoco River from this port to the sea allows ocean-going vessels to dock here and take on cargo which they will discharge later at Morrisville, Pennsylvania, or Mobile, Alabama. Almost all Venezuelan ore is thus exported. In addition, West Germany and the United Kingdom receive small amounts, and a tiny fraction is diverted to a domestic iron-and-steel mill in the vicinity of San Félix and Puerto Ordaz.

Production in Communist China

Until very recently, Communist China was a minor producer of iron ore. Now official sources in the United States and the United Nations credit the country with about 10 per cent of the world output;

The fledgling port of Seven Islands is now one of Canada's leaders in tonnage. Its commerce is almost entirely iron ore moving from the Quebec-Labrador fields to the United States and other importing nations. (National Film Board of Canada)

only the United States, the Soviet Union, and France produce more. Even if allowance is made for possible exaggeration, this nation appears to be moving rapidly into the front ranks of iron-ore producers. The procuring of ore, like the production of iron and steel, takes place chiefly in Manchuria, in the vicinity and hinterland of Peking, and in focal places on the Yangtze River.

Other producing nations

With more than four-fifths of the world's yield of iron ore accounted for by the leading producers, not much remains for the fifty countries, more or less, which also are listed as active in iron-ore output. Seventeen of these secondary producers are in Europe. Of the others, India, Brazil, and Australia appear to be foremost.

Production in technically advanced and underdeveloped nations

Technically advanced nations thus far have been able to procure sufficient ore within their own or their neighbors' territory to satisfy much of their increasingly voracious appetites for iron. Only comparatively small amounts now are taken from the ground in underdeveloped countries, and most of these move to technically advanced nations, whose capital investment makes its obtainment possible. However, Communist China appears to be increasing its output rapidly, and India and Brazil and a few other underdeveloped countries are making some progress toward increased production for home use.

Non-Communist and Communist production

Non-Communist nations presently originate more than two-thirds of the world's iron ore. However, the Communist share is increasing, chiefly as a result of activity in the Soviet Union and Communist China. It would appear that Communist nations will mine an even higher share in the foreseeable future, with the most pronounced increases occurring in Communist China.

The location of iron-ore mining

As the best iron-ore reserves continue to disappear in lands where they are consumed most actively, man will be faced with an increased measure of responsibility concerning his future actions in its procurement. Government policy will be a key consideration and will vary with individuals, time, and place, for men sometimes and in some places conduct themselves foolishly in such matters and at other times and places act quite reasonably. The imposition of a sharp export or import tariff, or a quota, could alter drastically what would otherwise appear to be a smooth situation; and, in contrast, the reduction of the adverse effects of such measures, as is now occurring in the European Coal and Steel Community, would have the opposite effect. Government policy aside, it would appear that key considerations, whatever the type of economy, will be the long-standing ones of production and transportation costs. The number of alternatives will be higher than formerly, because there will be more fields of intermediate and low-grade deposits to consider than there were of the high-quality deposits. Costs versus advantages of beneficiation also will have to be considered. Policies will vary, too, according to who does the considering; if some of the underdeveloped nations begin to achieve their dreams of substantial economic growth, the balance of political and economic power may shift somewhat away from the technically advanced nations. This, however, does not loom as an immediate prospect.

INTERNATIONAL TRADE

Over 1 ton in 4 of usable iron ore, concentrates, etc.,[8] enters into international trade (Fig. 27.1).

[8] The U.S. Bureau of Mines distinguishes crude iron ore from usable iron ore, the former involving all ore as it comes from the mines and the latter direct-shipping ore plus the output of beneficiation plants (except those located directly at the iron and steel mills). The difference between the two terms is marked: in 1957, for example, the United States is credited with nearly 160 million long tons of crude ore but only about 105 million long tons of usable ore.

Movement among European nations accounts for more than half of this trade, with France forwarding the product mainly to Belgium-Luxembourg and West Germany, and Sweden sending it to West Germany, the United Kingdom, and Belgium-Luxembourg. The establishment of the Coal and Steel Community has not affected the movement of iron ore so much as the movement of finished products, chiefly because there were few tariffs, quotas, and similar restrictions on iron-ore movement before the community came into being.

The overwhelming significance of the United States in world economic affairs is emphasized by the fact that it is by now the leading import nation of iron ore, despite the thriving domestic output which supplies three-fourths of the nation's demand. Canada, Venezuela, and lesser producers in the Western Hemisphere forward most of this incoming ore, with Sweden, Liberia, the Philippines, and Morocco contributing from the other half of the world. Canada, paradoxically, imports a rather small quantity of ore from the United States. Japan and Czechoslovakia also are importers, albeit minor ones, the former receiving its iron ore mainly from southeastern Asia, and the latter from the Soviet Union.

OTHER INDUSTRIAL METALS

RELATIVE SUBORDINATION TO IRON

Considered in terms of amounts of metal actually produced and consumed each year, industrial metals other than iron are less significant. Table 27.4 generalizes the 1959 output of some of the world's leading industrial metals. The total for all of the lesser metals shown amounts to less than 9 per cent of that for iron. This is an extremely important fact; it places the world's metals in perspective—even if the perspective is the somewhat unsatisfactory one of quantity.

PATTERNS OF CONSUMPTION, PRODUCTION, AND TRADE

An overview of the consumption, production, and trade of bauxite is shown in Figure 27.5, and a summary of output of other industrial metals is shown in Figure 27.6. The drawings emphasize what by now has become a familiar situation to the reader: dominance of consumption by technically advanced nations, particularly those with sizable populations; domestic production on the part of consuming nations in so far as is eco-

TABLE 27.4

World output of selected industrial metals, 1959, metal content

Metal	*Output in million short tons*
Iron	246.3
Ferroalloys	
Manganese	5.6
Chromium	1.7
Nickel	0.312
Tungsten	0.056
Molybdenum	0.039
Cobalt	0.018
Vanadium	0.005
Metals seldom alloyed with iron	
Aluminum	4.5
Copper	4.0
Zinc	3.4
Lead	2.5
Tin	0.19
Magnesium	0.10

SOURCE: Calculated by the author from data supplied by the Division of Foreign Activities of the Bureau of Mines. Data for manganese and chromium assume a 40 per cent average metal content of ore. The figures above do not necessarily include portions of some commodities mined for such nonmetallic uses as paint pigment.

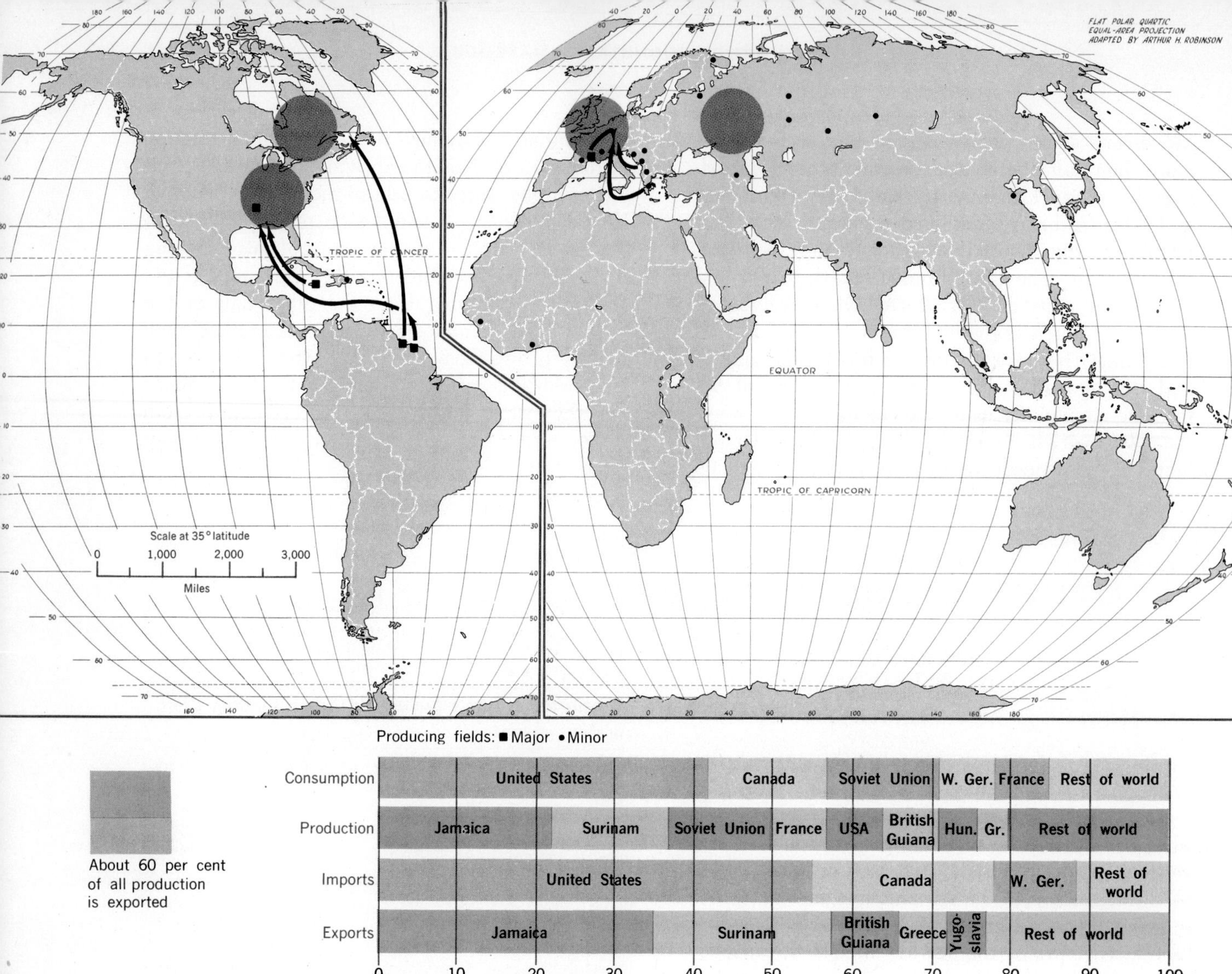

Figure 27.5 ***Consumption, production, import, and export of bauxite, the primary source of aluminum.*** *Circles show nations or regions of heaviest consumption (in this case, factory consumption by smelters). Leading producing fields are shown by symbols. The United States and Canada are the dominant importers, and several underdeveloped economies in Caribbean America are the leading exporters.*

nomically feasible; reliance upon imports when absolutely necessary. Where imports must be relied upon, underdeveloped countries and lightly populated technically advanced nations that are well endowed naturally are given careful attention if foreign investment is needed to obtain desired materials, but trading with other heavily populated technically advanced nations is not overlooked, particularly in Europe. As a group, the world's underdeveloped nations have as yet made little progress in producing industrial metals for their own use. Except in the Soviet Union and some eastern Euro-

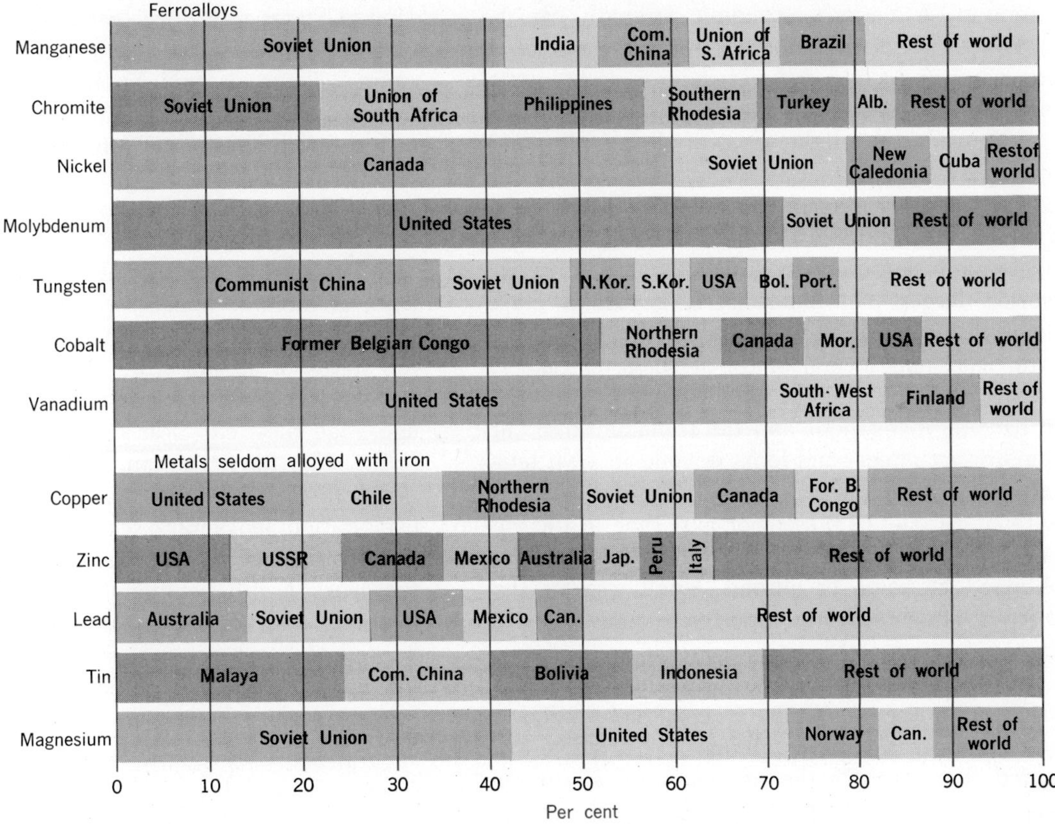

Figure 27.6 ***Leading nations in the production of selected metallic ores. For the total amounts produced, see Table 27.4.***

pean nations, the Communist bloc also has been somewhat slow to advance the mine productivity of these materials. Particularly in the Soviet Union, however, the rate of extraction has increased impressively since the First Five-Year Plan was initiated in 1928. Communist China also is rising in importance.

INDUSTRIAL METALS AND ECONOMIC GEOGRAPHY

Concern in economic geography with industrial metals involves more than the simple mechanics of their extraction, transportation, and use; for these materials represent the foundation of technically advanced economies. No nation can claim even modest economic strength unless it engages in the factory production of these materials. However, no technically advanced nation possesses sufficiently large and varied natural resources to boast a complete domestic supply for its needs, and some, like Japan and the United Kingdom, import surprisingly large quantities of their total raw-material consumption. A nation's economic strength can be measured, in no small degree, by the volume of its domestic production and net imports of industrial metals.

Viewed in this light, the overwhelmingly dominant position of the United States in world economic affairs once again comes to the fore. Here is a nation which supplies three-fourths of its domestic iron-ore consumption and yet has become the world's largest net importer! It is also a major domestic producer and importer of mined copper, lead, zinc, and several of the ferroalloys. Like all nations, it is deficient in some metallic minerals—in bauxite, manganese, and tin, to name three outstanding examples—and looks beyond its own territory in acquiring these. All in all, however, it is without parallel in present or past time in the volume of its utilization of industrial metals, whether obtained at home or abroad. Small wonder that there is an acute, world-wide interest in its day-to-day economic health!

Also significant are two trends in the procurement of industrial metals. One is the prodigious growth in world consumption. It has been estimated that by 1975 the utilization of aluminum, lead, iron, manganese, copper, and zinc in the United States will have increased, respectively, by 358, 61, 54, 50, 45, and 38 per cent over 1950 volumes.[9] These, it will be noted, are the leaders among industrial metals. Consumption increases in a resurging Western Europe and an expanding Soviet Union also are pronounced, and those in some other parts of the world are worthy of more than passing notice.

The second trend is toward more international trade in metallic minerals. The United States, particularly, is now experiencing a transition toward the status of an importing nation of consequence. Britain and Japan, of course, experienced it so long ago that they can scarcely remember any other status. The Soviet Union, largest of all nations in physical size and only recently interested in active exploitation, looks more securely to its own reserves than do most countries. However, the Soviet Union too lacks a full complement of desired metallic minerals, and, for the few currently in short supply as well as for the several in only modest supply, it too appears destined to enter more actively into international exchange.

[9] *Resources for Freedom:* vol. 2, *The Outlook for Key Commodities,* President's Materials Policy Commission, 1952, p. 118.

REFERENCES

Clark, Mills Gardner: *The Economics of Soviet Steel,* Harvard University Press, Cambridge, Mass., 1956.

Diebold, William, Jr.: *The Schuman Plan: A Study in Economic Cooperation, 1950–1959,* Frederick A. Praeger Press for the Council on Foreign Relations, New York, 1959. (Especially chaps. 6–8.)

Eldon, Donald: *American Influence in the Canadian Iron and Steel Industry,* University of Rochester Press, Rochester, New York, 1954.

Hoffman, John N.: *Manganese: Its Minerals, Deposits, and Uses,* Pennsylvania State University Press, University Park, Pa., 1957.

Humphrys, Graham: "Schefferville, Quebec: A New Pioneering Town," *Geographical Review,* **48:**151–166, 1958.

"Iron Ore Beneficiation: Fifty Years Old and Still Growing," *Minneapolis Federal Reserve,* October, 1957.

Jarret, H. Reginald: "Lunsar: A Study of an Iron Ore Mining Center in Sierra Leone," *Economic Geography,* **32:**153–161, 1956.

Karan, Pradyumna P.: "Iron Mining Industry in Singhbhum-Mayurbhanj Region of India," *Economic Geography,* **33:**349–361, 1957.

Kerr, Donald: "The Geography of the Canadian Iron and Steel Industry," *Economic Geography,* **35:** 151–163, 1959.

Kohn, Clyde F., and Raymond E. Specht: "The Mining of Taconite, Lake Superior Iron Mining District," *Geographical Review,* **48:**528–539, 1958.

Langdon, George: "The Mesabi Range: A Fabulous

Iron Ore Producer Shows Evidence of Decline," *Journal of Geography,* **57:**119–129, 1958.

Loewegren, Gunnar: *Swedish Iron and Steel: A Historical Survey,* Svenska Handelsbanken, Stockholm, 1948.

Mining and Mineral Processing in Canada, Royal Commission on Canada's Economic Prospects, Ottawa, 1957.

Nordenson, Jonas: "The International Iron Ore Market Since the War," *Skandinavaska Banken Quarterly Review,* **39:**47–52, 1958.

Parsons, Arthur B.: *The Porphory Coppers in 1956,* American Institute of Mining, Metallurgical, and Petroleum Engineers, New York, 1957.

Pearson, Ross: "The Jamaica Bauxite Industry," *Journal of Geography,* **56:**377–384, 1957.

Pounds, Norman J. G., and William N. Parker: *Coal and Steel in Western Europe,* Indiana University Press, Bloomington, Ind., 1957.

Roe, Lawrence A.: *Iron Ore Beneficiation,* Minerals Publishing Company, Lake Bluff, Ill., 1957.

Survey of World Iron Ore Resources, United Nations Department of Economic and Social Affairs, New York, 1955.

Thoman, Richard S.: *The Changing Occupance Pattern of the Tri-state Area: Missouri, Kansas, and Oklahoma,* University of Chicago Department of Geography Research Paper 31, Chicago, 1953.

28 MANUFACTURING AS AN ECONOMIC ACTIVITY

THE WORD "MANUFACTURE" IS DERIVED FROM THE MEDIEVAL LATIN TERM *manufactura,* which in turn involves a combination of the Latin words *manus* (hand) and *factura* (a making). Some dictionaries solemnly assure us that this is an obsolete interpretation; and in the current Age of Semiautomation in the world's technically advanced societies such an assurance appears plausible. However, a probable one-half of the world's manufacturing labor force is still engaged in handicrafts, and we cannot omit these workers from a world-wide overview of the occupation.

CONSUMPTION

Significance of the consumption of manufactured goods

We have noted that many products of agriculture, grazing, forest-products industries, fishing and hunting, and mining tend to move to manufacturing plants for further processing before eventual use. Once through the final stage of processing, however, a commodity is ready to be consumed—either as a producer good or as a consumer good. When we speak of the importance of consumption to the functioning of economies, therefore, we are thinking especially of the consumption of manufactured products. This is notably true in technically advanced economies, where the production specialist is replacing the Jack-of-all-trades and the factory is replacing the home workshop. Inasmuch as most of the world's economies, whatever their present status, are either becoming more technically advanced or hoping to become so, we can anticipate confidently that the consumption of manufactured products will play an even more vital future role in the functioning of the world's economies than has been true in the past.

Consumption in technically advanced economies

We have mentioned earlier the need for high levels of consumption in technically advanced nations—that such nations are reapproaching a garden-of-Eden status in their economic history, with the important differences that millions of people have replaced the original two and that complex, highly mechanized, semiautomated economies have replaced the garden's provident trees. The trees presumably could be harvested selectively, or even not at all, and nothing except the actual fruit would be lost; but the economies which have replaced them must be "harvested" continuously, or they will get out of kilter. Interestingly, this means that technically advanced nations have reached a status almost the opposite of that foreseen by the gloomy Malthus—for in such nations, the rate of consumption is being stimulated to use up the produced goods, which is the reverse of Malthus's prediction.

The commodities consumed in technically advanced economies involve high percentages of finished metals, fabricated metal products, chemicals, and—more recently—electronics and related equipment. Actual uses vary appreciably. In the United States, for example, a high percentage of the steel output goes into automobiles; in most European nations, this percentage is not so high, although prominent; and in the Soviet Union, where steel is being converted to producer goods, it is very low.

Consumption in underdeveloped economies

The volume of consumption of manufactured goods is much lower in technically underdeveloped economies than in the technically advanced group. Furthermore, the composition is quite different. Textiles are predominant, and food is usually second. (Of course, food is a very important item in actual consumption, but most is prepared in individual households rather than in factories.) Several of the larger or more active technically underdeveloped nations now have some iron and steel facilities producing for the home markets, but these, as yet, are minor on the world scene. Latest reports suggest that Communist China may be increasing its output and consumption of manufactured products. However, much time will probably pass before even the total volume of consumption (much less per capita consumption) of manufactured goods in underdeveloped economies becomes impressive.

PRODUCTION AND INTERNATIONAL TRADE

We have noted previously that about one-fifth of the world's labor force is engaged in manufacturing including handicrafts (Table 7.1), that almost one-half of all available energy is consumed in manufacturing (page 208, and that manufacturing facilities are punctiform—that they occupy very small amounts of space in comparison with the value of their output (page 137). The world's manufacturing is concentrated in a few of the world's nations and in relatively small regions or districts within those nations; the United States and Canada account for nearly 40 per cent of the annual value of all manufactured goods, Europe for nearly 30 per cent, and the Soviet Union for slightly less than 20 per cent (page 140). Manufacturing is expanding very rapidly—notably in the world's technically advanced economies and embryonically in the technically underdeveloped economies (page 140). Much emphasis is being placed upon manufacturing by Communist nations, but only the Soviet Union, East Germany, Czechoslovakia, and possibly Poland among this group can be considered as technically advanced. Finished and semifinished products account for slightly over one-half of the value of a total world trade that is focused sharply on the leading technically advanced nations (pages 202 to 203).

CHANGE IN APPROACH

Because of the importance of consumption in the functioning and location of the world's economic activities, we have emphasized it heretofore in this section and placed it first in each chapter. Unfortunately, consumption of the world's manufactured products often involves the use of an amalgam of wholly unlike semiprocessed and processed materials. Consider, for example, the amount and variety of different materials in an automobile! We shall continue to emphasize consumption in the following chapters, but the emphasis will be more general and will not be focused quite so forcefully upon individual commodities.

Two additional aspects of economic geography —process and time—are given more weight in the forthcoming chapters than in those which have gone before. We have noted that manufacturing is not so nature-oriented as the other five productive occupations (see page 5), and an insight into the processes of given industries provides some understanding as to why man has located them where they now are and why they function as they now do. Historical background provides the fourth dimension of time to these same aspects of economic geography.

29 MANUFACTURING: IRON AND STEEL AND LESSER INDUSTRIAL METALS

ALTHOUGH CONJECTURE ALWAYS INVOLVES DOUBT, IT WOULD APPEAR THAT without iron and steel, manufacturing as we know it would not exist today. Certainly a modern technology based upon wood is unthinkable. Of metals other than iron, few exist in sufficiently large quantity or with sufficiently versatile properties to be considered as substitutes. In total output and use, none offers even token competition with iron (Table 27.4). Aluminum, as we have noted, is more plentiful in the earth's crust than iron, but a sophisticated technology is necessary to detect and extract it, whereas small amounts of crude iron ore long have been available almost for the taking. This fact is significant, for as a human civilization evolves, it can make use only of known materials, methods, and tools. Under such conditions, the advantages of a readily available material are self-evident. Moreover, there is reason to believe that, despite its increased use, aluminum will never achieve the volume of application now enjoyed by iron and its alloyed derivatives.

CONSUMPTION

Over 330 million short tons of steel are produced and consumed each year, most of it without leaving the nations of manufacture (Fig. 29.1). Only about one-eighth of all finished steel is exported, and no single nation is so marked an importer that its status as a consumer differs much from that as a producer. Currently, the United States consumes about 28 per cent of all steel; the Soviet Union, 20 per cent; West Germany, 8 per cent; the United Kingdom, 7 per cent; France, 6 per cent; Japan, 6 per cent; Communist China, 4.5 per cent; and all other countries, the remaining 20.5 per cent. Trends indicate a growing importance of the Communist bloc, even if allowance is made for possible exaggeration in their reports. Communist China now is involved in a high-productivity–low-utilization-of-consumer-

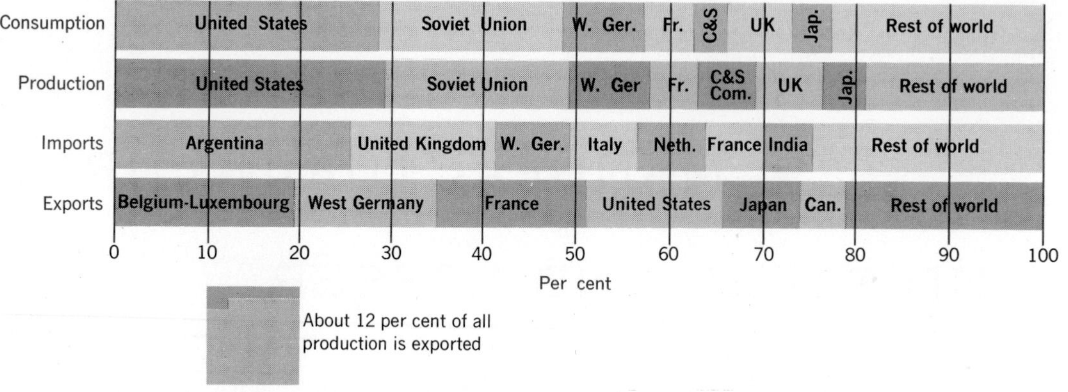

Figure 29.1 ***Consumption, production, import, and export of steel.*** *Why is Western Europe so active in both imports and exports?*

goods program like that initiated within the Soviet Union in 1928. Each year's steel output in Communist China is diverted almost entirely to machines, factories, and other producer goods. In 1957, that country consumed and produced about 5.5 million short tons of steel. Two years later, the figure stood at 14.7 million short tons. This rate of increase is unparalleled among the leading consumers and producers—indeed, scarcely paralleled among all producing nations.

THE PROCESSES

We are concerned in this chapter primarily with the making of iron and steel, and not with the numerous fabricative or other productive processes to which those materials later are subjected. We assume that beneficiation has occurred, and our interest is mainly in the conversion of iron ore and beneficiated concentrates into *pig iron, wrought iron,* and various grades of *steel.* To secure pig iron, the ores and concentrates are subjected to a smelting operation which removes most of their impurities. Essentially all iron-smelting operations use coke as a fuel, and some carbon thus passes from the coke to the molten metal. Because of the presence of the carbon, which may range from 3 to 5 per cent of the total mass, pig iron is very brittle and difficult to work when solidified. If the carbon is removed by refining, the product becomes wrought iron, which is much more workable but too soft for most purposes. Most steel is produced by first withdrawing the carbon and other impurities from pig iron and subsequently readding the carbon in carefully measured amounts. Low-carbon steels contain 0.8 per cent or less of the element, and high-carbon steels between 0.8 and 2 per cent. Manganese usually is added also, even in nonalloy steels. To other steel, known as *alloy steel,* are added manganese (in larger amounts than in nonalloy steel), nickel, chromium, vanadium, and other metals which may be combined readily with iron and carbon and used to obtain such special qualities as resistance to abrasion or corrosion under specific conditions. Manganese dominates this group of *ferroalloys* (Table 27.4). Low-carbon steel is utilized especially for structural purposes, and high-carbon and alloy steel for machinery, tools, etc.

Iron manufacture

The Blast Furnace. Nearly all iron ore is now smelted into pig iron in blast furnaces—steel shells 80 to 100 feet high and 20 to 30 feet in diameter containing an inner lining of firebrick (Fig. 29.2). Supplementary units include stoves for heating and blowing air and dust catchers. Charges of limestone, ore and/or concentrates, and coke are injected continuously at the top, where temperatures are a mild 400°F. Molten slag and iron are drawn off at the bottom, where temperatures are over

3000°F. Average daily pig-iron capacity per furnace ranges from 250 to 1,800 tons. The furnace and its operation have been described by one authority as follows:[1]

The modern blast furnace has become a large unit, expensive to construct, but by far the most economically operated of the various iron producing methods. Its size has resulted largely from efforts to economize on the consumption of coke, the most expensive component of the charge. Loss of heat and gas generated from coke is much greater in the smaller furnaces, and higher thermal efficiency is the prime goal of today's blast furnace operators.

Essentially, a blast furnace receives through its top a continuing series of charges composed of ore, coke and limestone. These move slowly downward through the stack, and molten pig iron and slag are discharged at the bottom and gas at the top. Ore is converted into metal by carbon reduction of the iron. In effect, carbon from the coke combines with oxygen from the ore, freeing the iron to accumulate at the bottom of the furnace. Coke has the important additional function of supplying heat, and stone is necessary to form a slag and eliminate impurities. Moreover, the formation of a slag progressively reduces the temperature necessary to melt the ore and stone. Mixed limestone and silica will melt at a lower temperature than either material alone. This is the fluxing action. Figure 29.2 is a diagram of a modern blast furnace plant.

A blast furnace using Lake Superior ore of approximately 50 per cent iron content, operating under average conditions, will use the following average quantities of raw materials per ton of pig iron product:

Ore, sinter, etc., 3,800 lb
Limestone, 800–1,200 lb
Coke, 1,700–1,900 lb
Air, 116,000 cu ft

In addition to the pig iron, 1,100 or more pounds of slag and 200 to 400 pounds of flue dust will be produced. The over-all recovery of iron, considering only the metal content of the pig iron, is about 93 per cent. Most producers now market their slag as a by-product for use as aggregate in road building and, to some extent, for agricultural purposes.

Top gas from the blast furnace, containing appreciable quantities of carbon monoxide, is usually burned during passage through one of the stoves. Fresh air to

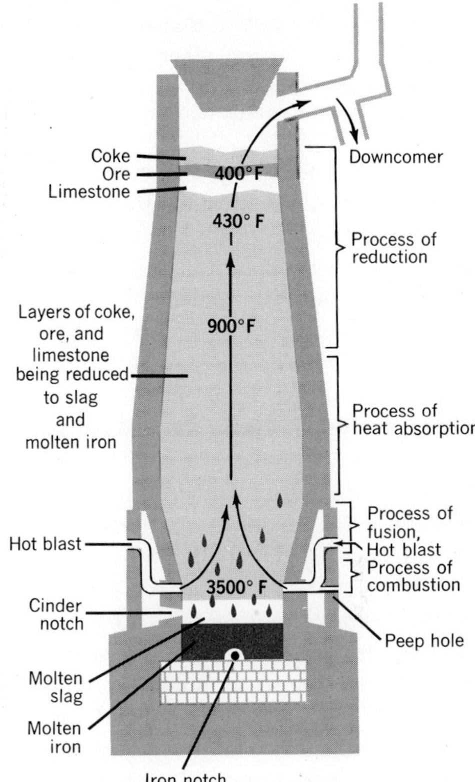

Figure 29.2 ***A modern blast furnace.*** *Coke, ore or concentrate, and limestone are inserted at the top in successive layers, and molten iron and slag are withdrawn at the bottom.*

be blown into the blast furnace is then drawn through the heated stove to be preheated before entrance into the furnace. The pig iron produced in the furnace is the basic raw material for refining processes used in the manufacture of steel as well as metal for gray-iron castings.

Over the years, research on furnace methods has been directed toward improving the physical nature of feeds; increasing reduction rates and efficiencies by pressurizing the furnace to provide better gas contact; developing improved methods of charging raw materials into the unit; better furnace design; improving blast generation; oxygen enrichment of blast; and other details of the complex operation. Almost all work has been directed primarily toward reduction of the coke requirements of the processes. However, modern blast furnaces are so large and expensive that experimentation proceeds with difficulty. It is logical that furnace foremen

[1] R. W. Holliday, *Iron,* U.S. Bureau of Mines Bulletin 556, 1956, pp. 16–18. (Preprint.)

tend to resist any radical changes in procedure, because a miscalculation or any other unexpected development can create great difficulties in operation, perhaps taking a furnace out of production several days.

Other Techniques of Pig-iron Manufacture. In Norway, Sweden, Finland, Italy, Japan, and some other countries or localities where coal is scarce and hydroelectricity plentiful and cheap, electric furnaces have partially replaced blast furnaces in pig-iron manufacture. They require only about one-half as much coke as do the blast furnaces, for electricity does much of the actual heating. Open-hearth furnaces, designed chiefly for making steel, also have been used to produce iron. Experiments are also being conducted in conversion of iron ore to metal without actual melting—a process which is expected to be less costly than reduction.

Wrought-iron Manufacture. Although pig iron may be used for products made by casting (pouring of molten metal into a mold), it is not malleable. Wrought iron, on the other hand, can be pounded and forged into a variety of shapes, does not rust easily, can be magnetized with an electric current, and possesses several other qualities rendering it useful in a variety of ways. Its manufacture is appreciably a hand operation surprisingly similar to methods of two or more centuries ago. A batch of molten pig iron is placed upon an open hearth near a flame. A workman known as a *puddler,* using a long rake, manipulates the molten iron, exposing different portions to the flame until the carbon content is essentially burned out—a condition signified when the mass becomes pasty. Deprived of its carbon, the iron is subjected to rolling and other processing. Recent efforts at mechanizing wrought-iron production have met with some success.

Steel manufacture

If pig iron is too brittle and wrought iron too soft for many uses, it would appear that a compromise is in order. That compromise is steel, generally containing less carbon than pig iron and more than wrought iron, and containing it in specific amounts that are evenly distributed. Steel may be made from pig iron or scrap iron or a combination of the two. Commercially, it is produced today chiefly in one of four processes: the *bessemer process,* the *open-hearth process,* the *electric process,* and the *basic oxygen process,*[2] to name them in order of historical discovery rather than of current importance.

The Bessemer Converter. The bessemer converter consists essentially of a large container in which air or oxygen is blasted from the bottom through the molten pig iron it holds (Fig. 29.3). Its capacity ranges from 15 to 60 tons, and processing takes only ten to twenty minutes. By combustion, the oxygen in the blast simply burns out the carbon, silicon, manganese, and certain other troublesome impurities, such as sulfur and phosphorus. The original bessemer converter, lined with sandstone or some other siliceous material capable of absorbing basic impurities, cannot process pig iron of higher than 0.10 per cent phosphorus. It is still used in some plants, where it is known as the *acid bessemer converter.* A variation in its use involves lining the converter with limestone or some other basic material which can neutralize phosphorus present in rather large amounts—2.0 per cent or higher of total charge content. This is known today as the *basic bessemer process,* or *Thomas process.* Unfortunately, neither technique is effective on pig iron with a phosphorus content of 0.1 to 2.0 per cent, and much of the world's pig iron falls within this range. The bessemer converter is also at a disadvantage in modern technology in that it can accept essentially no scrap, which is an important ingredient in the world's steel industry.

The Open-hearth Furnace. The open-hearth furnace is preferred by many steelmakers because: (1) individual units can be constructed to handle very large amounts of metal; (2) it readily accepts scrap as well as pig iron; and (3) it accepts phosphorous and sulfurous ores which the bessemer con-

[2] In addition to these four, the crucible process is still used, although sparingly. This is largely a hand operation in which carbon is added to melted wrought iron in a panlike crucible.

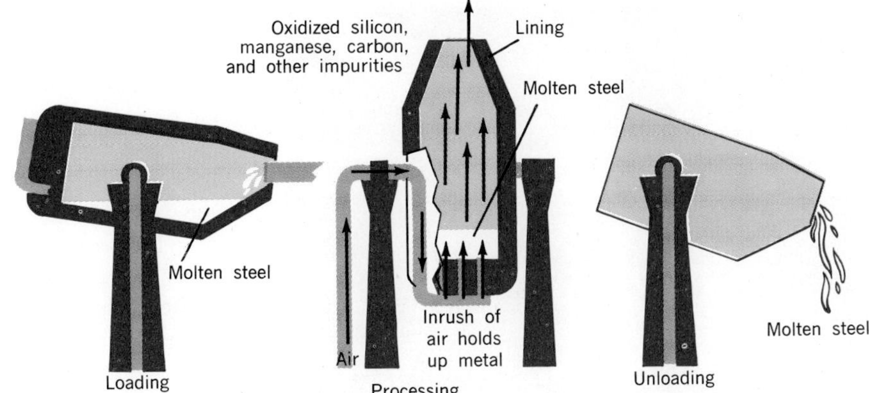

Figure 29.3 ***A bessemer converter.***

verter cannot process. Constructed of steel and brick, the hearth is broad but not deep, so that a batch of molten metal poured into it will spread rather thinly and expose a substantial upper surface (Fig. 29.4). Over this surface pass preheated air and gas, and the carbon and other impurities of the metal thus are oxidized. The direction of the air current is reversed periodically to increase the efficiency of the impurity removal. Recently oxygen has been substituted for air in some units. Both basic and acid processes are employed. As in bessemer converters, the difference is essentially in the material with which the furnace is lined. Open-hearth furnaces have been built with individual capacities ranging from 10 to 600 tons of steel, with the average unit capable of working 200 to 300 tons at one time. It usually takes between eight and twelve hours to process a single charge.

The Electric Furnace. We have noted that electric furnaces are used to produce small amounts of pig iron. A similar unit is used to make steel. In either situation, the sole contribution of the electric current appears to be very high and even heat—at least 3000°F in pig-iron manufacture and 2800°F in steel production. The furnaces are usually somewhat cylindrical in form, with spouts on their upper sections to facilitate pouring the processed metal. In

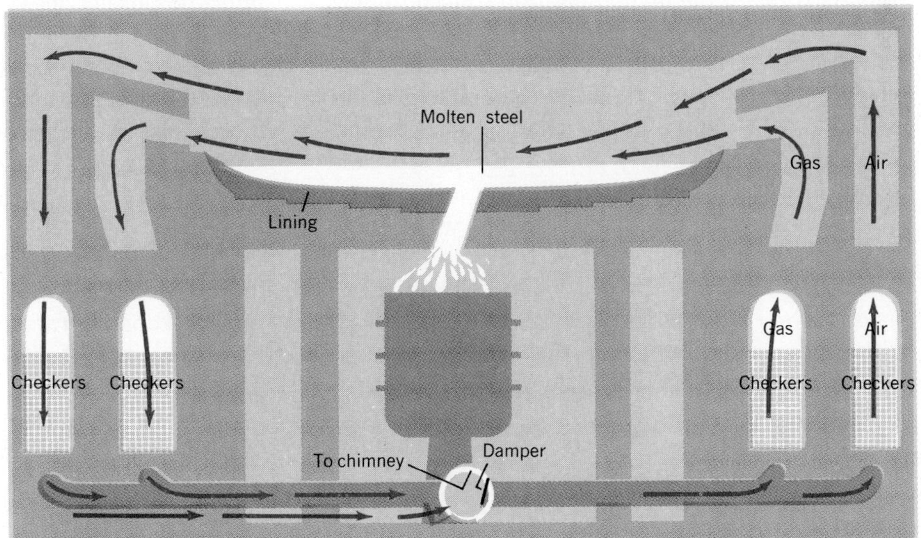

Figure 29.4 ***An open-hearth furnace.***

Tapping an electric furnace (Bethlehem Steel Company).

the arc-type furnace, an electric current passes directly through the molten pig iron from terminals usually suspended from the top. In the induction type, the current passes through a series of coils which create a magnetic field around a crucible containing the molten iron. Average units have capacities of 100 tons. They process pig iron in three to five hours and scrap iron in five to seven hours. Chiefly because of the close degree to which their temperatures can be regulated, they are excellent for making alloy steels and are also efficient utilizers of scrap. However, they are in close competition with open-hearth furnaces, the temperatures of which can be regulated with increasing exactness.

The Basic Oxygen Process. Oxygen in air long has been used in steelmaking, but commercial oxygen has been expensive to produce until recently. It has now become generally available at sufficiently reduced cost so that it can be used more actively. To a degree, it has come to be consumed in all three of the above-named processes, usually mixed with air or moisture. Since the last war, however, there has been developed in Austria a new method known by such different terms as the *basic oxygen process*, the *Linz-Donawitz process*, and the *Brassert process*. The equipment of this process consists essentially of a large, kettlelike converter which holds the molten pig iron (Fig. 29.5). A jet of oxygen is directed from above upon the molten iron at the center of the container. The jet stream quickly oxidizes the metal upon which it is focused, causing an increase in weight. The now heavier liquid sinks, reacts chemically to oxidize some of the molten pig iron with which it comes in contact at lower levels, and at the same time is replaced at the surface by more molten iron to be processed. Unlike the bessemer converter, the basic oxygen converter can accept scrap up to as much as one-fourth of its total charge and can process iron of intermediate phosphorus content (0.10 to 2.0 per cent). It also removes other impurities satisfactorily. Most units now in use hold 30 to 40 tons and process a charge in ten to twenty minutes. Since it makes steel equal in quality to open-hearth steel, since it is faster than any other process, and since it requires only small capital investment, the basic oxygen process offers promise of active competition.

Subsequent Processing. Molten steel usually is poured into molds and allowed to harden as ingots, which are made into sheets, slabs, billets, and blooms. Many are further worked into plates, beams, channels, wires, etc. The continuous rolling mill makes for high efficiency and low labor costs in such of these operations as it performs. Most of the finished products involve carbon steels, but a small portion—in the United States, less than 10 per cent—are made of alloy steels.

Importance of Scrap. In 1915, the world's output of steel began to exceed that of iron. The difference, which subsequently has increased steadily in favor of steel, is due chiefly to consumption of scrap in steel furnaces. Nearly one-third of all newly made steel now comes from scrap (Fig. 29-6). The actual ratio of scrap to pig iron varies pronouncedly from factory to factory and even from nation to nation; Italy consumes over four times as much scrap as pig iron; whereas nearby Belgium depends very slightly upon scrap. Among leading nations of production, the ratio ranges only slightly above or below the world average.

Scrap has the advantage of being already refined and thus free of all impurities except those which man has added in previous manufacturing. Furthermore, it is usually easily available. The world's iron and steel industry is generally located within or close to complex areas of other manufacturing, of intricate transportation facilities, and of heavy population pressures. This means that *prompt industrial scrap* is continuously forthcoming from stamping, cutting, boring, and other milling and fabrication processes to which newly refined steel is subjected. *Obsolete scrap*—old machines, automobiles, ships, etc.—also is to be had in quantity in such areas. Prompt industrial scrap tends to be recycled quickly into the furnaces, and obsolete scrap acts as a cushion against periods of short supply in pig iron or prompt industrial scrap. Nations which have been making steel for a long time by now are quite well endowed with obsolete scrap, which tends to be rare in some newly industrialized economies. Scrap availability is now sufficiently important to the iron and steel industry to be given serious consideration in new plant location, even in a government-owned economy like that of the Soviet Union.

Locational considerations

The current *regional* trends in the location of the world's iron and steel industry, certainly in non-Communist lands, reflect the magnetism of large numbers of people and clusters of other manufacturing—especially as markets, as sources of scrap and other raw materials, and as sources of labor. Markets probably are the most significant of these, but all merit serious consideration in the pages to follow, where attention is given to actual location in specific countries. Neither raw materials nor fuels appear to be so forceful as markets.

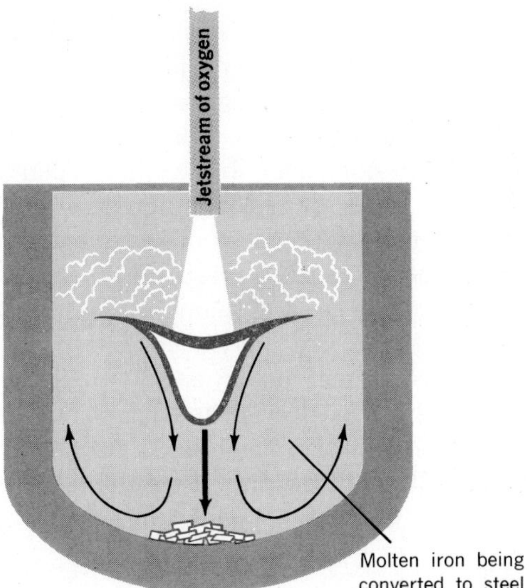

Figure 29.5 ***A basic oxygen converter*** *(after* Mineral Facts and Problems, *p. 775).*

Figure 29.6 ***Per cent of pig iron and scrap iron in the finished steel of selected nations.***

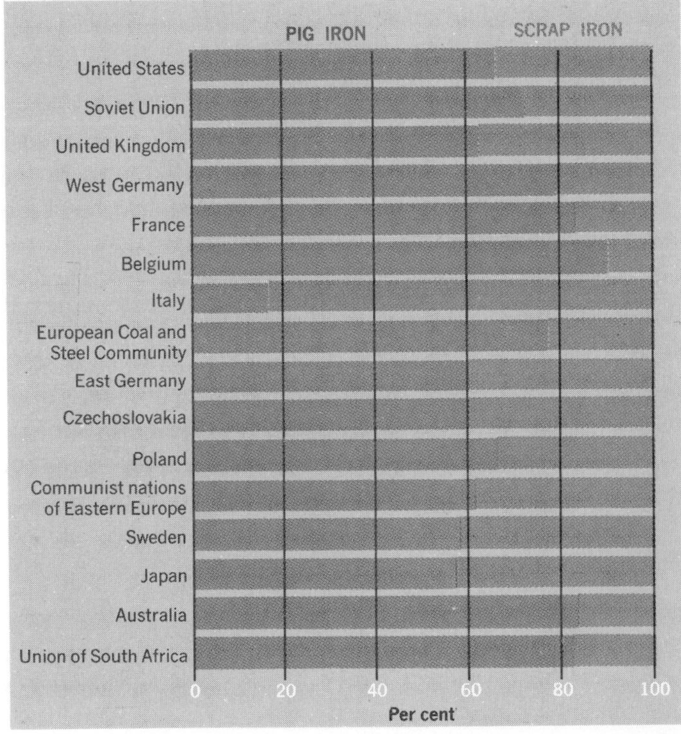

At the *local* level (specific sites within regions), water supply is a very important consideration. Nearly every processing stage in the iron and steel industry involves large quantities of water, which is used in quenching and washing operations, boilers and condensers, cooling equipment, etc. All in all, as many as 200 tons of water may be used for each ton of finished steel. Fortunately, untreated water can be used in many of these processes, but purification is sometimes necessary.

Government policy is important at both the regional and local levels, and in both non-Communist and Communist economies, as we shall note from time to time in the discussion to follow.

HISTORICAL DEVELOPMENT OF IRON AND STEEL MANUFACTURING

Early production

Iron appears to have been utilized some six thousand years ago in isolated places south and east of the Mediterranean Sea. Some three thousand years later, the metal was in sufficiently common use that an Age of Iron can be said to have begun in Greece and the neighboring classical lands. (Note that as much time elapsed between these two dates as from the beginning of the Age of Iron to the present day!) Iron processing had become sufficiently sophisticated in Greece at that time for cast iron, requiring melting and resolidification, to be achieved. The Romans, after they had conquered southern Britain during the first and second centuries A.D., set up iron-working districts in what is now Sussex and Gloucestershire in the southern half of England. They cannot be said to have introduced iron processing to the island, but they did leave an indelible stamp on operations there. Paradoxically, one of the motives for the Roman conquest appears to have been the desire for mineral wealth—not only for precious meals, but also for industrial metals. Here we have an excellent example, some two thousand years old, of exploitation on the part of a "technically advanced" nation of minerals located in an "underdeveloped" land!

In the Far East, iron may have been used at an earlier time than in the Mediterranean lands. China is believed by some authorities to have known the metal since the sixth century B.C., to have produced cast iron since the fourth century B.C., and to have made steel since the second century B.C.[3] Interestingly, much of their steelmaking involved the selective removal of carbon from pig iron by cold-air processes, instead of reduction to wrought iron and subsequent readding of the carbon. Other areas in southern and eastern Asia likewise were producing some iron and steel. In India, iron has been worked since the second century B.C., and a product known as *wootz steel* was refined in a manner similar to the crucible process developed much later in Britain. Among the buyers of the steel were the famed artisans of Damascus.

European production

Before the Nineteenth Century. After the fall of the Roman Empire, century followed upon century without witnessing major changes in European iron and steel technology or output. As late as A.D. 1300, it is estimated that not more than 900 tons of iron were produced annually in all of England, Scotland, and Wales—and this by hand methods not remarkably unlike those of the Rome-dominated era.[4] Although both iron and steel were recognized and produced, their respective carbon contents were not carefully controlled, and a given implement might contain both. Small blast furnaces for iron-ore smelting appeared in the fifteenth century, heralding the two-stage technique of iron and steel production which has continued to the present day. Prior to the appearance of the blast furnace, iron ore had been treated in a single operation in crude hearths to make either iron or steel, the type of product depending largely upon the skill of the workman. The early blast furnaces, like those today, melted the iron but mixed it with carbon and some

[3] Joseph Needham, *The Development of Iron and Steel Technology in China*, Newcomen Society, London, 1958, pp. 46–47.

[4] H. R. Schubert, *History of the British Iron and Steel Industry from 450 B.C. to A.D. 1775*, Routledge & Kegan Paul, Ltd., London, 1957, p. 109.

other impurities. Subsequent refining, today accomplished in the open-hearth furnace, electric furnace, or bessemer converter, was then achieved in small, crude forges. However, the chemistry and metallurgy of transforming iron into steel were not understood. The process was an art, not a science. Indeed, steel frequently was obtained simply by treating certain ores that happened to be high in manganese and within acceptable limits of carbon content.

Prior to the eighteenth century, the treatment of iron depended chiefly upon charcoal for fuel. Processes were inefficient, and much charcoal was used. This meant locating the small furnaces and forges near forests, the source of charcoal; and when the wood supply of a vicinity was depleted, entire operations were sometimes transferred, like those of today's portable sawmills, to new positions close to timber. Coal long had been used experimentally in iron refining—possibly even during the time of the Roman occupation of southern Britain—but never with success. Several undesired impurities in the coal were transmitted to the hot iron while in the furnaces. The sulfur in coal particularly caused difficulty. Distilling coal into coke to drive off these unwanted materials prior to refining became known early in the eighteenth century and was a common practice in England some three decades later. The process was also adopted in the Silesian district and other producing areas of central Europe by the end of the eighteenth century but was not fully accepted for another fifty years in what is now the Ruhr-Lorraine industrial complex of Western Europe. The combination of its general acceptance with other technological change that raised levels of both demand and supply resulted in a marked boost in European production, as is indicated in Table 29.1. Also shown in the table are the commanding positions assumed by England and France as the eighteenth century drew to a close.

TABLE 29.1

Production of iron in eighteenth-century Europe, in tons

Country	*Pig-iron output early in the century*	*Pig-iron output late in the century*
France	25,000	140,000
Great Britain	17,000	125,000
Sweden	45,000	70,000
Russian Empire	5,000	65,000
Germany	(30,000)	(50,000)
Austrian Empire	(20,000)	(25,000)
Low Countries	15,000	22,000
Spain	10,000	11,000
Other countries	(2,000)	(4,000)

SOURCE: Norman J. G. Pounds and William N. Parker, *Coal and Steel in Western Europe,* Indiana University Press, Bloomington, 1957, p. 27. Figures in parentheses are not supported by documentary evidence. In addition to the output shown above, some 12,000 tons of wrought iron are known to have been produced in Great Britain, and some 36,000 tons of wrought iron are known to have been produced in Sweden, early in the century. By permission of publisher.

During and since the Nineteenth Century. The transition from the eighteenth to the nineteenth century was marked by a shift of Europe's iron and steel industry from the forests to the coal fields. The twentieth century brought the possibility of its migration away from those fields to such purely economic attractions as markets and break-of-bulk transportation terminals. As the eighteenth century waned, numerous technical innovations affected the industry. Two of the most significant were Watt's steam engine, which stimulated the development of the railroad, steamship, and other sources of voracious demand for iron and steel, and Cort's puddling process, which permitted refining of pig iron on an expanded scale. Far-reaching technological changes also occurred in the nineteenth century, including the invention of Bessemer's converter in 1855 and of Siemens's open-hearth furnace a year later; the discovery in 1878 of the Thomas process for treating pig iron high in phosphorus content; and the appearance in 1899 of Héroult's electric furnace. The basic oxygen furnace was developed during the 1950s. These were largely improvements in the making of steel rather than of iron, and they marked the first time the commodity could be produced in sufficient quantity to be considered a vital ingredient of the Industrial Age. There followed still other improvements, notably those relating to the amount of

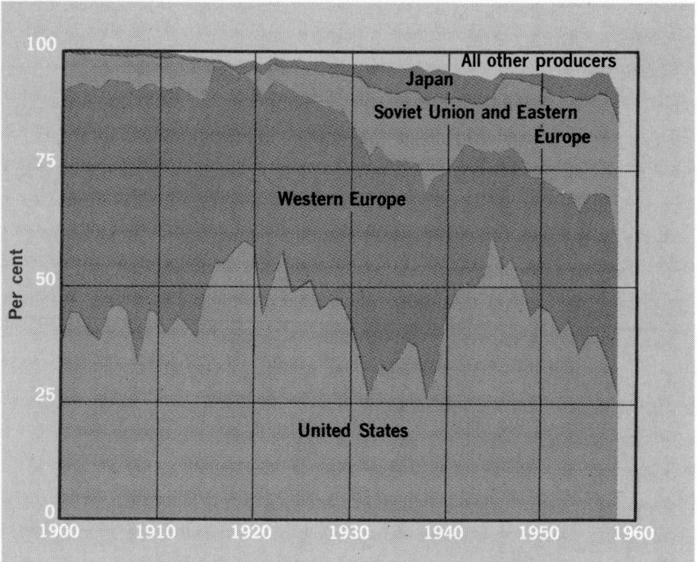

Figure 29.7 ***Leading nations and regions in world steel output for this century*** *(American Iron and Steel Institute).*

energy necessary for smelting ore. Whereas in the early 1800s the tonnage ratio of fuel consumed to iron produced was approximately 3:1, it is currently about 1:1, or even 0.75:1. This has meant a relaxing of the once strong locational ties binding the industry to energy, particularly to coal. Only in the twentieth century, however, has this development become apparent in plant location, and then largely in nations and localities where the market and other advantages prove to be definitely superior. But cultural lag is a potent force, and much of the iron and steel industry of Europe remains rather firmly rooted over the coal fields whose nearness once was vital.

During this time the tonnage of both iron and steel rose each year to almost unprecedented levels. Europe achieved and maintained a dominance in both metals, although since the late 1800s it has been forced into relative retreat by the rapidly expanding economy of the United States as well as of Japan and, since 1928, of the Soviet Union (Fig. 29.7). World output of iron rose from fewer than 500,000 short tons in 1800 to nearly 250 million short tons in 1959. Steel production, which almost can be said to have commenced in the 1850s with the invention of the bessemer and open-hearth processes, caught up with iron output in 1915 and by 1959 amounted to over 330 million short tons—more than 40 per cent above the figure for iron! As late as 1880 Europe (excluding Russia) produced nearly 70 per cent of all iron and 55 per cent of all steel; the United Kingdom alone accounted for over 40 per cent of the iron and 30 per cent of the steel. By 1959, Europe's share had declined to about one-third of each product. Even today, however, no single nation outproduces Europe.

Production in the United States

Before the Nineteenth Century. Colonization of what is now the United States took place during a comparatively early stage in the development of modern iron and steel technology. Small blast furnaces were known, operated by charcoal; the bessemer and open-hearth converters were not to be invented until two hundred years later. Interest in iron manufacture was shown by some colonists almost immediately upon arrival; the Virginia Company, for example, built a furnace on the James River in 1621—a furnace soon destroyed by Indians apparently motivated either by instinct or by remarkable foresight. Some twenty years later, however, a successful furnace began operation in Lynn, Massachusetts, and the United States iron and steel industry was born. By 1775, the iron output of this almost independent nation was about 30,000 tons—an amount easily exceeded by any of several European countries (Table 29.1).

During and since the Nineteenth Century. The nineteenth-century iron and steel industry of the United States was characterized not so much by indigenous invention as by prodigious growth. By 1860, only the United Kingdom was outproducing the United States, and thirty years later even that nation had relinquished its position as a world leader in both iron and steel.

At the outset the United States, like contemporary Europe, used charcoal as a fuel. In the nineteenth century, however, anthracite began to be substituted for charcoal—a technique which, although never practiced widely in Europe, gained such acceptance in the United States that by the outbreak of the Civil War anthracite was responsible for twice as much of this country's iron as charcoal was. Europe, meanwhile, shifted almost exclusively to coke in its blast furnaces, and, soon after the Civil War, the United States also came to rely upon coke, which contains far fewer impurities than anthracite. This meant a westward shift by the industry from eastern locations to western Pennsylvania and eastern Ohio, where the very extensive deposits of high-grade bituminous coking coal in the Appalachian plateau became mainstays of fuel supply and have remained so to the present day. Later, when Lake Superior iron ore began to be utilized, components of the industry appeared at current locations along the lower Great Lakes. During and since the Second World War, the lower-lakes sites grew at rates exceeding those in the Pittsburgh-Youngstown vicinity. On the Atlantic seaboard, some new plants and enlarged facilities, mainly oriented to incoming foreign ores, also were constructed, and this area regained a portion of its once declining iron-and-steel status. Meanwhile, iron and steel operations in the South, notably at Birmingham, Alabama, had grown to their present modest proportions, and those in the West became at least noteworthy, largely because of the emergency stimulus of the Second World War. In the aftermath of that war, this country has experienced a relative decline on the world scene, chiefly because of the increased output of the Soviet Union and Western Europe (Fig. 29.7).

Although the remarkable growth of metallurgical technology involved use of basic techniques originating in Europe, the United States rapidly became a leader. In the iron and steel industry, this leadership has found expression not so much in single, far-reaching inventions like the open-hearth furnace as in numerous but aggregately important improvements, such as the making of alloy steels to exact specifications. An outstanding exception to this generalization is the continuous rolling mill by which some steel ingots are shaped into beams, rails, etc.—a United States achievement which can take its place beside the open-hearth furnace as an outstanding step forward in the progress of iron and steel technology.

Production in the Soviet Union

Iron is known to have been obtained from charcoal-fired blast furnaces in Russia as early as the seventeenth century. During the early eighteenth century, Russia ranked lowest among European producers for which data are available, but its output rose substantially as that century neared its close (Table 29.1). However, czarist Russia was never a dynamic producer of iron or steel, and its economy was turning out only somewhat over 4 million short tons annually of either metal shortly before the 1917 revolution—and this was during the stimulus of involvement in the First World War. Production essentially halted during the revolution and its immediate aftermath, and it was not until 1928, the year of initiation of the First Five-Year Plan, that the 1913 output level was again reached. Under this and succeeding plans, however, priority was given to expansion of iron and steel facilities, and, despite the destruction wrought in European Russia by the Second World War, the Soviet Union now ranks behind only the United States as an iron and steel manufacturer (Figs. 29.1 and 29.7). A substantial portion of this increase has resulted from expansion of facilities in the Ukraine and in European Russia, but credit must be given also to activity in the Urals, Kuznets, and lesser producing districts or places developed by the Soviet government. The temporary loss of the Ukraine to the Germans in the Second World War motivated a rapid expansion of these more easterly districts, but in all probability they would have grown rapidly even if that invasion had not occurred.

Production elsewhere in the world

Japan, although a minor iron and steel manufacturer at the beginning of the twentieth century, began marked expansion of these activities at the close of the Sino-Russian War in 1905. Steel output was particularly emphasized—based on heavy consumption of imported scrap. Despite a paucity of both domestic iron ore and good coking coal, the steel industry became sufficiently dynamic to sustain the country in the early years of the Second World War, and, despite defeat in that war, Japan now produces almost as much steel annually as in 1939 (Fig. 29.7).

Meanwhile, at least noteworthy production has appeared in many widely separated countries such as Communist China, Canada, and Australia. In each, production is a kind of miniature version of that in the leading nations; and historical development usually has been closely associated with such nations—in some cases as neighbors, in others as political or economic affiliates, and in still others as both.

IRON AND STEEL PRODUCTION TODAY

The United States

The United States currently has the capacity to produce substantially more iron and steel than any other nation. Ordinarily, over one-fourth of the world output of both metals actually comes from this one country, which, since the end of the Second World War, generally has not operated to an expanding capacity.

Iron Production. PLANT LOCATION. The United States is capable of producing about 95 million short tons of pig iron annually. Over one-third of this capacity is located along the shores of the lower Great Lakes—chiefly at Chicago in Illinois; East Chicago and Gary in Indiana; Dearborn, River Rouge, and Trenton in Michigan; Toledo, Lorain, and Cleveland in Ohio; Erie in Pennsylvania; and Buffalo, Lackawanna, Tonawanda, and North Tonawanda in New York (Figs. 29.8 and 29.9). These are scattered locations; but they merit a common classification because they all are at, or very near, lower-lakes ports situated on neither iron nor coal, but depending largely upon Great Lakes transportation to bring the one commodity and land transportation to bring the other. Equally important, they are near markets in the nation's manufacturing belt.

Within a radius of 80 miles of Pittsburgh is another group of blast furnaces with an aggregate capacity nearly equal to that along the lower Great Lakes. Some thirteen of these are in the immediate vicinities of Pittsburgh and Youngstown, and many of the others are along the upper Ohio River.

Eastern furnaces involving eight sites in Pennsylvania, one (Baltimore–Sparrows Point) in Maryland, one (Troy) in New York, and one (Everett) in Massachusetts provide more than one-eighth of the nation's capacity, and seven Alabama plants account for yet another one-twelfth. The remaining furnaces are scattered rather widely throughout the country.

LOCATIONAL TRENDS. The geographic distribution of blast furnaces is undergoing change, with lower Great Lakes and Eastern seaboard sites gaining at the relative expense of some inland locations. This change involves different rates of growth—i.e., establishment of new works in some areas faster than in others—rather than an outright shift of the furnaces from one site to another. In the Great Lakes, the most dramatic increases from 1952 to 1959 have occurred in the Detroit automobile area, where one sizable new plant has been added and the capacity of a second has been doubled. The Chicago–East Chicago–Gary district also has experienced growth, notably in its Indiana segment. Additions along central and lower Lake Erie, while not so marked, nonetheless have been substantial. Except in Michigan, this growth in Great Lakes output largely represents expansion of existing facilities rather than establishment of new plants.

Increases in capacity on the Eastern seaboard are due in no small measure to the building of a single plant by the United States Steel Corporation and the enlarging of several of Bethlehem Steel's Eastern facilities. The new United States Steel plant is at Fairless Hills, near Morrisville, Pennsylvania, on the Delaware River, and the Bethlehem plant which has been the most greatly enlarged is at Sparrows Point in Baltimore. As we noted in the preceding chapter, both these companies have iron-ore mining operations in Venezuela and elsewhere, and their seaport locations are designed especially to process incoming foreign ore.

Along and near the central Ohio River is a

Figure 29.8 ***Distribution of blast furnaces in the United States.***

series of plants also experiencing growth, although not so vigorously as those on the Great Lakes and Eastern seaboard. This river and the Mississippi make available both ore and coal to these locations; ore is transshipped from deep-water vessels at Chicago, and coal is obtained primarily in the Appalachian field. Overland shipment of both coal and ore is also practiced by some companies in this group.

Growth rates from 1952 to 1959 in the producing areas described above have been higher than the national average, as are such rates in some of the outlying producing centers in the nation's South and West.[5] In the immediate vicinity of Pittsburgh, recent growth appears to have taken place at, or slightly below, the national average rate, and in Youngstown expansion has been considerably slower. Absolute decline, however, has not occurred in either vicinity.

In the future, the shore-line cities probably will continue to acquire an increasing share of national capacity at the relative expense of inland locations. This will be especially true in the lower Great Lakes ports which, now that the Great Lakes–St. Lawrence Seaway is a reality, are favorably located regarding domestic and foreign ore, coal, and

[5] It should be remembered that the rate of growth in this case is calculated by subtracting 1952 output from that in 1959 and dividing the difference by the 1952 figure. The results, while useful, tend to favor places with small 1952 production. For example, from 1952 to 1959 the Chicago-Gary district increased its blast-furnace capacity from 15,-122,670 to 17,590,900 net tons—a growth rate of 16.3 per cent, compared to the national average of 14.6 per cent. Kaiser's Fontana plant in California, representing the total blast-furnace capacity in that state, increased its output from 876,000 to 1,912,100 net tons in the same time period, thus realizing a growth rate of 118 per cent. However, the actual, or absolute, increase in the Chicago-Gary district of 2,468,230 net tons was substantially more than the 1,036,000 net tons added in California.

Figure 29.9 ***Value of shipments from blast furnaces in the United States.***

Each dot approximates 1 per cent of the national total. Because figures are rounded off and minor producers are sometimes omitted, dots do not always total 100.

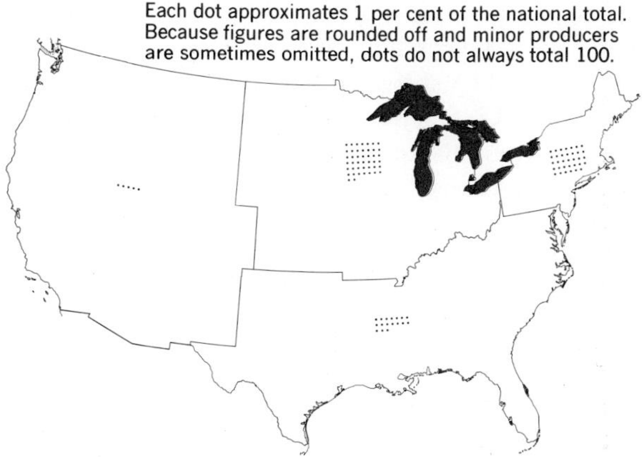

This large Bethlehem Steel Company plant is situated on tidewater at Sparrows Point in Baltimore. It utilizes iron ore inbound primarily from Venezuela, and Chile, but also accepts ore from other parts of the world. (Bethlehem Steel Company)

home and foreign markets. Additional expansion also can be anticipated along the Eastern seaboard.

ASSEMBLY COSTS. Further insight into the location and operation of blast furnaces can be gained through examination of assembly costs—chiefly mining and transportation costs—of coal, iron ore, and limestone per net ton of pig iron. These are shown in Table 29.2. Significantly, such costs are about the same at the Pittsburgh and lower Great Lakes locations; are lowest at Geneva, Utah, in the Rocky Mountain West; and highest at Houston, Texas, and along the Ohio River.

CLOSE FUNCTIONAL ASSOCIATION WITH STEEL. If assembly costs do not reveal a monetary advantage for producing sites which are gaining relatively in the nation's pig-iron production, the answer may lie in steel output, with which iron manufacture is very closely associated. Nearly all pig iron is converted into steel, usually in the same plant producing the iron itself. A small amount, less than 5 per cent, is cast as pig iron or made into wrought iron.

Steel Production. LOCATION. Although steel manufacturing usually occurs in the same plants which produce iron, the nation's steel capacity of nearly 148 million tons is in one way slightly more concentrated than its blast-furnace capacity, for the districts of heaviest steel production, while coinciding quite closely with those producing the most iron, generally account for a slightly higher percentage of the nation's steel than of its iron. On the other hand, steel production is slightly more dispersed spatially, in that some fourteen states, representing in total almost every section of the country,

TABLE 29.2

Assembly cost of raw materials per net ton of pig iron at selected blast-furnace locations, 1952

Location	*Ore*	*Coal*	*Limestone*	*Total*
Houston, Tex.	$10.28	$14.26	$1.53	$26.07
Ohio River area	13.87	9.02	1.27	24.16
Birmingham, Ala.	9.91	13.17	0.29	23.37
Granite City, Ill.	10.36	10.19	2.30	22.85
Bethlehem, Pa.	12.35	9.22	0.37	21.94
Chicago, Ill.	9.01	12.16	0.61	21.78
Lone Star, Tex.	8.19	11.53	2.00	21.72
Buffalo, N.Y.	9.04	11.38	1.07	21.49
Fontana, Calif.	7.12	13.81	0.50	21.43
Pittsburgh, Pa.	12.52	7.94	0.92	21.38
Duluth, Minn.	7.80	11.37	0.71	19.88
Baltimore, Md.	10.29	8.77	0.76	19.82
Geneva, Utah	6.87	9.40	0.63	16.90

SOURCE: Compiled from Marvin J. Barloon, "The Expansion of Blast Furnace Capacity, 1938–1952: A Study in Geographical Cost Differentials," *The Business History Review*, **28**, (1), 1954, p. 17. For each commodity shown, the relative costs of mining and transportation vary surprisingly from location to location.

produce no iron but refine steel (Figs. 29.8 and 29.10).

ROLE OF SCRAP. A partial explanation for the situation described above rests in the consumption of scrap, which now makes up over one-third of the furnace and converter charge of the nation as a whole. In the complex, multi-industry areas of heaviest steel production, much scrap is available to mix with the pig iron. In outlying areas where little or no pig iron is locally forthcoming, scrap can comprise the entire furnace charge. In the United States, about two-thirds of all scrap consumption involves prompt industrial scrap, and the remainder obsolete scrap.

Figure 29.10 ***Distribution of steel works and rolling mills in the United States.***

PROCESSES. About 85 per cent of the steel capacity of the United States involves open-hearth facilities; 9 per cent is made up of electric furnaces; slightly over 3 per cent, of basic oxygen units; and somewhat under 3 per cent, of bessemer converters. Open-hearth and electric furnaces are distributed throughout the nation more or less in accordance with the total iron and steel industry. Basic oxygen units are found chiefly in new plants—notably in Michigan and California. Bessemer converters are located mainly in western Pennsylvania and Ohio. Since the turn of the century, the open-hearth and electric furnaces have gained at the relative expense of the bessemer converter, which is not suitable for refining much of the nation's pig iron—iron which is of intermediate range (0.10 to 2.0 per cent) in phosphorus content. Increased use of scrap also has been to the disadvantage of the bessemer converter. The basic oxygen process, a newcomer, may well become important.

STEEL MARKETS. The relative uniformity in assembly costs for blast-furnace raw materials in the leading producing districts would suggest that the volume and location of market demand for finished steel and the costs of its transportation exert pressures on the location and functioning of the iron and steel industry. The domestic market for steel lies primarily in other manufacturing—in the automobile industry (nearly 25 per cent); oil, gas, and other warehouses (nearly 20 per cent); other construction and maintenance (nearly 12 per cent); containers (8 per cent); miscellaneous machinery, industrial equipment, and tools (6 per cent); and railroads (4 per cent). These, as we shall emphasize later, are located particularly within the nation's manufacturing belt, notably along the lower Great Lakes and Eastern seaboard. The newest and currently most rapidly expanding portion of this belt is its western portion, including the states of Illinois, Indiana, Michigan, and Ohio. Such expansion encourages a similar trend in the nation's iron and steel industry.

TRANSPORTATION COSTS AND FREIGHT RATES. The sensitivity of the nation's iron and steel industry to markets is partially the result of comparatively high freight rates on finished steel products—rates which per ton-mile may be as high as three times those for pig iron or coal.[6] Also important has been a change in freight-rate policy. Prior to 1924, the domestic freight rates for all steel were calculated as if the steel were manufactured in Pittsburgh. This was the so-called Pittsburgh Plus system. Thus, a Chicago steel-plant manager selling to a Chicago buyer necessarily added freight charges which would have been assessed if the product had been made in Pittsburgh. Contrarily, if he sold steel in Pittsburgh, he found it necessary to absorb the cost of shipment to that city. Needless to say, Pittsburgh did not object to this arrangement, but many of the other steel-manufacturing cities did. From 1924 until 1948, a multiple-point basing system was substituted for Pittsburgh Plus, but in 1948 this, also, had to be abandoned. Now steel is shipped f.o.b. the factory of its production. Many authorities feel that this change of policy has favored steel producers other than those in the Pittsburgh-Youngstown vicinity.

Centralized administration and economies of scale

One of the most important aspects of the United States iron and steel industry is the degree to which it is concentrated in administration. As is shown in Table 29.3, well over one-half of the industry is controlled by the leading four companies, and over two-fifths by the United States Steel and Bethlehem Steel corporations. Such centralization makes possible large-scale administrative integration of the industry, so that single companies can control mines, beneficiation plants, blast furnaces, steel furnaces, and final processing. Over 90 per cent of the na-

[6] See especially Allan Rodgers, "Industrial Inertia: A Major Factor in the Location of the Steel Industry in the United States," *Geographical Review*, 42:56–66, 1952. Rodgers points out in this article that the sensitivity to markets is offset partially by *industrial inertia*—by the tendency to produce even in an obsolete plant because of heavy capital investment in it, and that movement of a plant from an unfavorable location may await the wearing down or wearing out of that plant's facilities and equipment. This point may account for continued prominence of Pittsburgh and Youngstown.

tion's steel capacity and nearly 95 per cent of its pig-iron capacity are controlled by twenty-two fully integrated companies.[7]

Trends

The actual output of steel in the United States, in contrast to capacity, has not risen substantially since 1950. Meanwhile, world production, which from the turn of this century through the Second World War was so closely in harmony with that of the United States that the two registered matching cyclical variations, has risen markedly since that war's end and now stands at about three times the United States figure (Fig. 29.7). This is a sobering reality, for it marks the end of overwhelming predominance on the part of a single nation with respect to the most important of the industrial metals. To a degree the United States has lost in relative position to a resurging Western Europe and Japan. To an even greater degree, it has lost to a growing productivity in the Soviet Union and its Eastern European satellites.

The Soviet Union

Location. The iron and steel output of the Soviet Union, largely from open hearths augmented by electric furnaces, bessemer converters, and the new basic oxygen converters, is concentrated in three regions, two of which are outstanding and one of which is noteworthy. The leader in both commodities is the Ukrainian or Donets region, situated to the north of the Black Sea. The densest clustering of facilities here reaches from the Donets River basin southward to the Sea of Azov (Fig. 29.11). It includes eight cities with integrated blast and steel furnaces as well as rolling mills, two with steel furnaces and rolling mills, one with blast furnaces only, and one with rolling mills only. Stalino, Voroshilovsk, Kramatorsk, Makeyevka, and Zhdanov are among the more outstanding of such cities. Some 200 miles to the west in the vicinity of Krivoi Rog are four more sites with integrated blast-furnace, steel-furnace, and rolling-mill plants, as well as one site with only a blast furnace specializing in manganese and two more with rolling mills only. Krivoi Rog, Dnepropetrovsk (the site of the famous dam across the Dnieper River), and Zaporozhe are among the more prominent urban units here. To the south and across the Sea of Azov is another fully integrated plant at Kerch on the Crimean peninsula. Despite its capture and temporary paralysis during and immediately after the Second World War, this Donets region now produces nearly one-half of all pig iron and slightly under two-fifths of all steel made in the Soviet Union.

On either side of the central and southern Ural Mountains is an industrial region which extends latitudinally for about 600 miles and longitudinally for over 300 miles. It is named after the mountains around which it has grown. Among the more prominent iron and steel centers are Magnitogorsk, Beloretsk, Chelyabinsk, Nizhni Tagil, Alapayevsk,

TABLE 29.3

Leading corporations in the United States iron and steel industry, January 1, 1959

Corporation	*Per cent of nation's blast-furnace capacity**	*Per cent of nation's steel capacity†*
United States Steel	32.8	28.3
Bethlehem Steel	15.8	15.5
Republic Steel	8.3	8.6
National Steel	6.1	4.7
Jones & Laughlin Steel	5.2	5.4
Youngstown Sheet & Tube	4.3	4.5
Inland Steel	3.5	4.4
Armco Steel	2.9	4.3
Wheeling Steel	2.0	1.6
Kaiser Steel	1.9	1.9
All others‡	17.2	21.8

* Total blast-furnace capacity, 94,634,850 net tons, including 877,500 tons of ferroalloys capacity.
† Total steel capacity, 147,633,670 net tons.
‡ Includes twenty-four companies producing pig iron and seventy-two producing steel. (Note that reference is to *companies*, not *plants*. Some of the smaller companies, like the ten leaders, produce both iron and steel.)
SOURCE: Computed from information supplied by the American Iron and Steel Institute.

[7] E. B. Alderfer and H. E. Michl, *Economics of American Industry*, McGraw-Hill Book Company, Inc., New York, 1957, p. 29.

Figure 29.11 ***Leading iron and steel regions and cities of the Soviet Union.***

Krasnouralsk, Serov, Sverdlovsk, Lysva, and Zlatoust. All but the last three produce both iron and steel, and these three concentrate on steel only. The Urals region, which grew rapidly as the Soviet armies were forced to retreat from the Ukraine in the last war, now accounts for over one-third of the country's pig iron and a slightly higher portion of its steel.

Some 1,000 miles eastward from the Urals industrial region is the much newer and smaller Kuznets region, centered on the integrated facilities at Stalinsk and the steel furnaces at Belovo. This region now produces about 7 per cent of the nation's iron and 10 per cent of its steel.

The remaining iron and steel capacity of the Soviet Union is largely in the European portion—at Leningrad (steel only); Cherepovets (iron and steel); Moscow (steel only); Tula (pig iron only); Lipetsk (pig iron only); Stalingrad (steel only); and Rustavi (iron and steel). A small amount of steel production occurs in Soviet Central Asia (at Begovat and Ust-Kamenogorsk), and in far eastern Siberia (especially Petrovsk-Zabaikalski and Komsomolsk).

Locational Trends. Some locational trends in the Soviet Union's iron and steel industry are suggested in Table 29.4. During the twenty-year period for which data are shown, the national output more than doubled, despite the ravages of the Second World War. Among the three producing regions, the Urals improved its position very decidedly, essentially doubling its share of pig-iron production and nearly doing the same for steel. Most of its relative increase in pig-iron output has been at the expense of the Ukraine, with the remainder of the nation retaining its relative position. Its gain in steel, however, has not been accompanied by a correspondingly relative decline in either the Ukraine or the Kuznets but in the numerous smaller producing centers, which in 1937 accounted for 30 per cent of all steel but in 1956 for only 18 per cent. It would appear that, particularly in the production of steel, the Soviet Union has found spatial concentration advantageous, as have the giant corporations of the United States. Soviet statistics also reveal the recent establishment of small steel-producing units in outlying areas of the Soviet Union. Thus that country exhibits also a dual tendency which we already have noted in the United States—a tendency for spatial concentration on the one hand and spatial dispersion on the other. Meanwhile, the newest of the producing regions, the Kuznets, has increased its iron output at a rate slightly below the national average, and its steel output at a rate slightly above that average. The Ukraine, oldest of the three and the only one being worked extensively at the time of the Communist revolution, has declined in relative position with respect to both metals—only modestly in steel, but rather dramatically in pig iron. It is perhaps needless to add that this decline has been caused partly by the Second World War.

Spatial Imbalance of Consumption and Production. Historically, effective Russia has been European Russia. As a result, a substantial portion of national demand for semimanufactured and manufactured products remains there. Concerning iron and steel, this demand in the south of European Russia is supplied rather easily from local or nearby production in the Ukrainian industrial region, and in the east by the Urals industrial complex. However, the north central and northwestern sections of the country, including Moscow and Leningrad, are not self-sufficient in these metals but depend appreciably upon freight arrivals from elsewhere—notably from the Ukraine and the Urals. As shown in Table 29.4, expansion in plant output of the Soviet Union during the past twenty years has occurred mainly in these two regions of heaviest output, plus the far-away Kuznets region in Asian Russia. Thus there exists in the Soviet Union a spatial imbalance of consumption and production of iron and steel, the north central and northwestern sections of European Russia exhibiting an appreciable excess of capacity to consume over that to produce. It remains to be seen whether this spatial imbalance will be corrected—at least regarding steel, for which scrap is a significant raw material. Such a situation is not duplicated in the United States, where most new iron and steel plants are being located quite closely in accord with market distribution.

TABLE 29.4

Production of iron and steel in the Soviet Union, 1937 and 1956, in millions of metric tons for national production and per cent for regional production

Producing areas	*Iron output*		*Steel output*	
	1937	*1956*	*1937*	*1956*
Soviet Union	14.5	35.8	17.7	48.6
Ukraine	64%	50%	39%	37%
Urals	18%	35%	22%	35%
Kuznets	10%	7%	9%	10%
Rest of country	8%	8%	30%	18%

SOURCE: For 1937 data: *Promyshlennost S.S.S.R., Statisticheskii Sbornik,* 1957, pp. 112–113; for 1956 data, *Narodnoe Khoziaistvo S.S.S.R., Statisticheskii Ezhegodnik,* 1957, p. 69.

Europe

The Coal and Steel Community. Ardent concern with iron and steel output of the United States and the Soviet Union may result in lack of appreciation for the economic achievements of other nations. The Coal and Steel Community, particularly, should not be overlooked in this context. Consisting of six member nations whose animosities are deeply rooted in time and yet sufficiently current that four of the six were among the victors and two among the defeated in the Second World War, this coalition was considered a precarious experiment when it began in 1952. Far from failing, however, it has gained beyond even the wildest hopes of many of its originators. Its output of both pig iron and steel has increased since the last war, notably during 1954–1958, when it grew at a rate almost equal to that in the Soviet Union (Table 29.5). It currently accounts for over one-third of the European

TABLE 29.5

Production of pig iron and steel in the European Coal and Steel Community and the Soviet Union, 1954 and 1958 (in millions of short tons)

Area	*Pig iron*		*Steel*	
	1954	*1958*	*1954*	*1958*
European Coal and Steel Community	36.9	48.3	48.3	63.8
Soviet Union	33.1	43.7	45.6	60.5

SOURCE: *Mineral Trade Notes,* **49,** (2):24–5, U.S. Bureau of Mines, 1959.

production of both metals, and its share is rising slightly.

West Germany and France are the outstanding European producers of both iron and steel, accounting for about two-thirds of the output (Table 29.6). Capital investment from these two countries amounts to almost three-fourths of that in the community.

Although the community reaches discontinuously from the Atlantic Ocean to the Mediterranean Sea, its core section is located in Western Europe, where the political boundaries of West Germany, France, Belgium, Luxembourg, and the Netherlands form a close network. More specifically, it includes the Ruhr and nearby sites in West Germany, the Lorraine and the northern producing districts of France, and industrial clusters in the Benelux countries—clusters which more or less form a bridge between the German and French industrial regions.

TABLE 29.6

Production of pig iron and steel by individual nations of the European Coal and Steel Community, 1958 (in millions of short tons)

Country	*Pig iron*	*Steel*
West Germany*	21.8	28.9
France	13.4	16.1
Belgium	6.1	6.6
Luxembourg	3.6	3.7
Italy	2.4	6.9
Netherlands	1.0	1.6
Total	48.3	63.8

* Includes production in the Saar.

SOURCE: *Mineral Trade Notes,* **49,** (2):24–5, U.S. Bureau of Mines, 1959.

Most of the manufacturing is located on coal or iron ore—the Ruhr and Saar coal fields of West Germany, the Sambre-Meuse coal fields in Belgium and their projections into the north of France, and the Minette iron ore of Lorraine province of France and in Luxembourg. Only in Italy and the Netherlands is the bulk of iron and steel manufacturing not located on coal. These countries are minor producers of pig iron, and the Netherlands produces a comparatively small amount of steel. Italy, third in the community in steel production, depends appreciably on scrap rather than pig iron to charge the steel furnaces and converters.

The comparatively high phosphorus content of the Minette ores has resulted in rather extensive use of the Thomas process in the bessemer converter in the production of steel. In Luxembourg, this process is relied upon for nearly all steelmaking; in Belgium, for nearly seven-eighths; in France, for about three-fifths of steelmaking; and in West Germany, for about two-fifths. Open-hearth furnaces refine most of the community's remaining steel, much of it from pig iron smelted from ores imported from Sweden or elsewhere. Electric furnaces, located primarily in Italy, account for a very small percentage of the steel yield of the six nations.

Only about one-fourth of the community's steel comes from scrap—less than in any other major producing nation or region (Fig. 29.6). Scrap was in surplus supply in Europe during the chaotic aftermath of the Second World War but now is becoming increasingly scarce. Despite more exchange among member nations, import from beyond the community is necessary. At present, most of this import comes from the United States. However, the United States must supply its own voracious demand for scrap and also is shipping to Japan and other importing nations. Anticipating a decline in available scrap supply, the community now is enlarging its blast-furnace capacity to curtail reliance upon scrap.

Growth rates in iron and steel output over the past forty years have not been markedly dissimilar for individual nations now in the community, although Belgium and Luxembourg have achieved increases somewhat above the community average. Unlike the Soviet Union and somewhat unlike the United States, the community has experienced an intensification of activity in places which have been mainstays of production over the past century, rather than the establishment of new industrial districts or regions.

An extremely important aspect of the community's existence is interdependence among the member nations. As much as 9 per cent of all coal, 13 per cent of all coke, 19 per cent of all iron ore, 13 per cent of all scrap, and 12 per cent of all iron and steel goods produced or otherwise made available by the six nations is traded among them.[8] Before the community came into being in 1952, the charges for transporting these commodities were sometimes raised by 25 per cent or more through discriminatory rating practices and the necessity to levy only short-haul rates because of the small sizes of the countries involved. The railroads carried nearly two-thirds of this freight, waterways about one-fifth, and trucks the remainder. Immediate efforts were focused upon lowering the railroad rates, with the results shown in Figure 29.12.

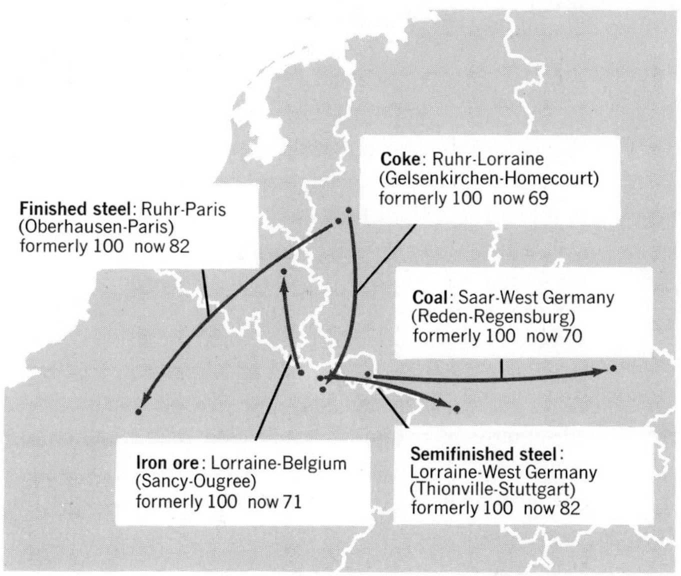

Figure 29.12 ***Railroad freight rates*** *(in index numbers) of selected products between selected places before and after action by the Coal and Steel Community to reduce discriminating practices by the six nations of that community.*

Concern with trade by the European Coal and Steel Community demonstrates that markets there, as in the United States and the Soviet Union, exert a strong force over the location and functioning of the industry. Indeed, one of the primary purposes in forming the community was that of creating a common market for the industry's products, and the adjusting of railway freight rates was done partly for that purpose.

The United Kingdom. Once supreme in steel production, the United Kingdom is now fourth on the world scene and second in Europe (Fig. 29.1). The rigors of the Second World War left their toll on this nation, which during the twentieth century has been unable to cope completely with such economic trends as declining world demand for coal and such political trends as pressure for more independence by political units once securely welded to the empire—trends coinciding with the emergence of economic and political giants in the forms of the United States and the Soviet Union. By 1953, the country's archrival, Germany—more accurately that part of Germany occupied by the Allies immediately after the war and subsequently converted into West Germany—surpassed the United Kingdom's output of pig iron and in 1955 moved ahead in its volume of steel production. Meanwhile, the United Kingdom found it necessary to adopt a program of domestic austerity in the postwar years. In effect, that nation returned partially to mercantilist-like economic thinking which advocated the maximum export of home-produced goods, including iron and steel products, in order to acquire revenue. (Fortunately, it did not simply hoard the results of such trading, as the mercantilists of old would have done, but invested them in rebuilding.) Changing government policy also left its mark on iron and steel. The Labor party came to power near the end

[8] Norman J. G. Pounds and William N. Parker, *Coal and Steel in Western Europe*, Indiana University Press, Bloomington, Ind., 1957, p. 361.

of the Second World War and nationalized most of the iron and steel facilities, and the Tory party returned to power in the next nationwide election and denationalized most of them again. Meanwhile, the country's rate of growth in the output of both iron and steel since the last war has been appreciably slower than that of the Coal and Steel Community, and even slower than that of Europe as a continent (excluding the Soviet Union).

As in continental Europe, the majority of the United Kingdom's iron and steel facilities are located on coal—east, south, and west of the Pennines; in the Scottish lowlands to the north; along the southern fringe of the Welsh peninsula to the southwest. Because of the country's elongated shape, no part of it is far from seaport facilities, and the substantial amounts of imported iron ore supplementing the Midlands' production are subjected to only short hauls before processing. The basic open-hearth process predominates; acid open-hearth processes, basic and acid bessemer converters, and electric processes also are represented.

Now that the United Kingdom's postwar recovery has been achieved, another problem has arisen in the form of the European Coal and Steel Community and, more serious, the European Economic Community, which is dedicated to creating a common market for all European products among the six member nations now belonging to the Coal and Steel Community. In essence the problem is: Can the United Kingdom compete with such a coalition in the production of iron and steel and other goods? Probably not. Then why not follow the old adage "If you can't lick 'em, join 'em"? There are several reasons, but the most important focus upon the incompatibility between the British Commonwealth, presently accounting for about one-half of all British foreign trade, and the community. The latter, while making every effort to remove internal trade restrictions, has set up substantial controls over the trade between itself and other countries. (Technically, the overseas affiliations of France, Belgium, and the Netherlands can be included in such an arrangement in that they are, for the most part, now merely overseas portions of domestic governments—just as Hawaii is an overseas state in the United States.) However, most of the actively trading members of the British Commonwealth are independent nations whose only tie to the Commonwealth is an allegiance—sometimes more theoretical than actual—to the Queen. The United Kingdom's joining the community, therefore, could mean the partial dissolution of the British Commonwealth as it is now constituted. We mentioned in Chapter 10 the creation of the Outer Seven, a loose trade alliance brought into being chiefly through efforts of the United Kingdom to offset the growing strength of the Coal and Steel Community and its cousin, the European Economic Community. Despite obstacles mentioned above, many Europeans hope that the six nations of the Coal and Steel Community and the European Economic Community will unite with the Outer Seven nations to form a common bloc.

Production Elsewhere in Europe. Excluding the microstates, every European nation except Greece, Albania, and Portugal produces some iron, and every nation but Albania and Portugal produces some steel. All in all, the volume of this production is not inconsequential, amounting to nearly one-third of that for the continent. Except in the famed Silesian district, which once was shared by Germany, Czechoslovakia, and Poland but since the Second World War is shared only by the latter two, this manufacturing tends to be oriented to single cities rather than urban clusters. Production is somewhat more intense in nations bordering the Coal and Steel Community than in the prevailingly agrarian countries in the southeast of Europe.

Japan

Japan, like West Germany, has recovered from the Second World War and now ranks sixth in global production of both iron and steel. Furthermore, the country has ambitious plans which, if realized in the target year of 1962, will increase iron and steel capacity by more than 50 per cent of that in 1957. The heaviest plant concentrations are in Kyushu and southern Honshu, with lesser works in northern

This new iron-and-steel plant near Mysore, India, is financed from public funds and is a state-owned enterprise. It employs over 6,000 workers. Through such efforts as this one, India can move to higher productivity and perhaps even a higher level of living. (Government of India Press Information Bureau)

Honshu and southern Hokkaido. Open-hearth furnaces process about four-fifths of the country's steel, with electric furnaces supplying nearly all of the remainder. The new basic oxygen process is being well received and soon may well account for a substantial output. The country is deficient in both coal and iron, importing nearly one-half of the domestic consumption of the former and about three-fifths of the latter. Scrap is vital, for from it comes well over 40 per cent of Japan's steel. About three-fifths of Japan's imported scrap and coking coal comes from the United States, as does one-eighth of the iron ore. Most of the latter, however, is procured from Malaya, India, the Philippines, and Goa. Finished steel products, amounting to less than one-tenth of Japanese production, move largely to eastern and southern Asia.

Other production

Among the lesser producers, Communist China is now the leader and the most aggressive. Data from that nation indicate very marked success, despite such futile schemes as making iron in little backyard furnaces like those in general use before the Industrial Revolution. A sizable plant series had been constructed in Manchuria by Japan and, although largely carted off to the Soviet Union by that nation's armies after their belated entrance into conflict with Japan during the Second World War, was returned in part when China became a Communist state. Most of the current output of Communist China is located in Manchuria and the neighboring northern section of Communist China proper. Canada, Australia, India, the Union of South Africa, and Brazil are among other leaders in this group of comparatively minor producers.

Production in technically advanced and underdeveloped lands

Slightly over one-half of the forty-two nations currently reporting production of iron and the forty-seven reporting an output of steel are classified as underdeveloped. However, they produce a total of less than one-tenth of all steel. Meanwhile some fifty underdeveloped nations, in addition to numerous political dependencies, manufacture essentially no steel. In contrast, all nations classified as technically advanced are steel producers with the possible exception of Ireland.

Production in non-Communist and Communist nations

Non-Communist nations now produce about two-thirds of the world's iron and steel, and Communist nations the remainder. Aside from the Soviet Union, which accounts for approximately two-thirds of Communist production, the leading nations in this group are Communist China, Poland, and Czechoslovakia. The increasing share of Communist nations in world production is shown in Figure 29.7.

INTERNATIONAL TRADE

About one-eighth of all steel products is exported before being subjected to further processing (Fig. 29.1). This fraction represents a marked decline from the late 1920s and early 1930s, when between one-fifth and one-fourth was exported (Fig. 29.13). The European Coal and Steel Community accounts for over 50 per cent of all steel exports; Belgium-Luxembourg, West Germany, and France are the leaders. This is appreciably a trade within the community. The United States, Canada, and distant Japan are also among the major world exporters. Most of the world's steel is further processed within the nations of its manufacture into transportation equipment, construction materials, machinery, and a host of additional materials. Some of these eventually may be exported, but by then they are sufficiently altered in form and contain a sufficiently large number and variety of new materials that they no longer can be classified as steel exports. The leading importing nations are Argentina, the United Kingdom, various members of the Coal and Steel Community, and India (Fig. 29.1).

Figure 29.13 ***World steel exports as a per cent of world steel production for years shown*** *(American Iron and Steel Institute).*

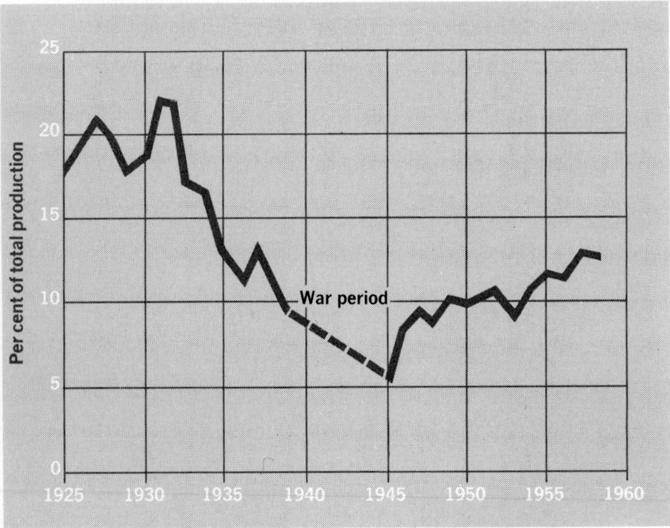

IRON, STEEL, AND OTHER INDUSTRIAL METALS IN ECONOMIC GEOGRAPHY

We have emphasized the heavy dependence upon industrial metals by technically advanced nations and the modest use of such metals by technically underdeveloped nations. We have noted also that steel is overwhelmingly predominant among the industrial metals when considered in terms of absolute consumption, since it is utilized especially for transportation equipment, construction, and machinery—uses where weight is no hindrance. The remaining industrial metals tend to have somewhat more specialized uses. The ferroalloys, as suggested by the term, are fused into steel to achieve highly specialized results and have other uses equally specialized for the most part. Copper is an excellent conductor of electricity, and hence in demand in a growing electrical industry for equipment ranging from generators and motors to transmission lines. It is malleable as well as ductile and is used for sheets, tubing, etc. Aluminum is also an excellent conductor of electricity and, when alloyed, is a strong but light metal, well suited to the increasing

This aluminum-rolling mill runs the metal through its facilities at a speed of 20 miles per hour (British Information Services).

number and variety of air and outer-space transportation equipment as well as for such less spectacular goods as cooking utensils. Zinc resists oxidation and makes a rust-resistant cover for other metals, and hence is used extensively in galvanizing. Alloyed, it is a very satisfactory metal for die-casting equipment and for commodities involving brass. Nonmetallic uses include making paint pigment. The strong resistance of lead to corrosion, including that of sulfuric acid, makes it notably valuable for wet-cell batteries. In addition, it is an excellent cable cover and construction material for plumbing fixtures, as well as an ingredient in nonmetallic products ranging from pigment to insecticide. Tin is consumed largely in plating (tin cans, etc.) but is utilized also in soldering metal, tin foil (now in sharp competition with aluminum foil), type metal, and a number of less important products. Magnesium is even lighter in weight than aluminum and hence of value when alloyed for certain components of aircraft as well as for other materials calling for a high strength-weight ratio. In different composition, it burns quickly and brilliantly and is a basic ingredient in flash bulbs, tracer bullets, flares, etc. There are many uses for each metal other than those noted.

It will be noted that nearly all the nonferrous metals are used for purposes which are highly specialized and which, although requiring increasing amounts of metal, do not offer evidence of expansion comparable to that which has occurred in steel. An important exception to this generalization might involve aluminum and magnesium, at present basic structural materials in various types of aircraft and

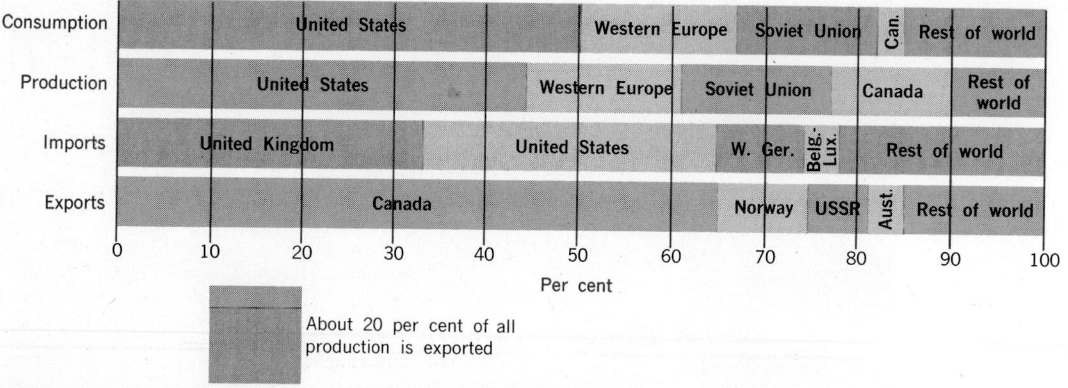

Figure 29.14 ***Consumption, production, import, and export of refined aluminum.*** *Three nations account for over three-fourths of all output. No underdeveloped nations are shown by name; all are too unimportant. Canada uses plentiful electricity to refine alumina that is smelted from bauxite which originates largely in British Guiana (Fig. 27.5). Aluminum is refined electrolytically (page 255), and the refineries almost invariably are located near the source of electric energy. The Canadian production is far above domestic demand, and the country dominates world exports overwhelmingly. The United Kingdom and United States are leading importers, despite the heavy domestic output of the latter.*

other space equipment. Continued rapid expansion in the demand for these appears almost inevitable as man continues to expand his missile-construction programs and begins to build stations in outer space. In the immediate future, however, most men and their creations will continue to be anchored rather firmly to the earth's surface, and the materials for their use can and probably will be the rather heavy iron and steel products, which do not offer evidence to date of relative decline with re-

Figure 29.15 ***Distribution of aluminum refineries in the United States.*** *The refineries in the Pacific Northwest are oriented to hydroelectricity there. Plants in Arkansas are oriented chiefly to raw materials—to domestic bauxite and alumina.*

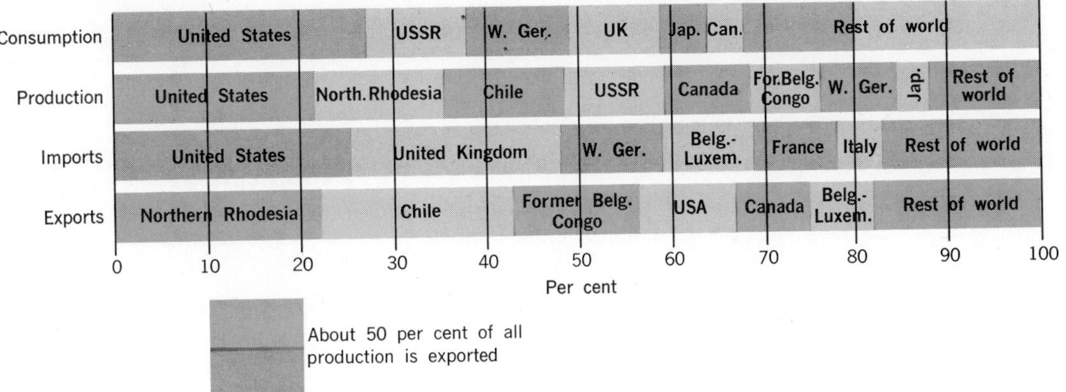

Figure 29.16 **Consumption, production, import, and export of smelted and refined copper.** *The United States is important in all four categories. Note the widely separated places of production. Production is located in both technically advanced and underdeveloped economies, but consumption is restricted almost entirely to technically advanced economies. The capital for exploiting deposits in Chile comes largely from the United States, and that for use in Africa comes from Europe and the United States.*

spect to either the lighter metals or the recently developed plastics. Inasmuch as the sophisticated yet widespread use of iron and steel is an important characteristic of technically advanced nations, we can anticipate with confidence their continued close association. The marked emphasis by Communist nations upon iron and steel production in their frenzied efforts to advance themselves technically is evidence of their appreciation of the significance of these metals in the Industrial Revolution in all its implications.

The total output of other leading industrial

Figure 29.17 **Distribution of primary copper smelters in the United States.** *Most copper ore is smelted in the Western states. It is extremely low-grade ore, sometimes containing 1 per cent or less copper content. Many smelters as well as concentrating mills are located near the source of the raw material to get rid of as much waste material as possible and hence save on shipping costs to the markets of the East.*

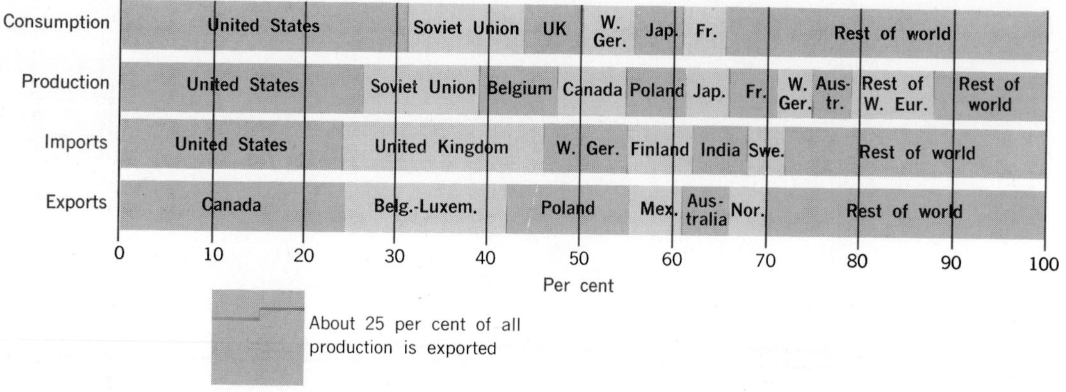

Figure 29.18 ***Consumption, production, import, and export of smelted and refined zinc.*** *There are many producing nations, and no single one is outstanding. Nearly every economy cited is technically advanced. The United States does not produce enough to meet its needs and, along with Western Europe, is a major importer.*

metals is indicated in Table 27.4, and national production of some is summarized in Figs. 29.14 to 29.21. As is indicated in respective captions, the details concerning each differ somewhat from those presented for iron and steel. Their general roles in the world economic scene, however, are not unlike that of iron and steel. Technically advanced nations dominate overwhelmingly in utilization, production, and imports. Where underdeveloped economies are important producers, their ranking frequently is due to capital investment from technically advanced nations. This is true particularly in the non-Communist countries. Among Communist nations, the Soviet Union and China tend to be rising rather rapidly, and certain Communist countries of Eastern Europe are important with respect to some commodities.

Figure 29.19 ***Distribution of primary zinc smelters in the United States.*** *Some are near the mines of the West, and some are near markets (plus some mines) of the East.*

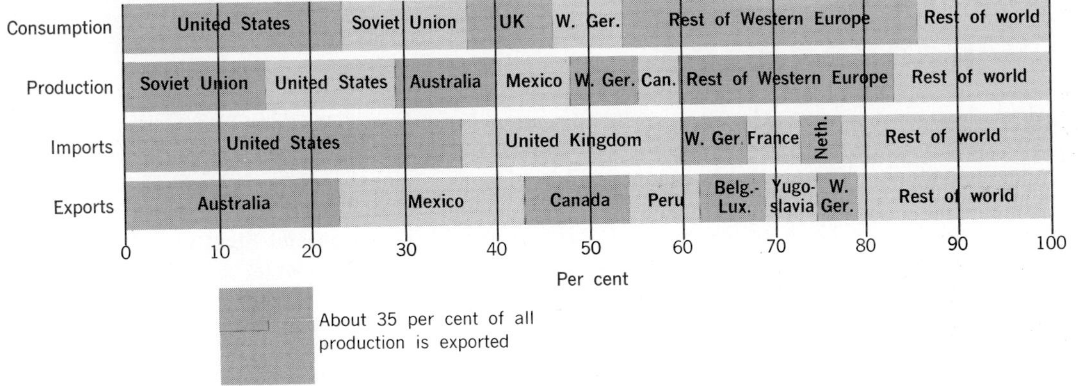

Figure 29.20 ***Consumption, production, import, and export of smelted and refined lead.*** *As with zinc, there are many producing nations, and none dominates. Again, technically advanced economies are almost the only important producers (except for Mexico, where capital from the United States has been invested heavily). Also as with zinc, the United States imports heavily.*

Figure 29.21 ***Distribution of primary lead smelters in the United States.*** *Most are near mines in the West. Some, like the one in Omaha, take advantage of in-transit freight-rate privileges (Chapter 8), and locate at a point between mine and market.*

REFERENCES

Alexandersson, Gunnar: "Changes in the Locational Pattern of the Anglo-American Steel Industry: 1948–1959," *Economic Geography,* **37:**95–114, 1961.

Bok, Derek Curtis: *The First Three Years of the Schuman Plan,* Princeton University Department of Economics and Sociology, Princeton, N.J., 1955.

Brush, John E.: "The Iron and Steel Industry in India," *Geographical Review,* **42:**37–55, 1952.

The Canadian Primary Iron and Steel Industry, Royal Commission on Canada's Economic Prospects, Ottawa, 1956.

Clark, Mills Gardner: *The Economics of Soviet Steel,* Harvard University Press, Cambridge, Mass., 1956.

Diebold, William, Jr.: *The Schuman Plan: A Study in Economic Cooperation, 1950–1959,* Frederick A. Praeger Press for the Council on Foreign Relations, New York, 1959.

"The European Coal and Steel Community," *University of Maryland Studies in Business and Economics,* **9** (3):1–19, 1955, and **10** (1):1–16, 1956, University of Maryland Bureau of Business and Economic Research.

Harris, James C. O.: "Trends in Steelmaking Processes," paper presented at the Pacific Northwest Regional Conference, American Institute of Mining, Metallurgical and Petroleum Engineers, Seattle, Washington, 1956. (Mimeographed.)

Isard, Walter, and John H. Cumberland: "New England as a Possible Location for an Integrated Iron and Steel Works," *Economic Geography,* **26:**245–259, 1950.

Japan's Iron and Steel Industry, 1958, Tokyo Foreign Service, Tokyo, 1958.

Kerr, Donald: "The Geography of the Canadian Iron and Steel Industry," *Economic Geography,* **35:** 151–163, 1959.

Pounds, Norman, J. G.: "Historical Geography of the Iron and Steel Industry of France," *Annals of the Association of American Geographers,* **47:**3–14, 1957.

Pounds, Norman J. G., and William N. Parker: *Coal and Steel in Western Europe,* Indiana University Press, Bloomington, Ind., 1957.

Rodgers, Allan: "Industrial Inertia: A Major Factor in the Location of the Steel Industry in the United States," *Geographical Review,* **42:**56–66, 1952.

Roepke, Howard G.: *Movements of the British Iron and Steel Industry: 1720–1951,* University of Illinois Studies in the Social Sciences, vol. 36, Urbana, Ill., 1956.

The Russian Iron and Steel Industry, Iron and Steel Institute, London, 1956.

Schroeder, Gertrude G.: *The Growth of Major Steel Companies, 1900–1950,* Johns Hopkins University Studies in Historical and Political Science, Baltimore, 1953.

Steel in the Soviet Union, American Iron and Steel Institute, New York, 1958.

Stocking, George W.: *Basing Point Pricing and Regional Development,* The University of North Carolina Press, Chapel Hill, N.C., 1954.

Tuemertekin, Erol: "The Iron and Steel Industry of Turkey," *Economic Geography,* **31:**179–184, 1955.

White, C. Langdon: "Water: A Neglected Factor in the Geographical Literature of Iron and Steel," *Geographical Review,* **47:**463–489, 1957.

30 MANUFACTURING: TRANSPORTATION EQUIPMENT

THE U.S. BUREAU OF THE BUDGET INCLUDES THE FOLLOWING INDUSTRIES IN ITS two-digit detail classification[1] of industries using primary metals:

Fabricated metal products, except ordnance, machinery, and transportation equipment

Machinery, except electrical

Electrical machinery, equipment, and supplies

Transportation equipment

Professional, scientific, and controlling instruments; photographic and optical goods; watches and clocks

Miscellaneous manufacturing

We have selected transportation equipment as representative of this group, which advances certain products from initial stages of manufacture described in the preceding chapter to various assembled commodities. No single group, of course, can be adequately representative of all. Transportation equipment is as representative as any listed above except in one very important respect: being what it is, transportation equipment is more mobile than most products in the other categories, and the costs and difficulties of getting it to market are not always so pronounced as, for example, the

[1] The Bureau of the Budget classifies the nation's industries and services by using "digit details," with the fewer digits indicating the coarse, more general classifications and the additional digits denoting subdivisions of those generalizations. For example, all transportation equipment manufacture is summarized in the Census of Manufactures in the two-digit detail number 37. (Other two-digit detail classifications include food and kindred products with the number 20; tobacco manufactures, 21; chemicals and allied products, 28; petroleum refining and related industries, 29, etc.) Subdivisions of transportation are summarized at the three-digit detail: motor vehicles and equipment (371); aircraft and parts (372); ship and boat building and repairing (373); making of railroad equipment (374), etc. Each of these, in turn, is further subdivided into the four-digit detail. Motor vehicles and equipment (371) is subclassified into motor vehicles (3711); passenger car bodies (3712); truck and bus bodies (3713); motor vehicle parts and accessories (3714), etc. We are discussing above the two-digit detail, or coarse classification. See *Standard Industrial Classification Manual,* Executive Office of the President, U.S. Bureau of the Budget, 1957.

moving of industrial machinery to its ultimate market area. Thus market attractions, while possibly as strong regarding transport equipment as with industries making the other products, may not result in physical location of producing plants in the market area to the same degree as might be true of some of the other industries.

The specific industries we shall examine in this chapter are those making motor vehicles, railway rolling stock, ships, and aircraft.

MOTOR VEHICLES

Of the more than one hundred million passenger cars and trucks now in use in the non-Communist world, about two-thirds are found in the United States (Fig. 30.1). Most of the remainder are in Europe, although no single country there contains over one-twentieth of the world total. Moreover, the vehicles in use in Europe tend to be smaller than their counterparts in the United States, and Europe would appear even less important if this comparison were not on a basis of sheer numbers. Canada and Australia also are noteworthy users of automobiles. As yet, most Communist nations are not emphasizing the making of motor vehicles; they prefer railways and ships as transport media. Where built in Communist countries, particularly the Soviet Union, motor vehicles involve mostly trucks rather than cars. Not over one-twentieth of the world's motor vehicles are to be found in Communist countries.

HISTORICAL BACKGROUND

We think of the motor vehicle as a twentieth-century product—and so it is. Many of us not past the prime of life (we hope) can remember the time of the horse and buggy—the time when, as youngsters, we rode behind old Dobbin over gravel roads (if we were lucky), heavily clothed and covered with blankets on days that were extra cold. At the sound of an approaching automobile—an unmistakable noise that carried far and wide on cold winter days—we would jump up from under our quilts to see this strange phenomenon as it lurched by. How different from the millions of fishtailed affairs that glut our freeways today!

However, like so many human creations, the motor vehicle is very much rooted in the past. One account of its development begins in 1678, with the use of a cylinder and piston to pump water.[2] Later came the development of the steam engine, of the self-propelled vehicle, of interchangeable parts, of toll roads, of time and motion studies, of crude, gasoline-powered buggies. In 1899 came what appears to have been the first United States factory devoted solely to car manufacture—the Olds Motor Works of Lansing, Michigan. In 1909 came the famed Model T, and by 1913 the output of the "tin lizzy" reached 1,000 vehicles per day. In that same year, used cars began to compete actively with new ones. By 1925, more closed than open automobiles were being made, and the groundwork for today's automobile and today's automobile industry was laid.

In a sense, the history of the automobile is like the history of the country with which it is now most closely identified. Both the vehicle and the nation have strong roots in Europe, but both have reached their present high levels of activity on the North American continent. In each case, Europe has continued to play an active role—but as a specialist, a dilettante on the edge of a whirlpool which has its focal center across the Atlantic in the New World.

CURRENT PRODUCTION

The making of motor vehicles involves the putting together of some fifteen thousand semifinished and finished materials into completed units. Some 64 per cent of all natural rubber, 63 per cent of all synthetic rubber, 39 per cent of all reclaimed rubber,

[2] Merrill Denison, *The Power to Go*, Doubleday & Company, Inc., New York, 1956, pp. 13–18.

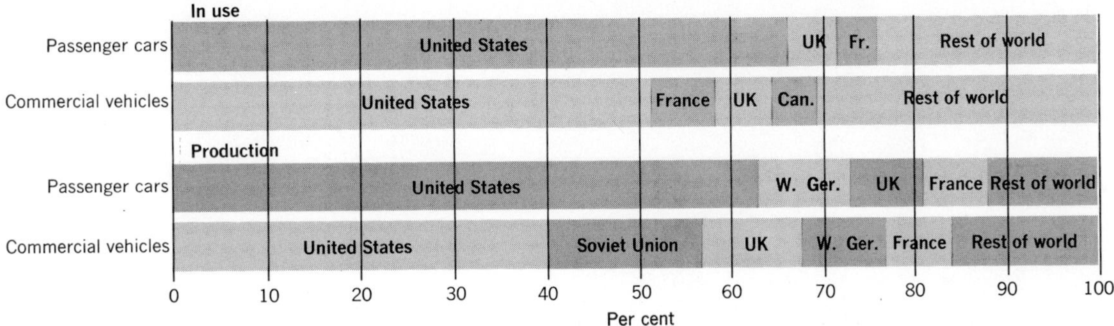

Figure 30.1 ***Utilization and production of motor vehicles.***

50 per cent of all malleable iron, 44 per cent of all lead, 44 per cent of all sheet steel, 35 per cent of all zinc, 33 per cent of all strip steel, 32 per cent of all alloy steel, 21 per cent of all bar steel, 18 per cent of all stainless steel, 16 per cent of all nickel, and 4 per cent of all cotton consumed in the United States are accounted for by the nation's motor-vehicle industry.[3] In so far as it is possible, assembly-line techniques are utilized in such manufacture—techniques aided increasingly by automatic or semiautomatic devices and equipment (Fig. 30.2). At one time, the various processes were integrated as far as possible, so that all or nearly all production of a given vehicle occurred under a single roof. To a degree, this is still true. However, at least in the United States, there has been a trend toward locating the final stage of assembly in proximity to market—a trend which we shall discuss in more detail later in this chapter.

Leading nations

It is for good reason that the motor vehicle and the United States have come to be so closely identified. This one nation produces about 60 per cent of the world's automobiles and nearly 40 per cent of its trucks (Table 30.1). If measured by weight, these figures would be even higher, for vehicles produced in the United States are heavier than the world average. The country's much lower share of the world output of buses, approximately 8 per cent, is further evidence of the predominance of the private automobile here. West Germany, the United Kingdom, France, Italy, Canada, Australia, the Soviet Union, Sweden, Japan, and Czechoslovakia are the major automobile producers other than the United States; these same countries, in different order, are leading manufacturers of trucks and buses. The major producers of buses, it will be noted, are the United Kingdom, the Soviet Union, Japan, and West Germany, each of which accounts for more of these vehicles per year than the United States.

Production in the United States

We have implied that the role of the automobile in the economy of the United States is unique in terms not only of consumption but also of livelihood. The automobile industry is the leading source of demand for steel, consuming almost 25 per cent of the country's annual output. It accounts for over 4 per cent of the nation's manufacturing labor force, and nearly 5 per cent of the value added by all manufacturing there. It leads in value added even when compared with aircraft and parts (the demand for which has been stimulated by military purchases) and the products of blast furnaces and steel mills.

Location. Although some forty-one states possess plants turning out motor vehicles or parts, over one-half of the industry's total labor force is in Michigan. About 10 per cent is employed in Ohio, and lesser percentages in New York, California, Wisconsin, Illinois, Pennsylvania, and Missouri. Many of the parts are first produced in some 25,000 plants of intermediate to small size, the majority of which

[3] Which in this book we shall consider as the making of automobiles, trucks, and buses.

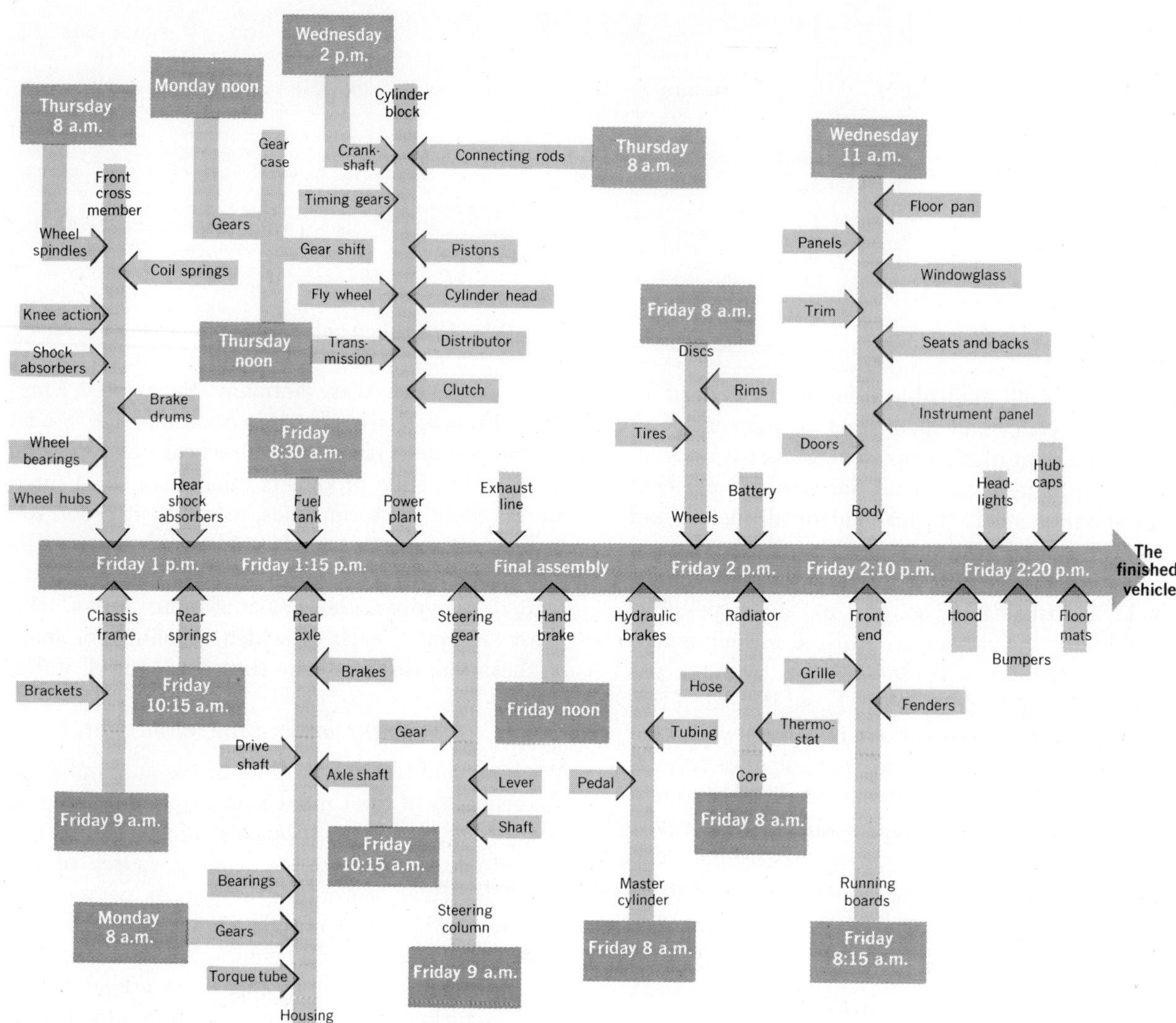

Figure 30.2 ***The assembly of an automobile in a modern factory of the United States.***

are located in the vicinities of Detroit and other automobile-assembly centers in Michigan (Fig. 30.3). From these, the parts are transferred to a relatively small number of rather large plants, where they are placed on assembly lines. In some cases, final products emerge from such plants and are shipped by rail, water, or special motor carrier to both local and distant customers. However, the cost of shipping a finished automobile by rail is at least twelve times as high as that of shipping the various parts in knocked down form, ready for final assembly.[4] Increasingly, therefore, the final assembly operations are being performed in special plants situated not far from the nation's more than forty-five thousand dealers. The dealers, in turn, have located with an eye on potential markets. The migration of the nation's population to cities and

[4] See especially Neil P. Hurley, "The Automotive Industry: A Study in Industrial Location," *Land Economics,* 35 (1):1–14, 1959.

TABLE 30.1

World motor-vehicle production, 1957

Country	Passenger cars	Trucks	Buses	Total
United States	6,113,344	1,103,343	3,833	7,220,520
West Germany	1,040,188	166,505	5,539	1,212,232
United Kingdom	860,842	280,624	9,498	1,150,964
France	724,662	198,177	3,043	925,882
Soviet Union	113,600	371,600	9,000	494,200
Canada	340,016	71,424	444	411,884
Italy	325,883	23,669	2,247	351,799
Japan	47,121	241,596	8,036	296,753
Australia	88,239	40,849	635	129,723
Sweden	52,367	17,339	1,948	71,654
Czechoslovakia	34,561	12,464	1,333	48,358
India	12,171	18,433	—	30,604
Spain	27,800	2,636	*	30,436
Austria	9,496	4,038	376	13,910
Yugoslavia	3,008	3,459	*	6,467
Netherlands	—	1,461	360	1,821
Finland	—	1,158	307	1,465
Switzerland	—	704	120	824†
Belgium	8	109	203	320
World total	9,793,306	2,559,588	46,922	12,399,816

* Buses included with trucks.

† Registrations of new Swiss-produced vehicles.

SOURCE: *Automobile Facts and Figures, 1958 Edition,* American Manufacturers Association, Detroit, 1958, p. 15.

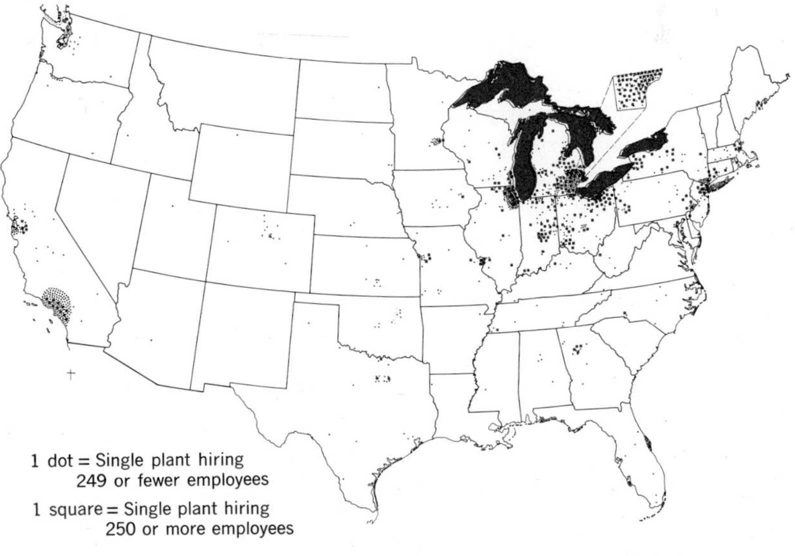

Figure 30.3 ***Distribution of plants making motor vehicles and parts in the United States.*** *The Great Lakes states, notably Michigan, predominate; yet there are many plants elsewhere. Note that most plants located outside the manufacturing belt tend to be somewhat small, hiring 249 or fewer workers. A sizable number of these are final-assembly plants located near regional markets. Some of the numerous small plants around Chicago, Detroit, and New York are final-assembly plants, and some supply plants.*

This is an integrated automobile plant, the famed Ford River Rouge Plant at Dearborn, Michigan. In the distance, near the white smoke in the upper right-hand corner, an ore ship is unloading. The tall structures to the left are blast furnaces and coke ovens. The center building houses the main plant, including stamping mills, engine-parts divisions, and final-assembly lines. (Ford Motor Company)

towns has meant an increased clustering tendency on the part of many dealer establishments, with such clusters especially prominent in the large metropolitan areas. The attraction of dealers to urban markets, and of final-assembly plants to dealers, has meant a decentralization of the final-assembly stages of the nation's automobile industry from the Michigan area to the vicinities of urban and a few rural markets. This decentralization, however, is not entirely due to market considerations and lower transport costs; it is as well a shift toward large numbers of people to provide market, labor, some raw materials, and still other advantages. The labor force of the automobile industry, for example, is comprised to a surprising degree of unskilled or semiskilled workers, for many operations of the industry are at least semiautomated.[5] Where sizable populations exist, such labor is easily available. Many of the "raw" materials of the automobile industry also are to be had most cheaply in areas of complex manufacturing activity and associated dense population, for the industry depends almost entirely upon other manufacturing to supply such materials.

[5] *Ibid.*, p. 7.

Europe, too, uses the assembly line to make automobiles. This is a factory at Luton in Bedfordshire, United Kingdom. (British Information Services)

Corporative Structure. The "Big Three" of the automobile industry—General Motors, Ford, and Chrysler Corporations—supply nearly 95 per cent of the automobile market. Because of the volume and far-flung national and global distribution of their operations, they are able to maximize economies of scale which smaller competitors cannot employ. Such economies reach beyond the production of automobiles: General Motors, for example, turns out some forty products, including diesel locomotive engines, refrigerators, spark plugs, and radios. The making of truck bodies and automobile trailers is not yet so centralized administratively in the United States.

Production outside the United States

We have noted that motor-vehicle production outside the United States is located chiefly in Europe, the Soviet Union, and Japan. Needless to say, nearly all these nations are technically advanced; yet India, Spain, and Yugoslavia, usually classified as technically underdeveloped, are motor-vehicle producers. Almost invariably, producing sites are in places of dense population, which frequently coincide globally with places of heaviest domestic steel output and of other active manufacturing, as well as with coal fields. Domestic markets, labor, and power thus are readily available. For nations which export rather heavily, seaports are not far away; however, the world's automobile plants, even those specializing only in final assembly, are not generally located in seaports. Market attractions pertain prevailingly to domestic outlets.

The United States is gradually losing a once overwhelming position in motor-vehicle output. From 1936 to 1938, this one country accounted for 72 per cent of all motor vehicles, compared with the slightly over 60 per cent it now produces. Relative gains in this twenty-year period have been scored most dramatically by Europe, which produced only 15 per cent of the world's automobiles from 1936 to 1938 but nearly 30 per cent in 1958. West Germany and France have been the leaders in this expansion. The Soviet Union, in contrast, is producing no higher a percentage of the world's motor vehicles than it did in 1938; the emphasis here has been upon fewer but larger vehicles—vehicles used as common carriers (Fig. 30.1).

International trade

The United States exports slightly more than 5 per cent of its motor-vehicle production and imports a slightly lower percentage. Its export of trucks is appreciably higher than that of automobiles, and its import of automobiles is appreciably higher than of trucks. Small European cars and *microbuses* recently have been accepted rather enthusiastically into the United States market, and these make up a large share of its imports. Our percentage of exports is exceeded by those from West Germany and the United Kingdom, each of which sends into the world markets some 40 per cent of its production. All in all, some 20 per cent of the world's motor-vehicle output is shipped to foreign lands, despite somewhat heavy import tariffs in most countries of receipt. To a degree, this is a movement within the currency blocs—from the United States to the dollar bloc and from the United Kingdom to the sterling bloc, etc. However, it is also a movement among producing nations; for example, the United States currently imports more motor vehicles than any other nation, followed by Belgium and Sweden.

RAILWAY ROLLING STOCK

Locomotives, freight cars, and passenger cars for the world's railways are largely common carriers used for public benefit. Their allocation among nations is discussed in Chapter 9. Unlike the automobile, which is a consumer product in rising demand wherever living levels stimulate its use, railway equipment is produced in comparatively small amounts except in times of rapid technical and economic change or of emergency. Shortly after the turn of this century, by which time the United States had become a truly transcontinental economic unit, demand for rolling stock was extremely high, because the railroad literally had made unification possible on a modern scale. In an opposite hemisphere, the Soviet Union of today is as dependent upon the railroad as the United States was fifty years ago, and demand for rolling stock there is currently high. Communist China, India, Brazil, and numerous other sizable but underdeveloped countries are now evidencing an increased interest in railway equipment, as their economies become more dynamic. Europe, well supplied with such equipment before the last war, experienced a renewed demand for replacement of destroyed material during and after that war. Decreases in demand assessable to technical change are primarily due to the use of increasingly large or more efficient equipment, so that fewer need be produced. For example, modern diesel and electric locomotives can pull substantially larger trains than could the old "iron horse," and fewer are needed to do the same jobs.

HISTORICAL BACKGROUND

The early entries in our chronology of the automobile are also milestones in the development of the railway train, which was stimulated by Trevithick's invention of a steam coach in 1801. The rapid growth of railways in Europe and in North America, and the construction of substantial networks in Russia, Communist China, India, Australia, southern Africa, and nodally arranged intermittent locations in South America, are well known. Technical change involving replacement of the steam engine by the diesel unit in the United States and, to a lesser degree, by the electric engine and diesel unit in Europe and the Soviet Union, also is a familiar story. The relative decline in the United States of the railroad as a freight carrier in competition with the truck and pipeline and as a passenger carrier in competition with the airplane and bus also has been related many times in many articles and a few books. Not so familiar is a somewhat general trend in Western Europe. In contrast, most Communist and most underdeveloped nations are utilizing railways and railway equipment to an unprecedented degree; for them, the automobile in every driveway is yet to come.

CURRENT PRODUCTION

Whereas millions of motor vehicles are produced in some countries each year, railway rolling stock is manufactured only in terms of thousands of units. In 1950, when approximately 7 million automobiles were turned out in the United States alone, only 4,750 locomotives and about 45,000 railway cars were manufactured by the same nation. As with motor vehicles, the "raw" materials of railway rolling stock are primarily semimanufactured commodities, especially from steel furnaces; but assembling is appreciably a custom operation involving much skilled labor.

Erratic output

Inasmuch as it is well built and carefully serviced, railway rolling stock lasts for a long time. Model changes, which carry so much appeal in some nations with respect to the automobile industry, enter less forcibly into marketing consideration unless something other than fashion is satisfied thereby. The production which replaces equipment that has succumbed to normal wear is comparatively light. However, sudden increases in production may result from a truly beneficial technical innovation, or a spurt of activity in a given econ-

TABLE 30.2

Production of railway rolling stock in the United States, number of units

Year	*Locomotives*	*Passenger cars*	*Freight cars*
1933	63	7	2,202
1937	570	557	78,819
1941	1,104	363	83,009
1948	3,152	822	114,885
1950	4,750	954	44,209
1952	2,042	128	79,398
1959	842	74	56,494

SOURCE: *Statistical Yearbook, 1952,* United Nations Department of Economic Affairs, New York, 1953, p. 242, for data up to and including 1952. Freight-car data for 1959 from the American Car Institute; locomotive and passenger-car data for 1959 from the Association of American Railroads.

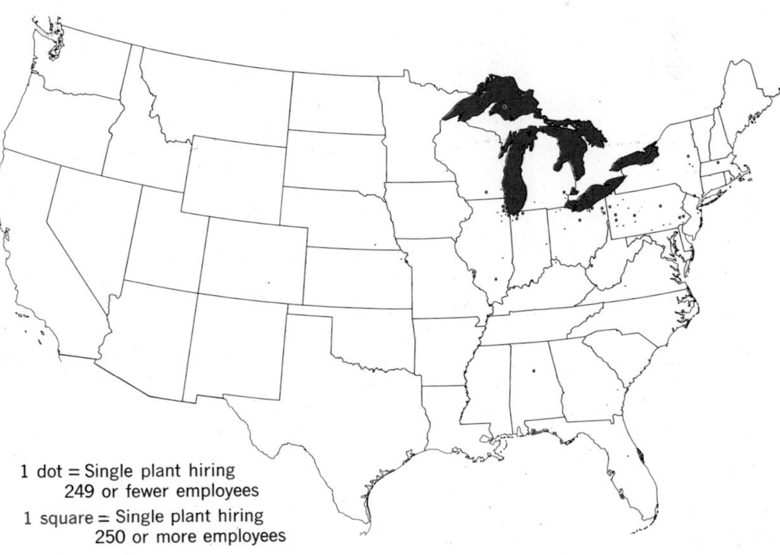

Figure 30.4 **Distribution in the United States of plants making locomotives, railroad and street cars, and parts.** *What is the orientation here? Markets? Raw materials (Fig. 29.10)? Other?*

TABLE 30.3

Production of railway locomotives and freight cars, 1952

Country	*Locomotives*	*Freight cars*
United States	2,042	79,526
United Kingdom	559	37,067
West Germany	503	2,829
Canada	226	11,458
Japan	134	3,924
France	104	6,091
All others except Soviet Union*	191	6,205

* Some other producing nations did not manufacture in 1952 and hence have also been excluded.

SOURCE: *Statistical Yearbook, 1953,* United Nations Department of Economic Affairs, New York, 1953, p. 242.

TABLE 30.4

Production of railway tires, wheels, and axles, 1954 (in thousands of tons)

Country	*Production*
Soviet Union	523
United Kingdom	291
United States	230
Czechoslovakia	143
West Germany	140
Poland	98
Italy	40
France	33
All others	111

SOURCE: *Railways and Steel,* United Nations Department of Economic and Social Affairs Document 296, Geneva, 1957, p. 2.

omy, or need for replacement of equipment ruined in wartime, etc. In practice, the output of rolling stock may be very light in one year, or even a series of years, and heavy in others, as is evidenced by the record of United States production in selected years of the past quarter century (Table 30.2).

Location

Most of the world's manufacturing of railway rolling stock is situated within or near major iron and steel districts—not infrequently in close juxtaposition with some of the older of such districts, for railroads and large-scale iron and steel production were once even more interdependent than they are at present. Railway-rolling-stock production is especially concentrated in areas of dense population and complex manufacturing. (For the location of such plants in the United States, see Fig. 30.4.) However, this does not necessarily imply a physical orientation to markets; for railway rolling stock, unlike automobiles, cannot be shipped any more cheaply in semiassembled condition than in completed form. When their manufacture is complete, they are simply hooked behind a locomotive and pulled to their first destination—sometimes loaded with their first commercial freight.

Leading nations of production

The two most recent United Nations estimates of output of railway rolling stock are given in Tables 30.3 and 30.4; the first excludes the Soviet Union and considers entire units (but excludes passenger cars), and the second includes the Soviet Union but considers only wheels, tires, and axles.

Although neither table tells an entire story, we can surmise by comparing them that the United States, the Soviet Union, the United Kingdom, West Germany, Canada, Japan, France, and Czechoslovakia are the world's leading producers of railway rolling stock but that their relative ranks shift somewhat pronouncedly each year because of the varying demand from within the industry. In all probability, demand is most constant within the Communist realm, where an emphasis upon railway building and intense use is combined with an equally strong emphasis upon continuous growth.

SHIPS

It is a commonplace that a ship is larger than a boat, although the specifications are not clearly defined. In this section we are interested only in ships, especially merchant ships of 100 gross registered tons or over. The allocation of such shipping among nations is discussed in Chapter 9.

HISTORICAL BACKGROUND

Shipbuilding dates back so far in time that its origin is not fully known. Wood was its basic construction material for millenniums, during which time man learned the superiority of wind to human or animal muscle as a mover of vessels, and his sails, rigging, and mast work became increasingly complex. With the Industrial Revolution came energy from coal and, later, petroleum, and came metals which could better withstand not only the traditional forces of nature but also the multiplications of those forces resulting from faster speeds.

Without the ship, the global expansion of certain civilizations as we now know them in all probability would not have taken place.

CURRENT PRODUCTION

Whereas most motor vehicles are built on assembly lines and most railway rolling stock is put together with the aid of some assembly-line techniques, most ships—certainly the larger ones—are custom built to shippers' specifications. These, in turn, vary with the cargo expected to be carried, the type of fuel to be consumed, the anticipated routes, and the prospective shipowner's own ideas. For each vessel, before actual construction is begun, detailed drawings are made that serve as the bases for patterns and models. The ship itself takes form slowly on a *way*—a foundation over which are built the skids that support the developing vessel and that eventually slide it into the water, and the scaffolding used in assembling the hull. Once the hull is constructed and the more complex installations, including heavy machinery, are in place, it is launched and sometimes towed to a different site for completion.

High labor and low materials costs

In comparison with the averages of all industries in the United States and also in comparison with railway rolling stock and aircraft in particular, shipbuilding involves very high labor costs and relatively low costs in materials (Table 30.5).[6]

TABLE 30.5

Relative costs in the United States of labor and raw materials in construction of selected transportation equipment, 1954

Type of equipment	*Per cent* attributable to labor*	*Per cent* attributable to materials*
Ships	46	37
Aircraft	28	46
Railway cars and streetcars	28	56
Locomotives	24	56

* Costs are expressed as percentages of final-product value. Data on motor vehicles were not available. There are, of course, costs to manufacturing other than labor or raw materials, so that the above percentage will not total 100. Energy is one major cost item, and entrepreneurship another. The value of product when shipped also includes profits.

SOURCE: Computed from *Census of Manufactures, 1954*, U.S. Bureau of the Census, 1957.

Location

Two aspects of industrial location are especially important to shipbuilding: site and labor. The significance of site is obvious: large ships cannot be transported feasibly overland and must therefore be constructed on the waterfronts of the rivers, lakes, or oceans upon which they later will travel. (For a view of the location and output of shipyards in the

[6] In their book *Economics of American Industry*, E. B. Alderfer and H. E. Michl have calculated from the Census of Manufactures of all United States industries the per cent of final-product value accounted for respectively by labor and materials. Their conclusions are:

Low-labor-cost industries: 9 per cent or less of the value of products are labor costs.

Medium-labor-cost industries: 10 to 20 per cent.

High-labor-cost industries: over 20 per cent.

Low-materials-cost industries: 49 per cent or less of the value of products are materials costs.

Medium-materials-cost industries: 50 to 59 per cent.

High-materials-cost industries: 60 per cent or more.

For details, see *Economics of American Industry*, McGraw-Hill Book Company, Inc., New York, 1957, pp. 11–12.

Figure 30.5 ***Distribution of active shipbuilding and -repairing yards in the United States.*** *Note the very large number of small yards in southeastern New York and at other places along the Atlantic Coast. In contrast, the yards fringing the Gulf and Pacific Coasts are fewer but larger. Why?*

United States, see Fig. 30.5 and Fig. 30.6.) A reservoir of skilled labor is important because of the high costs of labor in shipbuilding. Demand for ships, like that for railway rolling stock, is erratic, and this adds to the difficulty of labor procurement, for no worker desires to ply a trade which does not assure steady employment. Materials costs, especially steel, are important, and most of the large shipyards are located where such materials can be made available to waterfront construction sites. Markets are comparatively unimportant in regard to location, as the finished ships, which can be moved easily and inexpensively, may be put to use in places far from the owner's nation of citizenship.

Figure 30.6 ***Value of shipments from shipbuilding and -repairing yards in the United States.*** *Despite smaller shipyards (Fig. 30.5), the East predominates.*

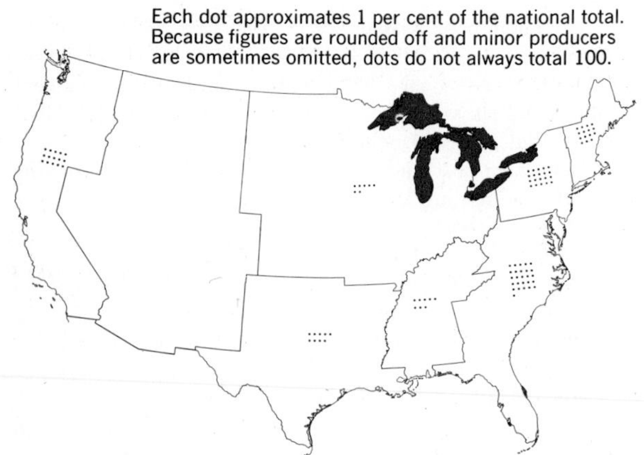

TABLE 30.6

Merchant vessels, tonnage launched, 1958 (in thousands of gross registered tons)*

Country	*Total*	*Tankers*
Japan	2,067	1,176
West Germany	1,429	492
United Kingdom	1,402	577
Sweden	760	521
United States	732	644
Netherlands	556	243
Italy	551	331
France	451	255
All others †	1,322	536
Total	9,270	4,775

* Vessels of 100 gross registered tons or over.
† Excluding the Soviet Union.
SOURCE: *Statistical Yearbook, 1959*, United Nations Department of Economic and Social Affairs, New York, 1959, p. 252.
For a discussion of ocean shipping including tankers and dry cargo vessels, see Chapter 9.

Leading nations of production

High labor costs and other handicaps have discouraged shipbuilding in the United States except during emergencies, during which time the nation's shipbuilding may expand more than twelvefold. This is true despite the payment by the Federal government of from 30 per cent to 50 per cent of construction costs of vessels qualifying for such subsidies under the Merchant Marine Act of 1936.

On the world scene, vessel construction varies rather markedly from year to year, not only in total amount but also in terms of leading nations. Japan, West Germany, and the United Kingdom are leaders in a merchant-marine construction that in 1958 totaled more than 9 million gross registered tons, of which over 50 per cent were tankers (Table 30.6). The Soviet Union, not included in the table, is probably also a leading producer.

AIRCRAFT

Aircraft and, more recently, missiles are utilized in large quantity by the military, especially of technically advanced nations, without whose demand the industry would be far less active than it now is. Nonmilitary demand for large planes springs mainly from commercial airlines, and for planes of intermediate to small size from such airlines and private and public organizations as can absorb their costs. Mass production of private planes for individuals, once considered a possibility, has not materialized.

HISTORICAL BACKGROUND

Whereas shipbuilding has been known for millenniums, railway rolling stock for centuries, and motor vehicles for nearly a century, the airplane has been known only for decades. The famous first flight of the Wright brothers occurred in 1903. Yet, despite its youth, aircraft manufacture is now very important to the functioning of economies of certain technically advanced nations: in the United States, for example, it accounts for over 5 per cent of the manufacturing labor force, leading all other industries classified at the three-digit level by the U.S. Bureau of the Census, and it is exceeded in value added to manufacture only by motor vehicles and parts. This outstanding growth has been partially a response to a mushrooming demand, particularly from the military. It has been aided measurably by reserve of technical knowledge accumulated over the centuries since the dawn of the Industrial Revolution.

CURRENT PRODUCTION

Airplane manufacture has been described as follows:[7]

> Aircraft manufacturing, in general, is similar to that of automobile manufacturing in that it calls for designing, machining, and assembly, but there are important differences. An airplane is infinitely more complicated and therefore requires much more engineering time, the machining operations require extreme accuracy and minute tolerances, inspection is frequent and critical, assembly must be done with great care, and the final product undergoes rigid testing before delivery to the customer.
>
> An unbelievable amount of work goes into the designing and engineering of a new type of airplane. For example, North American's F-100A Super Sabre, a fighter with swept-back wings capable of supersonic speed at both level and climbing flight, required almost 5 million man-hours of designing and engineering and 4½ years to develop. "Lead time" is a frequently heard term in the shop talk of the industry because of the very long designing and manufacturing cycle.
>
> Machining operations in an aircraft plant are performed on some of the strangest-looking machine tools. Airframe sections are made on huge extrusion and forging presses. Immense dies and general-purpose machine tools are used with highly specialized jigs and fixtures. Numerous parts must be made to the greatest accuracy

[7] E. B. Alderfer and H. E. Michl, *Economics of American Industry*, McGraw-Hill Book Company, Inc., New York, 1957, pp. 173–175.

Figure 30.7 ***Distribution in the United States of plants making aircraft.*** *Southern California is especially active. The aircraft industry is new, and most plants are large and modern; only a few hire 249 workers or fewer.*

humanly possible; moreover, jet engines generate temperatures too high to permit use of ordinary metals like alloy steel and aluminum. Consequently, manufacturers resort to newer metals like titanium, which, in turn, creates entirely new problems of design and machining. Professional, semiprofessional, and technical workers in the aircraft industry make up about 15 per cent of the total work force, which is much higher than in most other industries.

The assembly operations in an aircraft factory depend partly upon the size of the plane being assembled and partly on the size of the order. Prior to World War II, airplane manufacturers scarcely ever had orders of sufficient size to utilize the economies of mass production. Accordingly, the assembly operations were somewhat analogous to the building technique practiced in the shipbuilding industry. But the aircraft industry has outgrown that stage. Numerous orders are now sufficiently large sized to justify the moving-assembly-line technique. It differs somewhat, however, from that used in the automobile industry. Instead of highly standardized mass production as in autos, aircraft manufacturers use what is called "flexible mass production." Because of the rapidly changing designs in aircraft there are usually only several hundred, or at best several thousand, planes of identical type manufactured before a new design pushes the current model off the drawing boards.

Figure 30.8 ***Value of shipments from aircraft plants in the United States.*** *The Pacific West still predominates, but not so much as we might expect from viewing Fig. 30.7.*

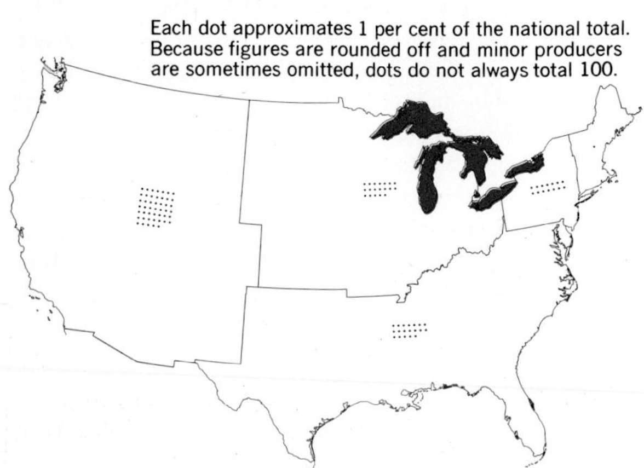

Erratic output

Perhaps to an even greater degree than is true of railway rolling stock and ships, the output of aircraft fluctuates markedly over a number of years. It is subjected to changes occasioned not only by economic cycles and such emergencies as wars but also by a technical change so rapid that some models are obsolescent almost before they come off the assembly lines. As yet, the airplane has not become a consumer good as has the automobile in

Figure 30.9 ***Distribution of aircraft-engine plants in the United States.*** *Most aircraft engines are produced in the manufacturing belt, then shipped to the plants making aircraft (Figs. 30.8 and 30.9). This is frequently a long-distance shipment of a finished product commanding high freight rates, so that shipping costs are high. In view of this, why are not more engine plants located near aircraft plants? One reason is industrial inertia; plants making such engines first located near the automobile market, and they have been slow to shift.*

technically advanced markets, and its sales depend largely upon demand from the military and from commercial carriers.

Location

In the United States, the aircraft industry is characterized by moderately high labor costs and low materials costs (Table 30.5 and footnote 6 of this chapter). Energy costs are small, and markets do not exert a strong pull toward specific regions or sites, because (1) the primary markets are the military and (2) the finished product can be transported easily and quickly to such markets. One authority has termed the aircraft industry as *footloose*—i.e., as oriented to no specific factor of production.[8] If the output of engines and propellers as well as airframes is taken into consideration, the industry is rather widely distributed throughout the country (Figs. 30.7, 30.8, 30.9, and 30.10). Actual assembly of the airplanes, however, appears to react sensitively to pools of labor, even though it is technically a footloose industry. As a partial result, such manufacture began in the nation's Northeast, where highly skilled labor was available, but many plants shifted to the Far West and the Middle West as the industry matured—seeking reservoirs of labor and other advantages. This was not so much differential growth as outright shift: whole plants were transferred, together with cadres of labor and management, to new locations. In 1940, over one-half of the industry's capacity was in locations other than the original choice of the companies concerned.[9]

[8] William Glenn Cunningham, *The Aircraft Industry: A Study in Industrial Location,* Lorrin L. Morrison, Los Angeles, 1951, pp. 191–199.

[9] *Ibid.,* p. 191.

Figure 30.10 ***Value of shipments from aircraft-engine plants in the United States.***

Each dot approximates 1 per cent of the national total. Because figures are rounded off and minor producers are sometimes omitted, dots do not always total 100.

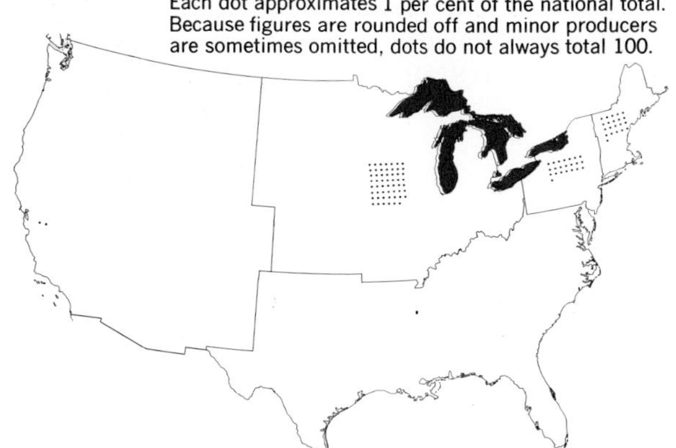

Climate appears to be a feature of serious concern in locating new plants, particularly in that milder and drier climates are conducive to more continuous flight testing and to lower maintenance costs. Locally, an airport demand exists for flat land which is near civic centers and yet sufficiently removed from the urban sprawl that buildings, etc., do not interfere with the take-off and arrival of aircraft. With the advent of the jet, a larger amount of such flat land is required per field for the longer runways that are required by this particular type of aircraft.

Leading nations of production

The United States, the Soviet Union, the United Kingdom, France, West Germany, Italy, Sweden, Switzerland, Japan, and India are producers of aircraft. Because of the importance of aircraft production to military operations, details are not so plentiful as with other types of transportation equipment. At least temporarily, however, that demand seems to be decreasing—largely because of the growing acceptance of the missile as an air weapon.

REFERENCES

Alderfer, E. B., and H. E. Michl: *Economics of American Industry,* McGraw-Hill Book Company, Inc., New York, 1957. (Especially chaps. 9–11.)

Allen, Peter: *Locomotives of Many Lands,* Locomotive Publishing Co., London, 1954.

Automobiles, 1959, Motors Trade Association of Japan, Tokyo, 1959.

The Canadian Automotive Industry, Royal Commission on Canada's Economic Prospects, Ottawa, 1956.

Cunningham, William Glenn: *The Aircraft Industry: A Study in Industrial Location,* Lorrin L. Morrison, Los Angeles, 1951.

Government of India, Tariff Commission: *Report on the Automobile Industry, 1956,* New Delhi, Government of India Press, 1957.

Hurley, Neil P.: "The Automotive Industry: A Study in Industrial Location," *Land Economics,* **35** (1):1–14, 1959.

Industrial Planning in the U.S.S.R.: The Automotive Industry as a Typical Branch of the Category of Machine Building, U.S. Department of the Air Force Directorate of Intelligence, 1954.

Lucas, Walter A.: *Locomotives and Cars since 1900,* Simmons-Boardman Publishing Corporation, New York, 1959.

Maxcy, George, and Aubrey Silberston: *The Motor Industry,* George Allen & Unwin, Ltd., London, 1959.

The Motor Industry of Great Britain, 1958, Society of Motor Manufacturers and Traders, Ltd., London, 1957.

Rae, John B.: *American Automobile Manufacturers: The First Forty Years,* Chilton Company, Philadelphia and New York, 1959.

Railways and Steel, United Nations Department of Economic and Social Affairs Document 296, Geneva, 1957.

Some Aspects of the Motor Vehicle Industry in the U.S.A., Organization for European Economic Cooperation, Paris, 1953.

Woytinsky, W. S., and E. S. Woytinsky: *World Population and Production,* The Twentieth Century Fund, Inc., New York, 1953. (Especially pp. 1158–1175.)

31 MANUFACTURING: CHEMICALS

THERE IS NOT JUST ONE CHEMICAL INDUSTRY BUT MANY, AND THE NUMBER increases in a generally inverse ratio to the degree of restraint in defining the term *chemical industry*. Despite appreciable effort, no universally acceptable definition has been set down, and considerable ambiguity results. Most definitions are based on products and focus on a hard core of commodities which largely are derived synthetically and, for the most part, involve few and radically altered natural materials—commodities like sulfuric acid, soda, and certain drugs. Around this core are arranged commodities easily traceable to natural raw materials but with ingredients that are as much a result of chemical processes as of natural-materials content—commodities like soap, cosmetics, paint, and solvent. Near the periphery in such definitions are products in which natural materials are even more easily recognizable but which are nonetheless subjected to some kind of chemical process—products like gum and wood chemicals, certain vegetable and animal oils, and certain types of paper.[1] At some point not yet agreed upon, some of the products which might well qualify for this last category find themselves classified as nonchemical—as beyond the pale of strictly chemical materials, although chemical processes remain important to their manufacture. The many products of this kind include iron and steel, aluminum, and petroleum.[2]

The U.S. Bureau of the Budget includes products from all three categories in its official classification, while classifying in other groups such

[1] There are, of course, many ways of classifying chemical products. One particularly incisive classification, by Alderfer and Michl, is as follows: (1) strictly chemical industries, involving (*a*) heavy chemicals (much bulk, low price per unit), (*b*) fine chemicals (small bulk, high price per unit), (*c*) miscellaneous chemicals; (2) allied chemical industries, mainly involving strictly chemical products mixed with products of nonchemical origin; (3) chemical-process industries which, as the term implies, chiefly apply chemical processes to natural materials. See E. B. Alderfer, and H. E. Michl, *Economics of American Industry*, McGraw-Hill Book Company, Inc., New York, 1957, pp. 239–240.

[2] However, petrochemicals, or chemical derivatives of petroleum, are usually included with the chemical industry.

commodities as pulp and paper and primary metals. Included under its two-digit detail classification "Chemicals and Allied Products" are the following three-digit detail categories:

Industrial inorganic and organic chemicals

Plastics materials and synthetic resins, synthetic rubber, synthetic and other man-made fibers except glass

Drugs

Soap, detergents and cleaning preparations, perfumes, cosmetics, and other toilet preparations

Paints, varnishes, lacquers, enamels, and allied products

Gum and wood chemicals

Agricultural chemicals

Miscellaneous chemical products

PROCESS

The number and kinds of processes employed within the world's chemical industry are as varied as the internal operational structure of the industry. Some of the chemical and physical processes most frequently utilized are shown in Table 31.1.

Although generalization concerning such a complex industry is difficult, four points appear especially relevant: (1) only a few natural materials are involved in most instances; (2) from these comparatively few materials—or man-made counterparts or substitutes—come a surprising array of end products, each almost tailored to demand, with several commodities usually produced at a given

TABLE 31.1

Chemical and physical processes most frequently utilized in the chemical industry

Chemical reactions	*Physical processes*
Combustion	Fluid dynamics
Oxidation	Heat transfer versus cooling
Neutralization	Evaporation versus evaporative cooling
Silicate formation	Humidification
Causticization	Gas absorption
Electrolysis	Solvent extraction
Double decomposition	Absorption
Calcination, dehydration	Distillation and sublimation
Nitration	Drying, high-vacuum distillation
Esterification (sulfation)	Mixing
Reduction	Classification or sedimentation versus fluidization
Ammonolysis	Filtration
Halogenation	Screening
Sulfonation	Crystallization versus extraction
Hydrolysis, hydration	Centrifugation
Hydrogenation, hydrogenolysis	Size reduction versus size enlargement
Alkylation	Materials handling
Condensation	
Polymerization	
Diazotization and coupling	
Fermentation	
Pyrolysis, cracking	
Aromatization	
Isomerization	
Hydroformylation (oxo)	
Ion exchange	

SOURCE: R. Norris Shreve, *The Chemical Process Industries*, McGraw-Hill Book Company, Inc., New York, 1956, p. 10.

plant; (3) the industry maintains a very large research staff, and innovations appear more frequently than in most industries; and (4) once set in motion, many chemical processes continue almost without the aid of human hands and under only modest supervision, so that a high level of automation is possible.

Comparatively small number of natural materials

The raw materials used in producing 150 leading chemicals of the United States are shown in Table 31.2. The first six materials—water, air, coal, sulfur, mineral salt, and limestone—are active ingredients in the production of from sixty-three to ninety-nine products. (However, the table should not be misconstrued to mean that *all* chemical products are derived from these few materials, for this is not the case; what is implied is that only a few natural materials are responsible for most of the *leading* products, measured quantitatively.)

Variety of products

Because of its ability to change the actual structure of commodities, the chemical industry frequently can move toward the obtainment of either widely differing products from given natural materials or identical end products from differing natural materials (Fig. 31.1). In petroleum refining, for example, the ratio of hydrogen to carbon can be increased by hydrogenation, through which process heavy oils are converted to lighter oils, and that ratio can be decreased by polymerization, through which process light oils may be made heavier. A somewhat different illustration is provided in the obtaining of sulfuric acid, the raw materials of which may be native sulfur deposits described in Chapter 25; or pyrites; or various lead, zinc, and copper sulfides; or petroleum and natural gas; or gypsum; or industrial gases from still other manufacturing.

Interestingly, many of these end products frequently are the raw materials for still other manufacturing. The author is familiar, for example, with a fertilizer plant belonging to one organization located immediately beside a lead refinery owned by a different organization. The lead enters the refinery as a compound with sulfur which, when removed, is forwarded as a raw material to the fertilizer plant. This type of cooperation, frequently much more

TABLE 31.2

Ultimate geologic raw materials used in producing 150 important industrial chemicals in the United States

Raw material	*Frequency of use in making 150 industrial chemicals*
Water	99
Air	96
Coal	91
Sulfur	88
Mineral salt	75
Limestone	63
Sulfide ores	32
Brines	24
Petroleum	23
Natural gas	16
Saltpeter	13
Potassium minerals	11
Gypsum	10
Lead ores	9
Sand	9
Aluminum minerals	8
Chromium ores	7
Iron ores	6
Phosphate rock	6
Sea water	5
Copper ores	4
Fluorine minerals	4
Arsenic minerals	3
Magnesium minerals	3
Mercury ores	3
Zinc ores	3
Antimony minerals	2
Barium minerals	2
Boron minerals	2
Manganese ores	2
Tin ores	2
Bismuth minerals	1
Silver ores	1
Titanium ores	1

SOURCE: R. Norris Shreve, *The Chemical Process Industries,* McGraw-Hill Book Company, Inc., New York, 1956, p. 6.

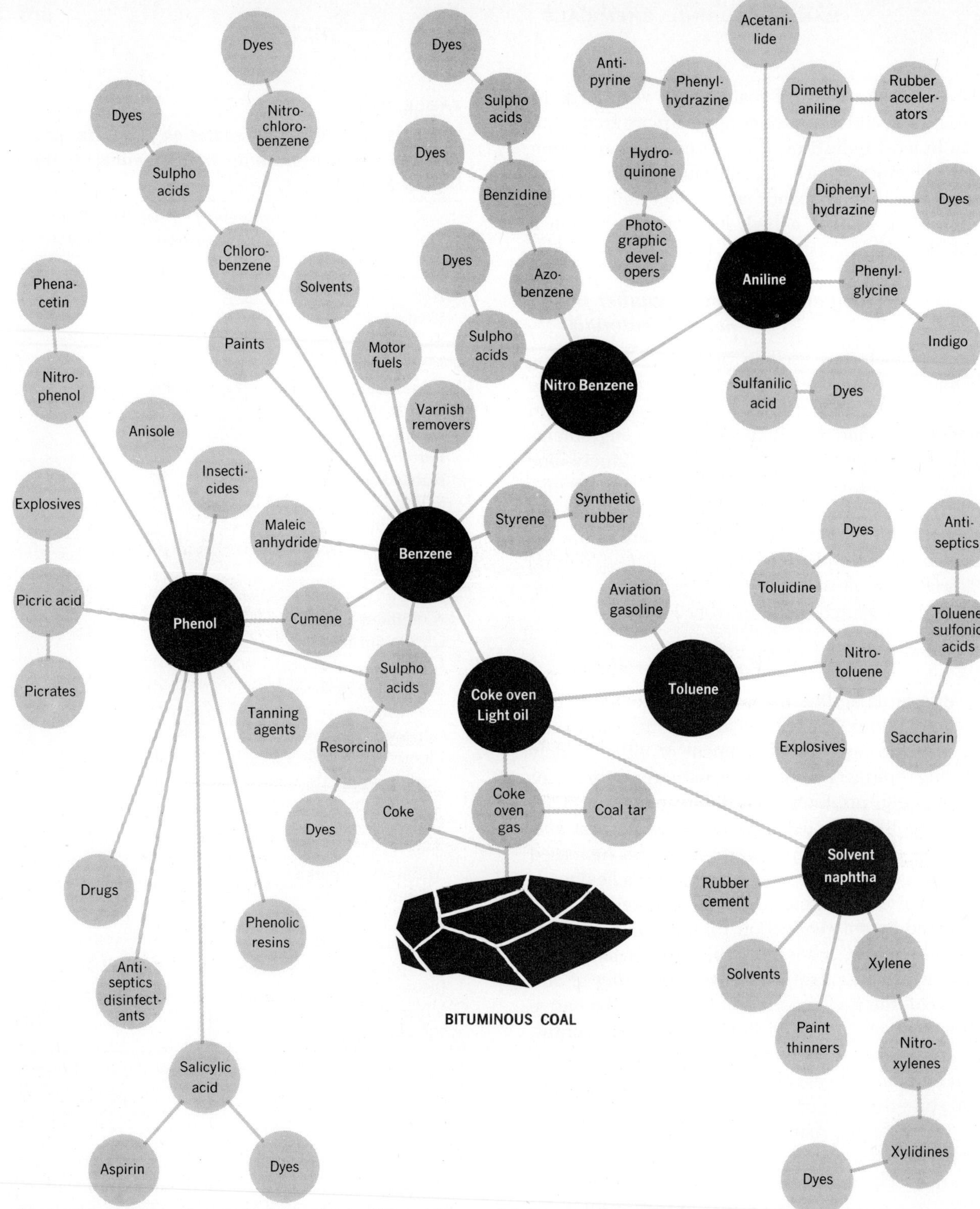

Figure 31.1 ***Some chemicals derived from bituminous coal*** *(after graph supplied by Allied Chemical Corporation).*

complex than in the illustration, is characteristic of much of an industry that utilizes from 25 to 75 per cent of its own output and, in addition, supplies some product to almost every other type of industry.

The total number and variety of chemical products is surprising. Before the last war, about fifteen thousand such products were being made, and about twenty thousand are being turned out today.[3]

Dynamic character of the industry

Change is more characteristic of the chemical industry than of most manufacturing. In the United States, nearly one-fifth of all chemical-industry employees are involved in research. Furthermore, the industry invests in research a percentage of its sales dollars approximately three times as high as that of all manufacturing. A partial result is that commodities which make their initial appearance today may be obsolescent tomorrow—superseded in some way by commodities which can do all that the earlier products can do but can do it better. A new commodity enters the chemical market almost every day. One major company in the United States has estimated that by 1970 three-fifths of its sales will be accounted for by items that are still largely unknown to the public and in early developmental stages.[4]

Such dynamism based upon scientifically demonstrated capacities may be one result of an interesting aspect of management in the chemical industry in the United States, and presumably elsewhere as well: a sizable portion of that management is made up of trained chemists, engineers, or other scientists who hold small brief for habit and traditionalism and who greet each innovation with an enthusiasm matching its exhibited advantages.

Automation

Automatic process control, or automation, is being applied increasingly to many different types of manufacturing. The production of chemicals, petroleum, energy, iron and steel, transportation equipment, and large and small household appliances are a few examples. Where manufacturing largely involves liquids and gases, or solids in either solution or suspension, automation becomes important to temperature, moisture, density, and pressure regulation, to flow of materials, and to time measurement of physical mixing and chemical reactions. Inasmuch as the chemical industry largely involves working with such easily flowing materials, sending them from one tank, vat, or reaction chamber to another via connecting channels—in other words, involves working with apparatus more than with machinery—much of it has been successfully automated (Fig. 31.2).

HISTORICAL BACKGROUND

Prescientific chemical industry

Given the broadest possible interpretation of the term *chemical industry* we can trace it as far back in time as man is known to have achieved—however accidentally or unknowingly—some sort of chemical reaction and to have made use of it. This would take us back to 2500 B.C., and probably earlier. Several historians concerned with the world's chemical industry begin their narratives at about this time, labeling the 4,200 years, or more, that elapsed between the dawn of the Bronze Age and the dawn of the Industrial Revolution as the period of *prescientific chemistry,* and subsequent time, involving approximately three centuries, as the period of *scientific chemistry.*

Scientific chemical industry

Until the eighteenth century, such chemical reactions as had been achieved were appreciably a result of accident, and knowledge about them, largely empirical, was a subject of interest mainly to craftsmen and artisans rather than scientists. During the century and five decades that passed after the onset of the Industrial Revolution, loose empirical methods were replaced in considerable degree by systematic recognition of ingredient and process—replaced, in other words, by the predeces-

[3] "The Chemical Industry: A Particularly Dynamic Industrial Branch," *Rotterdamsche Bank N. V.*, 14–15:8, June, 1957.

[4] *Ibid.*, p. 9.

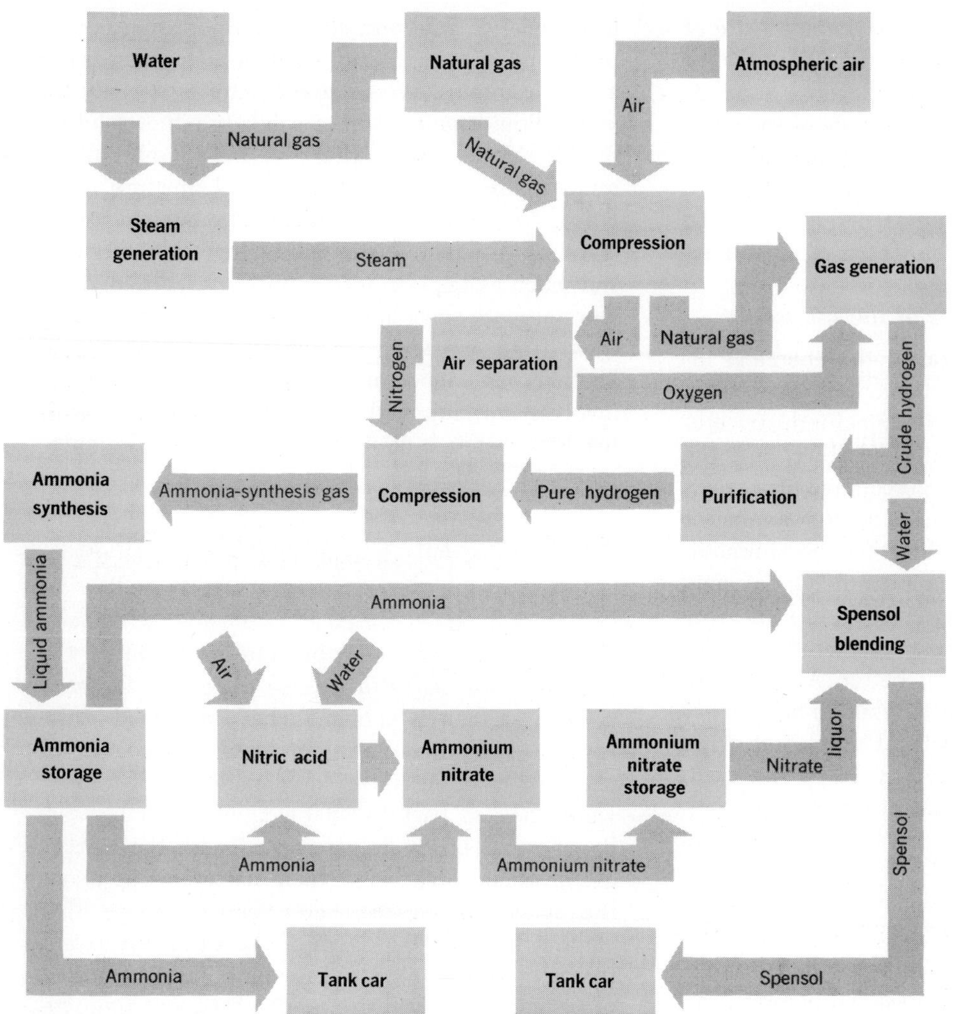

Figure 31.2 ***Production flow chart of the Vicksburg, Mississippi, works of the Spencer Chemical Company.*** *Spensol is the trade name for a chemical product. Production is by means of apparatus rather than machinery, and automation generally is easier than with machinery. (After graph supplied by Spencer Chemical Company)*

sor of science as we know it today. By the middle of the nineteenth century, industrial processes involving chemical reactions could be explained rationally and in explicit terms, and the groundwork thus was laid for the mushrooming chemical industry of the present.

Scientific Pioneers. This change was wrought primarily by a comparatively few brilliant minds, some of whom were blotted out prematurely by the actions of more ignorant minds who happened to enjoy positions of political power. The British scientist Robert Boyle (1627–1691) distinguished chemical elements from compounds, defined chemical reactions clearly, and gave his name to the famous law of gases. The French pioneer Antoine Lavoisier (1743–1794) introduced quantitative methods to the study of chemical reactions, classified substances on the basis of element and compound, gained insight into the importance of oxygen in animal and plant respiration, and was responsible for so many other lasting chemical innovations that the field can never repay its debt to him—and he died on the guillotine in the Reign of Terror that followed the French Revolution! The French chemist and surgeon Nicolas Leblanc (1742–1806) invented a process for recovering soda from common salt. The English chemist and physicist John Dalton (1766–1844) and the Swedish researcher Baron J. J. Berzelius (1779–1848) perfected the atomic theory and utilized equivalents and atomic weights of elements in making quantitative chemical predictions. The German Baron Justus von Liebig (1803–1873) made remarkable advances in producing artificial fertilizers. The Swedish chemist and inventor Alfred Nobel (1833–1896) perfected the manufacture of nitroglycerine and dynamite (and later endowed funds for excellence in physics, science, chemistry, medicine, literature, and sincere efforts to bring about world peace). The English chemist Sir William Henry Perkin (1838–1907) discovered aniline dyes. The Belgian industrial chemist Ernest Solvay (1838–1922) discovered a more efficient process than Leblanc's for producing soda. These are but a few names; the list is long, and growing more or less in geometric progression as the number of scientists and the reserve of knowledge increase. It is significant that the products associated with the names of "pure" researchers tend to outnumber those of "applied" chemists, most of whom have been responsible for a single product only.

Historical Overview. The emergence of a scientific chemical industry from its prescientific roots and its development during subsequent centuries have been described by one source as follows:[5]

> Chemistry emerged as a science in its own right at the close of the eighteenth century and laid the foundation for the development, in the nineteenth and twentieth centuries, of the present chemical industries.
>
> Long before chemistry was regarded as a distinct science, there were chemical industries in which materials were converted into other substances. These industries included the manufacture of soap and candles, the production of various paints and beverages, the glass and paper industries. Production of these oldest branches of what may be termed the prehistoric period of the chemical industry took place, as one might say, unconsciously—purely empirically and without any systematic application of the scientific methods of work which characterize the chemical industry of modern times. In the old days, chemistry was, in fact, alchemy from which subsequently evolved what is now known as the science of chemistry.
>
> Looked at from the historical point of view, the development of the chemical industry and that of industrialization generally reacted upon each other. The rise of the modern big industries brought in its wake a very substantial demand for certain chemical raw and other materials. On the other hand, the general expansion of industry was very largely based on, and promoted by, the enormous growth of chemical science and its practical application in an ever increasing number of new fields.
>
> The chief starting point of the modern chemical industry was the first big Industrial Revolution ushered in by the birth of the textile industry. For a long time the discoveries made in the field of chemistry were exclusively applied to textiles (cleaning, bleaching, dyeing). The first product of the chemical industry as a branch of applied science was sulfuric acid. It could be used in the treatment of textiles, more particularly for the purpose of substantially shortening the bleaching process. It turned out to be an extensive basic product and it has remained up to the present time one of the most vital chemical products.
>
> The second most important basic product for the chemical industry was soda, which was also required for the textile industry. The process for the manufacture of soda from common salt evolved towards the end of the eighteenth century.
>
> The sixties of the nineteenth century saw the beginning of the heavy chemical industry. In course of time ever larger quantities of sulfuric acid, soda, caustic soda, hydrochloric acid, nitric acid and superphosphate were manufactured.
>
> The first blast furnaces and gasworks are traceable to the middle of the nineteenth century. These works need the coke derived from coal, tar being a residuum. The latter was the starting point for very important industrial branches, like the manufacture of dyes and pharmaceutics.
>
> The next stage of development was heralded by the production of cheap electric power which at the beginning of the twentieth century rendered possible electrochemistry; this, in its turn, led to new manufacturing processes for caustic soda and chlorine. Electricity was also used for the production of carbide from

[5] "The Chemical Industry: A Particularly Dynamic Industrial Branch," *Rotterdamsche Bank N. V.*, 14–15:5–7, June, 1957. By permission of the publisher. Spelling has been altered to conform with usage in the United States.

which were derived acetylene and a number of other products including calcium cyanamide and acetic acid.

In the interwar period, the development of the chemical industry was marked by the rise of organic chemistry, of plastic materials and of synthetic rubber. This new development in the chemical industry made possible the manufacture of synthetic petrol from coal, as well as the spectacular progress registered in the field of photography. It was a period not only of hectic expansion but also of refined production, of improvement and modernization in the chemical industry.

This evolution made great strides after the Second World War, the rise of the petrochemical industry and the striking growth made in the sphere of plastics particularly attracting attention.

Generally speaking, since the end of the war very great progress can also be recorded with respect to already existing products. This was reflected in improved apparatus and manufacturing processes and in an ever greater variety of products. An outstanding example of this development may be found in the pharmaceutical industry (vitamins, antibiotics, hormones, and so on), as well as in the field of derivatives to combat plant diseases and of nutrients to promote the growth of plants.

Modern industrial chemistry started in England, the country where the Industrial Revolution took place and the textile branch first assumed enormous proportions. England where interest centered more especially on heavy chemicals, which turned out bulk products, maintained its lead in the world's chemical industry up to the eighties of the nineteenth century, when it was outdistanced by Germany whose dyestuffs for textiles and pharmaceutical industry made remarkable progress. The triumphant advance of the German chemical industry was primarily based on the use of tar as a starting point for the manufacture of a large number of articles. In 1880 or thereabouts, the coke factories were not yet yielding either tar or gas, both of which were burned in the cooling process and used to fuel the coke-ovens. Prominent German chemists chose tar for their experiments and discovered its virtually inexhaustible possibilities for the use of the manifold compounds tar contains. Other chemicals being also necessary for the processing of tar, the manufacture of tar drove Germany in the direction of the heavy chemical industry. The incredibly large number of experiments carried out in innumerable fields played a major role in the preponderant position of the German chemical industry, which position the latter was able to hold up to the First World War.

During the latter, however, Germany lost its hegemony in the field of chemicals. This industry rapidly advanced in America, whilst both England and France witnessed a big revival of this branch. Being cut off from German imports these countries were compelled to manufacture a large number of products which had so far been made virtually only in Germany.

Between the two wars, the chemical industry in all the producing countries developed rapidly. The 1939–1945 war led to a tremendous expansion of the chemical industry in the United States, as a result of which there occurred a very important shift in regard to the countries' respective strength in world industry. This is most clearly illustrated by the circumstance that the American chemical industry now produces more than the combined chemical industries of western Europe. In the new and exceptionally important branch of the chemical industry which sprang up after the Second World War, viz. petrochemicals, the United States grasped the lead, a fact to which great significance may be attached considering the enormous possibilities in store for this industry which, in reality, is still in its infancy.

A capstone to this discussion can well take the form of still another quotation, by an observer writing some thirty-five years ago:[6]

This century will see changes that will dwarf those of the nineteenth century, as those of the nineteenth dwarf those of the eighteenth.

LOCATIONAL CONSIDERATIONS

Labor and raw-materials costs

Although the Census of Manufactures does not provide sufficient data for the entire chemical industry of the United States to make possible an evaluation by Alderfer and Michl criteria (page 499), some data are available on subproduct operations. We can conclude that the industry is medium- to low-cost with respect to materials, and medium- to high-cost regarding labor. We have mentioned that the industry is appreciably automated; blue-collar employment consists in no small measure of watchmen who look after either entire factories or specific processes. Much of the labor costs involve highly

[6] Allerton S. Cushman, *Chemistry and Civilization*, E. P. Dutton & Co., Inc., New York, 1925, p. 131.

paid researchers and technicians who develop and maintain the apparatus—employees who are somewhat more mobile than most labor and whose present-day places of residence therefore need not be considered as a major factor in the location of plants.

Tendency for physical clustering of plants

In giving attention to the "Why?" of chemical plant location, we should not lose sight of the manifold and many-sided nature of the industry, and of the associated difficulty of generalization. Nevertheless, as we have noted, a tendency exists for physical clustering of plants because of complementarity of product—i.e., a tendency of one plant to use as a raw material the end product of another plant. When this realization is coupled with the thoughts that each plant customarily produces several products and that many such products are troublesome to transport for long distances, some insight is gained into the tendency for physical clustering of plants.[7]

Regional markets

Within limits allowed by the preceding paragraph, we can best generalize the chemical industry as footloose—as oriented physically to none of the traditionally accepted forces of attraction. Raw materials tend to be few and rather easily obtainable and, except for some petrochemicals, do not appear to attract industrial plants. Many of the processes are automated, and little of the labor involved in the actual output needs to be highly skilled. Considerable energy is consumed, but usually not in such large or costly quantities per unit that plants must be located at energy sources. If there is any single overriding attraction, it would appear to be regional markets, coupled with excellent transportational access to such markets.[8]

Importance of water availability

We have noted in Table 31.2 that water enters the most frequently into the production of 150 leading chemicals. Chemical plants generally use large amounts of water—one in Ohio, for example, consumes well over 130 million gallons per day! Some of this water can be taken directly from surface sources and utilized without further treatment. Some, however, must meet exact specifications and must be treated very carefully. Some, meeting specifications between these two extremes, need not be treated in precise detail but nonetheless require some treatment. Rivers, streams, lakes, ponds, rainy wells (dug under these surface sources, so as to tap their water after it has filtered through the ground for an appreciable distance), and normal wells of varying depths are the sources of most water for chemical plants. Generally those plants needing large amounts of water locate near a surface supply.

LEADING NATIONS OF PRODUCTION

Since complete world-wide data for the production of all chemicals are either not as yet forthcoming or not wholly reliable, we have indicated in Table 31.3 and Fig. 31.3 the world output of sulfuric acid only. This one commodity is frequently used as

[7] The Woytinskys have shown that the chemical industry is its own best customer—that, at least in the United States, some three-fourths of the products of the chemical and chemical-process industries are recycled into plants of those industries. See W. S. Woytinsky and E. S. Woytinsky, *World Population and Production,* The Twentieth Century Fund, Inc., New York, 1953, p. 1180. Others report a much smaller percentage, the difference being due to a different interpretation of the term *chemical industries.*

[8] In a special study conducted by the author, regional market and transportational-access considerations were emphasized above all others by chemical-plant managers interviewed. This conclusion is substantiated in the latest edition of *The Chemical Industry Facts Book,* which lists the following considerations in the order in which they are given here, while specifying that this does not necessarily imply order of importance: markets, raw materials, transportation services, communication facilities, utilities, taxes, regulatory laws and practices, competitors, construction costs, labor, living conditions, recreational facilities, climate, police and fire protection, neighbors, and community planning. See *The Chemical Industry Facts Book, 1960–61,* Manufacturing Chemists' Association, Washington, D.C., 1959, p. 47.

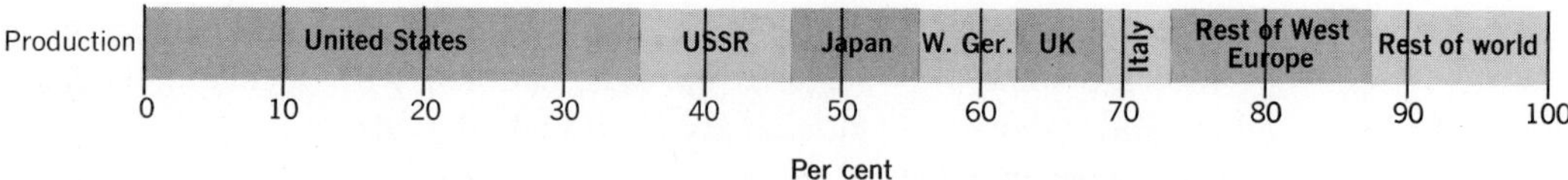

Figure 31.3 ***World output of sulfuric acid.*** *Only a few technically advanced nations, of which the United States is easily in the fore, are important producers.*

such an indicator, because the intensity of its use in the derivation of other chemical products is exceeded only by that of water, air, and coal—is exceeded, in other words, only by materials which are so freely available that data concerning their use are not tabulated on a world-wide basis or by materials which are used mainly for fuel.

As represented by sulfuric acid, the world's chemical industries have (1) increased in output by over 2.5 times between 1937 and 1958; (2) increased in reported number of producing countries from 32 to 45 in that same time span; (3) changed somewhat with respect to the importance of the leading producers, with the United States and the Soviet Union gaining at the relative expense of Europe and Japan. The largest gains have been registered in the United States, which rose from supplying 29 per cent of all the world's sulfuric acid in 1937 to furnishing 35 per cent in 1958. Growth in the Soviet Union has been about one-half as fast. Both leading European nations and Japan have declined relatively, although in each case the decline has been very small. Nations other than the leaders are supplying a percentage of the world's sulfuric acid that is slightly higher now than it was twenty years ago.

TABLE 31.3

World and national output of sulfuric acid (in millions of metric tons and per cent)

Area	*1937*	*1958*
World	16.5*	41.8†
United States	29	35
Soviet Union	8	11
Japan	12	9
Germany	12	
West Germany		7
East Germany		2
United Kingdom	6	5
Italy	6	5
France	7	4
Rest of Europe	13‡	13§
Rest of the world	7¶	9‖

* 21 countries (plus 11 which did not report in 1937 but reported in 1938).
† 37 countries (plus 8 which did not report in 1958 but reported in 1957).
‡ 10 countries.
§ 15 countries.
¶ 6 countries.
‖ 14 countries.
SOURCE: Calculated from data in *Statistical Yearbook, 1958,* United Nations, New York, 1958, pp. 213–214, and *Statistical Yearbook, 1959,* United Nations, New York, 1959, pp. 221–222.

The United States

Growth and Present Size. The chemical industry is one of the most rapidly growing activities in the nation—paralleled only by electronics. Whereas the nation's population increased nearly one-fourth between 1947 and 1959 and its total industrial production rose approximately 40 per cent, the output of chemicals and allied products grew by 90 per cent and of allied chemicals alone by about 110 per cent of respective 1947 levels. In 1958, the chemical industry ranked fourth in the nation when compared as to value of total assets, and fifth when viewed as to total sales (Table 31.4).

Present Composition. The United States is unexcelled as to variety as well as volume of chemically produced materials. It accounts for a share of almost every chemical manufactured on the world scene. The total number of end products ranges from 10,000 to 20,000, depending upon the degree of rigidity with which certain types of chemicals are defined.

One of the most rapidly growing branches of the industry is the petrochemical branch, which

TABLE 31.4

Rank of the chemical industry among manufacturing industries of the United States (in billions of dollars)

In terms of total assets as of Dec. 31, 1958		*In terms of total sales for the year 1958*	
Petroleum refining and related industries	$35.1	Food and kindred products	$50.9
Primary metal industries	26.9	Transportation equipment	36.3
Transportation equipment	23.9	Petroleum refining and related industries	26.9
Chemicals and allied products	21.5	Primary metal industries	24.2
Food and kindred products	20.8	Chemicals and allied products	23.7
Machinery other than electrical	19.2	Machinery other than electrical	23.3
Electrical machinery, equipment, and supplies	15.0	Electrical machinery, equipment, and supplies	23.2
Fabricated metal products other than machinery	10.0	Fabricated metal products other than machinery	15.9
Paper and allied products	9.2	Textile mill products	12.0
Textile mill products	7.8	Paper and allied products	10.7
Stone, clay, and glass	7.1	Apparel and other finished products	9.8
Rubber and miscellaneous plastic products	4.8	Stone, clay, and glass	7.6
Printing and publishing except newspapers	4.3	Rubber and miscellaneous plastic products	7.5
Lumber and wood products except furniture	4.2	Printing and publishing except newspapers	7.3
Apparel and other finished products	3.5	Lumber and wood products except furniture	5.5
Instruments and related products	3.3	Tobacco manufactures	4.6
Tobacco manufactures	3.2	Miscellaneous manufacturing and ordnance	4.6
Miscellaneous manufacturing and ordnance	2.8	Instruments and related products	4.3
Furniture and fixtures	1.9	Furniture and fixtures	3.7
Leather and leather products	1.7	Leather and leather products	3.4

SOURCE: *The Chemical Industry Facts Book, 1960–61,* Manufacturing Chemists' Association, Washington, D.C., 1959, p. 15. The above classifications are at the two-digit detail.

essentially did not exist before the last world war but now accounts for about one-fourth of the nation's chemical output. Involving organic chemicals largely traceable to natural gas, petroleum, and industrial gases, this group turns out a wide variety of end products.

Plant Size. Although there are more than 12,500 chemical plants in the United States, the comparatively small number of larger units dominate the industry, as is indicated in Table 31.5.

Distribution. The geographical distribution and output of some plants in the United States are indicated in Table 31.6 and Figs. 31.4 and 31.5. The table refers to a variety of chemicals and allied products, and the maps refer only to sulfuric acid. The table indicates a rather pronounced orientation of the industry to places of heavy population and other manufacturing. This could be an orientation to markets—but it also could be an orientation to

TABLE 31.5

Relative size of chemical plants in the United States, 1956

Number of employees per plant	*Percentage of all plants represented*	*Percentage of all employees represented*
1–19 employees	64.4	6.3
20–99 employees	25.1	17.2
100–249 employees	5.9	14.0
250–499 employees	2.3	12.0
500 or more employees	2.3	50.5

SOURCE: *The Chemical Industry Facts Book, 1960–61,* Manufacturing Chemists' Association, Washington, D.C., 1959, p. 48.

Figure 31.4 ***Distribution of sulfuric acid plants in the United States.*** *The process is semiautomated, so most plants need hire only a few workers. There is no pronounced concentration of plants in any section of the country.*

raw materials, because much of the chemical industry involves intermediate and late stages of processing and hence is dependent upon other manufacturing plants for raw materials. The maps suggest that sulfuric acid plants predominate slightly in the South. One reason for this is the ready availability there of native sulfur (Chapter 25). However, this industry also is located not far from its markets. It would appear that the chemical industry of the United States is oriented mainly to both raw materials and markets.

Figure 31.5 ***Value of shipments from sulfuric acid plants in the United States.*** *The South is in the lead. Why?*

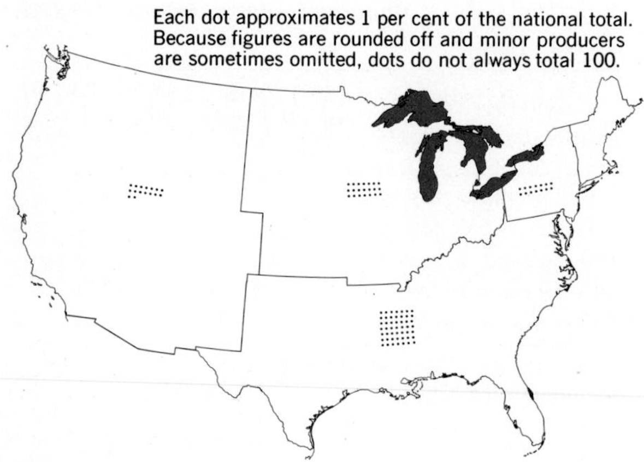

New Construction. However, the pattern of new construction is not similar to that of current plant distribution (Fig. 31.6). Over 61 per cent of the new plants, measured by value, are being built in the South (including Texas, Oklahoma, Maryland, and Delaware), and only 23 per cent in the main part of the manufacturing belt. Some 36 per cent involve only Texas, Louisiana, Arkansas, and Oklahoma. A major explanation for this apparent shift in focus of interest is associated with the growth of the petrochemical industry, in which many plant owners prefer to build near the source of the raw materials. With respect to most petrochemicals, however, there is no logically demonstrated superiority to locating plant sites near the raw materials, and there is reason to believe that the current emphasis upon the South will not continue—certainly not at its present intensity.

The Soviet Union

Increasing the output of chemicals has been a major objective of the various plans of the Soviet Union. The degree to which this objective has been realized is suggested in Table 31.3: despite the damages of the Second World War, the country is now second in the world among individual producing nations of sulfuric acid, although accounting for less than one-third of the output of the United

States. The latest plan, the Seven-Year Plan ending in 1965, envisions a doubling in output of ammonia, caustic soda, soda ash, and sulfuric acid over the 1958 figure. Other aspects of the chemical industry also are receiving attention in this plan, which places an unprecedented measure of emphasis upon the industry. The chemical plants are scattered rather widely throughout the effective territory of the Soviet Union, with small concentrations in the Ukraine and the Urals industrial regions.

Europe

Once predominant in the chemical industry, Europe is experiencing a slow but sure decline in that predominance. Among single nations, only the United Kingdom produces about as high a percentage of the world output of sulfuric acid as it did in 1937; all others have not kept pace with the world growth rate. Lesser as well as major producing nations are in a poorer relative position than in 1937: in that year, some ten lesser European producers accounted for 13 per cent of the world's supply of sulfuric acid, whereas by 1958 some fifteen lesser producers supplied 13 per cent of the world's output (Table 31.3).

Despite its loss in relative position, however, Europe is still a major producer, responsible for over one-third of the world's annual yield of sulfuric acid and excelled only by the United States.

Japan

Lacking a multiplicity of raw materials, Japan turned early to the chemical industry to supply many of them and by 1937 was producing 12 per cent of the world's annual yield of sulfuric acid. Today, despite defeat in the Second World War, the nation produces 9 per cent of all sulfuric acid —in other words, almost has kept pace with a world growth rate dominated by the burgeoning chemical industry in the United States, which did not feel the physical pangs of the last war.

Other producing nations

The production of chemicals is restricted quite closely to technically advanced nations discussed above. Besides this group, only Canada stands out as a dynamic producer; and Canada's output, amounting to about 2 per cent of that for the world, is so closely tied to United States production in terms of both physical location and capital investment that it almost can be considered as an adjunct to that production.

TABLE 31.6
Production of chemicals and allied products in twenty-five leading states

State	*Value added by manufacture, 1957 (in thousands)*	*Number of employees*
New Jersey	$1,408,162	83,851
New York	1,054,441	68,201
Texas	1,044,832	39,587
Illinois	827,724	52,370
Pennsylvania	714,434	46,686
Ohio	693,853	49,109
Michigan	610,518	40,614
California	564,837	36,292
Tennessee	546,458	42,149
Indiana	482,987	24,792
Virginia	444,831	33,624
West Virginia	426,248	23,491
South Carolina (1956)	337,490	14,252
Louisiana	300,281	16,915
Missouri	283,915	19,151
Kentucky	200,360	10,331
Massachusetts	194,451	16,360
Florida	188,803	13,631
Maryland	185,545	13,321
Connecticut	157,718	11,709
North Carolina	138,914	11,560
Washington	137,017	11,208
Minnesota	119,826	6,329
Georgia	117,494	11,169
Kansas	108,711	7,420

SOURCE: *The Chemical Industry Facts Book, 1960–61*, Manufacturing Chemists' Association, Washington, D.C., 1959, p. 50.

CENTRALIZATION OF AUTHORITY

Almost since its inception, the world's chemical industry has been tightly organized. In the Communist bloc, of course, the industry is but one more state-owned enterprise. In the non-Communist

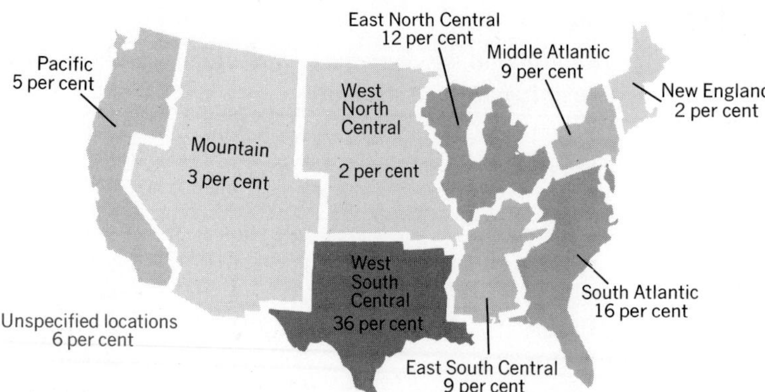

Figure 31.6 ***Investment in new chemical plants of the United States, 1959–1960.*** *The South leads, the manufacturing belt is second, and the Pacific West is third.* (*After* The Chemical Industry Facts Book, 1960–1961, *p. 47*)

realm, however, where the industry came to maturity, the organization has been by large corporations and cartels. In the United States, three companies accounted for about 64 per cent of the assets of all chemical companies in 1939 and predominate today.[9] One cartel dominates chemical production in West Germany, another in the United Kingdom, another in France, another in Italy, and another in Belgium. Close liaison is maintained among these various organizations, with the result that competition frequently is replaced by quasi-monopolistic cooperation.

INTERNATIONAL TRADE

Approximately 8 per cent of all produced chemicals enter into international trade. The United States, so predominant in production, is also the leading trading nation, accounting for about 30 per cent of all exports and 25 per cent of all imports. The United Kingdom, West Germany, and other dynamic producers of Europe account for most of the remaining trade; Canada is also considered active in this respect. Most such trade is among technically advanced nations outside the Communist bloc. The Soviet Union, East Germany, and lesser Communist producing nations as yet are consuming most of their respective output domestically.

[9] George W. Stocking and Myron W. Watkins, *Cartels in Action,* The Twentieth Century Fund, Inc., New York, 1946, pp. 363–429.

THE CHEMICAL INDUSTRY IN ECONOMIC GEOGRAPHY

Heretofore in this section we have indicated a range of several industries which we considered to be represented by the chemical industry. However, the chemical industry is unique in that it scarcely can stand for any other group of industries; it must represent itself only. It is, however, of such growing importance to economic geography that any general statement almost becomes dated at the moment it appears. A suggestion of this has been set down in the latest edition of *The Chemical Industry Facts Book,* which lists the following possible developments within the industry, and their application to the world at large:[10]

> Here are some of the possibilities now being discussed, planned or developed that could bring the U.S. closer to the truly Chemical Age. All will rely on chemistry's contributions and many will be predominantly chemical in character.
>
> —World-wide broadcasts of television images.
> —Global control of weather and climate.
> —Many synthetic foods, such as synthetic products with built-in characteristics of meat or milk.
> —Homes constructed largely of plastics and special adhesives.
> —Girders made of limestone, sea water and air—stronger than steel.

[10] *The Chemical Industry Facts Book, 1960–61,* Manufacturing Chemists' Association, Washington, D.C., 1959, pp. 34–35.

–Lightweight clothing treated to protect the wearer against cold, heat and toxic agents.
–Farming in over-populated land-poor regions on beds of crushed stone, water and chemicals.
–Chemicals to control heredity and animal behavior.
–Chemicals to remove or prevent many physical disorders common in infancy and old age.
–The addition of chemicals to soils to make them waterproof and strong enough to serve many types of transportation.
–Production of electricity in fuel or thermoelectric cells, which require chemical components.
–Food harvested from the ocean.
–A neutral white photosensitive pigment paint for automobiles which can be tinted to desired colors by exposure to electromagnetic radiation.
–Homes lighted, heated or cooled by special plastic panels.
–Precise duplication of hand-carved stone work with vinyl plastisols.
–Application of electrically conductive plastics to many special uses.
–An automobile with no engine; power would come from a small cylinder on each wheel holding oxygen and hydrogen gases.
–New pain-killing drugs that are many times more powerful than morphine, but are nonhabit forming.
–Plastic coatings for moving parts of machinery, a plastic so slick the parts never need be oiled or greased.
–Plastic domes to place over entire houses and yards for year-round climate control.
–A writing pen in which atmospheric nitrogen is combined with a solid chemical compound to produce a writing fluid.
–Transistor radios run by solar power; pocket radios about the size of a watch.
–Cordless electric clocks that will have no moving parts, yet be accurate to the split second. Clocks will use an electronic circuit based on tiny transistors and miniaturized batteries.

This list contains relatively few of the developments that may be introduced to the American scene in the near future. These and products like them should keep the nation's chemical plants working near capacity at least for several years to come.

REFERENCES

The Canadian Chemical Industry, Royal Commission on Canada's Economic Prospects, Ottawa, 1957.

Cushman, Allerton S.: *Chemistry and Civilization*, E. P. Dutton & Co., Inc., New York, 1925.

Eckman, Donald P.: *Automatic Process Control*, New York: John Wiley & Sons, Inc., New York, 1958.

Faith, W. L., et al.: *Industrial Chemicals*, John Wiley & Sons, Inc., New York, 1957.

Happel, John: *Chemical Process Economics*, John Wiley & Sons, Inc., New York, 1958.

Reichl, Anny: *Chemische Industrie und Chemieaussenhandel*, Ludwigshafen-am-Rhein, 1957.

Shreve, R. Norris: *The Chemical Process Industries*, McGraw-Hill Book Company, Inc., New York, 1956.

Stocking, George W., and Myron W. Watkins: *Cartels in Action*, The Twentieth Century Fund, Inc., New York, 1946.

——— and ———: *Cartels or Competition?* The Twentieth Century Fund, Inc., New York, 1948.

——— and ———: *Monopoly and Free Enterprise*, The Twentieth Century Fund, Inc., New York, 1951.

Taylor, F. Sherwood: *A History of Industrial Chemistry*, Abelard-Schuman, Inc., Publishers, New York, 1957.

32 MANUFACTURING: PULP AND PAPER

THE PULP AND PAPER INDUSTRY IS OF INTEREST TO ECONOMIC GEOGRAPHERS FOR several reasons. In the first place, most of its raw materials come from the world's forests, and it thus represents advanced manufacturing stages based upon forest-products industries rather than upon mining, as are the products discussed in Chapter 29, or upon quasi-synthetic manufacturing, as are the products discussed in Chapter 31. Second, it involves the application of chemicals to forest-derived raw materials in some of its processes and hence is closely related to the chemical industry. More specifically, it is a chemical-process industry in that some chemicals are needed in some of its processing operations, but these chemicals are not basic raw materials. Third, it provides a basis for further discussion of technically advanced and underdeveloped economies, as well as of the non-Communist and Communist realms of influence.

PROCESS

Basic ingredients

Nearly all paper comes from *cellulose,* found in the cell walls of the fibrous portions of a wide variety of plant life. Cellulose is available in cotton, corn, sugar cane, wheat, bamboo, and many other botanical forms, including wood, which is the primary commercial source. It comprises an average of from 55 to 56 per cent of the weight of growing timber. Cellulose occurs almost invariably with *lignin,* an imperfectly understood combination of compounds which bind the cellulose fibers together, and with *pentosan,* a complex combination of carbohydrates. Both lignin and pentosan are essentially removed in the making of high-quality papers.

Pulp and paper making

In its simplest sense, the making of paper from pulpwood involves removing the cellulose fibers from their sources and intertwining them into even sheets which, when dried, become paper. Extraction of the cellulose from the wood is known as *pulping,* and many mills specialize only in this aspect of manufacture. Beating the fibers so that they are more flexible and aggregately form a continuous sheet, refining them, and bonding them into specific thicknesses and processing them further into different grades—all these are papermaking operations. It is not uncommon for pulp making and papermaking to take place under the same roof; however, it also is not uncommon for each operation to exist independently. An important consideration here is the utilization of waste paper. In the United States, nearly one-third of all newly processed paper and paper products comes from waste paper, and the remainder is supplied from pulpwood sources. The waste paper is made into lower grades of paper.

Pulping processes

Mechanical. Certainly the simplest of the pulping processes is that of mechanical pulping, or grinding. The pulpwood is ground to small fragments, usually by placing it against a turning grindstone. The cellulose fibers, together with the lignin and pentosan, are then beaten together in the papermaking operation to form newsprint and other cheap paper. The actual cellulose content of newsprint is scarcely higher than that of the wood from which it came. Newsprint is bulky, low in tensile strength, and yellows quickly with the passing of time, but it fills an obvious need.

Chemical. Three chemical processes are generally recognized—the *sulfite,* the *sulfate,* and the *soda.* The first two are used most commonly. All involve the chemical "cooking" of wood which has been ground into chips, the major objective being the removal of lignin and pentosan. The sulfite process, which is an acid reaction, is particularly effective upon spruce and most other softwoods except pine, the resins of which are not removable by this process. The sulfate and soda processes are alkaline in reaction, the difference between them being appreciably a matter of the amount of sulfur present in the cooking solution. They can utilize pine as well as other softwoods. Besides high-quality papers, the sulfate process is particularly important for the production of kraft (usually brown) wrapping paper, most of which, in the United States, comes from the pulp of the southern pine.

Pulp produced chemically is of a much higher cellulose content than mechanically produced pulp and consequently forms papers that are smoother, stronger, and more durable. However, its unit-for-unit yield compared to input is much less than that of the mechanical pulp, which largely consists of ground-up pulpwood. In contrast, less than one-half the weight of the initial pulpwood is retained in chemical pulp.

After removal from the pulping machines, the chemically produced pulp may or may not be chemically bleached, depending upon its ultimate use. Subsequently, it is forwarded to the papermaking machinery—either in the same building or many miles away.

Semichemical. As its name implies, semichemical pulping involves the partial treatment of pulpwood utilizing any of the three chemical processes and subsequent mechanical processing. The resultant pulp is intermediate between chemical and mechanical pulp in quality, and higher in unit-for-unit yield than chemical pulp but lower than mechanical pulp. It is used chiefly for the making of cardboard and wrapping paper.

Although used on both softwoods and hardwoods, these processes have been developed especially for the former, which are consumed more actively by the pulp and paper industry. For hardwoods, the soda process is commonly used, mainly to produce a semichemical pulp.

Papermaking processes

Beating and Refining. The beating operation involves the mechanical rolling of pulp under water, so that the cellulose fibers break up and intermesh still further than when they were in pulp. Dyes, chalk fibers, and other substances designed for special purposes also may be added during beating. The product is then refined, so that density of the slushy material becomes more even and the fiber lengths more or less uniform. In this condition the slush passes to the next stage of manufacture.

Papermaking. The slush then enters the papermaking machines, where it is poured evenly over a series of continuously moving belts, pressed, dried, sized, sometimes *calendered,* and finally rolled into huge cylinders for shipment. Calendering involves the passing of the paper over huge rollers with glossy surfaces so that it becomes "slick"—a condition highly desired by the so-called slick magazines. An even higher gloss can be obtained if a coat of fine clay is added to the paper before calendering.

Types of wood utilized

Most pulp mills prefer softwoods other than resinous pines. However, these are in increasingly short supply in some nations of high consumption—notably the United States—so that pine and the various hardwoods are being used increasingly.

HISTORICAL BACKGROUND

Premechanical papermaking

Making paper from plant fiber is a very old art—at least 2,000 years old. It may well have been a Chinese discovery, and knowledge of it may have filtered slowly from China to the Middle East, to southern Europe, to northern Europe, and finally to European colonial empires. Not until the fifteenth century, however, did paper exceed vellum (animal skin, especially lambskin) as a writing material. Cheap as well as quality paper soon came to be known and, by the time of European colonization, papermaking had been thoroughly integrated into European culture, so that it was soon carried overseas by the colonists. The first paper mill in the United States, for example, was constructed in Germantown, Pennsylvania, in 1690.

The coming of the machine

Prior to the beginning of the nineteenth century, papermaking was appreciably a hand operation, dependent upon rags for fibers. However, the invention of papermaking machinery in 1799 resulted in a demand for new sources of fiber, and wood was one of the first to be given serious consideration. By 1850, the early imprints of today's pulp and paper industry had made their appearances, and subsequent developments have involved technological improvement and expansion of capital equipment. Modern machinery can produce paper in continuous sheets at the rate of over 20 miles per hour.

LOCATIONAL CONSIDERATIONS

Relative costs of labor and raw materials

By Alderfer and Michl criteria as applied to the United States only, the making of pulp involves intermediate levels of both raw-materials costs and labor costs, whereas the making of paper involves high raw-materials costs and intermediate labor costs, (page 499). In either industry, raw-materials costs are key considerations in plant location.

Pulp mills

The pulp mills, which report raw-materials costs of only intermediate levels with respect to the national average for all manufacturing, nevertheless locate with a careful eye toward raw materials, the world's stands of timber. The pulpwood usually is cut to standard lengths of 6 to 8 feet at or near the spot of initial tree felling. In many situations, the felling occurs in sufficient proximity to waterways or seacoasts for the wood to be floated downstream or rafted along the coast to the pulp mill. The pulp mill, on the one hand, is located as close as possible to the paper mills and ultimate consuming markets and, on the other hand, is located as favorably as possible with respect to the most inexpensive means of receiving the pulpwood—usually water transportation. The problem, then, is to find a site which has access both to the more remote outreaches where forests tend to occur, and to regional markets. This is becoming increasingly difficult in countries which rely predominantly upon exploitation of natural reserves, because the sites of tree felling necessarily shift outward and away from markets as the nearby stands become depleted. Countries which maintain a careful program of cut-and-growth balance, however, frequently have important producing areas not far from densely settled areas; and since such a program involves stability and an assured annual harvest of trees, the locational relationship between source and market becomes more or less permanent.

Paper mills

Paper mills, which are more than twice as numerous in the United States as pulp mills, are found prevailingly in and near heavily populated areas, which provide markets, labor, inexpensive power (because of cheaper bulk rates serving many households and factories), and about one-third of all raw materials in the form of waste paper.

Pulp-and-paper mills

For combined pulp-and-paper mills sites are preferred which on the one hand can receive pulpwood at minimum transportation costs and on the other are near clusters of population and other manufacturing. Not infrequently, they are on the outer margins of densely settled areas, but they may be located, like the pulp mills, with favorable reference to forests, or they may be located, like the paper mills, in good position with respect to market, labor, etc.

Importance of water

Water as an agent in manufacture is vital to both pulp and paper making, and sites in localities are chosen accordingly. Water must be not only ample in amount but within rather closely specified standards in composition. Continuous availability is also important, and sites where freezing can halt water flow or where drought is sufficiently frequent to diminish it are generally avoided.

LEADING NATIONS

The primary producing nations of both pulp and paper are indicated in Fig. 32.1. The familiar pattern of dominance by technically advanced nations is in evidence once again. However, the dominance in this case narrows essentially to two nations—the United States and Canada, which in 1958 were jointly responsible for at least one-half of the output of both pulp and paper. Such a dominance reflects not only the much larger amount of journal and newspaper material available to residents of these two countries than to residents of other technically advanced nations and all underdeveloped nations, but also the increasing tendency on the part of both nations to substitute paperboard for wood, etc., in packaging. Newsprint, paperboard, wrapping paper, and tissue are the primary products which are consumed on a much grander scale in the United States and Canada than elsewhere. With respect to the finer papers, the imbalance is somewhat redressed in that other technically advanced nations consume what might be labeled their "fair share." Canada, it will be noted, predominates in the output of newsprint and the United States in paper other than newsprint.

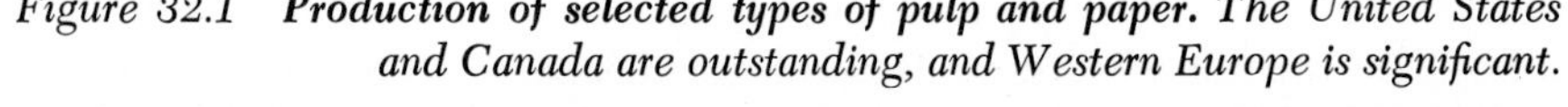

Figure 32.1 ***Production of selected types of pulp and paper.*** *The United States and Canada are outstanding, and Western Europe is significant.*

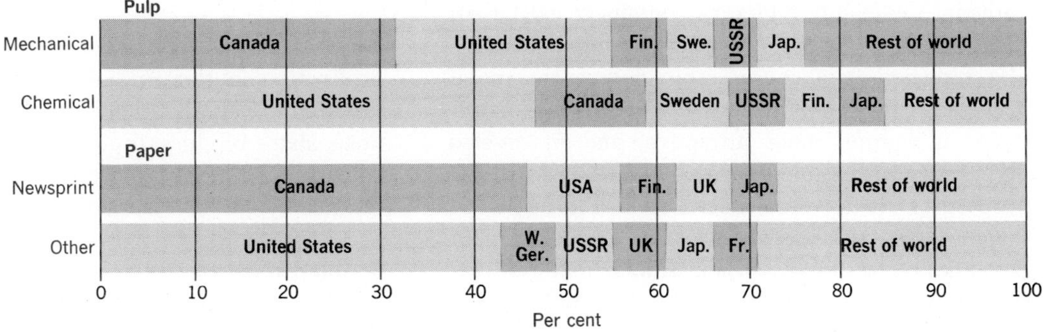

TABLE 32.1

Per capita consumption of paper and paperboard for selected nations

Nation	*Pounds consumed per person*
United States*	386.4
Canada*	280.3
Sweden*	193.2
Norway*	185.0
United Kingdom*	161.1
Australia*	141.5
Belgium*	101.5
Japan*	48.4
Mexico	20.2
Hungary	13.9
Former Belgian Congo	3.4
Ethiopia	0.3

* Usually considered technically advanced.
SOURCE: *The Statistics of Paper, 1957,* American Pulp and Paper Association, New York, 1957, p. 35.

The United States

Consumption. The predominant position of the United States in per capita consumption of paper and paperboard is suggested in Table 32.1. That consumption has approximately quadrupled since 1920, and during the same time the nation's total population has grown by over 70 per cent of the 1920 figure. This has meant a voracious increase in domestic demand for paper and paperboard. The most marked increase has been for paperboard, used for packaging individual items, for shipping cartons, and for numerous other purposes. The emphasis upon semiprepared packaged foods has been a boon for the paperboard industry, for no cheaper and more efficient single-use containers exist than those made of paperboard. Such containers have also replaced to a considerable degree the metal and glass containers for liquids. For cartons, paperboard is lighter, more attractive, and in diverse other ways preferable to wood, and its use for this purpose is rising. Paperboard is also growing in demand for building construction, particularly in combination with gypsum and similar materials for interior walls and partitions. All in all, paperboard alone accounts for over 45 per cent of the total amount of paper and paperboard products consumed in the United States. Newsprint ranks second, being responsible for about 20 per cent of all consumption. Books and printing paper other than newsprint utilize 12 per cent, coarse paper 11 per cent, tissue paper 5 per cent, fine paper 4 per cent, and miscellaneous papers the remainder. The country finds it necessary to be a net importer of both pulp and paper. Net pulp imports amount to approximately 8 per cent of total consumption, and net paper imports, consisting almost entirely of newsprint, amount to approximately 15 per cent of total consumption.

Production. The Census of Manufactures for 1954 lists 252 pulp mills and 680 paper, paperboard, and building-paper-and-board mills in the United States. Although separated for purposes of classification, many pulp and paper mills actually are combined. As is indicated in Fig. 32.1, the United States leads the world in chemically produced wood pulp and in paper other than newsprint. Over one-half of the country's wood-pulp production involves the sulfate process, and nearly one-fifth the sulfite process. The former, it will be remembered, is particularly important in the production of kraft paper and paperboard. In other words, the heaviest emphasis in the nation's pulp and paper production is upon coarse paper and paperboard, particularly the latter—a logical response to demand conditions.

The industry's labor force of some 530,000 places it slightly below the median level in a ranking of two-digit detail industries as classified by the U.S. Bureau of the Budget.

Geographic Distribution of Production. Wood-pulp production in the United States is very unevenly distributed. The Southern states now command the lion's share of the output and offer promise of becoming even more important (Figs. 32.2 and 32.3). Over one-half of the nation's output now comes from the Southern states, which have more than doubled their production since the end of the last world war. Indeed, the postwar growth of the pulp

Figure 32.2 ***Distribution of pulp mills in the United States.*** *There are more small plants than large ones in New England, the Middle Atlantic, and Great Lakes states, but more large than small plants in the South. Why?*

industry has been largely in the Southern states and in the Far West, which ranks a poor second in sectional output. The industry has grown also in the country's Northeast and North Central sections but at a rate beneath that for the nation as a whole.

In paper and paperboard production too, the South recently has come into a position of increased importance, although its output is as yet far below the production of the Northeastern and North Central sections, where waste paper is so important as a raw material (Figs. 32.4 and 32.5). The growth rate in the Far West's paper industry has been markedly above that for the entire nation, but it still lags substantially behind the remainder of the country in total output. However, current growth rates concerning both the pulp and the paper industries of the nation indicate an emergence of the South and of the West to the comparative disadvantage of the manufacturing belt and its adjacent countrysides to the north.

Canada

Although Canada's relatively high per capita consumption of pulp and paperboard places it in a category generally like that of the United States, the country's pulp and paper industry has a significance in its economy that is wholly different from that of the United States. Whereas domestic production in the United States has not kept pace with consumption, Canada's pulp and paper output is considerably in excess of domestic demand, and the nation is a net exporter. Furthermore, the value of its shipments to other lands, currently amounting to over one-fifth of the country's total export revenue, is exceeded by no other commodity. In addi-

Figure 32.3 ***Value of shipments from pulp mills in the United States.*** *Southern and southeastern states lead.*

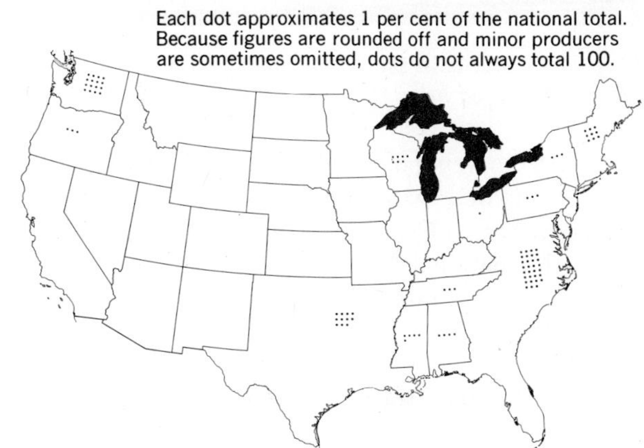

This paper mill is in the Great Smoky Mountains, near Canton in North Carolina. Why is it located here? (Standard Oil Company of New Jersey)

tion, far from being of only intermediate importance when compared with other industries, as in the United States, in Canada the pulp and paper industry is the national leader, whether measured by value of finished product, value added by manufacture, or labor force.

Type of Product. As is indicated in Fig. 32.1, Canada is outstanding on the world scene in the production of mechanical pulp and newsprint. Most of the pulp is made into newsprint by Canadian firms, but almost five-sixths of the newsprint then is exported to the United States. Two-thirds of the remainder goes to other foreign nations, and one-third is retained for domestic use. Of the total pulp production, less than one-half is chemically produced, and about one-half of this is exported—largely to the United States—before further processing. The industry thus depends heavily upon markets in the United States.

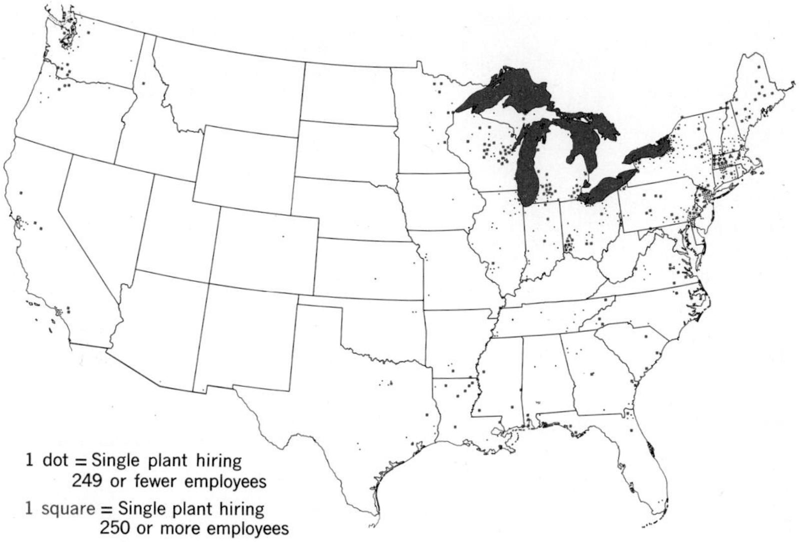

Figure 32.4 **Distribution of paper and paperboard mills in the United States.** *Some are at sites of pulp mills (Fig. 32.2). However, this industry is much more market-oriented than the pulp industry. Why?*

1 dot = Single plant hiring 249 or fewer employees
1 square = Single plant hiring 250 or more employees

Geographical Distribution of the Industry. Of the country's 126 pulp and paper mills, 56 are in Quebec province; 41 in Ontario; 12 in British Columbia; 13 in New Brunswick, Novia Scotia, and Newfoundland; and 4 in the Prairie Provinces. Canada's leading producing section is thus both a mirror image and a continuation, in terms of location, of the producing section in the Northeastern United States. (Or we might say that the reverse is true, depending upon the viewpoint.) However, the Canadian section is fortunate in that it does not have to compete domestically with a section characterized by mild climates and quickly growing trees such as is the case in the Southern states of the United States, and its predominance probably will continue into at least the immediately foreseeable future. To the Far West, production in British Columbia is like that in the Far Western United States, except that Canadian local markets are much smaller and prospects for rapid growth not so bright.

Close Liaison with the United States. Over 80 per cent of the tonnage of Canadian pulp and paper exports goes to the United States. Furthermore, United States capital has been invested in some Canadian pulp and paper enterprises (although not so heavily as in petroleum recovery, certain mining undertakings, and certain chemical industries). Inasmuch as the pulp and paper industry is Canada's largest, and as pulp and paper account for the greatest export revenues, the dependence upon the United States by that sector of Canada's economy is self-evident.

Figure 32.5 **Value of shipments from paper and paperboard mills.** *The South and Far West are expanding, but as yet they are far behind the manufacturing belt. One important reason is that waste paper is an important raw material for this industry, and it is available in greatest quantities within the manufacturing belt.*

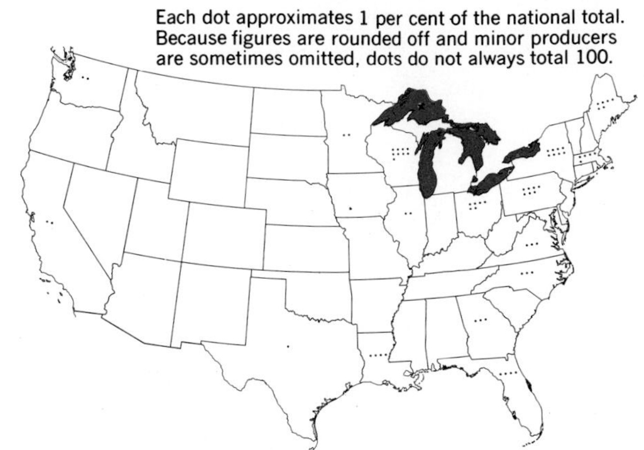

A view of a pulp-and-paper mill at Three Rivers, Quebec Province, Canada. The pulpwood, cut to length, is stored first in the water, then in piles beside the plant. The large amount of water needed in processing is readily available. (Photographic Surveys, Ltd.)

Production elsewhere

Europe, the Soviet Union, and Japan are the leading producers of pulp and paper outside the United States and Canada. The first accounts for about one-fourth of all mechanical pulp, chemical pulp, and newsprint, and about one-third of all paper other than newsprint. No single country can be classed with the United States as a major producer; West Germany, for example, although ranking immediately behind the United States in the output of paper other than newsprint, produces less than one-fifth of the output of the United States. Communist nations as yet are minor producers of pulp and paper, especially the more costly chemical pulps and high-grade papers.

Several northern European nations—Sweden, Finland, and Norway—are noteworthy manufacturers of pulp and paper, especially of pulp. This activity is based upon the presence there of considerably large amounts of forest lands.

However, the small per capita consumption and production in all European countries in comparison with the United States and Canada is a reflection of the lesser reliance in Europe upon packaged goods and upon numerous and large newspapers and popular journals, all replete with advertisements.

There is also a small production of pulp and paper in technically advanced nations other than those discussed above, and in the world's technically underdeveloped lands. Australia, Argentina, Brazil, the Union of South Africa, and India are among the leaders.

INTERNATIONAL TRADE

About one-sixth of all wood pulp enters into international trade before being processed into paper. This movement is largely from Canada to the United States, and from Sweden, Finland, and Norway to Europe and the Soviet Union. Nearly one-fourth of all paper and paperboard products enters international markets. This is overwhelmingly a traffic in newsprint from Canada to the United

States, with lesser flows involving Canadian shipments to the United Kingdom and other European countries, and Fennoscandian shipments to other European nations.

There is a tendency for nations with heavy consumption to levy rather heavy tariffs on incoming finished products if they compete with commodities produced at home, but to admit raw materials and semimanufactured items with little or no duty. The United States admits pulpwood, wood pulp, and newsprint free of duty but assesses a 10 per cent tariff on book and printing paper and a 25 per cent tariff on writing paper. Tariff policies among importing European nations vary in detail but generally follow the pattern outlined above.

REFERENCES

Casey, James P.: *Pulp and Paper: Chemistry and Chemical Technology,* 2 vols., Interscience Publishers, Inc., New York, 1952.

Eddison, John C.: *A Case Study in Industrial Development—The Growth of the Pulp and Paper Industry in India,* Massachusetts Institute of Technology, Cambridge, Mass., 1955.

Final Report, Royal Commission on Canada's Economic Prospects, Ottawa, 1957.

The Future for Paper in the United States, Stanford Research Institute, Menlo Park, Calif., 1956. (Appendixes published separately.)

Our $1,000,000 Pulp and Paper Markets in the Proposed Free Trade Area Countries, American Pulp and Paper Association Export Committee, New York, 1959.

The Outlook for Canadian Forest Industries, Royal Commission on Canada's Economic Prospects, Forestry Study Group, Ottawa, 1957.

Prunty, Merle, Jr.: "Recent Expansion in the Southern Pulp-Paper Industries," *Economic Geography,* **32:** 51–57, 1956.

The Pulp and Paper Industry in the USA, Organization for European Economic Cooperation, Paris, 1951.

Reference Tables, Canadian Pulp and Paper Association, published annually.

Shepard, H. B.: *Hardwood Pulp,* The New England Council, Boston, 1956.

Stafford, Howard A., Jr.: "Factors in the Location of the Paperboard Container Industry," *Economic Geography,* **36:**260–266, 1960.

The Statistics of Paper, 1959, American Pulp and Paper Association, New York, 1959.

Stephenson, J. N., (ed.): *Pulp and Paper Manufacture Series,* 4 vols., McGraw-Hill Book Company, Inc., New York, 1950–1955.

The Western Hemisphere as a Market for U.S. Paper, Board and Paper Products, American Pulp and Paper Association, New York, 1959.

33 MANUFACTURING: TEXTILES

THE TERM "TEXTILE" ACTUALLY MEANS WOVEN FABRIC, MADE BY INTERLACING two separate series of parallel yarns. In practice, it also includes knitted goods, made by interlocking loops into a single yarn; felt goods, made by crushing and intermeshing individual fibers in a method suggestive of newsprint manufacture; bonded goods, made by gluing fibers together; and such other items as lace goods, cordage, and twine. The U.S. Bureau of the Budget has made the following breakdown of textile-mill products:

Cotton, man-made fiber, woolen, and silk fabrics

Knitted materials

Dyed and finished textiles

Woven, tufted, and twisted carpets, mats, and similar floor covers

Yarn and thread

Miscellaneous textile goods, including felt, lace, padding and upholstery filling, processed waste, artificial leather and oilcloth, tire and cord fabric, scoured wool, cordage and twine, and diverse smaller items

In this chapter we shall be concerned primarily with textiles destined for the apparel and cloth-goods industry. Particular emphasis will be on textiles made from cotton, man-made fibers, jute, and wool, which aggregately account for over three-fourths of the world output.

PROCESS

There are many processes in the textile industry, but they can be classified as (1) fiber preparation and yarn manufacture or (2) textile and other end-product manufacture.

Fiber preparation

Nearly all vegetable and animal fibers must first be cleaned and carded. Such processes remove foreign material and excessively short fibers, and align the desired fibers so that they are roughly parallel to each other. These last are then combined into loosely structured ropes called *slivers*, which gradually are drawn, or stretched, until they become exceedingly but uniformly thin. The final stages of drawing take place on the spinning machine, which also twists the fibers into yarn and winds the yarn on a spool. The spindles on the spinning machine thus do the same kind of work as is done by the spindle on a spinning wheel. The end-product yarns may contain as few as eight fiber strands, or as many as one hundred or even more, depending upon their ultimate uses. Specific techniques vary, of course, with the type and condition of the initial fibers.[1] Raw-cotton fibers, or staples, are from ½ inch or less to over 2 inches long, whereas raw-wool fibers range from less than 1 inch to several inches and have been known to exceed 3 feet in length. Man-made fibers, on the other hand, are manufactured by forcing a liquid through extremely tiny holes and are continuous, although they may be chopped later into desired staple lengths (footnote 1).

Whatever the technique of its manufacture, most yarn is then forwarded to weaving *looms*. Before being so forwarded, some cotton and woolen yarns are *sized* (starched) and *beamed* (spooled), and some may be dyed. Not all yarn moves directly to looms; some may be stored or even shipped to another country for weaving.

The processes of fiber preparation, once carried on by hand, now largely are mechanized in technically advanced nations and in some underdeveloped nations as well. However, a sizable labor force, customarily dominated in numbers by women, is needed to initiate and supervise specific operations and to inspect finished products.

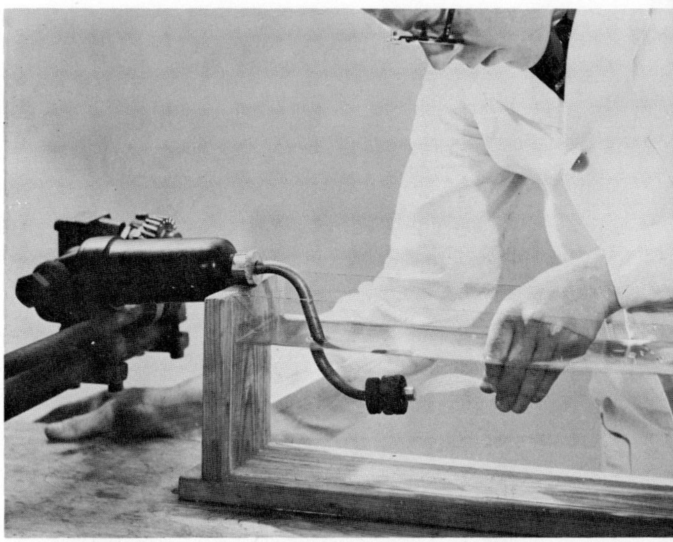

In wet-process rayon making the liquid is extruded through the tiny holes of the spinneret, and becomes a thread on contact with the acid bath. The operation replaces the agricultural production that is necessary for most natural fibers, so that in the man-made-fiber industry we have one extra manufacturing process instead of an agricultural activity in procuring the raw materials. (British Information Services)

Conversion into fabric

Technically advanced weaving processes basically are like those in handicrafts except for the use of much inanimate energy and quasi-automatic machinery. Most of the world's mechanized looms are single-shuttle types, in which a shuttle containing a bobbin of yarn flies under and over consecutive warp strands, leaving in its wake the weft strands that complete the weave. In technically advanced equipment, shuttles change bobbins automatically and with essentially no slowing of motion, so that the weaving is almost continuous. A single operator may be able to tend from seventy-five to one hundred looms in a modern plant. The *single-shuttle*

[1] There is a slight ambiguity in terminology within the textile industry in that the word *fiber* is used on the one hand to refer to individual staples in a cotton boll or individual fleece in wool, etc., and on the other to refer to the continuous, threadlike strands resulting from the intermeshing of the staples or fleece. The continuous strands subsequently are twisted together to make yarn. Man-made fibers are continuous, threadlike strands at the outset. These are called *continuous filament* fibers and may be combined with little or no twisting into a yarn of the same name. When more such fibers are involved and the twist is tighter, the resulting yarn is called *tow*. Sometimes the continuous filament fibers are chopped up into short lengths, like natural staples, and then remeshed into a *staple* fiber, which subsequently is spun into yarn. The lengths of the staples vary appreciably and usually are cut to customer requirements. Still other man-made fibers are known as *monofilaments*. These are essentially continuous filament fibers which are quite thick and are sometimes irregular in cross section, and are converted into bristles for brushes, strands in window screening, and other nontextile commodities.

Spun wool is being wound upon rollers from which it will be transferred eventually to looms (British Information Services).

loom produces the plain, twill, and satin weaves that dominate current industrial output. Special weaves come from *dobby looms,* which turn out geometric designs; *box looms,* which insert different colors in the weft threads; and *jacquard looms,* which produce intricate floral and other unusual patterns that are not necessarily geometric.

The woven fabric may or may not be subjected to chemical bleaching and dyeing or other finishing before being converted into apparel and other finished products. Most fabrics so treated are from single-shuttle looms. Flat fabrics like sheets and blankets require so little additional labor that these are frequently completed at the textile mills.

Felting and bonding

The processes of felting and bonding account for only a small amount of finished goods. In felting, the fibers are pounded until they intermesh into a fabric. In bonding, the fibers are bonded together with resin, a kind of glue. Felting is used particularly for hats, and bonded materials for miscellaneous purposes requiring somewhat thick fabrics.

HISTORICAL BACKGROUND

Process

Spinning and weaving as handicrafts date back at least to 3000 B.C. Until the seventeenth century, wool was the principal fiber of recorded use, although others, notably cotton, doubtless were utilized much more than current records indicate. Western Europe—England, particularly—became interested in cotton at this time and by the middle of the following century was importing cotton in amounts sufficiently large to threaten established status of wool. The early antecedents of modern textile machinery soon appeared, and the famed cotton industry of England and Western Europe was launched. Technological improvement followed immediately, notably in spinning. Meanwhile, other nations also became interested in cotton making. The first United States mill was built in New England in 1790. Not until 1894, however, was the first fully automatic loom invented, and this took place at Burlington, Vermont.

Woolen fabric is being made on the hand loom at the left. Knitted wool comes off the machine at the right. (British Information Services)

Expansion and change in techniques and materials

Once the application of inanimate energy and machinery to textile manufacture had become feasible, the industry expanded rapidly, for textiles are a consumer good needed by every member of so-called civilized society. Mechanized production is currently a reality not only in those nations that are technically advanced but in many of the world's underdeveloped nations, as well. (However, as we shall soon see, handicraft weaving is by no means extinct.)

Perhaps the most dramatic changes in the textile industry have involved raw materials. At the dawn of the nineteenth century, nearly 80 per cent

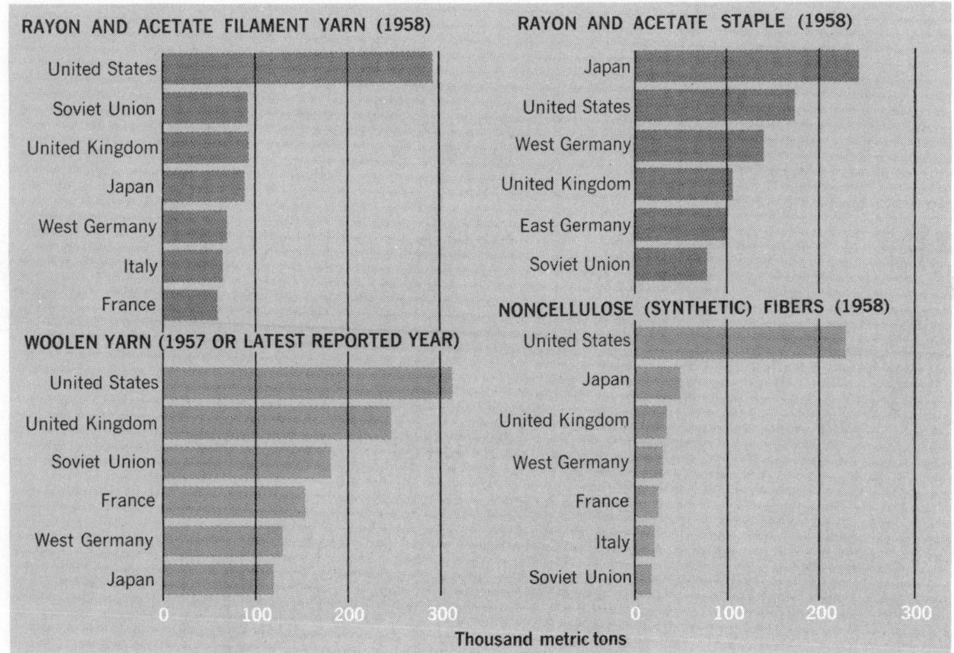

Figure 33.1 ***Leading nations in the production of selected fibers, staple, yarn, and fabric.*** *As used here, staple is continuous filament fiber cut into short lengths to simulate natural staples. Except in cotton yarn and fabrics, only technically advanced nations are shown. Why?*

of all recorded industrial-fiber consumption involved wool, and the remainder was chiefly flax. In all probability, cotton was more important at that time than can now be determined, because many producing countries did not keep adequate census records. One century later, cotton accounted for over 60 per cent of all recorded industrial-fiber consumption, and wool was only one of several lesser fibers that included jute, hemp, silk, and the emerging man-made fibers. Today, cotton accounts for only about 50 per cent of the world industrial-fiber consumption, and the rapidly growing man-man fibers are in second place with over 15 per cent.

Early man-made fibers, rayon and acetate, were derived from cellulose. Since the 1930s, a new group has appeared, of which nylon is the best known. These are made synthetically from combinations and recombinations of molecules occurring initially in petroleum, natural gas, coal tars, corn cobs, molasses, and still other sources, but so altered during several stages of chemical change and combination that they are considered to be synthetic.

LOCATIONAL CONSIDERATIONS

By Alderfer and Michl criteria, the textile industry of the United States can be considered to be high in the cost of both raw materials and labor. (It will be remembered that, by such criteria, any industry with more than 60 per cent of its end-product value attributable to raw-materials costs is termed a high-materials-cost industry, and one with more than 20 per cent of such value due to labor costs is designated a high-labor-cost industry.) This generalization applies to nearly all branches of the industry and to nearly all stages of manufacture. Raw-materials costs amount consistently to 60 per cent or more of the value of product shipped. Labor costs are especially high with respect to cotton broadwoven fabric, the leading product of the entire textile industry in the United States, and amount to over 28 per cent of the value of shipments. Only the industries making cotton and woolen yarn cannot be considered as high-labor-cost industries by the above criteria, and these almost qualify.

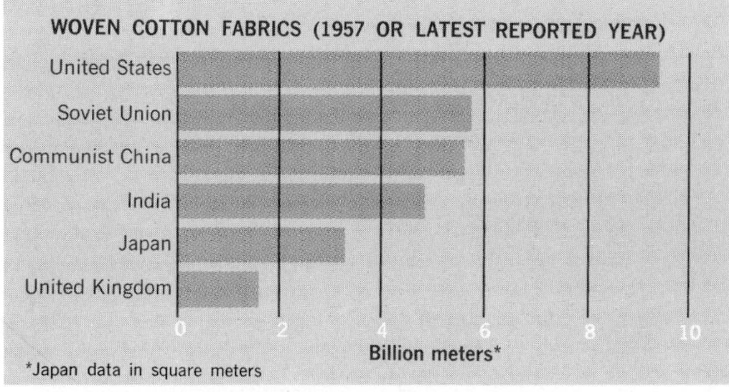

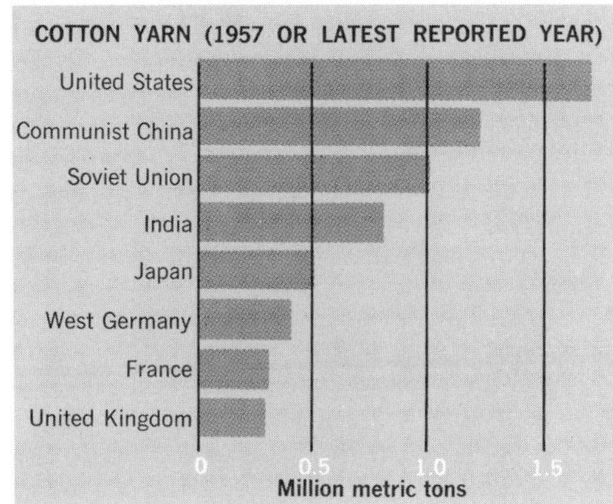

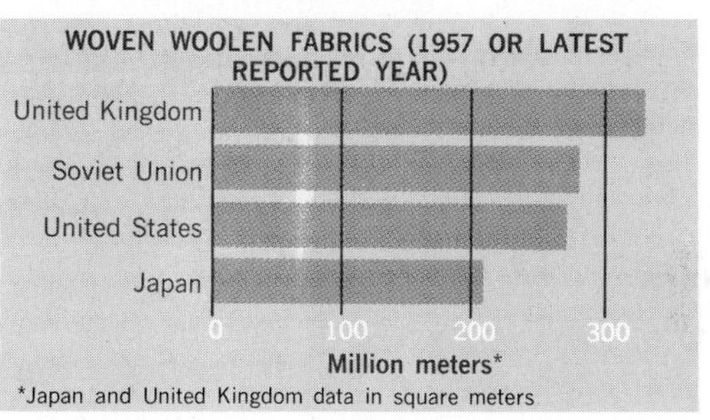

Textile mills hence are located with careful consideration to costs of raw materials and labor. Whether such consideration results in physical location near supplies of raw materials and/or labor, and whether individual plants will be clustered or isolated, depend upon specific requirements of individual establishments. Also important is the type of economy within which each new plant is to function, and how soon an investment is expected to be amortized. The conclusions drawn from conditions in the United States probably are applicable to a degree in Western Europe, as well as in other non-Communist, technically advanced countries, but not so applicable to the planned economies or to nations of low labor costs.

LEADING NATIONS

In the discussion to follow, individual countries will be ranked according to their production of the leading fabric, cotton, and discussed, with respect to cotton, man-made fibers, wool, and occasional lesser fibers. Ranked thus according to cotton-textile production, the leading nations are the United States, the Soviet Union, Communist China, India, Japan, and the United Kingdom (Fig. 33.1). All in all, some forty countries record at least a noteworthy output of cotton textiles; of these, nineteen are usually considered to be technically advanced and twenty-one technically underdeveloped. With its emphasis upon consumer products, the cotton-textile industry obviously is important to technically underdeveloped as well as advanced economies. Even among the six leaders are two, Communist China and India, which usually are classified as underdeveloped.

The United States

Cotton. IMPORTANCE OF DOMESTIC CONSUMPTION. Cotton-textile manufacture in the United States largely satisfies a domestic market that is structured upon both very high per capita consumption (Table 33.1) and a rapidly growing population. As implied in the table, domestic demand for cotton is active despite competition from the man-made fibers, and per capita annual consumption is twice that of any other major world division. Nearly all United States cotton-textile production is chan-

TABLE 33.1

Per capita consumption of cotton, wool, rayon, and acetate in major world divisions, 1938 and 1957 (in pounds)

Years	*United States and Canada*	*Western Europe*	*Oceania*	*Soviet Union and Eastern Europe*	*Latin America*	*Asia*	*Africa*	*World average*
Cotton								
1938	20.7	8.8	8.4	6.8	6.4	4.2	2.4	6.4
1957	21.8	10.8	8.8	10.6	7.3	4.8	3.1	7.5
Wool								
1938	2.4	3.3	5.7	1.3	0.9	0.2	0.2	1.0
1957	2.4	3.7	6.0	1.8	0.9	0.2	0.2	1.1
Rayon and acetate								
1938	2.2	2.9	2.9	0.2	0.4	0.4	0.2	0.9
1957	6.4	5.1	3.4	3.3	1.4	0.6	1.4	2.0
Total cotton, wool, and rayon fibers								
1938	25.3	15.0	17.0	8.3	7.7	4.8	2.8	8.3
1957	30.6	19.6	18.2	15.7	9.6	5.6	4.7	10.6

SOURCE: *Changes in the American Textile Industry,* U.S. Department of Agriculture Marketing Research Division Technical Bulletin 1210, 1959, p. 8. Note that per capita increases have occurred in nearly every fiber and every world division between 1938 and 1957. By and large, however, the most dramatic increases have been registered in technically advanced portions of the world. Despite competition with man-made fibers, per capita consumption of cotton in the United States and Canada is over four times that in Asia and over five times that in Africa. Why should Asia experience the smallest per capita increase in total fiber consumption during the twenty-year period?

Figure 33.2 ***How a bale of cotton is used in the United States cotton-textile industry*** *(after* Changes in the American Textile Industry, *U.S. Department of Agriculture Marketing Research Division Technical Bulletin 1210, 1959).*

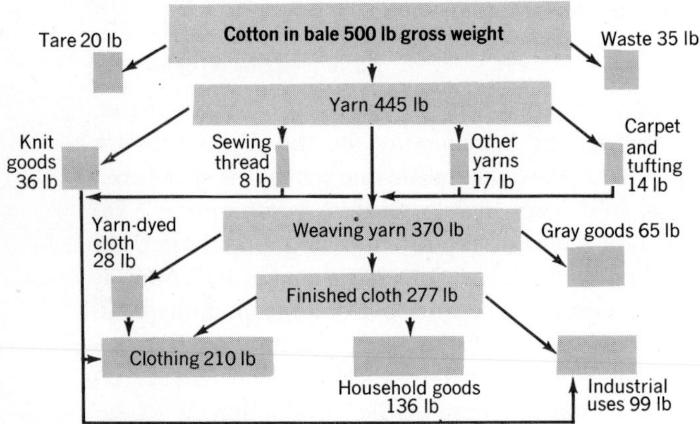

neled into its domestic market, which purchases over one-fifth of the world cotton-textile output. Meanwhile, an import tariff of 20 to 25 per cent on cotton yarn and 30 per cent on cotton cloth discourages the tapping of this market by foreign concerns.

IMPORTANCE AMONG OTHER INDUSTRIES. Cotton yarn, fabrics, and related products account for about two-thirds of the output of all textile products in the United States. In turn, the entire textile industry is one of the more important among the twenty industries classified at the two-digit detail (page 489), by the Bureau of the Budget. Considered by value of sales, that industry ranks ninth among the twenty industries (Table 31.4). Measured by labor force, it ranks sixth, being exceeded only by transportation equipment, food and kindred products, nonelectric machinery, apparel and related products, and primary metals. The textile industry thus is important in terms of both output and livelihood, and the cotton-textile branch is its leading subdivision.

ULTIMATE USE. How is this cotton used in the United States? As indicated in Figure 33.2, about nine-tenths of an average bale goes into yarn, mostly weaving yarn. Ultimately, nearly one-half of all yarn is manufactured into apparel, slightly less than one-third into miscellaneous household goods, and the remainder into diverse industrial commodities.

TRENDS. Cotton, man-made fibers, and wool are the leading fibers consumed in the United States.[2] Their respective percentages of total mill consumption in 1925 and 1958 are shown in Table 33.2.

Cotton's relative position is obviously on the decline; even more than wool, it has lost ground in this sense in competition with man-made fibers. In absolute terms, neither cotton nor wool has lost substantially, but neither have they expanded much over the same time period, as is shown in Table 33.3.

Meanwhile, as we have shown in Chapter 20, agricultural production of cotton has continued to exceed domestic and foreign demand, so that cotton has become a surplus commodity, stockpiled because of oversupply.

LOCATION. The manufacture of cotton yarn and fabric at one time was appreciably a New England enterprise but now is found overwhelmingly in certain cotton-growing states (Table 33.4 and Figs. 33.3 and 33.4). This change has been essentially a migration rather than a differential growth—a building of new plants in the cotton-growing states and an abandoning of old plants in New England and elsewhere rather than a persistent expansion in one part of the country without any decline in another. Interestingly, the trend to the South is still continuing, despite the near-monopoly now enjoyed by the so-called cotton-growing states. Whether national production will stabilize with this heavy concentration in the South, especially the Southeast, despite the generally westward movement of the country's center of gravity with respect to population, remains to be seen.

Why has such a differential rate of growth occurred? One might suspect a physical orientation to raw materials—a suspicion reinforced by the term *cotton-growing states* used frequently for the Southern states by official sources. However, the majority of spindles and the most active consumption of raw cotton are to be found in North and South Carolina and Georgia, notably on the Piedmont. These states are not heavy cotton growers. In contrast, the leading cotton-growing states—Texas, California, Mississippi, and Arkansas—are rather modest mill consumers. Rather long hauls thus are still involved in sending much of the raw cotton to the mill—not so far as to New England, but still not short.[3] Some saving in costs results from the newer arrangements in that nearly all points of cotton-freight origin and destination are within the same freight-rate classification territory (see Chapter 8).

[2] The many lesser fibers manufactured into twine or textiles in the United States include sisal and henequen, jute, abaca, silk, flax, kapok, and hemp. All these account for a total of about one-eighth of all mill fiber consumption.

[3] In the 1956–1957 season, it cost approximately $5.60 to ship a bale of cotton by rail from Dallas, Texas, to the Carolina mills, and $7.05 to the New England mills.

TABLE 33.2

Percentages of total mill consumption of cotton, wool, and man-made fibers in the United States

Commodity	*1925*	*1958*
Cotton	88.3	65.7
Man-made fibers	1.7	28.6
Wool	10.0	5.7

TABLE 33.3

Total mill consumption of cotton, wool, and man-made fibers (in millions of pounds)

Commodity	*1925*	*1958*
Cotton	3,075	3,863
Man-made fibers	58	1,686
Wool	350	336*

* 1957—370

Figure 33.3 ***Distribution of cotton-broadwoven-fabric mills in the United States.*** *The new, large mills are largely in the Piedmont states and the old, smaller ones are in southern New England and in New York and New Jersey.*

The primary motive for the spectacular rise of the Southern mills appears to have been associated with labor costs and degree of unionization. Although a sizable labor force is necessary to supervise cotton-textile operations, that force in general need not be highly skilled. Yet Alderfer and Michl show that labor costs are high (page 499). At one time, labor was far less expensive and less organized into unions in the South than in New England and although the imbalance is somewhat redressed today, it still exists. In addition, some Southern states and localities initially offered special inducements in the forms of reduced taxes and added services. A not inconsiderable attraction is the South's natural environment. Water for processing and generation of hydroelectricity is as available here as farther north and furthermore is not frozen during winter. In addition, the costs of plant and domestic heating are measurably reduced in the comparatively mild subtropical climate of the South.

Figure 33.4 ***Value of shipments from cotton-broadwoven-fabric mills, 1954.*** *The Piedmont states predominate.*

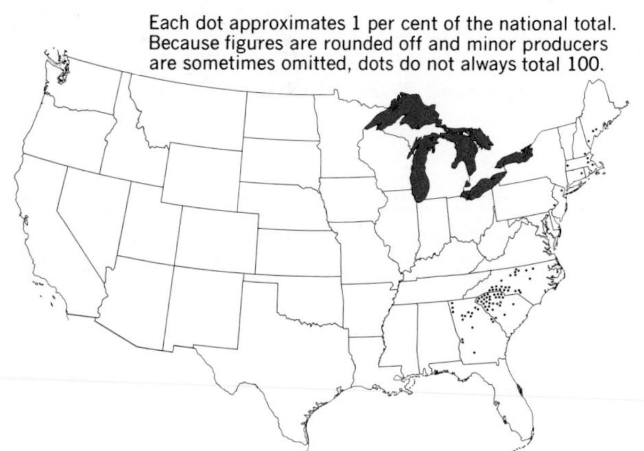

Man-made Fibers. RISING IMPORTANCE. As shown in Tables 33.2 and 33.3, man-made fibers have risen quickly to a position of significance in the United States economy. Currently, they account for approximately one-fourth of the nation's total fiber consumption. A recent survey suggests that by 1975 they may account for over one-half of a total consumption that, in turn, will have increased by over 25 per cent of its 1960 level.[4]

CELLULOSE AND SYNTHETIC FIBERS. We have indicated previously that some man-made fibers are derived from the cellulose of wood (particularly

[4] Joseph Airov, *The Location of the Synthetic Fiber Industry*, Massachusetts Institute of Technology, Cambridge, Mass., and John Wiley & Sons, Inc., New York, 1959, p. 153.

spruce), cotton linters, and other vegetable sources, whereas others are termed *synthetic.* These latter have their initial origin in some natural substance such as coal, natural gas, or petroleum but have been altered so drastically in varying chemical combinations and recombinations that the term *synthetic* describes them more satisfactorily than any other would. Today, textile products from cellulose fibers are termed *rayon* or *acetate,* the former designating regenerated cellulose. The synthetic group includes a wide variety of end products, of which the more common are known by such terms as *Nylon, Dacron,* and *Orlon.*

In the United States, which is a leading producer and consumer of both types, about twice as much rayon and acetate as synthetic fiber is currently being produced. The latter is expanding rapidly, however; it more than doubled its output between 1953 and 1958, during which time domestic production of rayon and acetate actually declined slightly. Synthetic fiber shortly may become the leading man-made fiber in this country.

USES. Rayon and acetate are used for tire cordage, woven materials, and knitted goods. The first of these outlets accounts for nearly one-half of the total output. Nylon and other synthetic fibers are used for knitted hosiery and woven apparel, as well as for cloth other than apparel and for cordage going into tires and other industrial products. Some man-made fibers are blended with natural fibers into woven fabrics.

TABLE 33.4

Cotton consumed by mills in selected divisions of the United States, 1890 to 1958, in per cent

Region	*1890*	*1910*	*1930*	*1958*
New England	60	43	19	4
Cotton-growing states	20	49	78	96
Other states	20	8	3	n

n = negligible.

SOURCE: Data before 1930 are computed from Erich W. Zimmerman, *World Resources and Industries,* Harper & Brothers, New York, 1951, p. 343; subsequent data from "Changes in the American Textile Industry," U.S. Department of Agriculture Marketing Research Divisions Technical Bulletin 1210, 1959, p. 72.

LOCATION OF PLANTS. The man-made-fiber industry involves an initial step in manufacture that is unnecessary in natural-fiber processing—namely, the making of the fiber itself. In other words, manufacturing replaces agriculture for this step. Virginia contains more fiber-making plants than any other state, in terms of either rayon and acetate fibers or synthetic fibers (Fig. 33.5). Tennessee, Alabama,

Figure 33.5 ***Distribution of synthetic-fiber plants in the United States.*** *These are plants not making use of cellulose as a raw material. The rayon, acetate, and other man-made-fiber mills making use of cellulose as a raw material are found chiefly in Tennessee, Maryland, Ohio, Pennsylvania, West Virginia, and Connecticut.*

Figure 33.6 ***Distribution of synthetic-broadwoven-fabric mills in the United States.*** *The fibers from the plants mapped or described in Fig. 33.5 come to these mills for processing into fabric. Older, smaller plants predominate in the northeastern states, and newer, larger plants predominate in the Piedmont South.*

Pennsylvania, and neighboring states in and near the Appalachians also are important. Plants producing both categories of man-made fibers appear to be oriented physically to labor and market. For rayon and acetate, the raw materials, in the form of forests and cotton, are comparatively near. Plants making synthetic fibers have easy access to coal and can obtain natural gas and petroleum relatively cheaply from the Texas and Louisiana fields. Markets, which are the spinning and weaving mills, also are an attraction. Their influence is manifested appreciably through savings in transportation costs rather than administrative structure, because not very many of the fiber-making plants are interlocked managerially with the spinning and weaving mills. These mills are found especially in the vicinity of the cotton-weaving and -spinning mills, with nearly one-half of the total labor force in North and South Carolina (Figs. 33.6 and 33.7). However, a not inconsequential number is located farther north, in New England (containing over one-fifth of the nation's synthetic-fabric labor force) and the Middle Atlantic states (over one-sixth). The industry's position remains virtually the same when measured by value of product.

Figure 33.7 ***Value of shipments from synthetic-broadwoven-fabric mills in the United States.***

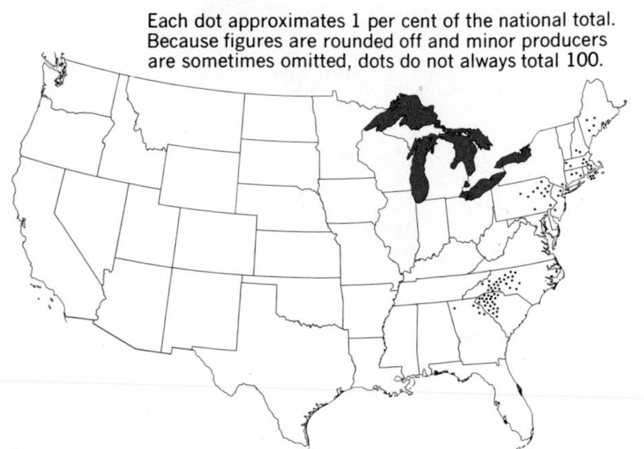

Wool. VOLUME OF PRODUCTION. The woolen-textile industry, like cotton, has just about maintained its average annual volume of output during the past thirty years but, like the cotton-textile industry, has declined relatively in competition with man-made fibers. Its role in the nation's textile industry for some twenty years is suggested in Table 33.5. Only in a comparatively small volume of miscellaneous consumer goods has wool's share increased. The importance of apparel, carpets and rugs, and knit goods as end products is shown in Figure 33.8.

LOCATION. Much of the nation's wool industry has remained in the Northeast. Over one-half of the labor force involved in the production of woven wool fabrics is found in New England, with over one-fifth in Massachusetts alone. New England remains the leader when the industry is considered by number of plants and value of shipments (Figs. 33.9 and 33.10). The Middle Atlantic states of New York, New Jersey, and Pennsylvania also are important, and the Piedmont South is significant. Knitting mills, especially, are generally farther south—in the Carolinas and the Middle Atlantic states. A southward shift of the center of gravity of wool manufacture is taking place, although it is delayed in comparison to that of cotton production and also is of much smaller proportions. By and large, locational considerations analogous to those of the cotton industry are also important with respect to wool. However, the attraction of raw materials, such as it is, is lacking, because most domestic wool comes from the West, and imported wool is as easily available at northerly coastal locations as at those farther south. The almost phenomenal growth of the man-made-fiber industry also has acted as a deterrent to southward expansion, for interest in setting up and equipping costly new establishments wanes when the total demand for the product is on the relative decline.

Organization of the Textile Industry. ADMINISTRATIVE STRUCTURE. By and large, the nation's textile industry is not dominated by a few corporations to the extent characteristic of some other industries. The 1958 Census of Manufactures indicates that approximately 28 per cent of all United States employment in cotton broad-woven fabrics is accounted for by the industry's eight largest companies. In comparison, 75 per cent of all employment in motor vehicles and parts, 69 per cent in steelworks and rolling mills, and 51 per cent in miscellaneous organic chemicals is concentrated in the eight largest companies of the respective industries. Wool and man-made-fiber firms also are in comparatively small concerns, except in so far as the latter is a part of the nation's chemical industry. (Actual making of man-made fibers frequently is carried on by chemical firms.) However, textile manufacture is not necessarily a highly deconcentrated industry administratively; other industries

TABLE 33.5

Types of fibers consumed in the manufacture of specified end products in the United States, in per cent

End use of fiber	*Cotton*	*Wool*	*Man-made fibers*
Apparel			
1937	70.1	17.8	12.1
1957	66.2	13.2	20.6
Home furnishings			
1937	81.0	16.1	2.9
1957	64.7	10.5	24.8
Other consumer goods			
1937	75.9	5.8	18.3
1957	68.8	10.0	21.2
Industrial uses			
1937	95.2	3.8	1.0
1957	53.8	2.6	43.6
All end uses			
1937	80.4	12.2	7.4
1957	63.5	10.0	26.5

SOURCE: "Changes in the American Textile industry," U.S. Department of Agriculture Marketing Research Divisions Technical Bulletin 1210, 1959, p. 12.

Figure 33.8 ***How a bale of wool is used in the United States woolen-textile industry*** *(after* Changes in the American Textile Industry, *U.S. Department of Agriculture Marketing Research Division Technical Bulletin 1210, 1959).*

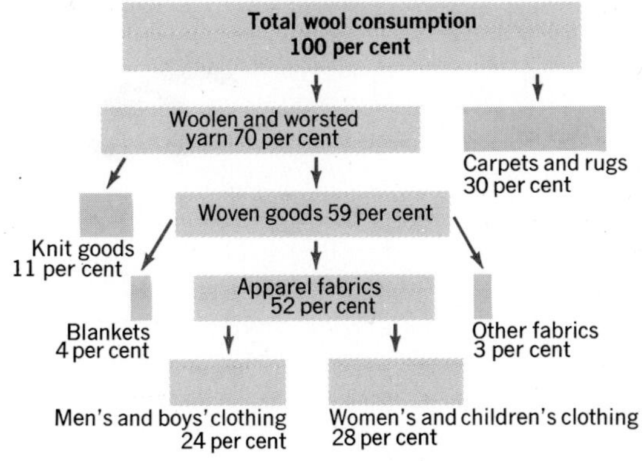

Figure 33.9 ***Distribution of woolen- and worsted-fabric mills in the United States.*** *Both new and old mills are found in New England, but chiefly newer, larger mills are to be seen elsewhere.*

are pyramided even less. For example, only 18 per cent of all employment in the making of men's and boys' suits, and only 7 per cent of all employment in sawmills and planing mills, is restricted to the eight largest companies in each industry.

PLANT SIZE. When the focus is narrowed from firms to plants, the making of textiles becomes a larger-scale activity. Using labor force as a yardstick, we find that an average of 130 workers are employed per plant in the entire textile industry. While this average is not so high as that for transportation equipment (321) or primary metals (200), it is much higher than that for fabricated metals (58) or apparel (38), and is much higher than the national average for all manufacturing (55).

Figure 33.10 ***Value of shipments from woolen- and worsted-fabric mills in the United States.***

INTEGRATION. The woolen-textile industry of the United States is rather thoroughly integrated—i.e., most of the various stages of manufacture are carried on within single mills rather than forwarded from one specializing mill to another. In the cotton industry, fiber preparation, spinning, and weaving frequently are done under a single roof, but finishing operations often are completed elsewhere. In contrast, the man-made-fiber industry tends to involve the making of the fibers by one set of mills and the spinning, weaving, and finishing elsewhere.

The Soviet Union

Textile products have not enjoyed a high priority in the series of plans through which the Soviet Union achieved its marked economic growth. As a result, the textile industry has not grown so rapidly there as have industries producing metals, metal products, chemicals, and energy. Nevertheless, per capita output and consumption have increased (Table 33.1), and the industry's growth rate in the current Seven-Year Plan is expected to be at least the equal of that for all manufacturing in the country. Among the specific fibers, primary attention is being given to man-made-fiber output, which, as an integral part of the chemical industry that has received more emphasis, has expanded rapidly. This heavy emphasis upon man-made fibers is documented in Table 33.1, as is the country's marked emphasis upon cotton and very moderate emphasis upon wool.

Historically, the textile industry of the Soviet Union has been in the west, particularly the vicinity of Moscow. The majority of such plants still are located there, with a heavy concentration in the city and its suburbs as well as immediately to the northeast. Other mills are found along the Baltic coast, in the Ukraine, and especially to the north of the Caucasus Mountains. Newer mills have been constructed in some oasis cities along southern Soviet Central Asia as well as in cities of the Urals and eastward along the general route of the Trans-Siberian Railway. Cotton-textile mills, which employ about one-half of the total textile labor force, are found in all areas of textile manufacturing. Woolen mills are especially numerous in the vicinity of Moscow, as are flax mills. Woolen mills also are conspicuously present along the middle Volga River and adjacent countrysides. Both the cotton and the woolen mills depend chiefly upon domestic supplies and markets.

Communist China

Communist China inherited from the deposed government and foreign investors a substantial cotton textile industry concentrated especially within and near the port city of Shanghai. Some mills also had been built by Japan in Manchuria, and there were still others in other parts of the country. All now have been placed under government ownership. Reportedly, the industry has been emphasized in Communist China's planned economic growth, processing largely for the immense domestic market but also exporting to an increasing degree. The country now ranks second in the world in output of cotton yarn, and third in cotton fabric (Fig. 33.1). In distribution, the industry continues to be concentrated in Shanghai but also exhibits a tendency toward an evenly patterned scattering of plants throughout effective Communist China and into the more sparsely populated sections of the country's bleak and inhospitable west. This is particularly true of the cotton-textile industry, the mainstay of the group. The silk industry is conspicuous in and near Shanghai and at other sites in the south central portions of the country but is represented at isolated sites elsewhere. The comparatively few linen and woolen mills are largely in the vicinity of Shanghai but also are found in a few other places.

The extent of mechanization and automation of the industry can be inferred from the data in Table 33.6. Each average yarn worker in Communist China tends only about one third as many spindles as his counterparts in the United States and Japan. Fabric workers fare better. Obviously, Communist China is emphasizing fabric more than yarn in the modernization of its textile industry.

Reportedly, textile production currently amounts to about one-fourth of all manufacturing output in Communist China. The country appears to be placing an emphasis upon this commodity, and the very latest preliminary reports indicate that it may now exceed the Soviet Union in cotton-textile output.

India

Both India and Communist China are substantial producers and consumers of cotton textiles. For a time after the Second World War, India was con-

TABLE 33.6

*Spindles and looms per worker in selected nations, 1953**

Nation	*Number of spindles (for yarn) per worker*	*Number of looms (for fabric) per worker*
United States	1,500–2,100	60 (automatic)
Japan	1,600–2,000	30–40 (automatic)
United Kingdom	800	6 (ordinary)
Communist China	674	23 (automatic)
India	380	2 (ordinary)

* Data for Communist China are for 1956.

SOURCE: *Economic Survey of Asia and the Far East, 1958*, United Nations Economic Commission for Asia and the Far East, Bangkok, 1959, p. 122.

Some manufacturing in underdeveloped economies is technically advanced. This is a view of the spinning section of a cotton-textile mill in India. (Government of India Press Information Bureau)

sidered to rank in third place in total world production, ahead of Communist China. Available data now assign India to the fourth-ranking position, even if allowance is made for considerable exaggeration in Communist Chinese reports. Furthermore, the rate of growth in Communist China's textile industry appears to be exceeding that of India's, and there is reason to expect the current ranking to continue into the foreseeable future.

Internal Technical Advance and Underdevelopment. Most classifications designate the Indian economy as underdeveloped. By and large, it is. However, just as a technically advanced economy can have pockets of underdevelopment, so can an underdeveloped economy have pockets of technical advance. Indeed, so can a given industry. The textile industry of India is a good example. Approximately ten million people in that country are engaged in hand-loom production—a work force so large that it is exceeded in India only by that in agriculture. These ten million people, however, are responsible for the output of only about one-fifth of India's total cotton cloth. Some 800,000 workers, employed in textile mills that have been inherited mainly from the recent historical period of British domination and that were constructed in general accordance with modern specifications, produce the remaining four-fifths.[5] The factory labor force, while small in comparison with that engaged in hand-loom work, is outstandingly large in comparison with other manufacturing in India. It makes up over 30 per cent of the country's manufacturing labor force. Ranking far behind is the second industry, food processing, which accounts for only 12 per cent.

Location. India's cotton-textile production first became important as a factory industry in Bombay

[5] In India, these data reflect also a basic difference in outlook between two influential leaders and close personal friends—Mohandas Gandhi and Jawaharlal Nehru. Once political independence was obtained, the former preferred an emphasis upon handicrafts and cottage industries as an adjunct to agriculture. In this championing of the rural way of life, Gandhi was a kind of twentieth-century Thomas Jefferson. Nehru, however, appreciated the inevitability of the Industrial Age, even in its implications to underdeveloped countries, and favored the factory system. The death of Gandhi just as India was commencing to function as an independent nation left Nehru's thinking without serious challenge on one of the few basic issues concerning which the two men differed seriously.

and Ahmadabad and adjacent places on the western coast. Subsequently, it has spread to its rather diffused location in many parts of the country, with an emphasis upon the Madras vicinity of the southern peninsula. Faced with competition from these newer mills, the Bombay-Ahmadabad mills have tended to specialize in finer materials, and to depend at least partially upon imported cotton fibers of medium to long staple. The other mills tend to use domestic cotton, most of which is short-staple. Hand looms are found throughout India but are especially numerous near Madras, where over one-third of the country's hand-loom workers are concentrated.

General Features of Production and Trade. Domestic cotton supplies approximately seven-eighths of total manufacturing and handicraft demand, and imported cotton the remainder. The present plans of the national government do not emphasize the increasing of current capacity but do stress the maximizing of production within that capacity. A major liability to the industry is old equipment, much of which is sufficiently worn that under other circumstances it would be discarded. Much of this machinery will have to be replaced soon. The domestic market consumes about nine-tenths of total output, and the remainder is exported. At present there is no tariff upon incoming foreign goods that compete with the domestic output, despite the possibility of competition from Japan and elsewhere. In contrast, a small export tariff has been levied upon coarser, lower-grade fabrics that are in general home demand, thus discouraging their export. All in all, there is little government intervention in the cotton-textile industry, even though that industry is very much a part of the short-term plans of over-all economic development. Other, more pressing aspects of the economy are receiving more careful official attention, and the cotton-textile industry is being allowed to function almost completely under private ownership and management. The government's relationship with hand-loom operators is somewhat dichotomous. On the one hand, provision has been made for the slow conversion of hand looms to power looms and mills—15,000 in the First Five-Year Plan, and 20,000 in the Second. On the other hand, the Gandhi concept of the desirability of rural self-sufficiency persists, and hand looms are considered to be a vital aspect of such self-sufficiency. So, in 1949, the government decreed that at least one-third of all textiles purchased by it should be hand-woven. Tax concessions and direct financial aid also have been made available to hand-loom operators by the government. The core point of governmental concern appears to be a desire to mechanize and yet a fear that such mechanization will add still more to the already high number of currently unemployed or underemployed persons.

Jute and Other Textiles. The manufacture of coarse cloth and sacking from jute is a secondary but important industry in India, accounting for nearly 10 per cent of the country's manufacturing labor force. Concentrated almost entirely within Calcutta and its immediate hinterland, the industry produces over two-thirds of the world's jute fabric. Traditionally, its raw material has been grown in the adjacent delta lowland of the Ganges and Brahmaputra Rivers, immediately to the east. However, as we have indicated in Chapter 20, the inclusion of most of that delta in East Pakistan left the Indian mills without a good source of domestic supply and the Pakistan growers without a satisfactory outlet for their raw jute. Political friction between the two countries thus interfered seriously with a once integrated activity. As a result of this friction, some fields in India that could be growing food crops are being planted to jute, and some new mills are being built in Pakistan to process jute. However, some jute continues to move from the fields of Pakistan to mills of India in the traditional manner.

Minor fabrics produced in India include wool and rayon, but neither is made in substantial quantities.

Japan

A century ago Japan had no modern textile mills. By 1938, it ranked second only to the United States in mill consumption of raw cotton. Losing more than three-fourths of its spindles during the Second World War, the country has largely replaced them with new and more modern equipment, and again is a world leader in cotton consumption, production, and exports.

There are many reasons for such phenomenal growth and regrowth; the most potent involves cheap labor costs, as is indicated in Table 33.7. Such costs result from a combination of low-wage but efficient labor with equally efficient machines. Female labor is utilized widely.

Japan's cotton-textile industry, essentially privately owned and dominated by ten leading corporations which own over three-fifths of all spindles and looms, is located chiefly in or near metropolitan areas and large cities. Tokyo, Nagoya, Osaka, and Okayama are outstanding among a sizable number that also includes Hiroshima, Kure, Kobe, Wakayama, and Shizuoka. Many of these are seaports, and access to foreign as well as home markets is thus assured.

Japan is not only a leading producer of cotton yarn and fabrics but also is an important producer of woolen yarns and fabrics and man-made fibers and cloth (Fig. 33.1). The woolen mills are located in more or less the same general areas as the cotton-textile units. At present, Japan ranks sixth in world production of woolen yarns and fourth in output of woolen fabrics. The man-made-fiber plants tend to be in somewhat smaller towns of the southern section of Honshu, the main island, as well as in similar towns in the southern islands of Kyushu and Shikoku. The country is foremost in world output of rayon and acetate fabrics, and second only to the United States in noncellulose (synthetic) fibers.

TABLE 33.7

Relationship of labor costs to total costs in cotton-textile industries of selected nations

Nation	*Per cent of total costs due to labor costs*
United States	28.1
India	23.4
Philippines	18.0
Japan	6.9

SOURCE: For the United States, Table 8.1; for other countries, *Economic Survey of Asia and the Far East, 1958*, United Nations Economic Commission for Asia and the Far East, Bangkok, 1959, p. 123.

As important as the *status quo* in Japanese production is the rapid rise in its output once recovery from war had been achieved. Continued expansion appears to be restricted only by markets. At present, one of every 3 tons of Japanese cotton cloth is exported. Competition from expanding Communist China and India as well as from Europe, the Soviet Union, and the United States will attempt to stabilize or even reduce this ratio. However, Japan has demonstrated a know-how of survival in world competition, and only sharply restrictive measures will keep her products from moving abroad. An increased measure of such restriction may well be in the offing, for many of the smaller underdeveloped countries to which Japan long has looked for markets are beginning to develop their own textile industries. With the countries' own population growth and resultant market reduced by a birth-control program, the selling of Japanese fabrics will become increasingly difficult. Difficulties, however, are not new to the dynamic Japanese textile industry.

The United Kingdom and Western Europe

In the United Kingdom and the rest of Western Europe, where the modern textile industry and the Industrial Revolution more or less were initiated together, the momentum of leadership has been surrendered appreciably to the producing areas discussed above. Only in woolen yarns and woolen woven fabrics does the production from individual European nations remain extremely high on the world scene, and even here there is a serious challenge or even a surpassing of that production by other nations. Considered as a single unit, however, Western Europe is an active contender in the production of all major yarns and fabrics.

The United Kingdom leads with respect to most textiles, being exceeded by other European producers only in cotton yarn and rayon and acetate staple (Fig. 33.1). Before the First World War, this one nation exported nearly two-thirds of the world's cotton cloth that entered international markets. Its Lancashire district, focused on Manchester, long has enjoyed a reputation for specialized output: the raw fibers entered mills farthest from that hub city and gradually made their way through a series of manufacturing stages—each stage providing livelihood for specific cities or towns grouped in arcs around Manchester—until finally they entered finished fabric plants of the central city itself. Of course, such production still continues, but it is no longer the monarch of world output that it once was. Among the advantages of location west of the Pennines is a climate with consistently high moisture content, so that individual threads do not dry out and break during processing. The woolen mills were and are concentrated in the same general latitudes but on the eastern limbs of the Pennines, as well as in the Glasgow vicinity to the north. The man-made-fiber industry is also conspicuous near the Pennines, especially to the west and south. All industries have scattered representations elsewhere in the United Kingdom.

Producing districts on the continent are found especially to the north of France and across the border in Belgium and Holland; along the Rhine River between France and West Germany; along the Rhone River and in the Alps Mountains to the east; in northern and central Italy; in the province of Saxony in East Germany; in southern Poland and across the border in northern Czechoslovakia. West Germany, France, and Italy appear most frequently on lists of leading producers.

The decline in cotton-textile output in Europe generally has been absolute as well as relative—dramatically so in the United Kingdom, which at mid-century produced only half as much cotton cloth as twenty years earlier. Wool output has increased modestly in most European nations. While these somewhat unfavorable conditions have been offset somewhat by a rise in man-made-fiber output, they have been due largely to competition from Japan, India, the Soviet Union, Communist China, and other large populations which once imported but now have sizable home industries to supply their domestic markets or may even export. (In other words, the comments in the preceding section relative to the growing competition faced by Japan apply also to Europe and the United States, but even more forcibly there, because of differences in labor and other production costs between the Occident and the Orient as well as differences in location relative to importing countries, many of which are in eastern and southern Asia.) There does not appear to be much expectation of an upturn in European textile output; a recent survey by the United Nations reveals a rate of growth between the 1926-to-1929 period and 1959 in the textile industry of ten Western European nations to be substantially beneath that of all manufacturing in the same nations.[6]

Production in other nations

Between 1913 and 1950, the amount of cotton consumed in the world increased by slightly more than 40 per cent. During the same time period, the number of producing nations for which reports are available more than doubled. Many of these newcomers have commenced operations since the Second World War, and several produce only small amounts of yarn, thread, and/or fabric; but there is a definite striving toward whole or partial self-sufficiency on the part of many technically underdeveloped nations. Eastern Europe, Latin America, the Middle East, and the Far East all are represented in the new producers, and we can anticipate with some confidence that some newly independent countries of Africa and elsewhere soon will be added.

INTERNATIONAL TRADE

Despite the many nations now engaged in textile production, only a few are active trading countries. Japan, the United States, and the United Kingdom account for nearly two-thirds of all cotton exports in the non-Communist realm, and Japan alone accounts for nearly two-fifths. About one-third of the Japanese production and almost as much of British

[6] *Economic Survey of Europe in 1959*, United Nations Economic Commission for Europe, Geneva, 1960, chap. 1, p. 24.

production is exported. The United States exports about 5 per cent of its output, and India sometimes exports as much as 15 per cent of its annual production. The British colony of Hong Kong is a major importer and exporter of cotton cloth. All in all, however, cotton exports are declining absolutely as well as relatively in non-Communist countries, having dropped from 610,000 metric tons in 1938 to 590,000 metric tons in 1956.[7]

[7] *Economic Survey of Asia and the Far East, 1958,* United Nations Economic Commission for Asia and the Far East, Bangkok, 1959, p. 125.

Among Communist nations, Communist China recently has emerged as an important exporter of cotton, which amounted in 1956 to over 12 per cent of the value of all exports to the Soviet Union and which is being sent also to Burma, Indonesia, Hong Kong, and other non-Communist areas. Such exportation has been partially a result of increased production and partially of a change in policy after 1952—a change emphasizing exports regardless of domestic demand.

The volume of trade in other finished textiles is minor compared to that in cotton. The leading nations produce largely for their domestic markets.

REFERENCES

Airov, Joseph: *The Location of the Synthetic Fiber Industry,* Massachusetts Institute of Technology, Cambridge, Mass., and John Wiley & Sons, Inc., New York, 1959.

Alderfer, E. B., and H. E. Michl: *Economics of American Industry,* McGraw-Hill Book Company, Inc., New York, 1957. (Especially chaps. 19–24.)

Changes in the American Textile Industry, U.S. Department of Agriculture Marketing Research Division Technical Bulletin 1210, 1959.

Economic Survey of Asia and the Far East in 1958, United Nations Economic Commission for Asia and the Far East, Bangkok, 1959. (Especially pp. 118–126.)

Economic Survey of Europe in 1959, United Nations Economic Commission for Europe, Geneva, 1960.

Economic Survey of Latin America in 1957, United Nations Economic Commission for Latin America, New York, 1959.

Hague, Douglas C.: *The Economics of Man-made Fibers,* Gerald Duckworth & Co., Ltd., London, 1957.

Hess, Katharine P.: *Textile Fibers and Their Use,* J. B. Lippincott Company, Philadelphia, 1958.

The Outlook for the Canadian Textile Industry, Royal Commission on Canada's Economic Prospects, Ottawa, 1956.

34 MANUFACTURING: FOODS

THE MODERN KITCHEN OF A TECHNICALLY ADVANCED HOME IS AN ANACHRONISM. On the one hand, it contains enough equipment to supply food to a small restaurant—electric or gas ranges, frequently with double ovens and automatic controls; refrigerators; freezer units; mixers; beaters; blenders; choppers; whittlers; disposal units; dishwashers. On the other hand, in very many homes this equipment appears surprisingly untarnished—scarcely used, except perhaps, for a burner or two on the range. The secret lies in still another piece of equipment found in every kitchen—a piece which, in truly modern kitchens, appropriately is powered electrically. This is the can opener, without which many a modern housewife would suffer frustration and despair. Time was when canned foods were not so tasty as home-cooked ones. Today canned foods are quite tasty, although their labels still evidence a need to assure us that the contents are "just as good as mother or grandmother used to make."

What is the import of all of this food processing? Simply that in technically advanced societies food processing largely has been taken out of the kitchen and placed in the factory. Moreover, there is every indication that the trend will continue into the future even more actively. Food processing is now a major industry in almost every technically advanced country. By and large, it is not so important as a livelihood occupation in many underdeveloped countries, because in those countries it is still appreciably a home activity, done as part of the daily chores. It is, however, important to the populations of some countries which export agricultural commodities—whether they are technically advanced or underdeveloped. We therefore have two overlapping aspects of commercial food processing: (1) the preparation of foods within technically advanced countries for their large domestic markets as well as for some foreign consumers and (2) the preparation of foods within both technically advanced and underdeveloped nations which export sizable quantities of agricultural commodities.

What specific industries and commodities are involved? The U.S. Bureau of the Budget has listed the following under the heading "Food and Kindred Products":

Meat products
Dairy products
Canned and preserved fruits, vegetables, sea food, etc.
Grain-mill products

Bakery products
Sugar
Confectionery and related products
Beverages
Miscellaneous food preparations and kindred products

This classification basically is similar to those of most other countries, although some include tobacco as a "kindred product" whereas the United States considers tobacco separately.

PROCESS

There are so many processes in food preparation that meaningful generalization is difficult. Cattle, hogs, and sheep are converted into meat and other products; milk is preserved for consumption while fresh after pasteurization, or changed to butter, cheese, ice cream, etc.; fruits and vegetables are canned; grains are separated into bran and kernels, and the latter ground into flour; bread and pastries are baked; sugar is derived from beets and cane; and each of the many other foods is obtained in a manner peculiar to its own requirements. There is, of course, some overlap in method, but, by and large, the processes are unique for each food industry and frequently for subbranches.

HISTORICAL BACKGROUND

The preservation of certain foods by salting and drying has long been practiced. Indeed, one of the major trade commodities in classical times as well as the comparatively recent age of the Hanseatic League was salt for food preservation. Such preservation, however, was carried on largely as a home activity. The basis for an industry was not present until the early part of the nineteenth century, when Nicolas Appert, a French confectioner and baker, invented rudimentary canning techniques in response to a prize offered by the French government. The subsequent work of Louis Pasteur placed the canning process on a more scientific basis by offering a rational explanation as to how it worked—i.e., that cooking foods removed bacteria and that, if the foods were sealed immediately in a can and thus prevented from having contact with the open, bacteria-laden air, they would remain unspoiled for long periods of time. By the middle of the nineteenth century, canning was being practiced in small factories of England, France, and the United States, and subsequently was adopted elsewhere. The advantages of freezing certain foods were known as early as 1870, but widespread utilization of this process did not occur until the 1930s, when techniques of quick freezing were developed. Now, there is experimentation in preservation of foods through radiation, and storage at normal temperatures in very inexpensive containers. Whether these will become trade practices remains to be seen.

Of course, the advent of food-processing industries was not necessarily entirely dependent upon development of techniques of food preservation. Many grain-mill products and sugar, for example, can be stored for quite long periods without excessive harm if natural temperature and moisture conditions are not unfavorable. It is perhaps more accurate to say that preservation techniques have been very important among a rather long list of developments, such as the increasing ease and decreasing cost of energy obtainment, the increasing efficiency of mechanized production, and the increasing specialization of labor—developments which affected all manufacturing as well as food processing. Nevertheless, food processing in factories is fundamentally a younger, newer industry than factory output of iron and steel, and can be said almost to have begun in the twentieth century and to have reached a grand scale of operation only since the Second World War.

SIZE AND LOCATION

Unlike many industries, food processing tends to be a small-company–small-plant industry (in economies where companies exist; in others, it is still a small-plant industry). This is especially true if food processing is compared with the making of transportation equipment, industrial metals, etc., and it obtains in technically advanced as well as underdeveloped economies. In the United States, for example, there are over forty-two thousand establishments involved in food processing, whereas there are only slightly more than fifty-three hundred establishments making transportation equipment—despite the fact that the total labor forces of each of these two industries are about equal. There is evidence that other technically advanced countries, as well as such underdeveloped ones as engage in the activity, also have many plants of moderate to small size.

The entire industry, in contrast, is large. More than 11 per cent of the total labor force of the United States is engaged in food processing—a percentage exceeded only by that of the transportation-equipment industry. Although these conditions are not exactly duplicated in other technically advanced countries, their statistics reveal consistently large labor forces in food processing. Even the United Kingdom, which imports much food, receives a substantial portion of it in raw or semifinished form, completing the processing in domestic plants. Although underdeveloped countries process many foods in households for the domestic market, many also have factory processing; the relative importance of factory processing varies sharply among economies in this category.

A very important locational consideration in the food-processing industry is that labor costs tend to be very low and raw-materials costs correspondingly high. This is especially true of processes which receive raw agricultural products and either complete the first stage of manufacturing or complete the entire process in a single stage. Processes which receive semifinished materials for further manufacture frequently involve later stages of manufacture in which labor costs are relatively higher and materials costs somewhat lower. You will remember that, by Alderfer and Michl criteria, an industry in which labor costs exceed 20 per cent of the value of products shipped from factories is considered to be a high-labor-cost industry, and one in which materials exceed 60 per cent of that value is termed a high-materials-cost industry. By these criteria, meat-packing plants of the United States are very low in labor costs (less than 9 per cent of the value of shipped products) and very high in materials costs (87 per cent). Dairy products and canned, preserved, and frozen food plants are medium in labor costs and high in materials costs. Flour mills are extremely low in labor costs and high in materials costs. With soft drinks and beer, we find labor costs to be comparatively high

Successful canning of food has been carried on for nearly a century and a half. Here are sealed cans of grapefruit nearing the end of an "assembly line." Today's food processing in technically advanced economies tends to be highly mechanized, and labor costs are low in comparison with such costs in many other industries. (U.S. Department of Agriculture)

(30 and 25 per cent, respectively, of the value of products shipped), and materials costs are relatively low (in each case, slightly above or below 40 per cent). This would suggest that the first group of food-processing industries may be located with an eye toward raw materials and markets. On the other hand, those food-processing industries which tend to be latter-stage industries, and so do not receive their raw materials directly from the farm, tend to locate with careful consideration to markets and labor. Indeed many of these, for reasons other than we have noted previously—the need for quick transfer to market or existence of high costs of such transfer—are located in nearly every city and town of any appreciable size. These are among the so-called *ubiquitous* industries, which are found in almost every town and city—industries which are key ingredients in the successful functioning of urban units and which one can expect to be present there.

In the surveys to follow, therefore, we shall look for the possibility of location near raw materials or at places intermediate between raw materials and markets on the part of early-stage or complete-stage plants, and for locations near clusters of people that provide both market and labor for plants involved in latter stages of plant operation. Of course, there will be exceptions to any generalizations we make; the basic question is, "Do the exceptions invalidate the generalization?"

SELECTED NATIONS OF PRODUCTION

Because the processing of food is such a widespread activity, necessarily found in some form—either factory or household—in every economy, a world-wide appraisal would be beyond the scope of this book. We therefore shall select two nations and examine the food processing industries of each. One, the United States, is a technically advanced nation producing largely for the domestic market. The second, Brazil, is usually designated as underdeveloped, contains a large population and therefore a large domestic market, but is also a major exporter of agricultural commodities.

The United States

We have noted that food processing is one of the largest industries in the United States and that it involves approximately 11 per cent of the total manufacturing labor force—more than any other two-digit detail industry except transportation equipment. In this section, we shall not be concerned with all food products in the United States, but only with meat products; grain-mill products; sugar; canned, preserved, and frozen foods; and beer and ale. We are omitting from the classification listed at the beginning of this chapter the following "Food and Kindred Products" industries: dairy products, bakery products, confectionery and related products, some beverages, and miscellaneous food preparations. By and large, we are omitting the ubiquitous industries and are focusing attention upon those food-processing activities which are somewhat unique in character and therefore located with respect to particular considerations.

Meat Packing. Meat is one of the major items in the diet of residents of the United States—regardless of their socioeconomic status. As the nation's population grows, so grows its demand for meat. Because of this large domestic demand, meat packing is the largest of the industries listed by the U.S. Bureau of the Budget under "Food and Kindred Products," accounting for about 21 per cent of all employees in this group. Nearly all the meat produced in this country is also consumed here; only a very, very small amount is exported. All in all, there were 2,367 meat-packing plants in the United States in 1954. Most of these are not large, each having a labor force of 249 or fewer. Indeed, over half have labor forces of 19 or fewer. A very small number of plants—155—have labor forces of 250 or more. Only 45 have 1,000 or more employees. Meat packing therefore can be considered as a small-plant industry when measured by labor force and number of establishments. Nevertheless, the few large plants account for a large portion of the total output.

LOCATION. Figure 34.1 shows the distribution throughout the nation in 1954 of all meat-packing

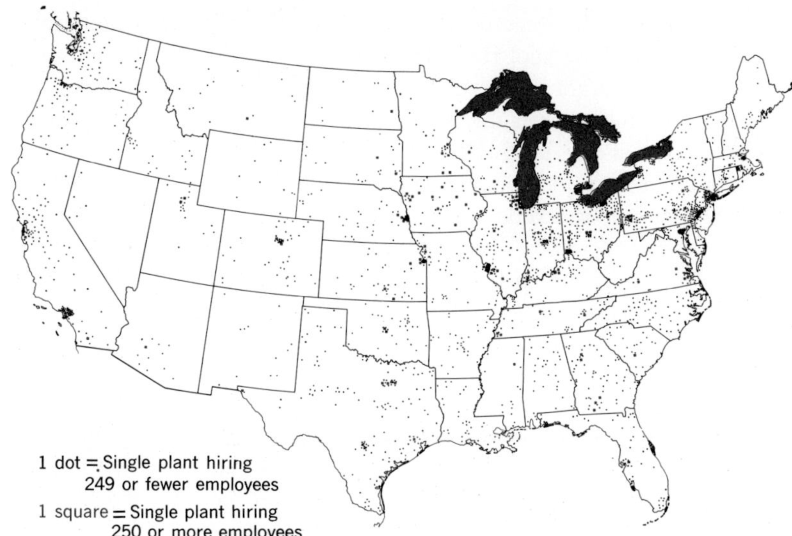

Figure 34.1 ***Distribution of meat-packing plants in the United States.***

plants. Both the large and small plants are located in general correspondence with over-all population distribution, and the suggestion therefore arises that most of these are market-oriented. This appears to be true especially of the small plants, which are clustered particularly in, or not far from, major metropolitan centers. Among the larger plants —those with labor forces of 250 or more—we find on the one hand a tendency toward clustering near the major metropolitan markets and on the other a tendency toward clustering in a few strategically placed cities such as Omaha, Kansas City, Chicago, and St. Louis—cities which are either on the edge of the major market or actually slightly removed from it but which are well located with respect to the supply of animals in the corn belt and the Great Plains. These major producers, for the most part, are at critical points between raw materials and markets (Figs. 34.1 and 34.2). Recently, there has been a tendency for plant movements to such cities as Omaha, and away from Chicago. Omaha lately has become the leading beef-packing center in the United States, measured by weight.

A further consideration in this shift of some larger plants to outlying metropolitan centers appears to involve labor costs and labor-union restriction—especially the latter—a consideration not unlike that involved in the migration of the cotton-textile industry away from New England and to the Piedmont states of the South. Such costs and restrictions are less troublesome in the outer reaches.

The meat packer is in an unusual situation in that his product is perishable both before and after processing. Unless animals are carefully tended before slaughter, they lose weight quite rapidly and yield unsatisfactory carcasses. After slaughter, the meat is subject to quick spoiling unless canned,

Figure 34.2 ***Value of shipments from meat-packing plants in the United States.***

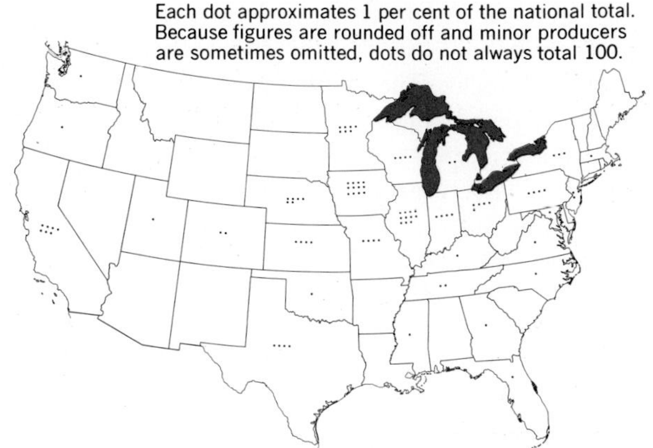

frozen, chilled, or treated in some way; if only chilled, it cannot be kept fresh for very long periods of time. The market orientation of the industry appears to be due appreciably to the high degree of perishability of the product—a disadvantage offset by modern techniques of preservation even during transportation to markets.

DECENTRALIZATION. Independent plants predominate in numbers in the meat-packing industry. These are small-capacity plants. The primary responsibility for meat packing is assumed by a comparatively small number of large, active plants owned by large corporations. Among these firms, the "Big Four"—Swift, Armour, Wilson, and Cudahy—account for over 40 per cent of the value of all shipments, and the twenty largest companies account for over 60 per cent of that value. However, the industry is decentralizing; as recently as 1947, the "Big Four" were responsible for 54 per cent of the value of all shipments, and the twenty largest companies for 85 per cent. The relative decline of the largest companies has resulted from an entry into the market of numerous smaller companies, rather than a withdrawal by the leaders. Here we find a reversal of the prevailing trend in the nation's manufacturing: here, the small firm appears to be not only holding its own but also moving ahead, in competition with larger companies.

Grain-mill products. The leading activities in grain-mill products include the making of flour and meal, preparation of animal feeds, preparation of breakfast foods, and other human food, the milling of rice, and the preparation of flour mixes. We shall concentrate on the first of these—the milling of flour and meal. The labor force involved here is much smaller than that in meat packing; it involves only about 6 per cent of the "Food and Kindred Products" manufacturing labor force. A total of 803 plants were engaged in this activity in 1954. Of these, 543 had labor forces of nineteen or fewer persons, and 789 had labor forces of 249 or fewer. Only fourteen had labor forces of 250 or more, and only one—near Springfield, Illinois—had a labor force of 1,000 or more.

LOCATION. At first glance, there appears to be a general similarity between the pattern of distribution of flour and meal mills and that of meat-packing plants (Figs. 34.1, 34.2, 34.3, and 34.4). Both have dense sprinklings of plants in the East, where the population is the heaviest, and both have concentrated clusters in the eastern margins of the Great Plains around a few metropolitan areas and large towns—locations between raw materials and markets. (We should keep in mind that the primary raw material for the flour and meal mills is wheat from the winter- and spring-wheat belts, from the Palouse country of eastern Washington and Oregon, and from the soft-wheat-growing area of the humid East.) There are, however, differences. In the first place, there is a concentration of small flour mills in the general farming region of the United States—in Virginia and North Carolina, Kentucky and Tennessee. Secondly, flour mills are not clustered so densely in the manufacturing belt as one might expect if the industry were truly market-oriented. Third, there are unusual clusters; Buffalo, for example, has three large plants. Finally, a high proportion of larger mills is found in locations somewhat removed from the market and nearer raw materials.

There are several possible explanations for this difference in pattern between flour-milling and meat-packing plants. In the first place, flour keeps quite easily unless moisture content of air is very high, and finished products can be shipped essentially as easily as raw materials—often at in-transit freight-rate privileges, so that the cost is no more than if they were raw materials. Second, flour mills are only part of many grain-mill operations, which also involve the preparation of animal feed. The market for the product of such mills, therefore, is not only the nation's people but also its animals. These latter are concentrated especially in the Middle West and the humid East, including the South. This accounts partially for the location of some plants away from the leading concentrations of people. Third, many of the smaller mills, especially in Virginia, North Carolina, Kentucky, and Tennessee, are active relics of the past century. However, they continue to process grain from nearby farms. Fourth, unlike meat products, well over one-fifth of all wheat

Figure 34.3 ***Distribution of mills processing flour and meal in the United States.***

grown in the United States currently is exported, and although a very small proportion of this is exported as flour, mills have located along the routes of wheat export. The most important of these routes involves the water transportation of the Great Lakes. Until recently when the Great Lakes–St. Lawrence Seaway was opened, much of the wheat was transferred from growing areas to the lakehead ports and carried by lake vessel to the lower part of Lake Erie. There, just before the water route entered Canada, much of the grain was transshipped at Buffalo to land carrier to be forwarded eastward to an Atlantic seaport. As we have mentioned in Chapter 9, wherever break of bulk occurs, expensive terminal charges result. It is logical, therefore, to process at such break-of-bulk centers, to avoid later terminal charges for manufacturing alone. Manufacturing plants, therefore, tend to locate in such break-of-bulk centers as Buffalo. The flour mills at Buffalo are assured a steady supply of grain, and they are also well located in relation to eastern domestic markets. They thus are oriented toward markets as well as transportation facilities.

In review: The processing of flour and meal—especially the numerous small plants in the eastern half of the United States—tends to be oriented to markets and to raw materials (grain) in the humid climates there. The clusters of mills in the Minneapolis–St. Paul area, Kansas City, Omaha, and other cities somewhat west of the major market but east of the grain supply are located with respect to both markets and raw materials, and transportation costs of each play an important role in their location. In the winter-wheat belt and in the Palouse country of eastern Washington and Oregon are some plants which appear to be closely

Figure 34.4 ***Value of factory shipments from mills processing flour and meal in the United States.***

Each dot approximates 1 per cent of the national total. Because figures are rounded off and minor producers are sometimes omitted, dots do not always total 100.

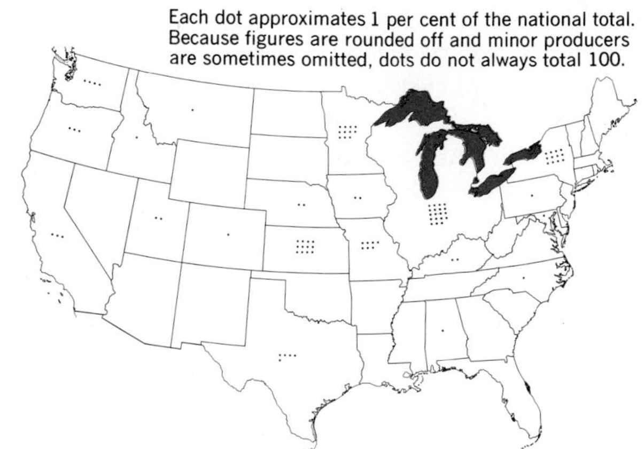

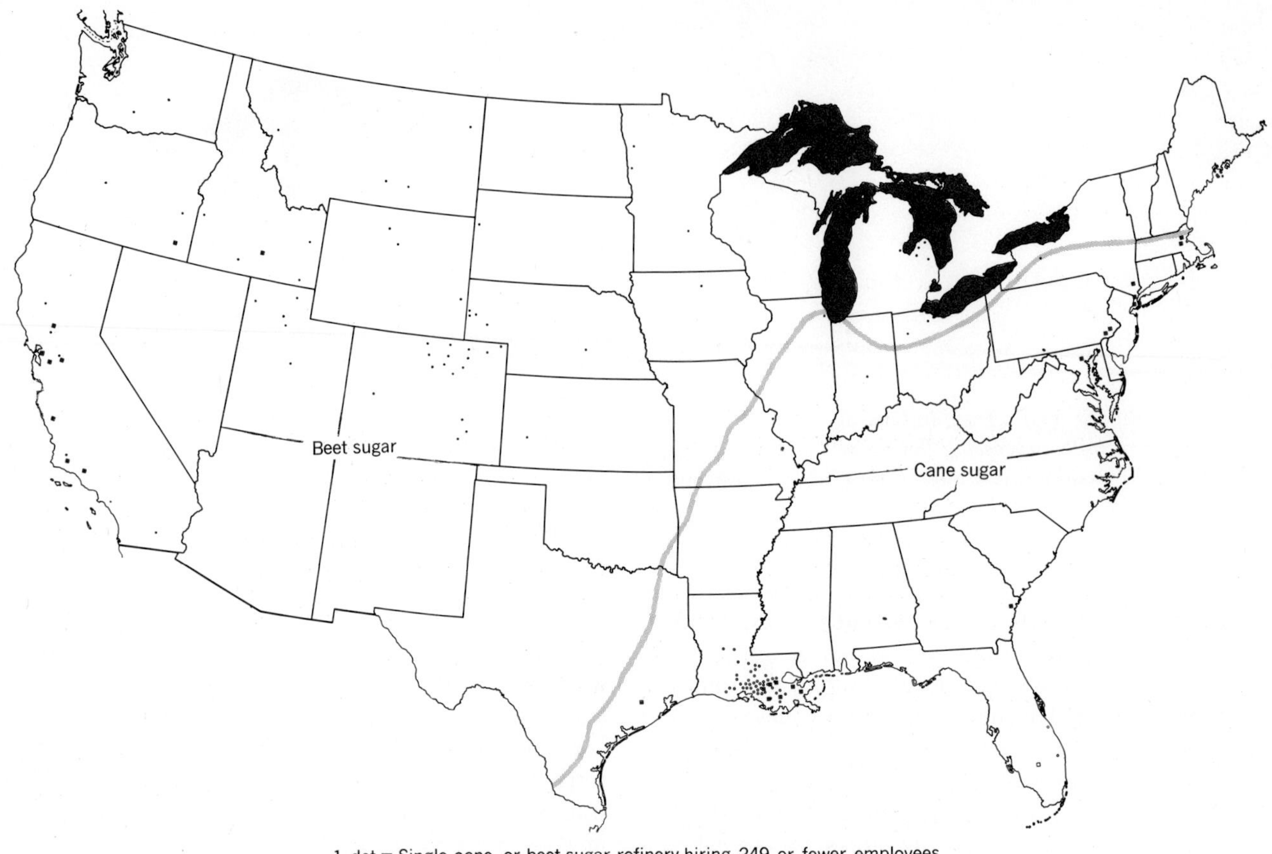

Figure 34.5 ***Distribution of cane-sugar mills and refineries and of beet-sugar plants in the United States.*** *The cane mills concentrate sugar, and the refineries purify it—a two-stage process frequently carried out in widely separated locations, with the mills located near raw materials and the refineries near markets. In contrast, the beet plants complete the entire process under a single roof. They are located mainly near raw materials.*

oriented toward raw materials, inasmuch as they are located very near those materials. Interestingly, the spring-wheat belt is almost devoid of both large and small plants; few people and animals live there (or few animals are fattened there), and its produce moves on to milling centers farther east.

CENTRALIZATION. In contrast to meat packing, the flour and meal industry of the United States is rapidly centralizing administratively. In 1947, the four largest companies accounted for 29 per cent of the value of all shipments, and the twenty largest companies for 57 per cent. In 1954, the leading four accounted for 40 per cent, and the leading twenty for 68 per cent.

Sugar Processing. The centrifugal refining of cane sugar and the processing of beets into sugar are comparatively small industries in the United States, accounting for less than 2 per cent of the total labor force engaged in the processing of "Food and Kindred Products." These industries also are small when viewed in terms of number of establishments: there are only twenty-three cane-sugar refineries and sixty-five beet-sugar plants in the United States. The cane-sugar refineries are mostly large-scale operations; of the twenty-three, only four have labor forces of 49 or less, and nineteen have labor forces of 250 or more, with seven actually employing over 1,000 workers. These plants are centrifugal refineries, processing sugar which has been concentrated in mills located near the growing fields. They are located either near those mills or in ports of import that are adjacent to markets (Fig. 34.5). A neat separation can be made between the raw-materials-oriented plants in Louisiana and Texas on the one hand, and the market-oriented plants on the other—plants which import crude sugar from Cuba and elsewhere, refining it for shipment to the domestic market. Operations are seasonal, reaching a peak activity when the cane is harvested in the summer and fall.

The processing of beet sugar is a single-stage operation, is highly seasonal, and definitely is raw-materials-oriented. Once they have been dug, sugar beets are subject to spoilage within a matter of months at the most, so that they must be sent to the processing plant quickly. At present, their shipment is not feasible for much farther than 100 miles from their place of growth. Processing plants therefore are located in the general vicinities of farm production. Activity begins in the fall when the beets are harvested, and continues at top speed during the next few months. The location of the plants, as shown in Figure 34.5, corresponds very closely with the growing of sugar beets. A large share of them is in the Far West, notably California.

Processing Canned Fruits and Vegetables. Measured by labor force, this industry is much larger than either the sugar or grain-mill-products industries, accounting for about 12 per cent of all employees in "Food and Kindred Products." It is essentially a small-plant industry: in 1954, 1,758 plants were operating; 760 of these had 19 employees or fewer, and 1,195 had 49 or fewer. A total of 1,670 establishments had 249 employees or fewer. Only 88 had more than 250 employees, and only 7 had 1,000 employees or more. It is also a highly seasonal industry, dependent upon part-time female labor. In location, there is a close association between these plants and agricultural fields producing their raw materials (Figs. 34.6 and 7.1). High product perishability almost necessitates plant location near sites of raw materials, unless transport arrangements are very efficient and thorough. However, the comparatively heavy concentrations in the manufacturing belt and other populous sections suggest that markets are not without influence. For example, there is quite a clustering of plants in east central Indiana and west central Ohio—areas which are not outstanding in production of fruits and vegetables. On the other hand, many irrigated sections of the arid and semiarid West that do specialize in growing such food do not have very many processing plants. Much of their produce is sent to plants in other places by refrigerated truck or railway car. Clearly, raw materials are the first attraction in the location of canned fruit and vegetable plants, but markets and labor supplies also are considered. Administratively, the canned fruit and vegetable industry is centralizing, but only slightly. In 1947, 27 per cent of the value of all shipments was accounted for by the four leading firms, and 46 per cent by the twenty leading firms. In 1954, the percentages were 28 and 52, respectively.

Processing of Beer and Ale. The beer and ale industry is also of intermediate significance in employment among the "Food and Kindred Products" industries, accounting for about 12 per cent of the labor force in that series. There were only 301 plants in the nation in 1954; and of these, 35 had 19 employees or fewer; 213 had 249 employees or fewer; 88 had 250 or more; and 13 had 1,000 or more. Beer and ale manufacture obviously is not a tiny-plant industry; it attracts plants of intermediate size.

In terms of administration, this industry is

Figure 34.6 ***Distribution of plants canning fruits and vegetables in the United States. Location is chiefly near raw materials.***

about as highly centralized as the canned fruits and vegetable industry. In 1954, 27 per cent of the value of shipments was accounted for by the four leading companies, and 60 per cent by the twenty leaders. This represents substantial gains, in each category, over the situation in 1947; centralization, rather than decentralization, is the trend. These plants are located in close accord with the distribution of the nation's population (Figs. 34.8 and 34.9). The manufacturing belt, the growing manufacturing areas of California, and the Gulf South all are reflected in the map of this population-oriented industry—an orientation largely to markets and labor. Many of the largest plants are in metropolitan centers.

Review. It would appear that our earlier generalizations regarding food processing are comparatively well borne out in an examination of plants in our selected industries. In each case, the pull of both markets and raw materials is distinguishable; actual location is nearer raw materials in those industries where materials costs are high. We have noted certain exceptions such as the flour mills of Buffalo and some meat packing plants; but, by and large, the generalization appears relatively valid as applied to these specific industries. The importance of location near raw materials for plants processing commodities subject to quick spoilage is also apparent. The pull of markets regarding such activities as some cane-sugar refining and the production of beer and ale also is quite clear.

Brazil

Whereas the United States is technically advanced and a moderate net importer of agricultural products, Brazil is usually considered to be underdevel-

Figure 34.7 ***Value of shipments from plants canning fruits and vegetables in the United States.***

Figure 34.8 ***Distribution of beer and ale breweries in the United States.***

oped and is a net exporter of such products. Indeed, Brazil depends overwhelmingly upon agricultural commodities, mostly beverages and foods, for total exports. Both countries have sizable domestic markets—the United States, about 180 million people and Brazil nearly 65 million.

Despite the fact that much of Brazil's food processing for the domestic market is carried on in individual households in the manner of quasi-subsistence economies, commercial food processing is a major industry there. A total of over fifteen thousand food-processing establishments are found there—a number totaling nearly one-third of all manufacturing establishments in the entire country. So considered, food processing is by far the largest nonagricultural industry; next in rank is the processing of nonmetallic minerals, which involves only about five thousand establishments. In terms of labor force, some 200,000 employees from a total manufacturing labor force of about 1,000,000—approximately one in five—are engaged in food processing activities. Only the textile industry, which employs about one-fourth of the manufacturing labor force, ranks higher. Historically, food processing has become more or less stabilized in competition with other activities. After the First World War, it was employing only about one-eighth of the nation's manufacturing workers. For the last twenty years, however, it has accounted for its present one-fifth of those workers. It also accounts for nearly one-third of the value of all manufactured products and by this criterion is also the leading industry of the nation. It has been responsible consistently for approximately one-third of the value of Brazil's manufactured products for the past forty years, despite its relative decline in labor force during that time. This would suggest increased mechanization and other means of raising output per worker.

Figure 34.9 ***Value of shipments from beer and ale breweries in the United States.***

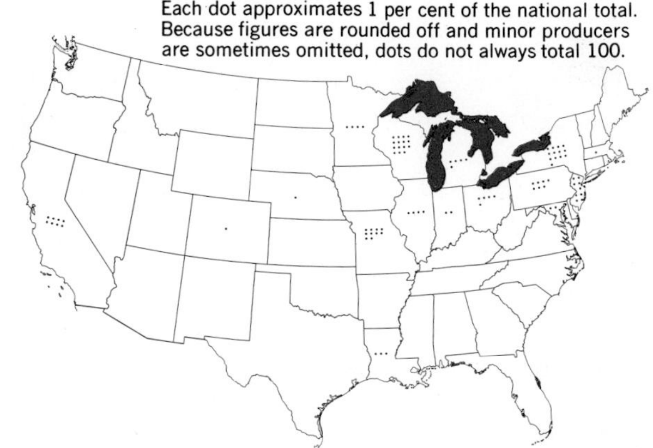

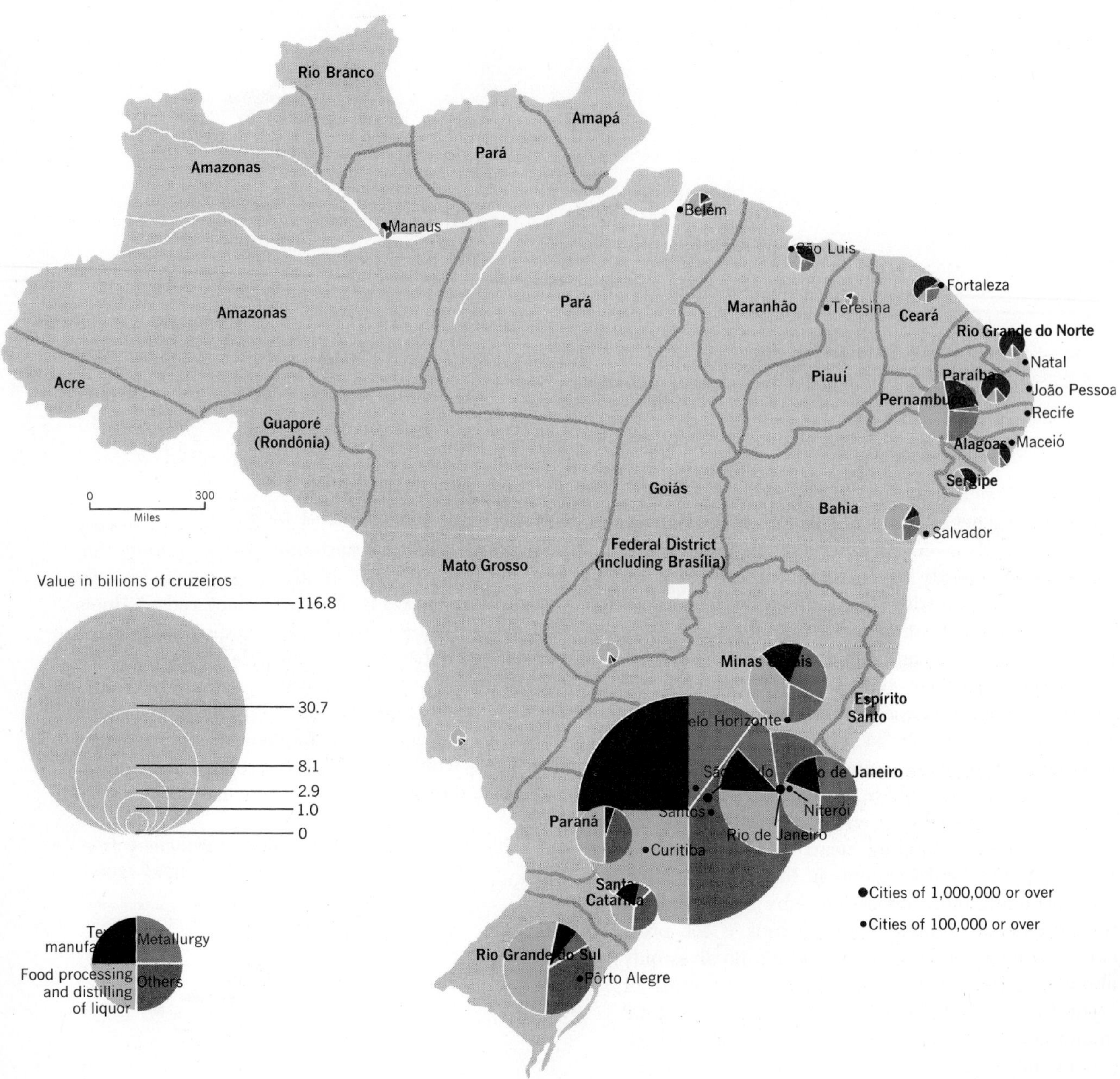

Figure 34.10 ***Distribution of Brazil's leading manufacturing industries, by state.*** *The small circle at the lower left indicates only the relative positions of the industries in the pie graphs, and is not indicative of a national average. (After maps in* Atlas Do Brasil (Geral e Regional), *Organizado Pela, Divisião de Geografia do Conselho Nacional de Geografia, 1959)*

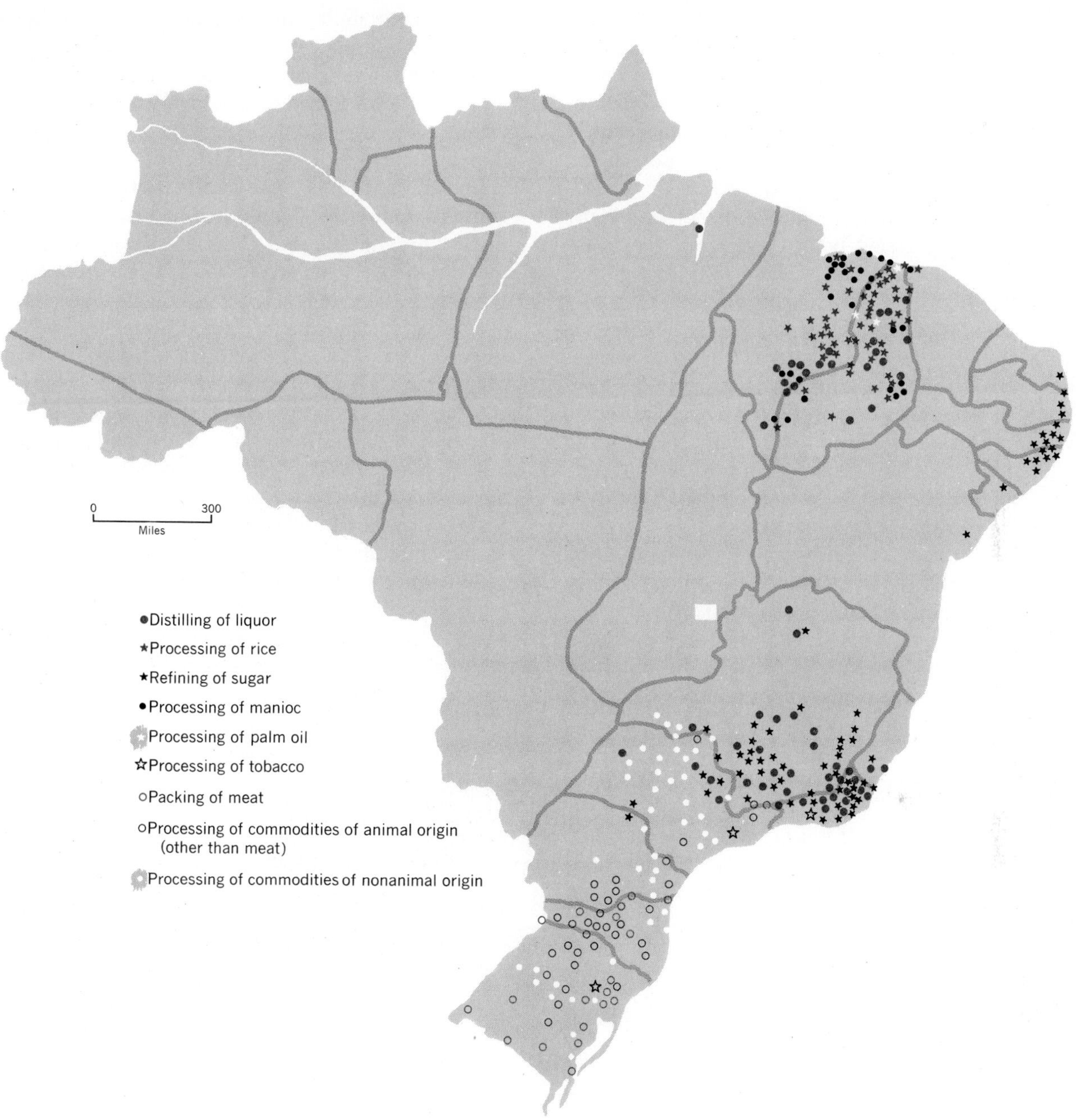

Figure 34.11 **Distribution of some of Brazil's leading food-processing industries.** *The map was compiled from several large-scale map sheets that were completed by different scholars and were not standardized as to detail. For this reason, in all probability, not all food processing is shown. (After maps in* Atlas Do Brasil (Geral e Regional), *Organizado Pela, Divisião de Geografia do Conselho Nacional de Geografia, 1959)*

Brazil's food processing also is significant when measured by value of output (Fig. 34.10). It dominates the manufacturing of most of the country's outlying area, and even accounts for one-fourth or more of the manufacturing output of the heavily populated states of São Paulo and Rio de Janeiro.

What specific industries are involved? Brazil's most important export, coffee, requires essentially no factory processing before shipment; the beans are merely dried, usually where they are grown, and shipped to local and seaport markets. Certainly the leading food-processing activity of the nation is meat packing. The cleaning of rice, the concentration of sugar, the making of a very popular alcoholic brew known as *cachaça* as well as wine, vermouth, and brandy, the pressing of palm oil, and the processing of manioc and other vegetable and animal products also are among the more outstanding food-processing industries.

That these establishments are distributed throughout the country more or less in accordance with population would suggest market orientation (Figs. 34.10 and 34.11). Yet there are sectional differences. Meat packing is particularly important in the south, where most of the country's cattle are raised. Sugar mills are numerous in the northeast and the hinterland of Rio de Janeiro, where the growing of cane is concentrated. Palm oil, manioc, and rice are processed most actively near the places where they are raised or extracted. These plants thus appear to be located first with respect to raw materials and only secondarily with respect to markets. Only the distilleries evidence a distinct market orientation, and these are second-stage industries, dependent largely on th sugar from other sections of the country.

More so than in the United States, the initial-stage or complete-stage industries display patterns suggesting the pull of raw materials as a locational consideration, and the second-stage industries display pull of domestic markets. This may be because much manufacturing in Brazil has not yet reached the sophisticated stage that it has in the United States—that small, independent producers, who act on hunch more than on mathematical equation, are yet in predominance. Perhaps we may be reading too much into the distribution patterns of their plants, therefore, to apply closely some of the theories developed from examples in technically advanced nations.

REFERENCES

Alderfer, E. B., and H. E. Michl: Economics of American Industry, McGraw-Hill Book Company, Inc., New York, 1957. (Especially chaps. 27–33.)

James, Preston E.: *Latin America,* The Odyssey Press, Inc., New York, 1959.

Malecki, George J.: *Survey of the Food Industry and Food Processing in Eastern Europe,* The Library of Congress Photoduplication Service, Microfilm 2551–334DR, 1956.

Webb, K.: "A Geography of Food Supply in Central Minas Gerais, Brazil," unpublished doctoral dissertation, Syracuse University, 1958.

Woytinsky, W. S., and E. S. Woytinsky: *World Population and Production,* The Twentieth Century Fund, Inc., New York, 1953. (Especially chap. 27.)

TRENDS AND OUTLOOK

Serious interruptions to the smooth functioning of economies usually are due not so much to natural obstacles as to human actions that frequently appear illogical when viewed objectively but are quite understandable when viewed in terms of current events. Vested interest is still very much with us.

(INTRODUCTION, PAGE 16)

TWENTIETH-CENTURY MAN IN MANY SOCIETIES IS EXPERIENCING CHANGE unprecedented in both pace and scope. Innovations appear so frequently and in so many and such varied forms that new machines have been known to be obsolescent before they are off assembly lines and new information to be out of date almost before it is released from the press. Particularly in technically advanced nations, such change affects nearly all realms of human endeavor, including those upon which this book has been focused. The resultant complexity means that prediction is increasingly difficult, despite the many and efficient methods and tools developed by science for that purpose. It means also that prediction pertaining to at least the immediate future is increasingly necessary, for today's decisions involve large numbers of people and things as never before and cannot be made in a vacuum.

Four trends, each of which has been either mentioned or discussed at some length in preceding chapters, have contributed pronouncedly to this complexity. The first, which scarcely can be overemphasized, is the population explosion. The recent acceleration in population increase and the probable doubling of the world's total population by the year 2000 have obvious connotations for students of economic geography, stimulating a number of sobering questions. Will aggregate consumption rise at a corresponding rate or—if underdeveloped nations especially are to improve their economic conditions—at an even higher rate? How will such an increase in numbers affect the world-wide location of economic activity, including consumption as well as the more familiar production and exchange? Will yet additional, heretofore unused, land be plowed under in large-scale schemes such as that which occurred in the Soviet Union in the middle 1950s? Will intensive subsistence agriculture, which now supports so many people in eastern and southern Asia, be introduced on a broad scale into generally similar natural environmental conditions of Africa and Latin America to provide for rapidly growing populations in some places in each of these areas? Perhaps more urgent, will the intensive subsistence farming methods of eastern and southern Asia be improved through the use of chemical fertilizers and more careful seed selection, so that they will provide food more adequately for the burgeoning populations in that section of the world? Will the oceans be combed more thoroughly for fish, and forests for edible plants and game? Will new urban complexes appear and the older ones become larger and even coalesce, as more people leave rural areas and turn to the cities for residence and support? Will existing and proposed transportation facilities be sufficient to carry the additional freight that certainly will result from the increased consumption associated with increasing populations? Or will the rate of population increase be curbed, as in Japan, so that many of the above questions will be less acute? These and still other basic questions in economic geography automatically accompany the very real and pronounced population increases now recognized even in the popular press.

A second major trend involves the role of the Industrial Revolution in the twentieth century. It is linked inextricably with the first trend and among other considerations offers a prime hope of relief from some of the more excessively adverse effects of population increase—if only for the simple reason that it makes possible a rising per capita output in both the productive and the service occupations. But the twentieth-century connotations of the Industrial Revolution differ somewhat from those of preceding centuries in that they are focused upon all occupations, productive and service, rather than upon manufacturing and transportation. Because the factory and technology rose together, they provided new means of livelihood as well as an unprecedented volume of output, and the upper levels of both the livelihood and the output have not as yet been established. This has continued into the twentieth century, when, even in the most technically advanced nations, the manufacturing labor force is on the wax rather than the wane. However, many of the methods and tools of the Industrial Revolution now are being applied on a grand scale to occupations other than manufacturing and its associated transportation. The other five productive occupations, unlike modern manufacturing, long have been established, and the methods and tools of the Industrial Revolution, while increasing their output, also are reducing their need for labor. As one result, the number of people actually engaged in many of the other productive occupations actually is decreasing, absolutely as well as relatively, in the world's most technically advanced nations. This is particularly true of agriculture, long the mainstay of population support. Replaced by machines, where do the surplus rural workers go? To the cities and towns; there is no other place for them to go. In such cities and towns they find employment either in manufacturing or in the rapidly growing service occupations. This rural-to-urban migration has meant a sharp areal focusing of consumption, which no longer is distributed in blanket-like fashion over a rural countryside but is clustered into urban units. Meanwhile, a few men and their newly developed machinery continue to make the countrysides produce at rates equal to or exceeding those of earlier years. The output of farms, ranches, mines, and forest-products industries thus has not declined, but its market has shifted notably to the world's urban units—again, particularly in technically advanced countries. At the same time, in most technically advanced societies, the levels of living are rising under the new conditions. The volume as well as the areal distribution of consumption thus is affected sharply by twentieth-century applications and developments of the Industrial Revolution. This, in turn, means a greater strain on the world's transportation facilities, whether engaged in domestic or international commerce. Goods which once were produced and consumed in localities now travel appreciable distances from trading areas to cities and possibly back again. They may be processed at some point en route, or may be merely packaged and marketed. International commerce likewise has benefited from the transfer of raw materials and finished products in this age of specialized production, and on an even grander scale than that of urban units and their trading territories.

Where applied, twentieth-century connotations of the Industrial Revolution thus have resulted in a sharp centralization of consumption and some production, as well as a marked growth in consumption, production, and exchange in the nations which have adopted them. We should not forget, however, that two-thirds of the world's people are considered to be living in underdeveloped economies, which have been only partially affected by the Industrial Revolution, and in some cases scarcely at all. The gap between the more technically advanced and the more underdeveloped economies in both the pace and volume of economic activity has been increasing rather than decreasing. Although some underdeveloped economies are now striving to change this trend, others appear to be making few if any efforts to do so. It appears probable, therefore, that the range from the most to the least dynamic of economies will widen rather than narrow in the immediate future and that only a few of the heretofore underdeveloped economies will approach and perhaps pass over the nebulous line separating them from technically advanced conditions.

A third major trend has been the economic growth of the Soviet Union, and the impact of this and other Communist economies upon the world distribution and functioning of economic activity. The combination of centralized control and police coercion with specific short-term plans that fit into a long-term pattern has resulted in a marked rate of economic growth in the Soviet Union and Communist China, and a noteworthy growth rate in much of Eastern Europe. Also important has been the planned development of such new industrial districts as the Urals and the Kuznets—development involving long-term capital outlay with no expectation of early return. Such thinking has altered drastically the location of economic activity in this part of the world. However abhorrent some of the methods—and no civilized mind can condone the ruthless sacrifice of one generation to the welfare of one yet unborn—the marked growth of economic activity in such nations is a documented reality, the impact of which has been and is being felt abroad as well as at home. This impact, ranging from the maintenance of aircraft, rocket, and other military-oriented industries and the hurried development of missile programs to the extension of loans, grants, and other forms of foreign aid to underdeveloped nations, has occurred on both sides of the iron curtain.

A fourth trend of major importance to the world's economic geography is that of political independence on the part of a sizable and growing number of countries, most of which are economically underdeveloped. This trend has taken form largely since the Second World War, and its effects are not yet fully apparent. Many of the nations involved are small in both area and population, and are incapable of economic self-sufficiency. A substantial portion are former members of European empires and appear willing to continue an economic affiliation with the former controlling country. Such an attitude probably will benefit these nations during their embryonic years, for drastic changes of economic partners sometimes can be unfortunate if not catastrophic. Specific changes, if any, in the pace and location of economic activity in these nations will vary sharply with the actual objectives of each, and with their respective capacities to reach those objectives. Generally, we can anticipate: (1) closer control of exported mineral resources and higher revenues to exporting nations from such resources as do leave; (2) some efforts to improve domestic agricultural efficiency and output; (3) some efforts to initiate or expand manufacturing, particularly of textiles and foods, but also of diverse other items, including iron and steel; and (4) some efforts to reduce the present ravages of hunger and disease now characterizing too many underdeveloped economies. It also appears probable that many such nations will take advantage of their particular locations and roles with respect to the cold war in order to obtain various forms of foreign aid from both sides of the iron curtain. The end result of their actions may be to lessen somewhat the present dominance of world economic activity by a few technically advanced nations.

All four of these trends give evidence of continuing into the immediate future. It appears likely that they and still other considerations will result in a quickened pace and an increased complexity of economic activity, particularly in technically advanced operations, wherever found. Man's economic ties with his fellow man and with nature are becoming increasingly intricate and perhaps increasingly intimate as well. At the same time, his outlook hopefully is becoming more sophisticated. Technical advance frequently results in a pushing back of what once were considered natural restrictions, and in a widening of the range of feasible human choices. The freedom to choose, however, is accompanied by an increased measure of responsibility.

In today's highly organized societies, the livelihood and well-being of many people depend pronouncedly upon the actions of a few decision makers, and a bad decision concerning the location of a manufacturing plant or farm or mine can be at least a temporary liability to people, organizations, and natural features somehow associated with it. Today's decisions, therefore, involve more than ever before the selection of what appears to be the best in a series of possibilities, and the alternatives to each must be weighed carefully before implementation. Actual costs of labor, raw materials, energy, capital equipment and marketing are key considerations to the location and functioning of any economic activity, as are the numerous other economic criteria outlined in Chapter 8. Also involved, however, are noneconomic considerations, if we are to avoid economic determinism. Should a town be allowed to wither and die because nationwide coal mining is no longer so active as it once was or because division points which once serviced the old steam locomotives are unneeded in diesel-motor maintenance? If the clustering of economic activity makes for more economic efficiency, as it seems to do, does this justify the jamming of millions of persons into metropolitan areas, sometimes creating "blackboard jungles"? Is such clustering sound thinking in an age when missiles can be "zeroed in" on urban complexes and destroy them in a single blast? (We are not attempting here a polemic against the centralization of economic activity but a suggestion of only a few noneconomic considerations that necessarily present themselves when the location of economic activity is given careful thought.)

It is important to remember also that natural conditions, while perhaps altered slightly by the multitude of methods and tools developed by man for that purpose, are yet very much with us. In the past a none-too-large population has used part of nature's bounty to excess. In some places, the best ores and forests and soils are gone. In many areas, our expanding economies will have to get by with the poorer stuff. This we can do, usually with greater efficiency than our forebears, because our science and technology are more exact and thorough than theirs were. But we cannot run rampant; we must still practice conservation—defined as wise use in our time. Alternative materials must be sought for those in short supply, especially for the natural features which are not replaceable. Alternative outlets need to be considered for those materials which are either easily replaceable or in very adequate supply. Very possibly, as in no other age, this is a time of the weighing of alternatives.

Thus far, we have considered only the viewpoint of the individual person, firm, or organization. Geographic features, however, do not exist individually but in intricate regional combinations. In the end analysis, man's economic and geographic use of the earth, which is the sum total of all regions, involves his considering the wisest use of all pertinent components in a given region, and ultimately of the earth itself. It is at this point that the selection of specific features and courses of action becomes increasingly difficult, that quantitative measurement needs to be carried as far as possible. It is this regional and world view, this considering of all persons and things germane to the optimal functioning of a specific part of the world and ultimately of the entire world, which maximizes the complexity of, and the necessity for more work in, economic geography and associated disciplines.

SELECTED DATA ON THE WORLD'S POLITICAL UNITS

SELECTED DATA ON THE WORLD'S POLITICAL UNITS

Political unit	*Political status*	*Area (thousands of square miles)*	*Population (millions)*	*Density per square mile (to nearest whole number)*	*Per cent of respective populations living in metropolitan areas of 100,000 or over*
Afghanistan	Kingdom	250.0	13.27	53	2.5
Albania	People's republic *	11.1	1.51	136	7.1
Andorra	Autonomous principality	0.175	0.007	40	—
Argentina	Republic	1,072.7	20.96	20	42.4
Austria	Republic	32.4	7.02	217	37.5
Bahrain	British protectorate	0.233	0.143	620	—
Belgium and affiliates					
Belgium	Constitutional monarchy	11.8	9.08	771	41.0
Ruanda-Urundi	United Nations trust territory	20.9	4.71	224	—
Bhutan	Protectorate of India	19.3	0.700	36	—
Bolivia	Republic	424.1	3.42	8	16.3
Brazil	Republic	3,286.9	66.31	20	17.6
Bulgaria	People's republic*	42.8	7.72	180	13.1
Burma	Republic	261.8	20.46	78	5.2
Cambodia	Kingdom	69.9	4.74	68	8.4
Cameroun	Republic	166.8	3.24	19	3.7
Chile	Republic	286.4	7.54	26	29.6
China (Communist)	People's republic*	3,768.7	700.00	186	7.4
China (Nationalist)	Republic	13.9	10.14	731	18.7
Colombia	Republic	439.5	13.82	32	20.3
Congo, Republic of the (former Belgian Congo)	Republic	904.9	13.56	15	4.1
Costa Rica	Republic	19.7	1.08	55	16.5
Cuba	Republic	44.3	6.47	146	25.1
Czechoslovakia	People's republic*	49.4	13.44	272	13.8
Dahomey	Republic	44.7	1.73	44	—
Denmark and affiliates					
Denmark	Constitutional monarchy	16.6	4.52	272	37.9
Greenland	Overseas department	840.0	0.028	0.03	—

Faeroe Islands	Autonomous part of Denmark	0.54	0.033	61	—
Dominican Republic	Republic	18.7	4.07	216	10.2
Ecuador	Republic	105.7	4.12	39	13.8
El Salvador	Republic	8.3	2.43	295	11.1
Ethiopia and affiliate					
Ethiopia	Empire	409.3	18.96	46	2.9
Eritrea	Autonomous state federated with Ethiopia	45.9	1.04	23	—
Finland	Republic	130.1	4.41	34	17.7
France and French Community					
France	Republic	212.8	45.4	213	33.6
African affiliates					
Algeria (incl. Sahara)	Overseas department	919.6	10.48	9	11.1
Central African Republic †	Republic	241.7	1.17	5	—
Chad †	Republic	495.4	2.58	5	—
Comoro Islands	Overseas territory	0.83	0.18	218	—
Congo †	Republic	134.7	0.76	6	—
Gabon †	Republic	103.1	0.41	4	—
Malagasy †	Republic	227.7	5.14	23	5.9
Réunion	Overseas department	0.97	0.318	328	—
Senegal †	Republic	76.1	2.3	30	10.0
Somaliland	Overseas territory	9.0	0.069	8	—
North American affiliates					
Guadeloupe	Overseas department	0.69	0.259	377	—
Martinique	Overseas department	0.43	0.265	615	—
St. Pierre and Miquelon	Overseas territory	0.093	0.005	53	—
South American affiliate					
French Guiana	Overseas department	35.14	0.030	0.9	—
Oceania affiliates					
French Polynesia	Overseas territory	1.4	0.079	55	—
New Caledonia and dependencies	Overseas territory	8.5	0.069	8	—
New Hebrides	French-British condominium	5.7	0.053	9	—
German Democratic Republic (East)	People's republic*	41.6	17.31	416	37.8
German Federal Republic (West)	Republic	95.9	55.36	575	50.1
Greece	Kingdom	51.2	8.22	161	21.9
Guatemala	Republic	42.0	3.55	84	10.4
Guinea	Republic	94.9	2.73	29	—
Haiti	Republic	10.7	3.46	323	6.8
Honduras	Republic	43.3	1.95	46	6.4

SELECTED DATA ON THE WORLD'S POLITICAL UNITS

Political unit	*Political status*	*Area (thousands of square miles)*	*Population (millions)*	*Density per square mile (to nearest whole number)*	*Per cent of respective populations living in metropolitan areas of 100,000 or over*
Hungary	People's republic*	35.9	9.98	276	20.2
Iceland	Republic	39.8	0.169	4	—
Indonesia	Republic	575.9	88.90	155	7.7
Iran	Kingdom	636.3	20.04	32	15.7
Iraq	Republic	171.6	6.96	40	15.0
Ireland	Republic	27.1	2.85	105	29.0
Israel	Republic	8.0	2.06	258	47.5
Italy	Republic	116.3	49.91	429	26.4
Ivory Coast	Republic	124.5	3.18	25	4.0
Japan	Constitutional monarchy	142.8	93.51	654	38.2
Jordan	Kingdom	37.3	1.61	43	10.6
Korea (North)	People's republic*	47.9	8.02	167	18.1
Korea (South)	Republic	37.4	23.61	628	18.0
Kuwait	Independent sheikdom	6.0	0.206	34	58.0
Laos	Kingdom	85.9	1.69	20	—
Lebanon	Republic	4.0	1.53	380	19.4
Liberia	Republic	43.0	1.25	29	—
Libya	Kingdom	679.3	1.15	2	11.3
Liechtenstein	Constitutional monarchy	0.061	0.015	250	—
Luxembourg	Grand duchy	1.0	0.322	322	—
Mali	Republic	464.9	4.29	9	—
Mauritania	Republic	450.6	0.656	2	—
Mexico	Republic	760.4	34.60	46	20.3
Monaco	Sovereign principality	0.0006	0.020	35,332	—
Mongolian People's Republic	People's republic*	591.1	0.910	2	—
Morocco	Kingdom	174.5	11.61	66	12.9
Muscat and Oman	Independent sultanates	82.3	0.550	7	—

Nepal	Kingdom	54.4	9.04	166	1.7
Netherlands and affiliates					
Netherlands	Kingdom	12.6	11.34	899	28.0
Asian affiliate					
Netherlands New Guinea	Overseas part of kingdom	160.6	0.700	4	—
North American affiliate					
Netherlands Antilles	Overseas part of kingdom	0.394	0.191	485	—
South American affiliate					
Surinam	Overseas part of kingdom	55.1	0.252	5	—
Nicaragua	Republic	57.1	1.38	24	13.1
Niger	Republic	489.2	2.56	5	—
Norway	Constitutional monarchy	149.2	3.58	24	21.4
Panama	Republic	28.8	1.02	36	22.1
Paraguay	Republic	157.0	1.68	11	14.0
Peru	Republic	496.2	10.52	21	12.6
Philippines	Republic	115.7	27.47	237	11.6
Poland	People's republic*	120.4	29.60	246	23.4
Portugal and affiliates					
Portugal	Republic	35.5	8.98	253	19.7
African affiliates					
Angola	Overseas province	481.4	4.51	9	4.9
Cape Verde Islands	Overseas province	1.6	0.192	124	—
Mozambique	Overseas province	303.1	6.23	21	—
Portuguese Guinea	Overseas province	13.9	0.559	40	—
São Tomé and Príncipe Islands	Overseas province	0.372	0.062	167	—
Asian affiliates					
Macao	Overseas province	0.006	0.188	31,333	100
Portuguese India	Overseas province	1.6	0.649	401	—
Portuguese Timor	Overseas province	7.3	0.493	67	—
Qatar	British protectorate*	8.5	0.040	5	—
Rumania	People's republic	91.7	18.06	197	14.2
San Marino	Republic	0.024	0.015	625	—
Saudi Arabia	Kingdom	872.7	6.04	7	5.8
Sikkim	Protectorate of India	2.7	0.150	55	—
Somali Republic (Somalia)	Republic	246.2	1.97	8	—
Spain and affiliates					
Spain	Monarchy	194.9	29.89	153	25.8
African affiliates					
Fernando Po	Overseas province	0.786	0.045	57	—

Political unit	*Political status*	*Area (thousands of square miles)*	*Population (millions)*	*Density per square mile (to nearest whole number)*	*Per cent of respective populations living in metropolitan areas of 100,000 or over*
Spain and affiliates—African affiliates (continued)					
Ifni	Overseas province	0.579	0.052	90	—
Río Muni	Overseas province	10.0	0.165	16	—
Spanish Sahara	Overseas province	102.7	0.019	0.2	—
Sudan	Republic	961.5	11.02	11	2.3
Sweden	Constitutional monarchy	173.6	7.44	43	22.8
Switzerland	Republic	15.9	5.19	325	29.0
Thailand	Kingdom	195.8	21.88	112	6.8
Togo	Republic	21.8	1.64	78	—
Trucial states	British protectorates	32.3	0.086	3	—
Tunisia	Republic	48.3	3.88	80	12.1
Turkey	Republic	301.4	25.93	86	9.8
Union of Soviet Socialist Republics (Soviet Union)	People's republic*	8,650.1	208.83	24	21.6
Union of South Africa and affiliate					
Union of South Africa	Republic	472.7	14.93	31	33.1
South-West Africa	United Nations mandated territory	317.7	0.56	2	—
United Arab Republic	Union of republics	457.3	29.45	64	19.9
Egypt	Republic	386.1	25.03	65	18.8
Syria	Republic	71.2	4.42	62	25.4
United Kingdom and Commonwealth of Nations					
United Kingdom of Great Britain and Northern Ireland	Constitutional monarchy	93.9	51.87	552	68.5
Australia and Commonwealth					
Australia	Parliamentary state	2,974.6	10.01	3	49.5
Christmas Island	External territory	0.062	0.0028	45	—
Nauru	United Nations trust territory	0.008	0.004	539	—
Norfolk Island	External territory	0.013	0.0011	82	—

Papua and New Guinea	External territory and United Nations trust territory	183.5	2.07	11	—
Canada	Parliamentary state	3,851.1	17.48	5	41.2
Ceylon	Parliamentary state	25.3	9.39	371	8.8
Cyprus	Republic	3.6	0.549	154	—
Ghana	Parliamentary state	91.8	6.69	73	5.8
India	Republic	1,259.8	407.91	322	8.3
Malaya	Constitutional monarchy	50.7	6.60	130	13.2
New Zealand and affiliates					
New Zealand	Parliamentary state	103.7	2.30	22	41.0
Western Samoa	United Nations trust territory	1.1	0.102	90	—
Nigeria	Republic	339.2	33.04	97	4.5
Pakistan	Republic	364.7	85.64	235	5.2
Sierra Leone	Republic	27.9	2.12	76	—
Singapore	Republic (with limitations)	0.225	1.63	7,279	81.1
United Kingdom dependencies and trusteeships					
Africa					
Basutoland	Colony	11.7	0.658	56	—
Bechuanaland	Protectorate	275.1	0.334	1	—
Cameroons	United Nations trust territory	34.1	1.59	47	—
Gambia	Colony and protectorate	4.0	0.292	73	—
Kenya	Colony and protectorate	225.0	6.45	29	3.4
Mauritius (including dependencies)	Colony	0.805	0.622	773	—
Rhodesia and Nyasaland, Federation of	Federation of two protectorates and a self-governing colony	484.5	7.99	16	4.4
St. Helena (including dependencies)	Colony	0.156	0.005	32	—
Seychelles	Colony	0.157	0.042	269	—
Swaziland	Protectorate	6.7	0.267	40	—
Tanganyika	United Nations trust territory	362.7	8.92	25	1.5
Uganda	Protectorate	93.9	5.85	62	—
Zanzibar	Protected sultanate	1.0	0.299	293	—
Asia					
Aden	Colony and protectorate	112.2	0.791	7	17.4
Brunei	Protected sultanate	2.2	0.073	33	—
Hong Kong	Colony	0.391	2.75	7,028	92.5
Maldive Islands	Protected sultanate	0.115	0.082	713	—
North Borneo	Colony	29.4	0.401	14	—
Sarawak	Colony	47.5	0.631	13	—
Europe					
Gibraltar	Colony	0.002	0.025	113	—

Political unit	*Political status*	*Area (thousands of square miles)*	*Population (millions)*	*Density per square mile (to nearest whole number)*	*Per cent of respective populations living in metropolitan areas of 100,000 or over*
United Kingdom dependencies and trusteeships—Europe (continued)					
Guernsey Island and dependencies	Crown dependency	0.030	0.043	1,433	—
Jersey Island	Crown dependency	0.045	0.057	1,267	—
Malta	Colony (self-governing)	0.122	0.324	266	61.1
Man, Isle of	Crown dependency	0.221	0.055	249	—
North America					
Bahama Islands	Colony	4.4	0.136	31	—
Bermuda	Colony	0.021	0.043	2,048	—
British Honduras	Colony	8.9	0.085	10	—
British Virgin Islands	Colony	0.059	0.008	129	—
West Indies	Federation of colonies moving toward independence	8.0	3.21	400	18.3
South America					
British Guiana	Colony	83.1	0.541	7	22.2
Falkland Islands and dependencies	Colony	8.1	0.003	0.3	—
Oceania					
Fiji	Colony	7.1	0.374	53	—
Gilbert and Ellice Islands	Colony	0.369	0.042	114	—
New Hebrides	British-French condominium	5.7	0.054	9	—
Pitcairn Island	Colony	0.019	0.0001	8	—
Solomon Islands	Protectorate	11.5	0.114	10	—
Tonga	Protected kingdom	0.270	0.060	222	—
United States and affiliates					
United States	Republic	3,615.2	183.12	50	54
Central American affiliates					
Panama Canal Zone	Leased territory	0.558	0.057	102	—
Puerto Rico	Commonwealth	3.4	2.35	681	31.2
Virgin Islands	Territory	0.133	0.031	235	—

Asian affiliates					
Bonin-Volcano Islands	Military government	0.040	0.0002	5	—
Ryukyu Islands	Military government	0.848	0.855	1,008	20.0
Oceania affiliates					
American Samoa	Territory	0.076	0.020	265	—
Guam	Territory	0.209	0.072	345	—
Marshall, Caroline, and Mariana Islands	United Nations trust territory	0.687	0.071	103	—
Upper Volta	Republic	105.8	3.47	33	—
Uruguay	Republic	72.2	2.80	39	33.2
Vatican City	Ecclesiastical state	0.0002	0.001	5,882	100.0
Venezuela	Republic	352.1	6.51	19	25.1
Vietnam					
Democratic Republic of (North)	People's republic*	60.2	15.24	254	3.2
Republic of (South)	Republic	65.9	13.96	212	17.1
Yemen	Kingdom	75.3	4.50	60	—
Yugoslavia	People's republic*	98.8	18.45	187	7.1

* All nations indicated as "people's republic" are Communist nations.

† Countries which have received independence from France but have remained within the French Community.

SOURCE: Area and population data from the latest published sources, chiefly publications of the United Nations and Encyclopaedia Britannica's *Book of the Year;* densities calculated by author; metropolitan area information calculated from *The World's Metropolitan Areas,* International Urban Research, Institute of International Studies, Berkeley, University of California Press, 1959, pp. 37–63.

INDEX